Danger In the Camp
An Analysis and Refutation of the Heresies of the Federal Vision

John M. Otis

Triumphant Publications

Scripture quotations are from the New American Standard Bible copyright 1960, 1963, 1971, 1973, 1975, 1977 by the Lockman Foundation.

References to the Westminster Confession and to the Larger and Shorter Catechisms is taken from the original 1646 unedited version published by Free Presbyterian Publications.

References to John Calvin's *Institutes of the Christian Religion* are taken from the McNeill and Battles translation.

References to the Knox Theological Seminary Colloquium are taken from a pre-published version of this work.

Triumphant Publications
4253 Mulligan Dr.
Corpus Christi, Texas 78413
E-mail: cjotis2@yahoo.com

Visit Triumphant Publications at: www.westminster-rpcus.org

ISBN: 9772800-0-4

Acknowlegements

I want to thank my wife, Christine, for all the years of being a faithful wife to this preacher. Her unwavering commitment to the Lord Jesus Christ and His precious Word has been a constant joy to me. She has been a constant source of encouragement to my ministry. She has been a most suitable helper. She has always been my own technician. She has put her talents to use by being the typesetter of this book.

I would like to thank David Martinez for his encouragement and zeal for the Reformed Faith. He is constantly seeking to proclaim the great truths of the Protestant Reformation.

I would like to thank Mike and Tricia Miller for their diligent work in the proof reading of the manuscript.

Dedicated To

Jennifer Martinez and Christopher Marks, two young rising and shining stars in the Reformed church, without whose persistent encouragement this project would never have been completed.

Those people who fail to understand the law aright, are blind; in their presumptuous way, they think they can fulfill it with works. They are unaware how much the law demands.

Martin Luther

Table of Contents

Chapter

Introduction 1
   A Brief History of the Controversy 3
   Prominent Proponents Of Federal Vision Theology 6
   The Betrayal 7
   Present Status 7
   Other Denominations Agree With the RPCUS Analysis 8

1   What Is A Heresy? 13
   Who Decides Who Is A Heretic? 22
   Indicating Marks of a Heretic 24
   The Necessity for Doctrinal Defense 25
   A General List of the errors of the Federal Vision 28
   Is The Federal Vision A Heresy? 29

2   Allegiance to the Reformed Standards? 33

3   A Denial of Justification by Faith Alone 39
   The Theology of Norman Shepherd 39
   Shepherd's History of Theological Controversy 40
   Shepherd's Problems with Westminster Seminary 41
   Errors in Shepherd's book The Call of Grace 51
   Shepherd's article in Reformation and Revival 67 74
   A Biblical and Reformed Understanding of James Chapter 2 .78

4   A Denial of Christ's Active Obedience in Justification 83
   Christ's Work of Imputation 83
   Christ's Passive Obedience 86
   We Must Be Reconciled To God 86
   God Needs To Be Propitiated 87
   Blood Must Be Shed 88
   Redemption through Christ's Blood 88
   Christ's Active Obedience 89
   References to Christ's Active Obedience 92
   The Covenant of Works 94
   The Covenant of Works and the Law of God 97
   Shepherd's Denial of Christ's Active Obedience 100
   Falsehoods Demonstrated In Shepherd's Lectures 107

The Federal Vision and Socinianism .126
The Canons of Dordt and Christ's Merits 127
Rich Lusk's Denial of Christ's Imputation 130
The Heidelberg Catechism and the Law of God 137

5 The Relationship of Works to Justification by Faith 153
A Restatement of the Federal Vision's View of Works 155
Biblical Passages Relating Works to Justification 158
Faith and Good Works In The Reformed Standards 184
The Three Forms of Unity 194
The Canons of Dordt 197

6 The Federal Vision's Concept of the Church 199
The Federal Vision and the Objectivity of the Covenant 201
Steve Wilkins' View of the Objectivity of the Covenant 201
Steve Wilkins Views in the Knox Seminary Colloquium 205
Position of Auburn Avenue Presbyterian Church 218
Doug Wilson's View of the Objectivity of the Covenant 221
John Barach's View of the Objectivity of the Covenant 225
Steve Schlissel's View of the Objectivity of the Covenant . . .232
Shepherd's View of the Objectivity of the Covenant 241
Rich Lusk's View of the Objectivity of the Covenant 249
Analysis of the Federal Vision's Objective Covenant 258
The Relationship of the Invisible to the Visible 275
The Federal Vision Distortion of John 15: 1-11 279

7 Modern Day Judaizers 287
Rich Lusk 287
Steve Schlissel 300
Steve Schlissel's Denial of Total Depravity 307
Schlissel's Views In The Knox Seminary Colloquium 315
Schlissel's Views in the Christian Renewal Magazine 29 . . .317
Excerpts from Schlissel's Church's Website 320
Schlissel's Understanding of Justification/Sanctification 322
Doug Wilson on the Nature of Justification By Faith 331
Auburn Avenue's position on Justification 346

8 Baptismal Regeneration 349
The Necessity of Baptism 352
Norman Shepherd Teaches Baptismal Regeneration 355
Steve Wilkins Teaches Baptismal Regeneration 357

Doug Wilson Teaches Baptismal Regeneration 360
John Barach Teaches Baptismal Regeneration 360
Steve Schlissel Teaches Baptismal Regeneration 363
Rich Lusk Teaches Baptismal Regeneration 364

9   A Denial of the Perseverance of the Saints 387
Various Articles of the Canons of Dordt 2 389
The Reformed Standards on the Perseverance of the Saints .392
Wilkins' Session Deny the Perseverance of the Saints 397
Doug Wilson Denies the Perseverance of the Saints 401
John Barach Denies The Perseverance of the Saints 404
Rich Lusk Denies The Perseverance of the Saints 405
Scriptures refuting the Federal Vision's views 410

10 A Hybrid Form of Roman Catholicism 419

11 Greg Bahnsen is Not in the Federal Vision Camp 431

12 Conclusion 453
We Have a Responsibility 453
What Should be Done to Those in The Federal Vision? 455
The Responsibility of Local Sessions 455
The Responsibility of Presbyteries and General Assemblies .456

Appendix A 461
Presbytery Questions for ministerial candidates 461

Scripture Index 469

Subject Index 479

Bibliography 517

Triumphant Publications' Books

The Reformed Bookshelf

About the Author

Danger in the Camp

Introduction

Theological controversy has been one of the unfortunate facts about the history of the visible church of the Lord Jesus Christ down through the centuries. It is unfortunate because Christian unity is an important doctrine of Scripture. This unity was on the heart of our Lord Jesus Christ just prior to His arrest and crucifixion, constituting an integral part of His intercessory prayer (John 17:17-24). One of the promises that Jesus gave to His disciples was that when the Holy Spirit came, the Spirit would guide them into all the truth (John 16:13-15). In John 17:17, Jesus prayed to His Father that his disciples down through the ages would be sanctified in the truth, and immediately stated that God's Word was truth.

It is the Holy Spirit who enlightens men's minds and hearts to the truth of God's Word. Without the Spirit's guidance, we would know nothing of God's mysteries. We must constantly be praying for the Spirit's enlightening ministry in our lives. At the same time, we must be diligent students of the Word of God, for we are exhorted to present ourselves as competent workman who handle accurately the word of truth (II Timothy 2:15). Even though the Holy Spirit is not restricted to means, He, nonetheless, often uses means to accomplish His purposes. As we diligently strive to read and study with great fervency, the Spirit reveals to us His marvelous truths that were inspired by Him so many centuries ago.

I have often asked the question, "If the Holy Spirit resides in the lives of every genuine Christian, and the Spirit is the conveyer of truth to us, then why is it that there is so much theological difference of opinion in His church?" I believe the answer is several fold. First, we must admit that we are hampered by our sinful tendencies. Even though the Christian has been set free from the bondage of sin, which has liberated his heart and mind, he is still not perfect. The remaining vestiges of sin often clouds his thinking.

Second, in light of II Timothy 2:15, we must be diligent students of the Word. Wisdom and knowledge must be pursued with the same fervency as treasure hunters. Proverbs 2:3-6 states, *"For if you cry for discernment, Lift your voice for understanding; If you seek her as silver, And search for her as for hidden treasures; Then you will discern the fear of the Lord, And discover the knowledge of God. For the Lord gives wisdom; From His mouth come knowledge and understanding."*

Many people will not come to a true and full understanding of God's Word simply because they don't spend sufficient time in the Word. They don't pursue wisdom and knowledge with the same intensity, dedication, and perseverance as one who pursues precious earthly treasure. Consequently, they are prone to make theological errors more often than others.

A third reason why sincere men differ in their understanding of Scripture is because they make false assumptions that cause them to go astray in their understanding of various doctrines. It is possible to reason logically from false assumptions. This is a pitfall that must be carefully avoided because a person can think to his dying breath that his views are correct, that they make logical sense, when all along they were derived from false beliefs.

Fourth, Christians, being still sinners, can succumb to the sin of pride. I believe this reason to be a major factor in the continuance of theological differences. Those of us that take our theological pursuits with great seriousness don't want to be found mistaken. Our pride becomes our greatest hindrance in understanding truth. We think, "Surely, all this study that I have made, the books that I have written, the years that I have spent can't be to no avail." When our views are questioned by others, we become defensive, and when others are not always gracious and tactful in their challenge, then we have a tendency to be more resistant to their criticisms.

Pride is a very dangerous sin in the life of a minister or teacher of God's Word. It can cause him to remain steadfast in an error, thus leading him to lead his congregation or audience astray. Even though others try to show him the error of his thinking, he refuses to believe that he may be wrong. This pride becomes even more dangerous in the lives of those who have developed notoriety because of their speaking or writing accomplishments. It would take great humility for such a man to admit his error, especially when he has made his views public. It is the sinful pride that keeps a man from admitting his error.

A fifth reason why men differ in their understanding of Scripture is because some are still in spiritual darkness despite their profession of faith. These are the wolves in sheep's clothing. The frightening thing is that the wolves are not necessarily those who know they are wolves. They are deluded to think that they are distinguished sheep who can lead other sheep. The Pharisees were deluded men whom Jesus had to rebuke often. In Matthew 15:14, Jesus referred to the Pharisees as blind guides who cause not only themselves to fall into the pit but also those whom they are leading. In Matthew 7:22-23, Jesus even said that there would be men who had prophesied in His name, cast out demons in His name, and performed miracles in His name, but who would be eternally lost because He never knew them.

It is possible to be a very intelligent person, who understands the logic of Scripture, who has a conceptual understanding of the Bible, who can reason from certain premises logically and be quite convincing in one's arguments, but who is still in the darkness of sin. The history of the church is full of such sad examples of such gifted men.

In Galatians 1:8-9 Paul stated quite clearly that if man preached a gospel contrary to what he had preached, then this man was accursed of God. To be accursed of God means that a man is lost forever in Hell. This should be a very sobering thought to those who preach a "gospel." It had better be the right gospel.

A Brief History of the Controversy

Those who attend Reformed churches are more than likely aware to some degree of a raging controversy in the Reformed community. This controversy revolves around the teaching of a certain group of men. The particular views of these men have been termed Auburn Theology or the Federal Vision.

The average church member is probably unsure what to make of this controversy. They may be thinking, Why all the fuss? This is probably one of those issues that the theologians like to wrangle about but which has no practical value whatsoever for us." I can assure you that this is no minor theological issue. The fundamental issue is the gospel itself. The controversy goes to the very heart of the Christian faith – how is a man saved?

One purpose of this book is to enable church members to have a thorough but not an exhaustive understanding of the nature of the controversy. One could easily read thousands of pages of material. My goal is to narrow down the essence of the arguments so that the reader can understand the nature of the theological errors and then see them in contrast to the truth of Scripture.

Another purpose of the book is to be a clarion call to Reformed churches throughout the world to resist this aberrant theology. I view the Federal Vision as a theological poison that will do inestimable damage to the churches that tolerate or adopt it. Already, several people that have been influenced by the Federal Vision have left their Reformed churches and returned to Roman Catholicism. This is not to say that every person who adopts the Federal Vision will necessarily become Roman Catholic; however, there are striking similarities with Roman Catholicism. If people are confused as to how they are justified before the living God, then we have an immense problem on our hands.

I have a keen interest in this controversy, seeing that I was the moderator of Covenant Presbytery of the Reformed Presbyterian Church in the United States (RPCUS) in June of 2002. On June 22, 2002, the RPCUS passed a resolution at its annual presbytery meeting condemning the views that were propagated at the 2002 pastors' conference at Auburn Avenue Presbyterian Church in Monroe, Louisiana. The resolution that was passed was termed "*A Call to Repentance,*" whereby we stated that the teachings of Steve Wilkins, Steve Schlissel, Doug Wilson, and John Barach were antithetical to the historic Reformed faith as set forth in the Protestant Reformation of the 16th Century.

The resolutions called for these men to repent of their views, and if repentance did not occur, then we called upon their respective ecclesiastical courts to discipline them accordingly. First, we did not carry out a trial against these men because we did not have the church jurisdiction to do so. This is why we called upon their church courts to discipline them.

Initially, The RPCUS was accused of being schismatic in the Reformed community. We were accused of violating the Matthew 18 principle of handling differences with professing brothers.

With regard to the Matthew 18 principle, even several of the proponents of the Federal Vision admit that the Matthew 18 principle did not apply here simply because this was not a private issue. One such proponent, Doug Wilson has written:

> This is as good a place as any to make note of the fact that public controversy is not bound by the rules of confrontation laid out for us in Matthew 18. When Peter sinned at Antioch, Paul rebuked him publicly, face to face (Gal. 2:11), and he did this on the spot. It is not necessary to take someone aside

privately if they have just done something publicly. I do not know how many times I have been asked about this. Let's say I have written criticism of a recently published book – "Did you contact Tony Campolo privately before you wrote that book review?"[1]

The 2002 pastors' conference was a public forum and they disseminated their audio tapes throughout the country. Dr. Joseph Pipa, the president of Greenville Theological Seminary who was invited to the Knox Seminary colloquium, said the following in his article of refutation against Steve Wilkins' article in the colloquium:

> Here again is a place where proponents of the Federal Vision have erred. They ought to have circulated papers for theolog- ical discussion amongst ministers, elders, and theologians. They chose to preempt this procedure with public confer- ences that have greatly disturbed the church.[2]

This was the same perspective of Covenant presbytery of the RPCUS in 2002. We responded to their new paradigm that was publicly disseminated. We believed that their views were an audacious innovation into the Reformed community. Why didn't they ask for input from their fellow Reformed brothers before advancing their views? Instead, they dropped a theological bomb upon the Reformed world.

The RPCUS was accused of being hasty in its condemnation of the Monroe Four. The reason we did not have a public forum for debate with these men was because we did not see the need to do so. We fully understood their theology. The tapes of the 2002 Auburn conference had been circulated among the ministers of the RPCUS for study. Additionally, Covenant presbytery had the entire conference lectures fully transcribed so that its ministers could carefully analyze the theology of the lectures. We tried to put these transcripts on our denominational website so that the world could see for itself what these men were teaching. The Monroe Four greatly opposed this attempt, claiming that we were violating copyright laws. We received counsel from lawyers that we

---

[1] Douglas Wilson, *A Serrated Edge: A Brief Defense of Biblical Satire and Trinitarian Skylarking.* (Moscow, Idaho: Canon Press, 2003), p. 64.

[2] Joseph Pipa, "A Response to 'Covenant, Baptism, and Salvation'", *Q*uoted in the Knox Theological Seminary Colloquium on the Federal Vision, August 11-13, 2003, published by Knox Theological Seminary, p 291.

were more than likely within legal bounds; however, rather than get into a squabble about copyrights, the presbytery decided to withdraw posting the transcripts. We did this graciously, but we wondered why the objection? Why not let the world see in print what they are teaching? If there is nothing wrong with it, what are they trying to hide? I find it interesting that since that time, the Monroe Four have agreed to put their teaching in print via their own website, the interview with the Christian Renewal magazine, the Knox Seminary colloquium, and other books.

Moreover, the discussion on the Federal Vision Theology at the June 2002 meeting of Covenant presbytery was augmented by virtue of a problem case in one of our mission works in Tennessee. A young man in that mission work had been persuaded by the theology of the 2002 pastors' conference and began challenging the views of our evangelist for that work. The evangelist brought the case before us for counsel. Interestingly, the young man eventually left the mission work, joining a church of another Reformed denomination, but he then shortly left that church, embracing Roman Catholicism as the logical extension of believing in Federal Vision Theology.

Covenant presbytery of the RPCUS saw the teaching of these men as extremely dangerous. Something had to be done to stop the spread of this theological cancer. This gave rise to our approving the resolutions. These resolutions were not rash. Our individual ministers had already spent months reviewing the tapes.

The problem facing the Reformed churches right now is that the proponents of the Federal Vision want us to accept their teaching as being an acceptable interpretation of the Reformed Standards and as an acceptable alternative understanding to many of the Scriptural texts pertaining to the doctrines in question.

Prominent Proponents Of Federal Vision Theology

Some of the figures who have promoted Federal Vision Theology are: Norman Shepherd, Steve Wilkins, Steve Schlissel, John Barach, Douglas Wilson, Peter Leithart, James B. Jordan, and Rich Lusk. This is not an exhaustive list, but these persons have either spoken at conferences where this theological perspective is advocated, or they have written books or articles defending this perspective.

The Betrayal

Most of these men subscribe to the historic Reformed Standards to some degree. To this day, they all believe that their views are still within the parameters of the Reformed faith. Seeing that they all believe this to be true, I will seek to demonstrate that they all have been guilty of betraying the Confessions and Catechism of the Reformed faith. More importantly, they have betrayed the sacred doctrines of Scripture and constitute a very serious threat to our churches. Their new paradigm constitutes a betrayal of the Gospel. It is a plague that must be eradicated.

Most, if not all of these men, took vows to uphold the teaching of the Reformed Standards that have served as the constitution of their churches. They vowed that if at any time that they found themselves out of accord with the doctrine of these Standards that they would voluntarily make known to their respective ecclesiastical courts their change in beliefs. Having read their articles and the transcripts of some of their public lectures, these men remain adamant that their views are still within the parameters of the Reformed faith. Therefore, they are not going to voluntarily admit that they have transgressed the Standards or the Scriptures. They have admitted that they are purporting a new paradigm, but this paradigm shift is not Reformed teaching. This belief that their teaching is consistent with the Reformed Standards only demonstrates the depth of their delusion. To adopt their radical views, trying to make them conform to the Scripture and the Reformed Standards demands that one severely distort the meaning of the Scripture and the intent of the Confessional Standards. It should become apparent to any serious student of the Confessional Standards that these views are wholly incompatible.

Present Status

As of the writing of this book, three years have elapsed since the 2002 resolutions of Covenant Presbytery of the RPCUS warned the Reformed world of these erroneous beliefs. During this period of time, the proponents of the Federal Vision have not only remained regimented in their views despite opposition from other sectors in the Reformed world, but they have become even more bold and aggressive. They continue to sponsor annual conferences purporting their views, they continue to write articles and books defending these views, and they continue to deny more fundamental truths of the Reformed Faith and of orthodox Christianity.

One of the most significant theological errors that has developed in their thinking over the past three years is the outright denial of the active obedience of Christ in our justification. Not only have they denied justification by Christ through faith alone, but they have now explicitly denied this vital aspect of orthodox Christianity.

The most disheartening thing is that these men still insist that their teaching is not only orthodox but Reformed. They keep claiming that they are being misunderstood. Other people from various denominations have met personally with them, challenging them about their views, but the Auburn proponents remain adamant. Nothing has changed in three years. The Auburn proponents still think that they are correct and misunderstood. This only goes to show the seriousness of their doctrinal errors. They cannot be reasoned with the Scriptures any longer.

Other Denominations Agree With the RPCUS Analysis

Over the past three years, other denominations and institutions have conducted their own studies and have come to virtually the same conclusions that the RPCUS came to in June 2002.

In the summer of 2002 Greenville Theological Seminary devoted their entire issue of the *Katekomen* to the subject of justification. Parts of the issue dealt with N. T. Wright and Norman Shepherd. In January 2003, Joseph Pipa, the president of Greenville Theological Seminary and Dr. Morton Smith, one of the founders of Greenville Seminary were invited to speak at the 2003 Auburn Avenue Pastors' Conference in Monroe, Louisiana in order to express their objections to what had been presented the year before. These men saw for themselves that the four Monroe speakers (Wilkins, Schlissel, Wilson, and Barach) were convinced of their new paradigm.

On August 11, 2003, Knox Theological Seminary in Fort Lauderdale, Florida sponsored its colloquium on the Federal Vision. This was one of the first public forums of its kind on this issue. There were fourteen participants, seven representatives of the Federal Vision and seven who represented mainline Reformed thought. Each person presented papers, and the other side had opportunity to respond. Those representing the Federal Vision perspective were: John Barach, Peter Leithart, Rich Lusk, Steve Schlissel, Tom Trouwborst, Steve Wilkins, and Douglas Wilson. Those on the other side were Calvin Beisner, Christopher Hutchinson, George Knight III, Richard Phillips, Joseph Pipa, Carl Robbins, R. Fowler White, and Morton Smith.

This colloquium was most illuminating because it revealed that the analysis of the RPCUS a year earlier was not a rash action. The colloquium demonstrated that the proponents were well entrenched in their doctrine; in fact, it was in one of the Federal Vision papers that it was becoming evident that the active obedience of Christ for our justification was being denied.

In August of 2003 Norman Shepherd gave two lectures at a conference entitled "Contemporary Perspectives on Covenant Theology" sponsored by the Southern California Center for Christian Studies. In these two lectures, Norman Shepherd explicitly denied the active obedience of Christ for justification and further explained his understanding of justification by faith. It became evident that Shepherd was demonstrating his further slide from a historical, biblical understanding of the Reformed Faith.

The August-September 2003 issue of *The Banner Of Truth* was dedicated to the subject of justification and was published to expose the departure of some in the Reformed community on the vital subject of justification by faith alone.

On May 10-13, 2004, a special committee of the Reformed Church in the United States (the RCUS) was appointed to study justification in light of the current justification controversy and presented its finding to the 258th Synod of the RCUS. This study focuses on Norman Shepherd's views of justification.

The committee's Resolution 2 states:

> **That we find that Rev. Norman Shepherd for many years has taught a confused doctrine of justification, contrary to the Heidelberg Catechism, The Belgic Confession and the Canons of Dordt.[3]**

> **The committee's Resolution 3 reads: Therefore, we also resolve that the teachings of Norman Shepherd on justification by faith are another gospel, and we admonish Reverend Shepherd and call on him to repent of his grievous errors.[4]**

> **The committee's Resolution 4 reads: That the Reformed Church in the United States recognize these Romish,**

---

[3] Report Of The Special Committee To Study Justification In Light Of The Current Justification Controversy. Presented to the 258th Synod of the Reformed Church in the United States (May 10-13, 2004), p. 43.

[4] Report Of The Special Committee To Study Justification. p. 45

Arminian, and Socinian errors for what they are and urge our brethren throughout the world to reject them and to refuse those who teach them.[5]

The committee's report was adopted by the synod. This was a bold proclamation of the RCUS and as one can see, its denunciation of Federal Vision Theology is quite pointed. The RCUS became the second American Reformed denomination to condemn the teachings of the Federal Vision.

The latest Presbyterian body to study the teachings of the Federal Vision was Mississippi Valley Presbytery of the Presbyterian Church In America (the PCA). On February 1, 2005 this presbytery unanimously adopted its study committee's report on this controversy. With regards to the various doctrines of the Federal Vision, the committee stated, "*All of these and more, we find to be out of the bounds of acceptable diversity in this presbytery and in the PCA. As such they should not be taught or countenanced as part of the public teaching of the church...No greater tragedy could befall the PCA today than to compromise the lucidity of her preaching of the glorious Gospel of grace, yet that is, we fear, precisely what we are facing. To that end, we here pledge again our commitment to the faith once delivered. By God's grace, it is our prayer that we would not preach a different Gospel, which is really not another and contrary to that which we have received, but rather that we would boldly proclaim that one true Gospel that is the power of God unto salvation to everyone who believes.*"[6]

In the ad hoc study committee's report of Mississippi Valley presbytery the committee noted that in the PCA, two presbyteries had refused to transfer PCA ministers sympathetic to the Federal Vision into their presbyteries. They noted that Evangel Presbytery's credentials committee of the PCA rejected for transfer into their bounds a PCA minister in good standing who embraced the Federal Vision. They found his views to be outside the pale of acceptable doctrinal diversity. The report noted that Central Carolina Presbytery of the PCA had sent communications asking for Louisiana Presbytery to conduct a thorough investigation of the Federal Vision within its own bounds.[7]

On May 11, 2005, Mississippi Valley Presbytery of the PCA sent overture 14 to the General Assembly of the PCA to send its report to the clerks of the PCA

---

[5] Report Of The Special Committee To Study Justification.

[6] Ad Hoc Committee Report: "The New Perspective on Paul", of Mississippi Valley Presbytery (PCA), February 1, 2005, pp. 4,5.

[7] Ad hoc Committee Report, p. 1.

presbyteries and make it available via various media, as a useful study aid in the ongoing discussion relating to the "New Perspectives on Paul," the theology of N.T. Wright, the theology of Norman Shepherd, and the theology of the so-called "Federal Vision" in the PCA.[8]

Observations

I trust that those who do know the Standards and the Scripture will come to realize that Federal Vision Theology can never be seen as a viable way to interpret the Scriptures. In fact, I will demonstrate that it is a twisting of the Scripture.

I still find it difficult to understand how these men could have departed so quickly from a truly Reformed and Orthodox position. To openly deny the imputation of Christ's active obedience to the believer as part of the basis for justification, to advocate baptismal regeneration, to alter the meaning of saving faith to mean faithful obedience to covenant stipulations, to advocate that a genuine Christian can lose his salvation are no minor deviations. It is the abandoning of the Faith once delivered to the saints.

These men have clearly demonstrated over the past three years an unteachable spirit. As Dr. Joseph Pipa of Greenville Theological Seminary stated, these men interjected their beliefs into the Reformed community without first consulting their Reformed brothers. They had to know that their views were not in the mainstream of Reformed thinking, yet they boldly proceeded to teach them.

They should not have been surprised that their Reformed brothers would call them "on the carpet" for this teaching. In fact, one of the speakers at the 2002 Auburn Avenue Pastors' Conference stated in his lecture that he had nearly been run out of town in Canada for saying the same things that he was lecturing on.

Throughout the controversy, the proponents of the Federal Vision have said they have wanted open dialogue with others on their views, but when those agreed to do so, there was no change in their views. People have gone to them in person, committee representatives have met them in person, and yet there is no change. These men remain steadfast in their views. After meeting with the proponents of the Federal Vision, some Reformed brothers and presbytery

---

[8] Overture 14 to the General Assembly of the PCA from Mississippi Valley Presbytery, May 11, 2005.

committees have informed them that their views are not Reformed and orthodox in several areas. What is the response of the Federal Vision? They retort back that they are misunderstood and unjustly maligned.

Probably the most discouraging thing is that these men are insistent that they are right despite having been reproved by brethren from various sectors in the Reformed community. Many in the Reformed community have exhorted, reproved, and called for their repentance. Denominations have called them to repent, but they stubbornly refuse. They are placing themselves as those who are right. They insist that the Reformed creeds are not necessarily the best expressions of biblical thought. They push for a new paradigm. They directly challenge Luther; they place themselves in opposition to great Reformed thinkers of the past 500 years. Everyone else is wrong, but they are right.

Proverbs 11:14-15 states: *"Where there is no guidance, the people fall, But in abundance of counselors there is victory."* Those in the Federal Vision camp have refused the counsel of their brothers.

Proverbs 15: 31-33 states: *"He whose ear listens to the life-giving reproof will dwell among the wise. He who neglects discipline despises himself, But he who listens to reproof acquires understanding. The fear of the Lord is the instruction for wisdom, And before honor comes humility."*

James 4:6 states, *"...God is opposed to the proud, but gives grace to the humble."*

The proponents of the Federal Vision for the past three years have stubbornly resisted the admonitions of their Reformed brethren. They have now demonstrated obstinacy to the truth. It is the duty of the church of the Lord Jesus Christ to rise up and defend the honor of Christ and protect the purity of the church from these wolves in sheep's clothing.

The ecclesiastical courts that have jurisdiction over these men must have the courage and moral fortitude to do what God demands. They must be tried and expelled from the ministry. Unless action is taken to eradicate these teachings from the church more and more spiritual damage will be done.

Chapter 1

What Is A Heresy?

It is imperative that I discuss the meaning and nature of "heresy." After all, I have subtitled my book: "An Analysis and Refutation of the Heresies of the Federal Vision." I am fully aware of the stigma that is often attached to this word "heresy," and I am also fully aware of the abuse of this idea throughout church history. Moreover, I have spent much time in thought over the controversy that has arisen in the Reformed community. I did not rashly choose to call the Federal Vision a heresy. I am quite aware of the gravity of referring to men as heretics. My decision to refer to the teaching of the Federal Vision as a heresy has come after considerable time of study over the past several years. I have not made this decision in isolation. I am not the only one who has declared Federal Vision dogma as heretical. It is a very sobering thing to declare various ministers of churches as heretics. However, in light of the meaning of "heresy," and in light of the doctrines that the Federal Vision propagates, I believe it is fully justified to view the Federal Vision as a heresy of the church, which must be eradicated from our churches in the Reformed world.

We are fully aware of the horrendous things that have been perpetrated in the name of the defense of the church down through the centuries. The Spanish Inquisition of the Roman Catholic Church and the assault upon the Scottish Covenanters are grim reminders that zeal in the name of the church can often be misguided. The Roman Catholic Church declared Protestantism a heresy. Rome's Council of Trent anathematized the blessed truths of justification by faith alone in Christ. Not everyone who is called and treated as a heretic is truly a heretic. This is why we must tread with great care before we declare men heretics. Nonetheless, the term "heresy" or "heretic" is a biblical word. The Bible does portray certain teachings as heresy, and it gives us the guidelines for making such a declaration.

There are those in the church today who shy away from declaring anyone a heretic. Unity in the church is one of the most important doctrines in Scripture, but unity must never be sought at the expense of truth. To fail to defend the Faith which was once and for all delivered to the saints is a serious sin. Unless we defend truth, all can be lost. The attitude that shuns theological debate for fear of upsetting people is not an admirable trait. In fact, if taken to an extreme, it is a betrayal of allegiance to the Lord Jesus Christ. Jesus did not shy away from saying hard things to those who corrupted the Word of God, to those who substituted their man made traditions for the Word of God (Matthew 15:1-9; 23: 13-39). For the Lord to call men white washed tombs and blind guides who lead themselves and others into destruction, is quite intense. For the apostle Paul to refer to the Judaizers as "dogs" and "evil workers" (Philippians 3:2) who are accursed of God (Galatians 1: 8), and to refer to the Galatians as "foolish" for having succumbed to the "bewitching" teachings of the Judaizers is also quite intense. In the cause of truth and in fidelity to the Lord Jesus Christ, we must be willing to declare some men to be heretics if they truly deserve it.

What is heresy? The English word "heresy" is derived from the Greek word "*hairesis*," and the English word "heretic" is derived from the Greek word "*hairetikos*." "*Hairesis*" is used four times in the New Testament (Acts 24:14; I Corinthians 11:19; Galatians 5:20; 2 Peter 2:1). "*Hairetikos*" is used once in the New Testament (Titus 3:10). I will obviously discuss these usages and their implications, but there are other passages that must be considered. For example, Galatians 1:6-9 is absolutely vital. Though the word "heresy" is not used specifically, the inference is definitely there because Paul calls the Judaizers anathematized or accursed of God. When Paul tells the Ephesians elders in Acts 20:29-31 that there would come in among themselves wolves in sheep's clothing who would not spare the flock, he is definitely inferring that these were heretics. The admonition to confront those bringing false doctrine is an inference to heretics.

Both "*hairesis*" and "*hairetikos*" have their derivation in the root word "*haireomai*" which means "to take for oneself, prefer, or choose." Let's take a look at all of the passages where the word "heresy" or "heretic" is used. Acts 24:14 states:

> But this I admit to you, that according to the Way which they call a **sect** I do serve the God of our fathers, believing every-thing that is in accordance with the Law, and that is written in the Prophets.

The word "sect" in the New American Standard Bible is the Greek word *"hairesis."* The King James Version translates the word as "heresy," which I believe to be a better rendition of the Greek word. The point here is that Paul states that Christianity in its early days was viewed as a faction of the Jewish faith. In other words the Jews saw Christians as heretics. We could say that Paul once believed this himself, which is why he zealously persecuted the Christians. He believed he was being a faithful Pharisee to rid the community of these factious Christians. This goes to show that one can be zealously mistaken just like Paul. The Christians were viewed as heretics when obviously they were not heretics from God's perspective.

When Paul was admonishing the Corinthians, he says in I Corinthians 11:18-19:

> For, in the first place, when you come together as a church, I hear
> that divisions exist among you; and in part, I believe it. For there
> must also be **factions** among you, in order that those who are
> approved may have become evident among you.

The word translated as "factions" in the New American Standard is the word *"hairesis."* The King James Version, again, does a better job of translating it as "heresies." The reason that the New American Standard translators used the word "factions" is probably because that is what the context conveys. In verse 18 Paul says that divisions existed among them.

We read in Galatians 5: 19- 20:

> Now the deeds of the flesh are evident, which are: immorality,
> impurity, sensuality, idolatry, sorcery, enmities, strife, jealousy,
> outbursts of anger, disputes, dissensions, **factions.**

The King James version translates the word "factions" as "heresies." Thus far, whether justified or not, the term "heresy" conveys "divisiveness or schism." When one studies the history of heresies over the centuries, one very obvious fact is seen: Heresies bring division and unrest to the unity of the Church. Professing Christians become confused and begin to take sides with one or the other. This tells us who inspires heresies doesn't it? Satan is the master deceiver who loves nothing more than to bring unrest to the church of the Lord Jesus Christ. Our arch-enemy relishes heresies. Satan wants to impede the onslaught of the church against the "gates of Hell." The Scripture promises victory ultimately to the church of Jesus. The enemies of Christ will "lick the dust" as the Old Testament puts it. In Matthew 16:18, Jesus promised that the "gates of Hell" could not resist the church's onslaught. In 2 Corinthians 10:3-5 we are told that the church possesses divinely powerful weapons to destroy the fortresses of Satan and bring all thoughts captive to the obedience of Christ. Satan is known as the great "deceiver" and "Abaddon, the destroyer." As the deceiver and destroyer, Satan will seek to manifest himself through his agents (false apostles) who disguise themselves as angels of light (2 Corinthians 11: 13, 14). Satan's objective? To bring men to destruction in the fires of Hell forever. If Satan can convince men of a lie as to how to be saved other than the way that God has prescribed, then he has achieved his devious plans. When heresies arise in the church, there will always be disunity. Heretics are troublemakers in Israel!

In 2 Peter 2:1- 2 we read:

> But false prophets also arose among the people, just as there will also be false teachers among you, who will secretly introduce destructive **heresies**, even denying the Master who bought them, bringing swift destruction upon themselves. And many will follow their sensuality, and because of them the way of the truth will be maligned.

In this passage the word "heresies" is translated the same in both the New American Standard and the King James Version. This is not an easy text to deal with because the Arminians historically have used this passage to support their belief that one can lose his salvation because it says that these false teachers who come with their heresies deny the Master who bought them and end up in destruction. Without going into a prolonged exegesis of this passage, it is noteworthy that the word for "Master" is the Greek word "*Despotes*." Arminianism and the Federal Vision both believe that "Master" is a reference to Jesus as redeemer. There is no exegetical support for this. The best interpretations view that "Master" refers to God as creator and the phrase "who bought them" pertains to the fact that all men are creatures of God and owe obligation to their creator. Another point to be made about this text is that even though this text says that these false teachers were "sensual" men, this should not be taken as something that is indicative of all "heretics."

Let's now turn our attention to the one usage of the word "hairetikos." It is only found in Titus 3:9-11:

> But shun foolish controversies and genealogies and strife and disputes about the Law; for they are unprofitable and worthless. Reject a **factious** man after a first and second warning, knowing that such a man is perverted and is sinning, being self-condemned.

The King James Version calls this man a "heretic" which is close to the Greek pronunciation. Again, we see that schism is at the heart of the heretic. The heretic in this context is one who relishes in theological speculation (v. 9). The result? Division occurs, and the Scripture gives an analysis of the heretic – he is perverted; he is sinning; and he is self-condemned (v. 11). One could say that a heretic is one who uses controversy to create a division in the Church.

This concludes an examination of all of the direct usages of the idea of heresy; however, as noted earlier, there are indirect references to heresy in other passages. We read in I Timothy 1: 3-7:

> As I urged you upon my departure for Macedonia, remain on at Ephesus, in order that you may instruct certain men not to teach strange doctrines, nor to pay attention to myths and endless genealogies, which give rise to mere speculation rather than furthering the administration of God which is by faith. But the goal of our instruction is love from a pure heart and a good conscience and a sincere faith. For some men, straying form these things, have turned aside to fruitless discussion, wanting to be teachers of the Law, even though they do not understand either what they are saying or the matters about which they make confident assertions.

These men teach strange doctrines, and what is strange about them? It does not correspond to that which the apostles have taught. I am reminded of what Calvin said to his short term pupil, Socinus, who would later deny essential elements of Christ's atonement and to whom Unitarianism has been traced. The church historian, Philip Schaff, comments that between 1548-49, Socinus came to Geneva seeking instruction from Calvin. Some of the questions he had pertained to whether it was lawful for Protestants to marry Roman Catholics; whether popish baptism was efficacious; and how the doctrine of the resurrection of the body could be explained. On July 25, 1549 Socinus wrote Calvin that he was troubled very much about the resurrection. In December of 1549 Calvin sent a letter to Socinus warning him against the dangers of his skeptical bent of mind. Then in 1554 Socinus presented to Calvin his objections to the doctrine of the vicarious atonement of Christ. Calvin replied at length, but to no avail of persuading Socinus. Later Socinus would depart from the biblical understanding of the sacraments and the Trinity, questioning the personality of the Holy Spirit and then the eternal divinity of Christ.[1] Where did the downhill slide begin with the young Socinus? It began with his questioning of

---

[1] Philip Schaff, *History of the Christian Church* (Grand Rapids, MI: Wm. B. Eerdmans Publishing Co., 1974) Vol 8, pp. 634- 636.

biblical truths. I Timothy 1:3-7 demonstrates also that these false teachers (heretics) want to be teachers of the Law, and they are given to "confident assertions" about their teaching that is not biblically consistent.

One of the most profound passages on the nature of false doctrine that can be seen as heresy is found in Galatians 1:6-9:

> I am amazed that you are so quickly deserting Him who called you by the grace of Christ, for a **different gospel**; which is really not another; only there are some who are disturbing you, and want to distort the gospel of Christ. But even though we, or an angel from heaven, should preach to you **a gospel contrary to that which we have preached to you, let him be accursed.** As we have said before, so I say again now, if any man is preaching to you **a gospel contrary to that which you received, let him be accursed**. (Emphasis mine)

John Calvin in his commentary on Galatians 1:6-9 has some very instructive comments about this passage:

> He commences by administering a rebuke, though a somewhat milder one than they deserved; but his greatest severity of language is directed, as we shall see, against the false apostles. He charges them with turning aside, not only from his gospel, but from Christ; for it was impossible for them to retain their attachment to Christ, without acknowledging that he has graciously delivered us from the bondage of the law.
>
> Thus, in our own times, the Papists, choosing to have a divided and mangled Christ, have none, and are therefore "removed from Christ." They are full of superstitions, which are directly at variance with the nature of Christ. Let it be carefully observed, that we are removed from Christ, when we fall into those views which are inconsistent with his mediatorial office; for light can have no fellowship with darkness.
>
> On the same principle, he calls it **another gospel**, that is, a gospel different from the true one. And yet the false apostles professed that they preached the gospel of Christ; but, mingling with it their own inventions, by which its principal efficacy was destroyed, they held a false, corrupt, and spurious gospel.[2] (Emphasis Calvin)

---

[2] John Calvin, *Calvin's New Testament Commentaries, Commentary on Galatians.* Translated by T.H. L. Parker (Grand Rapids, Michigan: Eerdman's Publishing Co., 1965), p. 13.

From Christ, who called you by grace … To revolt from the Son of God under any circumstances, is unworthy and disgraceful; but to revolt from him, after being invited to partake salvation by grace, is more eminently base. His goodness to us renders our ingratitude to him more dreadfully heinous … Which is not another thing … for he speaks contemptuously of the doctrine of the false apostles, as being nothing else than a mass of confusion and destruction…He declares that it is not a gospel, but a mere disturbance.[3]

He charges them with the additional crime of doing an injury to Christ, by endeavoring to subvert his gospel. Subversion is an enormous crime. It is worse than corruption. And with good reason does he fasten on them this charge. When the glow of justification is ascribed to another, and a snare is laid for the consciences of men, the Savior no longer occupies his place, and the doctrine of the gospel is utterly ruined.

To know what are the leading points of the gospel, is a matter of unceasing importance. When these are attacked, the gospel is destroyed. When he adds the words, of Christ, this may be explained in two ways; either that it has come from Christ as its author, or that it purely exhibits Christ. The apostle's reason for employing that expression unquestionably was to describe the true and genuine gospel, which alone is worthy of the name.

Of what avail was it to profess respect for the gospel, and not to know what it meant? With Papists, who hold themselves bound to render implicit faith, that might be perfectly sufficient; but with Christians, where there is no knowledge, there is no faith. That the Galatians, who were otherwise disposed to obey the gospel, might not wander hither and thither, and "find no rest for the sole of their foot," (Genesis 8:9) Paul enjoins them to stand steadfastly by his doctrine. He demands such unhesitating belief of his preaching, that he pronounces a curse on all who dared to contradict it.[4]

---

[3] *Calvin's New Testament Commentaries, Commentary on Galatians*, p. 14.

[4] *Calvin's New Testament Commentaries, Commentary on Galatians*, pp. 14, 15.

When he says, "let him be accursed," the meaning must be, "let him be held by you as accursed." In expounding 1 Corinthians 12:3, we had occasion to speak of the word "*anathema*." Here it denotes cursing, and answers to the Hebrew word, "*herem*."[5]

What, then, must be the consequence, if ignorance of the nature and character of the gospel shall lead to hesitation? Accordingly he enjoins them to regard as devils those who shall dare to bring forward a gospel different from his, — meaning by **another gospel**, one to which the inventions of other men are added; for the doctrine of the false apostles was not entirely contrary, or even different, from that of Paul, but corrupted by false additions.[6] (Emphasis Calvin)

The reason that I have quoted Calvin extensively on this passage is because of its enormous ramifications for this book. Paul sees an attack on the doctrine of justification by faith alone in Christ as being another gospel. The Judaizers had come in and sought to undermine Paul's apostleship and teach that the Galatians had to submit to all the laws of Moses in order to be justified. As Paul writes in Galatians 5:4, if they buy into this false doctrine of the Judaizers, then they have been severed from Christ and fallen from grace, meaning that if one makes justification contingent upon works, then salvation is not of grace but of works. **We can assuredly affirm that maintaining justification by faith alone is a fundamental doctrine. Any doctrine that denies this is truly a heresy, making the teaching and teacher accursed of God.**

We now turn our attention to I John 2: 18–24:

Children, it is the last hour; and just as you heard that antichrist is coming, even now many antichrists have arisen; from this we know that it is the last hour. They went out from us, but they were not really of us; for if they had been of us, they would have remained with us; but they went out, in order that it might be shown that they all are not of us. But you have an anointing from the Holy One, and you all know. I have not written to you because you do not know the truth, but because you do know it, and because no lie is of the truth. Who is the liar but the one who denies that Jesus is the

---

[5] *Calvin's New Testament Commentaries, Commentary on Galatians,* p. 15.

[6] *Calvin's New Testament Commentaries, Commentary on Galatians,* p. 16.

Christ? This is the antichrist, the one who denies the Father and the Son. Whoever denies the Son does not have the Father; the one who confesses the Son has the Father also. As for you, let that abide in you which you heard from the beginning. If what you heard from the beginning abides in you, you also will abide in the Son and in the Father.

We learn from this passage that there are many antichrists. Antichrist is anyone who denies the true nature of the Father and the Son. This would entail any deviation regarding the Trinity, that all persons of the Trinity are co-equal in power and glory. It would declare anyone who does not believe in the Trinity as an antichrist – a heretic. Anyone not believing the deity of the Son of God in its fullest sense is antichrist – a heretic. Anyone who mishandles the work of the Son who is the Redeemer is antichrist – a heretic. To deny that Jesus is the only way of salvation between sinners and God is antichrist – a heretic. Anyone who denies the imputation of Christ's righteousness to sinners as that which is necessary to inherit eternal life is antichrist – a heretic. The belief that man is basically good and can keep the law for justification is antichrist – a heretic.

Although one could argue that not all false doctrine is necessarily identical to heresy. Technically, any doctrine that is not reflective of the truth is a false doctrine. Not all false or erroneous doctrines strike at the fundamental understanding of God and His redemptive work. Marcion of the 2nd Century A.D. taught that the God of the Old Testament was a God of hate, but then the God of the New Testament was a God of love. The heresy of Arianism was condemned at the Council of Nicea in 325 A.D.; Arius' teaching challenged the very nature God. Arius did not believe that the Son of God was co-equal in essence or glory with the Father. He saw the Son of God as the first born of God, that there was a time that the Son of God was non-existent. Our modern day Arians would be Jehovah's Witnesses and Mormons to name a few. Pelagius did theological battle with Augustine in the 5th Century. Pelagius denied the biblical doctrine of original sin. He taught that every man was born in the same state that Adam was created that is without sin. Pelagius believed that man could choose to obey God's commandments and be sinless. Socinus during the time of Calvin came to challenge the nature of the atonement. When we commonly think of heresies in church history, we think of those doctrines that challenged the nature of the Trinity, the fundamental nature of man, and the atoning work of Christ. Differences in understanding the nature of the mode of baptism (sprinkling/pouring vs. immersion), the nature of church government (Congregationalist vs. Presbyterian) would not be viewed as heresies because the nature of God and the gospel are not jeopardized. Heresy then would be a challenge to the direct witness of the Scriptures pertaining to God's being, Christ's person, the nature of man, and the plan of salvation.

Who Decides Who Is A Heretic?

First and foremost the **Scripture** decides who is a heretic. The Bible is inerrant and the only infallible interpreter of its own doctrines. Yes, it is men or the church who make declarative statements as to who are heretics, but this is in conformity with the teaching of the Word of God. Because men choose not to believe one denomination's teaching does not necessarily make one a heretic. The fact that men are fallible and can err as did Roman Catholicism in its declaration of Martin Luther as a heretic, does not detract from the responsibility of the elders of Christ's church to guard the doctrines of Scripture with great tenacity. Paul wrote to young Timothy in I Timothy 6:3-5:

> If anyone advocates a different doctrine, and does not agree with sound words, those of our Lord Jesus Christ, and with the doctrine conforming to godliness, he is conceited and understands nothing; but he has a morbid interest in controversial questions and disputes about words, out of which arise envy, strife, abusive language, evil suspicions, and constant friction between men of depraved mind and deprived of the truth, who suppose that godliness is a means of gain.

Paul further encourages young Timothy in 2 Timothy 3:14-17:

> You, however, continue in the things you have learned and become convinced of, knowing from whom you have learned them; and that from childhood you have known the sacred writings which are able to give you the wisdom that leads to salvation through faith which is in Christ Jesus. All Scripture is inspired by God and profitable for teaching, for reproof, for correction, for training in righteousness; that the man of God may be adequate, equipped for every good work.

Earlier in his second epistle to Timothy Paul had exhorted Timothy with the words of 2 Timothy 2:15:

> Be diligent to present yourself approved to God as a workman who does not need to be ashamed, handling accurately the word of truth.

A conscious, wholehearted commitment to the Bible is that which is necessary to discern truth from error.

From a human standpoint the **Church at large is a determiner of that which constitutes heresy, subordinate to the Scripture.** This is the importance of church councils. The early councils of the Christian church made definitive statements as to what the Scripture taught as orthodox doctrine. Not that human councils are infallible, but the Scripture does say that in the multitude of many counselors there is safety. After all, Jesus recognized the fallibility of men, but this did not stop Him from entrusting to elders of His visible church the keys of the kingdom to open and shut the doors to the kingdom (Matthew 16:19; 18:15-20). The Westminster Confession of Faith was one such gathering of elders of the church to set forth biblical truth. For our understanding of the role of such councils, Chapter 31 Sections 3 and 4 of the Westminster Confession has some instructive comments:

> It belongs to synods and councils, ministerially to determine controversies of faith and cases of conscience; to set down rules and directions for the better ordering of the public worship of God, and government of his Church; to receive complaints in cases of maladministration, and authoritatively to determine the same: which decrees and determinations, if consonant to the Word of God, are to be received with reverence and submission; not only for their agreement with the Word, but also for the power whereby they are made, as being an ordinance of God appointed thereunto in His Word.

> All synods or councils, since the Apostles' times, whether general or particular, may err; and many have erred. Therefore they are not to be made the rule of faith or practice; but to be used as a help in both.

The Scripture set the pattern for church councils in Acts 15. When Paul found himself entangled with the Judaizers in the church of Antioch of Syria, the theological debate was ecclesiastically settled in Jerusalem. We read in Acts 15:1-2:

> And some men came down from Judea and began teaching the brethren, "Unless you are circumcised according to the custom of Moses, you cannot be saved." And when Paul and Barnabas **had great dissension and debate with them,** the brethren determined that Paul and Barnabas and certain

others of them should go up to Jerusalem to the apostles and
elders concerning the issue. (Emphasis mine)

In the rest of Acts 15 we see that the Council of Jerusalem determined the issue
and sent a decree to the churches at large instructing what they should do. As
one examines the decision of the Council of Jerusalem, one notices that
decisions were made in conformity with the Scripture. Scriptural
understanding led to the decision of the Council. The apostle James quotes
from Amos 9 (Acts 15:13-16).

When ecclesiastical bodies convene and pass judgments on certain doctrines,
it should be taken very seriously. When godly men meet in the name of the
Lord Jesus as a court of the church and inquire of the Lord using the Scripture
to settle theological issues, this is no minor thing. When a court of the church
makes a judgment with reference to the theological aberrations of certain men,
those to whom it is directed should take this very seriously. To slough it off as
the mere opinions of men is not a godly, humble attitude. One should ask himself a sobering question, "Is there something that I have failed to see properly
that an ecclesiastical body, especially one of a sister denomination, should react
so strongly?" To ignore creeds and confessions is the height of theological arro-
gance.

Indicating Marks of a Heretic

1.   Their teaching runs counter to Scripture as delineated in the historic
creeds and confessions of the church, challenging doctrines regarding the
nature of God, the nature of man, and the redemptive work of Christ.

2.   They believe that they have a new teaching that the church of the past
centuries has missed.

3.   They operate with deception; often reinterpreting words with different
meanings. They appear as wolves in sheep's clothing (Acts 20: 29-31).

4.   Their teaching creates confusion and schism in the visible church.

5.   They attempt to not appear divisive, and they often seek to make their
opponents appear divisive or judgmental.

6.   They are often proud, seeking to make names for themselves (2 Peter
2:13, 18-19), and they stubbornly spurn the reproofs of the church courts.

In making the previous comments, it needs to be fully understood that the
underlying assumption is that the teaching of certain men is indeed in error and

that the reproofs given are in conformity with the Scripture alone and not the traditions of men.

The Necessity for Doctrinal Defense

It is very unfortunate that we live in an age that generally disdains the notion of doctrine. There are many Christians who are being taught that there is a separation between doctrine and practical Christianity. People say, "I don't like doctrine that much; I emphasize the practical side of the Faith. It is application that is important." The truth is that the Bible does not make such a separation between doctrine and practical application. The Scripture emphasizes both because they go hand in hand. Doctrine is simply biblical truth in any area, and every doctrine has its proper practical application. Of course there is false doctrine with its accompanying ungodly application. If we don't see the application, then we haven't understood the doctrine properly. For example, let us consider the doctrine of Jesus Christ's deity, that He is true God in human flesh. Colossians 1:16-19 teaches us that Jesus has total dominion over the universe because He was the agent of creation (v.16) and all the fullness of deity dwelt in Him (v.19). In Colossians 2:3 we are told that in Christ are hidden the treasures of wisdom and knowledge. Jesus possesses this because He is God in the flesh. In Colossians 2:4-8 we see the direct application of this biblical truth.

It is impossible to separate doctrine from practical Christianity and be faithful to Scripture; therefore, it is incumbent upon us to endeavor to discern biblical doctrine and its application for godly living. Simply put, I really don't know how to faithfully serve the Lord without simultaneously knowing what God has said. Therefore, doctrine is essential.

The Scripture emphasizes the necessity for sound doctrine and the need to guard against false doctrine. The Greek word for "doctrine" is the word, *"didaskalia."* This word belongs to the word *"disaskalos,"* meaning "teacher." Mark 7:5-8 reads:

> And the Pharisees and the scribes asked Him, "Why do Your disciples not walk according to the tradition of the elders, but eat their bread with impure hands?" And He said them, "Rightly did Isaiah prophesy of you hypocrites, as it is written, 'This people honors Me with their lips, But their heart is far away from Me.' But in vain do they worship Me, Teaching as doctrines the precepts of men. "Neglecting the commandment of God, you hold to the tradition of men."

In this passage, the doctrines of the Pharisees and scribes were the doctrines or teachings of man in distinction from the commandments of God. False doctrine will always be the doctrines of men and not of God.

In Romans 12:7 we read: *"If service, in his serving; or he who teaches in his teaching."* Hence, doctrine in a passive sense is what a teacher teaches. Doctrine is the teaching of the teacher; therefore, we cannot escape doctrine. Teachers are either teaching sound doctrine or false doctrine. Paul stressed to Timothy and Titus the necessity for maintaining sound doctrine. In I Timothy 4:16 we read, *"Pay close attention to yourself and to your teaching; persevere in these things; for as you do this you will insure salvation both for yourself and for those who hear you."* The word translated as "teaching" is our Greek word "didaskalia." In I Timothy 6:1-5, Paul speaks of "our doctrine" as opposed to those who advocate a different doctrine that leads to the disunity of the body of Christ. The text states:

> Let all who are under the yoke as slaves regard their own masters as worthy of all honor so that the name of God and our doctrine may not be spoken against. And let those who have believers as their masters not be disrespectful to them because they are brethren, but let them serve them all the more, because those who partake of the benefit are believers and beloved. Teach and preach these principles. If anyone advocates a different doctrine, and does not agree with sound words, those of our Lord Jesus Christ, and with the doctrine conforming to godliness, he is conceited and understands nothing; but he has a morbid interest in controversial questions and disputes about words, out of which arise envy, strife, abusive language, evil suspicions, and constant friction between men of depraved mind and deprived of the truth, who suppose that godliness is a means of gain.

Verse 3 states that his doctrine is a "doctrine conforming to godliness." This demonstrates the point that I made earlier that every biblical doctrine has its proper application, namely that of godliness. As we have said, teachers will either teach sound doctrine or false doctrine, but they will teach **some** doctrine.

In Ephesians 4:14-16 we read:

> As a result, we are no longer to be children, tossed here and there by waves, and carried about by every wind of doctrine, by the trickery of men, by craftiness in deceitful scheming; but speaking the truth in love, we are to grow up in all aspects

into Him, who is the head even Christ, from who the whole body being fitted and held together by that which every joint supplies, according to the proper working of each individual part, causes the growth of the body for the building up of itself in love.

Paul stresses that the church is not to be carried away by every wind of doctrine by the trickery of men, by craftiness in deceitful scheming. Verses 15-16 speak of the body growing together in unity, which presupposes a sound doctrine.

There is always the danger of false doctrine creeping into the church and causing chaos. The church must always be vigilant to guard against false doctrine that will spiritually damage it. The false teachers in the church are called wolves in sheep's clothing, which is what makes them so dangerous. They come in the guise of purporting biblical truth when in reality it is not truth; hence, the sheep, the people of God are led into spiritual disaster. Acts 20:28-31 is quite enlightening:

Be on guard for yourselves and for all the flock, among which the Holy Spirit has made you overseers, to shepherd the church of God which He purchased with His own blood. I know that after my departure savage wolves will come in among you, not sparing the flock; and from among your own selves men will arise, speaking perverse things, to draw away the disciples after them. Therefore be on the alert, remembering that night and day for a period of three years I did not cease to admonish each one with tears.

The frightening thing is that Paul said in v. 30 that "among your own selves" men will arise to draw away disciples after them. Paul was speaking to the Ephesians elders! There would arise false elders, particularly false pastors. Titus 1:9-10 sets forth the qualifications for church elders when it says:

"holding fast the faithful word which is in accordance with the teaching, that he may be able both to exhort in sound doctrine and to refute those who contradict. **For there are many rebellious men, empty talkers and deceivers, especially those of the circumcision, who must be silenced because they are upsetting whole families, teaching things they should not teach, for the sake of sordid gain.**" (Emphasis mine)

The reason that I emphasized a certain portion of the previous passage is due to the nature of the present controversy in the Reformed camp. "Those of the circumcision" are the Judaizers who were espousing a works based salvation. In other words, they were denying justification by faith alone. Federal Vision proponents are our modern Judaizers.

The responsibility of an elder is two fold. He must be able to exhort in sound doctrine, and he must be able to refute those who contradict. The elder must know the Word of God and be equipped to discern false teaching, demonstrating its errors. The primary responsibility of the elders according to Acts 20:28 is the guarding, the overseeing, and the shepherding of the flock, which is the church purchased by Jesus' blood. We must not miss a vital point. A church that does not seek to maintain sound doctrine and refute those who teach false doctrine is an unfaithful church. Our Lord Jesus Christ will personally hold responsible those elders who do not spiritually guard His church from these false teachers. A false teacher must be exposed so that he can be refuted.

The RPCUS did not pass its resolutions out of spite, trying to be theological hair-splitters, for we know according to the sacred Scriptures that false doctrine will have serious, even soul destroying consequences. Our denomination could not idly sit by and allow this false doctrine to be propagated.

A General List of the errors of the Federal Vision

The errors of the Federal Vision are not only a systematic denial of several of the historic doctrines of the Reformed faith, but more importantly, some of the errors are a denial of historic, orthodox Christianity.

These errors are:
- A faulty view of the covenant
- A faulty view of the church
- A faulty view of election
- A faulty view of baptism
- A faulty view of eternal security and assurance of salvation
- A faulty view of man's depravity
- A faulty view of justification
- A faulty view of sanctification
- A faulty view of regeneration
- A faulty view of Christ's atoning work

The two most serious doctrines that demonstrate that the Federal Vision is outside the parameters of historic, orthodox Christianity are: **1) a denial of justi-**

fication by faith alone in Christ, 2) a denial of the imputation of Christ's righteousness to the believer.

These two aberrant doctrines attack the very heart of the Gospel of Jesus Christ, constituting a false gospel as delineated by the apostle Paul in Galatians 1:6-8.

The errors of the Federal Vision can be summarized as follows:

Entrance into God's covenant is objective via our water baptism. There is no distinction between the visible and invisible church. The term "elect" applies corporately to those who are objectively in the covenant. Water baptism is the distinguishing mark of those who constitute the elect of God. Our water baptism, be it infant baptism or adult baptism constitutes true union with Christ, meaning that we have all of the saving graces at our baptism. Since we are in genuine union with Christ at our baptism and since apostasy is a real warning in Scripture, those who renounce the Faith or who live rebellious lives with regard to God's commandments can lose their salvation. This means that one loses his initial justification. There is a final justification that must be maintained by faithful obedience to God's Law throughout one's lifetime. Justification is seen in terms of "obedient faith" or as "faithfulness." Good works are not merely the genuine fruit or evidence of saving faith; it is seen as the essence of faith. We are justified by covenant faithfulness, and justification is progressive in the sense that we will be declared justified on the Day of Judgment as long as we did not apostatize during our lifetime. The covenant of works is non-existent. Jesus' active obedience or His righteous keeping of the Law has nothing to do with the basis of our justification on the final Day of Judgment. Christ's obedience to the Law enabled Him to be the worthy, sinless sacrifice, giving Him a right standing before God the Father so that union with Christ in His resurrected and glorified life is what is credited to us, not His meritorious works on our behalf.

I will demonstrate these beliefs by quoting directly from the proponents of these views. I will allow them to speak for themselves. I will demonstrate that the RPCUS did not over react to the teaching of these men. Their own written testimony will show them to be out of accord with the historic Reformed Standards and out of accord with evangelical, orthodox Christianity.

Is The Federal Vision A Heresy?

Absolutely! The errors of the Federal Vision attack the very nature of the gospel. Are those who dogmatically teach these errors to be considered heretics? Yes! Are they wolves in sheep's clothing? Yes. Those who genuinely believe in their hearts the theology of the Federal Vision are in very serious trouble. When I was in seminary, I once had my systematic theology professor give the following answer to a question as to whether a person could be saved if he was in the Roman Catholic Church. His answer was: "It is possible to truly be trusting Christ and happen to be on the rolls of the Roman Catholic Church. However, if one genuinely believes in Roman Catholic doctrine, then one cannot be saved." My professor did go on to elaborate that he believed that God would in time lead the genuine Christian out of this false church.

One cannot genuinely believe that one's works is necessary for one's salvation and be saved. This is why Paul said that the Judaizers of Galatians 1:6-9 have another gospel, and belief in that other gospel places one under the curse of God. There is only one gospel that saves. It is the gospel that teaches that faith alone in Jesus Christ's work on our behalf in His active and passive obedience is the only basis for salvation.

I am not the only minister of the gospel who believes that the Federal Vision is a heresy. One of my fellow ministers in the RPCUS, Henry Johnson, believes the teaching of the Federal Vision to be heretical regarding its views of justification. In an interview with Gerry Wisz for the *Christian Renewal* magazine, Mr. Wisz asked Pastor Johnson as to whether he believed the views of the 2002 Auburn Avenue Pastors' Conference were heretical. The question was: "And you believe them to be erroneous and heretical?" Pastor Johnson's reply was "Yes."[7] Pastor Johnson had indicated that prior to the RPCUS' resolutions in June 2002 he had called pastor Steve Wilkins, calling upon him to repent of circulating views that were contrary to the Standards of the church. Pastor Johnson went on to say:

> One of Wilson's addresses at Monroe in 2002 was about dealing with heresy. He said, "the faithful individuals who address it (heresy) should address it as churchmen. They should address it as members of the church rather than addressing it as individuals who have a personal problem with what this guy is teaching." I mentioned this to Wilkins because these men were **publicly declaring a new gospel**. They were teaching a justification not in accord with the confessions, and the doctrines of grace were under attack by

---

[7] "The Monroe Four Speak Out (with a Response)", *The Counsel of Chalcedon* (May 2004), Article reprinted with permission from Christian Renewal magazine and Gerry Wisz, Interviewer.

implication, baptism and many other doctrines were being redefined by their new teaching. I asked him to say publicly that they needed to go back and do some work, and to go back to their church courts. I find it ironic that these men have accused us of trying and convicting them when we sought their church courts to look at these teachings. They are out of accord with the historic Reformed confessional faith and they are the ones acting as individuals without regard for the courts of the church.[8] (Emphasis mine)

In his article on the views of the Federal Vision, Pastor Brian Schwertley said the following about Norman Shepherd's views on justification:

> If Shepherd was willing to say that true saving faith **leads to** an obedient life, or is **always accompanied by** faithfulness, or that it **results in** good works which are **evidence** of a true living faith, then he would be in line with the Reformed symbols and there would be no controversy. But, his insistence on a faith/works combination in justification is non-confessional, Romanizing, heretical, and deadly. Shepherd and his followers are wolves in sheep's clothing and therefore must be defrocked and excommunicated for the safety of the sheep and the preservation of the Reformation against Romanism.[9] (Emphasis Schwertley).

The RCUS (not to be confused with this author's denomination of the RPCUS) declared in its synod report on the current justification controversy:

> *Resolution 3: Therefore, we also resolve that the teachings of Norman Shepherd on justification by faith are **another gospel**, and we admonish Reverend Shepherd and call on him to repent of his grievous errors.*[10] *(Emphasis mine)*

It is the duty of faithful elders to rise up and earnestly contend for the faith. All elders must heed the exhortation in Jude 3:

---

[8] Johnson, "Against the Tradition."

[9] Brian Schwertley, A Refutation of the Auburn Avenue Theology's Rejection of Justification by Faith Alone. This article was derived off of the internet.

[10] Report of the Special Committee To Study Justification In Light of the Current Justification Controversy. Presented to 258th Synod of the Reformed Church of the United States. May 10-13, 2004. The article was obtained off of the internet.

Beloved, while I was making every effort to write you about our common salvation, I felt the necessity to write to you appealing that you contend earnestly for the faith which was once for all delivered to the saints.

Chapter 2

Allegiance to the Reformed Standards?

As we examine the views of the Monroe Four on the subject of the covenant and the church, we shall see that they openly reject what the Confessional Standards teach; hence, several of these men have deliberately contravened the oaths that they took upon entering the ministry with reference to allegiance to their respective creedal formulations, be they the Westminster Standards or the Three Forms of Unity (Belgic Confession, Heidelberg Catechism, and the Synod of Dordt).

Since the Confessional Standards are but the system of doctrine that the Scripture teaches, we shall see that the Monroe Four openly distort the Scriptural texts supporting the creedal statements. In one sense, these men give lip service to the Reformed Standards, but in other instances they are critical of those who want to want to maintain strict subscription to those standards. Consider Steve Schlissel's comments:

> We continue, I'm afraid as Reformed and Presbyterian people, to think that time was frozen if not in the sixteenth then at least in the seventeenth century. That truth we're to develop in our understanding and the application of Scripture that that's necessarily an act of apostasy because once the Westminster Standards were written, truth was frozen and we can never go back and look at anything. We have this notion that we will go back in time that we will go back, by the way, the only reason that these things were successful is that they were building on Catholic capital in a Christianized Europe. [1]

---

[1] Steve Schlissel, *Covenant Reading,* Lecture given at 2002 Auburn Avenue Pastors' Conference.

Schlissel continues:

> And this Pollyanna notion that there is a frozen moment in histo-
> ry that has become the norm for now is false and dangerous. We
> must not think that the high point of all Christian history was
> reached at that time and that every act of reformation is simply a
> return to that point in time. It is not, that's false. Reformation is a
> return to the word of God and the Holy Spirit enlightening us to
> understand what our responsibilities are, in our generation, in
> every generation we might find ourselves.
>
> We have gotten to a point where we have abstracted the word of
> God, set it up on flash cards into various propositions and
> deceived ourselves into thinking that simply to return to these par-
> ticular *solas* or what have you is all that is necessary for us to
> make the progress that God would have us make and I just want
> to say that's not the case, it's not true.[2]

Schlissel sets up a false dichotomy between the Reformed Standards and the
Scripture itself by implying that if one is a strict subscriptionist to the
Standards, then somehow this person has abandoned Scripture for man made
formulations. Schlissel creates a straw man and associates that straw man with
all those who will seek to criticize him by using the Reformed Standards.
Schlissel states:

> Can I say something? Don't trust in deceptive words, we are
> reformed, we are reformed. Don't trust in deceptive words,
> Westminster Confession, Westminster Confession. You have to
> have the whole word of God and the fear of God in your heart and
> in your home. That's what God wants. If you really change your
> ways and your actions and deal with each other justly, if you don't
> oppress the alien, the fatherless or the widow and you don't shed
> innocent blood, if you don't follow other gods to your own harm,
> then I will let you live.[3]

Schlissel continues to argue against his straw man as it relates to his critics:

> I desire mercy not sacrifice. Acknowledgment of God rather
> than burnt offerings. I desire mercy not discrete propositions
> and acknowledgment of God rather than the right solas. God
> says, I hate, I despise your religious feasts… Now listen, we

[2] Schlissel, *Covenant Reading*.

[3] Schlissel, *Covenant Reading*.

are a confessional church in Brooklyn, I know it is hard to believe but we do need to make contrasts of things. And this is a biblical way of speaking. Remember in Amos, God said, "I hate, I despise your religious feasts, I cannot stand your assemblies." Well who authorized those assemblies? God did. Why is he saying he hates them? Because they were not accompanied by a wholehearted fear of God in conforming to his word. It is just as easy for God to say today, "I hate, I despise your confessions of faith.

We have a magnificent book, the Bible; it is God's own word. In this book we have bookends, it opens up with the creation, it concludes with a new creation… Here in between these bookends is the covenant of God. This book is not reducible to solas. It is not reducible to abstraction. It is not reducible to proposition. This book is your life. Eat it and live. Eat it, as God told the prophets. Take it and absorb it. We don't just use it in a way that serves our purposes, but rather we use it in a way to know how we can serve God's purposes.[4]

On his website for Messiah's congregation Schlissel states:

A problem with some modern Reformers is that they have no abiding interest in reforming. They have come to equate "continuing reformation" with liberalism, a petrifying error. Such brothers are more tightly wrapped up in their tradition than any arch-Romanist opponent of their ancestors, yet they deny it. Chanting *sola scriptura* rings hollow when what is really meant is "sola-those-parts-of – scriptura that serve the system I bring to the Bible.

It would be good if our generation at least resolved to learn from Scripture to ask the right questions. That would be progress. For we have spent 400 years breaking the Scripture down into propositions. It's past time for us to see all the Word's words as comprising one perfect story.[5]

In his continued diatribe against strict subscriptionism to the Reformed Standards, Schlissel states:

We had been saying that now is the time for Christians to be more

---

[4] Schlissel, *Covenant Reading.*

[5] "True Confessions" (September 21, 2002) <www.messiahnyc.org/Articles>

> Jewish: not in our festal celebrations but in our orientation, our
> thinking, our tilt, our way of seeing. The work of the Reformation
> has been stymied by our stubborn retention of Greek categories
> ... We have reduced its message to "spiritual laws" and proposi-
> tions.[6]

One of Steve Schlissel's greatest problems is this dichotomy that he places
between a Hebrew mindset and a Greek mindset, which has supposedly influenced the Reformation and its confessional standards. The real problem is that
this perspective is an entirely arbitrary imposition. It is a view that is propagated by the adherents to the New Perspective on Paul, which demonstrates
Schlissel's agreement with it on this point at least.

The interesting thing about Steve Schlissel is that he likes to make an appeal to the
Reformed Standards when he wants to, when it makes him sound Reformed to his
audience. For example, on his website for Messiah's Congregation, he makes the
statement that his readers ought to check out the form of subscription that his church
adheres to, which is the Three Forms of Unity.[7]

In his article that he wrote for the Knox Seminary Colloquium, Schlissel
writes:

> The charges made against "the Monroe Doctrine" rely not
> upon Scripture alone, but rather upon an alleged departure
> from secondary standards. So disturbing is this perceived dif-
> ference in the minds of a few, that these seem unable to hear
> the responses of the four speakers from the original 2002
> conference. "We affirm the Reformed Standards."[8]

Doug Wilson insists that the Federal Vision's views are consistent with the
Reformed Standards when he says:

> We have cautioned against an abuse of systematic and con-
> fessional theology, which abuse is present whenever we are
> not permitted to speak in scriptural language. Nevertheless,
> we do understand ourselves to be in the middle of the main-
> stream of historic Reformed orthodoxy. In the various papers
> we present in this volume, numerous citations from our con-

---

[6] "Faith Works" (March 24, 2002) <www.messiahnyc.org/Articles>

[7] "True Confessions"

[8] Steve Schlissel, *A New Way of Seeing,* The Auburn Avenue Theology, Pros and Cons:
Debating The Federal Vision, The Knox Theological Seminary Colloquium on the
Federal Vision, August 11-13, 2003, p. 21.

fessions and our Reformed forefathers will be found that make this point.

As was made clear earlier, we are bound to Scripture and are more than willing to reject our confessional tradition if allegiance to the Bible requires it. But at the same time, we are glad that we do not have to do this. These issues that we are debating have been debated numerous times before in Protestant history, and it is easy to cite many respected names from Reformed history, not to mention various confessions and catechism, that say in substance what we are saying. For the particulars, we would refer the reader to the various papers.[9]

Wilson wants us to believe that the views of the Federal Vision are clearly within the parameters of the Reformed Standards. As I shall demonstrate throughout this book, this is not the case. There is no way that one can maintain their views and square them with the Reformed Standards and with the Scripture. This is what makes the Federal Vision so dangerous. It comes to us with the guise of being Reformed and biblical. However, terms are consistently redefined to fit their views. The unsuspecting and theologically untrained are deceived. Such practice is common to those who have taught false doctrine throughout the centuries. This is why they are termed "wolves in sheep's clothing." This is how heresy creeps into the church.

At the 2002 AAPC pastors' conference, during the question and answer session the following question was asked to Steve Wilkins to which he gave this reply:

> **Q: [Steve Wilkins]** The next question- what exceptions, if any, would these views require a PCA minister to take from the Westminster Confession Standards?
> **A: [Steve Wilkins]** The only exception, I think, if you agree with paedocommunion, that is clearly an exception, I think, to the larger catechism and so, I think, you should, you ought to make that known if you have it. It is not right to hold views contrary to the Confession when we are in a confessional church and not acknowledge those things or try to keep them to yourself. That's wrong, it's subversive and it's not honest and it's the wrong thing to do. It undermines the integrity of

---

[9] Doug Wilson, *Union with Christ: Broad Concerns of the Federal Vision,* Knox Seminary Colloquium on the Federal Vision.

our confessional stance and we don't want to do that. What we want is reformation. Now the other side is we, some of our friends don't think the Standards can be improved and they make it equivalent, practically to the Bible. That's the other problem. We don't want that either, but you have to make, you have to operate with honesty under your confession or you have nothing.

As of the writing of this book, neither Steve Wilkins nor any of the other men who subscribe to the Auburn views have done this. If only Wilkins would heed his own admonition and encourage others who hold similar views to act with integrity. It is apparent that they will not do this; hence, it is incumbent upon the ecclesiastical bodies that they are within to force them to either recant of their aberrant views or leave their denominations. If they do not voluntarily leave, then they should be tried for heresy and demitted from the ministry.

Chapter 3

A Denial of Justification by Faith Alone

The Theology of Norman Shepherd

It is important that I discuss the theological views of Norman Shepherd. He was scheduled to be one of the original speakers at the 2002 Auburn Avenue Pastors' Conference (hereafter designated as the AAPC). When he was unable to attend, John Barach was designated as his replacement. At this conference, during question and answers, someone asked Steve Wilkins what books that he recommended on the covenant. One of the books that he recommended was Shepherd's book, *"The Call Of Grace: How the Covenant Illuminates Salvation and Evangelism."*

Though he was not one of the featured speakers at the 2005 Auburn Avenue Pastors' Conference, Shepherd did speak at a service at Auburn Avenue Presbyterian Church just prior to the conference.

Norman Shepherd must be considered as one of the dominant figures of the Federal Vision movement. Those at the 2002 AAPC have virtually agreed with him in all his various theological views such as: his theological perspective on the covenant, his understanding of baptism as it pertains to the covenant, his views of election, his understanding of the relationship of works with justification, and his denial of the imputation of Christ's merits to the believer.

His two most glaring theological errors, or should we say heresies, are:

- **he has denied the biblical doctrine of justification through faith alone**
- **he has denied the imputation of Christ's righteousness to the believer**

As other Reformed thinkers have noted, these errors constitute a departure from historic, orthodox Christianity. It is "another gospel" under the censure of the apostle Paul in Galatians 1:8-9.

Norman Shepherd, just like the others in the Federal Vision, insists that he is Reformed and that he is in conformity with the Reformed Confessional documents such as the Westminster Confession with its Larger and Shorter Catechisms, the Belgic Confession with its Heidelberg Catechism, and the Canons of Dordt. And of course he believes that he has interpreted the Scriptures correctly in all these matters.

In analyzing Norman Shepherd, I will demonstrate that he is not in conformity with the Reformed Standards and has twisted their meaning. The reader can decide for himself as to whether Shepherd has accurately understood the Scriptures. In directly quoting him and then comparing his public comments and writings with the Scripture and the Reformed Standards, it should become apparent that Shepherd has departed from the faith which was once for all delivered to the saints.

Shepherd's History of Theological Controversy

A fine historical sketch of Shepherd's theological controversy can be found in the Reformed Church in the United States' special committee report on the justification controversy. They stated:

> "The 'justification issue' came to the attention of the Faculty of Westminster Theological Seminary in 1975, when certain students were reported to have set forth a position that justification was by faith and works when being examined by various church bodies." This subsequently led to a seven year investigation into the teaching of Norman Shepherd, which eventually resulted in him being dismissed from his teaching post at Westminster "as of January 1, 1982." In May 1982 charges were filed against Shepherd and presented before the Presbytery of Philadelphia of the OPC, but "Mr. Shepherd was transferred out of the Philadelphia Presbytery before charges filed against him could be heard. He was received into the Christian Reformed denomination ... without notation that charges had been filed against him." "He served pastorates in the CRC in Minnesota and Illinois before retiring in 1998."[1]

---

[1] *The Report of the Special Committee To Study Justification of the RCUS.*

Just because a person has charges filed against him does not automatically mean that a person is guilty, but it does raise serious questions why fellow ministers would take this serious step. We will see that the evidence will be convincing that Shepherd's views are not Reformed and are not orthodox.

In 2000, Shepherd published his book *The Call Of Grace.* I will demonstrate that this is simply a regurgitation of his views twenty years earlier. The problem is that Shepherd's book found fertile ground among some preachers such as Steve Wilkins, Steve Schlissel, Douglas Wilson, and John Barach, to name a few. I will demonstrate that these men express themselves using virtually the same terminology as Norman Shepherd.

Shepherd's Problems with Westminster Seminary

The problem revolved around the relationship of good works to justification. The biblical doctrine of justification does not entail any good works that a person can do in order to be justified before a holy God. This concept is stated clearly in the Westminster Confession of Faith, Chapter 11, Section 1, reads:

> Those whom God effectually calleth, He also freely justifieth: not by infusing righteousness into them, but by pardoning their sins, and by accounting and accepting their persons as righteous, not for anything wrought in them, or done by them, but for Christ's sake alone; nor by imputing faith itself, the act of believing, or any other evangelical obedience to them, as their righteousness, but by imputing the obedience and satisfaction of Christ unto them, they receiving and resting on Him and His righteousness by faith; which faith they have not of themselves, it is the gift of God.

It is quite apparent that justification does not infuse righteousness or obedience into men. Justification pardons men of their sins. Men who are justified are declared righteous, not made righteous inwardly. The righteousness that is given to them is the righteousness of Christ, freely bestowed. The Confessional statement expressly states that the righteousness that men possess is not rooted in faith itself or in any kind of evangelical obedience. The obedience that justified men possess is said to be the obedience and satisfaction of Christ that is credited to their account.

Faith is simply the instrument whereby men appropriate Christ's work done for them. It is the means of our justification, not the cause of it. This is very important to understand.

Chapter 11, Section 2 of the Westminster Confession of Faith states:

> Faith, thus receiving and resting on Christ and His righteousness, is the alone instrument of justification; yet is it not alone in the person justified, but is ever accompanied with all other saving graces, and is no dead faith, but worketh by love.

Where do good works come in? Chapter 16, Section 2 of the Westminster Confession Of Faith states:

> These good works, done in obedience to God's commandments, are the fruits and evidences of a true and lively faith.

Chapter 16, Section 5 of the Westminster Confession of Faith states:

> We cannot, by our best works, merit pardon of sin, or eternal life at the hand of God, by reason of the great disproportion that is between them and the glory to come; and the infinite distance that is between us and God, whom, by them, we can neither profit, nor satisfy for the debt of our former sins, but when we have done all we can, we have done but our duty, and are unprofitable servants; and because, as they are good, they proceed from His Spirit; and as they are wrought by us, they are defiled, and mixed with so much weakness and imperfection, that they cannot endure the severity of God's judgment.

It is clear from this section of the Westminster Confession that good works cannot pardon sin because even the best of works done by a Christian is tainted with sin so as to fall short of what God demands. The very nature of justification is the act of God pardoning our sins.

It is also important to note that faith is the **alone** instrument of justification. This faith, which is the only instrument, is said to be **accompanied** by other saving graces, which demonstrates this faith to be lively and not dead. It is very important that we understand that accompanying graces do not imply that they are the essence of faith.

The trouble with Norman Shepherd's views is that he has joined good works or evangelical obedience with justification. Good works are not simply the fruits or evidence of justification but part and parcel with it.

In 1978 Shepherd presented to the Presbytery of Philadelphia of the Orthodox Presbyterian Church his *Thirty-four Theses on Justification in Relation to Faith, Repentance, and Good Works.*

Thesis 20 states:

> The Pauline affirmation in Romans 2:13, "the doers of the Law will be justified," is not to be understood hypothetically in the sense that there are no persons who fall into that class, but in the sense that faithful disciples of the Lord Jesus Christ will be justified (Compare Luke 8:21; James 1:22-25).[2]

To show that Shepherd has completely misunderstood and twisted this passage, I simply quote John Calvin at this point. To understand the context of verse 13 it is necessary to tie in the relationship of verse 12 with verse 13. Calvin's comments are as follows:

> As the Gentiles, being led by the errors of their own reason, go headlong into ruin, so the Jews possess a law by which they are condemned; for this sentence has been long ago pronounced, "Cursed are all they who continue not in all its precepts." (Deuteronomy 27:26)

> A worse condition then awaits the Jewish sinners, since their condemnation is already pronounced in their own law. Paul anticipates the objection which the Jews might have adduced. As they had heard that the law was the rule of righteousness, (Deuteronomy 4:1,) they gloried in the mere knowledge of it: to obviate this mistake, he declares that the hearing of the law or any knowledge of it is of no such consequence, that any one should on that account lay claim to righteousness, but that works must be produced, according to this saying, "He who will do these shall live in them." The import then of this verse is the following, — "That if righteousness be sought from the law, the law must be fulfilled; for the righteousness of the law consists in the perfection of works." They who pervert this passage for the purpose of building up justification by works, deserve universal contempt.[3]

---

[2] Norman Shepherd, *Thirty-four Theses on Justification in Relation to Faith, Repentance, and Good Works*, (November 18, 1978) <www.hornes.org/theologia/content/norman_shepherd/the_34_theses.htm>

[3] John Calvin, *Calvin's New Testament Commentaries: The Epistles of Paul to the Romans and Thessalonians,* translated by R. Mackenzie (Grand Rapids, Michigan: Eerdman's Publishing Company, 1960) pp. 46, 47.

Calvin is quite blunt about those who seek to use this passage to use obedience to God's law as a basis for justification. They deserve universal contempt! Shepherd has completely distorted the passage, making it the exact opposite of its intent.

Norman Shepherd stated in thesis 21:

> The exclusive ground of the justification of the believer in the state of justification is the righteousness of Jesus Christ, but his obedience, which is simply the perseverance of the saints in the way of truth and righteousness, is necessary to his continuing in a state of justification (Heb. 3:6,14).[4]

It is quite apparent from this thesis that the believer's justification is linked with his own persevering obedience. Rather than justification being a one time act that is definitive in space and time, at the moment of faith, Shepherd presents justification as something that one must continue in, inferring that the person might not continue in it. This opens the door to the idea that one might fall from his state of justification. As we shall see in our further analysis of the Federal Vision, this is exactly what they believe. They explicitly deny the historic Reformed doctrine of the perseverance of the saints.

Norman Shepherd stated in thesis 22:

> The righteousness of Jesus Christ ever remains the exclusive ground of the believer's justification, but the personal godliness of the believer is also necessary for his justification in the judgment of the last day (Matt.7:21-23; 25:31-46; Heb.12:14).[5]

In this thesis, Shepherd gives lip service to the idea that Jesus is the sole ground for justification, but then he states that the personal holiness of the believer is also necessary for justification. The problem is that Shepherd is confusing the relationship of sanctification with justification. These two doctrines are intimately related, but they are not identical. One must maintain the distinction between the two lest one make sanctification as an equal basis of a man's justification.

Question 77 of the Westminster Larger Catechism asks: Wherein do justification and sanctification differ? The answer is:

---

[4] Shepherd, *Thirty-four Theses on Justification*
[5] Shepherd, *Thirty-four Theses on Justification.*

> Although sanctification be inseparably joined with justification, yet they differ, in that God in justification imputeth the righteousness of Christ; in sanctification his Spirit infuseth grace, and enableth to the exercise thereof; in the former, sin is pardoned; in the other, it is subdued: the one doth equally free all believers from the revenging wrath of God, and that perfectly in this life, that they never fall into condemnation; the other is neither equal in all, nor in this life perfect in any, but growing up to perfection.

One of the fundamental serious errors of the Federal Vision is that it blurs this distinction between justification and sanctification. To blur this distinction is no minor error; it is heresy. It adopts the view of Roman Catholicism as we shall demonstrate in a later chapter.

Norman Shepherd states in thesis 15:

> The forgiveness of sin which repentance is an indispensable necessity is the forgiveness of sin included in justification, and therefore there is no justification without repentance.[6]

Norman Shepherd states in thesis 23:

> Because faith which is not obedient faith is dead faith, and because repentance is necessary for the pardon of sin included in justification, and because abiding in Christ by keeping his commandments (John 15:5; 10; I John 3:13; 24) are all necessary for continuing in the state of justification, good works, works done from true faith, according to the law of God, and for his glory, being the new obedience wrought by the Holy Spirit in the life of the believer united to Christ, though not the ground of his justification, are nevertheless necessary for salvation from eternal condemnation and therefore for justification (Rom. 6:16, 22; Gal. 6:7-9).[7]

There are several very important things about Shepherd's views on the relationship of repentance to justification. His great error is that he makes the pardoning of sin or the forgiveness of sin, which is involved in justification, directly dependent upon repentance.

---

[6] Shepherd, *Thirty-four Theses on Justification*
[7] Shepherd, *Thirty-four Theses on Justification*

Shepherd clearly states that repentance is "**necessary** for the pardon of sin included in justification" (emphasis mine). Shepherd does not mean that repentance flows out of saving faith or that it is closely associated with it; he clearly makes repentance necessary to justification. This is a very serious theological error. This is not what the Scripture says, nor is it what our Confessional Standards teach in keeping with Scripture.

One of the biblical references that Shepherd uses to tie in repentance with justification is Romans 6:16, 22 which says, "*Do you not know that when you present yourselves to someone as slaves for obedience, you are slaves of the one whom you obey, either of sin resulting in death, or of obedience resulting in righteousness...But now having been freed from sin and enslaved to God, you derive your benefit, resulting in sanctification, and the outcome, eternal life.*" Shepherd has greatly erred by associating this passage with justification. As verse 22 indicates, the obedience to Christ has to do with sanctification, not justification. The text says explicitly, sanctification. Our obedience has nothing to do with our justification, none whatsoever. The only obedience that is involved in justification is Christ's obedience or righteousness that is imputed to us. Of course, we will discover that Shepherd explicitly denies the imputation of Christ's righteousness or His merits to us. Shepherd has completely twisted the meaning of Romans 6:16, 22.

The Westminster Confession of Faith states in Chapter 15, Section 3 "Of Repentance Unto Life":

> Although repentance be not to be rested in, as any satisfaction for sin, or any cause of the pardon thereof, which is the act of God's free grace in Christ; yet is it of such necessity to all sinners, that none may expect pardon without it.

Robert Shaw comments upon this portion of the *Confession*:

> ... our Confession asserts, that repentance is not to be rested in as any satisfaction for sin, or a cause of the pardon thereof...Repentance is never supposed to be a legal ground for remitting the punishment due to crimes committed against a civil State. How unreasonable, then, to suppose that it can form a sufficient ground for the pardon of sin as committed against God! Christ has fully satisfied the justice of God by the sacrifice of himself, and his blood alone cleanseth us from all sin – I John 1:7. To us the pardon of sin is wholly gratuitous- "an act of God's free grace in Christ" – and, if it be of

grace, then it is no more of works, therefore, not by repentance, as a satisfaction for sin.

True repentance and pardon are inseparably connected. Though no one is pardoned for his repentance, yet repentance is of such indispensable necessity, that an impenitent sinner cannot be a pardoned sinner. "They are connected in the economy of salvation, not as cause and effect, but to show the consistency of a gratuitous pardon with the interests of holiness.

... for the vindication of the honour of the plan of mercy, has so connected pardon with repentance and confession- the expression of repentance- that they are the only certain evidences that we are in a pardoned state; while pardon and repentance are equally the gift of God through Jesus Christ our Lord.[8]

Robert Shaw reflects an historic understanding of the interrelationship of various doctrines. Though pardoning of sin and repentance are inseparably linked, the two theological truths are not so linked that one is the cause of the other. The Westminster Confession clearly states that repentance does not cause the pardoning of sin. We know that in justification the believer is pardoned of his sins. Shepherd is clearly wrong when he says that repentance is necessary for justification. This is very akin to the Roman Catholic idea of penance. As Shaw states, repentance is the **evidence** that one is in a pardoned state, which means that one is in a justified state. Evidence is **not** the cause or basis of something. The relationship of repentance to justification is no different than the relationship of sanctification to justification. They are both the evidences of a justified state, not the cause of it, as Shepherd would lead us to believe.

John Calvin has some insightful comments regarding the relationship of repentance to a pardoned state. Calvin states:

Now it ought to be a fact beyond controversy that repentance not only constantly follows faith, but is also born of faith.[9]

---

[8] Robert Shaw, *An Exposition Of The Westminster Confession of Faith,* (Christian Focus Publications, 1992), pp. 158,159.

[9] John Calvin, *Institutes of the Christian Religion,* translated by Ford Lewis Battles, ed. John T. McNeill, Library of Christian Classics (Philadelphia: The Westminster Press, 1975) Book 3, Chapter 3, Section 1, p. 593.

There he reckons repentance and faith as two different things. What then? Can true repentance stand, apart from faith? Not at all. But even though they cannot be separated, they ought to be distinguished.[10]

I interpret repentance as regeneration, whose sole end is to restore in us the image of God that had been disfigured and all but obliterated through Adam's transgression.[11]

Likewise, "Turn again, and repent, that your sins may be blotted out." (Acts 3:19). Yet we must note that this condition is **not so laid down as if our repentance were the basis of our deserving pardon,** but rather, because the Lord has determined to have pity on men to the end that they may repent, he indicates in what direction men should proceed if they wish to obtain grace.[12] (Emphasis mine)

Whomsoever God wills to snatch from death, he quickens by the Spirit of regeneration. **Not that repentance, properly speaking, is the cause of salvation**, but because it is already seen to be inseparable from faith and from God's mercy... [13] (Emphasis mine)

It is very clear that Calvin states that even though repentance and pardon of sin are inseparably linked, they are not so linked that repentance is the cause of salvation. Calvin understands repentance to be regeneration in the sense that no one will ever repent who has not been regenerated or born of God by the Spirit. Seeing that regeneration and repentance are said to be gifts of God in the Scripture, one cannot attribute them as causes or necessities for justification.

Calvin made it clear that repentance follows faith or is born of faith. We will see that the Scripture and the Confessional Standards never make saving faith as the basis of justification but only the instrument of justification. If repentance flows from faith, it cannot be necessary for the pardon of sin. Hence, Shepherd is clearly wrong in insisting that repentance is the cause or basis of justification, which is the pardoning of sin. It is clear that Shepherd is anti-Confessional and completely disagrees with Calvin.

---

[10] *Institutes*, Book 3, Chapter 3, Section 5, p. 597.

[11] *Institutes*, Book 3, Chapter 3, Section 8, p. 601.

[12] *Institutes*, Book 3, Chapter 3, Section 20, p. 614.

[13] *Institutes*, Book 3, Chapter 3, Section 21, p. 615.

Theological errors that are not dealt with sufficiently will resurface to plague the church, and this is what has happened with Norman Shepherd. In 1977 the faculty of Westminster Theological Seminary in Philadelphia did not come to a unified consensus regarding Shepherd's teachings. The faculty requested that Shepherd prepare a paper explaining his views of justification by faith alone. Shepherd presented a fifty-three page paper titled, *"The Relation of Good Works to Justification in the Westminster Standards."* After reading the paper, the Board of the Seminary was troubled by some of the expressions of how Shepherd phrased the relationship of works to justification. In May of 1977, a more complete report was made to the Seminary Board, which said:

> The Faculty report specified four areas where modifications of the language and formulations of Mr. Shepherd were to be desired. These concerned his broad use of the term justification, his language of requirement for good works in relation to justification, his reluctance to make faith prior to justification even in a logical sense; and his strategy of explaining the 'alone' function of faith as separating it from meritorious works rather than from other graces.[14]

Although six members of the Faculty "believed that these criticisms were not severe enough," and "held Mr. Shepherd's views to be erroneous," a majority of the Faculty concluded that "although Mr. Shepherd's 'structure of argumentation seems bound to create misunderstanding,' his formulations fell within the toleration limits of the Westminster Standards (April 25, 1978, Report to the Board)."[15]

A dissent to the faculty's majority decision was registered by visiting professor of New Testament to the Seminary, Phillip Hughes. The RCUS committee report gives this synopsis of Hughes dissent:

> Hughes expressed concerns, which to him crystallized the issue facing the Seminary. Hughes' major concern was that the Faculty in its report on Shepherd spoke approvingly of the necessity of good works for salvation. No one denies that the root of faith produces good works, and that without per-

---

[14] *Report Of The Special Committee To Study Justification.* The RCUS report quoted this from *Reason and Specifications,* p. 137.

[15] *Report Of The Special Committee To Study Justification,* p. 5. This quote of the RCUS report was documented from Reasons *and Specifications,* p. 137 and from O. Palmer Robertson's book *The Current Justification Controversy,* p. 26.

sonal subjective holiness no one will see the Lord (Hebrews 12:14). "But the attempt is being made to connect these good works with faith in such a way that though defined as non-meritorious they are regarded as necessary to our future (or final or eschatological) justification: no good works, no Heaven!" Endorsement is given to the idea that justification is "a process in three stages: initial ('this initial entry into God's favor'), continuing ('the continued enjoyment of God's favor'), and consummating ('the consummation of God's favor at the Judgment')." The problem with this idea is that it "has the effect of calling in question the perfection and the once-for-all character of the initial – and I would insist, the only – justification of the sinner who puts his trust in Christ and to whom the perfect righteousness of Christ is fully and indefectibly imputed." It also "implies that the sinner's justification is in some real sense dependent on what he does, on the nature of his works, following his 'initial' justification."[16]

Hughes marks with emphasis:

> **Where justification is concerned** (and this is the essential qualification) I do indeed isolate faith from good works and I do indeed regard good works as intrinsically in competition with the unique role of faith. I deprecate the extension of justification into the sphere of sanctification, for it is precisely this procedure that leads to the notion that the good works of the Christian have a necessary part to play in his justification. ... This is the whole point of the Biblical and Reformed emphasis on **faith alone** where our justification is concerned; for justification by faith alone (**sola fide**) means justification by faith in isolation, and particularly in isolation from works.[17]

In February of 1982, the Executive Committee of the Board dismissed Shepherd and wrote an eighteen page paper titled "Reason and Specifications Supporting the Action of the Board of Trustees in Removing Professor Shepherd." Part of this report states:

---

[16] *The Report Of The Special Committee To Study Justification,* p. 5, which quotes from John Robbin's *Companion to the Current Justification Constroversy*, p. 106.

[17] *The Report Of The Special Committee To Study Justification*, p. 5.

> While the Board has not judged that his views are in error, the
> Board has come to the conviction that his views are not clear-
> ly in accord with the standards of the Seminary; for this rea-
> son it has acted within its authority to remove him from his
> office for the best interests of the Seminary.[18]

Twenty-three years have elapsed since Shepherd was dismissed from Westminster
Seminary in 1982. As I noted earlier, the Orthodox Presbyterian Church, of which
Shepherd was a minister in, had charges pending against him, but nothing was offi-
cially done when Shepherd left for another denomination.

Heresies, like infectious diseases, have a tendency to crop up over the years.
Shepherd's publishing of his book, *The Call Of Grace* in 2000, has once again
plagued the church with false teachings on the nature of justification by faith alone.

Errors in Shepherd's book *The Call of Grace*

In this book, Shepherd sets forth many views that are consistent with his thirty-
four theses on justification. His view of the covenant, baptism, election, and the
nature of justifying faith are all explained. We will see that his views have all
been adopted by the other major figures in the Federal Vision. There is no coincidence that Shepherd and these other men use the same terminology.

In his conclusion to Part I of his book, Shepherd makes this incredible statement:

> The time has now come for us to return to the subject with which
> we began. Is there any hope for a common understanding
> between Roman Catholicism and evangelical Protestantism
> regarding the way of salvation? May I suggest that there is at least
> a glimmer of hope if both sides are willing to embrace a covenan-
> tal understanding of the way of salvation.[19]

Any Reformed person ought to be shocked by this statement. There is no common ground between Roman Catholicism and Protestantism on the issue of the
way of salvation! The two views are completely antithetical. Rome has made
it very clear and has never changed its declaration from the Council of Trent
that the Protestant understanding of salvation is an anathema. Shepherd's com-

---

[18] *The Report Of The Special Committee To Study Justification*, pp. 8, 9.

[19] Norman Shepherd, *The Call Of Grace. How The Covenant Illuminates Salvation
and Evangelism* (Phillisburg, New Jersey: Presbyterian and Reformed Publishing,
2000), p. 59.

ment ought to send an alarm to anyone that there is a very serious problem. We will see that Shepherd's plan of reconciliation between Rome and Protestantism is virtually a return to Rome!

It is no coincidence that there have been several people who have embraced the Federal Vision who have abandoned a Protestant understanding and joined the Roman Catholic religion. I personally know two young men. One of these young men said that Romanism is the logical extension of the Federal Vision. As sad as it is, this young man accurately sees the inevitable conclusion in believing this theology.

These two young men and the others that have defected back to Rome will not be the last. We should expect to see many more. This is why the Reformed community must unite to condemn this theological poison before it spreads further.

In the preface of his book, Shepherd states:

> The Reformed faith makes clear that salvation is all of divine grace from the beginning to end. But if that is so, where and how does human responsibility enter in? The presentations that follow are an attempt to shed light on two separate but related aspects of that question from the perspective of covenant. The first part deals with the problem of faith and works, or grace and merit. This issue has come to the fore once again in recent discussions between evangelical Protestants and Roman Catholics, as well as among evangelicals themselves.[20]

The kind of human responsibility that Shepherd supposedly will enlighten us with is most grievous. Shepherd teaches that the **essence of saving faith is covenantal obedience**. This is no compromise between Rome and Protestantism. This is essentially Romanism!

In his discussion regarding the historic debate between Rome and Protestantism, Shepherd says that there are some unresolved questions that are really the legacy of the Protestant Reformation.[21] Shepherd tells us that Rome emphasized good works as what merited us eternal life, while Luther emphasized grace through faith alone. Shepherd comments, *"We are saved by grace through faith. We are not saved by good works through merit."*[22] Shepherd continues, *"We are profoundly grateful for*

---

[20] Shepherd, *The Call Of Grace*, viii.

[21] Shepherd, *The Call Of Grace*, p. 4.

[22] Shepherd, *The Call Of Grace*, p. 5.

the progress that was made by the Reformation. We were led into a more biblical understanding of the way of salvation. Nonetheless, unresolved issues remain."[23]

For Shepherd these unresolved issues had to do with the long-standing difference of Rome with Luther regarding the use of the law of God. A very serious error that Shepherd makes is his analysis of the Protestant Reformation. Shepherd states, *"Children of the Reformation insist that salvation is by grace alone. There is nothing that you can do or should try to do to save yourself. For some, salvation by grace means that you make a decision for Christ."*[24]

Shepherd goes on to describe how these people emphasize receiving Jesus as Savior but not as Lord and that all that matters is faith independent of works. Shepherd refers to this kind of thinking as antinomianism, which means against the law. Shepherd states, *"The term brings out the fact that law keeping plays no role in the way of salvation. The strength of antinomianism is its appeal to what is at the heart of the Protestant Reformation: salvation by grace through faith, not by merit through works."*[25]

His view is quite perplexing. Shepherd leaves the definite impression that the Protestant Reformation was somewhat antinomian. Reformed thinkers are not those who advocate an antinomian thought. There are many Reformed brethren, including myself, who would agree that one must accept Jesus as Lord and not merely as a Savior. Shepherd has given a definition of antinomianism that is illegitimate as it pertains to the Protestant Reformation. It is a false statement to say that the heart of the Protestant Reformation was antinomian. Shepherd explicitly states that the phrase, *"salvation by grace through faith, not by merit through works,"* is an antinomian statement. Shepherd in the next paragraph says, *"Over against the antinomians, others point out that it isn't quite that simple. According to the teaching of James in the second chapter of his letter, faith without works is dead. Such faith is of no use. It will not save."*[26]

Shepherd states that the teaching of James 2 is somehow distinct from the Protestant Reformation's teaching of salvation by grace through faith. Shepherd says that the Protestant Reformation's emphasis on faith apart from works is inadequate. He thinks that the Protestant Reformation was antinomian. He defines antinomianism:

---

[23] Shepherd, *The Call Of Grace.*

[24] Shepherd, *The Call Of Grace*, p.6.

[25] Shepherd, *The Call Of Grace*, pp.6, 7.

[26] Shepherd, *The Call Of Grace*, p. 7.

The word means, literally, 'against law.' The term brings out the fact that law keeping plays no role in the way of salvation. The strength of antinomianism is its appeal to what is at the heart of the Protestant Reformation: salvation by grace through faith, not by merit through works.[27]

Shepherd sets the stage for the rest of his book when he says, *"How do you preach grace without being antinomian? On the other hand, how do you preach repentance without calling into question salvation by grace apart from works? How do you insist on obedience without being legalistic?"*[28]

The answers that Shepherd provides us with are not encouraging. His answers will demonstrate that he is outside the pale of not only the Reformed Faith, but he is outside of the pale of orthodox Christianity. His answers will reveal that he has, indeed, denied the biblical and Reformed blessed truth of salvation by Christ through faith alone. Shepherd's views are heretical, and these views have not bridged the gap between Rome and Protestantism; they have brought us back to Rome, despite what he says! And when the Federal Vision proponents endorse Shepherd's book and promotes his lectures at their conferences, they are aligning themselves with his heretical views.

Shepherd's view about saving faith is explained in his chapter on the Abrahamic covenant. Shepherd asks the question, *"Would the promises be fulfilled irrespective of any response on the part of Abraham and his children? The biblical record shows that conditions were, indeed, attached to the fulfillment of the promises made to Abraham. There are at least six considerations that serve to demonstrate this point."*[29]

Shepherd lists circumcision as one of the conditions. He says, *"Circumcision was clearly a condition for inheriting what was promised."*[30]

He does mention that this circumcision was not restricted to an outward ceremony but it must refer to an inward circumcision of the heart as well. Shepherd says, *"In requiring circumcision, God was requiring the full scope of covenantal loyalty and obedience all along the line."*[31]

---

[27] Shepherd, *The Call Of Grace*, pp. 6, 7.

[28] Shepherd, *The Call Of Grace*, pp. 8, 9.

[29] Shepherd, *The Call Of Grace*, p. 14.

[30] Shepherd, *The Call Of Grace*.

[31] Shepherd, *The Call Of Grace*, p. 15.

Shepherd then goes on to make the connection with baptism of the New Testament.stating, "*We may note in passing that baptism has the same significance in the new covenant. In the Great Commission, Jesus teaches us to disciple the nations by baptizing them and teaching them to obey everything he has commanded ... Baptism has come in the place of circumcision. Just as circumcision obliged Israel to obey God under the old covenant, so also baptism obliges believers to obey him under the new covenant.*"[32]

Before I continue, I must draw attention that Shepherd is not really talking about obedience being the fruit of God's saving promises; **he is clearly referring to obedience as the condition of those promises.** In other words, we must do something in order to get God's promises. How much more plain can Shepherd say it? He is advocating obedience or works as the **basis or cause** of receiving the promises.

The second condition that Shepherd believes God requires to obtain the promises is that of faith. Now, one might think that Shepherd has returned to orthodoxy by this comment until one reads how he explains the essence of faith. Shepherd then makes this perplexing and confusing comment, "*In fact, Genesis 15:6 says that Abraham's faith was so significant that it was credited to him as righteousness! If so, then righteousness was a condition to be met, and faith met that condition.*"[33]

What sounded so orthodox a moment ago is now stated as an unbiblical concept. Shepherd says that Abraham's faith was credited to him as righteousness, but he then says that righteousness was a condition for Abraham to meet. This is where Shepherd further corrupts the gospel. Shepherd has now made Abraham's righteousness as the basis for receiving the promises of God. This is not the gospel! The gospel applies Christ's righteousness to Abraham (God's people). But Shepherd says no, it is Abraham's own righteousness.

In Shepherd's third condition for receiving God's promises, he says: "*The faith that was credited to Abraham as righteousness was a living and active faith.*"[34]

Shepherd will now explain for his readers what the righteousness consisted of in being credited to him. Faith is now said to be **living and active.** He then quotes passages from James 2, namely verse 24, stating that Abraham was justified by what he did and not by faith alone. Shepherd says, "*The faith credited to Abraham as righteousness was a living and active faith ... This connec-*

---

[32] Shepherd, *The Call Of Grace.*

[33] Shepherd, *The Call Of Grace.*

[34] Shepherd, *The Call Of Grace,* p. 16

tion between a blameless walk and confirmation of the covenant is not artificial."[35]

The great blunder and heresy that Shepherd makes here is that he is severely confused about James' discourse on faith. James is merely stating what justifying faith looks like, not that works are the conditions for justification. I will clearly demonstrate what the Reformed Confessional Standards have stated in this regard at a later point. Remember, Shepherd has been discussing the conditions for receiving the promises. There is no question that Shepherd is making Abraham's own righteousness as the basis. Shepherd continues, *"I will make your descendants as numerous as the stars in the sky and will give them all these lands, and through your offspring all nations on earth will be blessed, **because Abraham obeyed me and kept my requirements, my commands, my decrees and my laws.**"*[36] (Emphasis Shepherd) Shepherd is **not** saying that Abraham's obedience is the fruit or the evidence; it is the very basis of justification. Shepherd has clearly made man's works as the grounds or basis of justification.

Shepherd states, *"We have the promise of children, the land, and the presence of God himself. God confirms these oath-bound promises. Notice why he does this: '**Because** Abraham obeyed me and kept my requirements, my commands, my decrees and my laws.'"*[37] (Emphasis Shepherd)

Shepherd states as his last condition for receiving the Abrahamic promises: *"The ultimate proof of the conditional character of the Abrahamic covenant resides in Jesus Christ ... All of this is made possible through the covenantal righteousness of Jesus Christ. His was a living, active, and obedient faith that took him all the way to the cross. This faith was credited to him as righteousness."*[38]

Herein lies the great deceptiveness of Shepherd and the Federal Vision. They use the same terminology as historic Reformed theology, but they change its meaning. One might think that the previous quote sounds biblical. On the surface it appears this way until Shepherd explains what he means. One might think that the righteousness being credited to believers is the righteousness of Jesus himself. But this is not what Shepherd means. One paragraph later Shepherd states:

---

[35] Shepherd, *The Call Of Grace.*

[36] Shepherd, *The Call Of Grace*, p. 17.

[37] Shepherd, *The Call Of Grace.*

[38] Shepherd, *The Call Of Grace*, pp. 18,19

Nothing demonstrates the conditional character of the Abrahamic covenant more clearly than the way in which the promises of that covenant are ultimately fulfilled. They are fulfilled through the covenantal loyalty and obedience of Jesus Christ. But just as Jesus was faithful in order to **guarantee** the blessing, so his followers must be faithful in order to **inherit** the blessing. According to the Great Commission, to be followers of Jesus we must learn to obey everything that he has commanded. We must become not only believers, but disciples! Or, to put it another way, to be a true believer is to be an obedient disciple. We must obey also by seeking to disciple others to Christ. This is the way in which the blessing promised to the nations in the Abrahamic covenant will be fulfilled![39](Emphasis Shepherd)

Just when we think that the righteousness of Jesus Christ is what is being credited to us, it is not His perfect righteousness. Jesus' righteousness enabled Him to be righteous for Himself, but we are told that we, like Jesus, must be faithful and obey everything in order to get the Abrahamic blessing. It is through covenant loyalty that the blessings come.

At this point, Shepherd has denied the imputation of Christ's righteousness as being the basis of our justification by inference. In chapter 4, I will give quotes from Shepherd whereby he openly denies this imputation to the believer.

His commitment to individual works righteousness is further seen in this comment: *"Abraham and his seed are obligated to demonstrate new obedience. They must walk with the Lord and before the Lord in the paths of faith, repentance, and obedience. In this way, the promises of the covenant are fulfilled.*[40]

Shepherd states that we must perform repentance and obedience in order to receive the blessings. This corresponds to Shepherd's thirty-four theses that he gave twenty years earlier. His views have never changed!

The next comments are extremely important because they demonstrate how Shepherd will conveniently twist words to fit into his system of thought. Shepherd states, *"Do the promises actually describe the reward merited by good works? Not at all! Fulfilling the obligations of the Abrahamic covenant is never represented as meritorious achievement...The obedience that leads to*

---

[39] Shepherd, *The Call Of Grace,* pp. 19, 20.

[40] Shepherd, *The Call Of Grace,* p. 20.

the fulfillment of promise is totally different. It is the expression of faith and trust in the Lord, not the expression of confidence in human effort. "[41]

Shepherd defines merit as an expression of confidence in human effort; however, effort done in exercising covenant loyalty and obedience to the terms of the covenant are okay! It is important to see the distinction that Shepherd makes because he is not opposed to effort being made in order to be justified; he is just opposed to the **wrong kind** of effort being made in order to be justified!

My friends, this is works salvation! This was the legalism that Paul was confronted with by the Judaizers. This is another gospel condemned by Paul under the inspiration of the Holy Spirit in Galatians 1: 8, 9. However, we are now told that Galatians had nothing to do with a condemnation of a works salvation, but that the whole book of Galatians is simply how the Gentiles are to be accepted with the Jews. Now enters the whole theology of the New Perspective on Paul of whom N.T. Wright is a major proponent.

As we can see, once one begins the downhill slide, there is nothing to stop the person into perverting all of Scripture. In one fell swoop, all the biblical texts exhorting men to embrace Christ by faith alone in His righteousness performed for us and imputed to us is no longer the real teaching of Scripture.

Shepherd ends his chapter on the Abrahamic Covenant by stating:

> The blessings of the covenant are the gifts of God's free grace, and they are received by way of a living and active faith. Salvation is by grace through faith. By **grace** and through **faith!**[42]

Shepherd is playing games with words. He uses grace and faith, indicating that we are saved by the gifts of God's free grace. However, he has spent an entire chapter telling us that this faith is really obedience to God's covenant stipulations and that this obedience is prior to receiving all the glorious promises of the Abrahamic covenant.

This is not grace! This is a works salvation, for gifts are not earned! Before moving on to another portion of Shepherd's book, I must demonstrate Shepherd's perversion of the gospel by looking at two passages: Genesis 15: 5-6 and Romans 4.

---

[41] Shepherd, *The Call Of Grace,* pp. 20, 21.

[42] Shepherd, *The Call Of Grace*, p. 22.

Genesis 15: 5-6 reads:

> And He took him outside and said, "Now look toward the
> heavens, and count the stars, if you are able to count them."
> And He said to him, "So shall your descendants be." Then he
> believed in the Lord; and He reckoned it to him as righteous-
> ness.

This is a vital passage because it is one of the passages whereby God reaffirms
His covenant with Abraham. In Genesis 15 God assures Abraham that one of
his offspring shall be his heir through whom all the families of the earth would
be blessed. God tells Abraham in verse 5 that his heirs would one day be as
numerous as the stars of the sky.

This is one of the fundamental blessings promised to Abraham. In fact, it contains the promise of God's redemption of a great people through Jesus Christ.
Essentially, Genesis 15:5-6 is a Messianic promise. In Genesis 12:3, God
promised Abraham that in him all the families of the earth would be blessed.
Abraham, in Genesis 15, is wondering how this blessing is going to happen
without an heir.

Galatians 3:8 is an incredible passage because it explicitly says that the gospel
was preached beforehand to Abraham. The passage reads:

> And the Scripture, foreseeing that God would justify the
> Gentiles by faith, preached the gospel beforehand to
> Abraham, saying, "All the nations shall be blessed in you."

In Galatians 3:16, 29 we are told that the seed promised to Abraham was none
other than the Lord Jesus Christ (v.16) and that all who believe in Jesus are also
referred to as the seed of Abraham according to the promise (v.29).

We must note that the gospel that was preached to Abraham was said to be
specifically the promise of – "All the nations shall be blessed in you." This
promise is the gospel itself. Jesus said to some Jews in John 8:56-59 that their
father Abraham rejoiced to see His day and was glad. When they were per-
plexed as to how Abraham could have seen Jesus' day, Jesus informed them
that before Abraham was "I AM." At this point the Jews went for stones to
stone Jesus to death because they fully understood Jesus' comments. Jesus
applied the sacred name of Jehovah to Himself, implying that He was God in
the flesh.

The main significance of Genesis 15:5-6 in our understanding of Norman
Shepherd's theology is that Shepherd, as we have noted in his quotes thus far,

insists that the promises of the covenant are based on conditions and that faith itself is this covenant obedience.

It is baffling why Shepherd cannot see the obvious point of Genesis 15. When Abraham was wondering how he was going to get a seed, God told him to look at the stars and that one day his seed would be this numerous. The text says that Abraham believed God, and his faith in the promise was reckoned to him as righteousness.

There is no covenantal obedience of Abraham mentioned here! There is no circumcision mentioned as a condition for the promise! Abraham did nothing except believe. Norman Shepherd has completely twisted the Word of God.

John Calvin has made insightful comments regarding Genesis 15:5-6:

> None of us would be able to conceive the rich and hidden doctrine which this passage contains, unless Paul had borne his torch before us (Romans 4:3). But it is strange, and seems like a prodigy, that when the Spirit of God has kindled so great a light, yet the greater part of interpreters wander with closed eyes, as in the darkness of night.
>
> But it is (as I have said) monstrous, that they who have had Paul as their luminous expositor; should so foolishly have depraved this place. However it hence appears, that in all ages, Satan has labored at nothing more assiduously than to extinguish, or to smother, the gratuitous justification of faith, which is here expressly asserted. The words of Moses are, "He believed in the Lord, and he counted it to him for righteousness." In the first place, the faith of Abram is commended, because by it he embraced the promise of God; it is commended, in the second place, because hence Abram obtained righteousness in the sight of God, and that by imputation.
>
> Just as we understand that they to whom iniquity is imputed are guilty before God; so those to whom he imputes righteousness are approved by him as just persons; wherefore Abram was received into the number and rank of just persons by the imputation of righteousness.
>
> Therefore, they foolishly trifle who apply this term to his character as an honest man; as if it meant that Abram was personally held to be a just and righteous man. They also, no less unskillfully, corrupt the text, who say that Abram is here

ascribing to God the glory of righteousness seeing that he ventures to acquiesce surely in His promises, acknowledging Him to be faithful and true; for although Moses does not expressly mention the name of God, yet the accustomed method of speaking in the Scriptures removes all ambiguity. Lastly, it is not less the part of stupor than of impudence, when this faith is said to have been imputed to him for righteousness, to mingle with it some other meaning, than that the faith of Abram was accepted in the place of righteousness with God.

Therefore, we do not say that Abram was justified because he laid hold on a single word, respecting the offspring to be brought forth, but because he embraced God as his Father. And truly faith does not justify us for any other reason, than that it reconciles us unto God; and that it does so, not by its own merit; but because we receive the grace offered to us in the promises, and have no doubt of eternal life, being fully persuaded that we are loved by God as sons. Therefore, Paul reasons from contraries, that he to whom faith is imputed for righteousness, has not been justified by works. (Romans 4:4)

Whence it follows, that the merit of works ceases when righteousness is sought by faith; for it is necessary that this righteousness should be freely given by God, and offered in his word, in order that any one may possess it by faith. To render this more intelligible, when Moses says that faith was imputed to Abram for righteousness, he does not mean that faith was that first cause of righteousness which is called the **efficient**, but only the **formal** cause; as if he had said, that Abram was therefore justified, because, relying on the paternal loving-kindness of God, he trusted to His mere goodness, and not to himself, nor to his own merits. For it is especially to be observed, that faith borrows a righteousness elsewhere, of which we, in ourselves, are destitute; otherwise it would be in vain for Paul to set faith in opposition to works, when speaking of the mode of obtaining righteousness. Besides, the mutual relation between the free promise and faith leaves no doubt upon the subject. (Emphasis Calvin)

Therefore, by a consideration of the time in which this was said to Abram, we certainly gather, that the righteousness of works is not to be substituted for the righteousness of faith, in any such way, that one should perfect what the other has begun; but that holy men are only justified by faith, as long as they live in the world.

Meanwhile, however, this is a settled point, that men are justified before God by believing not by working; while they obtain grace by faith, because they are unable to deserve a reward by works. Paul also, in hence contending, that Abram did not merit by works the righteousness which he had received before his circumcision, does not impugn the above doctrine. The argument of Paul is of this kind: The circumcision of Abram was posterior to his justification in the order of time, and therefore could not be its cause, for of necessity the cause precedes its effect. I also grant, that Paul, for this reason, contends that works are not meritorious, except under the covenant of the law, of which covenant, circumcision is put as the earnest and the symbol.

Both arguments are therefore of force; first, that the righteousness of Abram cannot be ascribed to the covenant of the law, because it preceded his circumcision; and, secondly, that the righteousness even of the most perfect characters perpetually consists in faith; since Abram, with all the excellency of his virtues, after his daily and even remarkable service of God, was, nevertheless, justified by faith. For this also is, in the last place, worthy of observation, that what is here related concerning one man, is applicable to all the sons of God. For since he was called the father of the faithful, not without reason; and since further, there is but one method of obtaining salvation; Paul properly teaches, that a real and not personal righteousness is in this place described.[43]

I have quoted from Calvin extensively because Calvin absolutely and unequivocally refutes Norman Shepherd's view of justification by faith. The fact that Shepherd believes that his views are in line with Reformed thinking is quite sad. It is significant that Calvin ties in Genesis 15:5-6 with Romans 4:3 because the Genesis passage is the basis for Paul's argument in Romans 4. I encourage the reader to go back and examine Shepherd's quote about Genesis

---

[43] John Calvin, *The Comprehensive John Calvin Collection.* Calvin's Commentary on Genesis 15. (Albany,OR: Sages Software, 1998), p. 279-283.

15:6, which is found in the second paragraph on page 55 of this chapter, and you will see the glaring error that Shepherd makes.

In Shepherd's fourth condition to receive the blessings of the Abrahamic covenant, he says that Abraham was commanded to walk blameless before the Lord and to be obedient. It is important that Shepherd insists on Abraham's obedience in order to receive the blessing of his seed being as numerous as the stars. He states:

> … I will make your descendants as numerous as the stars in the sky and will give them all these lands, and through your offspring all nations on earth will be blessed, because Abraham obeyed me and kept my requirements, my commands, my decrees and my laws.[44]

I will let Calvin respond to Shepherd's erroneous thinking regarding Shepherd's interpretation of Genesis 26:4-5:

> Moses does not mean that Abraham's obedience was the reason why the promise of God was confirmed and ratified to him; but from what has been said before, (Genesis 22:18) where we have a similar expression, we learn, that what God freely bestows upon the faithful is sometimes, beyond their desert, ascribed to themselves; that they, knowing their intention to be approved by the Lord, may the more ardently addict and devote themselves entirely to his service: so he now commends the obedience of Abraham, in order that Isaac may be stimulated to an imitation of his example.[45]

Romans 4

Let's now examine Romans 4 and demonstrate from this part of God's word just how Shepherd has completely misunderstood the Word of God and has advocated a works salvation.

Romans 4:1-5 states:

> What then shall we say that Abraham, our forefather according to the flesh, has found? For if Abraham was justified by works, he has something to boast about; but not before God. For what does the Scripture say? And Abraham believed

---

[44] Shepherd, *The Call Of Grace*, p. 17.
[45] Calvin, Commentary On Genesis 26:5, p. 464.

God, and it was reckoned to him as righteousness. Now to the one who works, his wage is not reckoned as a favor, but as what is due. But to the one who does not work, but believes in Him who justifies the ungodly, his faith is reckoned as righteousness.

Romans 4:9-16 states:

Is this blessing then upon the circumcised, or upon the uncircumcised also? For we say, "Faith was reckoned to Abraham as righteousness." How then was it reckoned? While he was circumcised, or uncircumcised? Not while circumcised, but while uncircumcised; and he received the sign of circumcision, a seal of the righteousness of the faith which he had while uncircumcised, that he might be the father of all who believe without being circumcised, that righteousness might be reckoned to them, and the father of circumcision to those who not only are of the circumcision, but who also follow in the steps of the faith of our father Abraham which he had while uncircumcised. For the promise to Abraham or to his descendants that he would be heir of the world was not through the Law, but through the righteousness of faith. For if those who are of the Law are heirs, faith is made void and the promise is nullified; for the Law brings about wrath, but where there is no law, neither is there violation. For this reason it is by faith, that it might be in accordance with grace, in order that the promise may be certain to all the descendants, not only to those who are of the Law, but also to those who are of the faith of Abraham, who is the father of us all.

It is vital that we understand Paul's argument in Romans 4 and where it differs from Shepherd's understanding. Let's reiterate the salient points that Shepherd has made thus far. Shepherd has stated that the promises of the Abrahamic covenant, such as the promise of a numerous seed, is a conditional promise. It is conditioned upon faith, a faith whose essence is faithful obedience to the covenant. Shepherd has argued that circumcision was a requirement for Abraham to receive the blessings, of which a numerous seed was one such vital promise.

Shepherd's understanding is a total corruption of Romans 4. His corruption constitutes a perversion of the gospel. Paul's polemic in Romans 4 is purposed as a refutation of the Judaizers, who were making salvation based upon obedience to the Law of Moses.

It is clear from Romans 4:1-5 that the contrast is between faith and works. Paul defines works as the receiving of wages for labor performed. Faith has nothing to do with any kind of work, for God's Word says, "*But to the one who does not work, but believes in Him who justifies the ungodly, his faith is reckoned as righteousness.*"

What Paul has done is to clearly affirm that the promise given to Abraham had nothing to do with any righteousness on Abraham's part. And remember, the promise being referred to is the promise of a seed as numerous as the stars in heaven. There was no obedience of Abraham that earned him God's favor.

When did Abraham have righteousness credited to his account? Before or after circumcision? Paul argues that circumcision came **after** his faith. Faith precedes the sacrament. Now, Shepherd has said that one of the conditions of the blessings is that circumcision is required, which would make it **before** the blessing.

Paul affirms in Romans 4:13 that the promise that Abraham would be heir of the world (this is the promise of a numerous seed) was not through law, which is obedience, but through faith. In Romans 4:14, Paul contrasts those of faith and those of the law. Any attempt to be an heir of the promise through personal righteousness in keeping the law is a vain attempt. Such attempts will get one nothing! Romans 4:16 clearly states that faith is in accord with grace. Grace and law keeping are contrasted in terms of acquiring the promises. Shepherd does not believe this because his says that grace and faith are two parts of the covenant. Again, notice what Shepherd says:

> The blessings of the covenant are the gifts of God's free grace, and they are received by way of a living and active faith. Salvation is by grace through faith. By **grace** and through **faith**! Those are the two parts of the covenant. (Emphasis is Shepherd).[46]

For Shepherd, faith is active in the sense that it entails obedience, which is why he defines faith as the "obedience of faith." This is not what God's Word says! Shepherd is explicitly in opposition to the Scripture. He has corrupted the gospel.

---

[46] Shepherd, *The Call Of Grace*, p. 22.

I must bring in Calvin's perspective on this issue by various quotes from his Institutes. He says:

> Let us also, to begin with, show that faith righteousness so differs from works righteousness that when one is established the other has to be overthrown.[47]

> When reward is made for works it is done out of debt, not of grace [Romans 4:4]. But righteousness according to grace is owed to faith. Therefore it does not arise from the merits of works. Farewell, then, to the dream of those who think up a righteousness flowing together out of faith and works.[48]

> The Sophists, who make game and sport in their corrupting of Scripture and their empty caviling, think they have a subtle evasion. For they explain "works" as meaning those which men not yet reborn do only according to the letter by the effort of their own free will, apart from Christ's grace. But they deny that these refer to spiritual works. For, according to them, man is justified by both faith and works provided they are not his own works but the gifts of Christ and the fruit of regeneration.[49]

At this point, allow me to again quote Shepherd so that the reader can see that Calvin is referring exactly to people like Shepherd.

Shepherd states:

> Abraham and his seed are obligated to demonstrate new obedience. They must walk with the Lord and before the Lord in the paths of faith, repentance, and obedience. In this way, the promises of the covenant are fulfilled.

> Do the promises actually describe the reward merited by good works? Not at all! Fulfilling the obligations of the Abrahamic covenant is never represented as meritorious achievement...The obedience that leads to the fulfillment of promise is totally different. It is the expression of faith and

---

[47] John Calvin, *Institutes of the Christian Religion,* translated by Ford Lewis Battles, ed. John T. McNeill, Library of Christian Classics. (Philadelphia: The Westminster Press, 1975). Book 3, Chapter 11, Section 13, p. 743.

[48] Calvin, *Institutes*, p. 744.

[49] Calvin, *Institutes*.

trust in the Lord, not the expression of confidence in human effort.[50]

Notice that Shepherd is calling the works, not meritorious, but the works are said to be obedience nonetheless. Calvin called this kind of reasoning as Sophistry. It is a play on words that Calvin calls empty caviling.

In referring to these Sophists, of which Shepherd is a modern day version, Calvin states:

> Still they do not observe that in the contrast between the righteousness of the law and of the gospel, which Paul else-where introduces, all works are excluded, whatever title may grace them [Galatians 3:11-12].[51]

> Moreover, we shall see afterward, in its proper place, that the benefits of Christ—sanctification and righteousness— are different. From this it follows that not even spiritual works come into account when the power of justifying is ascribed to faith. The statement of Paul where he denies that Abraham had any reason to boast before God—a passage that we have just cited —because he was not righteous by his works, ought not to be restricted to a literal and outward appearance of virtues or to the effort of free will. But even though the life of the patriarch was spiritual and well nigh angelic, he did not have sufficient merit of works to acquire righteousness before God.[52]

Calvin could have been speaking directly to Norman Shepherd when he said:

> As regards the rank and the of the papists or Schoolmen, they are doubly deceived here both because they call faith an assurance of conscience in awaiting from God their reward for merits and because they interpret the grace of God not as the imputation of free righteousness but as the Spirit helping in the pursuit of holiness.

> It is clear from their own writings that in using the term "grace" they are deluded. For Lombard explains that justifi-cation is given to us through Christ in two ways. First, he

---

[50] Shepherd, *The Call Of Grace*, pp. 20, 21.

[51] Calvin, *Institutes*, p. 744.

[52] Calvin, *Institutes*.

says, Christ's death justifies us, while love is aroused through
it in our hearts and makes us righteous. Second, because
through the same love, sin is extinguished by which the devil
held us captive, so that he no longer has the wherewithal to
condemn us. You see how he views God's grace especially in
justification, in so far as we are directed through the grace of
the Holy Spirit to good works. Obviously, he intended to follow Augustine's opinion, but he follows it at a distance and
even departs considerably from the right imitation of it. For
when Augustine says anything clearly, Lombard obscures it,
and if there was anything slightly contaminated in Augustine,
he corrupts it.[53]

Shepherd and the Federal Vision proponents like to talk about "faith working
through love" as meaning that love is not simply the fruit of faith but that it is
the essence of it. As one will note from the above quote, Calvin recognizes that
argument for what it is – salvation by works, which he says is a Papist argument.

Calvin speaks directly to this idea of justifying faith incorporating the work of
love. He states:

Also, they pointlessly strive after the foolish subtlety that we
are justified by faith alone, which acts through love, so that
righteousness depends upon love. Indeed, we confess with
Paul that no other faith justifies" but faith working through
love" (Galatians 5:6). But it does not take its power to justify
from that working of love. Indeed, it justifies in no other way
but in that it leads us into fellowship with the righteousness
of Christ.[54]

As I noted in the earlier part of this chapter, Shepherd's view returns us to
Roman Catholicism. His desire to bridge the gap between Romanism and
Protestantism is really a one-way bridge back to Rome.

Calvin continues:

But Scripture, when it speaks of faith righteousness, leads us
to something far different: namely, to turn aside from the con-

---

[53] Calvin, *Institutes*, p. 745.

[54] Calvin, *Institutes*, p. 750.

templation of our own works and look solely upon God's mercy and Christ's perfection.[55]

As I have noted previously, Shepherd affirmed that grace and faith were two parts of the covenant and that faith was active, living, and obedient. Well, Calvin has something to say about this:

> From this relation it is clear that those who are justified by faith are justified apart from the merit of works—in fact, without the merit of works. For faith receives that righteousness which the gospel bestows. Now the gospel differs from the law in that it does not link righteousness to works but lodges it solely in God's mercy.[56]

In the following quote, Calvin might as well have had the Federal Vision books in hand when he said:

> Now the reader sees how fairly the Sophists today cavil against our doctrine when we say that man is justified by faith alone (Romans 3: 28). They dare not deny that man is justified by faith because it recurs so often in Scripture. But since the word "alone" is nowhere expressed, they do not allow this addition to be made. Is it so? But what will they reply to these words of Paul where he contends that righteousness cannot be of faith unless it be free (Romans 4:2 ff.)? How will a free gift agree with works? With what chicaneries will they elude what he says in another passage, that God's righteousness is revealed in the gospel (Romans 1:17)? If righteousness is revealed in the gospel, surely no mutilated or half righteousness but a full and perfect righteousness is contained there. The law therefore has no place in it. Not only by a false but by an obviously ridiculous shift they insist upon excluding this adjective.[57]

Norman Shepherd simply cannot get away from incorporating obedience as the very nature of saving faith. He continually insists that the term "the righteousness of faith" is linked with personal obedience, which the Scripture rejects. Shepherd states:

---

[55] Calvin, *Institute,* p. 746.

[56] Calvin, *Institutes,* p. 748.

[57] Calvin, *Institutes*, pp. 748,749.

The obedience required of Israel is not the obedience of merit, but the obedience of faith. It is the fullness of faith. Obedience is simply faithfulness to the Lord; it is the right-eousness of faith (compare Rom. 9:32)...Obedience in the Mosaic covenant is not meritorious achievement, but the expression of faith.[58]

In his chapter entitled "The New Covenant" in his book *Call Of Grace*, Shepherd makes this incredible statement about the Great Commission:

In giving this missionary mandate, Jesus told his followers to make disciples of the nations. Disciples not only believe with their minds, but also obey with their hands and feet. Jesus says that his disciples must be taught "to obey everything I have commanded you" (Matt. 28:19, 20). "You are my friends if you do what I command" (John 15:14). "If you obey my commands, you will remain in my love, just as I have obeyed my Father's commands and remain in his love" (John 15:10).

Those who claim to live in him and to have life in him "must walk as Jesus did" (I John 2:6). They must become obedient, as he was obedient. "The man who says, 'I know him,' but does not do what he commands is a liar, and the truth is not in him" (I John 2:4). "And this is his command: to believe in the name of his Son, Jesus Christ, and to love one another as he commanded us" (I John 3:23). This last verse is most striking. **Even faith itself is a matter of obedience to the command of our Lord.**[59] (Emphasis mine)

In these quotes, Shepherd makes it very clear that the gospel of the Lord Jesus is linked to obedience to the commandments of God, not as works being the evidence of a person who has faith but as the very essence of faith. Once again, he has perverted the word of God by teaching a works salvation. This works salvation paradigm of Shepherd is further seen in the following quote:

Eternal life is promised as an undeserved gift from the Lord. He forgives our sins and receives us as righteous because of Jesus Christ and his redemptive accomplishment on our behalf. At the same time, faith, repentance, obedience, and

---

[58] Shepherd, *The Call of Grace,* pp. 39, 41.

[59] Shepherd, *The Call of Grace,* p. 48.

perseverance are indispensable to the enjoyment of these blessings. They are conditions, but they are not meritorious conditions. Faith is required, but faith looks away from personal merit to the promises of God. Repentance and obedience flow from faith as the fullness of faith. This is faithfulness, and faithfulness is perseverance in faith. A living, active, and abiding faith is the way in which the believer enters into eternal life.

Even here in James 2, eternal life is a free gift, unearned and unmerited, but it must be received by a penitent and obedient faith. Repentance and obedience are necessary, but they are not the meritorious grounds of our acceptance with God. Salvation remains a gift of God's free grace.[60]

False teachers, historically, have always couched their heresies by using biblical terms but totally changing their meaning. Shepherd uses the words, "faith," "gift of God's free grace," but they do not mean what orthodox Christianity has understood them. We have already documented that Shepherd understands "meritorious" as works stemming from our own thoughts and efforts, which he defines as "personal merit." But, works, as seen in Scripture are any kind of works, including the works of the law of God. Shepherd calls repentance and obedience as the "fullness" of faith. This is simply another expression for calling faith – the obedience of faith. In order to remain justified, one must exercise faithfulness and persevere in it. In a later chapter, I will examine where Shepherd and other Federal Vision proponents have abandoned the Reformed doctrine of the perseverance of the saints and openly teach that one can lose what they once genuinely possessed in Christ. Notice in Shepherd's quote that faithfulness is the way we enter into eternal life!

Several times Shepherd mentions the following quote in his book *The Call Of Grace:*

Salvation is both by **grace** and through **faith**. These are the two parts of the covenant: grace and faith, promise and obligation. Grace is not without conditions, and a living and active faith is not meritorious achievement.[61] (Emphasis Shepherd)

---

[60] Shepherd, *The Call of Grace*, pp. 50, 51.

[61] Shepherd, *The Call of Grace*, p. 63.

Notice Shepherd's grammatical construction. Grace corresponds with promise and faith corresponds with obligation. Of course, he says, we are not talking about meritorious achievement, but we know how he has defined that. The idea that **grace with conditions** is not Reformed doctrine!

Shepherd shows great confusion and distorts Romans 1:5 when he says:

> For Abraham, the sign of both covenant privilege and covenant responsibility was circumcision. Paul calls circumcision "a seal of the righteousness that he had by faith" (Rom. 4:11). The righteousness of faith is the obedience of faith (Rom. 1:5; 16:26), and is therefore simultaneously covenant privilege and responsibility.[62]

It is clear from Shepherd's comment that he understands the phrase "the obedience of faith" found in Romans 1:5 and 16:26 to mean the believer's covenant responsibility, one of which was circumcision.

To demonstrate his misinterpretation of the text we refer to Calvin, John Murray, and Lenski. Calvin's commentary on Romans 1:5 in regard to the phrase "the obedience of faith" is as follows:

> That is, we have received a command to preach the gospel among all nations, and this gospel they obey by faith... We must also notice here what faith is; the name of obedience is given to it, and for this reason — because the Lord calls us by his gospel; we respond to his call by faith; as on the other hand, the chief act of disobedience to God is unbelief, I prefer rendering the sentence, "For the obedience of faith," rather than, "In order that they may obey the faith;" for the last is not strictly correct, except taken figuratively, though it be found once in the Acts 6:7. Faith is properly that by which we obey the gospel.[63]

Calvin simply understood the phrase "the obedience of faith" to be the act of obeying the call of the gospel, which is to have faith in Christ. It has nothing to do with explaining faith's essence as being obedience to God's commands.

John Murray refers to the phrase, "the obedience of faith" to mean:

---

[62] Shepherd, *The Call of Grace,* p. 76.

[63] John Calvin, *The Comprehensive John Calvin Collection.* Calvin's Commentary on Romans 1:5. (Albany, OR: Sages Software, 1998), p. 34.

Faith is regarded as an act of obedience, of commitment to the gospel of Christ. Hence the implications of this expression "obedience of faith" are far reaching. For the faith which the apostleship was intended to promote was not an evanescent act of emotion but the commitment of wholehearted devotion to Christ and to the truth of his gospel. It is to such faith that all nations are called.[64]

And finally, R. C. H. Lenski makes these comments on the phrase "the obedience of faith":

The view that it is the subjective genitive is usually rejected because the obedience which faith renders is thought to be that of works (Zahn, for instance, referring to Gal.5: 6; James 2:14, 22). The same objection would hold good against "faith-obedience" if works were referred to. But here the obedience lies in the very act of believing and not in the category of works. God's gospel calls on us to acknowledge, receive, and appropriate it as what it is; and doing this by the power and the grace coming to us in the gospel, in full confidence and trust, is this essential obedience of faith.[65]

If it isn't clear by now that Norman Shepherd has turned the Gospel into a works oriented paradigm, then this comment near the end of his book should seal it. He says:

It is both striking and significant that the Great Commission in neither Matthew nor Luke speaks of calling upon sinners to believe. Faith is not mentioned specifically, but only by implication. What is explicitly asserted is the call to repentance and obedience. When the call to faith is isolated from the call to obedience, as it frequently is, the effect is to make good works a supplement to salvation or simply the evidence of salvation ... According to the Great Commission, however, they belong to the essence of salvation, which is freedom from sin and not simply freedom from eternal condemnation

---

[64] John Murray, *The New International Commentary on the New Testament,* Epistle To The Romans. (Grand Rapids, Michigan: Eerdman's Publishing Company, 1968), pp. 13,14.

[65] R.C.H. Lenski, *Interpretation of Romans,*(Minneapolis, Minnesota: Augsburg Publishing House, 1961), p. 47.

as the consequence of sin. Because good works are done in obedience to all that Christ commanded, they are suffused with and qualified by faith, with which no one can please God (Heb. 11:6).[66]

Shepherd's article in Reformation and Revival [67]

Norman Shepherd does not like the term "justification by faith alone," and he gives his explanation why the Westminster Standards does not use that particular phraseology. Although, Larger Catechism answer number 70 uses the phrase "received by faith alone." He thinks that the Westminster fathers wanted to avoid serious misunderstanding of the gospel. (p. 85) However, we will see in a subsequent chapter that the Westminster Standards definitely teach the theology of "justification by faith alone."

Shepherd takes issue with Martin Luther's insertion of the word "alone" in Luther's translation of Romans 3:28, which would make the text to read, "For we hold that one is justified by faith **alone** apart from works of the law." Shepherd says that this distorts Paul's meaning. (p. 87) Shepherd is no real friend of Luther and neither is Federal Vision proponent Steve Schlissel. In another chapter, one will definitely see that Schlissel has great disdain for Luther's formulations.

Shepherd states: "*there is no such thing as a faith that exists alone, all by itself.*" (p. 83) He states: "*faith and repentance are inseparable twins.*" (p.84) Shepherd continues: "*It is not an adequate answer to say that justification is by faith alone, meaning faith without repentance, but that repentance will inevitably follow as the fruit and evidence of faith and justification.*" (p. 85) "*We must not resort to the idea that repentance and obedience automatically follow upon justification as evidence of salvation that is granted by faith alone apart from repentance and obedience.*" (p. 87)

From these comments, Shepherd has clearly put himself at odds with the Scripture and the Confessional Standards. This is where people simply think that Shepherd is merely stating that obedience is the fruit of faith. This is **not** what he is saying. He clearly stated that we should not think this way. Shepherd has stated:

---

[66] Shepherd, *The Call of Grace,* p. 104.

[67] Norman, Shepherd, "Justification By Faith Alone," *Reformation and Revival* 11:2 (Spring 2002), pp. 75-90.

… justifying faith does not have the other gifts and graces **added to it at a later point**, after it has brought about justification. (p. 81) (Emphasis mine)

Shepherd states that "*the sequence is of fundamental importance.*" (p. 81) The sequence that is wrong according to Shepherd is the placing of covenantal obedience as a fruit or evidence of faith, making it come after faith.

I agree with David H. Linden's comment about Shepherd's understanding of justifying faith when he states:

The question is this: does the Confession teach that justifying faith includes the other saving graces at the moment when a person is justified? What he is teaching is this: when a person is justified by faith, that justifying faith has in it already all these other graces.[68]

Let's look carefully at what the Westminster Confession of Faith says in Chapter 11 Section 2:

Faith, thus receiving and resting on Christ and His righteousness, is the alone instrument of justification; yet is it not alone in the person justified, but is ever accompanied with all other saving graces.

We must carefully note that the Confession states that all the other saving graces **accompany** the faith **in the person justified.** The Confession clearly teaches that these saving graces, of which obedience to God's commands is one, are an attachment or fruit or evidence of justifying faith. Shepherd is completely distorting the meaning of the Confession. Let's think what Shepherd's view is implying. If covenantal obedience is part of the means by which a person is justified, then the gospel preacher must demand that these graces be present in the one who is being preached to. The Confession clearly states that these accompanying graces are **in a justified person**. This means that the graces cannot be the instrument of justification. What it means is that the accompanying graces are expressed naturally in a person who has already been justified. It is very important that we get this straight because the difference is between biblical Christianity and heresy. It is heresy to state that obedience to God's laws is part and parcel with justifying faith.

---

[68] Norman, Shepherd, "Justification By Faith Alone," Review by Faith Alone" by David H. Linden (Reformation and Revival Journal Vol. 11, Number 2, Spring 2002) p.4

The Westminster Confession of Faith, Chapter 14, Section 2 states:

> By this faith, a **Christian** believeth to be true whatsoever is revealed in the Word, for the authority of God Himself speaking therein; and acteth differently upon that which each particular passage thereof containeth; yielding obedience to the commands trembling at the threatenings, and embracing the promises of God for this life, and that which is to come. But the principal acts of saving faith are accepting, receiving, and resting upon Christ alone for justification, sanctification, and eternal life, by virtue of the covenant of grace. (Emphasis mine)

Looking at this closely, we note that it is a Christian who yields obedience to God's commands, who trembles at God's warnings, who embraces the promises of God. The Christian is one who is already justified. Hence, obedience cannot be that which defines the nature of justifying faith. David Linden states very well the implications of Shepherd's views:

> In other words he takes the virtue of a person already justified and vitally united to Christ, and he then makes that a condition up front for a justification that is supposed to be by faith alone according to the catechisms. It is a massive confusion that destroys justification by taking the faith of a poor sinner with no righteousness and demands that he come with obedience. Shepherd might as well say that to become a Christian you have to be one first.[69]

When Shepherd emphasizes repentance, he greatly errs by making the fruits of repentance as a condition for justification. David Linden observes:

> Change from sinfulness is not optional to God, but it is simply not the point of justification. We are accepted in Christ, we are justified only in His righteousness. By modifying faith, as he has to include our obedience, the attention of real faith is adulterously diverted from the true righteousness. It is only because of Jesus' law keeping and only because of Jesus' obedience that God can ever justify any sinner. Shepherd cannot get out of his peculiar covenantal thinking that we are justified in our covenantal faithfulness.

---

[69] Linden's review of Shepherd, p. 5.

Faithfulness is required of us as covenant people; it is not required for justification.[70]

One of the inevitable results of Shepherd's association of Christian graces being tied with the nature of justifying faith is that **it makes justification a process.** This is why Shepherd says in his original Thesis 23 that good works are necessary for **continuing in the state of justification.** Here we see Shepherd's utter confusion of the relationship of justification with sanctification. Reformed thinkers for centuries have made it a point to help students realize that justification is an **act** of God's free grace, stressing that it is a completed action, whereby sanctification is a **work** of God's free grace, stressing that it is a life time process that is encumbered with imperfection.

Shepherd has made these incredible statements:

> Regeneration initiated the process of sanctification, and saving faith, emerges in the believer in the process of sanctification. This process brings to life not only faith but also repentance and obedience. Just this priority of regeneration to faith explains why faith can never be alone "but is ever accompanied with all the other saving graces, and is no dead faith, but worketh by love.
>
> Faith is logically prior to justification. We believe with a view to being justified. Because regeneration is prior to faith and is the initiation of sanctification, **we have to say that the process of sanctification begun is prior to justification.**[71] (Emphasis mine)
>
> … the personal godliness of the believer is also necessary for his justification in the judgment of the last day (Matt. 7:21-23; 25:31-46; Heb. 12:14)… abiding in Christ by keeping his commandments (John 15:5, 10; I John 3:13; 24) are all necessary for continuing in the state of justification.[72]

Shepherd has totally corrupted the biblical and Reformed ordo salutis (the order of salvation). In Shepherd's thinking, justification is in a continual state of process, and seeing that the process of justification is linked with our covenantal faithfulness, then we really don't know what the outcome of our

---

[70] Linden's review of Shepherd, p. 8.

[71] Shepherd, "Justification By Faith Alone," p. 83

[72] Shepherd, *"Thirty-four Theses on Justification in Relation to Faith, Repentance, and Good Works,"* Theses 22 and 23

salvation is until the day we die. Shepherd's erroneous views open wide the doors for the explicit denial of the doctrine of the perseverance of the saints. This denial is exactly what he does, as well as other proponents of the Federal Vision. We shall demonstrate this fact in another chapter.

A Biblical and Reformed Understanding of James Chapter 2

Norman Shepherd and the other proponents of the Federal Vision have a particular understanding of James chapter 2. They cannot envision how a man can be justified by faith alone apart from obedience or works. This passage is supposedly one of the great proofs that the essence of faith is obedience. This interpretation is one that is espoused by Roman Catholicism, which only goes to demonstrate that the Federal Vision is a downhill slope to Romanism.

Shepherd states:

> By faith, Abraham obeyed the voice of God and left his homeland in order to inherit a Promised Land. By faith, he was ready to offer Isaac as a sacrifice, confident that God would nevertheless fulfill his promise. James 2 is even more explicit. Verse 21 says that Abraham was considered righteous for what he did when he offered his son Isaac on the altar. His faith and his actions were working together, and his faith was made complete by what he did. Verse 23 says, "And the scripture was fulfilled that says, 'Abraham believed God, and it was credited to him as righteousness,' and he was called God's friend." James goes on to say that faith without deeds is dead. For that reason, he can also say in verse 24 that "a person is justified by what he does and not by faith alone." The faith credited to Abraham as righteousness was a living and active faith.[73]

James 2:17 says, "Even so faith, if it has no works, is dead, being by itself." Calvin makes this comment about this verse:

> He says that faith is dead, being by itself, that is, when destitute of good works. We hence conclude that it is indeed no faith, for when dead, it does not properly retain the name. The Sophists plead this expression and say, that some sort of faith is found by itself; but this frivolous caviling is easily refuted;

---

[73] Shepherd, *Call of Grace,* pp. 15-16.

for it is sufficiently evident that the Apostle reasons from what is impossible, as Paul calls an angel anathema, if he attempted to subvert the gospel (Gal. 1:8).[74]

James 2:18 states, *"But someone may well say, 'You have faith, and I have works; show me your faith without the works, and I will show you my faith by my works'."* Calvin comments:

> The meaning then is, "Unless thy faith brings forth fruits, I deny that thou hast any faith." But it may be asked, whether the outward uprightness of life is a sure evidence of faith? For James says, "I will shew thee my faith by my works." To this I reply, that the unbelieving sometimes excel in specious virtues, and lead an honorable life free from every crime; and hence works apparently excellent may exist apart from faith. Nor indeed does James maintain that every one who seems good possesses faith. This only he means, that faith, without the evidence of good works, is vainly pretended, because fruit ever comes from the living root of a good tree.[75]

James 2:21 says, *"Was not Abraham our father justified by works, when he offered up Isaac his son on the altar?"* Calvin says:

> The Sophists lay hold on the word justified, and then they cry out as being victorious, that justification is partly by works. But we ought to seek out a right interpretation according to the general drift of the whole passage. We have already said that James does not speak here of the cause of justification, or of the manner how men obtain righteousness, and this is plain to every one; but that his object was only to shew that good works are always connected with faith; and, therefore, since he declares that Abraham was justified by works, he is speaking of the proof he gave of his justification. When, therefore, the Sophists set up James against Paul, they go astray through the ambiguous meaning of a term. When Paul says that we are justified by faith, he means no other thing than that by faith we are counted righteous before God. But James has quite another thing in view, even to shew that he who professes that he has faith, must prove the reality of his

---

[74] John Calvin, *The Comprehensive John Calvin Collection.* Calvin's Commentary on James 2:17. (Albany, OR: Sages Software, 1998).

[75] Calvin on James 2:18.

faith by his works. Doubtless James did not mean to teach us here the ground on which our hope of salvation ought to rest; and it is this alone that Paul dwells upon.

That we may not then fall into that false reasoning which has deceived the Sophists, we must take notice of the two-fold meaning, of the word justified. Paul means by it the gratuitous imputation of righteousness before the tribunal of God; and James, the manifestation of righteousness by the conduct, and that before men, as we may gather from the preceding words, "Shew to me thy faith," etc. In this sense we fully allow that man is justified by works, as when any one says that a man is enriched by the purchase of a large and valuable chest, because his riches, before hid, shut up in a chest, were thus made known.[76]

James 2:22-23 states: *"You see that faith was working with his works, and as a result of the works, faith was perfected; and the Scripture was fulfilled which says, 'And Abraham believed God, and it was reckoned to Him as righteousness, and he was called the friend of God.'"*

They who seek to prove from this passage of James that the works of Abraham were imputed for righteousness, must necessarily confess that Scripture is perverted by him; for however they may turn and twist, they can never make the effect to be its own cause. The passage is quoted from Moses. (Genesis 15:6) The imputation of righteousness which Moses mentions, preceded more than thirty years the work by which they would have Abraham to have been justified. Since faith was imputed to Abraham fifteen years before the birth of Isaac, this could not surely have been done through the work of sacrificing him. I consider that all those are bound fast by an indissoluble knot, who imagine that righteousness was imputed to Abraham before God, because he sacrificed his son Isaac, who was not yet born when the Holy Spirit declared that Abraham was justified.

Why then does James say that it was fulfilled? Even because he intended to shew what sort of faith that was which justified Abraham; that is, that it was not idle or evanescent, but

---

[76] Calvin on James 2:21.

rendered him obedient to God, as also we find in Hebrews 11:8. The conclusion, which is immediately added, as it depends on this, has no other meaning. Man is not justified by faith alone, that is, by a bare and empty knowledge of God; he is justified by works, that is, his righteousness is known and proved by its fruits.[77]

Regarding James 2 and Romans 3, there is no contradiction between James and Paul. Their emphases were completely different. Paul is addressing the **grounds or basis** of man's justification and how Christ's perfect righteousness is imputed to him. James is addressing the **demonstration** of a man's faith. James is concerned with easy-believism and hypocrisy. James is refuting the idea that one can simply assent to certain propositions but never act upon them. James mentions in 2:19 that the demons believe in certain biblical facts, but this does not save them. A similar intellectual faith or mere assent will not save men either.

James is distinguishing between genuine faith and false faith. A profession of faith without the fruit or evidence to demonstrate its validity is not saving faith at all. This is James' point. For Shepherd and the Federal Vision to import into James 2 the idea that obedience to God's law is the very essence and definition of faith is a foreign teaching to the Word of God.

Good works always accompany genuine faith, but this does not mean that faith itself is the good work. Good works are not the conditions for faith as Shepherd leads us to believe.

---

[77] Calvin on James 2:22, 23.

Chapter 4

A Denial of Christ's Active Obedience in Justification

When one begins the downhill slide into heresy, one heresy leads to another. I have already demonstrated that Norman Shepherd, who is a leading proponent of the Federal Vision, has corrupted the biblical doctrine of justification by faith alone. This corruption has led him to advocate a works salvation paradigm. Justifying faith has been redefined as covenantal obedience to God's commandments. This heresy inevitably leads to another heresy – the outright denial of Christ's active obedience in the justification of the believer. In this denial, the Federal Vision has denied the covenant of works; hence, I must set forth the salient elements of this covenant and its bearing on the doctrine of Christ's active obedience.

In this chapter, I will demonstrate from Shepherd's lectures that he has openly denied this vital aspect of biblical, orthodox Christianity. I will demonstrate where other Federal Vision adherents have denied this doctrine as well. I will use some of the Reformers and other Reformed thinkers to refute their statements such as John Calvin and John Owen. In this chapter, I will positively set forth the biblical, Reformed doctrine of Christ's active obedience in man's justification and the support for this doctrine from the Reformed Standards and Scripture.

Christ's Work of Imputation

Before I get into the details of the departure of the Federal Vision from this precious doctrine, I must give a brief description of the Reformed doctrine of Christ's work of imputation so that one can have a general concept of how the Federal Vision distorts the doctrine.

What do we mean by the word "imputation?" It means to credit to another's account; to lay to one's charge; to reckon to. In has been customary in the Reformed Faith to recognize a two-fold imputation. The first imputation is the imputation of Adam's guilt to all mankind because he is the representative head of the human race. Romans 5:12-14 says, "*Therefore, just as through one man sin entered into the world, and death through sin, and so death spread to all men, because all sinned ...Nevertheless death reigned from Adam until Moses, even over those who had not sinned in the likeness of the offense of Adam, who is a type of Him who was to come.*" The second imputation is the imputation of Christ's obedience to believers. This imputation is seen in Romans 5:16-19. See the text in a later section in this chapter.

When we speak of Christ's imputation to believers, the historic Reformed Faith has understood this to entail two important aspects that came to be known as the **passive** and **active** obedience of Christ. The passive obedience refers to Christ's atoning work on the cross whereby He suffered and died for His people. The active obedience refers to His imparting of His righteous Law keeping to the account of His people, giving them title to eternal life. Some Reformers have used different names such as the **penal** and **prescriptive** work of Christ, referring to the passive and active obedience respectively.

In speaking about the passive obedience of Christ, I don't want to leave the impression that Jesus was inactive in His death. Jesus obeyed the Father in His suffering. Hebrews 5:8 says that Jesus learned obedience from the things that he suffered. Philippians 2:6-8 states that in His incarnation, the Son of God became obedient unto death, even the death on the cross. Acts 20:28 says that God purchased the church with His own blood – a reference of course to Jesus. In Hebrews 7:27, Jesus offered up Himself to be the sacrifice of sins. Jesus said in John 10:17 that he willingly laid down His own life. As we can see, Jesus was, in this sense, very active in His suffering and death. Probably the reason why this work of Jesus came to be known as the passive obedience was because Jesus allowed Himself to be led like a lamb to the slaughter (Isaiah 53:7). He remained quiet before His accusers. Jesus allowed Himself to be arrested, beaten, and crucified.

When a sinner stands before the tribunal of God on that great and terrible Day of Judgment, he must show that he should not justly be condemned and why he should be declared entitled to eternal life.[1] We are dealing with the **ground**

---

[1] Charles Hodge, *Systematic Theology*, Volume 3, Chapter 17, "Justification" (Grand Rapids, Michigan: Eerdman's Publishing Company, 1977), p. 142.

of a man's justification. The ground or basis of a man's justification can be no other than the righteousness of Christ. Regarding the overall work of imputation, Charles Hodge states:

> Imputation never changes the inward, subjective state of the person to whom the imputation is made. When sin is imputed to a man he is not made sinful; ...When you impute theft to a man, you do not make him a thief. When you impute goodness to a man, you do not make him good. So when righteousness is imputed to the believer, he does not thereby become subjectively righteous.[2]

We must ask, "Why does mankind need the imputation of Christ's righteousness? It is because we are sinners and cannot live up to the demands of God's justice. The Law of God requires two things of man. First, God being a just God does not simply overlook our sins. The violation of His covenant must be penalized. Payment must be made. The Scripture says that the penalty for this violation is death (Gen. 2:17; Rom. 6:23). All mankind stands under the curse of the Law (Gal. 3:10; Deut. 27:26). Mankind is separated from a Holy God because of sin (Isa. 59:2; Rom. 3:23). All those outside of Christ are under God's wrath (John 3:36). In short, mankind is **guilty** before a Holy God. In order to go to Heaven, a man's guilt and sin's curse must be removed.

Second, God's Law **requires perfect obedience.** We must understand the nature of sin. Sin is simply the transgression of God's Law (I John 3:4; Rom. 3:19-20; 7:5-11). "Under the Law" is a common biblical phrase and that is, "under the law." To be under the law means to be under the domination of sin (Rom. 6:14); that man cannot commit one sin (James 2:10); to be under a curse if one cannot keep all of it (Gal. 3:10). Man is to be holy as God is holy (Lev. 11:44; I Peter 1:16). Perfect obedience is required in thought, word, and deed. Jesus indicated that the thoughts of hatred and lust were the sins of murder and adultery respectively. All of our righteous deeds are as filthy rags before God and no one calls on God's name, or arouses himself to take hold of God, for God hides His face from all sinners (Isa. 64:6-7). In speaking to both Jew and Gentile, which encompasses all of the human race, none are righteous, none understand, all have turned aside, their speech is wicked, they are swift to run to evil, they are violent, and there is no fear in their eyes (Rom. 3:9-18).

---

[2] Hodge, *Systematic Theology*, p. 145.

Christ's Passive Obedience

Since man cannot render to God what God demands, man's only help is in a perfect substitute, who was not only God in the flesh but also a true human being. The Westminster Larger Catechism questions 38 and 39 speak directly to this issue.

> Question 38 asks, why was it requisite that the Mediator should be God?
>
> **Answer:** It was requisite that the Mediator should be God, that he might sustain and keep the human nature from sinking under the infinite wrath of God, and the power of death, give worth and efficacy to his sufferings, obedience, and intercession; and to satisfy God's justice, procure his favor, purchase a peculiar people, give his Spirit to them, conquer all their enemies, and bring them to everlasting salvation.

> Question 39 asks: Why was it requisite that the Mediator should be man?
>
> **Answer:** It was requisite that the Mediator should be man, that he might advance our nature, perform obedience to the law, suffer and make intercession for us in our nature, have a fellow-feeling of our infirmities; that we might receive the adoption of sons, and have comfort and access with boldness unto the throne of grace.

We learn that the Mediator had to be God in order to render a sacrifice so great that it could save all of His people; only God can accomplish something of this magnitude. Moreover, the Mediator had to render perfect obedience to the Law's demands and only God is perfect. The Mediator had to have a real human body in order to shed real blood to pay the penalty for those whom He is their substitute. Adam, in whose guilt all humans stand guilty before God, was a real man; hence, the second Adam must likewise be a real man (Rom. 5:12-19; Heb.10: 5-7).

We Must Be Reconciled To God

Because of our sin, we are separated from God (Isa. 59:2). We are said to be enemies of God because of sin (Rom.5:8). The amazing thing is that men can do nothing in themselves to be reconciled to God. It is God who initiates reconciliation. Romans 5:8 says that God demonstrates His love for us in that God the Father provides Jesus for sinners. II Corinthians 5:18-21 says that God was reconciling the world to Himself through Christ. In this reconciliation, God does not count our sins against us, that is, in Christ, sin's guilt is erased. If there is to be peace between God and man, then something needs to be done about sin. Jesus was made sin in a representative fashion for us in order that we might become the righteousness of God in Him. This is imputation. Christ's payment of sin's penalty on our behalf is credited to us as righteousness.

God Needs To Be Propitiated

The Bible says that God is a righteous judge, who is angry with sinners (Ps. 7:11). The Psalmist pleads with God not to rebuke him in His wrath and chasten him according to His anger (Ps.6:1; 38:1). Why is God angry with men? It is because they violate His holy law (Ex. 32: 8-10). On several occasions, Moses had to intercede as a mediator for Israel to turn away God's wrath from destroying Israel (Ex. 32:11-14; Deut. 9:25-29). We learn from the Old Testament that a mediator was necessary to turn away God's wrath.

While the Bible maintains the reality of God's wrath, it does not picture this as God's dominant feature. Micah 7:18-19 demonstrates that God is unmatched in His desire to pardon sin: "*Who is a God like Thee, who pardons iniquity and passes over the rebellious act of the remnant of His possession? He does not retain His anger forever, Because He delights in unchanging love. He will again have compassion on us; He will tread our iniquities under foot. Yes, Thou will cast all their sins into the depths of the sea.*"

The word "propitiation" does not occur that frequently in the New Testament, but it is a powerful concept. In Romans 3:24-25 we see that our redemption in Christ Jesus is displayed through propitiation in blood. In Hebrews 2:17, Jesus as our faithful and merciful High Priest makes propitiation for the sins of His people. In I John 2:1-2 Jesus is our advocate (literally meaning one who comes along side of) with the Father to make propitiation for our sins. And finally in I John 4:10 we see that the supreme demonstration of God's love for His people is that He sent His only begotten Son to be the propitiation for their sins.

So, what does propitiation mean? It is the satisfaction of God's justice by means of a bloody sacrifice. God's justice demands punishment for sin for the violation of His holy Law; it demands perfect obedience. Jesus is the perfect bloody sacrifice that satisfies God's justice that demands the penalty of death for violators. As our substitute, He averts the wrath of God toward us because of our sins. Jesus is the greater Moses who intercedes for the sins of His people. The most significant fact is that God is the one who initiates and provides the means to placate His wrath. What a glorious God!

Blood Must Be Shed

In Jesus we are said to be justified in His blood (Rom. 5:9). The elect of God (Eph.1:13) are said to be redeemed through His blood (Eph. 1:7; I Peter 1:19). There is no forgiveness of sins without the shedding of blood (Heb. 9:14, 22).

Redemption through Christ's Blood

In Romans 3:24, we are told that we are freely justified through the redemption that is in Christ Jesus. The cost for this redemption was nothing less than the blood of Christ. We are told in I Corinthians 6:20 that we were bought with a price which is why we must glorify God in our bodies. In Colossians 1:13-14, we find that the redemption that we have in Christ is **the forgiveness of sins**. We should note that this redemption is from the domain of darkness where we have been held captive.

The idea of deliverance by means of **a ransom** is a dominant idea in redemption. The payment of the ransom price secures the release of the captive. Mark 10:45 says that Jesus gave His life as a ransom for many. In Revelation 5:9, we learn that Jesus was slain in order to purchase unto God with His blood a people from every tribe, and tongue, and nation.

In Galatians 4:4 we see that in space and time, God sent His Son to be born of a woman (which means that He assumed to Himself a true human nature), and born under the Law (which means to be accountable to the Law in terms of its penalty and its perfect obedience). God did this in order to redeem those who were under the Law so that we could be adopted by God. As noted earlier, to be under the law means that we are under obligation to keep it perfectly, and if we don't, then we must die. Dominant in this text is the idea of **substitution**. Jesus performs actions on our behalf. He does for us what we cannot do for ourselves.

A very important question is: To whom is the ransom price paid to secure the release of the captive? Even though we are held captive by Satan to do his will and are in his dark domain, the ransom price is paid to God the Father. Our bondage to Satan is the result of our sin. God is the one who is offended; it is His law that has been transgressed; it is His justice that needs to be satisfied.

Christ's Active Obedience

Even though the Bible does speak about Christ's death as being a basis for our justification, it is not the totality of it. The other aspect of Christ's imputation for His people is known as His active or prescriptive obedience. By this kind of obedience, **Jesus gives us title to eternal life.** Charles Hodge stated it quite well:

> The mere expiation of guilt confers no title to eternal life. The condition of the covenant under which man was placed was perfect obedience. This, from all that appears in Scripture, the perfection of God requires. As He never pardons sins unless the demands of justice be satisfied, so He never grants eternal life unless perfect obedience be rendered. Heaven is always represented as a purchased possession. In the covenant between the Father and the Son the salvation of his people was promised as the reward of his humiliation, obedience, and death. Having performed the stipulated conditions, He has a claim to the promised recompense. And this claim inures to the benefit of his people. But besides this, as the work of Christ consisted in his doing all that the law of God, or covenant of works requires for the salvation of men, and as that righteousness is freely offered to every one that believes, every such believer has as valid a claim to eternal life as he would have had, had he personally done all that the law demands.[3]

John Owen, one of the great English Puritans of the 17th Century stressed the importance of Christ's active obedience. In discussing the importance of both the passive and active obedience of Christ, Owen states:

> These things, I confess, are inseparably connected in the ordinance, appointment, and covenant of God. Whosoever has his sins pardoned is accepted with God, has right unto eternal blessedness. These things are inseparable; but they are not one and the same. And by reason of their relation are they so put together by the apostle, Rom. 4:6-8, but it is one thing to be freed from being liable unto eternal death, and another to have right and title unto a blessed and eternal life. It is one thing to be redeemed from under the law, that is, the curse of

---

[3] Hodge, *Systematic Theology*, pp. 164-165.

it; another, to receive the adoption of sons; - one thing to be freed from the curse; another, to have the blessing of Abraham come upon us.

For by the imputation of the sufferings of Christ our sins are remitted or pardoned, and we are delivered from the curse of the law, which he underwent; but we are not thence esteemed just or righteous, which we cannot bed without respect unto the fulfilling of the commands of the law, or the obedience by it required.

Neither do sufferings give satisfaction unto the commands of the law, which requires only obedience. And hence it will unavoidably follow, that we have need of more than the mere sufferings of Christ, whereby we may be justified before God, if so be that any righteousness be required thereunto; but the whole of what I intend is, that Christ's fulfilling of the law, in obedience unto its commands, is no less imputed unto us for our justification than his undergoing the penalty of it is.[4]

John Dick made these instructive comments:

In the case of a sinner, therefore, the imputation of righteousness is pre-supposed as the ground of his justification, which, consequently, implies something more than simple remission...If he (i.e, the sinner) cannot himself fulfill the law, another, taking his place, and coming under his obligations, may fulfill it in his name, and the obedience of this surety may be placed to his account.[5]

If a man is to make it into heaven, then he needs the perfect obedience of a substitute. W.G.T. Shedd writes:

When a criminal has suffered the penalty affixed to this crime, he has done a part, but not all that the law requires of him. He still owes a perfect obedience to the law, in addition

---

[4] John Owen, *"The Imputation for Christ's Obedience,"* taken from his works on Justification, volume 5.

[5] Brian Schwertley, *"A Defense Of The 'Active Obedience' Of Jesus Christ in The Justification Of Sinners: A Biblical Refutation of Norman Shepherd on the Preceptive Obedience of the Savior"* in the *"New Southern Presbyterian Review"*, Fall 2004, p. 24.

to the endurance of the penalty…Consequently, the justification of a sinner must not only deliver him from the penalty due to disobedience, but provide for him an equivalent to personal obedience.[6]

The law is not completely fulfilled by the endurance of penalty only. It must also be obeyed. Christ both endured the penalty due to man for disobedience, and perfectly obeyed the law for him; so that He was a vicarious substitute in reference to both the precept and the penalty of the law. By his active obedience He obeyed the law, and by his passive obedience He endured the penalty. In this way his vicarious work is complete.[7]

Charles Hodge quotes President Edwards (apparently the president of Princeton Seminary where Hodge was professor) who gave a sermon on justification. Hodge states:

"To suppose," he says, "that a man is justified by his own virtue or obedience, derogates from the honour of the Mediator, and ascribes that to man's virtue that belongs only to the righteousness of Christ. It puts man in Christ's stead, and makes him his own saviour, in a respect in which Christ only is the Saviour: and so it is a doctrine contrary to the nature and design of the Gospel, which is to abase man, and to ascribe all the glory of our salvation to Christ the Redeemer. It is inconsistent with the doctrine of the imputation of Christ's righteousness, which is a gospel doctrine."[8]

First, I would explain what we mean by the imputation of Christ's righteousness. Sometimes the expression is taken by our divines in a larger sense, for the imputation of all that Christ did and suffered for our redemption, whereby we are free from guilt, and stand righteous in the sight of God; and so implies the imputation both of Christ's satisfaction and obedience. But here I intend it in a stricter sense, for the imputation of that righteousness or moral goodness that consists in the obedience of Christ. And by that righteousness

---

[6] Schwertley, "*A Defense Of The 'Active Obedience' Of Jesus Christ*", p. 11.

[7] Hodge, *Systematic Theology,* Vol. III, p. 149.

[8] Hodge, *Systematic Theology,* p. 148.

being imputed to us, is meant no other than this, that that righteousness of Christ is accepted for us, and admitted instead of that perfect inherent righteousness that ought to be in ourselves: Christ's perfect obedience shall be reckoned to our account so that we shall have the benefit of it, as though we had performed it ourselves: and so we suppose that a title to eternal life is given us as the reward of this righteousness.[9]

References to Christ's Active Obedience

Romans 5:16-19

And the gift is not like that which came through the one who sinned; for on the one hand the judgment arose from one transgression resulting in condemnation, but on the other hand the free gift arose from many transgressions resulting in justification. For if by the transgression of the one, death reigned through the one, much more those who receive the abundance of grace and of the gift of righteousness will reign in life through the One, Jesus Christ. So then as through one transgression there resulted condemnation to all men, even so through one act of righteousness there resulted justification of life to all men. For as through the one man's disobedience the many were made sinners, even so through the obedience of the One the many will be made righteous.

In this passage, there is a direct parallel being made between Adam and Jesus Christ. There is an analogy regarding our relationship to both of these. In Adam we have all sinned due to his one transgression. This one sin was the basis for all of mankind's condemnation. We are all guilty in him. In the same manner, all those for whom Christ represents by his one act of obedience will reign in life and be made righteous. We must observe that this one act of righteousness is said to be a gift of righteousness. Whereas Adam did not perfectly obey the Law of God (to not eat of the tree of the knowledge of good and evil), Jesus did perfectly obey God's Law and thereby merit righteousness for those whom He represented. Jesus, and Jesus alone, is our righteousness. Jesus' righteous-

---

[9] Hodge, *Systematic Theology.*

ness, performed in our behalf as our substitute, is the basis for our justification. This one act of righteousness is seen in both His passive and active obedience.

I Corinthians 1:30, 31

But by His doing you are in Christ Jesus, who became to us wisdom from God, and righteousness and sanctification, and redemption, that, just as it is written, "Let him who boasts, boast in the Lord."

Calvin relates this passage to Christ's active and passive obedience:

Secondly, he says that he is made unto us righteousness, by which he means that we are on his account acceptable to God, inasmuch as he expiated our sins by his death, and his obedience is imputed to us for righteousness. For as the righteousness of faith consists in remission of sins and a gracious acceptance, we obtain both through Christ.[10]

Philippians 3:8-9

More than that, I count all things to be loss in view of the surpassing value of knowing Christ Jesus my Lord, for whom I have suffered the loss of all things, and count them but rubbish in order that I may gain Christ, and may be found in Him, not having a righteousness of my own derived from the Law, but that which is through faith in Christ, the righteousness which comes from God on the basis of faith.

We looked at this passage in the previous chapter, emphasizing the contrast between individual righteousness according to the Law and God's righteousness. For our purposes here, the emphasis is upon whose righteousness that believers are clothed with. Calvin states:

He thus, in a general way, places man's merit in opposition to Christ's grace; for while the law brings works, faith presents man before God as naked, that he may be clothed with the righteousness of Christ. When, therefore, he declares that the righteousness of faith is from God, it is not simply because

---

[10] John Calvin, *Calvin's New Testament Commentaries, The First Epistle of Paul to the Corinthians,* translated by John Frazer (Grand Rapids, MI: Eerdman's Publishing Co., 1960), p. 46.

faith is the gift of God, but because God justifies us by his goodness, or because we receive by faith the righteousness which he has conferred upon us.[11]

The Covenant of Works

It is crucial that I discuss the covenant of works in my analysis of the Federal Vision because it has denied the existence of this covenant. For sometime I did not fully understand why these men were denying this covenant, but now I understand. There is a common thread that runs throughout their theology. Since they have redefined the meaning of justifying faith to incorporate the essence of covenantal faithfulness or obedience, they must by necessity deny the covenant of works. The doctrine of the active obedience of Christ finds its roots in the covenant of works. Romans 5:12-21 finds its analogy in the covenant of works. The second Adam, Jesus Christ, is able to perfectly obey what Adam was unable to do. In the mindset of the Federal Vision, if Adam's eternal life was not bound to a perfect compliance to God's commands, then there is no need for a perfect obedience for us in the covenant of grace. We do not need a perfect substitute to keep the law for us.

For them our imperfect obedience done in the power of the Holy Spirit is what is acceptable to God. Brian Schwertley would concur with this analysis when he says this about the Federal Vision's view of the covenant of works, "*Ironically, those who reject the active obedience of Christ in justification always seek obedience from some other source. Such righteousness, however, is always imperfect.*"[12]

As I stated earlier, one heresy leads to another. The heresy of making justifying faith to mean the essence of obedience to God's moral law will inevitably lead to the heresy of denying Christ's perfect obedience as a necessity for man's justification. In their denial of the covenant of works, the Federal Vision continues to reveal its ugly gospel. It is a gospel that glorifies man and robs Jesus Christ of His glory. The Federal Vision is a man-centered theology through and through. It is not the gospel of the Lord Jesus Christ, and it must be fervently resisted.

Let us now take a look into the nature of the covenant of works and its vital necessity. Wilhelmus a Brakel once said:

---

[11] Calvin, *The Comprehensive John Calvin Collection*. Calvin's Commentary On Philippians 3:9.

[12] Brian Schwertley, "*A Defense Of The 'Active Obedience' Of Jesus Christ*", p. 12.

> Acquaintance with this covenant is of the greatest impor-
> tance, for whoever errs here or denies the existence of the
> covenant of works, will not understand the covenant of grace,
> and will readily err concerning the mediatorship of the Lord
> Jesus.[13]

The Westminster Confession of Faith has made this comment about the
covenant of works in Chapter 7, section 2:

> The first covenant made with man was a covenant of works,
> wherein life was promised to Adam, and in him to his poster-
> ity, upon condition of perfect and personal obedience.

Question 20 of the Westminster Larger Catechism states:

> What was the providence of God toward man in the estate in
> which he was created?
> **Answer:** The providence of God toward man in the estate in
> which he was created, was the placing him in paradise,
> appointing him to dress it, giving him liberty to eat of the fruit
> of the earth; putting the creatures under his dominion, and
> ordaining marriage for his help; affording him communion
> with himself; instituting the Sabbath; entering into a
> **covenant of life with him, upon condition of personal,
> perfect, and perpetual obedience**, of which the tree of life
> was a pledge; and forbidding to eat of the tree of knowledge
> of good and evil, upon the pain of death. (Emphasis mine)

Robert Shaw has made these comments about the covenant of works as set
forth in the Westminster Confession:

> That this covenant was made with Adam, not only for him-
> self, but also for all his natural posterity, is a doctrine which
> has met with much opposition. It is denied by Pelagians and
> Socinians, who maintain that he acted for himself alone, and
> that the effects of his fall terminated upon himself.[14]

This is not good company for the Federal Vision to be with – Pelagians and
Socinians. I will demonstrate later in the chapter where others, especially John

---

[13] Joe Morecraft III, "The Covenant Of Works," in *The New Southern Presbyterian
Journal,* Vol. 1, Number 2, Fall 2002 (Cumming, GA: Chalcedon Presbyterian
Church), p. 112.

[14] Shaw, *An Exposition Of The Westminster Confession of Faith,* p. 86.

Owen, refers to the theology which the Federal Vision now espouses as essentially the views of the Socinians. Heresies die hard.

Shaw's perspective of the covenant of works continues:

> The Scripture represents Adam as a figure or type of Christ, Rom. 5:14; and wherein does the resemblance between them consist? Simply in this, that as Christ was a federal head, representing all his spiritual seed in the covenant of grace, so Adam was a federal head representing all his natural seed in the covenant of works. In I Cor. 15:45, 47, the one is called the **first Adam**, the other, the **last Adam**; the one the **first man**, the other the **second man**) .... The conclusion is inevitable, that, in the covenant of works, our first parent not only acted for himself, but represented all his natural posterity. [15] (Emphasis is Shaw)

> ... we would have readily agreed that it was more eligible and safe for us to have our everlasting felicity insured by the obedience of our first parent, as our covenant head, than that it should depend upon our own personal behavior. And who would complain of this being represented by Adam in the covenant of works, since God has opened up a way for our recovery from the consequences of the breach of that covenant, by another and a superior covenant.[16]

Hosea 6:7 refers to a covenant that Adam transgressed, *"But like Adam they have transgressed the covenant; There they have dealt treacherously against Me."* We know from Romans 5:12-21 that there was a covenant that existed with Adam because of the analogy between Adam and Jesus as respective representative heads, even though the word "covenant" is not found in the passage. There are some differences in the application of the work performed by each representative head. When Adam sinned, condemnation and death came upon Adam and all his posterity. Christ's benefits in his perfect life and atoning sacrifice are imputed to **all who believe**. With Christ as our covenant head, we have gained far more than what was lost by Adam. Adam's holiness was capable of being lost, which is what happened. Those in Christ cannot be lost, ever.

---

[15] Shaw, *An Exposition Of The Westminster Confession of Faith.*

[16] Shaw, *An Exposition Of The Westminster Confession of Faith*, p. 87.

The Covenant of Works and the Law of God

It is important that we see this connection when we ask the questions, "Does the covenant of works have any force for man today? Does God still require of man perfect obedience as a requirement for fellowship with Him?" The answer is yes. I Peter 1:16 tells us that we are to be holy as He is holy, and Galatians 3:10 tells us that we are cursed if we do not abide by all things in the Law to perform them. Answering yes to these questions does not mean that anybody **can** keep them perfectly. This fact only magnifies the beauty of the work of the second Adam, Jesus, on behalf of all whom He represents. The fact that the covenant of works is still in force for mankind is an essential part of the gospel. The good news of the gospel is that there is a remedy for the problem of our inability to keep the law perfectly. We have our champion representative in Jesus Christ who kept that law perfectly, and His law keeping is credited to our account as if we had done it ourselves.

The Westminster Confession speaks directly to this issue in Chapter 19 "Of The Law Of God" in Sections 1 and 2:

> God gave to Adam a law, as a covenant of works, by which He bound him and all his posterity to personal, entire, exact, and perpetual obedience; promised life upon the fulfilling, and threatened death upon the breach of it: and endued him with power and ability to keep it.

> This law, after his fall, continued to be a perfect rule of righteousness, and, as such, was delivered by God upon Mount Sinai, in ten commandments, and written in two tables: the four first commandments containing our duty towards God; and the other six our duty to man.

Robert Shaw has some insightful comments on this section in the Confession:

> God having formed man an intelligent creature, and a subject of moral government, he gave him a law for the rule of his conduct... The law, as thus inscribed on the heart of the first man, is often styled **the law of creation**, because it was the will of the sovereign Creator, revealed to the reasonable creature, by impressing it upon his mind and heart at his creation. It is called the **moral law**, because it was a revelation of the will of God, as his moral governor, and was the standard and rule of man's moral actions. Adam was originally placed under his law in its natural form, as merely directing and

obliging him to perfect obedience. He was brought under it in a **covenant form**, an express threatening of death, and a gracious promise of life, was annexed to it. (Emphasis is Shaw)

That this covenant was made with the first man, not as a single person, but as the federal representative of all his natural posterity, has been formerly shown. The law, as invested with a covenant form, is called, by the Apostle Paul, "The law of works" (Rom. 3:27); that is, the law as a covenant of works. In this form, the law is to be viewed as not only prescribing duty, but as promising life as the reward of obedience, and denouncing death as the punishment of transgression...It prescribes terms which we are incapable of performing; and instead of being encouraged to seek life by our own obedience to the law as a covenant, we are required to renounce all hopes of salvation in that way, and to seek it by faith in Christ.

The covenant being made with Adam, not only for himself, but also for all his posterity, when he violated it, he left them all under it as a broken covenant. Most miserable, therefore, is the condition of all men by nature; for "as many as are of the works of the law are under the curse." – Gal. 3:10. Truly infatuated are they who seek for righteousness by the works of the law; for "by the deeds of the law shall no flesh be justified in the sight of God."[17]

Regarding 19:2 of the Confession, Shaw states:

Upon the fall of man, the law, considered as a covenant of works, was disannulled and set aside; but, considered as moral, it continued to be a perfect rule of righteousness...But the original edition of the law being greatly obliterated, God was graciously pleased to give a new and complete copy of it. He delivered it to the Israelites from Mount Sinai, with awful solemnity. In this promulgation of the law, he summed it up in Ten Commandments; and, therefore, it is commonly styled the Law of the Ten Commandments.[18]

---

[17] Shaw, *An Exposition Of The Westminster Confession of Faith*, pp. 192,193.
[18] Shaw, *An Exposition Of The Westminster Confession of Faith*, p. 194.

It may be remarked, that the law of the Ten Commandments was promulgated to Israel from Sinai in the form of a covenant of works. Not that it was the design of God to renew a covenant of works with Israel, or to put them upon seeking life by their own obedience to the law; but the law was published to them as a covenant of works, to show them that without a perfect righteousness, answering to all the demands of the law, they could not be justified before God; and that, finding themselves wholly destitute of that righteousness, they might be excited to take hold of the covenant of grace, in which a perfect righteousness for their justification is graciously provided.[19]

The Sinai transaction was a mixed dispensation. In it the covenant of grace was published ... But the moral law, as a covenant of works, was also displayed, to convince the Israelites of their sinfulness and misery, to teach them the necessity of an atonement, and lead them to embrace by faith the blessed Mediator, the Seed promised to Abraham, in whom all the families of the earth were to be blessed. The law, therefore, was published at Sinai as a covenant of works, in subservience to the covenant of grace. And the law is still published in subservience to the gospel, as "a schoolmaster to bring sinners to Christ, that they may be justified by faith."[20] (Gal. 3:24)

I trust that you can see that the covenant of works instituted by God with Adam and reaffirmed in the Mosaic covenant as being subservient to the covenant of grace is crucial to our understanding of the gospel of the Lord Jesus. When the Federal Vision denies the existence of this covenant of works, trying to portray everything as a covenant of grace as Shepherd does, it actually advocates a works salvation that is hostile to the gospel. Shepherd's book *The Call Of Grace* is a terrible misnomer. It militates against the biblical teaching of grace; it is the championing of a works paradigm. The fact that Shepherd would dare refer to his book as a call of grace is a tragedy, and it is a twisting of glorious biblical truths into a man sustained religion.

---

[19] Shaw, *An Exposition Of The Westminster Confession of Faith*, p. 195.
[20] Shaw, *An Exposition Of The Westminster Confession of Faith*.

Shepherd's Denial of Christ's Active Obedience

In this section, I will demonstrate with quotes from Shepherd's lectures at the Southern California Center for Christian Studies on the covenant that he has explicitly denied the existence of the active obedience of Christ as understood by the Reformed Faith for the past 500 years. I will demonstrate that he has presented outright falsehoods about what the early Reformers believed. His scholarship in these lectures is dismal. He will insist that the early Reformers such as Calvin and others did not believe in the active obedience of Christ as it came to be known. He will insist that Ursinus, the one who is credited with most of the formulation of the Heidelberg Catechism did not teach the active obedience of Christ. His use of the Reformed Standards is tragic in trying to get them to demonstrate his perspective. I will demonstrate from John Owen's comments regarding the teachings of Socinianism that Shepherd has embraced similar views when it comes to Socinianism's view of justification.

The following lengthy series of quotes are excerpts of my transcription of Shepherd's two lectures:[21]

> We inherit eternal life by way of a living, penitent, obedient faith just like the Lord led Israel into the Promised Land by way of a living, penitent, and obedient life.
>
> This is biblical and Pauline theology. Lord's Day 23, question 60 says, "How are you right with God?" What is the righteousness imputed to us?
>
> Ursinus says, "the Law requires obedience to its requirements or punishment for its disobedience. Either or, but not both."
>
> Evangelical righteousness is the fulfillment of law performed not by us but by another in our stead, all imputed to one who believes. This is really legal righteousness performed by another imputed to one who believes. In the Gospel, that other is Jesus Christ.
>
> Now how did Christ perform this legal righteousness for us? Did He do it by fulfilling the law during the course of His life,

---

[21] Norman Shepherd, Lectures on Contemporary Issues of Covenant Theology: "Justification by Faith and Pauline Theology" and "Justification by Works in Reformed Theology." SCCCS (The Southern California Center for Christian Studies) Summer Conference, 2003.

what theologians refer to ordinarily as His active obedience, or did he do it by submitting to punishment prescribed in the law for transgressors of the law, what theologians refer to as His passive obedience?

Now for Ursinus, it has to be one or another but not both. For Ursinus legal justification is simply what we call regeneration or sanctification. What does Ursinus mean by evangelical justification? He writes, "evangelical justification is the application of evangelical righteousness or the application of the righteousness of another, which is without us in Christ or it is the imputation and application of that righteousness which Christ wrought out for us by His death upon the cross and by His resurrection from the dead." And in that, Ursinus makes clear that the legal righteousness imputed to us in evangelical justification is the righteousness Jesus performed for us when he submitted to the punishment prescribed in the Law. The righteousness Christ wrought out for us was not the fulfillment of the demands of the law during the course of His life, but His death and resurrection to pay the penalty for sin. In other words, the righteousness of Christ imputed to us for our justification is not the active obedience of Christ but his passive obedience.

Therefore, when Ursinus goes on in the same paragraph to define justification as he defines it as the forgiveness of sins. Justification is not a transfusion of righteousness or the qualities thereof and that would be the Roman Catholic view, but justification is the acquitting or the declaring us free from sin in the judgment of God and on the ground of the righteousness of another. Justification and the forgiveness of sins are therefore the same, for to justify is that God should not impute sin to us and accept us as righteous on the ground of the righteousness of Christ made over to us.

We can summarize the position of Ursinus on justification with three observations: First, justification consists of the remission of sins. Secondly, sins are remitted on the grounds of the righteousness of Christ imputed to the believer. Thirdly, the righteousness imputed is the suffering and death of our Lord to pay the penalty for sin.

The view of Ursinus is also the view we find in the Heidelberg Catechism. Now what does the catechism mean by the perfect satisfaction, righteousness, and holiness of Christ? These words are often referred to include the active obedience of Christ, His law keeping throughout His life. However, this cannot be the case for the following reason. The satisfaction, righteousness, and holiness of Christ are the ground of pardon; therefore, they refer to His substitutionary suffering and death. This is obedience to His father's will that obtains the forgiveness of sins.

The second word that the catechism uses is the word, "righteousness." What is this referring to? Lord's Day 21 of the Heidelberg Catechism asks what do we mean by the forgiveness of sin. This is what we have seen to be what is justification. The answer is God because of Christ's atonement will never hold against me any of my sins nor my sinful nature which I need to struggle against all my life.

The third word, "holiness" in Lord's Day 15 says that holiness refers to the suffering and death of our Lord- and it is this that justifies the sinner and obtains the title to eternal life. The word, "satisfaction" can refer to all that Jesus suffered for us, the entire course of His humiliation throughout His life. The word cannot refer to anything less than the death of our Lord on the cross to pay the penalty for sin.

Does the preaching of the gospel focus on faith on the cross of Christ as the only ground of our salvation and the answer of the Catechism gives a resounding, yes. The answer read this way. Right. In the gospel the Holy Spirit teaches us and through the holy sacraments answers us that our entire salvation rests on Christ's one sacrifice for us on the cross. That is to say, that our entire salvation rests upon but one ground, not a double ground, active and passive obedience, but one ground. According to the Heidelberg Catechism, the cross of Christ is the only ground of our salvation.

This brings us to Lord's Day 1 of point C of your outline. We can place this teaching of justification in a broader setting by reference to Lord's Day 1 of the Catechism. Lord's Day 1 is the best known and most widely known section of the

Heidelberg Catechism. And this is how the gospel is summarized right at the beginning. As you know "what is your only comfort in life and in death, and the answer begins this way- that I am not my own but belong body, soul, in life, in death to my faithful savior Jesus Christ. That is to say, union with Christ lies at the heart of the application of redemption. So then we ask, "What is it that Jesus has done for me"? And what do I gain from this union with Christ? The catechism goes on by saying – He has fully paid for all my sins with His precious blood and has set me free from the tyranny of the devil, and you notice these two elements that constitute the sum and substance of my salvation. First of all, he has fully paid for all my sins with His precious blood and on that ground my sins are forgiven. I am justified and in a right relationship to God with the title to eternal life. Second, he has set me free from the tyranny of the devil and that is a succinct and powerful way of referring to satisfaction.

Justification is simply the forgiveness of sins grounded in the death and the resurrection of Christ and that explains the concurrence between Luther and Calvin on the doctrine of justification. There were significant differences between Luther and Calvin when it comes to the nature of justifying faith and I alluded to one of those last evening. They are differences that still play a role in the discussion today. The Lutheran doctrine of justification by faith alone excludes the Reformed doctrine of justification by a penitent and obedient faith. But Luther and Calvin were agreed that justification was not an infusion of righteousness as Rome taught; justification is the remission of sin on the ground of the righteousness of Christ imputed to the believer, and this righteousness was His suffering and death for us, what later theologians called His passive obedience. But as time went on there was what I call a paradigm shift in Reformed theology, and I call it a shift from grace/faith paradigm which I find in the apostle Paul and also in early Reformed theology – a shift from that grace/faith paradigm to a works/merit paradigm.

Now this is the situation. John Calvin defined justification as the remission of sin. Ursinus and the Heidelberg Catechism do the same. John Dick called this view a mistake. Why? Because a person cannot be pronounced just, that is, he can-

not be justified, unless he be possessed of justice or righteousness and with that statement we see a shift from a
Reformational grace/faith paradigm to a pre-Reformational
works/merit paradigm. A person cannot be justified unless
there be in him a meritorious ground in the performance of
good works that warrant the justifying verdict. Remember
that Ursinus maintained that legal righteousness is performed
either by obedience to the law or by punishment. Law
requires one or another. John Dick maintained that both are
necessary.

This brings us to point B: the structural similarity to Rome.
This shift to a works/merit paradigm is really to the same paradigm that Rome uses to structure its doctrine of justification,
and you can easily see the structural similarity between the
view of John Dick and the Roman Catholic view, which of
course John Dick rejects. But Roman Catholicism understood the Reformation to be saying that justification consisted merely in remission of sin, and in this understanding
Rome was correct. This is what Luther and Calvin, Ursinus,
the Heidelberg Catechism were saying. Rome no less clearly
rejects this view and insists that justification consists in the
transformation of an unjust man into a just man because without this transformation there is no ground for the justifying
verdict in the final judgment.

In effect, John Dick is in consensus with this view of Rome
when he says, quote "no man can be pronounced just by Him
who judges according to truth unless he be possessed of justice or righteousness." Structurally, the two views are the
same. They represent what I call a works/merit paradigm.
The Council of Trent, John Dick, and R.C. Sproul Sr. are all
in agreement that, quote, "ultimately the only way that one
can be justified is by works." And this is what I am referring
to in the title of this lecture as justification by works in
Reformed theology.

Therefore instead of an infused righteousness, Reformed
writers insisted on an imparted righteousness. Jesus kept all
the requirements of the Law perfectly during His life and His
perfect righteousness is imparted to the believer in his justification. So then, the believer is justified not only according to

the ground of the suffering and death of our Lord but also on the ground of His active obedience. It is this dependence upon the merit of Christ rather than on one's own personal merit that makes this view even evangelical and not Romanist. Salvation is by grace through faith but this Reformational and evangelical breakthrough is now grafted onto an alien works/merit paradigm. The imputation of the active obedience of Christ is absolutely essential to an evangelical view based on the works/merit paradigm. With it there is there either no justification or justification takes place on the ground of a personal, whether infused, performed righteousness. We are then back with Rome and have rejected the Reformation and that is why it is for some Reformed teachers today, the gospel itself stands or falls with a belief in the imputation or active obedience, not looking beyond the works/merit paradigm.

We do not find a belief in the imputation of active obedience in Calvin or Ursinus, or the Heidelberg Catechism all the reason for this is simply that they did not find this belief in the Bible. The very few Bible texts quoted by later theologians refer to the imputation and the righteousness of Christ wrought in His suffering and death for His people. And I want to point out that even the Westminster Confession as late as 1647 was written in such a way as to accommodate the views of three prominent members of the Westminster Assembly who did not subscribe to the imputation of active obedience. We do find language that has been interpreted affirming the imputation of active obedience. (Emphasis mine)

Early Reformed doctrine had no doctrine of active obedience because it defined soteric justification as the forgiveness of sin. Justification meant that God forgives our sins and on that basis accepts us as righteous and gives us the title to eternal life. There is no imputation of active obedience because the grace/faith paradigm is that they understood justification did not require it and no Bible text taught it.

The next step was to cast the works/merit paradigm into covenant theology. Ursinus says, quote, "Legal righteousness was the righteousness of Adam before the Fall. That idea became the covenant of works with justification on the grounds of an inherent righteousness. Adam failed and so Christ as the second Adam is placed in a covenant of works and that covenant of works in which Christ was placed is often called a covenant of redemption, but I call this covenant of redemption a wondrous theological invention. His success in fulfilling this covenant of works is then imputed to the believer so that ultimately the believer is justified by works. Now, it is interesting to see how that in a doctrine of justification based on works/merit paradigm, the merit of works moves into the foreground and the cross of Christ retreats into the background.

Norman Shepherd's Description of the Plan of Salvation:

I am still quoting from Norman Shepherd's lectures:

> Salvation comes ultimately through Jesus Christ who does two things. Jesus deals definitively with the guilt of sin and he deals definitively with the corruption of sin. By His death and resurrection, He pays the penalty for sin and on this ground he bestows the gift of forgiveness. This is justification. By His death and resurrection, He destroys the corruption of sin so that we are recreated in righteousness and holiness. This is sanctification. Those who are justified and sanctified in union with Christ are the righteous who inherit the kingdom and enter into eternal life.
>
> The good news of the gospel centers on the person and work of Jesus Christ and tells us what He has done to save us from the guilt and corruption of sin. The focal point of His mediatorial work for us is His death and resurrection. This is the gospel that we find in the gospels of Matthew, Mark, Luke, and John. The gospel calls us to look to Jesus Christ in faith, to turn away from sin in repentance and to obey all that Jesus has commanded because of the regenerating and sanctifying work of the Holy Spirit. Sinners can and do respond to this call. They believe in Christ and walk according to His Word. They trust and obey for there is no other way to be happy in Jesus but to trust and obey. They are forgiven and renewed. These are the righteous who will inherit the kingdom and enter into eternal life.

The great commission commends us to make disciples by how? By baptizing and teaching them to obey everything that Jesus commanded. As we see from Peter's words on the day of Pentecost, the baptism is a baptism of repentance for the forgiveness of sins- that's justification. Repentance is inseparable from obedience and that's why the evangelism mandate includes teaching people everything that Jesus has commanded – that's sanctification. On a works/merit paradigm, the great commission conflicts with a commonly received understanding of justification by faith alone. On a works/merit paradigm, repentance and obedience are all inevitable by products of faith and justification, but they cannot be constitutive for the gospel call without jeopardizing sole dependence on the imputed active obedience of Jesus Christ reward by faith alone.

Brothers and sisters, in order to be faithful to our Lord and to carry out the great commission, we need to abandon the works/merit paradigm as a well intentioned but misguided attempt to understand the biblical way of salvation. Well intentioned because it seeks to proclaim salvation by grace through faith but misguided because it grafts this Reformational breakthrough onto an alien works/merit structure. We need to return to a biblical paradigm of faith and grace. Our salvation from beginning to end is fully and exclusively the gift of God's sovereign grace and the Lord leads us into possession of eternal life in the way of faith, and this faith is specifically faith in Jesus and His shed blood. Faith is ever and always a living and active response to the gospel message. The way of faith is also the way of repentance and obedience because true faith inevitably and invariably expresses itself in faithfulness. We are justified ultimately by works as R.C. Sproul Sr. contends, but we are justified ultimately by the death and resurrection of Jesus.

Falsehoods Demonstrated In Shepherd's Lectures

From these lectures, Shepherd reveals his total misunderstanding and misuse of the Reformed Standards, particularly the Heidelberg Catechism. I find it very discouraging to see someone mishandle these documents in order to advance a false theology. Is Norman Shepherd deliberately manipulating the

Reformed documents in order to persuade people to his views? Or, is he simply blinded by his own preconceived ideas, his presuppositions that cause him to distort the Scripture? His handling of the Heidelberg Catechism and Ursinus's teachings is grievous, as I shall demonstrate.

There is no doubt that Shepherd is convinced that the Heidelberg Catechism, and Ursinus' teaching support his contention that our justification is grounded **only** in the passive obedience of Christ. Shepherd argues that the entire scope of man's justification is the forgiveness of his sins; it has nothing to do with Jesus' imputing of His righteous Law keeping to the believer's account. He thinks that any kind of imputation of Christ's righteousness is akin to Roman Catholicism's view of a works/merit paradigm. Shepherd actually believes that the early Reformers only believed in Christ's passive obedience. He actually believes that post Reformation Reformed thinkers have abandoned a faith/grace paradigm for a works/merit paradigm in their insistence on the value and necessity of the active obedience of Christ. Shepherd recoils at any kind of "merit," even that of Jesus done on His part for His people.

Shepherd has stated in his lecture that the terms, satisfaction, righteousness, and the holiness of Christ can **only** refer to Christ's suffering and death. He argues by saying the term "righteousness" in Lord's Day 21, question 56 can only mean the forgiveness of sins. Let's look at this statement in the Heidelberg Catechism:

> In Lord's Day 21 of the Heidelberg Catechism, Question 56 asks:
> What do you believe concerning "the forgiveness of sins"?
> **Answer:** That God, for the sake of Christ's satisfaction will no more remember my sins, neither my corrupt nature, against which I have to struggle all my life long; but will graciously impute to me the righteousness of Christ; that I may never be condemned before the tribunal of God.

Shepherd believes that this proves conclusively that the imputation of Christ's righteousness can **only** mean the forgiveness of sins. Is this what the catechism says? Where is the word "only" in the answer? Shepherd reads more into the answer than what is there. Yes, it does say that the righteousness of Christ forgives sin, **but it does not say that the righteousness of Christ is identical or exclusive to the forgiveness of sins.** This is a serious error. This is a classic example of fallacious reasoning. Shepherd said in his lecture, *"The word "righteousness" cannot refer to anything less than the death of our Lord on the cross to pay the penalty."*[22] Shepherd is guilty of adding a meaning to the cat-

---

[22] Shepherd, Lectures on the covenant.

echism that it does not explicitly say. And, we will see that it cannot even be logically inferred.

Shepherd states: *"The third word "holiness" in Lord's Day 15 refers to the suffering and death of our Lord – and it is this that justifies the sinner and obtains the title to eternal life."*[23]

In Lord's Day 15 of the Heidelberg Catechism, Question 37 asks"

> What do you understand by the word "suffered"?
> **Answer:** That he, all the time that he lived on earth, but especially at the end of His life, sustained in body and soul, the wrath of God against the sins of all mankind: that so by his passion, as the only propitiatory sacrifice, he might redeem our body and soul from everlasting damnation, and obtain for us the favor of God, righteousness and eternal life.

Where is the word "holiness" found in the answer? It is not there! Shepherd inserts the word "holiness" into the catechism to make the listener think that Christ's suffering is tied to Christ's holiness, as if the term "holiness" has nothing to do with Christ's keeping of the Law on behalf of believers.

To show you how Shepherd performs some theological gymnastics, he pulls the word "holiness" from Lord's Day 23, question 60 and inserts it into Lord's Day 15, question 37. Actually, Lord's Day 23, question 60 is a devastating rebuttal to Shepherd's thesis that imputation pertains only to Christ's suffering and death.

In Lord's Day 23 of the Heidelberg Catechism, question 60 states:

> How are you right with God?
> **Answer:** Only by a true faith in Jesus Christ; so that though my conscience accuse me, that I have grossly transgressed all the commandments of God, and kept none of them, and am still inclined to all evil; notwithstanding, God, without any merit of mine, but only of mere grace, grants and imputes to me, the perfect satisfaction, righteousness and holiness of Christ; even so, as if I never had, nor committed any sin: yea, as if I had fully accomplished all that obedience which Christ has accomplished for me; inasmuch as I embrace such benefit with a believing heart.

---

[23] Shepherd, Lectures on the covenant.

If you will notice, it is from this question that Shepherd gets his three terms: satisfaction, righteousness, and holiness. His terrible fallacy is to argue that all three terms refer to the same thing. A close examination of the answer to question 60 reveals that imputation refers not only to Christ's satisfaction, but it speaks of the imputation of Christ's righteousness and holiness that has reference to the keeping of all the commandments of God. **The conscience of the believer recognizes that he has grossly transgressed all the commandments of God, having kept none of them.** Moreover the phrase **"as if I had fully accomplished all that obedience which Christ accomplished for me"** refutes Shepherd's argument that Christ's obedience can only mean suffering. The answer has already stated, "as if I never had, nor committed any sin: yea…" The second phrase that I have highlighted is the second aspect of Christ's imputation. Question 60 actually teaches a double imputation, contrary to Shepherd's contention. If one were to look up all the proof texts that are given for each point in this catechism answer, one would realize that many of the passages refer to Christ's active obedience by obeying the Law in our stead.

In his lecture, Shepherd stated, "*Lord's Day 23, question 60 says, How are you right with God*"? *What is the righteousness imputed to us?*" Ursinus says, "the Law requires obedience to its requirements or punishment for its disobedience. Either or, but not both." Shepherd continues to argue that Ursinus meant only the punishment for its disobedience. In a moment, I will demonstrate from Ursinus' own commentary on the Heidelberg catechism that this is completely false. Actually, if one takes the context and sequence of the questions in the Heidelberg Catechism, one can see what Ursinus meant by "all that obedience which Christ accomplished for me."

In question 61, Ursinus continues the topic of being "right with God." In this question, he relates it to faith. Question 61 states:

> Why do you say that by faith alone you are right with God?
> **Answer:** Not that I am acceptable to God, on account of the worthiness of my faith; but because only the satisfaction, righteousness, and holiness of Christ, is my righteousness before God; and that I cannot receive and apply the same to myself any other way than by faith only.

Actually, this question refutes Shepherd's comments in his lecture where he says, "*we inherit eternal life by way of a living, penitent, obedient faith just like the Lord led Israel into the Promised Land by way of a living, penitent, and obedient life.*"[24] Question 61 explicitly states that we are not acceptable on

---

[24] Shepherd, Lectures on the covenant.

account of the worthiness of our faith. So much for Shepherd's living, penitent, obedient faith! Shepherd speaks of a worthy faith that inherits God's promises while the Heidelberg Catechism insists on an **unworthy** faith. Saving faith simply accepts Christ's satisfaction, righteousness, and holiness as his own. There is nothing to glory in; however, Shepherd glories in the nature of man's faith. It is Shepherd who has returned us back to Rome!

Ursinus continues in the development of the idea of being right with God in question 62:

> Why can't the good we do make us right with God, or at least help make us right with Him?
> **Answer:** Because, that the righteousness, which can be approved of before the tribunal of God, must be absolutely perfect, and in all respects conformable to the divine law; and also, that our best works in this life are all imperfect and defiled with sin.

Shepherd's idea that "righteousness" refers only to Christ's suffering and death is obviously wrong because the catechism answer relates the righteousness as absolutely perfect, conforming to the divine law. The proof texts used are Deut. 17:26 and Gal. 3:10 which uses righteousness with reference to obeying the commandments of God.

Not only did Shepherd not read very carefully the Heidelberg Catechism, he was not very thorough and careful with his reference to Ursinus's commentary on the Heidelberg Catechism.

The following quotes are from Ursinus' commentary that Shepherd failed to mention. Ursinus wrote: *"Legal righteousness is performed, either by obedience to the law, or by punishment. The law requires one or the other."*[25] Shepherd stated in his lecture that Christ's legal righteousness cannot entail both obedience to the Law and punishment. Shepherd uses this quote from Ursinus to argue that he meant it to be only Christ's passive obedience (his suffering and death). To demonstrate how Shepherd totally misread Ursinus, let's refer to some other Ursinus quotes.

Shepherd interprets Ursinus to mean that Christ's fulfillment of the Law simply meant to pay the Law's penalty. For Shepherd, Christ's perfect fulfillment of the Law was to enable Christ to be worthy as the mediator for Himself; it

---

[25] Zacharias Ursinus, *The Commentary of Dr. Zacharias Ursinus on the Heidelberg Catechism,* Translated by Rev. G.W. Willard (Phillipsburg, NJ: Presbyterian and Reformed Publishing Company), p. 325.

had nothing to do for us in terms of it being imputed to our account. To reiterate Shepherd's lecture comment, he says:

> Ursinus makes clear that the legal righteousness imputed to us in evangelical justification is the righteousness Jesus performed for us when he submitted to the punishment prescribed in the Law. The righteousness Christ wrought out for us was not the fulfillment of the demands of the law during the course of His life, but His death and resurrection to pay the penalty for sin. In other words, the righteousness of Christ imputed to us for our justification is not the active obedience of Christ but his passive obedience.[26]

The very foundation of Shepherd's view of justification, namely, that eternal life does not need to be merited, has never been seriously entertained in the Church. As Charles Hodge said, *"The Church in all ages has recognized this truth. ... They have ever regarded it as intuitively true that heaven must be merited. The only question was, whether that merit was in them or in Christ."*[27]

I want to give a lengthy series of quotes from the RCUS study report that gives a very good analysis of Shepherd's distortion of Ursinus when it says:

> It is not difficult to show that Shepherd is guilty of misunderstanding Ursinus. This "either obedience or punishment" paradigm does not indicate two alternatives that were facing Christ, but rather it indicates the nature of man's subjection to the law – apart from Christ. Apart from Christ, man has only two choices: obey the law perfectly, or suffer its eternal punishment. Ursinus explains: "The law binds all to obedience, and if this is not performed, to eternal punishment and condemnation. But no one renders this obedience. Therefore, the law binds all men to eternal condemnation."[28]
>
> Again, the law binds either to obedience or punishment. But satisfaction cannot be made through obedience, because our past obedience is already impaired, and that which follows cannot make satisfaction for past offenses. We are bound to render exact obedience every moment to the law, as a present

---

[26] Shepherd, Lectures on the covenant.

[27] Report of the Special Committee To Study Justification.

[28] Report of the Special Committee To Study Justification, p. 29.

debt. Hence, obedience being once impaired, there is no other way of making satisfaction except by punishment.[29]

Note again, it is man – not Christ – that has two mutually exclusive choices: either obedience or punishment. And since perfect obedience is not possible, man must be punished.

Since man himself has ruined the option of making satisfaction by perfect obedience, it does not follow that Christ did not have to make satisfaction for man by His perfect obedience, and that all He had to do was to make satisfaction by punishment. Quite the contrary, Ursinus says that Christ's perfect obedience was necessary to satisfy the law's requirement of perfect obedience. He wrote, *"although we are not able to make satisfaction through obedience, we are, nevertheless, able to make it through the endurance of a sufficient punishment, not in ourselves, but in Christ, who has satisfied the law **both by obedience and punishment**"* (Emphasis RCUS report)[30] Shepherd gives the impression that, for Ursinus, Christ satisfied the law only by punishment, and yet Ursinus clearly said it was by **obedience** and punishment. For Ursinus, obedience, and not merely suffering punishment, is a necessary component of the fulfillment of the law for us. This is clear from his definition of righteousness as conformity with the law:

...righteousness is the fulfillment of the law, and a conformity with the law is righteousness itself. This must be observed and held fast to, because **our justification can only be effected by fulfilling the law.** Evangelical righteousness is the fulfilling of the law, and does not conflict with it in the least. The gospel does not abolish the law, but establishes it. [31] (Emphasis RCUS report)

Since "our justification can only be effected by fulfilling the law," only Christ's perfect obedience can effect our justification. Ursinus wrote:

---

[29] Report of the Special Committee To Study Justification, p. 82.

[30] Report of the Special Committee To Study Justification, p. 88.

[31] Report of the Special Committee To Study Justification p. 325.

The law promises life to those who are righteous in themselves, or on the condition of righteousness, and perfect obedience. 'He that doeth them, shall live in them.' 'If thou wilt
enter into life, keep the commandments.' (Lev. 18:5. Matt.
19:17). The gospel, on the other hand, promises life by faith
in Christ, or on the condition of the righteousness of Christ,
applied unto us by faith. The law and gospel are, however,
not opposed to each other in these respects; **for although the
law requires us to keep the commandments if we would
enter into life, yet it does not exclude us from life if another perform these things for us.** [32] (Emphasis RCUS report)

We have a right to life because Christ kept the commandments for us! Though more quotes could be multiplied, one
more will suffice.

The law promises eternal life and all good things upon the
condition of our own and perfect righteousness, and of obedience in us: the gospel promises the same blessings upon the
condition that we exercise faith in Christ, by which we
embrace the obedience which another, even Christ, has performed in our behalf.[33]

It is quite apparent that Shepherd failed to quote substantial
explanations by Ursinus. Again, this is indicative of not only
terrible scholarship, but one wonders if he did not do this
deliberately. Shepherd's theology of a penitent, obedient saving faith does not fit into a biblical scheme of Christ's imputation of His merits by perfect law keeping. It is fully understandable why Shepherd is silent about this; it does not
advance his cause.

Francis Turretin was one of the great reformers of the 17th
century in Italy. Among Reformed scholars past and present,
he is considered one the most gifted Reformed thinkers that
has ever lived. In those places in Scripture where our salvation is ascribed to the death of Christ, Turretin said:

This is not done to the exclusion of the obedience of life
because nowhere is such a restriction found. ... Rather it

---

[32] Report of the Special Committee To Study Justification, p. 104.
[33] Report of the Special Committee To Study Justification, p. 497.

must be understood by a synechdoche by which what belongs to the whole is ascribed to the better part because it was the last degree of his humiliation, the crown and completion of his obedience.[34]

Louis Berkhof in his *Systematic Theology* comments on the idea that Christ merely paid the penalty for sin:

If Christ "had merely paid the penalty, without meeting the original demands of the law, He would have left man in the position of Adam before the fall, still confronted with the task of obtaining eternal life in the way of obedience."[35]

Shepherd makes this incredible statement in his lecture:

We do not find a belief in the imputation of active obedience in Calvin or Ursinus, or the Heidelberg Catechism all the reason for this is simply that they did not find this belief in the Bible ... And I want to point out that even the Westminster Confession as late as 1647 was written in such a way as to accommodate the views of three prominent members of the Westminster Assembly who did not subscribe to the imputation of active obedience. We do not find language that has been interpreted affirming the imputation of active obedience...Early Reformed doctrine had no doctrine of active obedience because it defined soteric justification as the forgiveness of sin.[36] (Emphasis mine)

When Shepherd made these unbelievable remarks, did he not think that anyone would not examine Calvin, the Form of Concord, and the Westminster Confession? Let's deal first with the *Form Of Concord*. This was produced by the Lutheran church in 1576, which is somewhat early considering that editions of Calvin's *Institutes of the Christian Religion* ranged from 1536 to 1559. The *Form of Concord* states:

That righteousness which is imputed to faith, or to believers, of mere grace, is the obedience, suffering, and resurrection of

---

[34] Francis Turretin, *InstitutesOf Elenctic Theology*, 3 vols. Translated by George M. Giger, edited by James T. Dennison, Jr. (Phillispburg, NJ: Presbyterian and Reformed Publishing, 1992), 2:452. Quoted in the RCUS study report, p. 31.

[35] Louis Berkhof, *Systematic Theology*, (Grand Rapids, MI: Eerdmans Publishing Company, 1939), p. 381.

[36] Shepherd's lecture at the 2003 SCCCS Summer Conference.

Christ, by which He satisfied the law for us, and expiated our sins…Hence, not only that obedience to God his Father which He exhibited in voluntarily subjecting Himself to the law and fulfilling it for our sakes, is imputed to us for righteousness, so that God on account of the total obedience which Christ accomplished for our sake before his heavenly Father, both in acting and in suffering, in life and in death, may remit our sins to us, regard us as good and righteous, and give us eternal salvation."[37]

Shepherd has boldly affirmed that Calvin did not teach the doctrine of active obedience whatsoever. Again, the doctrine of the active obedience of Christ is the biblical teaching that Christ kept the Law of God perfectly, demonstrating Himself as the sinless mediator, but He also kept God's Law in order to credit it to our account as if we had done it ourselves and thereby meriting for every believer the title to eternal life.

Calvin did affirm the doctrine of the active obedience of Christ even though he did not use that terminology. He agreed with his contemporaries and later Reformed thinkers. Calvin was in agreement with Ursinus and his Heidelberg Catechism that was published in 1563, which makes it a virtual contemporary work with Calvin's Institutes. Ursinus, in his commentary on the Heidelberg Catechism as we have noted, was explicit in his affirmation of the doctrine of Christ's active obedience.

What did Calvin teach in these matters? Regarding the doctrine of justification he said:

First let us explain what these expressions mean: that man is justified in God's sight, and that he is justified by faith or works. He is said to be justified in God's sight who is both reckoned righteous in God's judgment and has been accepted on account of his righteousness…Therefore, we explain justification simply as the acceptance with which God receives us into his favor as righteous men. **And we say that it consists in the remission of sins and the imputation of Christ's righteousness.**[38] (Emphasis mine)

---

[37] Hodge, *Systematic Theology*, Vol 3, p. 149.

[38] Calvin, *Institutes Of The Christian Religion*, Book 3, Chapter 11:2, pp. 726-727.

Shepherd has insisted that imputation of righteousness can only be understood as the forgiveness of sins. Calvin intimates that imputation is in addition to the remission of sins.

Calvin also states:

> The second requirement of our reconciliation with God was this: that man, who by his disobedience had become lost, should by way of remedy counter it **with obedience**, satisfy God's judgment, and pay the penalties for sin. Accordingly, our Lord came forth as true man and took the person and the name of Adam in order to take Adam's place in obeying the Father, to present our flesh as the price of satisfaction to God's righteous judgment, and, in the same flesh, to pay the penalty that we had deserved.[39] (emphasis mine)

From this comment, Calvin refers to three things that he pictures as separate items in Christ's reconciliation of us with God. These three things are: (1) obedience, (2) satisfying God's judgment, and (3) paying the penalties for sin. Calvin goes on to say that Jesus came as a true man to take Adam's place in obeying the Father, in satisfaction of God's righteous judgment, and to pay the penalty that we deserved.

Calvin discusses the way that we receive the grace of Christ:

> From this it is also evident that we are justified before God solely by the intercession of Christ's righteousness. This is equivalent to saying that man is not righteous in himself but because the righteousness of Christ is communicated to him by imputation—something worth carefully noting. Indeed, that frivolous notion disappears, that man is justified by faith because by Christ's righteousness he shares the Spirit of God, by whom he is rendered righteous.
>
> You see that our righteousness is not in us but in Christ, that we possess it only because we are partakers in Christ; indeed, with him we possess all its riches. And this does not contradict what he teaches elsewhere, that sin has been condemned for sin in Christ's flesh that the righteousness of the law might be fulfilled in us (Romans 8:3-4). The only fulfillment he alludes to is that which we obtain through imputation.

---

[39] Calvin, *Institutes Of The Christian Religion*, Book 2 Chapter 12:3, p. 466

> It is quite clear that Paul means exactly the same thing in
> another statement, which he had put a little before: "As we
> were made sinners by one man's disobedience, so we have
> been justified by one man's obedience" (Romans 5:19). To
> declare that by him alone we are accounted righteous, what
> else is this but to lodge our righteousness in Christ's obedi-
> ence, because **the obedience of Christ is reckoned to us as
> if it were our own?**[40] (Emphasis mine)

Calvin clearly sates that the law's righteousness can only be fulfilled in us
through imputation. Calvin appeals to Romans 5:19, stating that our righteousness is via Christ's obedience done for us as if we had done it ourselves.

Calvin discusses the purpose of the Law of God to drive us to Christ, seeing
that we cannot fulfill the moral Law. Calvin states:

> But, in order that our guilt may arouse us to seek pardon, it
> behooves us, briefly, to know how by our instruction in the
> moral law we are rendered more inexcusable. If it is true that
> in the law we are taught the perfection of righteousness, this
> also follows: the complete observance of the law is perfect
> righteousness before God. By it man would evidently be
> deemed and reckoned righteous before the heavenly judg-
> ment seat. Therefore Moses, after he had published the law,
> did not hesitate to call heaven and earth to witness that he had
> "set before Israel life and death, good and evil
> [Deuteronomy 30:19]. **We cannot gainsay that the
> reward of eternal salvation awaits complete obedience to
> the law, as the Lord has promised. On the other hand, it
> behooves us to examine whether we fulfill that obedience,
> through whose merit we ought to derive assurance of that
> reward.** What point is there to see in the observance of the
> law the proffered reward of eternal life if, furthermore, it is
> not clear whether by this path we may attain eternal life.
> (Emphasis mine)

> Therefore if we look only upon the law, we can only be
> despondent, confused, and despairing in mind, since from it
> all of us are condemned and accursed (Galatians 3:10). And
> it holds us far away from the blessedness that it promises to

---

[40] Calvin, *Institutes Of The Christian Religion*, Book 3 Chapter 11:23, p. 753.

its keepers. Is the Lord, you will ask, mocking us in this way? How little different from mockery is it to show forth the hope of happiness, to invite and attract us to it, to assure us that it is available, when all the while it is shut off and inaccessible? **I reply: even if the promises of the law, in so far as they are conditional, depend upon perfect obedience to the law — which can nowhere be found — they have not been given in vain.** For when we have learned that they will be fruitless and ineffectual for us unless God, out of his free goodness, shall receive us without looking at our works, and we in faith embrace that same goodness held forth to us by the gospel, the promises do not lack effectiveness even with the condition attached. **For the Lord then freely bestows all things upon us so as to add to the full measure of his kindness this gift also: that not rejecting our imperfect obedience, but rather supplying what is lacking to complete it, he causes us to receive the benefit of the promises of the law as if we had fulfilled their condition.**[41] (Emphasis mine)

There is no question that Calvin is advocating the doctrine of the active obedience of Christ. Notice that Calvin says that the Law causes us to have a confused, despairing mind. Why? It is because we cannot live up to the Law's perfect obedience. Calvin then states that God by His free goodness has given us the promises in the gospel by supplying what was lacking in us. And what was lacking in us? Perfect obedience. In Jesus, we have His perfect obedience as if we had fulfilled the Law's demands. Here is the doctrine of the active obedience of Christ, whose righteousness is given to us, enabling us to have the title of eternal life.

Norman Shepherd also confidently asserted that the Westminster Confession of Faith did not use language commonly associated with the doctrine of the active obedience of Christ because of some alleged accommodation to three Westminster delegates. First, who are these three delegates? Shepherd never mentions them. Second, let's see if the Confession uses language that teaches the active obedience of Christ.

Let's look at Chapter 11, Section 1 of the Westminster Confession on justification:

---

[41] Calvin, *Institutes Of The Christian Religion*, Book 2 Chapter 7:3, pp. 351, 352.

> Those whom God effectually calleth, He also freely
> justifieth; not by infusing righteousness into them, but by par-
> doning their sins, and by accounting and accepting their per-
> sons as righteous, not for anything wrought in them, or done
> by them, but for Christ's sake alone; nor by imputing faith
> itself, the act of believing, or any other evangelical obedience
> to them, as their righteousness, **but by imputing the obedi-
> ence and satisfaction of Christ unto them**, they receiving
> and resting on Him and His righteousness by faith; which
> faith they have not of themselves, it is the gift of God.
> (Emphasis mine)

The Confession makes a distinction between the imputation of Christ's obedience and the imputation of Christ's satisfaction. Herein is the active and
passive obedience of Christ respectively. Both imputations are involved in
man's justification.

Notice what the Westminster Confession Chapter 11, Section 3, states:

> Christ, by **His obedience and death**, did fully discharge the
> debt of all those that are thus justified, and did make a prop-
> er, real, and full satisfaction to His Father's justice in their
> behalf. Yet, inasmuch as He was given by the Father for
> them; and **His obedience and satisfaction accepted in their
> stead**; and **both** freely, not for anything in them; their justifi-
> cation is only of free grace; that both the exact justice, and
> rich grace of God, might be glorified in the justification of
> sinners. (Emphasis mine)

This section is about as clear as one can get in affirming that Christ's work of
imputation was two-fold. It entailed His obedience **and** His death or satisfaction. The fact that these were seen as separate imputations, the Westminster
delegates used the word "both" as referring to Christ's obedience and satisfaction.

In Chapter 16, Section 5, of the Westminster Confession, we read:

> We cannot, by our best works, **merit pardon of sin, or eter-
> nal life** at the hand of God, by reason of the great dispropor-
> tion that is between them and the glory to come; and the infi-
> nite distance that is between us and God, whom, by them, we
> can neither profit, nor satisfy for the debt of our former sins,
> but when we have done all we can, we have done but our

duty, and are unprofitable servants and because, as they are good, they proceed from His Spirit; and as they are wrought by us, they are defiled, and mixed with so much weakness and imperfection, that they cannot endure the severity of God's judgment. (Emphasis mine)

We see in this section that there is again the differentiation between the pardoning of sin and eternal life. It is interesting that the word "merit" is used to refer to these two facets. Shepherd maintains that the idea of "merit" that is used by Reformed writers is an espousing of Roman Catholicism. Is this portion an adoption of Romanist doctrine?

Let's look at Chapter 17, Section 2, of the Westminster Confession:

This perseverance of the saints depends not upon their own free will, but upon the immutability of the decree of election, flowing from the free and unchangeable love of God the Father; **upon the efficacy of the merit and intercession of Jesus Christ**; the abiding of the Spirit, and of the seed of God within them; and the nature of the covenant of grace from all which ariseth also the certainty and infallibility thereof. (Emphasis mine)

Here again the Westminster Assembly uses the word "merit" to refer to Christ's work on behalf of God's elect. This section deals with the perseverance of the saints. The reason that the saints, those who are effectually called and sanctified, cannot be lost but will persevere to eternal life is because Christ's merits are applied to them.

As I will show in another chapter of this book, the Federal Vision explicitly denies the Reformed doctrine of the perseverance of the saints. The Federal Vision in agreement with Roman Catholicism believes that it is possible to lose one's salvation. Part of the theological basis of the Federal Vision's denial of the perseverance of the saints is because of its rejection of the idea of the merits of Christ's atoning work!

I demonstrated earlier that Shepherd's living, penitent, and obedient faith is an outright denial of the precious doctrine of justification by faith alone. If the covenant of works does not exist, if the merits of Christ's perfect obedience are not imputed to the believer, then our perseverance must be dependent upon our own abilities to remain faithful. As you can see, one heresy leads to another and to another.

As noted earlier in this chapter in the section pertaining to the covenant of works, I quoted the Westminster Confession in Chapter 19:1 that this covenant bound the human race, represented by Adam, to personal, entire, exact, and perpetual obedience. Life was promised for fulfillment and death was threatened for failure to obey.

In Chapter 19, Section 6, we learn that the true believer in Jesus is not under the covenant of works to be justified or condemned, but the covenant of works is of great value to the Christian:

> … so as, examining themselves thereby, they may come to further conviction of, humiliation for, and hatred against sin; together with a clearer sight **of the need they have of Christ, and the perfection of His obedience.** (Emphasis mine)

The Christian recognizes that he cannot render God the perfection that God demands; therefore, he recognizes the need for Christ's perfect obedience. This is but another place that the imputation of Christ's righteousness is taught.

I noted earlier in questions 38 and 39 of the Westminster Larger Catechism (see the entire question and answer), that the Mediator must be both God and man so as to render for His representatives an efficacious suffering and obedience. As the Mediator, Jesus, according to LQ 39, **performed obedience to the law for us in our nature**. Here is but another example of Christ's active obedience.

Question 55 of the Westminster Larger Catechism states:

> How does Christ make intercession?
> **Answer:** Christ maketh intercession, by his appearing in our nature continually before the Father in heaven, **in the merit of his obedience and sacrifice on earth**, declaring his will to have it applied to all believers; answering all accusations against them, and procuring for them quiet of conscience, notwithstanding daily failings, access with boldness to the throne of grace, and acceptance of their persons and services. (emphasis mine)

Here again we see the term "merit" being used with reference to Christ's obedience and sacrifice. Here is but another instance of double imputation.

Regarding justification, question 70 of the Westminster Larger Catechism states:

> What is justification?

> **Answer:** Justification is an act of God's free grace unto sinners, in which he **pardoneth all their sins, accepteth and accounteth their persons righteous in his sight**; not for any thing wrought in them, or done by them, **but only for the perfect obedience and full satisfaction of Christ, by God imputed to them**, and received by faith alone. (Emphasis mine)

Question 71 of the Westminster Larger Catechism states:

> How is justification an act of God's free grace?
> **Answer:** Although Christ, **by his obedience and death**, did make a proper, real, and full satisfaction to God's justice **in the behalf of them that are justified**; yet in as much as God accepteth the satisfaction from a surety, which he might have demanded of them, and did provide this surety, his own only Son, **imputing his righteousness to them**, and requiring nothing of them for their justification but faith, which also is his gift, their justification is to them of free grace. (Emphasis mine)

Question 72 of the Westminster Larger Catechism states:

> What is justifying faith?
> **Answer:** Justifying faith is a saving grace, wrought in the heart of a sinner by the Spirit and Word of God, whereby he, being convinced of his sin and misery, and of the disability in himself and all other creatures to recover him out of his lost condition, not only assenteth to the truth of the promise of the gospel, but receiveth and resteth upon **Christ and his righteousness, therein held forth, for pardon of sin, and for the accepting and accounting of his person righteous in the sight of God for salvation**. (Emphasis mine)

Shepherd was wrong about Calvin; he was wrong about Ursinus; he was wrong about all the Reformed Confessions regarding the active obedience of Christ. I trust that the reader can see the depth of Shepherd's departure from orthodox Christianity.

In Norman Shepherd's lecture at the Southern California Christian Studies Conference in 2003, he openly denied one of the precious aspects of Christ's mediatorial work. He denied the imputation of Christ's perfect obedience to God's Law on behalf of God's children. In this lecture, as in his book *The Call*

of Grace, Shepherd separated himself from 500 years of evangelical and
Reformed thought. Everyone is wrong but him! Federal Vision proponents
have enthusiastically endorsed Shepherd's thought here, and in so doing, these
men have joined Shepherd in his heresy.

Shepherd Believes the Idea of Merit to Be Roman Catholic

In his lecture in Southern California, Norman Shepherd tried to portray any use
of "merit" with reference to Christ was akin to Roman Catholic tendencies.
This is an amazing comment, seeing that it is Shepherd's views that end up
being a version of Roman Catholicism. It is true that Romanism has its adherence to human merit as that which justifies man, but for Shepherd to state that
the idea of Christ's active obedience gives credence to Romanist views is
absurd.

When Norman Shepherd confidently declared that the idea of "merit" as it
applied to Christ's imputation was "a wondrous theological invention" and
"that in a doctrine of justification based on works/merit paradigm, the merit of
works moves into the foreground and the cross of Christ retreats into the background," he declared war on the history of Reformed thought spanning five
centuries. Shepherd and the rest of the adherents of the Federal Vision stand
below an avalanche of biblical and Reformed teaching.

In his lecture, Shepherd said:

> The imputation of the active obedience of Christ is absolute-
> ly essential to an evangelical view based on the works/merit
> paradigm. With it there, there is either no justification or jus-
> tification takes place on the ground of a personal, whether
> infused, performed righteousness. We are then back with
> Rome and have rejected the Reformation and that is why it is
> for some Reformed teachers today, the gospel itself stands or
> falls with a belief in the imputation or active obedience, not
> looking beyond the works/merit paradigm.[42]

As we saw in the quotes regarding the teaching of the Westminster Standards,
the Westminster Assembly had no problem using the term "merit" with reference to Christ's work. The Belgic Confession in Article 22 had no problem
speaking about Christ's merits being imputed to us. Even John Calvin uses this
terminology in his *Institutes.* He says:

---

[42] Shepherd, Lectures on the covenant.

By way of addition this question also should be explained. There are certain perversely subtle men who — even though they confess that we receive salvation through Christ — cannot bear to hear the word" merit," for they think that it obscures God's grace. Hence, they would have Christ as a mere instrument or minister, not as the Author or leader and prince of life, as Peter calls him (Acts 3:15).[43]

In discussing Christ's merit, we do not consider the beginning of merit to be in him, but we go back to God's ordinance, the first cause. For God solely of his own good pleasure appointed him Mediator to obtain salvation for us. Hence it is absurd to set Christ's merit against God's mercy. For it is a common rule that a thing subordinate to another is not in conflict with it. For this reason nothing hinders us from asserting that men are freely justified by God's mercy alone, and at the same time that Christ's merit, subordinate to God's mercy, also intervenes on our behalf. Both God's free favor and Christ's obedience, each in its degree, are fitly opposed to our works. Apart from God's good pleasure Christ could not merit anything; but did so because he had been appointed to appease God's wrath with his sacrifice, and to blot out our transgressions with his obedience. To sum up: inasmuch as Christ's merit depends upon God's grace alone, which has ordained this manner of salvation for us, it is just as properly opposed to all human righteousness as God's grace is.[44]

By his obedience, however, Christ truly acquired and merited grace for us with his Father. Many passages of Scripture surely and firmly attest this. I take it to be a commonplace that if Christ made satisfaction for our sins, if he paid the penalty owed by us, if he appeased God by his obedience —in short, if as a righteous man he suffered for unrighteous men — then he acquired salvation for us by his righteousness, which is tantamount to deserving it.[45]

---

[43] Calvin, *Institutes Of The Christian Religion,* Book 2, Chapter 1, p. 528.

[44] Calvin, *Institutes Of The Christian Religion,* p. 529.

[45] Calvin, *Institutes Of The Christian Religion,* pp. 530-531.

When Calvin made the comment that he did in footnote reference 55, we could insert the names Norman Shepherd and others of our day, and Calvin's comment would still be apt.

It was the great Puritan, John Owen, who accurately portrayed those who espoused views identical to Shepherd. Owen sets forth the views of Socinianism. Decide for yourself if Shepherd and company are modern day Socinians.

The Federal Vision and Socinianism

In May of 2004, The Reformed Church in the United States (not to be confused with the RPCUS) adopted at its 258th Synod a special committee report on the justification controversy. In their resolution 4, they state: *That the Reformed Church in the United States recognize these Romish, Arminian, and Socinian errors for what they are and urge our brethren throughout the world to reject them and to refuse those who teach them.*[46]

Philip Schaff in his *History of the Christian Church*, speaks of Calvin's interaction with Laelius Socinus (1525-1562). Socinus came to Geneva seeking instruction from Calvin, expressing various doubts that he had on certain doctrines such as the resurrection, predestination, original sin, the trinity, the atonement, and the sacraments.[47] Calvin would write letters to Socinus warning him of the dangers of a skeptical bent of mind. Philip Schaff indicates that Socinus visited Calvin a second time in 1554 and "soon afterwards he opened to Calvin, in four questions, his objections to the doctrine of the vicarious atonement. Calvin went through the trouble to answer them at length, with solid arguments in June, 1555.[48]

John Owen lays out the particular views of Socinus with reference to the atonement of Christ. Owen writes:

> There are two grand parties by whom the doctrine of justification by the imputation of the righteousness of Christ is opposed,—namely, the Papists and the Socinians; but they proceed on different principles, and unto different ends. The design of the one is to exalt their own merits; of the other, to destroy the merit of Christ.

---

[46] Report of the Special Committee To Study Justification, p. 45

[47] Schaff, *History of the Christian Church*, Vol.8, p. 634.

[48] Schaff, *History of the Christian Church*, p. 635.

So speak all the Socinians constantly; for they deny our obedience unto Christ to be either the meritorious or efficient cause of our justification; **only they say it is the condition of it**, without which God has decreed that we shall not be made partakers of the benefit thereof. [49] (Emphasis mine)

And in all their discourses to this purpose they assert our personal righteousness and holiness, or our obedience unto the commands of Christ, which they make to be the form and essence of faith, to be the condition whereon we obtain justification, or the remission of sins. And indeed, considering what their opinion is concerning the person of Christ, with their denial of his satisfaction and merit, it is impossible they should frame any other idea of justification in their minds.[50] (Emphasis mine)

And gospel faith is the soul's acting according to the mind of God, for deliverance from that state and condition which it is cast under by the law. **Concerning this faith and trust, it is earnestly pleaded by many that obedience is included in it**; but as to the way and manner thereof, they variously express themselves. **Socinus, and those who follow him absolutely, do make obedience to be the essential form of faith; which is denied by Episcopius. For the Socinians do not make obedience to be the essence of faith absolutely, but as it justifies. And so they plead unto this purpose, that "faith without works is dead."** [51] (Emphasis mine)

The similarity of Socinus' view of the nature of faith with today's Federal Vision is absolutely uncanny. Socinianism viewed obedience as the essence of faith as does Shepherd and company. Socinianism denied the active obedience of Christ as does the Federal Vision.

The Canons of Dordt and Christ's Merits

The Canons of Dordt are considered the third great body of Reformed material along side of the Belgic Confession and Heidelberg Catechism. These three confessional formulations are known as the Three Forms Of Unity to many

---

[49] Owen, Volume 5 on Justification.

[50] Owen, Volume 5 on Justification.

[51] Owen, Volume 5 on Justification.

Protestant and Reformed churches throughout the world. In 1618 the great
Synod of Dordt took place to address the growing tide of Arminianism in the
churches of the Netherlands. From this synod, the canons of Dordt arose. The
main issue at Dordt was to refute the errors of the Arminians. We will see that
there are definite parallels between Arminianism and the Federal Vision's
views of faith, and certain aspects of Christ's atonement. My primary purpose
in this section is to demonstrate that the Canons of Dordt were not afraid to use
the term "merit" when setting forth the Reformed doctrine of Christ's work.
The Federal Vision's antipathy toward "the merits of Christ" is contrary to yet
another Reformed expression.

In the heading of the section dealing with the death of Christ: Rejection of
Errors, Paragraph III, we read:

> Who teach: That Christ by his satisfaction merited neither salva-
> tion itself for anyone, nor faith, whereby this satisfaction of Christ
> is effectually appropriated but that he merited for the Father only
> the authority or the perfect will to deal again with man, and to pre-
> scribe new conditions as he might desire.[52]

Hoeksema makes the following comments about this section:

> In this third article it becomes still plainer in which direction
> the Arminian wants to go. The covenant which God wants to
> establish is not one of grace, but of works. Christ **merited** for
> no one either salvation or faith, but only the authority and will
> to prescribe new conditions (not the old one of complete obe-
> dience to the law, but new ones of faith and obedience; but
> conditions nevertheless)... Reformed truth maintains that
> Christ with certainty merited salvation for all those whom the
> Father gave Him from before the foundation of the world.[53]
> (Emphasis mine)

> The Arminian does not simply teach that Christ merited sal-
> vation, and that it is up to man to accept the salvation which
> Christ merited. He even denies that Christ really merited sal-
> vation for anyone.[54]

---

[52] Homer C. Hoeksema, *The Voice Of Our Fathers,* Of The Death Of Christ: Rejection
of Errors, Paragraph III, (Grand Rapids, MI: Reformed Free Publishing Association,
1980), p. 395.

[53] Hoeksema, *The Voice Of Our Fathers,* pp. 395-396.

[54] Hoeksema, *The Voice Of Our Fathers,* p. 398.

The Canons state in of The Death of Christ, Rejection of Errors, Paragraph IV:

> Who teach: That the new covenant of grace, which God the Father, through the mediation of the death of Christ, made with man, does not herein consist, that we by faith, inasmuch as it accepts the merits of Christ, are justified before God and saved, but in the fact that God having revoked the demand of perfect obedience of the law, regards faith itself and the obedience of faith, although imperfect, as the perfect obedience of the law, and does esteem it worthy of the reward of eternal life through grace.[55]

Hoeksema comments:

> For it is made evident that the Arminian by his wicked doctrine, while he mouths the terms of the truth of Scripture, such as "faith" and "the obedience of faith" and "grace," nevertheless maintains to the full the comfortless error of salvation by works. For note that here we have the next link in the Arminian chain of error. In Paragraph III we read to the Father's authority to prescribe new conditions, the fulfillment of which conditions is dependent upon the free will of man. In Paragraph IV we find those new conditions are faith and the obedience of faith. But because they are **conditions** – and this the fathers saw with penetrating insight – this faith and obedience of faith have an entirely different meaning and significance than the Reformed churches attach to them.[56] (Emphasis Hoeksema)

> According to the fathers, **faith was such that it accepts the merits of Christ**. This is noteworthy in this connection. About the fact that faith **accepts** (and is indeed very active in accepting) there is no quarrel. But notice: faith accepts of **the merits Christ**. That means that faith itself has no value, no merit...Those works or obedience of faith do not **precede** our justification, but follow it. All the merit, all the value, the sole righteousness on account of which we are justified before God, the absolutely unique ground of our justification, and therefore of our entire salvation, is Christ alone. And faith **accepts** this ... **Faith always receives, accepts, lays hold on**

---

[55] Hoeksema, *The Voice Of Our Fathers,* p. 401.
[56] Hoeksema, *The Voice Of Our Fathers,* pp. 401-402.

the merits and righteousness of Another. Faith accepts and appropriates the righteousness of God in Christ. Faith is such that it clings to the God of our salvation Christ Jesus.[57] (Emphasis Hoeksema)

In elucidating the errors of the Arminians, Hoeksema makes this needed observation about Arminianism's understanding of faith:

Faith itself and the obedience of faith (not the merits of Christ) are worthy of eternal life. Faith and the obedience of faith are therefore substitute works for the works of the law.[58]

Rich Lusk's Denial of Christ's Imputation

On August 11-13, 2003, Knox Theological Seminary in Ft. Lauderdale, Florida sponsored a face to face meeting of representatives of the Federal Vision with various men of mainstream Reformed thinking. By mainstream, I mean those men who believe that the historical Reformed Standards (The Westminster Confession of Faith with its Larger and Shorter Catechism, the Belgic Confession with its Heidelberg Catechism, and the Canons of Dordt) are faithful interpretations of the doctrines of Scripture. Both sides wrote papers, and there were opportunities for rebuttal papers. The compiled document was called *The Auburn Avenue Theology, Pros and Cons: Debating the Federal Vision.*[59]

One of the papers submitted was by Dr. Morton Smith. His paper was titled, *"The Biblical Plan of Salvation, with Reference to The Covenant of Works, Imputation, and Justification by Faith."* In this article, Dr. Smith sets forth the historic Reformed position regarding these doctrines. Rich Lusk wrote a rebuttal to this. Lusk's article was titled, *"A Response to The Biblical Plan of Salvation."* The significance of this article for myself and others in the Reformed community was that this was the first indication that the Federal Vision adherents were denying the active obedience of Christ. Earlier in the month of August 2003, Norman Shepherd had lectured at the Southern California Center for Christian Studies where he explicitly denied the active obedience of Christ.

---

[57] Hoeksema, *The Voice Of Our Fathers,* pp. 402- 403.

[58] Hoeksema, *The Voice Of Our Fathers,* p. 403.

[59] One can obtain copies of this work through Knox Theological Seminary. It is now available in book form.

In his article, Rich Lusk challenges Dr. Smith's article by saying *"But just on the surface of it, this pattern of argumentation seems flawed ... All sides must admit that the covenant of works is a relatively recent theological doctrine."*[60]

Lusk goes on to say, *"Luther himself never even so much as hinted at it. The Three Forms of Unity, the confessional basis of the Dutch Reformed branch of the Reformation, also uphold justification without presupposing a covenant of works in any explicit way."*[61]

This is simply not true! I have endeavored in this chapter to give a significant amount of direct quotes from all three forms of unity, in addition to direct quotes from the Westminster Confession and its Larger and Shorter Catechism. I will let the readers decide for themselves if Lusk's claims are true or not. Lusk continued to state, *"Even proponents of the meritorious covenant of works admit their position is a minority report in the Reformed world today. So the notion that the gospel falls to the ground if it isn't rooted in a covenant of works seems to be a highly suspicious claim."*[62] Lusk even asserts in a footnote quote, *"A veritable All-Star team of Reformed heroes have subscribed to one or both of those points, asserting or implying grace in the covenant of works: William Ames, the Westminster Divines, Francis Turretin, John Owen, Thomas Boston, R.L. Dabney, John Murray, Louis Berkhof, Anthony Hoeksema"*[63]

Lusk wants to leave the impression with his reader that the salient elements of the covenant of works were not taught by these confessional documents and that the men that he quoted are in agreement with the Federal Vision. This is a tragedy! Either Lusk is deliberately misleading people, hoping that they will not bother to read these documents and these men, or he simply is incapable of understanding what the documents are explicitly teaching. This veritable All-Star team refutes the position of the Federal Vision. Virtually all of these men explicitly referred to the merits of Christ's work being imputed to us. The Westminster Standards are very explicit in its adherence to the covenant of works. Lusk gives the misleading impression that he says that the covenant of works does not have elements of grace in it. The historic Reformed position has not been that God was not gracious to enter into that covenant with Adam, but this does not detract from the fundamental features of that covenant that

---

[60] Knox Theological Seminary Colloquium on the Federal Vision, August 11-13, 2003, published by Knox Theological Seminary, p. 119.

[61] Colloquium on the Federal Vision.

[62] Colloquium on the Federal Vision, pp. 119-120.

[63] Colloquium on the Federal Vision, p. 120. See footnote 7 in Colloquium.

entailed merit of which Jesus is the second Adam, accomplishing for us what Adam failed to do for us.

We must remember that Lusk is challenging the idea of the imputation of Christ's merits to the believer. He is directly challenging the active obedience of Christ. Lusk stated, "*As will be suggested below, when the Reformers threw out the medieval understanding of salvation, they should have gone the whole way and thrown out the antiquated concept of merit as well.*"[64]

The problem with Rich Lusk, Norman Shepherd and others is that they simply cannot read the confessional standards at face value. For example, Rich Lusk states, "*God certainly did require perfect and perpetual obedience of Adam. But, sadly, reading the Confession through the lens of merit theology misses–or at least obscures–the basic ethos of the pre-fall relation between Adam and his God.*"[65] This is where the Federal Vision is entirely mistaken. **Reformed thinkers, who espouse the covenant of works, do not interpret the Reformed Standards from the presupposition of merit theology of the Roman Catholic sort.** This is the fundamental argument of Shepherd; he thinks any kind of use of "merit" is an adoption of Romanist belief that human merit is sufficient to earn salvation. The Reformed Standards are very clear when they speak of the "merits of Christ" imputed to us and received by faith alone. It is incredible that the Federal Vision proponents cannot see this simple truth. But, as I have said earlier, the Federal Vision has its agenda. It must deny the covenant of works; it cannot have Jesus' imputed obedience given to us in a forensic or declarative way because the Federal Vision must pave the way for its active, penitent, and obedient faith. In its redefinition of saving faith, the Federal Vision has espoused a works salvation paradigm. The present Reformed world is now realizing that this is the implication of the theology of the Federal Vision. Is it any surprise that some people have rejected the Reformed Faith and returned to Romanism because of Federal Vision theology? Norman Shepherd boldly asserts in his book *The Call of Grace* that there is a bridge between Protestantism and Roman Catholicism. That bridge is his understanding of covenant. This understanding is that saving faith is an active, penitent, obedient faith. My friends, this is Romanism! It is ironic that those who want to denigrate us for holding to the covenant of works, saying that it denies grace, are the very ones who lead us to Romanism's merit theology.

The Federal Vision will not accept the fact that the Mosaic Law demanded perfect obedience, after all it has denied the existence of the covenant of works.

---

[64] Colloquium on the Federal Vision, p. 120.

[65] Colloquium on the Federal Vision, p. 121.

The Federal Vision continues to demonstrate its theological bankruptcy and heresy at this point. Rich Lusk states, *"Third, the law did not require perfect obedience. It was designed for sinners, not unfallen creatures. Thus, the basic requirement of the law was covenant loyalty and trust, not sinless perfection. This is why numerous sinful but redeemed people are regarded as law keepers in Scripture…Moses was right: this law was not too hard to keep, for it was a law of faith (Deut. 30:1ff; cf Romans 10:1-12)."*[66]

As incredible as the previous comment is, Lusk goes on to give us his understanding of the story of the young rich ruler. Lusk states:

> The story of the rich young ruler also presents an interesting slant on the keep-ability of the law. Jesus did not give commands to the young man as a hypothetical "covenant of works" to show him he was really a lawbreaker. Rather, Jesus is outlining the way of discipleship for this man, which at this particular juncture in redemptive history would have included selling all his possessions and journeying with Jesus to Jerusalem. We know this the way this story should be read because immediately afterwards, Peter indicates that he and the other disciples have done precisely what the young man refused to do (Matthew 19:27). Jesus does not correct Peter's claim; in fact he agrees with it, and then goes on to remind the disciples that they should not feel self-pity over the sacrifices they have made for the kingdom because it will all be paid back to them many times over.[67]
>
> Paul's statement in Galatians 3:12 that the law is "not of faith" does not contradict this point. In Galatians 3, Paul uses faith in a specific eschatological (New Covenant) sense (cf. Galatians 3:23, in which the coming of "faith" is equated with the coming of Christ into history). Certainly Paul would not have disputed the presence of faith on the part of saints under the administration of the law (cf. Hebrews 11). In a broader sense, the law was of faith. In fact, it was precisely Israel's failure to observe the law out of faith that prevented her from recognizing her Messiah (cf. Romans 9:30ff).[68]

---

[66] Colloquium on the Federal Vision, p. 128.

[67] Colloquium on the Federal Vision, p. 128. Quoted in footnote 29 and 30.

[68] Colloquium on the Federal Vision.

Let's first deal with Lusk's interpretation of the young rich ruler. Lusk gives the same interpretation that Steve Schlissel will give. Lusk's view demonstrates his inability to be an accurate interpreter of the Word of God. In fact, his view, which is consistent with the Federal Vision, only demonstrates its heresy of denying justification by faith alone. Lusk and company is advocating a works salvation, plain and simple.

Since Lusk thinks that Calvin would be in his camp on the issue of merit theology, let's take a look at what Calvin says about this story in Matthew 19: 16-26:

> Now, the meaning will be quite clear if we take into account to whom these words are addressed, something we should always heed in all Christ's discourses. A young man asks by what works he shall enter into eternal life [Matthew 19:16; cf. Luke 10:25]. Christ, because the question concerned works, refers him to the law [Matthew 19:17-19]. And rightly! For, considered in itself, it is the way of eternal life; and, except for our depravity, is capable of bringing salvation to us. By this reply Christ declared that he taught no other plan of life than what had been taught of old in the law of the Lord. So also he attested God's law to be the doctrine of perfect righteousness, and at the same time confuted false reports so he might not seem by some new rule of life to incite the people to desert the law.[69]

> The young man, not from evil intent, but puffed up with vain confidence, replies that he has kept all the precepts of the law from childhood [Matthew 19:20]. It is quite certain that he was an immeasurable distance away from what he boasted of having reached. And if his boasting had been true, he would have lacked nothing toward attaining the highest perfection. For we have shown above that the law in itself contains perfect righteousness; and this appears from the fact that its observance is called the way of eternal salvation. To teach him how little he had advanced toward that righteousness which he too boldly replied he had fulfilled, it was worthwhile to search out his intimate shortcoming. Since he abounded in riches, he had his heart fixed upon them. Therefore, because he did not feel this secret wound, Christ probes it. "Go," he says, "sell all you have." [Matthew

---

[69] Calvin, *Institutes of the Christian Religion,* Book 4, Chapter 13:13, p. 1267.

19:21.] If he had been as good a keeper of the law as he thought, he would not have gone away in sorrow on hearing this word [Matthew 19:22]. For the man who loves God with all his heart not only counts as refuse whatever opposes love of Him, but flees it like the plague.[70]

Calvin utterly refutes Lusk's interpretation. Lusk and the Federal Vision have their agenda. They must deny the law's requirement of perfect righteousness to push their new works paradigm. Notice, earlier, that Lusk blatantly said, "**the law did not require perfect obedience.**"[71]

To further demonstrate how Lusk does not understand the Westminster Confession, I simply quote Larger Catechism questions and answers 93-99. Remember, Lusk asserts that those pushing for a "merit" paradigm have misunderstood the Confession. Decide for yourself who is wrong.

Question 93 of the Westminster Larger Catechism states:

> What is the moral law?
> **Answer:** The moral law is the declaration of the will of God to mankind, directing and **binding every one to personal, perfect, and perpetual conformity and obedience thereunto**, in the frame and disposition of the whole man, soul and body, and in performance of all those duties of holiness and righteousness which he oweth to God and man: promising life upon the fulfilling, and threatening death upon the breach of it. (Emphasis mine)

Question 94 of the Westminster Larger Catechism states:

> Is there any use of the moral law to man since the fall?
> **Answer:** Although no man, since the fall, can attain to righteousness and life by the moral law: yet there is great use thereof, as well common to all men, as peculiar either to the unregenerate, or the regenerate.

Question 95 of the Westminster Larger Catechism states:

> Of what use is the moral law to all men?
> **Answer:** The moral law is of use to all men, to inform them of the holy nature and the will of God, and of their duty, bind-

---

[70] Calvin, *Institutes of the Christian Religion*, pp. 1267, 1268.

[71] Colloquium on the Federal Vision, pp. 119-120.

ing them to walk accordingly; to convince them of their disability to keep it, and of the sinful pollution of their nature, hearts, and lives: **to humble them in the sense of their sin and misery, and thereby help them to a clearer sight of the need they have of Christ, and of the perfection of his obedience**. (Emphasis mine)

Question 96 of the Westminster Larger Catechism states:

What particular use is there of the moral law to unregenerate men?

Answer: The moral law is of use to unregenerate men, to awaken their consciences to flee from wrath to come, and to drive them to Christ; or, upon their continuance in the estate and way of sin, to leave them inexcusable, and under the curse thereof.

Question 97 of the Westminster Larger Catechism states:

Question 97. What special use is there of the moral law to the regenerate?

Answer: Although they that are regenerate, and believe in Christ, be delivered from the moral law as a covenant of works, so as thereby they are neither justified nor condemned; yet, besides the general uses thereof common to them with all men, it is of special use, **to show them how much they are bound to Christ for his fulfilling it**, and enduring the curse thereof in their stead, and for their good; and thereby to provoke them to more thankfulness, and to express the same in their greater care to conform themselves thereunto as the rule of their obedience. (Emphasis mine)

Question 98 of the Westminster Larger Catechism states:

Where is the moral law summarily comprehended?

Answer: The moral law is summarily comprehended in the ten commandments, which were delivered by the voice of God upon Mount Sinai, and written by him in two tables of stone; and are recorded in the twentieth chapter of Exodus. The four first commandments containing our duty to God, and the other six our duty to man. (Emphasis mine)

Question 99 of the Westminster Larger Catechism states:

What rules are to be observed for the right understanding of the ten commandments?

Answer: For the right understanding of the ten commandments, these rules are to be observed:

1. **That the law is perfect, and bindeth everyone to full conformity in the whole man unto the righteousness thereof, and unto entire obedience forever; so as to require the utmost perfection of every duty, and to forbid the least degree of every sin.** (Emphasis mine).

The Heidelberg Catechism and the Law of God

Rich Lusk maintains that his views are in conformity with the Heidelberg Catechism. He claims that the Mosaic Law never did demand perfect obedience and that righteous people can keep it. Let's see how these views stack up with the Heidelberg Catechism.

In Lord's Day 2, Question 3, the Heidelberg Catechism asks:

> Whence knowest thou thy misery?
> **Answer:** Out of the law of God.

In Lord's Day's 2, Question 4, the Heidelberg Catechism asks:

> What doth the law of God require of us?
> **Answer:** Christ teaches us that briefly, Matt. 22: 37-40, "Thou shalt love the Lord thy God with all thy heart, with all thy soul, and with all thy mind, and with all thy strength. This is the first and the great commandment; and the second is like unto it, Thou shalt love thy neighbor as thyself. On these two commandments hang all the law and the prophets."

In Lord's Day 2, Question 5, the Heidelberg Catechism then asks a very important question:

> Canst thou keep all these things perfectly?
> **Answer:** In no wise; for I am prone by nature to hate God and my neighbor.

The Heidelberg Catechism is in stark opposition to Rich Lusk and the other Federal Vision adherent's belief that the Mosaic Law did not require perfect obedience. How they can maintain that their beliefs are compatible with the Reformed Standards is beyond me. The fact that Luke 10:27 and Romans 3:20 are used as proof texts demonstrates that the Moral Law of God is in view, not the ceremonial law. Moreover, so much for this New Perspective on Paul theology that insists that none of these passages are relevant to a person's individual relationship to the Law of God.

In building upon this inability to perfectly keep the Law, in Lord's Day 3, Question 8, the Heidelberg Catechism asks:

> Are we then so corrupt that we are wholly incapable of doing any good, and inclined to all wickedness?
> **Answer:** Indeed we are; except that we are regenerated by the Spirit of God.

The Heidelberg then follows up with an important question in Lord's Day 4, Question 9:

> Doth not God then do injustice to man, by requiring from him in his law, that which he cannot perform?
> **Answer:** Not at all; for God made man capable of performing it; but man, by the instigation of the devil, and his own willful disobedience, deprived himself and all his posterity of those divine gifts.

The Heidelberg Catechism continues in Lord's Day 4, Question 10:

> Will God suffer such disobedience and rebellion to go unpunished?
> **Answer:** By no means; but is terribly displeased with our original was well as actual sins; and will punish them in his just judgment temporally and eternally, and he hath declared, "Cursed is every one that continueth not in all things, which are written in the book of the law, to do them."

The Heidelberg Catechism has been biblically building a case. The Law of God was given to man as to how he should live. This law demands perfect obedience, but man cannot render this perfect obedience because man is a sinner. As a result of his sin, God will bring judgment upon man. Notice that the answer to question 10 contains two very important passages – Deuteronomy 27:27 and Galatians 3:10. It is being made very clear that judgment comes as a result of failure to obey perfectly. The Federal Vision explicitly denies this biblical truth.

The next Heidelberg question wonders if there is any mercy to be found in light of such harsh judgment. It asks in Lord's Day 4, Question 11:

> Is not God then also merciful?

> **Answer:** God is indeed merciful, but also just; therefore his justice requires, that sin which is committed against the most high majesty of God, be also punished with extreme, that is, with everlasting punishment of body and soul.

In its wonderful presentation from point to point, the Heidelberg then asks in Lord's Day 5, Question 12:

> Since then, by the righteous judgment of God, we deserved temporal and eternal punishment, is there no way by which we may escape that punishment, and be again received into favor?
> **Answer:** God will have his justice satisfied; and therefore we must make this full satisfaction, either by ourselves, or by another.

It is very important that we understand that we must make **full satisfaction of God's justice.** The Heidelberg Catechism has been very thorough and logical in its questions and answers. What is the full satisfaction of God's justice? Perfect obedience to all of God's law! Since man cannot give God this full satisfaction, man stands under a terrible curse and impending eternal judgment. Praise God, however, there is mercy. With reference to this need for satisfaction of justice, the Heidelberg continues in Lord's Day 5, Question 13:

> Can we ourselves then make this satisfaction?
> **Answer:** By no means; but on the contrary we daily increase our debt.

In Lord's Day 5, Question 14, the Heidelberg Catechism then asks:

> Can there be found anywhere, one, who is a mere creature, able to satisfy for us?
> **Answer:** None; for, first, God will not punish any other creature for the sin which man hath committed; and further, no mere creature can sustain the burden of God's eternal wrath against sin, so as to deliver others from it.

It is very important that we understand that there is **no man on earth** who can remedy our sin problem. This obviously includes ourselves! No man is capable of sustaining such an increasing debt. Every day it gets worse and worse. The debt grows bigger and bigger. However, Rich Lusk has said that the Law of God never demanded perfect obedience and that it is possible to keep.

Since no mere man is able to satisfy the immensity of his sin debt, the Catechism provides the answer in Lord's Day 5, Question 15:

> What sort of a mediator and deliverer then must we seek for?
> **Answer:** For one who is very man, and perfectly righteous; and yet more powerful than all creatures; that is, one who is also very God.

The Catechism states very clearly that the mediator/deliverer must be **perfectly righteous.** The Catechism continues to add in Lord's Day 6, Question 16:

> Why must he be very man, and also perfectly righteous?
> **Answer:** Because the justice of God requires that the same human nature which hath sinned, should likewise make satisfaction for sin; and one, who is himself a sinner, cannot satisfy for others.

Not only must the mediator be a real man in order to shed real blood for atonement, but the mediator must be God in order to render a death and an imputation of immeasurable value. The Catechism states in Lord's Day 6, Question 17:

> Why must he in one person be also very God?
> **Answer:** That he might, by the power of his Godhead sustain in his human nature, the burden of God's wrath; and might obtain for, and restore to us, righteousness and life.

It is vital for us to note that the mediator must be able to sustain this immense and unpayable debt **for us and restore to us, righteousness and life.** This is the imputation of Christ's passive and active obedience to us. We must have His righteousness for **our** sake, not His. Lusk and others emphatically deny the imputation of Christ's righteousness for us in order for the perfect demands of the Law to be satisfied.

The necessity for this imputation of Christ is further brought out in Lord's Day 6, Question 18:

> Who then is that Mediator, who is in one person both very God, and a real righteous man?
> **Answer:** Our Lord Jesus Christ: "who of God is made unto us wisdom, and righteousness, and sanctification, and redemption."

I have taken up much space quoting from the Westminster Larger Catechism and the Heidelberg Catechism in order to show that these Reformed documents understand the Bible far better than Rich Lusk and company. It is amazing that Rich Lusk and later Steve Schlissel agree that the law of God as given by Moses can be kept. If it can be kept, then we don't need the merits of Christ. Our feeble attempts are good enough to please God. Such thinking is why we must declare this Federal Vision theology a heresy. Now, they may retort, "We never said that we keep it perfectly." To this I say, "Then what you are saying is that an imperfect law keeping is good enough."

Lusk continues in his misunderstanding of the Mosaic covenant when he says:

> How, then, did some come to see the Mosaic covenant as a covenant of works? And how did this come to relate to the original covenant with Adam? It was simple, really. Luther took Paul's critique of the law in an abstract sense, as though the apostle was concerned with a generic moralism, rather than a specifically Jewish, redemptive-historical issue. Luther assumed Paul's Judaizing opponents were basically medieval merit mongers. Thus, Luther developed his infamous law/grace antithesis. Law per se is bad because it tempts the sinner to think he can and should earn salvation by being good. The gospel, by contrast, reveals a way of salvation apart from human effort. Law always condemns; gospel always comforts. Law is conditioned by strict justice; gospel is a matter of free grace.[72]

This comment puts Rich Lusk firmly into the New Perspective on Paul theology, popularized (though not exclusively) by N.T. Wright. Since N.T. Wright was the keynote speaker at the 2005 Auburn Avenue Pastors' Conference, which is hosted by the church that Rich Lusk was once the assistant pastor of, one ought not to be surprised. N.T. Wright, also denies the active obedience of Christ. This comment by Lusk also reveals his low view of Luther. Moreover, his comment reveals his complete misunderstanding of Luther. Luther did not view the Law as bad, tempting man to try to keep it in his flesh. Luther kept insisting that the Law's demands are so great that it drives men to Christ to receive grace.

The Federal Vision has purported that Luther's law/grace antithesis is a perversion of the gospel. I am sorry, Luther had it right; the Federal Vision has perverted the gospel. The Federal Vision has championed an imperfect, man sustained obedience as the way to eternal life. The Federal Vision completely distorts the meaning of "grace." They want to tout it, but they are the ones who

---

[72] Colloquium on the Federal Vision, p. 130.

have created a works paradigm, an ugly one that is void of the merits of Christ imputed to us by grace.

Rich Lusk reveals that he is squarely in the New Perspective on Paul Movement when he says:

> Paul's anti-Judaic polemic thus cannot be equated with the Reformers anti-Romish polemic. **No doubt at certain points the Reformers succumbed to eisegetically reading their debates with Rome back into Paul's debates with the Judaizers.** While there are analogies, there are also important differences. The Reformers were concerned with matters of individual soteriology and assurance. Paul's concerns included those things but were much broader. He was concerned to show that the great redemptive historical transition had taken place and the Judaic, typological, childhood phase of redemptive history had given way to the worldwide, fulfillment, mature phase. He was concerned with the new identity and configuration of the people of God. In Christ, all things were new; old things–including the good, but temporary Torah – were passing away.[73] (Emphasis Mine)

I trust that my reader caught the swipe that Rich Lusk took at the Reformers. He said that at certain points they were guilty of eisegesis, meaning reading into a text what they wanted it to say rather than exegesis, bringing out what it actually says. The Reformers, Luther especially, were unable to read the New Testament correctly. Paul's scathing attacks on the Judaizers had nothing to do with their human attempts to keep the Mosaic Law, thinking that by their imperfect obedience they could inherit eternal life. As the New Perspective on Paul Movement says, Romans and Galatians had to do with accepting the Gentiles into the covenant.

Lusk goes on to say:

> So, how does Paul's argument in Galatians 3-4 work? We cannot thoroughly exegete this passage, of course, but we can give a broad overview of the issues. It will become clear that Paul was not battling legalism per se; rather he is concerned to show **what time it is** on God's redemptive clock and **what covenant** God's people are now under. (Emphasis Lusk)

---

[73] Colloquium on the Federal Vision, pp. 132-133.

> There is no evidence the Judaizers were suggesting that cir-
> cumcision or other marks of Jewishness were good works an
> individual could do to earn or merit status before God; rather
> they were suggesting submission to the old covenant identity
> badges as the way of entrance into the true people of God, the
> promised family of Abraham.[74]

These comments, to put it bluntly, are New Perspective on Paul trash! I know that this comment is rather harsh, but we must come to grips as to what is at stake in this controversy in the Reformed community. The gospel is on the line! The Federal Vision tells us that they are bringing a new paradigm. Actually they are trying to convince us that most other Reformed thinkers were simply wrong. In Lusk's paper, he has tried to convince us that the great Reformed thinkers for the past 500 years saw it like he sees it. And if we read the Confessional Standards and think that it doesn't seem to say what Lusk insists, then we are simply reading into it our preconceived misconceptions. So, when the Westminster Larger Catechism question 93 explicitly states that the Mosaic Law bound all men to *personal, perfect, and perpetual conformity and obedience,* that it means something else?

Lusk, openly identifies himself with the New Perspective on Paul Movement when he says:

> Going the corporate, redemptive-historical route with Paul
> does not mean the sixteenth century soteriological concerns
> get lost in the shuffle. Rather, it means they get recontextual-
> ized in a much larger, more holistic framework ... The best
> theologians in the so-called "New Perspective on Paul"
> movement are simply recalling to us to the original meaning
> of the texts in their historical setting.[75]

In his footnote 53 of his Colloquium article, Lusk states that my denomination, the RPCUS, exhibited an appalling ignorance of the New Perspective on Paul debates when we condemned the 2002 Auburn Avenue Pastors' Conference. Well, looking at what Lusk has already stated in his article, does the reader think that the RPCUS has misunderstood the issues?

In his section on Christ and merit, Lusk accurately summarizes Morton Smith's covenant construction when he says, "*The covenant of grace is simply the covenant of works fulfilled by a sinless substitute provided by God himself.*

---

[74] Colloquium on the Federal Vision, p. 133.

[75] Colloquium on the Federal Vision, p. 135.

While there is much to appreciate about the symmetry of such a covenantal scheme, it seems fraught with biblical difficulties. "[76] So that the reader understands the impact of this quote, Rich Lusk has just taken issue with what the Reformed Faith has understood to be the gospel for the past 500 years.

Lusk goes on to say:

> It ends up looking something like this: In Genesis 1-2, God constructed Pelagian machinery for man to earn his way to blessing. Adam rendered himself incapable of operating that machinery when he sinned. But now God sends his Son into the world as One who can work the machinery flawlessly. In other words, Jesus is the successful Pelagian, the One Guy in the history of the world who succeeded in pulling off the works righteousness plan. Jesus covered our demerits by dying on the cross and provides all the merits we need by keeping the legal terms of the covenant of works perfectly. Those merits are then imputed to us by faith alone.[77]

One of the most frustrating things in dealing with the Federal Vision proponents is that they continue to say after three years now that people are misreading their viewpoints, and we do not understand their fine nuances. Others have said that some criticism directed toward them has been guilty of not giving them the benefit of the doubt. I encourage the reader to look again at the above quote and ask yourself, "Is there something vague here?" Lusk has just denied the gospel! He doesn't believe that Jesus' righteousness is imputed to us.

I don't understand why presbytery charges have not been filed against him and others for these kinds of comments. This minister took vows to uphold the system of doctrine as taught in the Westminster Standards. He has openly denied these vows.

Lusk states:

> The entire ministry of Jesus up to his resurrection took place under the Old Covenant, under the Torah (Galatians 4:4). Jesus was given initial life, like Adam, but unlike Adam persevered in it by faith. Moreover, he paid for Adam's sin on the cross. Finally, he entered into glorious eschatological,

---

[76] Colloquium on the Federal Vision, pp. 136-137.

[77] Colloquium on the Federal Vision.

mature life at his resurrection. He became the first man to enter God's new age.[78]

Of course, for us what matters most is that he took us with him on his journey into eschatological life. If all Jesus did was satisfy the requirements of an Adamic covenant of works (his "active obedience" as it is sometimes called), we'd still be living under the old creation. He could've gotten us back to square one, but no further. We'd still be in need of new creation, glorified life. We'd still be in need of maturation into full sonship.

At his resurrection, Jesus becomes the first mature man, the first graduate out of the old world into the new. He attains to wisdom and maturity. He completed his course of learning obedience through his suffering (cf. Hebrews 5:8-9) ... The incarnate Son has matured into full Father-like-ness. He has ascended to the Ancient of Days (Daniel 7) and become like him.[79]

The following comment is a lengthy quote, but it captures the essence of Lusk and the Federal Vision's departure from the Faith once delivered to the saints:

Those who advocate a meritorious covenant of works put a great deal of weight on the so-called "active obedience" of Christ. I remember hearing sermons in which I was told "Jesus' thirty-three years of law-keeping are your righteousness. They were credited to you! He kept the law, the covenant of works, on your behalf!" Similarly, but more formally, Dr. Smith writes, "It is Christ's active fulfillment of the law that becomes the ground of our acceptance with God. It is this righteousness that is imputed to us" (lines 520-521).

Several things need to be said about this sort of theologizing. First, there is no question the perfect obedience of Jesus played a vital role in his salvific work on our behalf. If he had sinned, he would have fallen under God's wrath and curse just like us, and wouldn't have been be able to rescue us. If he hadn't obeyed perfectly, he could not have been the spotless Lamb of God who went to the cross in fulfillment of the

---

[78] Colloquium on the Federal Vision, p. 138.

[79] Colloquium on the Federal Vision, p. 139.

entire sacrificial system. So his active obedience is necessary to guarantee the efficacy and worth of his death and to guarantee his resurrection on the other side.

But the notion of his thirty-three years of Torah-keeping being imputed to me is problematic. After all, as a Gentile, I was never under Torah and therefore never under obligation to keep many of the commands Jesus performed. Moreover, much of what Jesus did was, in the nature of the case, not required of others. Surely God does not require everyone to work as a carpenter or to turn water into wine or to raise a twelve year old girl from the dead.[80]

Lusk goes on to describe what he really understands imputation to mean. In the Colloquium, Lusk makes this comment:

That there is a double imputation of our sins to Jesus and His glory to us is certainly beyond question, and I am **not** disagreeing with the general doctrine of imputation, or of double imputation. But merit theology often assumes that Jesus' **earthly** works and merits are somehow given to us, and there is no foundation for this notion. It is, in fact, hard to comprehend what is meant by it. What does it have to do with my life that Jesus raised Lazarus from the dead and this good deed is given to me? The miracles that Jesus did were not required of **me** to satisfy God's justice. Salvation does not return us to the Old Adamic Covenant, even in a good and perfect way. Salvation gives us the glory of Jesus Christ, so that we do greater things than He did during his Adamic earthly life (Matthew 11:11; John 14:12). The New Testament is clear throughout that what is given to the saints is the Spirit, who comes from the glorified Jesus. It is not Jesus' earthly life and "works and merits" that are transferred to us, but His glorified and resurrected life in the Spirit that is transferred to us. There seems to be nothing in the Bible to imply that we receive Jesus' earthly life and then also His death. His earthly life was "for us" in the sense that it was the precondition for His death, but it is not given "to us." What we receive is not His earthly life and His death, but His death

---

[80] Colloquium on the Federal Vision, pp. 139, 130.

> and His glorified life. What we receive is not Jesus' merits,
> but His maturity, His glorification.[81] (Emphasis Lusk)

Notice what Lusk has done to Christ's imputation. His adherence to a double imputation is not the historic Reformed affirmation of double imputation. Lusk talks about an imputation of Christ's glory. This is not Reformed double imputation. Notice that Lusk says that Jesus' imputation was "for us" and not "to us." This is a fine nuance but one that is immense. The orthodox and Reformed position is an imputation done "to us." The idea of an imputation "for us" is some kind of union with Jesus whereby we receive His maturity and glorification.

Rich Lusk continues in his assault upon the active obedience of Christ when he says:

> This may rub a lot of Reformed folks the wrong way since the active obedience of Christ is a cherished doctrine. Many of us have heard the touching story of a dying Gresham Machen telegramming John Murray, "I'm so thankful for [the] active obedience of Christ. No hope without it."
>
> I would suggest (I hope with appropriate humility!) that Machen would have been more true to Paul if he had had telegrammed, "I'm so thankful for [the] resurrection of Christ. No hope without it." The resurrection is the real centerpiece of the gospel since it is the **new** thing God has done. (Emphasis mine).
>
> This seems to be the thrust of Romans 4:25. It is not Christ's life-long obedience per se that is credited to us. Rather, it is his right standing before the Father, manifested in his resurrection. His resurrection justifies us because it justified him. Again, it is not that his law-keeping or miracle-working are imputed to our account; rather, Christ shares his legal status in God's court with us as the One who propitiated God's wrath on the cross and was resurrected into a vindicated, glorified form of life.
>
> The problem with the "active obedience" model is that it de-eschatologizes the work of Christ. The new age is not brought him by his fulfillment of the old law; it is inaugurated in his

---

[81] Colloquium on the Federal Vision. See Lusk's footnote 59 on p. 140.

resurrection. The gospel, in other words, is thoroughly eschatological.

Paul says the gospel reveals God's righteousness (Romans 1:16-17) because it reveals how God has kept his covenant oath: namely, in and through Christ. Paul is not identifying the gospel with the doctrine of imputed righteousness.[82]

Lusk appeals to N.T. Wright as one theologian who helps us rethink our old ways when he states:

These theologians focus on union with Christ. They suggest justification presupposes union with Christ. If I am **in Christ**, he is my substitute and representative. All he suffered and accomplished was for me. All he has belongs to me. (Emphasis Lusk)

With regards to justification, this means my right standing before the Father is grounded in Christ's own right standing before the Father. So long as I abide in Christ, I can no more come under the Father's negative judgment than Jesus himself can!

I have this assurance because Jesus died in my stead, taking the penalty my sins deserved to secure my forgiveness. On the third day, he was raised to life for my justification. His resurrection was his own justification, as the Father reversed the Jewish and Gentile death sentences passed against him. But it was the justification of all those who are in him as well. He was raised up **on the basis of** his flawless obedience to the Father. Death could not hold him because he was a righteous man. His status is now my status. (Emphasis Lusk)

Rather, because I am in the Righteous One and the Vindicated One, I am righteous and vindicated. My in-Christness makes imputation redundant. I do not need the moral content of his life of righteousness transferred to me; what I need is a share in the forensic verdict passed over him at the resurrection. Union with Christ is therefore the key ... I am justified because the **status** he has as The Sinless One, and

---

[82] Colloquium on the Federal Vision p. 141.

> now as The Crucified and Vindicated One, has been
> bestowed upon me as well.[83] (Emphasis Lusk)

Lusk will now have the audacity to claim that Calvin would be supportive of him, for Lusk says, *"For Calvin, the central motif of Pauline theology is not "imputation," but union with Christ."*[84]

Lusk has not understood Calvin at all.

Lusk is arguing that the great reformer really did not believe in "merit" even though he uses the term. Lusk states, *"Later on Calvin makes it clear that Christ merited nothing for Himself (2.17.6), citing Philippians 2:9."*[85] The quote that Lusk is referring to is this:

> But to ask whether Christ merited anything for himself, as
> Lombard and the Schoolmen do, is no less stupid curiosity
> than their temerity in making such a definition. What need
> was there for God's only Son to come down in order to
> acquire something new for himself?[86]

Calvin is referring to those who are saying that Christ needed to merit something for Himself. This text occurs later in the paragraph, and Calvin's use of it is to prove that it demonstrates Christ's merits for us, humans, not for Himself, as the Mediator.

Calvin, in this paragraph, with the proper use of Philippians 2:9 states:

> For he who gave away the fruit of his holiness to others tes-
> tifies that he acquired nothing for himself. And this is indeed
> worth noting: to devote himself completely to saving us,
> Christ in a way forgot himself. But they absurdly apply Paul's
> testimony to this: "Therefore the Father has highly exalted
> him and bestowed on him the name," etc. (Philippians
> 2:9).[87]

To further demonstrate Rich Lusk's complete distortion and misinterpretation of the use of original sources, I simply direct the reader to the section just prior

---

[83] Colloquium on the Federal Vision, p. 142.

[84] Colloquium on the Federal Vision, p. 143.

[85] Colloquium on the Federal Vision, p. 145.

[86] Calvin, *Institutes of the Christian Religion,* Book 2, Chapter 17:6, p. 534.

[87] Calvin, *Institutes of the Christian Religion.*

to the one that Lusk refers to. In Chapter 17, section 5, Calvin discusses the price that Christ paid for our redemption. In this section Calvin states:

> "If we are justified through the works of the law, then Christ died for nothing (Galatians 2:21). From this we infer that we must seek from Christ what the law would give if anyone could fulfill it; or, what is the same thing, that we obtain through Christ's grace what God promised in the law for our works: "He who will do these things, will live in them (Leviticus 18:5, cf. Comm.). This is no less clearly confirmed in the sermon delivered at Antioch, which asserts that by believing in Christ "we are justified from everything from which we could not be justified by the law of Moses" (Acts 13:39; cf. Vg., ch. 13:38).[88]

> For if righteousness consists in the observance of the law, who will deny that Christ merited favor for us when, by taking that burden upon himself, he reconciled us to God as if we had kept the law? What he afterward taught the Galatians has the same purpose: "God sent forth his Son … subject to the law, to redeem those who were under the law" (Galatians 4:4-5). What was the purpose of this subjection of Christ to the law but to acquire righteousness for us, undertaking to pay what we could not pay? Hence, that imputation of righteousness without works which Paul discusses (Romans ch. 4). For the righteousness found in Christ alone is reckoned as ours.[89]

It is quite evident that either Rich Lusk never bothered to check his original sources in any kind of a thorough way, which would be ineptitude, or he has deliberately twisted it to say what he wants it to say. The latter part would be vicious, which I don't believe to be the problem. I believe that the problem lies in the fact that he and others of the Federal Vision have gotten a preconceived idea in their minds and that they are blinded by their own presuppositions. But one thing is certain. They are blinded to the truth, and their ability to interpret the Scriptures is seriously skewed. They cannot be trusted.

Well, let's see what Calvin would say about Rich Lusk and all the rest of the Federal Vision. Nearly 500 years ago Calvin said:

---

[88] Calvin, *Institutes of the Christian Religion*, Book 2, Chapter 17:5, p. 533.

[89] Calvin, *Institutes of the Christian Religion*.

What nonsense will the Pelagians chatter here? That Adam's sin was propagated by imitation? Then does Christ's righteousness benefit us only as an example set before us to imitate? Who can bear such sacrilege![90]

Indeed, that frivolous notion disappears, that man is justified by faith because by Christ's righteousness he shares the Spirit of God, by whom he is rendered righteous.[91]

Calvin and the other Reformers have already condemned the views of the Federal Vision on justification; there is nothing new under the sun. Heresies often die hard!

---

[90] Calvin, Institutes of the Christian Religion, Book 2, Chapter 1:6, p. 248.
[91] Calvin, Institutes of the Christian Religion, Book 3, Chapter 11:23, p. 753.

Chapter 5

The Relationship of Works to Justification by Faith

In chapter 3 regarding the Federal Vision's denial of justification by faith alone, I spent considerable time with Norman Shepherd and his book *The Call Of Grace*. I sought to lay out the precise nature of his views on works as they pertain to justification. In this chapter, the goal is to set forth some of the biblical texts relevant to this issue. I will quote several renowned Reformed commentators, and I want to set forth the relevant statements from the Reformed confessional documents. These would include: The Westminster Confession with its Larger and Shorter Catechisms; the Belgic Confession with its Heidelberg Catechism, and the Canons of Dordt. I will clearly demonstrate that the Federal Vision is totally out of accord with these Reformed documents and most importantly that it is out of accord with the teaching of the Word of God.

The Federal Vision claims that it is within the parameters of the Reformed Standards and that it is consistent with biblical teaching. This claim is false. While the Federal Vision claims allegiance to the Reformed Standards, several of its proponents have openly advocated that we must not be regimented in the views of the 17th Century. These Federal Vision critics such as Steve Schlissel are insistent that we must not think that truth has been frozen in these expressions. He and others insist that the church must always be reforming and that new paradigms should be considered. While it is true that the church of the Lord Jesus must always be reforming itself to be faithful to Scripture, we must carefully examine any theological view to determine its validity. While the Reformed Standards are not an exhaustive presentation of biblical truth, these expressions are nonetheless the compilation of some of the most godly and brilliant Christian minds the world has ever known. Though these expressions are not exhaustive, they are thorough. The Westminster Assembly was in session from 1643–1649.

John Murray sums up very well the importance of the Westminster Assembly.
He states:

> The work produced by the Westminster Assembly has lived
> and will permanently live. The reason is obvious. The work
> was wrought with superb care, patience, precision, and above
> all with earnest and intelligent devotion to the Word of God
> and zeal for His glory. Sanctified theological learning has
> never been brought to bear with greater effect upon the for-
> mulation of the Christian Faith. While it would be dishonor-
> ing to the Holy Spirit to accord to these documents a place in
> any way equal to the Word of God either in principle or in
> practical effect, yet it would also be dishonoring to the Holy
> Spirit, who has promised to be with His church to the end, to
> undervalue or neglect what is the product of His illumination
> and direction in the hearts and minds of His faithful servants.
> Other men labored and we have entered into their labors.[1]

Any time someone comes along and wants to argue that truth should not be
viewed as being regimented in these Reformed expressions, we should ask the
question, "Why are they saying this?" In the case of those among the Federal
Vision belief, it is obvious why they make these kinds of comments. They want
us to be more open to their new paradigms. When these men are challenged,
they simply say, "Oh, you think that truth is frozen in the 17th Century, how
narrow minded you must be." The Federal Vision wants to have free reign in
its proliferation of its theology. However, in their attempt to persuade people
that their views are really Reformed, they say, "Our views are Confessional, if
it is read the right way." I have already demonstrated in other chapters, I trust,
that the Federal Vision's handling of the Reformed Standards is dismal, to say
the least. I have shown that Norman Shepherd has taken expressions from one
catechism question and inserted them into other questions in an attempt to try
to prove that his views are Confessional. Rich Lusk, I have shown, wants us to
view the Westminster Standards apart from the lens of merit theology, as if that
is what the Westminster delegates were doing in the first place. Despite what
the Confession says, Lusk wants us to think that is not what it really means. We
then can get bogged down in an endless sea of subjective opinions. These
approaches are not new in the history of the church. Any time that a person is
criticized about his views, it is not unusual for that person to say, "Oh, you have

---

[1] John Murray, *The Work of the Westminster Assembly,* derived online at http://mem-
bers.aol.com/RSICHURCH/assembl2.html, p. 4.

misinterpreted me, or that is not what it really says." And so, the debate continues because people are not willing to accept that they may be wrong in their understanding. When there is a theological dispute, the best thing to do is to set forth arguments, seeking to encourage the audience to look at the data and determine who has done the best job of utilizing the Scripture.

My approach in this book has been simply this: Let's look at the Scriptural data; let's look at the Reformed Standards and compare Federal Vision theology with how it stacks up in comparison to the Word of God. Let's compare Federal Vision theology to the opinions of godly men down through the centuries and see if there is a consensus among these theologians. After all, the Holy Spirit is the Spirit of truth, who does guide His people into all truth. My conclusion is that Federal Vision theology has been found wanting, that it teaches a theology that is another gospel. I seek to persuade the reader that this is the case.

I still make this challenge to all those ministers and elders in the Presbyterian Church In America (PCA) who favor Federal Vision theology to take their theology to the General Assembly and submit it to the scrutiny of that ecclesiastical body.[2] If you are confident that your interpretation is correct and that multitudes of others are wrong, then convince your theological peers that this is the case. In saying this, I do not know for sure what the General Assembly of the PCA would do. You want your podium, then this is your opportunity.

A Restatement of the Federal Vision's View of Works

In this restatement, I will make frequent reference to Norman Shepherd not because he is the main spokesperson for the Federal Vision but because the other men hold him in such high regard; they recommend his book and invite him to lecture for them. This is an endorsement of his views. While I have seen comments on several occasions from various Federal Vision adherents that

---

[2] This is not to say that all those ministers and elders belong to the PCA. Good portions of them belong to other denominations. Federal Vision theology is not restricted to those in the PCA. It is dispersed throughout the Reformed community. My point in this challenge is that those who hold to Federal Vision theology, who are in the PCA, ought to be willing to have their views openly debated in the courts of the church. Since these ministers and elders took vows to uphold the Westminster Standards, then they are obligated to prove that they are in conformity with those Standards. Moreover, they took vows that they would submit to their brethren in the Lord. If there is any question about a theological view, then it behooves them to seek the counsel of their theological peers.

there is no monolithic position of the Federal Vision, I have yet to see any of them specify where they disagree from one another on the basic issues or any issue for that matter. I have found these comments to be an evasive maneuver.[3] I will document in another chapter where the Monroe Four: Steve Wilkins, Steve Schlissel, Douglas Wilson, and John Barach agree with Shepherd's views as being summarized below.

Shepherd believes:

- Justifying faith is itself a living and obedient faith. Obedience is the essence of faith (*The Call of Grace, p. 48)*.

- This obedient faith is seen in keeping the commandments of God (*The Call Of Grace*, pp. 47, 48).

- This obedient faith is necessary for justification (Shepherd's Thesis 23 in "Thirty-four Theses on Justification in relation to Faith, Repentance, and Good Works" and *The* Call Of Grace, p. 15).

- Faithful disciples will be justified (Shepherd Thesis 20).

- Repentance is a necessary element in justification itself (Shepherd Thesis 15).

- Grace is not without conditions (*The Call Of Grace*, p. 63).

---

[3] As recent as December 2004, the session of Auburn Avenue Presbyterian Church (PCA), where Steve Wilkins is the pastor and Rich Lusk was once an assistant pastor, responded to a critical study report done by the Mississippi Valley Presbytery (PCA). In this response, the Auburn session in point 2 insisted that there is no monolithic Federal Vision movement. The Auburn response also said, "The differences that exist between the positions held by the individuals involved must be identified if any meaningful critique is to be offered." Personally, I see this as an attempt to dodge a theological bullet. The session of Auburn Avenue has sponsored conferences where the lectures espoused various views that have come to be known as the Federal Vision. Auburn Avenue church has never published any article distancing itself from any of the speakers of these conferences. Additionally, Auburn Avenue has had Norman Shepherd speak in its pulpit; it has invited N.T. Wright to be one of its keynote speakers at the 2005 AAPC. Steve Wilkins and Rich Lusk participated in the Knox Seminary Colloquium in 2003. Nowhere in those papers did they ever specify where they differed from any others. Nowhere has Auburn church said that it does not agree with anything in Shepherd's book *The Call Of Grace.* One can obtain the response of Auburn Avenue Presbyterian Church to the Mississippi Valley Presbytery's report at <www. auburnavenue.org/Position Papers/missvalleypres.htm>

- Circumcision in the Old Covenant and baptism in the New Covenant were and are necessary conditions for the blessings of the Covenant in terms of justification (*The* Call *Of Grace,* p. 14-15, 94).

- Certain graces of the Christian life must be part of justification, not simply added later as fruit or evidences (Shepherd article, *"Justification By Faith Alone"* in *Reformation and Revival,* p. 87)

- The process of sanctification which includes repentance and obedience is begun prior to justification (Shepherd, *"Justification By Faith Alone"* in *Reformation and Revival,* p. 83)

- Justification is a life long process (Shepherd Thesis 21 and 23).

Those very familiar with the Scripture, especially those studied in the Reformed Faith, should recognize serious problems with the above-mentioned summary of the Federal Vision's stance regarding justification. Again, the Monroe Four have not disagreed in any public forum, either in lecture or in writing, to any of these statements.

One can look at the quotes again in the chapter dealing with the Federal Vision's Denial of Justification by Faith Alone. Again, my goal is to lay out the pertinent biblical passages that refute the Federal Vision's position, give the perspective of some well known Reformed theologians on these passages, and then set forth the statements in the historic Reformed Confessional documents pertaining to these issues. It should become apparent that the Federal Vision constitutes a departure from the faith once delivered to the saints.

Norman Shepherd is very clear that "works" are not the results, fruit, or evidences of justifying faith; it is the very essence of it. And, when he speaks about conditions for justifying faith, such as faithfully following God's commandments, he has advocated a works salvation paradigm. O. Palmer Robertson has recognized this fact about Shepherd's views for a long time. Robertson writes, *"Wherever Mr. Shepherd says a person is justified by 'obedient faith,' it is possible to substitute the idea that a person is justified by 'faithful obedience.' Instead of affirming that a man is justified by faith that always has accompanying graces, he affirms that man is justified by a faith that always is works."*[4]

---

[4] Joe Morecraft III, *"Faith and Works,"* The New Southern Presbyterian Review, Summer 2002, p. 237.

Biblical Passages Relating Works to Justification

Romans 2:11-13

> For there is no partiality with God. For all who have sinned
> without the Law will also perish without the Law; and all
> who have sinned under the Law will be judged by the Law;
> for not the hearers of the Law are just before God, but the
> doers of the Law will be justified.

Norman Shepherd has used this passage to support his thesis 20 which says:

> The Pauline affirmation in Romans 2:13, "the doers of the
> Law will be justified," is not to be understood hypothetically
> in the sense that there are no persons who fall into that class,
> but in the sense that faithful disciples of the Lord Jesus Christ
> will be justified.[5] (Compare Luke 8:21; James 1:22-25)

John Calvin had these comments regarding Romans 2:13:

> This anticipates an objection which the Jews might have
> adduced. As they had heard that the law was the rule of
> righteousness, (Deuteronomy 4:1,) they gloried in the
> mere knowledge of it: to obviate this mistake, he declares
> that the hearing of the law or any knowledge of it is of no
> such consequence, that any one should on that account
> lay claim to righteousness, but that works must be pro-
> duced, according to this saying, "He who will do these
> shall live in them." The import then of this verse is the
> following, — "That if righteousness be sought from the
> law, the law must be fulfilled; for the righteousness of the
> law consists in the perfection of works." They who per-
> vert this passage for the purpose of building up justifica-
> tion by works, deserve most fully to be laughed at even
> by children.
>
> It is therefore improper and beyond what is needful, to
> introduce here a long discussion on the subject, with the
> view of exposing so futile a sophistry: for the Apostle
> only urges here on the Jews what he had mentioned, the
> decision of the law, — That by the law they could not be

---

[5] Norman Shepherd, *Thirty-four Theses on Justification in Relation to Faith, Repentance, and Good Works,* found on the website <www. homes.org/theologia/The 34 Theses>

justified, except they fulfilled the law, that if they transgressed it, a curse was instantly pronounced on them.
Now we do not deny but that perfect righteousness is prescribed in the law: but as all are convicted of transgression, we say that another righteousness must be sought.
Still more, we can prove from this passage that no one is
justified by works; for if they alone are justified by the
law who fulfill the law, it follows that no one is justified;
for no one can be found who can boast of having fulfilled
the law.[6]

The sad reality is that Shepherd and the Federal Vision actually think that we
can be "doers of the law" as a means of being justified. As Calvin pointed out,
unless we can render a perfect obedience we cannot be justified. Who can live
perfectly? Yet, the Federal Vision would say that an imperfect obedience is
good enough to be justified. After all, one seeks to be a faithful disciple.

The problem is not that Christians should seek obedience to the law; but simply be sure that they are not mere hearers. The Reformed position has always
been that good works accompany salvation as the necessary fruit or evidence
of justification. To make obedience as part of justification is a works salvation
paradigm; this is the heresy of the Federal Vision.

Romans 3:19-31

Now we know that whatever the Law says, it speaks to those
who are under the Law, that every mouth may be closed, and
all the world may become accountable to God; because by
the works of the Law no flesh will be justified in His sight;
for through the Law comes the knowledge of sin. But now
apart from the Law the righteousness of God has been manifested, being witnessed by the Law and the Prophets, even
the righteousness of God through faith in Jesus Christ for all
those who believe; for there is no distinction; for all have
sinned and fall short of the glory of God, being justified as a
gift by His grace through the redemption which is in Christ
Jesus; whom God displayed publicly as a propitiation in His
blood through faith. This was to demonstrate His righteousness, because in the forbearance of God He passed over the
sins previously committed; for the demonstration, I say, of

---

[6] Calvin, *Calvin's New Testament Commentaries, The Epistle of Paul To The Romans*,
p. 47.

His righteousness at the present time, that He might be just
and the justifier of the one who has faith in Jesus. Where then
is boasting? It is excluded. By what kind of law? Of works?
No, but by a law of faith. For we maintain that a man is justified by faith apart from works of Law. Or is God the God of
Jews only? Is He not the God of Gentiles also? Yes, of
Gentiles also. Since indeed God who will justify the circumcised by faith and the uncircumcised through faith is one. Do
we then nullify the Law through faith? May it never be! On
the contrary, we establish the Law.

This is one of the great classic passages in the Word of God demonstrating that
no human being can be justified by the keeping of the Law of God, and the reason is that every person has sinned. To demonstrate Shepherd's distortion of
the text, he says:

The law does not set forth a works merit principle in opposition to grace and faith. It testifies to the grace of God revealed
in Jesus Christ. The Mosaic covenant embodies promises,
and promises can be received only by faith. For Israel, the
promises came wrapped in the garment of the Mosaic Law.
That is why faith in these promises also entailed faithfulness
with respect to the commandments. Obedience is simply an
expression of faith in the promises of God, not an alternative
to faith."[7]

Shepherd's view is very cumbersome. On one hand, he talks about grace and
faith. He talks about not obeying the law in terms of a merit/works principle,
and then, he turns around and explicitly states that this grace which is by faith
is actually obedience to the Mosaic Law. What does Shepherd really mean by
merit or works? Shepherd explains further:

The sacrificial system is a revelation of the grace of God,
enjoyed in the way of faith. Without a living, active, and obedient faith, it is an offense against God simply to go through
the motions of offering sacrifice ... The Lord will not be
pleased with thousands of rams and ten thousand rivers of oil.
He is seeking men who will act justly, love mercy, and walk
humbly with their God (Micah 6:7-8). Such men are men of
faith. Without faith, sacrifices and other religious ceremonies
amount to nothing. They are the "righteous acts" that are

---

[7] Shepherd, *The Call Of Grace*, pp. 31- 32.

called "filthy rags" in Isaiah 64:6. The sacrificial system is a leading feature of the Mosaic covenant. It does not exhibit a works/merit principle whereby we obtain forgiveness on the basis of something we have done. It leads us to Christ and to salvation by grace through faith in him.[8]

Shepherd reveals what he really means by not depending upon a law as a works/merit principle. One might think that Shepherd is against all kinds of works, viewing them as intrinsically a works mentality. But that is not the case at all. He explains how the Mosaic covenant was intended to function. He states:

> The Promised Land was exactly that- a **promised** land. In Deuteronomy 9:4-6, Moses reminds the Israelites that they must never say that they have taken possession of their inheritance because of their own righteousness. Rather, it is because of the Lord's righteousness in remembering his covenant that the Israelites possess the land.[9] (Emphasis Shepherd)

Now, we understand how Shepherd thinks. Law keeping in conformity with the Mosaic Law is acceptable while any other righteousness is unacceptable. If we were talking about law keeping as the natural fruit flowing out of saving faith, we would have no problem with such comments. However, Shepherd is using it with reference to justification. He immediately relates this to the grace of God revealed in Jesus Christ, and the grace is that God gave Israel such a wonderful law to keep.

Herein lies the slipperiness of Shepherd and the rest of the Federal Vision. It sounds okay, but then it doesn't. You're left scratching your head thinking, "Justification is not of works, but then it is." Herein is the key:

The Federal Vision says that justification is not by going through mere ritual, apart from conscious faith in Christ, but rather keeping the law as an act of obedient faith in Christ. This obedience would be done in the power of the Spirit, of course.

The Federal Vision says that the justified man is the one who truly keeps the law; the unjustified man is the one who tries to keep the law apart from faith in Christ. But think about this for a moment. This is still works salvation!

---

[8] Shepherd, *The Call Of Grace,* pp. 34-35.

[9] Shepherd, *The Call Of Grace,* p. 30.

Romans 3:19-31 is referring to **any attempt to obey the law as a means of justification**. The point is that no one can keep the law because every one has sinned; the righteousness of God is a gift, not earned by trying to faithfully keep it. There is no boasting at all, by anybody, including those seeking to do it by faith in Jesus. This portion of Scripture draws a contrast between keeping the law and faith in Jesus. Verse 28 is quite clear, *"For we maintain that a man is justified by faith apart from works of the law."* The Federal Vision denies this contrast because they insist that the faith in Jesus itself is an obedient faith. They have introduced a foreign concept into the passage.

Rich Lusk, the former assistant pastor to Steve Wilkins at Auburn Avenue Presbyterian Church, has adopted the exact same concept of merit. Lusk too, talks about the "obedience of faith" and argues exactly on the same grounds as Shepherd. To get a full grasp of Lusk's ideas, I refer you to chapter 4 in this book dealing with the Federal Vision's denial of the active obedience of Christ. The fact that Lusk uses the same terminology and adopts the exact same meaning of many of the texts that Shepherd uses only demonstrates that there is unanimity of thought. We can speak of a Federal Vision movement. Auburn Avenue Presbyterian Church's insistence that there is no monolithic theology is simply an attempt to steer people away from pinpointing them with theological error. Remember, this church has enthusiastically endorsed Shepherd.

Concerning the meaning of the phrase, "apart from the law," John Murray makes this comment that refutes Shepherd's view:

> In the expression, apart from the Law, the term "law" is used
> in the sense of works of the Law (v.20) and the thought is
> simply that law as commandment or as constraining to and
> producing works contributes nothing to our justification.[10]

The Romans 3:19-31 passage is one in which thousands of pages have been written since the days of the Reformation. It is almost incomprehensible that the Federal Vision would challenge the Reformed understanding of this passage. Once one understands that obedience to the law is okay for justification as long as you do it in "faith" in Jesus, then one begins to understand why the Federal Vision is against the idea of the imputation of the merits or the righteousness of Christ being imputed to the believer. It takes away obedience to the law on an individual basis. To the Federal Vision people, this is too simple; it sounds antinomian; it sounds like easy-believism.

---

[10] John Murray, *The New International Commentary on the New Testament, The Epistle To The Romans*, (Grand Rapids, MI: Eerdmans Publishing Co. 1959), p. 110.

Romans 9:30-33

> What shall we say then? That Gentiles, who did not pursue righteousness, attained righteousness, even the righteousness which is by faith; but Israel, pursuing a law of righteousness, did not arrive at that law. Why? Because they did not pursue it by faith, but as though it were by works. They stumbled over the stumbling stone, just as it is written, "Behold, I lay in Zion a stone of stumbling and a rock of offense, and he who believes in Him will not be disappointed."

Shepherd uses Romans 9:32 to make this comment:

> The obedience required of Israel is not the obedience of merit, but the obedience of faith. It is the fullness of faith. Obedience is simply faithfulness to the Lord; it is the right-eousness of faith (compare Rom. 9:32). This point comes out with special clarity in Hebrews 11, where we see what the patriarchs accomplished by faith ... we see that those who lived under the Mosaic covenant were obedient to the Lord and through faith "gained what was promised." (v. 33).[11]

Calvin states:

> That Israel, depending on the righteousness of the law, even that which is prescribed in the law, did not understand the true method of justification...This example of the Jews ought indeed justly to terrify all those who strive to obtain the king-dom of God by works. Nor does he understand by the works of the law, ceremonial observances, as it has been before shown, but the merits of those works to which faith is opposed, which looks, as I may say, with both eyes on the mercy of God alone, without casting one glance on any wor-thiness of its own.[12]

What Shepherd cannot accept is simply a justification totally independent of any kind of law keeping. From his comment, he still wants to make faith some kind of obedience to the Mosaic Law, but he doesn't want to call it the obedi-ence of merit. He calls it the obedience of faith. The Scripture, on the other

---

[11] Shepherd, *The Call Of Grace,* pp. 39- 40.

[12] Calvin, *Calvin's New Testament Commentaries, The Epistle of Paul To The Romans,* p. 218.

hand, is contrasting faith from any kind of pursuing of the law. The Jews thought that by strict law keeping they could become righteous. They misunderstood the purpose of the law in that regard. Pursuing it with zeal will not make them righteous. They needed to learn that righteousness could not be obtained by personal pursuits of it, no matter what their motive was. As Paul states in Philippians 3, there was no greater zealot for the Law than he, but it did him no good. The great contrast is between the Gentiles and the Jews. The Gentiles who had no concept of law keeping ended up getting the prize of righteousness because they obtained it by faith. On the other hand, the zeal of the Jews was inadequate. If we accept Shepherd's argument that the Jews pursued the Law in the wrong way, but if they had pursued it in the right way by seeing that obedience to the Law through Christ is okay, then the passage makes no sense. Where was the Gentiles covenant faithfulness?

Romans 10: 3-6

> For not knowing about God's righteousness, and seeking to
> establish their own, they did not subject themselves to the
> righteousness of God. For Christ is the end of the law for
> righteousness to everyone who believes. For Moses writes
> that the man who practices the righteousness which is based
> on law shall live by that righteousness. But the righteousness
> based on faith...

Jesus is the end of the Law, that is, He is the righteousness in its fullest expression of what the Law demands. He is the goal. Verse 5 reveals the righteousness that the Law demands of those who are under it. Due to our sin, all men cannot keep the demands of the Law and are thereby condemned for failure to do so. Jesus, on the other hand, is the very righteousness that the Law expects; therefore, His righteousness belongs to all those who have simple faith in Him. Romans 9:30-33 indicated that the Jews did not arrive at the goal, which was personal righteousness. It is because they sought it in their own strength, thinking they could keep it. The Law's demands were intended to reveal that we could not keep it by directly pursuing it so that it would drive us to Christ to receive the righteousness by faith as Galatians 3:22-24 reveals.

This is not what the Federal Vision believes. Shepherd says:

The law is a gracious gift that embodies wisdom for living. "Now choose life, so that you and your children may live … The Lord is your life" (Deut. 30:19-20). This is also the thrust of Leviticus 18:5, "Keep my decrees and laws, for the man who obey them will live by them. I am the Lord." This verse does not challenge Israelites to earn their salvation by their good works. Rather, it offers to all who are covenantally loyal and faithful the encouragement and assurance that they will live and prosper in the land. This is the Lord's promise to them, a promised received with a living and active faith.[13] (Emphasis mine)

When the Federal Vision thinks of Leviticus 18:5 or Deuteronomy 30, it views these things are absolutely possible for men to do. This is called covenantal faithfulness. Shepherd's living and active faith is obedience to the commandments of God. He says that the promise is obtained by this obedient faith, which we know to be keeping God's commandments. This idea of Israelites not earning their salvation by their good works is double talk. The Federal Vision is pursuing the Law's righteousness exactly like the Jews tried to. The only difference is that the Federal Vision says this obedience to the Law for justification is actually what faith in Jesus really is. But think! There is no contrast between works and faith then. What the Federal Vision is saying is: we cannot earn salvation by our works but we receive it by our works. Notice in Shepherd's quote that the "graciousness" is the fact that the Law is a gift to us by God, for it embodies wisdom for us, and that wisdom tells us to obey the Law. The grace is the Law given for us to obey. Paul makes it very clear in Romans 4:3-6 that grace is the very opposite of works. We have seen that Shepherd has the same twist on that passage as well, making Abraham's own righteousness the cause for God's blessing. **The Federal Vision believes in a works salvation, plain and simple. Calling the essence of faith in Jesus to be obedience to God's commandments is not grace!**

Galatians 3: 21-26

For if the inheritance is based on law, it is no longer based on a promise; but God has granted it to Abraham by means of a promise, Why the Law then? It was added because of transgressions, having been ordained through angels by the agency of a mediator, until the seed should come to whom the promise had been made. Now a mediator is not for one party

---

[13] Shepherd, *The Call Of Grace,* p. 36.

only; whereas God is only one. Is the Law then contrary to
the promises of God? May it never be! For if a law had been
given which was able to impart life, then righteousness
would indeed have been based on law. But the Scripture has
shut up all men under sin, that the promise by faith in Jesus
Christ might be given to those who believe. But before faith
came, we were kept in custody under the law, being shut up
to the faith which was later revealed. Therefore the Law has
become our tutor to lead us to Christ, that we may be justified by faith. But now that faith has come, we are no longer
under a tutor. For you are all sons of God through faith in
Christ Jesus.

This portion of the Bible so clearly lays out for us one of the primary purposes of God's law and the necessity of faith in Jesus. Essentially, this passage
contains the gospel. First, verse 18 differentiates between receiving the inheritance of God by the Law or by a promise. The Law could not deliver the promise, but Abraham got the promise. Verse 19 sets forth the purpose of the Law.
The law was given because of transgressions or because of sin; sin is the transgression of the Law (I John 3:4). In other words, it was given to expose sin for
what it really is. See Romans 7 for a wonderful presentation of why the Law
was given. The Law makes us guilty because we violate its requirements. In
Galatians 3:21, Paul makes it clear that the Law is not contrary to God's promises, that is, His inheritance. In fact, if God wanted to impart life by the Law,
then righteousness would have been based upon it. But that was not God's
intent. Verse 22 states that all men are under sin so that by faith in Jesus men
might receive the promise. How are men under sin? It is because the Law
exposes their sin by their failure to obey its very demands. As Paul says in
Romans 7:7 that he "*would not have come to know sin except through the
Law.*" In verse 23 it says that "***before faith came, we were kept in custody
under the law, being shut up to the faith which was later to be revealed.***" This
means that obedience to the Mosaic Law was seen as distinct from faith in
Jesus. Now this is a vital point to realize because the Federal Vision does not
believe that point. What was the purpose of the Law? It was a tutor, a schoolmaster, to lead us to Christ so that we could be justified by faith. Verse 25 states
that since faith has come, we are no longer under its curse - the curse being the
fact that we are judged guilty by not obeying every letter of the Law.

Calvin has some very helpful comments. Regarding verse 22 he says:

By the word Scripture is chiefly intended the law itself. It
"hath concluded all under sin," and therefore, instead of giv-

ing, it takes away righteousness from all. The reasoning is most powerful." You seek righteousness in the law: but the law itself, with the whole of Scripture, leaves nothing to men but condemnation; for all men, with their works, are pronounced to be unrighteous: who then shall live by the law?" He alludes to these words, " He who shall do these things, shall live in them." (Leviticus 18:5.) Shut out by it, says he, from life through guilt, in vain should we seek salvation by the law.[14]

Concerning verse 24 Calvin says:

But a question arises, what was the instruction or education of this schoolmaster? First, the law, by displaying the justice of God, convinced them that in themselves they were unrighteous; for in the commandments of God, as in a mirror, they might see how far they were distant from true righteousness. They were thus reminded that righteousness must be sought in some other quarter. The promises of the law served the same purpose, and might lead to such reflections as these: "If you cannot obtain life by works but by fulfilling the law, some new and different method must be sought. Your weakness will never allow you to ascend so high; nay, though you desire and strive ever so much, you will fall far short of the object." The threatenings, on the other hand, pressed and entreated them to seek refuge from the wrath and curse of God, and gave them no rest till they were constrained to seek the grace of Christ.

In what respect, then, is it abolished? Paul, we have said, looks at the law as possessing certain qualities, and those qualities we shall enumerate. It annexes to works a reward and a punishment; that is, it promises life to those who keep it, and curses all transgressors. **Meanwhile, it requires from man the highest perfection and most exact obedience. It makes no abatement, gives no pardon, but calls to a severe reckoning the smallest offenses.** It does not openly exhibit Christ and his grace, but points him out at a distance, and only when hidden by the covering of ceremonies. All such qualities of the law, Paul tells us, are abolished; so that

---

[14] Calvin, *Commentary on Galatians,* p. 64.

> the office of Moses is now at an end, so far as it differs in out-
> ward aspect from a covenant of grace.[15] (Emphasis mine)

This passage beautifully shows us our need of a Savior who gives us what we cannot obtain through the Law of Moses. The promise comes by faith, not by trying to be obedient to the Law. These truths are completely denied by Shepherd. Here is what he says about this section of Scripture:

> The thought here is not simply that the Mosaic covenant comes alongside the Abrahamic covenant to function concurrently with it. **The idea is not that the law reveals our sin so that we will be driven to seek grace apart from the Mosaic covenant**...Paul is saying in Galatians 3 that the Mosaic covenant is a further unfolding of the Abrahamic covenant. The Mosaic covenant is a revelation of salvation by grace through faith. Why was the law added to the Abrahamic covenant? It was not added to propose an alternative way of salvation that was bound to fail. Paul says it was added because of transgressions (v. 19). **The law was designed to counter the devastating effect of sin in the world. The law makes clear the kind of behavior that is pleasing and honoring to the Lord and is in the best interests of humanity.**[16] (Emphasis mine)

Shepherd and the rest of the Federal Vision would agree that the Mosaic law was not given to convict us to search for grace elsewhere, but that the Law was given to show us how to have the right behavior. This quote is consistent with everything else Shepherd has said. Grace is the Law! Faith is not separate from the Law; it is obedience to the Law! I trust that one can see that this is a butchering of the Word of God and an outright denial of the true gospel.

Matthew 19: 16-26

> And behold, one came to Him and said, "Teacher, what good thing shall I do that I may obtain eternal life? And He said to him, "Why are you asking Me about what is good? There is only One who is good; but if you wish to enter into life, keep the commandments." He said to Him, "Which ones?" And Jesus said, "You shall not commit murder; You shall not com-
> mit adultery; You shall not steal; You shall not bear false wit-

---

[15] Calvin, *Commentary on Galatians*, p. 66-67.

[16] Shepherd, *The Call Of Grace,* pp. 28-29.

ness; Honor your father and mother; and You shall love your neighbor as yourself. The young man said to Him, "All these things I have kept; what am I still lacking?" Jesus said to him, If you wish to be complete, go and sell your possessions and give to the poor, and you shall have treasure in heaven; and come, follow Me. But when the young man heard this statement, he went away grieved; for he was one who owned much property. And Jesus said to His disciples, Truly I say to you , it is hard for a rich man to enter the kingdom of heaven. And again I say to you, it is easier for a camel to go through the eye of a needle, than for a rich man to enter the kingdom of God. And when the disciples heard this, they were very astonished and said, Then who can be saved?" And looking upon them Jesus said to them, "With men this is impossible, but with God all things are possible.

In chapter 4 regarding the Federal Vision's denial of the active obedience of Christ, I noted that Rich Lusk, completely distorts this passage. The biblical and historic Reformed understanding of this passage has been that Jesus correctly told him that eternal life was the reward for any who kept the Law. This would be in keeping with what Leviticus 18:5 and Galatians 3:12 affirms. When the young man said that he had kept all of them and was there anything else, Jesus tells him to go sell everything and come follow Him. When the young man is unwilling to do this, Jesus said that it is hard for a rich man to enter the kingdom of God. The disciples, in shock, wonder who can really be saved. Jesus then says something very crucial to the whole story. Jesus says what is impossible with men is possible with God.

What was Jesus doing? He was seeking to show this deluded, sincere man that **he really was not keeping the Law.** When Jesus told him to sell all that he had and follow Him, Jesus was testing him to see if the young man could keep even the first commandment which was "You shall have no other gods before Me." The fact that the young man refused to do this, meant that money was his god. Hence, he failed the test and could not enter the kingdom of God because he didn't keep the law perfectly. When the disciples asked, "Then who can be saved"? Jesus said that this can only be accomplished by God. This is true because only God can remedy the sin problem of mankind who must obey perfectly or suffer the consequences. God, by His sovereign grace, gives Jesus to us so that through faith in Jesus we can have Jesus' righteousness credited to our account as if we had done it ourselves.

The Federal Vision denies all that I have said above. It believes that the Law can be kept; that the Law does not demand perfect obedience; that there is no imputing righteousness to our account so that we can enter eternal life. How do they interpret the passage? Rich Lusk says that the problem with the young rich ruler was that he wasn't willing to sacrifice and be a disciple. Lusk states that at this point in redemptive history this meant to sell all your possessions and follow Jesus, which the disciples of Jesus did do. **So, from Lusk's point of view, salvation (which is what this point in redemptive history means) is based on works of self-denial. The disciples are saved because they did sell all to follow Jesus.** [17] This is the teaching of Roman Catholicism! This is one of the bases for the monastic movement in Catholicism. This is what Calvin explicitly addressed in his commentary on this passage. The Federal Vision teaches a works salvation that is akin to Roman Catholicism. Is there any wonder why certain people who have embraced Federal Vision theology have defected to Romanism? In this paradigm presented by the Federal Vision, the disciples showed that their faith was an active, obedient faith by selling all their possessions and following Jesus. The young rich ruler did not have justifying faith because his faith was defective in lacking discipleship. I will say this, at least the Federal Vision is consistent; it's just that their consistency in these matters reveals the heresy of this movement.

Luke 10: 25-29

> And behold, a certain lawyer stood up and put Him to the test, saying, "Teacher, what shall I do to inherit eternal life?" And He said to him, "What is written in the Law? How does it read to you?" And he answered and said, 'You shall love the Lord your God with all your heart, and with all your soul, and with all your strength, and with all your mind; and your neighbor as yourself." And He said to him, "You have answered correctly; Do this, and you will live." But wishing to justify himself, he said to Jesus, "And who is my neighbor."

We have already seen how Rich Lusk, a Federal Vision proponent, has terribly misunderstood the story of the young rich ruler. The Federal Vision sees this story, which includes Jesus' parable of the good Samaritan as a reply to the lawyer as to who is his neighbor, as something that is doable in order to inherit eternal life. After Jesus tells his parable, Jesus asks the lawyer which one in the story really is the neighbor to the victim. In verse 37 we find the lawyer's

---

[17] Knox Theological Seminary Colloquium on the Federal Vision, p. 128.

response and Jesus' response – "*And he said, 'The one who showed mercy toward him.' And Jesus said to him, 'Go, and do the same.'*"

The Federal Vision reveals its advocacy of a works salvation mentality by believing that keeping God's law is an actual possibility on our part in order to inherit eternal life. The Federal Vision refuses to admit that the Mosaic Law demanded perfect obedience as the criterion for inheriting eternal life. The Federal Vision refuses to accept Christ's merits as the basis of perfect Law keeping in our stead. The Federal vision will not accept the fact that Jesus is seeking to show men that they cannot keep the Law perfectly.

William Hendrikson has some insightful comments about this story in Luke 10. Concerning Jesus' reply to the lawyer that constant keeping of the command to love God with all your heart and your neighbor as yourself as the way to inherit eternal life, Hendrikson makes this comment on verse 28:

> The answer is clear. If any human being would actually fulfill this law of love to perfection, he would indeed obtain everlasting life. There was nothing wrong with this high requirement of the law: "The law is holy, and the commandment is holy and righteous and good" (Rom. 7:12). "The man who does these things will live by them" (Gal. 3:12). The trouble is not with the divine principle that perfect obedience results in everlasting life. What, then, is wrong? Paul answers in these words, "We know that the law is spiritual; but I am carnal, sold under sin" (Rom. 7:14). If only the law-expert will now admit this. If only he will cry out, "O God, be merciful to me, the sinner!" If he will do this, Jesus can supply the further answer to the lawyer's question, that answer being, "Come to **me** you who are weary and burdened, and I will give you rest." What the law expert does, however, is the very opposite. He knows, of course, that he has by no means "arrived," has not at all reached the goal of perfection. So he tries to exculpate himself, "The law is not very clear, especially in the matter of loving the neighbor. Who is my neighbor anyway?"[18]

Contrary to the Federal Vision's interpretation, Hendrikson, in keeping with all other Reformed commentators, gives an accurate biblical understanding of the passage. Hendrikson comments on the meaning of Luke 10:37 by saying:

---

[18] Hendrikson, *New Testament Commentary on Luke*, p. 592.

It may be asked, "Does this answer of our Lord shed any light on the law-expert's original question, "What must I do to inherit everlasting life?" The answer would have to be, "Yes, it does." Not as if "being a good neighbor" would all by itself assure salvation. But proving oneself to be a neighbor, and doing this **to perfection**, and besides, loving God with a love that is also **perfect**, would indeed result in everlasting life. We hasten to add, however, that such perfection is impossible on this sinful earth. Yet, the demand of God's law is not abrogated. The solution of this problem has been furnished by God himself. Jesus Christ, by the substitutionary sacrifice of himself and by his life of **perfect** obedience, has done for us what we ourselves would never have been able to do. See Rom. 8:1-3; II Cor. 5:21; Gal. 3:13; Therefore: a) We must sincerely confess that it is forever impossible for us, by our own action, to fulfill the demands of God's law: "By the works of the law shall no flesh be justified (Gal. 2:16), b) We must, by God's grace and the power of his Spirit, place our trust in Christ (John 3:16, 36), c) **Out of gratitude** for the salvation which, because of Christ's merits, we have received as a free gift, we must now, guided and empowered by the Holy Spirit, live a life to the glory of God Triune. This means that even though while on earth we cannot love God and the neighbor perfectly, yet **in principle** we begin to live in accordance with this law. The law of love has not been abrogated. See Rom. 13:8-10.[19] (Emphasis is Hendrikson)

The Federal Vision absolutely, unequivocally denies the above understanding put forth by William Hendrikson. Norman Shepherd denies it, Rich Lusk denies it, and Steve Schlissel denies it. All who deny the active obedience of Christ as the imputation of His righteousness credited to us on our behalf denies the above comment. This is the position of the Federal Vision, which position states – the Mosaic Law never demanded perfect obedience, Christ's merits in this sense do not apply to any of us, the Mosaic Law can be kept by us as a means to eternal life, and this law keeping is the essence of faith whereby we are justified. Dear reader, this is why the Federal Vision is a heresy that must be eradicated from our churches.

---

[19] Hendrikson, *New Testament Commentary on Luke*, p. 596.

Galatians 3:10-12

> For as many as are of the works of the Law are under a curse,
> for it is written, "Cursed is everyone who does not abide by
> all things written in the Book of the Law, to perform them."
> Now that no one is justified by the Law before God is evi-
> dent; for, "The righteous man shall live by faith." However,
> the Law is not of faith; on the contrary, "He who practices
> them shall live by them."

This is a crucial passage because it clearly states that the Mosaic Law demands
perfect obedience contrary to the contentions of the Federal Vision proponents.
The text states that every man is cursed who does not abide by all things in the
Law. Since no one can claim perfect obedience to all things, this is why the
righteous man must live by faith. Verse 12 clearly states that the law is not of
faith! Here we see the bankruptcy of the Federal Vision's belief that the Mosaic
Law can be kept for eternal life. If one remembers, I made reference to all the
quotes of Norman Shepherd where he expresses that the very essence of faith
is obedience to the Mosaic Law. The Federal Vision replaces the perfect keeping of the Mosaic Law by Jesus imputed to us as if we had done it ourselves
with an individual, imperfect attempt to keep the Mosaic Law in order to be
justified. This is an insult to the Lord Jesus. This is what the Pharisees attempted to do with little success.

John Calvin makes the following comments on Galatians 3:10-12:

> The law holds all living men under its curse; and from the law,
> therefore, it is in vain to expect a blessing. They are declared to be
> of the works of the law who place their trust for salvation in those
> works; for such modes of expression must always be interpreted
> by the state of the question. Now, we know that the controversy
> here relates to righteousness. All who wish to be justified by the
> works of the law are declared to be liable to the curse. But how
> does he prove this? The sentence of the law is, that all who have
> transgressed any part of the law are cursed. Let us now see if there
> be any living man who fulfills the law. But no such person, it is
> evident, has been, or ever can be found. All to a man are here con-
> demned. The minor and the conclusion are wanting, for the any
> part of the law is cursed; all are held chargeable with this guilt;
> therefore all are cursed."

> This argument of Paul would not stand, if we had sufficient
> strength to fulfill the law; for there would then be a fatal

objection to the minor proposition. Either Paul reasons badly, or it is the law.

An antagonist might now object: "I admit that all transgressors are accursed; what then? Men will be found who keep the law; for they are free to choose good or evil." But Paul places here beyond controversy, what the Papists at this day hold to be a detestable doctrine, that men are destitute of strength to keep the law. And so he concludes boldly that all are cursed, because all have been commanded to keep the law perfectly; which implies that in the present corruption of our nature the power of keeping it perfectly is wanting. Hence we conclude that the curse which the law pronounces, though, in the phrase of logicians, it is accidental, is here perpetual and inseparable from its nature. The blessing which it offers to us is excluded by our depravity, so that the curse alone remains.

But that no man, is justified by the law. He again argues from a comparison of contradictory schemes. "If we are justified by faith, it is not by the law: but we are justified by faith therefore it is not by the law." The minor is proved by a passage from Habakkuk, which is also quoted in the Epistle to the Romans. (Habakkuk 2:4; Romans 1:17) The major is proved by the difference in the methods of justification. The law justifies him who fulfills all its precepts, while faith justifies those who are destitute of the merit of works, and who rely on Christ alone. To be justified by our own merit, and to be justified by the grace of another, are two schemes which cannot be reconciled: one of them must be overturned by the other.

The just shall live by faith…There is therefore no weight in the scornful reproaches of our adversaries, who allege that the prophet there employs the word Faith in a wider acceptation than Paul does in this passage. By Faith he evidently means the exercise of a calm, steady conscience, relying on God alone; so that Paul's quotation is properly applied.

And the law is not of faith. The law evidently is not contrary to faith; otherwise God would be unlike himself; but we must return to a principle already noticed, that Paul's language is modified by the present aspect of the case. The contradiction between the law and faith lies in the matter of justification. You will more easily unite fire and water, than reconcile these two statements, that men are justified by faith, and that they are justified by the law. "The law is not of faith;" that is, it has a method of justifying a man which is wholly at variance with faith. But the man who shall do these things. The difference lies in this, that man, when he fulfills the law, is reckoned righteous by a legal righteousness, which he proves by a quotation from Moses. (Leviticus 18:5.) Now, what is the righteousness of faith? He defines it in the Epistle to the Romans, If thou shalt confess with thy mouth the Lord Jesus, and shalt believe in thine heart that God hath raised him from the dead, thou shalt be saved." (Romans 10:9)

And yet it does not follow from this, that faith is inactive, or that it sets believers free from good works. For the present question is not, whether believers ought to keep the law as far as they can, (which is beyond all doubt,) but whether they can obtain righteousness by works, which is impossible. But since God promises life to the doers of the law, why does Paul affirm that they are not righteous? The reply to this objection is easy.

There are none righteous by the works of the law, because there are none who do those works. We admit that the doers of the law, if there were any such, are righteous; but since that is a conditional agreement, all are excluded from life, because no man performs that righteousness which he ought. We must bear in memory what I have already stated, that to do the law is not to obey it in part, but to fulfill everything which belongs to righteousness; and all are at the greatest distance from such perfection.[20]

---

[20] Calvin, *Calvin's New Testament Commentaries On Galatians, Ephesians, Philippians, and Colossians*, p. 53. If one looks up my references and compares them to the quotes listed, you will find some difference in wording only because my quotes are taken from a computer software program which utilized a different translator than my hard copy version; however, you will see that the meaning is fundamentally the same, pp. 54-55.

The above quotes are extensive from Calvin. The reason that I have done so is to demonstrate that Calvin bluntly refutes the theology of the Federal Vision. Shepherd insisted in his lecture in California in 2003 that Calvin agreed with his viewpoints. This is glaringly false. There is no similarity between the two whatsoever. There is nothing Reformed in the Federal Vision's theology of justification. It is a hybrid of Roman Catholicism, as I shall demonstrate in another chapter.

Galatians 2:15-21

> We are Jews by nature, and not sinners from among the Gentiles; nevertheless knowing that a man is not justified by the works of the Law but through faith in Christ Jesus, even we have believed in Christ Jesus, that we may be justified by faith in Christ, and not by the works of the Law since by the works of the Law shall no flesh be justified. But if, while seeking to be justified in Christ, we ourselves have also been found sinners, is Christ then a minister of sin? May it never be! For if I rebuild what I have once destroyed, I prove myself to be a transgressor. For through the Law I died to the Law, that I might live to God. I have been crucified with Christ; and it is no longer I who live, but Christ lives in me; and the life which I now live in the flesh I live by faith in the Son of God, who loved me, and delivered Himself up for me. I do not nullify the grace of God; for if righteousness comes through the Law, then Christ died needlessly.

There is a clear distinction or contrast being made between justification by the works of the Law and justification by faith in Christ. Men cannot be declared righteous by their efforts to keep the Mosaic Law. It is impossible because the Law kills us just like Paul states in Romans 7:8-12. Our failure to keep the Law's demands due to our sin demonstrates our utter helplessness in ourselves. This drives us to Christ to find remedy. It is faith in Jesus that gives us the righteousness of God that the Law demands, but it is not the "faith itself" that saves us; it is Christ who saves us. The faith is simply the instrument by which we receive the benefits of Christ. It is the merits of Christ imputed to us that grants us the privilege of eternal life.

The Federal Vision has completely distorted the relationship of the Mosaic Law to the Christian. Its position makes this passage self-contradictory. I quoted Norman Shepherd earlier (See first quote on page 168) where he states, **"The idea is not that the law reveals our sin so that we will be driven to**

seek grace apart from the Mosaic covenant." But this is the major thrust of the Law as demonstrated by Galatians 3:15-29. The Federal Vision's insistence that "faith" is simply "obedience to the Mosaic Law out of love for Jesus" is still an attempt to be justified by the works of the Law. Defining faith as obedience to the Law makes no sense whatsoever in this text. It would make Galatians 2:16 say something like this – "knowing that a man is not justified by the works of the Law, but through obedience to the Law in Christ Jesus." One cannot make "faith" synonymous with obedience to the Law.

There are some in the Federal Vision camp who have bought into the "New Perspective On Paul" error that Paul was not referring to the Judaizers as those who sought justification by obedience to the moral Law, but as those who simply wanted the Gentiles to conform to the ceremonial parts of the Mosaic Law. There is a very good reason for the Federal Vision camp to espouse this belief. By this interpretation, it allows them to promote justification through obedience to the moral demands of the Law.

John Calvin has some very helpful comments regarding the meaning of this Galatians passage:

> The first thing to be noticed is, that we must seek justification by the faith of Christ, because we cannot be justified by works. Now, the question is, what is meant by the works of the law? The Papists, misled by Origen and Jerome, are of opinion, and lay it down as certain, that the dispute relates to shadows; and accordingly assert, that by "the works of the law" are meant ceremonies. As if Paul were not reasoning about the free justification which is bestowed on us by Christ. For they see no absurdity in maintaining that" no man is justified by the works of the law," and yet that, by the merit of works, we are accounted righteous in the sight of God. In short, they hold that no mention is here made of the works of the moral law. **But the context clearly proves that the moral law is also comprehended in these words; for almost everything which Paul afterwards advances belongs more properly to the moral than to the ceremonial law; and** he is continually employed in contrasting the righteousness of the law with the free acceptance which God is pleased to bestow.

Hence it appears with what silly trifling the Papists of our day dispute with us about the word, as if it had been a word of our contrivance. But Paul was unacquainted with the theology of the Papists, who declare that a man is justified by faith, and yet make a part of justification to consist in works. Of such half-justification Paul knew nothing. For, when he instructs us that we are justified by faith, because we cannot be justified by works, he takes for granted what is true, that we cannot be justified through the righteousness of Christ, unless we are poor and destitute of a righteousness of our own. Consequently, either nothing or all must be ascribed to faith or to works.[21] (Emphasis mine)

If Calvin were alive today, he would be doing battle with the Federal Vision proponents. He would see them as hybrid Papists at best. Keep in mind, Norman Shepherd did say in his book *The Call Of Grace* on page 59 that there is hope for a common understanding between Roman Catholicism and Protestantism regarding the way of salvation by adopting his understanding of the covenant. Whatever Calvin addresses to the Papists applies to the Federal Vision. Shepherd insists that his view of an obedient faith is not rooted in a works/merit paradigm. This is simply a play on words, for the resultant meaning is the same. The moment that Shepherd stated that obedience is not something that follows justification, or that it flows out of justification he adopted a Romanist position. When Shepherd stated that faithful disciples of Jesus will be justified (Shepherd Thesis 20), he adopted a Romanist position.

Regarding Galatians 2: 15- 21, Calvin is very clear that none of us can keep the Law for justification:

He had already appealed to the consciences of Peter and others, and now confirms it more fully by affirming that such is the actual truth, that by the works of the law no mortal will obtain justification. This is the foundation of a freely bestowed righteousness, when we are stripped of a righteousness of our own. Besides, when he asserts that no mortal is justified by the righteousness of the law, the assertion amounts to this, that from such a mode of justification all mortals are excluded, and that none can possibly reach it.[22]

---

[21] *Calvin's New Testament Commentaries*, pp. 38-40.

[22] *Calvin's New Testament Commentaries*, p. 40.

Galatians 5:1-6

> It was for freedom that Christ set us free; therefore keep standing firm and do not be subject again to a yoke of slavery; Behold I, Paul, say to you that if you receive circumcision, Christ will be of no benefit to you. And I testify again to every man who receives circumcision, that he is under obligation to keep the whole Law. You have been severed from Christ, you who are seeking to be justified by law; you have fallen from grace. For we through the Spirit, by faith, are waiting for the hope of righteousness. For in Christ Jesus neither circumcision nor uncircumcision means anything, but faith working through love.

The Federal Vision makes much of the phrase "faith working through love." The "obedience of faith," which is a common catch phrase of the Federal Vision, is seen as love being a part of the essence of faith. In other words, the obedient faith is the loving faith. If the Federal Vision simply saw love as the accompanying, inevitable fruit or evidence of saving faith, there would be no problem. But, the Federal Vision makes love as the very "essence" of faith, which means that works are the basis of our justification.

The main thrust of this passage is Paul's refutation of the Judaizer's belief that outward ceremonies of the Mosaic Law, such as circumcision, are necessary for justification. Paul makes it very clear that outward ceremonies mean nothing when it comes to justification. The only thing that matters is Christ Jesus and a faith in Him that works through love.

John Calvin explains the role of "faith working through love" that does not commit the error of the Papists and that of the Federal Vision by comparison. He says:

> There would be no difficulty in this passage, were it not for the dishonest manner in which it has been tortured by the Papists to uphold the righteousness of works. When they attempt to refute our doctrine, that we are justified by faith alone, they take this line of argument. If the faith which justifies us be that "which worketh by love," then faith alone does not justify. I answer, they do not comprehend their own silly talk; still less do they comprehend our statements. **It is not our doctrine that the faith which justifies is alone; we maintain that it is invariably accompanied by good works; only we contend**

that faith alone is sufficient for justification. The Papists themselves are accustomed to tear faith after a murderous fashion, sometimes presenting it out of all shape and unaccompanied by love, and at other times, in its true character. **We, again, refuse to admit that, in any case, faith can be separated from the Spirit of regeneration; but when the question comes to be in what manner we are justified, we then set aside all works.** (Emphasis mine)

With respect to the present passage, Paul enters into no dispute whether love cooperates with faith in justification; but, in order to avoid the appearance of representing Christians as idle and as resembling blocks of wood, he points out what are the true exercises of believers. **When you are engaged in discussing the question of justification, beware of allowing any mention to be made of love or of works, but resolutely adhere to the exclusive particle. Paul does not here treat of justification, or assign any part of the praise of it to love.** Had he done so, the same argument would prove that circumcision and ceremonies, at a former period, had some share in justifying a sinner. As in Christ Jesus **he commends faith accompanied by love,** so before the coming of Christ ceremonies were required. But this has nothing to do with obtaining righteousness, as the Papists themselves allow; and neither must it be supposed that love possesses any such influence.[23] (Emphasis mine)

It is clear from Calvin's comments that good works **accompany or cooperate** with faith, but he is clear that one must never make love as the essence of faith. As Shepherd has made clear, he does not consider the works of faith as accompanying it but as its very essence; therefore, what Calvin attributes as the error of the Papists applies likewise to the Federal Vision.

When Shepherd discusses Galatians 5:6 in his book *The Call Of Grace* he mentions that Roman Catholicism likes to use this passage against Protestantism. Shepherd states that Rome's error is that it makes this passage an issue of "merit."[24] The idea of merit involves boasting of something earned, which he says is wrong, and Shepherd quotes Ephesians 2:8-9 as a refutation

---

[23] *Calvin's New Testament Commentaries,* p. 96.

[24] Shepherd, *Call Of Grace,* p. 60.

of the idea of earning our salvation. In this sense, Shepherd is correct in his analysis that Rome makes Galatians 5:6 as an issue of meriting salvation, but the problem is that Shepherd turns around and commits the same error, only he doesn't use the word "merit." Notice what Shepherd says:

> The biblical texts to which Rome appeals must be read in the light of the covenant. Then the biblical demands for repentance and obedience, together with the warnings against disobedience, can be seen for what they are. They are not an invitation to achieve salvation by human merit. They are a call to find salvation wholly and exclusively in Jesus Christ through faith in him ... What is required from Rome is a change from a works/merit paradigm for understanding the way of salvation to a covenantal paradigm ... At the same time, this change in paradigm would provide a proper basis for Rome's legitimate insistence that full credence be given to James 2:24, Galatians 5:6, and similar passages. In light of the covenant, these texts do function in our understanding of the way of salvation without a lapse into the error of legalism.[25]

> Passages like Galatians 5:6 and James 2:24, to which Rome appeals, are almost uniformly treated as problem texts because they do not fit into a noncovenantal paradigm of salvation by grace ... The answer to this dilemma is to be found in the doctrine of the covenant, with its two parts, promise and obligation ... All of the blessings of the covenant are ours as gifts of sovereign grace. The covenantal demand for faith, repentance, and obedience is simply the way in which the Lord leads us into possession of these blessings.[26]

> Salvation is both by **grace** and through **faith.** These are the two parts of the covenant: grace and faith, promise and obligation. Grace is not without conditions, and a living and active faith is not meritorious achievement.

> The covenant plays almost no role, either in the Roman Catholic doctrine of salvation, or in the thinking of many evangelical Christians. Progress can be made in the discus-

---

[25] Shepherd, *Call Of Grace*, pp. 60-61.

[26] Shepherd, *Call Of Grace*, pp. 62-63.

sion among evangelicals by letting the light of the covenant shine on the way of salvation.[27]

Though Shepherd doesn't like nor use the word "merit," this doesn't mean that he has avoided the heresy of advocating a works salvation. Notice that he said that **grace is not without conditions**. Faith is seen as the obedience that leads us to the promise. As I have noted earlier, Shepherd has said that circumcision in the Old Covenant and baptism in the New Covenant were both conditions in order to receive the promise of God's blessings.[28] I also noted earlier that Shepherd viewed the grace of God as the giving of the Mosaic Law in order for us to keep it, which is what a living and active faith is – it is covenantal loyalty and faithfulness.[29] Shepherd made clear that the faith that was credited to Abraham as righteousness in Genesis 15:6 was so significant that it was a condition to be met in order to receive the promise.[30]

I hope this sinks in. According to Federal Vision theology, one must meet a condition of obedience in order to get grace! Shepherd immediately says that these conditions are not meritorious. This is double talk. According to him, grace is the promise of the covenant, but one must meet conditions in order to receive the grace or promise. This is not grace!

Now that we know how Shepherd defines his terms, it is understandable why he thinks that his understanding of the covenant is able to bridge the gap between Roman Catholicism and Protestantism regarding the way of salvation. Rome sees our obedience as meritorious works; Shepherd and the Federal Vision sees it as covenantal faithfulness to the law of God. What's the real difference? The upsetting thing to me is that the Federal Vision seeks to disguise their works salvation paradigm by using orthodox terminology and by being critical of Roman Catholicism. The unwary reader is sucked in to believe that Federal Vision theology is acceptable. For example, consider Shepherd's title to his book – *The Call Of Grace*. He has totally redefined grace to being a works provision. The Reformed Faith has never defined grace this way. Just like Calvin, the Reformed Faith has always maintained that good works accompany saving faith, not that they are the very essence of it.

---

[27] Shepherd, *Call Of Grace*, p. 63.

[28] Shepherd, *Call Of Grace*, pp. 14-15.

[29] Shepherd, *Call Of Grace*, p. 36.

[30] Shepherd, *Call Of Grace*, pp. 15-16.

John 3:14-16

> And as Moses lifted up the serpent in the wilderness, even so must the Son of Man be lifted up; that whoever believes may in Him have eternal life. For God so loved the world, that He gave His only begotten Son, that whoever believes in Him should not perish but have eternal life.

The passage contains probably the most famous verse in the entire Bible (verse 16). This whole passage is devastating to the Federal Vision with its insistence that saving faith is actually covenantal obedience to God's Law. An analogy is made between the bronze serpent lifted up by Moses and the Son of Man being lifted up. The analogy is fundamental in understanding the nature of faith. The story of the bronze serpent is found in Numbers 21. The setting is Israel's complaint against God and Moses for their perceived lack of food and water in the wilderness, and it is said that Israel loathed "the miserable bread," which is a reference to the manna from heaven that God fed Israel.

As a result of their complaint against God and His anointed leader Moses, God sent fiery (poisonous) serpents among the people who bit many so that a multitude died. The people soon realized that complaining was a big mistake, and in so doing they had sinned against the Lord. They pleaded with Moses to intercede to the Lord on their behalf so that the serpents could be removed (Numbers 21:7). Moses did intercede and God told Moses what to do which is recorded in verses 8 and 9:

> Then the Lord said to Moses, "Make a fiery serpent, and set it on a standard; and it shall come about, that everyone who is bitten, **when he looks at it, he shall live.**" And Moses made a bronze serpent and set it on the standard; **and it came about, that if a serpent bit any man, when he looked to the bronze serpent, he lived**.

The absolutely vital thing for us to note is that healing came about by only a look! This was all that was required; there was no penance, there were no conditions of obedient living. Only a look! The analogy has tremendous import for our understanding of John 3:14-16 regarding the nature of faith. All that the ancient Israelites had to do was have faith so that looking would save them. What do we in the New Covenant have to do in order to be saved from our sins, which will surely kill us too? All we have to do is to look to Christ lifted up for us. Jesus was lifted up on Calvary for the atonement of our sins. He was the substitutionary provision for our dilemma. If we believe in Jesus by trusting that His death can heal us from sin's curse, then we can have eternal life.

Saving faith is simply a look to Christ for salvation. There is nothing special in the "faith." The faith does not save; it is Christ who saves. Faith is merely the instrument by which we appropriate the free gift that is offered. *"By faith we look away from ourselves, from all that we are or could ever accomplish, and we reach out empty hands to Christ. We depend on him and make him our only plea before God's throne. Faith as an instrument is the link between sinner and Savior, the channel through which the benefits of his life and death are imputed to us."*[31]

There are no conditions to grace as Shepherd insists. There is no demand for obedience to the Mosaic Law in order to secure eternal life. The Federal Vision's understanding of faith is a direct insult to the Triune God; it is a direct assault on the atonement of Christ.

Faith and Good Works In The Reformed Standards

The Federal Vision adherents want to be seen as still being Reformed; they still insist that their new paradigm is consistent with the Reformed Standards, which include the Westminster Confession Of Faith with its Larger and Shorter Catechisms, the Belgic Confession with its Heidelberg Catechism, and the Canons of Dordt. I have noted in other chapters where Federal Vision theology is out of accord with these documents concerning the meaning of justification, faith, and Christ's active obedience. The purpose in this chapter is to show that the Federal Vision is completely out of accord with the Reformed Standards on the relationship of justifying faith and good works. Having pointed out with various quotes the teaching of Federal Vision theology, I will simply quote the relevant portions of these documents to show where the Federal Vision has departed from the Reformed Faith and from Christian orthodoxy.

The Westminster Confession and Larger Catechism

Chapter 11, Section 1, "Of Justification" states:

> Those whom God effectually calleth, He also freely justifieth; **not by infusing righteousness into them,** but by pardoning their sins, and by accounting and accepting their persons as righteous, **not for anything wrought in them, or done by them,** but for Christ's sake alone; nor by imputing faith itself, the act of believing, **or any other evangelical obedience to them, as their righteousness,** but by imputing

---

[31] Donnelly, Edward, Justification By Faith Alone, *The Banner of Truth,* August-September 2003, p. 46.

the obedience and satisfaction of Christ unto them, they receiving and resting on Him and His righteousness by faith; which faith they have not of themselves, it is the gift of God. (Emphasis mine)

Federal Vision theology is completely out of accord with the Confession's statement on justification. Good works done on the part of the person who has faith has absolutely nothing to do with his justification. First, the Confession states that there is no infusion of righteousness into the person. Second, the Confession clearly states that the pardoning of sins and the acceptance of the person as righteous is totally independent of any thing in the person or done by the person. This rules out all conditions for receiving God's pardoning of sins. It rules out all obedience to any kind of law as that which leads to pardoning of sins. Even the faith that embraces Christ has nothing to do with the pardoning of sins. Pardoning of sins is due to Christ's sake alone. The contrast is made between Christ's sake alone and all evangelical obedience and its righteousness. The contrast is between Christ's obedience and satisfaction with man's acts of obedience. **The Confession clearly states that there is absolutely, unequivocally no relationship whatsoever between justification and our good works as the basis for the pardon of sins.** Norman Shepherd made it clear in his Thesis 23 (See page 45) that repentance, abiding in Christ by keeping his commandments, and good works done from true faith according to the law of God are all necessary for justification.

Robert Shaw makes these observations on this section of the Westminster Confession:

> But though justification and sanctification be inseparably connected, yet they are totally distinct, and the blending of them together perverts both the law and the gospel. Justification, according to the use of the word in Scripture, must be understood forensically; it is a law term, derived from human courts of judicature, and signifies, not the making of a person righteous, but the holding and declaring him to be righteous in law.[32]

The Westminster Confession continues to say in Chapter 11, Section 2:

> Faith, thus receiving and resting on Christ and His righteousness, is the alone instrument of justification; yet is it not alone in the person justified, **but is ever accompanied with all**

---

[32] Shaw, *An Exposition of the Westminster Confession of Faith*, p. 125.

other saving graces, and is no dead faith, but worketh by love.

The Confession explicitly states that other saving graces accompany faith; they are not the essence of this faith. This section differentiates between faith as the alone instrument of justification and the graces that accompany in the person already justified. So much for the Federal Visions insistence that justifying faith is "the obedience of faith" that is seen as covenant loyalty and faithfulness as conditions to receive God's promises.

Robert Shaw comments on this section of the Westminster Confession:

> No man can be justified before God, in whole or in part, on the ground of a personal righteousness of any kind. Romanists, Socinians, and Pelagians, maintain that we are justified either by a personal inherent righteousness, or by our own works. In opposition to this, our Confession teaches that persons are not justified "for anything wrought in them, or done by them, but for Christ's sake alone…Because we can only be justified on the ground of a perfect righteousness, and our inherent righteousness is imperfect.[33]

> That we cannot be justified by our own works is no less manifest, - 1. Because our personal obedience falls far short of the requirements of the law. The law demands obedience in all respects perfect; but "in many things we offend all" – James 3:22. Because our obedience, though it were commensurate to the high demands of the law, could not satisfy for our past transgressions. The law requires not only the fulfillment of its precept, but also the endurance of its penalty.[34]

> Neonomians allege, that though we cannot fulfill that **perfect** obedience which the law of works demanded, yet God has been graciously pleased, for Christ's sake, to give us a **new law**; according to which, **sincere obedience**, or faith, repentance, and sincere obedience, are accepted as our justifying righteousness…The gospel was never designed to teach sinners that God will now accept of a **sincere** instead of a **perfect** obedience, but to direct them to Jesus Christ as "the end of the law for righteousness to every one that believeth…None

---

[33] Shaw, *An Exposition of the Westminster Confession of Faith*, p. 126.

[34] Shaw, *An Exposition of the Westminster Confession of Faith*, p. 127.

can be justified without a **perfect** righteousness; for the demands of the law cannot be set aside or relaxed.[35] (Emphasis Shaw)

The incredible observation by Robert Shaw is that he wrote these words 150 years before Norman Shepherd wrote his thesis 23, but it is as if Shaw had Shepherd's thesis and book before him as he made these observations. Shepherd even uses the term "new obedience wrought by the Holy Spirit" as that which leads to justification.

The Westminster Confession in Chapter 11, Section 3 states:

> Christ, by His obedience and death, did fully discharge the debt of all those that are thus justified, and did make a proper, real, and full satisfaction to His Father's justice in their behalf. Yet, inasmuch as He was given by the Father for them; and His obedience and satisfaction accepted in their stead; and both freely, not for anything in them; their justification is only of free grace; that both the exact justice, and rich grace of God, might be glorified in the justification of sinners.

This section brings out that the sole ground of a sinner's justification before God is the righteousness of Jesus Christ. Jesus' righteousness is contrasted with anything done in us. The Confession defines grace as the free gift of Jesus' righteousness given to us. Jesus' righteousness in done in our stead. Norman Shepherd made it very clear in his book *The Call Of Grace* that Jesus' obedience to death served as the **pattern** for us to keep the covenant just like Abraham did.[36] Shepherd also said that grace is not without conditions.[37] Shepherd also said that the Mosaic Law is the grace of God given to us to obey as the essence of a living and active faith.[38] And to think that Norman Shepherd has the audacity to claim that the Westminster Confession supports his theology.

The Westminster Confession in Chapter 14, Section 2 "Of Saving Faith" reads:

> By this faith, a Christian believeth to be true whatsoever is revealed in the Word, for the authority of God Himself speaking therein; and acteth differently upon that which each particular passage thereof containeth; **yielding obedience to the**

---

[35] Shaw, *An Exposition of the Westminster Confession of Faith*, pp. 128, 129.

[36] Shepherd, *The Call Of Grace*, p. 75.

[37] Shepherd, *The Call Of Grace*, p. 63.

[38] Shepherd, *The Call Of Grace*, p. 36.

commands, trembling at the threatenings, and embracing the promises of God for this life, and that which is to come. But the principal acts of saving faith are accepting, receiving, and resting upon Christ alone for justification, sanctification, and eternal life, by virtue of the covenant of grace (Emphasis mine).

The Confession is clear. Saving faith **yields obedience** to God's commands, but it is not the essence of faith, being identical with it.

The Westminster Confession in Chapter 16, Section 2 "Of Good Works" states:

These good works, done in obedience to God's commandments, are the **fruits and evidences** of a true and lively faith: and by them believers **manifest their thankfulness,** strengthen their assurance, edify their brethren, adorn the profession of the gospel, stop the mouths of the adversaries and glorify God, whose workmanship they are, created in Christ Jesus thereunto; that, having their **fruit** unto holiness, they may have the end, eternal life. (Emphasis mine)

The Confession clearly states that good works are fruits and evidences of faith and that they manifest a thankful heart in the Christian. Shepherd and others have refused to say that good works are fruit or evidences of justifying faith. They do not see them as accompanying faith but as the very essence of it. In doing so, they have totally distanced themselves from the Westminster Confession.

Robert Shaw comments on the role of faith as the alone instrument of justification:

Faith is the alone instrument of the sinner's justification. That we are justified **by faith** is so frequently and expressly declared in the Scriptures, that on who professes to receive the Word of God as the rule of his faith can venture to deny it…Some have said, that faith is to be considered as the **condition** of our justification. The "condition" of anything usually signifies that which, being done, gives us a right and title to it, because it possesses either intrinsic or conventional merit. To call faith, in this sense, the condition of our justification, would introduce human merit, to the dishonor of divine grace, and would entirely subvert the gospel. (Emphasis Shaw).[39]

---

[39] Shaw, *An Exposition of the Westminster Confession of Faith*, p. 131.

We are reminded of Shepherd's insistence in his book *The Call Of Grace* that grace has conditions of which the sacrament of baptism is one and obedience to the Law is another. Of course, Shepherd says that this is not meritorious.

Robert Shaw quotes Martin Luther regarding the issue of works being the condition of our justification. Shaw says:

> Commenting on Gal. 2:16, he (Luther) says: "This is the true mean of becoming a Christian, even to be justified by faith in Jesus Christ, and not by the works of the law. Here we must stand, not upon the wicked gloss of the schoolmen, which say, that faith justifieth when charity and good works are joined withal. With this pestilent gloss, the sophisters have darkened and corrupted this and other like sentences in Paul, wherein he manifestly attributeth justification to faith only in Christ.[40]

In commenting upon the nature of faith as the alone instrument of justification Shaw states:

> In opposition to these various views of the relation which faith bears to justification, our Confession teaches that "faith, receiving and resting on Christ and his righteousness, is the **alone instrument** of justification." Some have misrepresented this expression, as if it meant that faith is the instrument wherewith God justifies. But it was never intended that faith is an instrument on the part of God, but on our part. Some have also inaccurately spoken of faith as the instrument by which we **receive justification.** Faith is more properly the instrument by which we receive Christ and his righteousness ... "Faith," says Mr. Haldane, "does not justify as an act of righteousness, but as the instrument by which we receive Christ and his righteousness.[41] (Emphasis Shaw)

Shaw makes a very important point that the Federal Vision has totally missed. Justification is Christ and His righteousness! Faith merely embraces Christ's righteousness. But, we have seen that the Federal Vision emphatically denies the imputation of Christ's righteousness to us; hence, the faith that justifies men is their own faith, an imperfect one at that. Again, I refer to Rich Lusk's horrendous comments that the perfect Law keeping of Jesus was not imputed to

---

[40] Shaw *An Exposition of the Westminster Confession of Faith,*.

[41] Shaw, *An Exposition of the Westminster Confession of Faith*, p. 132.

any Christian as Lusk had heard while growing up but that Jesus' Law keeping was for Himself only. See quote beginning at the bottom of page 145 through 146.

Shaw makes an excellent comment on the relationship of good works to saving faith when he says:

> The advocates to the doctrine of justification by faith **alone** were grossly calumniated, as if they had denied the necessity of good works. To guard against this injurious misrepresentation, our Confession teaches, that though "faith is the alone instrument of justification, yet it is not alone in the person justified." The faith that justifies is a living and active principle, which works by love, purifies the heart, and excites to universal obedience. It is accompanied with every Christian grace, and productive of good works. "Works," says Luther, "are not taken into consideration when the question respects justification. But true faith will no more fail to produce them, than the sun can cease to give light."[42]

The Westminster Confession in Chapter 16, Section 5 "Of Good Works" states:

> We cannot, by our best works, merit pardon of sin, or eternal life at the hand of God, by reason of the great disproportion that is between them and the glory to come; and the infinite distance that is between us and God, whom, by them, we can neither profit, nor satisfy for the debt of our former sins, but when we have done all we can, we have done but our duty, and are unprofitable servants and because, as they are good, they proceed from His Spirit; and as they are wrought by us, they are defiled, and mixed with so much weakness and imperfection, that they cannot endure the severity of God's judgment.

The Confession affirms that our **best works** are not good enough to merit pardon of sin and that even our best works are still defiled with weakness and imperfection that they cannot stand up in Judgment Day. But, this is not what Shepherd says. Shepherd says in his Thesis 22: *"The righteousness of Jesus Christ ever remains the exclusive ground of the believer's justification but the personal godliness of the believer is also necessary for his justification in the judgment of the last day."*[43]

---

[42] Shaw, *An Exposition of the Westminster Confession of Faith*, p. 133.

[43] Norman Shepherd, Thesis 22. *Thirty-four Theses on Justification in Relation to Faith, Repentance, and Good Works.* as found on the Theologia website.

The fundamental problem with Federal Vision theology is that it blurs the doctrines of justification and sanctification. The fact that Matthew 25 relates that the reason that the sheep, who are the righteous, are going into glory because of their good works lends one to think that the good works of the believer are the basis for this inheritance. The Westminster Confession emphasizes that good works (personal godliness) always accompany justification. As Hebrews 12:14 indicates, without sanctification no one will see the Lord. The fact that good works must be in the life of the Christian does not mean that they constitute the reason that a man is justified. The Federal Vision simply cannot grasp this truth, and in its confusion, it has championed a works salvation paradigm.

The Westminster Confession in Chapter 16, Section 6 addresses why God accepts the good works of believers when it states:

> Yet notwithstanding, the persons of believers being accepted through Christ, their good works also are accepted in Him, not as though they were in this life wholly unblamable and unreproveable in God's sight; but that He, looking upon them in His Son, is pleased to accept and reward that which is sincere, although accompanied with many weaknesses and imperfections.

The Confession clearly states that the imperfect works of Christians are accepted only because they are viewed as being in Jesus. It is Jesus' righteousness that matters. Robert Shaw makes this comment on this section of the Confession:

> Adorned with the glorious robe of the Redeemer's righteousness, he shall stand before the judgment-seat undismayed, while the exalted Saviour and Judge shall bid him welcome to that state of final and everlasting blessedness which God hath prepared for him, saying, "Come, ye blessed of my Father, inherit the kingdom prepared for you from the foundation of the world." ... Renouncing all dependence on their own works of righteousness, let them, like Paul, desire to "win Christ, and be found in him, not having their own righteousness, but that which is through the faith of Christ, the righteousness which is of God by faith."[44]

Question 71 of the Westminster Larger Catechism states:

> How is justification an act of God's free grace?

---

[44] Shaw, *An Exposition of the Westminster Confession of Faith*, pp. 136,137.

Answer: Although Christ, by his obedience and death, did make a proper, real, and full satisfaction to God's justice in the behalf of them that are justified; yet in as much as God accepteth the satisfaction from a surety, which he might have demanded of them, and did provide this surety, his own only Son, **imputing his righteousness to them, and requiring nothing of them for their justification but faith, which also is his gift, their justification is to them of free grace.** (Emphasis mine)

The Larger Catechism emphatically teaches that justification is a fee gift of grace totally independent of anything in the person justified. The righteousness that the person possesses is Jesus' righteousness imputed to them. So much for the Federal Vision's theology that there is no imputation of Christ's righteousness to us and that grace has conditions of obedience to the Law of God.

Question 72 of the Westminster Larger Catechism states:

What is justifying faith?
Answer: Justifying faith is a saving grace, wrought in the heart of a sinner by the Spirit and Word of God, whereby he, being convinced of his sin and misery, and of the disability in himself and all other creatures to recover him out of his lost condition, not only assenteth to the truth of the promise of the gospel, but receiveth and resteth upon Christ and his righteousness, therein held forth, for pardon of sin, and for the accepting and accounting of his person righteous in the sight of God for salvation.

The Larger Catechism emphasizes that saving faith recognizes the inability in himself to remedy his lost condition. Justifying faith is an **assent** to the promise of the gospel. Saving faith **receives and rests upon Christ and His righteousness for the pardon of sin.** This Catechism answer is in direct opposition to Shepherd's thesis 23. Saving faith is not covenant loyalty and faithfulness to God's Law. It is an assent. This assent is in conformity with the John 3:14-16 passage about believing in Christ who is lifted up. This assent or act of believing brings eternal life just like looking or assenting to the proposition that healing from the poisonous serpents is possible by simply looking in faith at the bronze serpent that Moses lifted up. The Catechism stresses that the assenting or faith rests upon Christ and His righteousness. It is not a faith which is an "obedient faith" that obeys God's commandments as that which grants pardon of sins as the Federal Vision insists.

Question 73 of the Westminster Larger Catechism states:

> How doth faith justify a sinner in the sight of God?
> **Answer:** Faith justifies a sinner in the sight of God, not
> because of those other graces which do always accompany it,
> or of good works that are the fruits of it, nor as if the grace of
> faith, or any act thereof, were imputed to him for his justifi-
> cation; but only as it is an instrument by which he receiveth
> and applieth Christ and his righteousness.

The Larger Catechism completely divorces all good works or other graces that accompany faith. The Catechism refers to good works as **fruits** of faith, and it refers to faith only as an instrument whereby it receives and applies Christ and His righteousness. There is no way that one can misconstrue that saving faith has works as its very essence. The righteousness that is received is Christ's, not our own . If one denies the imputation of Christ's righteousness, as does the Federal Vision does, what righteousness is left? Our own! The Federal Vision refuses to acknowledge that good works are the fruits of faith; they insist that they are the essence of saving faith.

Question 77 of the Westminster Larger Catechism states:

> Wherein do justification and sanctification differ?
> **Answer:** Although sanctification be inseparably joined with
> justification, yet they differ, in that God in justification
> imputeth the righteousness of Christ; in sanctification of his
> Spirit infuseth grace, and enableth to the exercise thereof; in
> the former, sin is pardoned; in the other, it is subdued: the one
> doth equally free all believers from the revenging wrath of
> God, and that perfectly in this life, that they never fall into
> condemnation; the other is neither equal in all, nor in this life
> perfect in any, but growing up to perfection.

The Larger Catechism clearly indicates that in justification Christ's righteous-ness is imputed to us while in sanctification grace is infused into us. Pardon of sin is associated with justification, not sanctification. In justification, the per-son is free from any condemnation, meaning that they are eternally secure in Christ. The Federal Vision is at complete odds with this Catechism. It denies the imputation of Christ's righteousness as the essence of justification. It asso-ciates pardoning of sin with our obedience to the Law of God. It denies the per-severance of the saints, believing that one can fall out of a state of justification. In its insistence that justifying faith is covenantal obedience to God's Law, it thoroughly blurs any distinction between justification and sanctification.

The Three Forms of Unity

These Reformed documents clearly set forth the relationship between faith and good works. This has important ramifications with reference to several of the Federal Vision proponents. For some, these are the documents that form the basis of their church constitution. Steve Schlissel's church, Messiah's Congregation, claims adherence to the three forms of Unity (The Belgic Confession, The Heidelberg Catechism, and the Canons of Dordt). When I get to a close examination of Schlissel's view in another chapter, I will document that he has adopted views that completely refute the Standards that his church says it upholds. In fact, all the others that comprise the Monroe Four are holding to views that deny the Standards that their church or denomination subscribe to. Steve Wilkins, being part of the PCA, is out of accord with numerous doctrines of the Westminster Confession. Doug Wilson's church, Christ's Church in Moscow, Idaho, is a member of the Confederation of Reformed Evangelicals. He claims that the confederation subscribes to the Westminster Standards and to the Three Forms of Unity. John Barach is part of the United Reformed Churches In North America, which holds to the Three Forms of Unity. I have already demonstrated that the Federal Vision theology is totally out of accord with the Westminster Standards. Now, I shall demonstrate that Federal Vision theology is totally out of accord with these Reformed documents regarding the relationship of faith with works.

Regarding the righteousness of faith, Article 22 of the Belgic Confession states:

> But Jesus Christ, imputing to us all his merits and so many holy works which he has done for us, and in our stead, is our Righteousness. And faith is an instrument that keeps us in communion with him in all his benefits, which, when become ours, are more than sufficient to acquit us of our sins.

The Belgic Confession clearly affirms the active obedience of Christ in that Christ's righteousness (called His merits) is given to us in our place. This is substitutionary righteousness; it is not the obedience of faith as taught by the Federal Vision.

Regarding the doctrine of sanctification, the Belgic Confession in Article 24 states:

> Therefore it is impossible that this holy faith can be unfruit-ful in man: for we do not speak of a vain faith, but of such a faith, which is called in Scripture, a faith that worketh by

love, which excites man to the practice of those works, which God has commanded in his Word. Which works, as they proceed from the good root of faith, are good and acceptable in the sight of God, forasmuch as they are all sanctified by his grace: **howbeit they are of no account towards our justification. For it is by faith in Christ that we are justified, even before we do good works; otherwise they could not be good works, any more than the fruit of a tree can be good, before the tree itself is good.** Therefore we do good works, but not to merit by them, (for what can they merit?) nay, we are beholden to God for the good works we do, and not he to us, since it is he that worketh in us both to will and to do of his good pleasure. Let us therefore attend to what is written: when ye shall have done all those things which are commanded you, say, we are unprofitable servants; we have done that which was our duty to do. (Emphasis mine)

The Confession sees good works as the fruit of a holy faith and that these good works do not count toward our justification. The contrast between good works and justifying faith is stark! The Belgic Confession thoroughly refutes Federal Vision theology that equates justifying faith with obedience to the Law of God.

In Lord's Day 7, Question 21, of the Heidelberg Catechism we find:

What is true faith?
Answer: True faith is not only a certain knowledge, whereby I hold for truth all that God has revealed to us in his word, but also an assured confidence, which the Holy Ghost works by the gospel, in my heart; that not only the others, but to me also, remission of sin, everlasting righteousness and salvation, are freely given by God, merely of grace, only for the sake of Christ's merits.

All the benefits that accrue to us as believers are due to sheer grace earned for us by Christ. There is none of this Federal Vision talk of grace that has conditions rooted in our covenantal obedience.

In Lord's Day 3, Question 60, of the Heidelberg Catechism it states:

How are you right with God?
Answer: Only by a true faith in Jesus Christ; so that though my conscience accuse me, that I have grossly transgressed all the commandments of God, and kept none of them, and am

still inclined to all evil; notwithstanding, God, without any
merit of mine, but only of mere grace, grants and imputes to
me, the perfect satisfaction, righteousness and holiness of
Christ; even so, as if I never had had, nor committed any sin:
yea, as if I had fully accomplished all that obedience which
Christ has accomplished for me; inasmuch as I embrace such
benefit with a believing heart.

This answer is devastating to Federal Vision theology. First, it declares that true
faith recognizes that it has transgressed all of God's commandments, keeping
none of them. Federal Vision theology believes that true faith is identical with
faithful keeping of God's commandments, out of a sincere heart of course.
Second, grace is contrasted to merit which is pictured as obedience to the Law
of God. Third, all of Christ's work is imputed to the believer, especially
Christ's righteousness and holiness. Fourth, this imputation of Christ's work to
us is substitutionary in that Christ's **perfect obedience** is done in the believer's
place as if he had done it. And fifth, all of Christ's benefits are embraced with
a believing heart. This rules out any idea of grace being conditional upon any
covenantal faithfulness.

Question 61 of the Heidelberg Catechism states:

Why do you say that by faith alone you are right with God?
Answer: Not that I am acceptable to God, on account of the
worthiness of my faith; but because only the satisfaction,
righteousness, and holiness of Christ, is my righteousness
before God; and that I cannot receive and apply the same to
myself any other way than by faith only.

The Catechism is now stressing the idea of faith alone. There is absolutely
nothing of value in our faith that pleases God. So much for the Federal Vision's
battle cry of "the obedience of faith" as the basis of our justification. Only
Christ's death, righteousness, and holiness can make me right with God.
Seeing that the Federal Vision denies the imputation of Christ's righteousness
and holiness to our account, then, according to the Heidelberg Catechism, there
is no way for a man to be right with God.

The Catechism gives the reason why our good works will fail to make us right
with God.

Question 62 of the Heidelberg Catechism asks:

Why can't the good we do make us right with God, or at least
help make us right with Him?

> **Answer:** Because, that the righteousness, which can be approved of before the tribunal of God, must be absolutely perfect, and in all respects conformable to the divine law; and also, that our best works in this life are all imperfect and defiled with sin.

The Federal Vision has stated that it does not believe that the law of God demanded perfect obedience; therefore, it believes that its imperfect obedience is good enough to be accepted by God. All those who are trusting in their imperfect obedience to make them justified before God are going to have a rude awakening on Judgment Day, especially those who have misled flocks to believe this lie.

Question 64 of the Heidelberg Catechism goes on to ask a very important question:

> How can you say that the good we do doesn't earn anything when God promises to reward it in this life and the next?
> **Answer:** The reward is not earned; it is a gift of grace.

Norman Shepherd said, *"We must not discount faith as a condition to be met for the fulfillment of promise. In fact, Genesis 15:6 says that Abraham's faith was so significant that it was credited to him as righteousness! If so, then righteousness was a condition to be met, and faith met that condition. The faith that was credited to Abraham as righteousness was a living and obedient faith."*[45] The fact that Shepherd thinks that his views are compatible with the Heidelberg Catechism is absolutely incredible.

The Canons of Dordt

The Canons of Dordt set forth with its articles a series of paragraphs rejecting various errors. One of these errors is as follows:

> Who teach: That the new covenant of grace, which God the Father through the mediation of the death of Christ, made with man, does not herein consist that we by faith, in as much as it accepts the merits of Christ, are justified before God and saved, but in the fact that God having revoked the demand of perfect obedience of the law, regards faith itself and the obedience of faith, although imperfect, as the perfect obedience of the law, and does esteem it worthy of the reward of eternal

---

[45] Shepherd, *The Call Of Grace*, p. 15.

life through grace. For these contradict the Scriptures: "Being justified freely by his grace through the redemption that is in Christ Jesus: whom God hath set forth to be a propitiation through faith in his blood," And these proclaim, as did the wicked Socinus, a new and strange justification of man before God, against the consensus of the whole church.[46]

The errors that this paragraph sets forth are: 1) a denial of the merits of Christ accepted by faith. The Federal Vision explicitly denies these merits. 2) a belief that God has revoked the perfect demands of the Law. The Federal Vision has explicitly denied that the Law demanded perfect obedience. 3) the belief that faith itself is seen as the "obedience of faith" and that this imperfect obedience of the law is worthy of inheriting eternal life. The Federal Vision champions the idea of "the obedience of faith" as that which does inherit eternal life.

---

[46] *The Canons of Dordt,* Second Head of Doctrine: Of the Death of Christ, and the Redemption of Men Thereby: Rejection of errors, paragraph 4.

Chapter 6

The Federal Vision's Concept of the Church

The Federal Vision has a unique view of the church of the Lord Jesus Christ. This view is at the heart of much of its theology. The Federal Vision argues for an understanding of the objectivity of the covenant. The subtitle to Norman Shepherd's book The Call of Grace is: *"How the Covenant Illuminates Salvation and Evangelism."* As noted in previous chapters, the Federal Vision argues for a particular view of God's covenant that accentuates covenant loyalty to God's commandments as that which constitutes the meaning of "saving faith."

The Federal Vision argues against the historic Reformed designation of the church of the Lord Jesus Christ into visible and invisible aspects. This denial has tremendous implications for other Reformed doctrines. Doug Wilson will argue for the adoption of new terms – the historic and eschatological church.

The Federal Vision will challenge the historic Reformed understanding of such doctrines as "election," "regeneration," "baptism," and "the perseverance of the saints." The Federal Vision's understanding of the church impacts all of these doctrines. Its understanding of the church is a significant departure from the Reformed Faith. I will demonstrate that the Federal Vision's views in each of the foregoing doctrines are not compatible with the historic Reformed Standards. The proponents of the Federal Vision have no right to claim to be within the pale of Reformed Theology. Its doctrinal commitments are more in line with Arminianism and aspects of Roman Catholicism. I will commit a chapter later in this book to the similarities of Federal Vision theology with Roman Catholic dogma.

The fatal flaw of the Federal Vision theology is precisely the fact that it seeks to be innovative. It admits to be a new paradigm. In his paper for the Knox

Theological Seminary Colloquium, Steve Wilkins made these illuminating comments:

> As Steve Schlissel has noted, this entire discussion revolves around a "way of seeing." It involves looking at the Scriptures from a covenant perspective and reading them straightforwardly from that perspective... But I (and the other men on the "Federal Vision" side) are suggesting that the Scriptures speak of the work of salvation in a much more concrete way — not contradictory to these truths as they are set forth in the Westminster Confession and Catechism but seeing these truths as overtones of the teaching of the Scripture. **The Scriptures seem to use the terms "covenant," "elect," and "regeneration," in a different way than the Westminster Confession uses them.**[1] (Emphasis mine)

Such a statement is at the heart of my assertion that these men are wolves in sheep's clothing. They are false shepherds in the truest sense. Wilkins gives lip service to the Westminster Standards. His statement is self-contradictory. On one hand he says that the Federal Vision's views are not contradictory to the Westminster Standards, but he then immediately turns around and says that the Scriptures use key terms differently than how the Westminster Standards use them. Think about this! He just pitted the Scriptures against the Westminster Standards. Wilkins took a vow to uphold the system of doctrine taught in the Westminster Standards, and then has the audacity to claim that the Federal Vision's views are Confessional. This is duplicity. It is a deliberate attempt to advance one's views at the expense of those in Presbyterian and Reformed churches. The Federal Vision wants to maintain the guise of being Reformed so as to influence more people. Their views have not brought clarity. They have brought confusion among people in our churches because of a redefinition of terms. As I have noted in other chapters, these men are completely redefining biblical words from the perspective of their new paradigm. They claim that they believe in justification by faith, but they say that "faith" means obedience to the Law of God. They talk about "election," but they then say that election is dependent upon our perseverance, thereby making it conditional. Confusion is always created when language is manipulated. Steve Wilkins complains that people are misunderstanding the Federal Vision. That is his fault! However, if one examines closely their theology, then it becomes crystal clear. It is not the Reformed Faith, and it is not orthodox Christianity! In the meantime, the average Christian in the pew is led down a false path. The sheep in the pews are fed

---

[1] Colloquium on the Federal Vision, p. 268.

"false food" that will lead to their spiritual starvation. But as the Scriptures state, be not deceived, whatever a man sows that he will also reap (Galatians 6:7). These false shepherds will receive their due punishment for their devious work in corrupting God's blessed truth.

My point is that their new paradigm is nothing new under the sun. It is a hybrid form of Roman Catholicism, outright Arminian in several of its doctrines, and is fundamentally heretical in its teaching on justification. The theology of the Federal Vision is essentially the false teachings that Calvin and Owen had to contend with.

In this chapter I will set forth the Federal Vision's position on the nature of the church as put forth by various proponents of the Federal Vision. I will then analyze these positions using the Reformed Standards and various Reformed theologians.

The Federal Vision and the Objectivity of the Covenant

Steve Wilkins' View of the Objectivity of the Covenant

Wilkins states: *Using the distinction that had grown up over the history of the church and been defined further and refined in the reformation. The distinction of the visible church that is the mixed multitude as we have heard it described, of elect and reprobate, and the invisible church, the elect. They (the Puritans) believed it was their duty to make the visible church conform as closely as possible to the invisible church.*[2]

> The Puritans came to believe that a mere profession of faith in the truth of the gospel and faithfulness of life were not sufficient to secure the purity of the church ... So they felt something more was needed than that and thus they added the requirement to a profession of faith and to a non-scandalous life, the requirement of the necessity to demonstrate that there in fact was the presence of true saving faith in the applicants for admission to membership.[3]
>
> Now this particular view led the Puritans then to embrace a different view of the covenant. What they called the covenant

---

[2] Steve Wilkins, *The Half-Way Covenant,* Lecture given at 2002 Auburn Avenue Pastors' Conference.

[3] Wilkins, *The Half-Way Covenant.*

of grace. The covenant of grace to them existed between God and the elect only, those who have saving faith. The church must be a reflection then of the covenant of grace. It should only consist of the elect and the elect can be identified as the possessors of saving faith. And the church should only, therefore, consist of those who are regenerate and born again.[4]

Now this theology of the covenant of grace became problematic, obviously, it is problematic in and of itself, but it became really problematic when they sought to apply it to their children. The Puritans were paedo-Baptists, of course, they viewed their children as subjects of baptism and believed that baptism admitted them into membership in the church but it didn't admit them into full membership. They were PCA Presbyterians in that sense. They were not allowed to vote, they were not allowed to partake of the Lord's Supper. That awaited their conversion. Now you see this is exactly the pattern that Presbyterians have adopted. That's exactly their position. That is the position of the halfway covenant, brothers. If you are going to accuse somebody of it, accuse yourself. This is the pattern. This is what they believe. You had to have a conversion, and when you did have a conversion, you met with the elders, you made a testimony, the elders admitted you to the Lord's Supper as a result of that. And that's how you got it. You became a full member rather than a half member.[5]

Now here is the problem. It is assumed, it was ignored, it was assumed first of all that the elect go through this common experience of conversion, that's the first thing. The second thing is it was assumed that that was the common experience of covenant children ... And so it was a great problem and the Puritans were sensitive enough to realize we have a dilemma here with our system. We are demanding an experience that they haven't had.[6]

The Puritans wanted to have a pure church and by their theology of conversion, their misunderstanding of the nature of

---

[4] Wilkins, *The Half-Way Covenant,* p. 160.

[5] Wilkins, *The Half-Way Covenant,* p. 163.

[6] Wilkins, *The Half-Way Covenant,* p. 164.

the church and salvation, they ended up undermining the very thing they sought. They ended up out "Phariseeing" the Pharisee.[7]

Now what were the problems here? Well, I hope you can see there were so many problems. Honestly I'm not a good shot, but I could be blindfolded with a rifle stuck between my legs and shoot and hit something. There are many, many problems here. But I only want to focus upon one which I think perhaps is the central one. They completely ignored the significance of baptism and consequently misunderstood the nature of salvation. Baptism was drained of all of its scriptural significance. And the biblical teaching of salvation coming to us by our union with Christ was lost in its true sense. Infant baptism to the New England Puritans and to most of their heirs in modern Protestantism and Presbyterianism is nothing more and was nothing more than a wet dedication service. That's all it was. It did nothing for the child. It did nothing more than bring the child into what they called an ecclesiastical covenant which was merely symbolic and actually accomplished nothing. This was also the view, as you know, and the dominant view in the southern Presbyterian Church in the nineteenth century, which was argued for by our heroes, and I mean that, I love those men, Thornwell and Dabney but they were arguing for this position and basically made baptism nothing more than a dedication.[8]

The Christian Renewal magazine interviewed the Monroe Four regarding the controversial issues taught at the 2002 Auburn Avenue Pastors' Conference. Gerry Wise asked various questions of the four speakers, and here are some of the questions and answers dealing with the covenant and the nature of the church.

> **Question**: Steve Wilkins, in your address you say that the Puritans and Presbyterians believe that baptism brings a child merely into ecclesiastical covenant. What else does it do?
>
> **Steve Wilkins**: Modern Presbyterian theology has made a distinction between external membership and real membership in the covenant. Obviously, by baptism we become

---

[7] Wilkins, *The Half-Way Covenant,* p. 166.

[8] Wilkins, *The Half-Way Covenant,* p. 167.

members of the church, but to be a member of the church is to be a member of the body of Christ and biblically speaking, that means that the baptized are united to Christ.[9]

Question: Can we be in the church but not united to Christ?
Steve Wilkins: That's a distinction the Bible doesn't make. I see what they're trying to preserve, but the distinction is not biblical. The visible, historic church is the body of Christ and thus, to be joined to it by baptism is to be united to Christ. By baptism God offers and gives Christ to us. But this good gift must be received by faith or our baptismal union with Christ will bring judgment not salvation. None of this undermines the sovereignty of God since faith is a gift from God and how we respond to His gifts is ultimately determined by His comprehensive decree.[10]

Wilkins clearly sees that water baptism is the objective reality that demonstrates that we are truly in Christ, experiencing all the blessings of God. He states:

The Bible teaches us that baptism unites us to Christ and by his, and to his body by the power of the Spirit. By one Spirit we were all baptized into one body whether Jews or Greeks, whether slaves of free, we've all been made to drink of one Spirit.[11]

Paul says that at baptism you are clothed with Christ Jesus. For as many of you as are baptized into Christ, have put on Christ. Union with Christ is a real, vital blessed union. The clothes make the man. With our union with Christ, we have all spiritual blessings. Union with Christ is union with the church, his body. We are members of his body, of his flesh and of his bones, Paul says, and then he says and don't you know that from marriage because the two, the Bible says, become one in marriage. And that is exactly the picture, marriage is a picture of the greater covenant that the church has with its divine bridegroom. The Church cannot be divorced from Christ and the blessings of the covenant and it is for this

---

[9] The Monroe Four Speak Out, *Christian Renewal Magazine* (2003).

[10] The Monroe Four Speak Out.

[11] Wilkins, *The Legacy of the Half-way Covenant.*

reason that our confession states that outside the church there is ordinarily no possibility of salvation. Now that's not a Roman Catholic confession I quoted that is the Westminster Confession and they are right, you see.[12]

Steve Wilkins Views in the Knox Seminary Colloquium

As noted elsewhere in this book, Knox Theological Seminary in Fort Lauderdale, Florida sponsored a colloquium on the Federal Vision theology. One of the papers that Steve Wilkins wrote for this was titled, "Covenant, Baptism, and Salvation." I will extensively quote from this article so that the reader will have a clear understanding of his views on the covenant. In his introduction to this paper, Wilkins acknowledges his heavy dependence upon others in the Federal Vision camp. In one of his footnotes, Wilkins states:

> Throughout this paper I am leaning heavily upon a number of contemporary essays as well as older works. In addition to the writings of Calvin, Nevin, Old, and others, I am indebted to the more recent work of Ralph Smith (in his paper published on the Internet titled "Trinity and Covenant: The Christian Worldview", online at http://www. berith.org/essays/tcv/); Jim Jordan's privately published "Thoughts on Sovereign Grace and Election"; and numerous papers by Dr. Peter Leithart, Dr. Joel Garver, Rich Lusk, and other more recent studies.[13]

This comment by Wilkins betrays the comments that he and his church has made over the past three years. Wilkins claims that there is no Federal Vision movement as such and that any criticism leveled must address individuals. As noted earlier, these men quote each other numerous times, invite one another to speak at their churches each year, recommend one another's books and sell them at conferences. Wilkins noted that he heavily relied on others in his paper for the colloquium. They do not depart from one another on any significant issues surrounding the controversy. These constant denials are but subtle ways to evade any kind of concerted effort against their theology.

Wilkins will express when a person becomes a new creation in Christ. It is no different than the rest of his Federal Vision cohorts. He states:

---

[12] Wilkins, *The Legacy of the Half-way Covenant.*

[13] Colloquium on the Federal Vision, p. 254.

In the first Adam we lost everything. Man now stands in need of a "second Adam" in whom all things can be restored. Of course, the Fall cannot be reversed by simply pretending it didn't happen and starting over. The "second Adam" inherits the circumstances of the Fall and must remedy them if mankind is to be restored to communion with God as His image-bearers. This demands that man first be freed from the dominion of sin and reconciled to God.

In order to restore man sin must first be dealt with. The curse of the covenant that hangs over mankind and all creation must be removed if man is to be reconciled to God and restored to His favor. Thus, the job of the second Adam is to undertake redemption by making atonement for sin and through death and resurrection to restore all things. This task was undertaken by the Second Person of the Godhead.

All the blessings and benefits of salvation therefore are found "in Christ." In the first Adam there is only death. In the second Adam there is life and peace. By virtue of union with the Second Adam we have wholeness and restoration–new birth, regeneration, new life. And by virtue of our union with Him who is the true image of God (Colossians 1:15), we are restored to full image-bearing (Romans 8:29). A new humanity is re-created in the Second Adam.

To be reconciled to God is to be restored back into covenant communion with Him. Christ is the only Mediator of the covenant–the one Mediator between God and man (1 Corinthians 2:4). Our covenant relationship with God is in and through Him. In Him we are granted all the promises of God and everything necessary for life and godliness (2 Corinthians 1:19-20).

The Bible teaches us that baptism unites us to Christ and His body by the power of the Holy Spirit (1 Corinthians 12:13). Baptism is an act of God (through His ministers) which signifies and seals our initiation into the Triune communion (we are "baptized into the name of the Father, Son, and Holy Spirit"). At baptism we are clothed with Christ, united to Him and to His Church which is His body (Ephesians 3:26-28). The church, therefore, is not to be divorced from Christ and the blessings of covenant. "We are members of His body, of His flesh and of His bones," Paul says (Ephesians 5:30). It is for this reason that the Westminster Confession states that outside the church there is no ordinary possibility of salvation (WCF 25.2). This is true simply because there is no salvation outside of Christ.

All that man must have is found in Him. He is the elect One of God, the chosen servant to accomplish for His people what they could not accomplish on their own. He is the well-beloved of the Father in whom we find acceptance in God's sight. He is the faithful and righteous One, in whose righteousness we are able to stand in God's presence. He was baptized and lived His life faithfully according to that baptism, keeping covenant as the second Adam, doing all that the first Adam failed to do, walking by faith in obedience in the power of the Spirit. Moreover, He did what the first Adam could not have done, taking our curse upon Himself, dying in our place, paying the penalty for our sins.

He is the justified One. At His resurrection He was vindicated by the Father, publicly declared to be the righteous One. We might say that by His resurrection He was the first One to be born again, born from above by the power of the Spirit as He died to sin and was raised in newness of life. In being delivered from death, He not only purchased salvation and secured it for His people, but we may also say that in one sense, He as our substitute, was the first to receive salvation in all its fullness. He receives it in the middle of history and thus becomes the surety that we too shall be made recipients of this salvation at the end of history.

By virtue of our union with Him, we are made recipients of all that is His. This is how we receive the grace of God. We often think of grace exclusively as the "unmerited favor" of God toward sinners. But the term refers to "favor, pleasure, or goodwill." Grace is not a thing or a substance, but the favor of God. Christ, in this sense was the object of God's grace–not that He had any sin which had to be forgiven, but in that He was the peculiar object of God's favor and good pleasure. He is the One who is "well-pleasing" to God and, thus, all God's favor or grace is found only in Him. We receive the grace of God "in Him." We are accepted in the Beloved (Ephesians 1:5-6). To be saved by grace then requires that we be united to Christ (Ephesians 2:5-6). Thus, Christians are called to persevere in the grace of God (Acts 13:43)–i.e., never forsake the Lord Jesus in Whom alone we may find grace and favor.

Salvation is relational. It is found only in covenant union with Christ. As we abide in Him, all that is true of Him is true of us. It has been the common practice in Reformed circles to use the term "elect" to refer only to those who are predestined to eternal salvation. Since God has ordained all things "whatsoever comes to pass" (Ephesians 1:11), He has certainly predestined the number of all who will be saved at the last day. This number is fixed and settled, not one of these will be lost. The Lord will accomplish all His holy will. But the term "elect" (or "chosen") as it is used in the Scriptures most often refers to those in covenant union with Christ who is the elect One.

In the Old Testament, Israel is called God's elect or chosen people (Deuteronomy 7:6; Psalm. 135:4; Isaiah 45:4). Consequently, Paul and the other apostles refer to the members of the Church, the "new Israel," as the "elect" as well (Colossians 3:12; 1 Peter 1:1-2; 2:9; 5:13; 2 John 1, 13).

Election was not something hidden or unknown to the apostles or the prophets but something that could be rightly attributed to all who were in covenant. Paul even addresses the Ephesians in startling language (Ephesians 1:3-5) saying that they were chosen in Christ "before the foundation of the world." We have to remind ourselves that he was not giving a theological lecture but stating what was objectively true of all those in the church in Ephesus. Being united to the Elect One, all who are baptized may be truthfully addressed as the "elect of God." Thus, if you were to ask Paul, "Do you know who the elect are?" he might have replied, "Of course! The elect are all who are in Christ!"

This is not to say that election is only "general" or "corporate" and not individual as Arminians like to say. It is both. No Israelite had the right to say, "God chose the nation, the class as a whole, but he didn't choose me." God chose each Israelite to belong to the nation. They couldn't take His promise to Israel as if it referred only to the nation as a whole but not to the particular individuals who made up the nation. Each Israelite was grafted by God into the body of His people as an act of His sovereign, electing love. Obviously, the promises were given to Israel as a whole, but that meant that every individual Israelite could say, "This belongs to me."

We see similar language in 2 Thessalonians 2:13-14 ("But we are bound to give thanks to God always for you, brethren beloved by the Lord, because God from the beginning chose you for salvation through sanctification by the Spirit and belief in the truth, to which He called you by our gospel, for the obtaining of the glory of our Lord Jesus Christ."). How could Paul say this? If someone insists that Paul was given special insight into whom God had chosen, then we must respond with John Barach, "we suddenly discover that we cannot learn from the apostle Paul, who told us to imitate him, how to talk to our churches."

The elect are those who are faithful in Christ Jesus. If they later reject the Savior, they are no longer elect–they are cut off from the Elect One and thus, lose their elect standing. But their falling away doesn't negate the reality of their standing prior to their apostasy. They were really and truly the elect of God because of their relationship with Christ.

Being "in Christ" is the key to understanding covenant … In fact, covenant is a real relationship, consisting of real communion with the triune God through union with Christ. The covenant is not some thing that exists apart from Christ or in addition to Him (another means of grace)–rather, the covenant is union with Christ. Thus, being in covenant gives all the blessings of being united to Christ. There is no salvation apart from covenant simply because there is no salvation apart from union with Christ. And without union with Christ there is no covenant at all. Because being in covenant with God means being in Christ, those who are in covenant have all spiritual blessings in the heavenly places. Union with Christ means that all that is true of Christ is true of us.

This seems clear by how the apostles address the churches.[14]

Wilkins discusses what it means to be "born again" through the gospel. He links it to being "in Christ." He links all of this to water baptism. He refers to Paul's addresses in I Corinthians:

> Through Paul's ministry, they have been "born" through the gospel (4:15 "in Christ Jesus I have begotten you [*gennao*] through the gospel."). Christ has been sacrificed for them (5:7). They have been washed (or baptized) which has brought about sanctification and justification in the name of Christ, by the Spirit of God (6:9-11).[15]

Regarding this last paragraph, Wilkins makes a comment in a footnote saying:

> Peter also speaks this way in his first epistle (1:22, 23-25). He uses the word "anagennao," which means "give new birth or life to." Peter speaks in the second person plural throughout without any qualifiers. All of the members of the Church have been "born again" by means of the word preached to them. Again, what is striking is that both Paul and Peter say this to the visible Church (even though they could not see the hearts of their hearers). Some commentators read I Corinthians 6:11 in this way: "But you received a justifying and sanctifying washing in the name of the Lord Jesus Christ and by the Spirit of our God." The grammar of the text may suggest the Spirit instrumentally confers justification and sanctification through the washing.

> They will, therefore, be raised up just as God raised up the Lord Jesus (6:14). The Holy Spirit is in the body and, therefore, they must remember that they are not their own; they have been bought with a price (6:19-20). The Corinthians are the "children" of the Fathers of Israel who were also "redeemed" out of Egypt, baptized in the Red Sea, and granted fellowship with God and communion with Christ—yet, God was not well-pleased with them; thus, they must not imitate them (10:1-5). These things were written to teach us not to do what Israel did in breaking covenant: lusting after evil

---

[14] Colloquium on the Federal Vision, pp. 259-262.

[15] Colloquium on the Federal Vision, p. 262.

things, becoming idolaters, committing sexual immorality, tempting Christ, murmuring against God (10:6-11). They have communion with the body and blood of Christ and are thus one body with Him (10:15-17). They have all been baptized into one body by the Spirit (whether Jews or Greeks) (12:13). He emphasizes that they are body of Christ and individually members of it (12:27). Paul emphasizes that Christ died for "our" sins (including those of his hearers; 15:3).

Paul declares these things to be true of the members of the Church in Corinth in spite of the fact that he knew of their sins. He was not able to speak like this because he had some special insight into the secret decrees of God. He was speaking about what was true of these objectively by virtue of their union with Christ in covenant. All this was true of each of the members, but, like Israel, they were required to persevere in faith. If they departed from Christ, they would perish like Israel of old. All their privileges and blessings would become like so many anchors to sink them into the lake of fire. This is his point in chapter 10. Note, however, Paul's method: he declares what is objectively true of them by virtue of their covenant union with Christ and then calls upon them to be faithful because of this union. "How can you who are members of Christ do these things?" (1 Corinthians 6:15-17).

The apostles did not view the covenant as a place of potential blessing or a place of fantastic opportunity–they viewed it as salvation, because it means fellowship and communion with the triune God. It is union with Christ in His obedient life, sacrificial, substitutionary death, triumphant resurrection, and glorious ascension and session at the right hand of the Father.

All in covenant are given all that is true of Christ. If they persevere in faith to the end, they enjoy these mercies eternally. If they fall away in unbelief, they lose these blessings and receive a greater condemnation than Sodom and Gomorrah. Covenant can be broken by unbelief and rebellion, but until it is, those in covenant with God belong to Him and are His. If they do not persevere, they lose the blessings that were given to them (and all of

this works out according to God's eternal decree which
He ordained before the foundation of the world).[16]

Steve Wilkins will advance the same view of apostasy as all the other proponents of the Federal Vision. As we will see, Wilkins believes that all these magnificent promises associated with the Christian life can all be lost if we do not
persevere in the faith. This is not a hypothetical apostasy, for there are some
who do apostatize and lose everything. His comments are as follows:

> Thus, when one breaks covenant, it can be truly said that he
> has turned away from grace and forfeited life, forgiveness,
> and salvation. For this reason the Scripture describe apostates
> as those who: "possessed the Kingdom" (Matthew 21:42-
> 45); received God's gifts (Matthew 25:14ff, the parable of
> the talents); received the word with joy (Matthew 13:20) and
> believe for a while (Luke 8:13); bore fruit (though not to
> maturity, Luke 8:14); had union with Christ as branches in a
> vine (John 15); had real communion with Christ (1
> Corinthians 10:4-5); had the Spirit's work within them
> (being "enlightened, tasted of the heavenly gift, made
> partakers of the Holy Spirit, tasted the Word and the powers
> of the world to come," Hebrews 6:4ff); received the knowl-
> edge of the truth (Hebrews 10:26 26); — had been sanctified
> by the blood of Christ (Hebrews 10:29); had been made
> members of the heavenly city, sprinkled by the blood of Jesus
> (Hebrews 12:22ff); had been cleansed from former sins (2
> Peter 1:9); were bought by the Lord (2 Peter 2:1); escaped
> the pollutions of the world (2 Peter 2:20); knew the way of
> righteousness (2 Peter 2:21); and had "the adoption, the
> glory, the covenants, the giving of the law, the service of God,
> and the promises" (Romans 9:4).

> The apostate fails to persevere in the grace of God and, thus,
> has his name removed from the book of life (Revelation 3:5:
> "He who overcomes shall be clothed in white garments, and
> I will not blot out his name from the Book of Life; but I will
> confess his name before My Father and before His angels.").
> The book of life is the book of the covenant (see also Exodus
> 32:31-33; Revelation 13:8; 17:8; 20:12, 15; 21:27). Those

---

[16] Colloquium on the Federal Vision, p. 263.

who "take away from the words of the book" will in turn be "taken away" from the Book of Life (Revelation 22:19).

This is not a hypothetical impossibility but a very real possibility for those who are in covenant with Christ and members of His Church. We must not view these and similar warnings as mere devices which are placed in the Scriptures in order to frighten the elect into heaven. The clear implication of these passages is that those who ultimately prove to be reprobate may be in covenant with God. They may enjoy for a season the blessings of the covenant, including the forgiveness of sins, adoption, possession of the kingdom, sanctification, etc., and yet apostatize and fall short of the grace of God.

The apostate, thus, forsakes the grace of God that was given to him by virtue of his union with Christ. It is not accurate to say that they only "appeared" to have these things but did not actually have them–if that were so, there would be nothing to "forsake" and apostasy is bled of its horror and severity. That which makes apostasy so horrendous is that these blessings actually belonged to the apostates–though they only had them temporarily they had them no less truly. The apostate doesn't forfeit "apparent blessings" that were never his in reality, but real blessings that were his in covenant with God.

This seems to be the point of John 15:1-8. Jesus here declares that He is the vine and His hearers are branches united to Him. He then exhorts them to continue abiding in Him so that they might bear fruit. If they refuse to abide in Him, they will be fruitless and incur the wrath of the Divine husbandman and, finally, will be cast into the fire. Here then we have those who are joined to Christ in a vital union (i.e. a union that could and should be fruitful) and yet who end up cursed and condemned.

Often this passage is interpreted along these lines: There are two kinds of branches. Some branches are not really in Christ "in a saving way," but only in an external sense–whatever fruit they bear is not genuine and they will eventually be destroyed. Other branches are truly joined to Christ inwardly and savingly, and they bear more and more fruit as they are pruned and cultivated by the Father." As Norman Shepherd has noted, "If this distinction is in the text, it is difficult to see what the point of the warning is. The outward ("external") branches cannot profit from it, because they cannot in any case bear genuine fruit. They are not related to Christ inwardly and draw no life from him. The inward branches do not need the warning, because they are vitalized by Christ and therefore cannot help but bear good fruit. Cultivation by the Father, with its attendant blessing, is guaranteed."

The Calvinist embraces this implausible interpretation because he (understandably) does not want to deny election, effectual calling, or the perseverance of the saints. The exegetical problems one must embrace with this position, however, are nearly insurmountable. If the branches are not truly joined to the vine, how can they be held accountable for their lack of fruit? The distinction of "external" and "internal" union seems to be invented and is not in the text. All the branches are truly and vitally joined to the vine. All can and should be fruitful. The pressure to preserve the Scriptural teaching of God's sovereignty in salvation ought not be allowed to push us to deny these obvious points. But in order to resist this pressure the text must be interpreted as it is intended to be interpreted–i.e., covenantally.

The picture of the vine and branches was a common way in which God referred to His covenant people Israel in the Old Testament (Psalm 80:8-16; Isaiah 5:1-7; Jeremiah 2:21). The Jews were used to thinking of themselves as the vineyard of Jehovah. "The vine" was a figure of God's chosen people. Here in John 15 Jesus says that "He is the real vine." He identifies Himself with His people. He is their covenant head. He is their life. He is not only their Creator but their Redeemer. They are His body, united to Him by God's gracious inclusion of them in covenant.

Covenant, therefore, is a gracious relationship, not a potentially gracious relationship. To be in covenant is to have the treasures of God's mercy and grace and the love which He has for His own Son given to you. But the covenant is not unconditional. It requires persevering faithfulness.[17]

---

[17] Colloquium on the Federal Vision, pp. 263-266.

The works salvation paradigm that all the other Federal Vision adherents promote is also promoted by Wilkins. With Shepherd and Schlissel particularly, Wilkins repudiates the biblical and Reformed doctrine of justification by faith alone in Christ. It is evident that we must learn to be faithful like Jesus was in order to be saved. Here are his comments:

> The covenant is dependent upon persevering faith. This is illustrated most clearly by Jesus acting as the Second Adam. Jesus came into the world with the same responsibility as Adam (He was to live as a man as He has always lived as the Second Person of the Trinity–i.e., denying Himself and seeking to glorify His Father). He was to walk by faith, entrusting Himself to the Father, believing His Word, and obeying. As with the first Adam, Satan tempted Him to doubt God's trustworthiness, seeking to get Jesus to satisfy His own desires and grasp at glory apart from the will of His Father. But Jesus continued to trust and remained faithful throughout His life, learning "obedience by the things which He suffered" (Hebrews 5:7-9). Even in death, He continued to entrust Himself to His Father (Luke 23:46). Through His sufferings He became mature, growing in wisdom, showing forth the image of the Godhead. And because He was faithful, He became the author of eternal salvation.

> His whole earthly life is the very embodiment of trust in God (Heb. 2:13–"And again: 'I will put My trust in Him.' And again: 'Here am I and the children whom God has given Me.'"). It is marked from start to finish by total dependence on the Father and complete attunement to his will (10:7,10). His faith expresses itself, necessarily, in prayer (5:7; John 17; Mk. 1:35, etc.), and is completely victorious as, surmounting all temptations and afflictions, he is made perfect through suffering (Heb. 2:10; 4:15), thus becoming "the source of eternal salvation to all who obey him" (5:8f.). In looking to Jesus, then, we are looking to him who is the supreme exponent of faith, the one who, beyond all others, not only set out on the course of faith but also pursued it without wavering to the end. He, accordingly, is uniquely qualified to be the supplier and sustainer of the faith of His followers.

> Covenant life is always founded upon persevering faith in the faithful One. If we are to abide in union with Him, we, by the

grace and power of the Spirit, must be faithful. Thus the elect
are marked by abiding in the Word of Christ (John 8:31-32).
Those who turn away and refuse to "hold fast to the word"
break covenant with Christ and are referred to by Paul as having "believed in vain" (1 Corinthians 15:1-2). The blessings
purchased by Christ are enjoyed only by those who "continue
in the faith" (Colossians 1:21-23).

We must embrace this straightforward covenantal framework
and allow it to direct our understanding of God's work of salvation as it unfolds in time. We cannot judge men based upon
the secret decrees of God or the hidden operations of the
Spirit. The secret things belong to God (Deuteronomy
29:29). We are to be concerned with those things that are
revealed. The questions of when a man is "regenerated," or
given "saving faith," or "truly converted," are ultimately
questions we cannot answer and, therefore, they cannot be
the basis upon which we define the Church or identify God's
people.

What we do know is whether or not a man is in covenant with
God. If he is not in covenant, he must repent of his sins and
believe in Christ Jesus, be joined to the people of God by
baptism, and persevere in faithfulness all his days (by the
power of the Holy Spirit who works in him "to will and do"
for God's good pleasure). If he has been baptized, he is in
covenant with God and is obligated to walk in faithfulness,
loving the Lord with all his heart, soul, mind, and strength. If
he is unfaithful, he is to be called to repentance. If he refuses
to repent, he is to be cut off from the body of Christ and delivered over to Satan with the prayer that he be taught not to
blaspheme.[18]

Steve Wilkins "reveals his hand" when he makes the following comments
about the meanings of "covenant," "election," and "regeneration." Wilkins
knows that the Federal Vision's theology on these points is out of accord with
the Westminster Standards, but he and the others of the Federal Vision movement think they are wiser than the Westminster delegates. Wilkins states:

As Steve Schlissel has noted, this entire discussion revolves

---

[18] Colloquium on the Federal Vision, pp. 266-267.

around a "way of seeing." It involves looking at the Scriptures from a covenant perspective and reading them straightforwardly from that perspective. The Westminster Confession of Faith deals with the work of salvation from the perspective of seeing what God does for those whom He has predestined to persevere in faith to the end. From this perspective we are able to speak about an infallible "effectual calling" (God giving faith and repentance) and His justifying, adopting, sanctifying and glorifying all those whom He has predestined unto life so that none of them fall away.

But I (and the other men on the "Federal Vision" side) are suggesting that the Scriptures speak of the work of salvation in a much more concrete way — not contradictory to these truths as they are set forth in the Westminster Confession and Catechism but seeing these truths as overtones of the teaching of the Scripture.

The Scriptures seem to use the terms "covenant," "elect," and "regeneration," in a different way than the Westminster Confession uses them. Thus, in the Scriptures, the Covenant is a structured relationship of love with the Triune God in which man participates in Christ Jesus. The elect are all those who are presently "in Christ" (as members of His body, the Church). Regeneration is the act of the Spirit of God whereby one is transferred from being united to the old Adam to union with the new (or second) Adam.

Biblically, to be in covenant is to be embraced within the circle of the eternal communion of the Trinity. We can only be accepted and welcomed into this divine fellowship by being united to Christ. Christ is the elect One, chosen and beloved by the Father, and to be united to Him is to be among the number of the elect. Thus, Christ, the whole Christ, Head and Body, constitutes the elect.

In Christ we are made recipients of the grace (favor) of God (we are renewed in covenant fellowship with Him). Thus, the Scriptures view salvation relationally. It is a matter of being in union with Christ. All who are in Christ are called upon to persevere in the grace of God (Acts 13:43; 11:23; 14:22) and endure in faith to the end (Matthew 10:22; 24:13; Mark

13:13), knowing that the blessings of life come only to those who "overcome" (Revelation 2:7, 11, 17, 26; 3:5, 12, 21; 21:7).[19]

Position of Auburn Avenue Presbyterian Church

On September 26, 2002 the session of Auburn Avenue Presbyterian Church, the church that Steve Wilkins pastors, passed a summary of its views on the covenant, baptism, and salvation. Since the elders of the church passed it, it stands as an official position held by this church. The summary statement is not a retraction of the views propagated at the conference in 2002, but it is actually a bold reaffirmation of those views. On April 3, 2005 the session of Auburn Avenue Presbyterian Church issued a revised statement of its 2002 position. It has a few modifications. Hence, not only do the Monroe Four stand in opposition to the Reformed faith, but a church now has denied the constitution that it swore to uphold, namely the Westminster Standards. Here are portions of what the session stated:

> God works out His eternal decree of salvation in history by means of His covenant. Salvation, therefore, may be viewed from two basic perspectives, the decretal/eternal and the covenantal/historical. The Bible ordinarily (though not always) views election through the lens of the covenant. This is why covenant members are addressed consistently as God's elect, even though some of those covenant members may apostatize, proving themselves in the end not to have been among the number of those whom God decreed to eternal salvation from before the foundation of the world. Thus, the basis for calling them God's "elect" was their standing as members of the Church (which is the body of Christ) and not some knowledge of God's secret decree. The visible Church is the place where the saints are "gathered and perfected" by means of "the ministry, oracles, and ordinances of God" (WCF 25.3).

> This covenant is made with believers and their children (Acts 2:39; WLC Q. 166). It is publicly manifested in the Church, the body of Christ to which we are solemnly admitted by means of baptism (WCF 28.1). The Church is not merely a human community, and the Church's enactments of the

---

[19] Colloquium on the Federal Vision, pp. 268-269.

means of grace are not merely human works. God works through the administration of the sacraments by the power of His Spirit and His word of promise (WCF 27.3). The Church herself is God's new creation, the city He promised to build for Abraham. The Church is not merely a means to salvation, a stepping-stone to a more ultimate goal. Rather, the Church herself is the historic manifestation of God's salvation (WCF 25.1-2), the partially-realized goal in history that will be brought to final fulfillment at the last day. When someone is united to the Church by baptism, he is incorporated into Christ and into His body; he becomes bone of Christ's bone and flesh of His flesh (Eph. 5:30). He becomes a member of "the house, family, and kingdom of God" (WCF 25.2). Until and unless that person breaks covenant, he is to be reckoned among God's elect and regenerate saints.

By baptism, one enters into covenantal union with Christ and is offered all his benefits (Gal. 3:27; Rom. 6:1ff; 2 Cor. 1:20). As Westminster Shorter Catechism #94 states, baptism signifies and seals "our ingrafting into Christ, and partaking of the benefits of the covenant of grace." Baptism in itself does not, however, guarantee final salvation. What is offered in baptism may not be received because of unbelief. Or, it may only be embraced for a season and later rejected (Matt. 13:20-22; Luke 8:13-14). Those who "believe for a while" enjoy blessings and privileges of the covenant only for a time and only in part, since their temporary faith is not true to Christ, as evidenced by its eventual failure and lack of fruit (1 Cor. 10:1ff; Hebrews 6:4-6). By their unbelief they "trample underfoot the Son of God, count the blood of the covenant by which they were sanctified an unholy thing, and do despite to the Spirit of grace" (Heb. 10:29) and thus bring greater condemnation upon themselves.

Salvation depends upon being united to Christ. Clearly, those who are eternally saved are those who continue to abide in Him by the grace of God. There are those, however, who are joined to Him as branches in the vine, but who because of unbelief are barren and fruitless and consequently are cut off from the vine and from salvation. Jesus says these "believe for a while" but do not bear fruit unto salvation. Why God would do this is a mystery, but the teaching of Scripture is clear: some whom He adopts into covenant relation, He later hardens (Rom. 9:4, 18, 11:1ff). In such instances God has not changed His decree regarding such people; to the contrary, He carries out His sovereign purposes in and through their unbelief and rebellion. Those elect unto eternal salvation are always distinguished by their perseverance in faith and obedience by the grace of God.

Once baptized, an individual may be truly called a "Christian" because he is a member of the household of faith and the body of Christ (I Cor. 12). However, not all who are "Christians" in this sense will persevere to the end. Some will "fall from grace" and be lost (Gal. 5:4; 1 Cor. 10:1-5). Though the difference between those who are predestined to eternal life and those who "believe for a while" is not merely one of duration (i.e., God works "effectually" in those whom He has predestined to eternal life so that they do not fall away in unbelief), the Bible does not explain the distinction between the nature of the work of the Spirit in the reprobate and the nature of His work in the elect, and even uses the same language for both.

None of those elect unto final salvation can lose that salvation, however much he may backslide (John 10; WCF 17). God preserves all those whom He has chosen to eternal salvation in covenant faithfulness. The Biblical language regarding salvation, however, is more complicated. Sometimes the term "salvation" is used in an eschatological sense with reference to its ultimate goal of eternal life. In that eschatological and final sense, of course, it would be most improper to speak of anyone "losing their salvation." All whom God has ordained to eternal life will surely be saved. But there is also another sense in which all those in the covenant are "saved." They have been delivered out of the world and brought into the glorious new creation of Christ (thus, the Scripture speaks of those who had "known the way of righteousness," "been cleansed from their former sins," "have tasted of the heavenly gift," etc.), but not all will persevere in that "salvation." Jesus spoke of those in the new covenant who were united to Him, but then cut off because they did not persevere in the fruit-bearing that is the evidence of a lively faith, by which we abide in Christ (John 15).

Whatever the precise complexion and content of that union for those who do not persevere, nonetheless, if Jesus Himself is salvation, must we not conclude that being cut off from Him means being cut off the from source of salvation and, in that specific sense, from salvation itself?

All covenant members are invited to attain to a full and robust confidence that they are God's eternally elect ones. Starting with their baptisms, they have every reason to believe God loves them and desires their eternal salvation. Baptism marks them out as God's elect people, a status they maintain so long as they persevere in faithfulness. By looking to Christ alone, the preeminently elect One, the One who kept covenant to the end and is the Author and Finisher of the faith of God's people, they may find infallible assurance (WCF 18.1-2). Those who take their eyes off Christ in unbelief, who desert the Church where His presence is found, will find that their false hopes and carnal presumptions have perished (WCF 18.1), having made a shipwreck of their faith and proven themselves to have received the grace of God in vain.[20]

Doug Wilson's View of the Objectivity of the Covenant

Regarding the issue of the objectivity of the covenant, Doug Wilson taught many unique ideas and explicitly denied the distinction that the Westminster Standards make concerning the visible and invisible church.

At the 2002 Auburn Avenue Pastors' Conference, Wilson made the following comments:

What is a Christian? After two thousand years, you would think that is something we had down. The church is the pillar and the ground of the truth. God has entrusted the truth to the church and yet for various reasons, we've gotten one of the fundamental questions all messed up all gummed up.

Who is a Christian, what is a Christian, is an objective question. You can photograph a Christian. A Christian in the New Testament is someone who is over there with those people

---

[20] Summary Statement of the Auburn Avenue Presbyterian Church's Position on Covenant, Baptism, and Salvation, passed by the session on September 26, 2002.

and he is associated with them because he is baptized in the triune name.

For 350 years in this country, we have been getting some of the fundamental issues with regard to the word of God, and the covenant, and the gospel, and what is a Christian, we have been getting them wrong.

We are accustomed in reformed circles to talk about the invisible and the visible church, but this is strange. Now I think there is a sense in which it is quite true, provided you qualify it in all the ways that we have not qualified it, and of course, if you ascribe to the Westminster Confession of Faith if you are a PCA minister or OPC minister, this is a confessional issue because the Confession talks about the visible, the distinction between the visible and the invisible church. And I believe it is a valuable distinction provided that it is qualified in the way we generally overwhelmingly do not qualify it.

When we said invisible church, people would stop us and say, what do you mean by that and then we would have to explain it. We are in the opposite situation, we have qualified visible and invisible so long that we have created a situation where people have assumed the wrong thing about it and that is what I want to get to this evening.

Now they knew that they had, they knew that there was such a thing as a false son, someone who was on good terms with the visible church and yet did not know God. And so they made this distinction between the visible and the invisible church. Now the question is why is it invisible and this is where the Hellenism that our brother Steve was speaking of has crept in and I think has really wrecked havoc with us on this point. When we say visible and invisible, we divide into categories, visible is down here and invisible is an ethereal church in the heavenlies. We create an ontological division between visible down here and invisible in heaven. Now in a visible sense, I have no problem with heaven and earth, but the Hellenistic problem is not heaven and earth because in Christ heaven and earth are united. But in the Greek mindset, the spiritual realm and the earthly realm were divided and the Hellenistic mind thought of the material world as inherently corrupt and irredeemable which is why the incarnation and the crucifixion gave them such difficulty. Well we say there is a invisible church up here and a visible church down here. If we are thinking like Platonists, if we are thinking like Hellenists, what we say is we have a invisible church composed of all the elect and then the visible church down here.

But we also know from our Bibles that there is only one church, one Lord, one faith, one baptism. But we've got two churches with two different rosters of names. All right the names of the elect and the names of all the church membership rolls stack up. And we say, well the names don't add up. The names down here don't match the names up there. There is significant overlap depending on the church, depending on the situation, but it is a different list of names. Now if you've got two churches existing at the same time with different names on their membership rolls, the question that comes up and it may not come up consciously, but the question that comes up is, "which one is the real church?" Which one is the true church? Our many decades, our centuries of American individualism have taught us to answer that question emphatically that the invisible church is the real church.

What we need to do is, I would like to submit two other terms for us to use to make the same distinction that is made by visible and invisible that doesn't create the same problem and doesn't create the temptation to go a Hellenistic route. And ... That is the historical church and the eschatological church. The historical church and the eschatological church. If we abandon the Hellenistic ontological division between invisible and visible and adopted a more Hebraic biblical way of thinking and toppled the whole thing on its side, the invisible church is the eschatological church and the visible church is the historical church. Now notice what this does, if I topple the whole thing on its side and it is now in history, the eschatological church is now the historical church and it is at the culmination of history, all right, and the visible church is that same church at an earlier point in time.

History is important, so we should think of the full number of the elect instead of the elect filling up this category in hyperspace, we should think of the full number of the elect as com-

posing the eschatological church, the church as it will visibly
be on the last glorious day of history. The eschatological
church is as visible as the church today. All right, it is not visible to us now because it is tomorrow. But that is the same
reason why the literal tomorrow is not visible to us. In other
words the eschatological church is visible in principal, it is
historically grounded. The resurrection of the dead will happen in history.

So rather than thinking of a visible church, we should think
of the historical church. Instead of thinking of an invisible
church, we should think of the eschatological church. And I
think a moments reflection will show that I'm giving away
nothing in terms of the confessional category. There are the
elect who will be there at the last day, glory to God. There
will be covenant members who fall away before that time.
But this is very important. Before they fall away, they are in
the church. Before they fall away, they are on the tree. Before
God's action cut Caiaphas out of the olive tree, Caiaphas was
in the olive tree and a wicked man. The sap flowed through
his branch, but he didn't bear fruit. But he was in the olive
tree.

This distinction between historical and eschatological church
helps us to understand the relationship of unconverted professing Christians to the church as well. And this is something that every pastor knows, the Apostle Paul speaks in
Romans 2, he says, a true Jew is one who is one inwardly, not
if you go through the motions, that doesn't mean that you are
converted to God, that doesn't mean you are submissive to
God, that doesn't mean that your heart's changed. And we
say, yes exactly, that person is not really a Christian. Well, no,
that's not what we do that's not the direction we must go. We
say he's truly a covenant member, he's genuinely a covenant
member, he really belongs.

And so what we do, we need to grab the Christian world by
its baptism. Now remember this returns to the earlier point
that I made that the word Christian is defined biblically in the
New Testament sense in an objective way.

So what is the true church? The true church is the church in history. The true church is the church on the corner. The church that you are connected with, the church as it exists in all its fragmented forms in your town that is the local expression of the bride of Christ.[21]

John Barach's View of the Objectivity of the Covenant

John Barach was a replacement speaker for Norman Shepherd at the 2002 Auburn Avenue Pastors' Conference. He also participated in the Knox Seminary Colloquium on the Federal Vision in August 2003. In January 2003, he became the pastor of Covenant Reformed Church in Grande Praire, Alberta, Canada, which is part of the United Reformed Churches in North America (URCNA).

Regarding the objectivity of the covenant, Barach has made the following comments as to who is in the covenant:

> Already now we have the beginnings of glorification because we have the spirit of the glorified Jesus. But who shares in those blessings? All those blessings are found in Christ, but who is in Christ? The answer that the Bible gives is that those people are in Christ who have been baptized into Christ. As in the old covenant, so in the new covenant, there is an objective covenant made with believers and their children. **Every baptized person is in covenant with God and is in union then with Christ and with the triune God.** (Emphasis mine)
>
> **The Bible doesn't know about a distinction between being internally in the covenant, really in the covenant, and being only externally in the covenant, just being in the sphere of the covenant.** The Bible speaks about reality, the efficacy of baptism. Every baptized person is truly a member of God's covenant. As it was in the old covenant, so it is in the new covenant. As it was with all the Adamic covenant, so it is now that those covenants have been fulfilled in Christ, **every baptized person is in Christ and therefore shares in his new life, shares in the new summons to life**

---

[21] Doug Wilson, *Visible and Invisible Church Revisited,* tape 2, 2002 Auburn Avenue Pastors' Conference. RPCUS transcription of the 2002 AAPC, p. 18-34.

and still receives, not only the covenant promises, but also the covenants demands and the covenant warning. (Emphasis mine)

But we need to be able to tell our congregations, we need to tell them and tell individual members, Jesus died for you, Jesus died for the elect, Jesus died for Christians. **We need to be able to say, "Jesus died for you personally and we mean it, to them, head for head, everyone of them." How do we know that? Because they are in covenant with God and we view them as brothers and sisters because that's who they really are.** (Emphasis mine)

But we look around the congregation and we see other people in the congregation, we do not give them a judgment of charity that says, well I don't know. Maybe he is a Christian, maybe he isn't, so I will be charitable, I will regard him as a Christian, I will treat him as a Christian, but I've got my doubts. Instead we go by God's promise. He has said that this person is in Christ and, therefore, believing God's promise, we treat that person as who he really is, someone who is in Christ.[22]

In his lecture on covenant and election, John Barach sets forth the relationship of the two. His view of the nature of the church is enlightening. Barach states:

How is election related to the covenant? It seems as if there are two possibilities, either God makes the covenant with the elect only or God makes the covenant with elect and non-elect people. A lot of reformed people opt for the former, God makes the covenant with the elect only. That has results, there are people who view the congregation as a mixed multitude which is actually an abuse of that term drawn from scripture, the mixed multitude in scripture were believers. But they regard the congregation as a mixed multitude. Some are in covenant with God, some aren't.

This afternoon I would like to argue for a third position. It is a modification of that second position I have outlined, the covenant is with believers and their children. But it is not

---

[22] John Barach, *Covenant and History,* tape 3, 2002 Auburn Avenue Pastors' Conference. The RPCUS transcription of the 2002 AAPC, p.46-47

exactly the same as that last view ... I would like to begin with something, perhaps we can call it, it has often been termed, as covenantal election, corporate election.

What about an individual Israelite? How should an individual Israelite standing there in Moab about to cross the Jordan, how should he have heard Moses' sermon here in Deut. 7 when Moses says, the Lord your God has chosen you, (plural), to be a people for his own possession ... As a part of the chosen people, he is in relationship to God, a relationship which is not grounded in anything in himself but solely on God's love. The Israelite standing there they should have taken this corporate election about which Moses speaks and he should have personalized it.

What does it mean though to be a church member? What does it mean to be one of God's covenant people? It means that you have been brought into relationship with God, you are in fellowship with the triune God, brought into his family life to share with Him in his love. God has brought you into the people on whom he has set his love, and therefore you personally are the object of God's love. You are among the people He has saved, the people he has "exodused," and the people He has committed to saving.

And so too as Christians we are united to Christ and we share in his story. We share in his death, in his resurrection, his ascension, all of that history which is our salvation. God has demonstrated his love and his faithfulness to us as part of his covenant people and we need as a member of the community, each one of us needs to personalize the corporate identity ... God has saved for himself a people and I am one of them and I apply that then to myself. God has chosen us and I am one of them and I apply that promise then to myself. I belong to his chosen people.

What kind of election is that, that he talks about when he says he chose us in Him before the foundation of the world? **People say well this covenant election that Israel enjoyed, that certainly didn't mean that everybody in Israel was going to be saved automatically. By the way, watch that word, automatically, that is a bit of a weasel word.** People use that in odd ways. But they will say, well look, covenant election, that doesn't guarantee that you are going to heaven no matter what. Covenant people fall away. And so they say what Paul was talking about here is the election of individuals to eternal life, special election, Paul says, you are going to be holy, you are going to be blameless. And this is not the same kind of election that Moses was talking about when he said God chose you. (Emphasis mine)

But then who is in Christ? Those who have been incorporated into Christ, brought into Christ, those who have been baptized into Christ. Covenant members are those who are in Christ. They are the ones that Paul is speaking to here in Ephesians when he says, he chose us in him before the foundation of the world... Covenantal election and individual election to salvation aren't actually all that far apart. We can distinguish them perhaps but we cannot and may not divide them completely. What is the connection? The connection has to do with God's promise, God's speech to us. (Emphasis mine)

God has promised every covenant member that he or she is elect in Christ. What do I mean when I talk about a covenantal promise? I don't mean a prediction. This is going to happen no matter what ... When God speaks to his people and calls them elect, he is not simply predicting that this will happen, he is making a pledge to them. God's promise comes in all of his speech. His promise is not simply something that will happen in the future that needs to be fulfilled later on.

And God in the gospel and **through baptism** promises us that he unites us to Christ, so that Paul can address the entire congregation men, women and children as those who are in Christ and who are chosen in Christ. And that's how we should view ourselves covenantally united to Jesus Christ and sharing in all of his riches. What's missing in Jesus? **In Him you have redemption, righteousness, justification, sanctification, the Holy Spirit, glorification and election. The whole package of salvation you could say from eternity past to eternity future is all found in Christ.** You need nothing beside Christ. He is the elect one and God tells you that you are united to Him. We may not feel that's true. Who feels elect? But we must believe that's true because God said so and to doubt God's promises is sin. We need to teach our congregation to be assured because doubting what God has said to us is sin. (Emphasis mine)

But you don't need a special dramatic revivalistic conversion to let you know that you are elect, you had the special experience that God gives you, it was called baptism. That's the special experience that lets you know that you are one of God's chosen people.[23] (Emphasis mine)

To demonstrate how Barach's presuppositions, that is, his faulty view of the covenant has affected his understanding of election, he discusses Esau. Barach conjectures **what would have happened if Esau had died in infancy before he lived his life of rebellion against God:**

For if he had died, then there would have been the seal of election for the Lord would not have rejected him eternally. But since he lived and was of the non-elect, he so lived so that we see in the fruit of his "unfaith", that he was rejected by the Lord. (Emphasis mine)

But what about those who fall away? Our election is unconditional. God doesn't choose us due to something in us. But our life in God's covenant including our enjoyment of that promise of election does have conditions, not everybody responds in faith. John 15 says that some in Christ are cut off and burned, there is no room in the covenant for presumption, "well I am elect, I can sin all I like." But those who fall away will be cut off from the church.

They will not be forever among the covenant people, the elect of God, the church of God. Jesus will say to them, I never knew you even if they call him Lord, Lord. And they will look back and discover that they were reprobate on that last day but they will also see that in history, and this is always God's plan for them, that in history God did graciously, really bring them into his church, that He really made them a part of his chosen people, that He gave them genuine promises that are just as real, just as dependable, just as trust-

---

[23] John Barach, *Covenant and Election*, tape 6, 2002 Auburn Avenue Pastors' Conference. The RPCUS transcription of the 2002 AAPC, p. 81-91.

worthy as the promises as the promises he gave to people
who do persevere to the end. He gave them real promises of
salvation, He united them to Christ in whom alone there is
salvation and they themselves willfully rejected it because
they didn't receive those promises mixed with faith. But for
a time they were really among God's chosen people.

**How do you know you are in Him? God gave you the sign
and seal of baptism. He gave you that rite that brought
you into Christ and you can look and you can trust that
God's promises are objective.** Some may fall away, some
do fall away, some are cut off. But that doesn't thwart God's
purposes. His purposes cannot be frustrated. (Emphasis
mine)

God chooses a church. It is amazing, the Heidelberg
Catechism links the doctrine of election and expresses that in
connection with the doctrine of the church and then teaches
all of its kids, the entire church community, to confess, the
son of God does this, gathers this church chosen and I am and
always will be a living member of it. That is the confession
of faith. God's election isn't a problem to worry about, it's a
promise to bank on. It's part of that whole package of salvation given to us in Christ.[24]

During the question and answer session at the 2002 AAPC, John Barach
responded:

Question: The question is, while it is true we must regard
all covenant members as covenant members, must we not
also maintain that there are some who are inwardly or
vitally connected to Christ and others who are only exter-
nally/legally related to Him though they are called to be
otherwise? And the person would like for me to read from
Romans 2:28-29. "A man is not a Jew if he is only one
outwardly nor is circumcision merely outward and physical. No a man is a Jew if he is one inwardly and circumcision is circumcision of the heart by the Spirit not by the
written code. Such a man's praise is not from man but
from God."

---

[24] Barach, *Covenant and Election,* p. 91-94.

John Barach: ... In Romans 2, what Paul is dealing with there when he talks about inwardly and outwardly, has to do with covenant keeping and covenant breaking ... We shouldn't take this distinction and apply it as if there is such a thing as an external covenant and us and all of our kids are in it and then there are some people who are really in the covenant. When we do that then the whole external, so called external covenant, becomes virtually meaningless. What does it matter if you are in the external covenant or not. What matters is that you are really in the covenant. This is tied also to the distinction between visible and invisible church. They feel, "Oh, what does it matter if you are in the visible church, what really matters is that you are in the invisible church?" We should be careful with using Paul's distinction here between outward, inward which has to do with faithfulness and applying that such that anybody unfaithful in your congregation is not really in the congregation. Well, yes he is and he needs to be dealt with as somebody who is not keeping covenant.[25]

Some might think that those who have been very critical of the teaching in the 2002 AAPC have misunderstood the Monroe Four that they did not listen to the tapes charitably. We shall see that the Monroe Four have not renounced their original teaching; in fact, they have reinforced their teaching in the Knox Theological Seminary Colloquium. John Barach submitted the following:

According to Scripture, not everyone who is in the covenant has been predestined to eternal glory with Christ. God establishes His covenant with believers and their households, including some who will later apostatize and be cut off from covenantal fellowship with Him. Put another way, all those who are baptized are genuinely baptized into Christ (Galatians 3:27), are brought into Christ's body, the church (1 Corinthians 12:13), and are members of God's covenant, at least until they are cut off, whether by Christ's church (excommunication) or directly by Christ (death as judgment).[26]

---

[25] *Question and Answer Session #1,* tape 8, 2002 Auburn Avenue Pastors' Conference. The RPCUS transcription of the 2002 AAPC, p. 120.

[26] Barach, *Covenant and Election,* p. 150.

And so the historic Reformed baptismal form links baptism with election. When we are baptized into the name of the Spirit, He promises to present us "without spot among the assembly of the elect in life eternal." If the Spirit promises that you will be among the elect in life eternal, you can bank on it and trust that you are among the elect now.[27]

Therefore, every member of the church can confess in faith the words the Heidelberg Catechism puts in the mouths of its students:

Question 54 states:

What do you believe concerning the "holy catholic church"?

Answer: I believe that the Son of God, through His Spirit and Word, out of the entire human race, from the beginning of the world to its end, gathers, protects, and preserves for Himself a community chosen for eternal life and united in true faith. And of this community I am and always will be, a living member.

The doctrine of election goes hand in hand with the doctrine of the church here. And in a warm and pastoral way, the Catechism teaches all the church's children–who have been grafted into the church through baptism (Q&A 74)–not to worry about their election ("Am I elect?") but to confess it together with the whole church: "The Son of God is gathering His elect church, and I am now and always will be a living member of it."[28]

Steve Schlissel's View of the Objectivity of the Covenant

I now turn attention to Steve Schlissel's view of the objectivity of the covenant. Schlissel is fundamentally in agreement with the three other speakers at the 2002 AAPC. Schlissel makes the point that one of our basic problems is that the church has pitted the idea of personal salvation and personal assurance with the idea of the objectivity of the covenant. The following quotes demonstrate this fact:

---

[27] Barach, *Covenant and Election* p. 155.

[28] Barach, *Covenant and Election*.

Luther had one foot on the Bible and used a broken lever and he shook the world. But imagine what he could have done if he had both feet on the Bible, that is the Old and the New Testament together without imagining an antipathy between them and that if he had a lever that was the covenant and not his mere personal salvation?

The world can be rocked but it has to be rocked by people standing solidly on the whole word of God who have the lever of the covenant in position to rock it. The Book as a whole is a covenantal book but I fear that we have brought our Greek ideas and Greek categories to it.

But what if we begin with the idea that we really need grace from God? And what if we begin with the radical idea that he has given it to us, and the even more radical idea that he has given it to our children? Then where do we begin? Teaching our children to doubt God afresh in every generation? Or to take what he has given us and to move it into action and into application in the world. Wash and make yourselves clean, take your evil deeds out of my sight, stop doing wrong, learn to do right, seek justice.

In our day, our people don't even know the Ten Commandments. We think we know the gospel because we have reduced it to four spiritual laws. But we don't know the Ten Commandments ... But this is the state of affairs because of our concern with our own personal salvation based upon a view that God really doesn't want to save anyone and that he is playing games, and that if it is not by works which we have done then it's by a kind of faith which we can't identify. And we are always looking, you know you see this, no offense, but this is especially prevalent in Southern Presbyterians for some reason who are essentially Baptists who don't refrain from sprinkling their babies. They think like Baptists. They address their children as Baptists. They don't believe their children are saved by the grace of God, they believe they are waiting for a decision, some sort of cogent, confessable experience of personal regeneration and transition from death to life because they believe their children are born in death. They have bought into the Baptistic way of thinking and it is just an abomination.

Does this mean there is no legitimacy to spiritual experience? Of course there is. Why should it be once? Why should it just be twice? It may not be at all. It may for a hundred times. There is growth and development ... And he has told us to look at his grace and that our children bear his name and really belong to him. Not maybe but truly and then what, then live for him. Well how do I do that, you got to learn his word.

"If you are willing and obedient, you will eat from the best of the land." This is what the Lord Almighty, the God of Israel says, reform your ways and your actions and I will let you live. Don't trust in deceptive words, the temple of the Lord, the temple of the Lord, the temple of the Lord." Can I say something? Don't trust in deceptive words, we are reformed, we are reformed. Don't' trust in deceptive words, Westminster Confession, Westminster Confession. You have to have the whole word of God and the fear of God in your heart and in your home. That's what God wants. If you really change your ways and your actions and deal with each other justly, if you don't oppress the alien, the fatherless or the widow and you don't shed innocent blood, if you don't follow other gods to your own harm, then I will let you live.

Was the problem of the unbelieving Jews of Jesus' day truly that they kept the Law? Does anybody seriously believe that their problem was that they kept the Law? That was what our Lord told them was exactly not the case... They did not love God, they did not keep his Law and that was their problem, not that they did. We have a magnificent book, the Bible, it is God's own word. In this book we have bookends, it opens up with the creation, it concludes with a new creation... Here in between these bookends is the covenant of God. This book is not reducible to solas. It is not reducible to abstraction. It is not reducible to proposition. This book is your life. Eat it and live. Eat it, as God told the prophets. Take it and absorb it.[29]

Schlissel, in his lecture, gives a succinct definition of the covenant:

Let me leave this session tonight with offering a definition of covenant. It is not an exhaustive one, it's not a complete one. I will just give it to you because I am hoping you will be dis-

---

[29] Schlissel, *Covenant Reading*, p. 8-13.

satisfied with the idea of a covenant as an agreement between two parties. Or a number of other less than desirable definitions. The covenant of scripture, the covenant that we read about in the Bible, the covenant that we possess is God's rescuing His people from that which would harm or destroy them, calling them and their children to live intimately with Him in faith, love and obedience, fearful of displeasing Him, lovingly with one another, distinct from, envied by and as a witness to the world, in humble expectation of receiving from Him, I will repeat it, at his appointed time, everything He has promised, signed and sealed in blood, through His appointed mediator.[30]

The covenant is God's gracious relationship that he has entered into with us in which our sins are forgiven and in which we are given new life, in which we are given a way to walk and to stay in that path of righteousness and not to depart from it. Not to depend on our own righteousness for eternal salvation but to stay in the path of righteousness for the glory of God.

We need to get back to that place where we can speak of the covenant people of God and address them as the righteous of the Lord to understand that they have a place in this world where they are to shine like the stars in the night as they hold forth the word of life. So that the gathered worshipers on a Sunday, on a Lord's Day, are built up in what God has made them and called them to be and not to be berated, belittled and stained and doubted and accused. This is so fundamentally important that if we don't agree that this is the way we have to go back to our congregations, then you might as well cash it in now and forget reformation, just give it up. If we can't speak to the people of God like God speaks to the people of God, if we can't speak to the people of God like Paul spoke to the people of God, then we have no right to be ministers of God. If we can't speak to the congregation of the Lord Jesus Christ as if they really are the congregation of the Lord Jesus Christ in whom he lives, in whom he dwells, in whom he has being in this world and a living testimony. If all we can do is

---

[30] Schlissel, *Covenant Reading*, p. 16.

berate and belittle and harangue, then we are working at cross purposes with the living God and woe be to that man.[31]

Schlissel, in one of his lectures, bemoans the fact that America has wandered from its Christian heritage. He explains why this has happened:

> At one time this nation was so manifestly Christian and in fact it was less than 100 years ago that an Associate Justice of the Supreme Court was able to give a series of public lectures entitled "America, a Christian Nation" without getting his head shot off or being put up for impeachment ... And yet since that time we have become an anti-Christian nation. And many of us are left scratching our heads saying, "How could it be that at one time we all basically confessed, as Pastor Wilson said, 75 years ago when we spoke about God, we basically knew the God of whom we were speaking. Now when we speak about God, He is the one who is self consciously excluded. We can speak about any other god but this God?"

> How did this come to be? I want to suggest that it is a failure of covenant consciousness that has led in large measure to this condition. A historian of note has written that, "The missionary expansion of the nineteenth century was everywhere based on the principle of individual conversion and this was marked by an introspective psychological approach and an intensely personal view of conversion and salvation. There is a fundamental contrast between this approach and the collective of communal or what we would call the covenantal form of expression, which had dominated the Christian world for upward of a thousand years. Western Christendom was not built up by the method of individual conversion, it was a way of life which the people accepted as a whole, often by the decision of their rulers. And which when accepted affected the whole life of society by the change of their institutions and laws. It is easy to condemn this type of corporate Christianity as superficial, external or even sub-Christian, but at least it means that Christianity is accepted as a social fact

---

[31] Schlissel, *Covenant Thinking*, tape 4, 2002 Auburn Avenue Pastors' Conference. The RPCUS transcription of the 2002 AAPC, p. 61.

which affects every side of life and not merely as an opinion or specialized group activity or even as a hobby."

If you want to know how it could have been that a nation that was once pretty much uniformly Christian in its self understanding has become anti-Christian, you need look no further than this individualized conception of God's dealing, so that it became every man for himself.[32]

Schlissel, in describing the objectivity of the covenant, places blame upon those who want to emphasize assurance of salvation in a way that Schlissel finds unacceptable. He says:

> Because these presuppositions governing this assurance doctrine that I was reading from all have certain ideas about God and about the Word that are basically false. In these doctrines you have a God who is manifestly reluctant to save and looking for excuses to forbid people entrance to the kingdom ... The presupposition is that the people of God are unknown and unknowable. The presupposition is that life should be lived on hold. Because in order to live your life fully for the glory of God, you have to have some sort of confidence of who you are in Him. Of whether you are His and accepted in the Beloved or whether you have to wait until you can become accepted and then begin your works which are acceptable to Him ... In all these ways, we are looking at the wrong presupposition. God in Christ has shown Himself to be anything but reluctant to save.
>
> God is not reluctant to say, we have a trustworthy Bible which we should teach our children to believe in every thing that God has told us about our identity in Him. That we should not accept for one moment the notion that Christianity is only legitimate when we first pass through the waters of internal torture. We should not believe that the people of God are few but rather that they are many and that everyone who is baptized is to be regarded as a person who belongs to Christ and has obligation to live in accordance with that covenant that they have been put in by the grace of God. We do not honor our mothers when we doubt that they are our

---

[32] Schlissel, *Covenant Hearing*, tape 9, 2002 Auburn Avenue Pastors' Conference. The RPCUS transcription of the 2002 AAPC, p. 128-129.

mothers. We do not honor our fathers when we doubt his paternity of ourselves. We do not honor our country when we doubt our citizenship.

God's testimony in baptism? Look at how the scriptures uniformly address the churches to whom the letters are written. They are prodigious in the descriptions and adjectives that these people are in fact the people who are heirs of the kingdom, who belong to Jesus Christ, who are sanctified by him, who are sure to persevere, who will continue, who have the Holy Spirit. This is the way Paul speaks to the churches. Yet in our day, we have been waylaid by introspectionists to the point they can't even truly pronounce the benediction upon the congregation without a string of qualifiers, that I don't mean you and I don't mean you and here is a whole bunch of other categories that I don't mean. Now go in peace. Right, go in peace. Pieces is more like it. These assurance hawkers remind me of good marketers who first create the desire and then are ready to stand by and fill the need. They create a job for themselves by making you miserable and unsure so that they can come along and keep that as a commodity that keeps them in business.[33]

Not only does Schlissel see water baptism as the primary, objective means of entering the covenant, he goes on to discuss what constitutes "calling." He relates "calling" with baptism with the following comment:

Calling is a covenant key. Paul says to the Ephesians, as a prisoner for the Lord, then I urge you to live life worthy of the calling you have received. That calling is objective and it is upon every single baptized person. When we bring our children to the font, when we bring our children for baptism to receive the name of the Father, the Son and the Holy Spirit, it is because they are under a calling from God that is as real as death, as real as a heart, as real as blood. That calling is upon them and we teach them to grow up and live in terms of it and to seek to honor God in that calling.

The Scriptures' teaching about calling is vitally important, a key to understanding the covenant. Covenant calling applies to everyone to tell us what our status is, what our obligations

---

[33] Schlissel, *Covenant Hearing*, p. 130-131.

are, it tells all covenant members who they are in an objective sense. Paul writes to the Thessalonians that he constantly prays for them that our God may count you worthy of his calling and that by His power He may fulfill every good purpose of yours and every act prompted by your faith. He wrote to Timothy about God who has saved us and called us to a holy life. The writer of Hebrews says, "Holy brothers who share in the heavenly calling. Fix your thoughts on Jesus, the apostle and high priest whom we confess." Peter tells us about the, "God of all grace who called you to His eternal glory in Christ." And Philippians we read about Paul's testimony, "I press on toward the goal to win the prize for which God has called me heavenward in Christ Jesus." Again Peter tells us, "That His divine power has given us everything we need for life in godliness to our knowledge of Him who called us by His own glory and goodness."

Those who reject their calling have the covenant curse resting upon them. Concerning Israel he says, all day long I have held out my hands to a disobedient and obstinate people. He says, the great speech of Stephen in Acts 7, concludes when he says, "You stiff-necked people with uncircumcised hearts and ears, you are just like your fathers, you always resist the Holy Spirit.

Remember Israel's problem was not the Law, it was that they didn't obey the law. It was not that they didn't have the Spirit, it was that they resisted the Holy Spirit. It's not that they didn't have a calling, it's that they didn't want their calling.

And yet we continue in this assurance problem to begin our enterprise in Christ with doubt. We begin our enterprise so that we never get a footing from which we can grow and develop in the consciousness of what we really are in Christ. How many times does God have to tell us how much we mean to Him? How much He loves us? And yet we spurn His love and we despise His overture, we don't believe them, we teach our children to doubt, we teach our congregations to doubt. We are the people of the living God.

Your identity is to be the people of God. God has called you to be His own. I will rescue you, He told Paul, from your own people and from the Gentiles. I'm sending you to open their eyes, to turn them from darkness to light from the power of Satan to God so that they may receive forgiveness of sins and a place among those who are sanctified by faith in Me. You were once darkness but now you are light in the Lord. Live as children of light. Don't you see how simple it is? This is who you are, you are children of light, live that way. What is so hard about this? I just can't, I can't go back to this old scholastic unbelieving way of reading the Bible, parsing it to death so that we miss the sentences. Here it is, you are God's children. Live like God's children. How simple can it be? Have pride in whom God has called you to be. Your identity is that you are the people of God and every pastor here has to address his people to inculcate this consciousness, to develop it, to nurture it, to feed it, to make it grow stronger not weaker.[34]

It is an affront of the first and capital sort to doubt this God and to go into this mindless nonsense about assurances of various sorts. God has spoken, let the world be silent and tremble before Him. He has told us who we are and we say, "Amen." He has told us what our portion is and we say, "Amen." He has told us what our future is and we say, "Amen, O God. We don't deserve it but O God, thank you, it's true."

People of God, cast away your doubts, they are unbecoming to you. Pastors, don't encourage your people to doubt. That's unbecoming of your calling. Let's listen closely to the whole word of God to recognize who we are. We are the people of the living God. He has called us his own and we only honor Him in the same way that Abraham did when God spoke, he "amen-ed" God and it was credited to him as righteousness. Let's hear the word of God and say, "Amen." Amen.[35]

In his article in the Knox Theological Seminary Colloquium, Schlissel writes this about the objectivity of the covenant:

Thinking that grace itself is dependent upon answering this

---

[34] Schlissel, *Covenant Hearing*, p. 131-135.
[35] Schlissel, *Covenant Hearing,* pp. 138-139.

question as they do, many AAPC critics have embraced the idea of a covenant status which essentially confers proximity to grace, but not grace itself. Children of believers, on their scheme, are brought near to Christ, but must not be regarded as being truly in Christ until they give evidence of some kind. Some go so far as to say that elect children who do not die in infancy must be sustained until they can have a faith moment (or a beginning of faith), marked by assent to a set of understood propositions about themselves and Jesus. Until then they are not justified. After all, one can only be justified by faith, and faith alone. Thus, for these men, the covenant status of the children of believers is a halfway sort of thing.[36]

Shepherd's View of the Objectivity of the Covenant

Shepherd makes an amazing comment when he says:

> Is there any hope for a common understanding between Roman Catholicism and evangelical Protestantism regarding the way of salvation? May I suggest that there is at least a glimmer of hope if both sides are willing to embrace a covenantal understanding of the way of salvation.[37]

Shepherd's criticism of Roman Catholicism is as follows:

> Roman Catholic teaching is faulty on two related but distinct levels. On one level, Rome's doctrine of salvation requires that place be given to human merit. This is clear from the decrees of the Council of Trent. But if there is place for human merit, then there is place for boasting about meritorious achievement ... But on a deeper level, what must be challenged in the Roman Catholic doctrine is the very idea of merit itself. God does not, and never did, relate to his people on the basis of a works/merit principle.[38]

What is required from Rome is a change from a works/merit paradigm for understanding the way of salvation to a covenantal

---

[36] Steve Schlissel, *A New Way of Seeing,* The Auburn Avenue Theology, Pros and Cons: Debating The Federal Vision, the Colloquium on the Federal Vision, August 11-13, 2003, p. 37.

[37] Shepherd, *The Call of Grace,* p. 59.

[38] Shepherd, *The Call of Grace,* p. 60.

paradigm ... this change in paradigm would provide a proper basis for Rome's legitimate insistence that full credence be
given to James 2:24 and Galatians 5:6, and similar passages.[39]

Regarding the Protestant approach to the way of salvation, Shepherd states:

We have rightly rejected the idea that a human being can do
anything to achieve his own salvation. We have rightly rejected the idea that a person can work to merit the reward of eternal life. However, we have not always rejected the very idea
of merit itself ... Passages like Galatians 5:6 and James 2:24
to which Rome appeals, are almost uniformly treated as problem texts because they do not fit into a noncovenantal paradigm of salvation by grace ... We want to ward off the clear
danger of legalism, but in doing so, we gravitate toward
antinomianism. Then, in order to ward off antinomianism, we
are compelled to introduce a measure of legalism.[40]

Shepherd tells us how we can bring together Roman Catholicism and
Protestantism by an emphasis on the covenant:

The answer to this dilemma is to be found in the doctrine of
the covenant, with its two parts, promise and obligation ...
All of the blessings of the covenant are ours as gifts of sovereign grace. The covenantal demand for faith, repentance,
and obedience is simply the way in which the Lord leads us
into possession of these blessings ... Salvation is both by
grace and through **faith**. These are the two parts of the
covenant: grace and faith, promise and obligation. Grace is
not without conditions, and a living and active faith is not
meritorious achievement.[41] (Emphasis Shepherd).

Shepherd explains the problem from the Reformed Protestant perspective by
stating that the common understanding of election and reprobation presents
tremendous problems for evangelism:

The doctrines of election and reprobation would appear to
make it inherently impossible to present the gospel as good

---

[39] Shepherd, *The Call of Grace,* p. 61.

[40] Shepherd, *The Call of Grace,* p. 62.

[41] Shepherd, *The Call of Grace,* p. 63.

news to modern man. The gospel would hardly appear to be good news to the reprobate, and since no one knows for sure who the elect are, no word of encouragement, comfort, or assurance can be addressed directly to them as such. As a result, we tend to proclaim the gospel in the third person, talking in terms of what Christ has done for "his own." But the question remains: What good news can a pastor give to this or that particular person? What good news does the gospel have for me?[42]

In any case, how can we demand faith or repentance or obedience when the basic response is not determined by the free will of the sinner, but by the sovereign choice of God, who elects whom he wills? Beyond that, how can we attain the assurance of being in a state of grace and salvation without a direct knowledge of our eternal election? We are told that the results of election and regeneration can be seen in the changed lifestyle of the believer, but then we are also reminded of the danger of misunderstanding and self-deception ... Honest and searching self-examination would appear to yield more reason for doubt than for assurance.[43]

Shepherd's answer to the supposed problem in Reformed theology as to who constitutes the "elect" of God is found in a supposed different approach to evangelism. He says:

In the process, we will have to compare and contrast what may be called "election-evangelism," or "regeneration-evangelism," with what may be called "covenant-evangelism."[44]

Covenant evangelism, according to Shepherd, must be carried out consistently with the Abrahamic covenant, and Shepherd explains what is involved in this:

The promise of the Holy Spirit and the promise of Christ's abiding presence with his people are the initial fulfillment of the heart of covenant privilege and blessing, union and communion with God ... At the same time, privilege entails responsibility, Abraham had to keep covenant with the Lord,

---

[42] Shepherd, *The Call of Grace,* p. 68.

[43] Shepherd, *The Call of Grace,* pp. 68-69.

[44] Shepherd, *The Call of Grace,* p. 70.

as did his descendants to whom the promises were also made. The preeminent covenant keeper is Jesus Christ. He is **the** seed of Abraham, "obedient to death – even death on a cross," (Phil.2:8). As covenant is kept, according to the pattern of Jesus Christ, the promises are fulfilled.[45] (Emphasis Shepherd)

Shepherd says that Jesus prescribed the same kind of evangelistic methodology as did Abraham:

Jesus prescribed the same methodology for his church when he said that all nations of the earth were to be discipled by "teaching them to obey everything I have commanded you" (Matt. 28:20). Just as the gospel of the Abrahamic covenant taught God's people to do what is right and just (Gen. 18:19), so the gospel of the new covenant teaches us to seek first the righteousness of the kingdom of God (Matt. 6:33). For Abraham, the sign of both covenant privilege and covenant responsibility was circumcision, Paul calls circumcision "a seal of the righteousness that he had by faith" (Rom. 4:11), the righteousness of faith is the obedience of faith (Rom. 1:5; 16:26), and is therefore simultaneously covenant privilege and responsibility.[46]

As already from the previous quotes of Shepherd, the objectivity of the covenant is seen in obedience to the covenant demands. Shepherd is going to argue for the further objectivity of the covenant by his redefinition of "election" and an emphasis on water baptism.

Shepherd begins his redefinition of the Reformed view of election by saying:

Furthermore, since Christ has died for particular persons (limited or definite atonement), whose identity can never be known with certainty, it is inconsistent with the Reformed faith to say to any specific person what Christ had done for him ... If his evangelistic methodology is oriented to the doctrine of election, the Reformed pastor can at best wait, hope, and pray for occasional seasons of revival. But if his evangelistic methodology is consciously oriented to the Great Commission and God's gracious covenant, he can and ought

---

[45] Shepherd, *The Call of Grace,* pp. 74-75.
[46] Shepherd, *The Call of Grace,* pp. 75-76.

to expect permanent vitality in the steady expansion of the church of Christ.[47]

To look at covenant from the perspective of election is ultimately to yield to the primal temptation to be as God. The proper stance for Adam and for all of us after him is a covenantal stance of faithful obedience. Only from that perspective can election be understood as grace.[48]

The Reformed evangelist can and must preach to everyone on the basis of John 3:16, "Christ died to save you." The death of Christ is inherently efficacious; otherwise, it would not be gracious ... If we look at this message, "Christ died to save you," from the perspective of election, it is only possibly true, and may well be false...Rather, John 3:16 is covenant truth. Its specific application- and this is what the proclamation of the gospel must be- in the declaration, "Christ died for you," is a demonstration of the grace of our Lord Jesus Christ opening the way to fellowship with God.[49]

Shepherd says that we must look at Ephesians 1:1-14 from a different perspective than what has been traditionally understood by the Reformed faith. He says:

When Paul says, "He chose us"(v.4), we must ask who "we" are. We could say that they are the saints in Ephesus and the faithful in Christ Jesus (v.1), and that because he was an organ of revelation, he knew that each and every member of that congregation was eternally elect of God. Grammatically and even theoretically, such an interpretation is possible. But it is utterly artificial, especially in view of the serious problems that Paul had to contend with in the churches he founded ... One could also argue that there were nonelect people in the congregation, but that the letter does not address them. Again, this is grammatically and theoretically possible. But are we to think that Paul was addressing only some of those on the roll of the Ephesian church and had nothing to say to the rest? How would these people know who they were?[50]

---

[47] Shepherd, *The Call of Grace*, pp. 81-82.

[48] Shepherd, *The Call of Grace*, p. 83.

[49] Shepherd, *The Call of Grace*, pp. 84-85.

[50] Shepherd, *The Call of Grace*, p. 87

> In Ephesians 1, Paul writes from the perspective of observable covenant reality and concludes from the visible faith and sanctity of the Ephesians that they are the elect of God. He addresses them as such and encourages them to think of themselves as elect. A Reformed pastor can and must do the same today ... It is true that some in the congregation may fall away and leave the church. Paul issues a warning in view of that possibility. Were some to fall away, he would no longer speak of them as the elect of God.[51]

It is clear that Shepherd believes that the objectivity of the covenant with regard to election is that the visible congregation of baptized people in its entirety constitutes the elect of God.

Shepherd also views John 15:1-8 as proof of the objectivity of the covenant. He says:

> A second passage that is illustrative of the covenant perspective on election is John 15:1-8. Jesus is clearly and unambiguously saying in this passage that he is the vine and that his hearers are branches abiding in him.[52]

Shepherd rejects the historic Reformed interpretation of this passage which states that there are some branches that are truly united to Him that bear fruit and there are some branches that are not truly united to Him and bear no fruit. The fruitful branches are genuine Christians while the unfruitful branches are only professing Christians but not elect because they are cut off and burned up. Shepherd states:

> The words **inward** and **outward** are often used in Reformed theology to resolve problems that arise because biblical texts are approached from the perspective of election ... The terms **outwardly** and **inwardly** are biblical terms, but when Paul uses them in Romans 2:28-29, he is not referring to the **elect** and the **reprobate**. The terms describe the difference between covenantally loyal Jews and disobedient transgressors of the law. The categories derive their meaning from the covenant, not from the decree.[53] (Emphasis Shepherd)

---

[51] Shepherd, *The Call of Grace,* pp. 87-88.

[52] Shepherd, *The Call of Grace,* pp. 88-89.

[53] Shepherd, *The Call of Grace,* p. 90.

Having reinterpreted the Reformed doctrine of election, Shepherd is now going to redefine the Reformed doctrine of regeneration:

> When Reformed evangelism is oriented to the doctrine of election, it is only a logical and natural extension of this method to orient evangelism also to regeneration. Regeneration is the new birth, the initial transformation of a sinner wrought by the Holy Spirit. The Holy Spirit renews the sinner in the innermost core of his being so that he can repent of sin and believe the gospel ... Regeneration is a secret operation of the Spirit, and through it the Spirit begins to apply to the elect what was granted to them in the secret counsel of God.[54]

> If evangelism is oriented to regeneration, the covenant is again viewed from the perspective of a secret work of God – now from the perspective of regeneration. But instead of looking at covenant from the perspective of regeneration, we ought to look at regeneration from the perspective of covenant. When that happens, baptism, the sign and seal of the covenant, marks the point of conversion. Baptism is the moment when we see the transition from death to life and a person is saved.[55]

> This is not to say that baptism accomplishes the transition from death to life, or that baptism causes a person to be born again. That is the doctrine of baptismal regeneration, which is rightly rejected by Reformed churches. The Holy Spirit works where, when, and how he pleases, not necessarily at the precise moment of baptism.

> From the perspective of election, regeneration is the point of conversion. Regeneration, however, is a secret work of the Holy Spirit, and so we do not know when it takes place. We do not have access to the moment of regeneration. What we hear from the converted sinner is a profession of faith, and what we see is his baptism into Christ. This covenant sign and seal marks his conversion and his entrance into the church as the body of Christ. From the perspective of the covenant, he is united to Christ when he is baptized.[56]

---

[54] Shepherd, *The Call of Grace,* p. 93.

[55] Shepherd, *The Call of Grace,* pp. 93- 94.

[56] Shepherd, *The Call of Grace,* p. 94.

In contrast to regeneration-evangelism, a methodology oriented to the covenant structure of Scripture and to the Great
Commission presents baptism as the transition point from
death to life ... According to the Great Commission, conversion without baptism is an anomaly. A sinner is not "really
converted" until he is baptized...Even in Reformed circles, it
is common to speak of the number of persons who are "really converted" or "Truly Christian," although the Bible itself
avoids such language and talks in terms of the number of
people baptized ... the Bible does not say when he was
regenerated, but it does say when he was baptized (Acts
9:18). His baptism marks the time when his sins were
washed away (Acts 22:16). When Paul exhorts the Romans
to obey God, he does not remind them that they were regenerated or suggest that they might not be regenerate, Rather, he
points to their baptism and calls them to live out of that experience. (Rom. 6:1-11)[57]

Christians are those who have been baptized ... Why does
baptism play such a minor role in modern evangelistic
methodology, when it holds the major place in the Great
Commission? The reason would appear to lie in the prefer-
ence for regeneration-evangelism over covenant-evangelism.

The covenantal focus on baptism does not mean that regeneration is discounted. Rather, the new birth is put in proper
perspective. The connection between baptism and regeneration comes to vivid expression when Paul says that we are
saved "through the washing of rebirth and renewal by the
Holy Spirit" (Titus 3:5). He also says that we are washed,
sanctified, and justified in the name of the Lord Jesus Christ
and by the Spirit of God (I Cor. 6:11).[58]

It is both striking and significant that the Great Commission
in neither Matthew nor Luke speaks of calling upon sinners
to believe. Faith is not mentioned specifically, but only by
implication. What is explicitly asserted is the call to repentance and obedience. When call to faith is isolated from the
call to obedience, as it frequently is, the effect is to make

---

[57] Shepherd, *The Call of Grace,* pp. 100-101.
[58] Shepherd, *The Call of Grace,* PP. 101-102.

good works a supplement to salvation or simply the evidence of salvation. Some would even make them an optional supplement. According to the Great Commission, however, they belong to the essence of salvation, which is freedom from sin and not simply freedom from eternal condemnation as the consequence of sin. Because good works are done in obedience to all that Christ has commanded, they are suffused with and qualified by faith, without which no one can please God (Heb. 11:6).[59]

Rich Lusk's View of the Objectivity of the Covenant

As discussed in chapter 5 dealing with justification and works, Rich Lusk was one of the most explicit writers in his denial of this orthodox doctrine. Regarding who is in the covenant, Lusk is equally explicit in his departure from Reformed theology.

Lusk states the relationship between the covenant and election:

> The covenant is God's administration of salvation in space and time, the historical outworking of His eternal plan. We have then two basic perspectives, the decretal/eternal and the covenantal/historical, through which to view salvation. As the handout above shows, the Bible ordinarily (though not always) views election through the lens of the covenant. (For more on this, see Norm Shepherd's book The Call of Grace.) This is why covenant members can be addressed consistently as God's eternally elect, even though some of those covenant members may apostatize and prove themselves to not be elected to eternal salvation·

> Sometimes Scripture simply conflates the elect and the covenant body, such as in Eph. 1:3ff and 2 Thess. 2:13. Other times, Scripture distinguishes the elect from the covenant community, such as when the biblical writers warn that some within the covenant will fall away (Rom. 11, 1 Cor. 10) ... The key to keeping election and covenant together is to remember that the covenant is the visible, historical context in which the eternal decree of election comes to fruition.

---

[59] Shepherd, *The Call of Grace,* p. 104.

In the Bible, election is always presented as good news – as pure gospel – for the covenant people of God. Yet, in many modern Calvinistic presentations, the doctrine takes on an ominous, threatening character. It raises the question, "Am I elect?," a question anxious souls want to have answered ... But here is a place where the Bible must be allowed to trump the deductions we might otherwise draw from premises provided by systematic theology. The inspired writers, after all, often speak of the covenant people of God as elect. And surely this knowledge of who is elect cannot be due simply to the fact that the Spirit is working in them as they write. Continually, the apostles address real words of comfort and assurance to visible churches – often very troubled visible churches! – and this is to serve as a model for pastors today.

If Paul had been writing Eph. 1 as a modern Calvinist, he would had to have said, "He chose some of us in Him before the foundation of the world, that we should be holy and without blame..." But Paul's theology of election permits him to speak of the whole covenant community as elect in Christ, even when he knows some members of that congregation will apostatize (cf. Acts 20:28-30)... I suggest 'viewing election through the lens of the covenant' is one helpful way of conceptualizing what Paul is doing in texts such as these... True, corporate election may not issue forth in final salvation, as the nation of Israel shows (cf. Dt. 7; Rom. 9-11). Apostasy is a real possibility for all covenant members, and is to be warned against. But corporate election is the context in which special election is worked out. There is indeed an election within an election (cf. Rom. 9:6), but for pastoral purposes, the two can and must be collapsed into one another. Thus, we are to regard all who are baptized and bear Christ's name as God's chosen ones.

We can truly derive comfort and encouragement from our covenant membership. God loves everyone in the covenant. Period. You don't have to wonder if God loves you or your baptized children. There is no reason to doubt God's love for you. You can tell your fellow, struggling Christian, "You're forgiven! Christ paid for your sins!" This is far more helpful than only being able to tell someone, "Well, Christ died for his elect, and hopefully you're one of them!" No, looking at election through the lens of the covenant, as Scripture does, allows us to really and truly apply the promises of Scripture to ourselves and our fellow covenant members.[60]

Rich Lusk defines the meaning of a non-elect covenant member:

> God has decreed from the foundation of the world all that comes to pass, including who would be saved and lost for all eternity. Included in his decree, however, is that some persons, not destined for final salvation, would be drawn to Christ and to his people for a time. These people, for a season, enjoy real blessings, purchased for them by Christ's cross and applied to them by the Holy Spirit through Word and Sacrament. (Reformed theologian John Murray makes it clear that whatever blessings reprobate experience in this life flow from Christ's work and the Spirit's work.) They may be said to be reconciled to God, adopted, granted new life, etc. But in the end, they fail to persevere, and because they fall away, they go to hell. Why would God do this? It's a mystery! ... Whatever the case, the teaching of Scripture is clear: some whom he adopts into covenant relation, he later hardens (Rom. 9:4, 18, 11:1ff).[61]

Lusk explains how perseverance relates to a covenant member who apostatizes:

> Saul and David look alike in the early phases of their careers; Judas looked like the other disciples for a time. No appeal to the decree can be allowed to soften or undercut this covenantal perspective on our salvation. It is only as history is lived, as God's plan unfolds, that we come to know who will persevere and who won't ... This means that at the outset of Saul's career, the biblical narrative itself draws no distinction between his initial experience of the Spirit and the experience of those who would enter into final salvation. Saul's apostasy was not due to any lack in God's grace given to him, but was his own fault ... Saul received the same initial covenantal

---

[60] Rich Lusk, *Covenant & Election FAQ's (Version 6.4)*, Quoted in *Theologia, 2002.* This article can be found at www. hornes.org/theolgia/Soteriology: *Covenant & Election FAQs.*

[61] Lusk, *Covenant & Election FAQ's (Version 6.4).*

grace that David, Gideon, and other saved men received, though God withheld from him continuance in that grace. At the same time, his failure to persevere was due to his own rebellion. Herein lies the great mystery of God's sovereignty and human responsibility (cf. WCF 3.1, 8).

While we as Calvinists like to make a sharp distinction between genuine regeneration and the common operations of the Spirit, we should be willing to recognize that this distinction does not enter into many biblical passages. Instead, we need to be willing to speak of the undifferentiated grace of God (or the generic, unspecified grace of God). For example, in Heb. 6:4-5, some Reformed theologians try to draw subtle distinctions, showing highly refined psychological differences between the blessings listed, which do not secure eternal salvation, and true regeneration, which does issue forth in final salvation. But it is highly unlikely the writer had such distinctions in view, for at least two reasons. For one thing, it is by no means certain that those who have received the blessings listed in 6:4-5 will fall away. The writer merely holds it out as a possibility, a danger they must beware of. In fact, he expects these people to persevere (6:9).

But if the blessings catalogued are less than regeneration, and these people might persevere after all, we are put in the awkward position of saying that non-regenerate persons persevered to the end (cf. 2 Cor. 6:1)! Second, the illustration immediately following the warning, in 6:7-8, indicates these people have received some kind of new life. Otherwise the plant metaphor makes no sense. The question raised does not concern the nature of grace received in the past (real regeneration vs. merely common operations of the Spirit), but whether or not the one who has received grace will persevere into the future. Thus, the solution to Heb. 6 is not developing two different psychologies of conversion, one for the truly regenerate and one for the future apostate, and then introspecting to see which kind of grace one has received. Rather, the solution is to turn away from ourselves, and keep our eyes fixed on Jesus, the Author and Finisher of our faith (Heb. 12:1ff). This is the 'secret' to persevering (and to assurance).[62]

---

[62] Lusk, *Covenant & Election FAQ's.*

Lusk addresses a potentially tough question regarding assurance. This is his vain attempt to deal with the Westminster Confession of Faith, Chapter 18, section 2:

> Assurance must never lead to presumption, complacency, or carelessness... Our Calvinistic pre-occupation with the decrees tends to make us rather complacent (the 'frozen chosen'!). There is a fine line between biblically-based assurance and presumption ... When I've talked to people who have had their assurance shaken by this kind of teaching, in virtually every case, after conversation with the person, it came out that the basis of their assurance was flawed.

> Some people who have been in the Reformed church for a while are startled by it because they thought that when they learned the TULIP, they had all they needed to know. But TULIP is not an exhaustive biblical theology, and systematic theology more generally cannot be treated as a substitute for actually getting your hands dirty with the text of Scripture. Sometimes we use systematics or a paradigm like TULIP to tame the Scriptures. This is a mistake. Systematic theology is a helpful check on our reading of Scripture. But it's like Cliff Notes – it really only does you good if you read the real text carefully. Moreover, there is great potential for confusion since the terminology of systematic theology doesn't always match the Bible's own terminology.

> I think many long time Reformed believers struggle with these things because they were taught election in abstraction from the covenant. The Reformed community has good books on election and good books on the covenant, but few that tie them together. Plus, the Reformed church has often paid inadequate attention to the OT in its theologizing (particularly about salvation), so a case like Saul is not studied closely enough and isn't allowed to properly refine our positions.

> For better and for worse, we have numerous popularizers of Reformed theology around today. The result is that what most of us think of as 'Reformed' is greatly truncated. American Reformed theology is like a bad cassette recording of the real thing. I'm simply trying to recover nuances that

were originally in the tradition, but have been lost. Yes, some
of it may seem trying, but in the end it is worth it.[63]

Lusk asks the question, "What does it mean to be in covenant?" He states two
views, and then gives an alternative view:

> On the one hand, some so totally identify covenant and elec-
> tion that to be in covenant and to be elect are one and the
> same. In other words, no non-elect persons ever enter the
> covenant. We don't know if someone becomes a covenant
> member at baptism because we don't know if that person is
> elect ... In the end, my local church affiliation doesn't really
> matter on this scheme; what counts is being a part of the
> 'invisible church', known only unto God.
>
> At the other extreme are those who identify the covenant with
> the visible church, but make covenant membership a matter
> of mere externals. Joining the church is no different than join-
> ing a social club of some sort ... Everyone baptized is a
> covenant member ... but so what? The covenant has no
> salvific value.
>
> Against both of these distortions, we must insist that the covenant
> is nothing less than union with the Triune God, nothing than
> less than salvation. The church is not merely a human com-
> munity and the church's enactments of the means of grace
> (Word and sacrament) are not mere human works. Rather, the
> church herself is God's new creation, the city he promised to
> build for Abraham. **The church is not merely a means to
> salvation, a stepping-stone on the way to a more ultimate
> goal. Rather, the church herself is God's salvation, the
> partially realized goal that will be brought to final fulfill-
> ment in the eschaton. So when someone is united to the
> church by baptism, that person is incorporated into
> Christ and into his body; that person becomes bone of
> Christ's bone and flesh of his flesh. Until and unless that
> person breaks covenant, he is to be reckoned as among
> God's elect and regenerate saints.**[64] (Emphasis mine)

Lusk describes a covenant breaker as one who breaks a marriage covenant:

---

[63] Lusk, *Covenant & Election FAQ's*.

[64] Lusk, *Covenant & Election FAQ's*.

Think of the covenant as a marriage. Baptism is your wedding ceremony, uniting you to your husband Christ (Rom. 6:1ff, Eph. 5:22ff). So long as you remain faithful, Christ will keep you under his protection and care, and share all he has with you. But if you become an adulterous spouse, an unfaithful spouse, Christ will cut you off and divorce you.

What, then, does it mean to be unfaithful to the terms of the covenant? Not all sins are grounds for divorce from Christ, just as not all sins are grounds for divorce in an earthly marriage ... **He does not demand perfection from us, only loyalty ... He is concerned with our direction, not perfection. A life of sustained faithfulness is what counts, however great or numerous our failings may be along the way ...** (Emphasis mine)

But just because the covenant can be broken does not mean it is not a real relationship, with real privileges granted and real obligations demanded... Just as we might call on a married man contemplating adultery to "be true to your wedding vows!" so we call on our fellow new covenant members to "be true to your baptisms!" In other words, "Be who you are!! You're united to Christ in baptism, dead to sin and alive to God – live like it!" Covenant breakers are untrue to the covenant relation into which they were baptized. But what makes covenant breaking so heinous (cf. the warnings in Hebrews) is the fact that it is sin against a gracious relationship with Christ.[65]

Lusk anticipates the question as to whether one can lose his salvation:

That depends. What do you mean by salvation? In many instances, the biblical writers view salvation as an eschatological concept – in this sense no one is saved till the last day. But salvation can also be understood as a past reality (you were saved in eternity past when God chose you in Christ, or when Christ died on the cross for you, or when the Spirit converted you) and a present and progressive reality (e.g., you are in the process of working out your salvation in fear and trembling, Phil. 2). No elect person can lose his salvation, however much he may backslide. This is the point of Jesus'

---

[65] Lusk, *Covenant & Election FAQ's.*

teaching in Jn. 10 – God the Father and God the Son will not lose their grip on those they have chosen for final salvation.

But the biblical language itself is more complicated. In one sense, all those in the covenant are 'saved'. They have been delivered out of the world and brought into the glorious new creation of Christ. But not all will persevere. Jude 5 speaks of the Israelites as having been saved, and then destroyed, because they did not persevere. The preface to the Ten Commandments addresses Israel as God's redeemed people. But many of those redeemed did not continue trusting their deliverer and perished. 2 Pt. 2 speaks of a similar class of people – redeemed by Christ, they then deny him, and are destroyed. To take another example, 1 Pt. 3 says eight people in all were saved from God's wrath in Noah's ark. But if we read the Genesis narrative, we find one of those saved, Ham, apostatized and came under a curse.[66]

Lusk has the notion, as faulty as it might be, that he stands in the tradition of the Reformers. He states:

Standing squarely in the tradition of Augustine and the best Reformers, my project is twofold: **First**, to make the biblical promises of salvation real to us. The people of God need to hear themselves spoken of and to as God's elect, as his children, as those bought with the price of Christ's blood, as those renewed and indwelt by the Spirit ... **Second**, to make the threats of apostasy real to us. We cannot hide behind the doctrine of election, or the 'invisible church,' and say these warnings are for other people, but not for us. They do apply to us, and we need to heed them. They do not undermine a properly grounded assurance, but they do keep us on our toes, spiritually speaking.[67] (Emphasis Lusk).

Lusk summarizes his views on the covenant and election as follows:

God, in eternity past, elected in Christ a great multitude to salvation. This election was wholly gracious and uncondi- tional, having its source only in the free mercy and good pleasure of God. Those the Father elected to eternal salvation,

---

[66] Lusk, *Covenant & Election FAQ's*.

[67] Lusk, *Covenant & Election FAQ's*.

he sent his Son to die for. His atoning work is fully sufficient for their salvation and completely accomplished their redemption. The Holy Spirit works in these same chosen ones to apply Christ's saving work to them and keep them faithful to Christ their whole lives. Because of the hardness of their hearts in sin, this work of grace must be, ultimately, irresistible. No elect person can be lost and no non-elect person can attain salvation.

However, God mysteriously has chosen to draw many into the covenant community who are not elect in the ultimate sense and who are not destined to receive final salvation. These non-elect covenant members are truly brought to Christ, united to him and the church in baptism, receive various gracious operations of the Holy Spirit, and may even be said to be loved by God for a time. Corporately, they are part of the chosen, redeemed, Spirit-indwelt people. But sooner or later, in the wise counsel of God, these fail to bear fruit and fall away. In some sense, they were really joined to the elect people, really sanctified by Christ's blood, really recipients of new life given by the Holy Spirit. But God withholds from them the gift of perseverance and all is lost. They break the gracious new covenant they entered into at baptism.

Thus, the covenant is a true revelation of God's salvation, for in the covenant community, all God's people, elect and non-elect, find gracious blessings. The covenant really is gospel – good news – through and through. Yet only those who continue to persevere in loyalty to the covenant and the Lord of the covenant inherit final salvation. Those who fall away lose the temporary covenantal blessings they had enjoyed. Ultimately, this is because God decreed that these covenant breakers would not share in the eschatological salvation of Christ. Of course, these apostates cannot blame God for their falling away – it's their own fault, since God's overtures of love towards them in the context of the covenant were sincere. And those who do persevere to the end cannot claim any credit or make any boast – all they have done has been because of God's grace at work in them to keep them faithful.

All covenant members are invited to attain to a full and robust confidence that they are God's eternally elect ones. Starting with their baptisms, they have every reason to believe God loves them and desires their eternal salvation. Baptism marks them out as God's elect people, a status they maintain so long as they persevere in faithfulness.

This, then, is the biblical picture. The TULIP is still in place, but has been enriched by a nuanced covenant theology. By framing the issues as we have, we are able to preserve God's sovereignty in salvation and hold covenant breakers accountable for their own apostasy. Plus, we can do justice to the Scripture's teaching on the nature of the church and efficacy of the sacraments, as well as the genuineness of the covenantal promises and threats. Nothing has been lost by our reformulation of the popular Reformed picture, and a great deal has been gained.[68]

Analysis of the Federal Vision's Objective Covenant

The theological aberrations of the Federal Vision find root in their understanding of the covenant. This is a classic example of how a dedication to false presuppositions can lead one down a perilous theological path. I have not been able to ascertain why these men began this journey. It is hard to understand their motives. Some might conjecture that they deliberately want to lead us back to Romanism. We know that Rome wants to recover her wayward children (Protestants). The Federal Vision proponents repeatedly claim that they dislike Roman Catholicism. Well, I will give them the benefit of the doubt even though their views are essentially a hybrid form of Roman Catholicism as I shall later demonstrate in a later chapter.

Personally, I cannot help but think that theological pride is at the basis of their new paradigm . Steve Schlissel has several times stated his outright opposition to Martin Luther. Schlissel wants to be rid of the constraints of the Reformed Standards if they don't serve his purposes. He thinks that any subscriptionist commitment to the Westminster Confession is a slavish regimentation in frozen truth. Schlissel insists that the church must always be reforming itself, and of course, he and the others of the Federal Vision will lead us to the promised land of new truth. He believes that Luther's law/gospel distinction is bunk. To quote Schlissel again from the 2002 AAPC, he says:

---

[68] Lusk, Covenant & Election FAQ's (Version 6.4).

> The gospel brought death in the hearer. This is what Lutherans claim the Law does. But that's what Paul said the gospel did. So I reject the distinction. I have nothing to do with it, it's false. The only way it has use is in theoretical construction to speak about people who want to be justified by the Law apart from faith in Christ. In other words they take Christ out of the Law which is no easy task.[69]

Schlissel and his fellow compatriots have given us supposedly new wonderful insight that Luther and others failed to see. The objectivity of the covenant as they understand it will enlighten us. Unfortunately, for Schlissel and the others, it has led them to deny the true gospel. They have misused the Reformed Standards, quoting them frequently in an attempt to persuade people in the pews that they have the key to unlock the mysteries. They, as I have shown already and will continue to show, have become false shepherds, wolves in sheep's clothing.

When the RPCUS formulated its resolutions in June of 2002 and sent them to all four of the Monroe speakers asking their respective church courts to discipline them, the response was alarming dismay on their part. They claimed that we misunderstood them; they wanted dialogue with us and others. When we did not grant them their request, they thought this was very wrong. Being the moderator of that Presbytery meeting when the RPCUS passed its resolutions, we did debate whether to join in further discussion with them, but our unanimous conclusion was that we were not going to give any kind of respectability to their heretical views. I believe their pride was hurt that we did not give them that kind of respectability. They publicly promoted their views at the 2002 AAPC for the whole world to see; we saw it and condemned it. Our perspective was that these men should have distributed their ideas to others in the Reformed world prior to going public with them so that there could be input from others. They deliberately chose a course of action that dropped a bombshell on the Reformed world at the 2002 AAPC.

A year later Knox Theological Seminary sponsored its colloquium on the subject, and the Federal Vision men got their forum. The result? It only showed that the Federal Vision was entrenched in its aberrations, and it demonstrated convincingly to those who took opposing views to the Federal Vision that the Federal Vision viewpoints were definitely out of accord with the Reformed Standards.

---

[69] Steve Schlissel, Questions and Answers Session # 2 (Tape 12) from the 2002 Auburn Avenue Pastors' Conference. The RPCUS transcription of the conference, p. 189.

The fundamental problem with the Federal Vision's concept of the church is their denial of the historic Reformed distinction between the visible and invisible church. The Federal Vision adamantly opposes such a distinction even though the Westminster Standards emphatically affirms that distinction. Hence, when Steve Wilkins, who has pledged allegiance to the Westminster as part of his ordination vows, diverges from this distinction, he is out of accord with a major theological point. Of course, he and his church session think they are in conformity with the Standards; however, I will show conclusively that they have corrupted the meaning of the Standards. We must keep in mind that Wilkins admitted that one must look at the Westminster Standards with his particular lens in order to understand it. In other words, as long as you accept his presuppositions about what is true, then one can make the Westminster Standards say anything that you want it to say.

I have extensively documented from their own statements earlier that the Federal Vision renounces any kind of distinction between the visible and invisible church. The Federal Vision interprets the "elect" as being those who receive full salvation and that the "elect" includes those who are objectively in the covenant via their water baptism. So, whenever Paul speaks to a church and mentions "election," it is applicable to **all persons who have been water baptized.** As Wilkins and Barach have said, the pastor can look out over the congregation and emphatically declare to all church members that God's loves you equally and that Jesus, really and truly, died for you and has forgiven your sins. Schlissel makes the point that it is wrong for me to wonder about the regeneration of the man in the pew next to me. Even though the Federal Vision has made explicitly clear that people can apostatize from the faith, all church members have really received all the saving graces of Christ through their baptisms.

Before I proceed further in my analysis, I need to set forth what the Reformed Standards have taught on the nature of the visible and invisible church. This should clearly show that the Reformed Standards are in opposition to the Federal Vision on the nature of the church.

Chapter 25 of the Westminster Confession reads:

> I. The catholic or universal Church which is invisible consists of the whole number of the elect that have been, are, or shall be gathered into one, under Christ the Head thereof; and is the spouse, the body, the fullness of Him that filleth all in all.

> II. The visible Church, which is also catholic or universal under the Gospel (not confined to one nation as before under the law), consists of all those throughout the world that pro-

fess the true religion; and of their children: and is the kingdom of the Lord Jesus Christ, the house and family of God,
out of which there is no ordinary possibility of salvation.

Question 30 of the Westminster Larger Catechism reads:

> Doth God leave all mankind to perish in the estate of sin and
> misery?
> **Answer:** God doth not leave all men to perish in the estate of
> sin and misery, into which they fell by the breach of the first
> covenant, commonly called the covenant of works; but of his
> mere love and mercy delivereth his elect out of it, and
> bringeth them into an estate of salvation by the second
> covenant, commonly called the covenant of grace.

Question 31 of the Westminster Larger Catechism reads:

> With whom was the covenant of grace made?
> **Answer:** The covenant of grace was made with Christ as the
> second Adam, and in him with all the elect as his seed.

Question 32 of the Westminster Larger Catechism reads:

> How is the grace of God manifested in the second covenant?
> **Answer:** The grace of God is manifested in the second
> covenant, in that he freely provideth and offereth to sinners a
> Mediator, and life and salvation by him; and requiring faith
> as the condition to interest them in him, promiseth and giveth
> his Holy Spirit to all his elect, to work in them that faith, with
> all other saving graces; and to enable them unto all holy obe-
> dience, as the evidence of the truth of their faith and thank-
> fulness to God, and as the way which he hath appointed them
> to salvation.

Question 57 of the Westminster Larger Catechism reads:

> What benefits hath Christ procured by his mediation?
> **Answer:** Christ, by his mediation, hath procured redemption,
> with all other benefits of the covenant of grace.

Question 58 of the Westminster Larger Catechism reads:

> How do we come to be made partakers of the benefits which
> Christ hath procured?
> **Answer:** We are made partakers of the benefits which Christ

hath procured, by the application of them unto us, which is the work especially of God the Holy Ghost.

Question 59 of the Westminster Larger Catechism reads:

Who are made partakers of redemption through Christ?
Answer: Redemption is certainly applied, and effectually communicated, to all those for whom Christ hath purchased it; who are in time by the Holy Ghost enabled to believe in Christ according to the gospel.

Question 60 of the Westminster Larger Catechism states:

Can they who have never heard the gospel, and so know not Jesus Christ, nor believe in him, be saved by their living according to the light of nature?
Answer: They who, having never heard the gospel, know not Jesus Christ, and believe not in him, cannot be saved, be they never so diligent to frame their lives according to the light of nature, or the laws of that religion which they profess; neither is there salvation in any other, but in Christ alone, who is the Savior only of his body the church.

Question 61 of the Westminster Larger Catechism states:

Are all they saved who hear the gospel, and live in the church?
Answer: All that hear the gospel, and live in the visible church, are not saved; but they only who are true members of the church invisible.

Question 62 of the Westminster Larger Catechism states:

What is the visible church?
Answer: The visible church is a society made up of all such as in all ages and places of the world do profess the true religion, and of their children.

Question 63 of the Westminster Larger Catechism states:

What are the special privileges of the visible church?
Answer: The visible church hath the privilege of being under God's special care and government; of being protected and preserved in all ages, notwithstanding the opposition of all enemies; and of enjoying the communion of saints, the ordi-

nary means of salvation, and offers of grace by Christ to all the members of it in the ministry of the gospel, testifying, that whosoever believes in him shall be saved, and excluding none that will come unto him.

Question 64 of the Westminster Larger Catechism states:

What is the invisible church?
Answer: The invisible church is the whole number of the elect that have been, are, or shall be gathered into one under Christ the head.

Question 65 of the Westminster Larger Catechism states:

What special benefits do the members of the invisible church enjoy by Christ?
Answer: The members of the invisible church by Christ enjoy union and communion with him in grace and glory.

Question 66 of the Westminster Larger Catechism states:

What is that union which the elect have with Christ?
Answer: The union which the elect have with Christ is the work of God's grace, whereby they are spiritually and mystically, yet really and inseparably, joined to Christ as their head and husband; which is done in their effectual calling.

Question 67 of the Westminster Larger Catechism states:

What is effectual calling?
Answer: Effectual calling is the work of God's almighty power and grace, whereby (out of his free and special love to his elect, and from nothing in them moving him thereunto) he doth, in his accepted time, invite and draw them to Jesus Christ, by his Word and Spirit; savingly enlightening their minds, renewing and powerfully determining their wills, so as they (although in themselves dead in sin) are hereby made willing and able freely to answer his call, and to accept and embrace the grace offered and conveyed therein.

Question 68 of the Westminster Larger Catechism states:

Are the elect only effectually called?
Answer: All the elect, and they only, are effectually called: although others may be, and often are, outwardly called by

the ministry of the Word, and have some common operations of the Spirit; who, for their willful neglect and contempt of the grace offered to them, being justly left in their unbelief, do never truly come to Jesus Christ.

Question 69 of the Westminster Larger Catechism states:

What is the communion in grace which the members of the invisible church have with Christ?

Answer: The communion in grace which the members of the invisible church have with Christ, is their partaking of the virtue of his mediation, in their justification, adoption, sanctification, and whatever else, in this life, manifests their union with him.

Some may not think this is that big a deal about understanding this theological point of the distinction between the invisible and visible church, but believe me it is a very big deal. The gospel is at stake! Blurring this distinction has tremendous theological ramifications because it determines who are genuinely the recipients of God's saving graces. Trusting in an outward profession of faith is a very dangerous thing to do. Trusting in one's water baptism as the mark of conversion from death to life as the Federal Vision says that it is can be spiritually fatal.

The importance of these quotes from the Westminster Standards is that it makes an explicit distinction between the visible and invisible church. It is very important to note the logical development of the Larger Catechism; it moves from one truth to another, building on what it has said. Its biblical development is absolutely devastating to the Federal Vision.

Let's follow the masterful development. First, Larger Catechism number 30 states that God's love and mercy applies only to the elect. Second, God's love brings about salvation only to the elect. Third, God's salvation that applies only to the elect is called the covenant of grace. It is very important that we note the proof texts that the Catechism gives for its answers. The proof texts provide the exegetical basis for the definitions given.[70]

One of the most important proof texts given in Larger Catechism number 30 is a reference to Titus 3:4-7. This text states: *"But when the kindness of God our*

---

[70] Let me reiterate what I said in another chapter about proof texts in the Reformed Standards. The Scripture references provide for us the theological truths conveyed. The definitions are not made up. When Doug Wilson's church

Savior and His love for mankind appeared, He saved us, not on the basis of deeds which we have done in righteousness, but according to His mercy, by the washing of regeneration and renewing by the Holy Spirit, whom He poured out upon us richly through Jesus Christ our Savior." The Westminster delegates understood this passage to refer only to the elect of God. Only the elect of God have been regenerated; and only the elect have the unique work of the Holy Spirit applied to them that saves them.

Larger Catechism number 31 explicitly states what Larger Catechism number 30 inferred. The covenant of grace is with Christ and his seed, which is the elect. It is important to note that the seed of Christ refers only to the elect. The proof text given is Galatians 3:16 which refers to Christ as the seed of Abraham. Now, they could have listed Galatians 3:29 that refers to all those who are joined to Christ by faith as His seed. One of the other proof texts given to support this truth is Romans 5:15-21 where Jesus is referred to as the second Adam whose imputation of righteousness gives the elect eternal life.

In Larger Catechism number 32, salvation is given only to the elect. Only the elect have the Holy Spirit given to them, who enables them not only to have saving faith but the obedience of life demanded by God. The proof texts given for this answer are John 3:16; I John 5:11-12; James 2:18: 9, 22 and Ephesians 2:18. All these references refer to salvation. Only the elect believe to the saving of their souls. Only the elect have eternal life, and only the elect have the Holy Spirit enabling them to obey God's Word.

The Larger Catechism discusses the two distinctions of the church of the Lord Jesus Christ. These two distinctions are the invisible church and the visible church. This distinction is not two separate churches that Doug Wilson claims that such a distinction makes. It is one true church seen from two aspects. Larger Catechism number 57 demonstrated that Christ's mediatorial work, which secures redemption and all other benefits, applies to the covenant of grace, which we know was made only to the elect; therefore, only the elect

---

in Moscow, Idaho said on their website that they accept all the Reformed Standards **without the proof texts**, this is a deliberate action on their part because they know the proof texts do not agree with their innovative theology. They must have a way to say the Scripture really means such and such. As an historical aside, the decline of the old Southern Presbyterian church, in part, began with the acceptance of the Standards without the proof texts. This allowed them to play loosely with the Confession. Without the proof texts we can make the Confession say anything we want, and those in the Federal Vision do exactly that, quoting frequently from them; however, they have redefined the terms to teach that which is foreign to the Standards.

have redemption. In Larger Catechism number 60 we learn that redemption is applied only to those who are redeemed by Christ, who are the only ones who believe by the power of the Holy Spirit. One of the proof texts given is Ephesians 1:13-14. The significance of this is that the Federal Visions believes that all of Ephesians chapter one applies to all who are objectively in the covenant by baptism. As the Federal Vision men say, this chapter belongs to all professing baptized Christians, even those who may later apostatize and never obtain final salvation, as they put it. What the Westminster Standards apply only to the elect of God, who can never apostatize and die in that state, the Federal Vision applies to all baptized persons indiscriminately.

Larger Catechism number 61 and Larger Catechism number 62 define the visible church and its significance. The most significant point about the visible church is that it consists of all those who profess Christianity with their children. Larger Catechism number 61 explicitly states that not all who are in the visible church are saved but only those who are true members of the invisible church. It is this truth that the Federal Vision flatly denies. Some Federal Vision men are quite adamant about this as you read the quotes that I have provided. A very important point is some of the proof texts given for Larger Catechism number 61. Romans 9:6 and 11:7 are significant passages that clearly indicate that not all who are objectively in the covenant are really of the covenant in a redemptive way. Romans 9:6 states, *"But it is not as though the Word of God has failed. For they are not all Israel who are descended from Israel."* Romans 11: 7 states: *"What then? That which Israel is seeking for, it has not obtained, but those who were chosen obtained it, and the rest were hardened."* What could be clearer? A distinction is being made between those who are simply the seed of Abraham by birth, who are circumcised with those who are the "chosen," who actually obtain the promises. Paul says that there is an "Israel" that sought the promises wrongly. They sought them by their attempts to obey the Law as a means of their own justification (Rom. 11:6). Does this sound terribly familiar? The Federal Vision believes that men are saved by obedience to God's Law as an expression of the essence of faith in Jesus. The Federal Vision believes that circumcision in the old covenant and baptism in the new covenant made men full recipients of God's salvation.

In Larger Catechism number 64, we see a definition of the invisible church. It explicitly teaches that only the elect shall be gathered to Christ under His headship. The Federal Vision emphatically denies this truth. The long list of quotes that I have provided demonstrate that the Federal Vision believes that the "elect nation" which is all who were circumcised and who professed faith were all recipients of every saving grace that God had to offer. Consequently, the distinction between "elect" and "professing Christians" is completely erased.

Everything that is true of the "elect" is true of everyone who is in the covenant by birth or profession of faith according to the Federal Vision.

Larger Catechism number 64 is supported by such proof texts as Ephesians 1:10; 22-23 and John 10:16. The Catechism applies these Scripture references to only the invisible church, not the visible church! This is very important. The Federal Vision dogmatically asserts that all of Ephesians 1 applies to the visible church; hence, all the redemptive aspects mentioned in this chapter apply totally to all who are in the congregation, even if they later apostatize. Hence, the full inheritance promised applies equally to every member of the church who has been baptized according to the Federal Vision. In John 10:16, the term "sheep" applies only to the elect of God, not those who profess but later apostatize. The Federal Vision believes that the term "sheep" applies to all who are in the covenant by birth and by simple profession of faith. This is not how Jesus uses the term sheep. We are told in John 10:11, 15 by the Lord Jesus that He laid down His life for the sheep, meaning that He came into this world to die only for the sheep. He did not die for the goats in any way whatsoever. Hence, on Judgment Day mentioned in Matthew 25, the goats will be sent into eternal destruction while the sheep are sent into everlasting life. Jesus secures salvation permanently for His sheep. None of His sheep will be in Hell. And nowhere in the Bible are we told that one can become a sheep initially but then make themselves a goat by apostatizing. Jesus said in John 10: 26 that those who don't believe are not His sheep, meaning only the sheep believe. So, those who profess Christ but later apostatize by denying the Faith cannot be said to be sheep. Apostates go to Hell and only goats go to Hell. In John 10:27, Jesus said that His sheep hear his voice because the sheep recognize the voice of their shepherd, and sheep will follow their shepherd. The sheep are obviously the elect of God who the Father had given to the Son of God from all eternity (John 6:37, 44). What is the promise that Jesus gives to His sheep? In John 10:28-29 Jesus says that He gives eternal life to His sheep and no one can snatch them out of His hand because they belong to the Father. The sheep will inherit eternal life! No doubt about it. They are eternally secure! However, the Federal Vision believes that one is a sheep by mere inclusion in the covenant by circumcision or baptism depending on whether they lived in the Old or New Testament period. The Federal Vision believes that one can truly be a sheep initially (initial salvation or justification) but then later deny Jesus (fail to achieve final salvation or final justification) and be lost for ever. This is one of the huge tragedies of the Federal Vision movement. It is insulting to the Savior! It believes that one, by his own unfaithfulness, can undo what Jesus supposedly died to accomplish. This is Arminianism through and through. All the proponents of the Federal Vision are seriously deluded if they think they are Reformed.

If as Jesus said, He died only for His sheep then what is another synomomous term for Jesus' sheep? It would be His church. But then it would be specifically the invisible church because only the elect constitute the invisible church. As the Reformed Standards indicate, the elect are the recipients of the benefits of Christ's death. Jesus shed His blood for His church. In Acts 20:28 Paul states, *"Be on guard for yourselves and for all the flock, among which the Holy Spirit has made you overseers, to shepherd the church of God which He purchased with His own blood."* Jesus purchased the church with His blood. Notice, it says that He purchased the church! I simply ask, " In light of the teaching of Scripture on the security of the sheep, how can any in this church fail to achieve glorification in the eternal state?" This church that Jesus purchases with His blood must be only the invisible church because the elect who are the sheep are the only ones who constitute the invisible church. Yes, the elect are in the visible church; they are part of the outward covenant which includes all who believe in Jesus with their children. We must maintain a distinction between the visible and invisible church otherwise we have Jesus dying for and purchasing redemption for some who will eventually deny the Faith by apostatizing. The unbelievable problem that emerges with Federal Vision theology is that in their denial of this two fold distinction of the church, they end up explicitly denying two cardinal doctrines of the Reformed Faith. They must by necessity deny the perseverance of the saints, and particular or limited atonement. They deny the perseverance of the saints in that they believe that one can truly be elect, regenerated, adopted, justified, and sanctified but then lose it all by their own actions, failing to achieve final salvation or final justification as they put it. They deny particular atonement because in believing that Jesus can purchase someone's redemption with His blood, but then this person not make it into Heaven means that someone is in Hell for whom Jesus died. This is impossible!

Actually the Federal Vision denies every one of the five points of Calvinism. Since the Federal Vision believes that men are saved by their faithful obedience to the Law, as imperfect as that obedience may be, and that there were supposedly righteous people all through the Scriptures that could obey God's Law, then the doctrine of total depravity falls to the wayside. The Bible maintains that none are righteous and that none are capable of keeping the law.

The Federal Vision denies unconditional election because in the final analysis it states that only those faithful to covenant obedience will become the "final elect." We must remember that the Federal Vision believes that all who are in the covenant by faith and by birth, receiving the sign of the covenant, are said to be elect. In this case, then election can not be unconditional. If final election is determined by my faithful obedience and contingent upon this, then election is conditional! As Shepherd and Wilkins stringently argued, grace does have conditions. One such condition is circumcision in the Old Testament and baptism in the New Testament. So, unconditional election also falls to the wayside.

Then what about the Reformed doctrine of irresistible grace? It is ultimately denied because this doctrine states that the Holy Spirit effectually calls the elect by regenerating their deadened hearts, enabling them to embrace Christ as He is offered in the gospel. Since effectual calling is linked in an inseparable sequence of redemptive events in Romans 8:28-30, then it is impossible for those who are called to salvation ever to fail to be glorified (enter into the eternal state with Christ forever). Since the Federal Vision maintains that it is possible for people to receive the Holy Spirit in all of His redemptive capacity but then this person be eventually lost due to apostasy, it denies the doctrine of irresistible grace. Rich Lusk has argued for the fact that the grace of God can be resisted (see second paragraph on page 252).

The Federal Vision champions the Arminian interpretation of Hebrews 6:4-6 and Hebrews 10:26-30. It maintains that the "partaking of the Holy Spirit" is full saving participation, but then this person can fall away, they say. In Hebrews 10:26-31 those who received the knowledge of the truth but then who go on sinning willfully and who regard as unclean the blood of the covenant by which they were sanctified (set apart) insult the Spirit of grace. Genuine Christians cannot insult the Spirit of Grace to the point that they deny the Spirit and go to Hell as the text states. Those guilty of all that is mentioned in verses 26-31 have the terrifying reality of falling into the hands of a wrathful God.

Moreover, Rich Lusk has cast dispersion on the five points of Calvinism by declaring that one cannot impose some sort of systematic theology upon the Scripture. He says that this is not a "substitute for actually getting your hands dirty with the text of Scripture" (see second paragraph on page 253). Where does he think the Reformed Faith got its five points of Scripture? Textual exegesis is at the heart of TULIP. It is Lusk and company who have imposed a foreign idea upon Scripture, not the Reformed Faith of the past 500 years.

Larger Catechism number 65 brings out another very important point in the controversy with the Federal Vision. The Catechism indicates that the invisible church, the elect, enjoy union and communion with Christ in grace and glory. This Catechism emphatically refutes the Federal Vision. Remember, the

Federal Vision insists that all who are in the covenant by baptism are in true union with Christ in all of its redemptive blessings (see third paragraphs on pages 204 and 206). The Federal Vision says that being in the objective covenant (the church) means that we are married to Christ and are bone of His bones and flesh of His flesh. Seeing that the Federal Vision completely obliterates the Reformed recognition of the distinction between the visible and invisible church, then true union with Christ is applied equally to some who will eventually apostatize; therefore, this union with Christ is incapable of sustaining some to eternal life. The Westminster Standards, in keeping with Biblical warrant, completely repudiate this notion of the Federal Vision on the nature of union with Christ. Only the invisible church, only the elect therefore, are in true saving union with Christ. The proof texts given to support the doctrine that only the invisible church is in union with Christ are John 17:21, 24 and Ephesians 2:5-6 which are all passages that the Federal Vision uses to refer to all who profess Christ and who are baptized. The real problem is that the Federal Vision's false doctrine blurs the distinction between the visible and invisible church. It interprets these passages as applying to the visible church as well. Of course, the Federal Vision does not use that term "visible." Doug Wilson prefers to call it the "historical" church.

Larger Catechism number 66 specifically states that it is the elect who are spiritually, mystically, and inseparably joined to Christ as their head and as His bride. Referring to the relationship between the church and Christ as a marriage is totally acceptable so far as one understands that it relates to the invisible church not the visible church. The Federal Vision totally misuses and corrupts the biblical passages. Yes, Ephesians 5:23-27 does use the analogy of marriage to describe the mystical union of Christ with His church. The context is very clear that it is a union that entails salvation in the fullest sense, a salvation that is destined for glorification. Christ makes His bride, the church, holy and blameless by sanctifying, cleansing, and perfecting her. This can only refer to the invisible church. The Federal Vision understands this passage to refer to all who are objectively in the covenant by baptism. In truly Reformed language the Federal Vision would make this passage inclusive of all who are in the visible church. This is clearly wrong. One cannot be truly joined with Christ and be saved but later apostatize and lose all the benefits of that union. Reformed Theology has always said that those who apostatize were never the elect and never part of the invisible church. In other words, they were those who were the "Israel" of God who were not really the "Israel of God" as Romans 9:6 states. John 10: 28 is one of the proof texts that the Larger Catechism gives for the fact that only the elect have union with Christ.

Larger Catechism number 67 discusses the meaning of effectual calling. Effectual calling is the same as "regeneration." This is the act of God, whereby God, by His Holy Spirit draws the elect to Jesus, savingly enlightening their eyes so that they can see and accept Christ as He is offered in the gospel. When God sovereignly calls the elect, they believe in Jesus because their hearts have been changed, and they will be glorified. They cannot be lost. Several of the proof texts provided in the Larger Catechism number 67 are Ephesians 1:18-20; 2 Timothy 1:8-9, and Titus 3:4-5. This means that all these verses pertain only to the invisible church, who are the elect, who are the sheep, who have the inheritance, who have been loved from all eternity, who have been renewed by the Holy Spirit, and who have been washed clean by regeneration. Now, all the terms that I have just used to refer to the elect of God who have been effectually called, the Federal Vision uses every single one to refer to those who are objectively in the covenant by profession of faith, even the apostates who have all of these blessings initially. John Barach stated that the Bible knows no distinction between some being internally in the covenant and some externally in the covenant. He emphatically denies the distinction that Romans 2:28-29 makes. Barach stated that in Christ the entire congregation gathered for worship who are baptized members have redemption, righteousness, justification, sanctification, the Holy Spirit, glorification, and election. He emphatically said that they had the "whole package of salvation from eternity past to eternity future. He says that we need to teach the entire congregation not to doubt any of this (see last paragraph on page 228). Now remember, Barach is applying all of this to professing, baptized persons of whom some can and will apostatize. It was Barach who made the absurd comment that if Esau had died in infancy before he proved himself unfaithful and unloved by God, he would have been saved (see third paragraph on page 229). I am sorry, but how he can still claim to be Reformed in his theology is beyond me. The men of the Federal Vision have so many inherent contradictions- it is absolutely astounding. Their undying fidelity to this objective covenant is their spiritual undoing. It is apparent that the Federal Vision men have not thought through their positions very well because if there are some who can be truly the recipients of God's saving activity by virtue of their mere profession of faith and baptism then they have a real problem with Matthew 7:21-23. In that passage there are those who not only profess Jesus but who, in His name, do some amazing things. Does this save them? No, Jesus in verse 23 says, *"I never knew you, depart from Me you lawless ones."* Jesus never knew them ever, meaning that they were never the elect. They were never the recipients of any of His saving graces despite their being in the covenant.

Larger Catechism number 68 asks the question: Are only the elect effectually called? The answer is a resounding yes. It emphasizes that only the elect are effectually called. It makes a big point that though others are outwardly called by common operations of the Spirit, they never truly come to Christ. These bold words are the words of the Catechism. The Federal Vision makes everyone externally in the covenant by profession and baptism as those who are effectually called. At least the effectively called have it initially until which time they may renounce it and lose everything. In this paradigm, the elect become the non-elect. The really saved become the unsaved; those really pardoned of all sins become unpardoned. Federal Vision theology is bankrupt.

Larger Catechism number 69 asks, "What is the communion in grace which the members of the invisible church have with Christ?" The Catechism states that Christ's mediation grants "justification, adoption, sanctification, and whatever else, in this life, manifests their union with Him." Reformed Theology insists that only the invisible church, those internally called by the Spirit, who are the elect, have the blessings of salvation that constitutes union with Christ. To say that external realities such as profession of faith and baptism constitute union with Christ in a saving sense perverts the Bible.

Doug Wilson, in his denial of the historic Reformed differentiation between the visible and invisible church, uses an analogy of people being members on two separate church rolls. He decries the idea that one can be a member on the church roll on earth while not being a member on a church roll in heaven. Wilson states that the problem with American Christianity is its emphasis on individualism, which has given the wrong idea that the invisible church is the real church (see first paragraph on page 223). The way that Wilson phrases his comment is awkward. The visible church according to Reformed theology is a real church. But in saying that the visible church is a real church, in no way infers that all those in the visible church are the elect of God. Wilson and company want to blur this fact, claiming that all in the covenant are in **the church** and in saving union with Christ for awhile until some prove themselves to be faithless and fail to achieve final salvation or as Wilson puts it, final eschatological election.

Romans 9:6-8 and the Church Visible and Invisible

Regarding the nature of the church, the Federal Vision goes astray. Their denial of the distinction of the visible and the invisible opens up Pandora's Box to all sorts of serious errors. Romans 9:6-8 clearly demonstrates that the textual exegesis demands a distinction in this passage. It reads:

> But it is not as though the word of God has failed. For they are not all Israel who are descended from Israel; neither are they all children because they are Abraham's descendants, but: "Through Isaac Your Descendants Will Be Named." That is, it is not the children of the flesh who are children of God, but the children of the promise are regarded as descendants.

Rich Lusk has written that there are some persons who for a time enjoy real blessings purchased for them by Christ and applied to them by the Holy Spirit but who later apostatize and are lost. He says that these apostates once really were "reconciled to God, adopted, granted new life, etc. But in the end, they fail to persevere, and because they fall away, they go to Hell" (see footnote 61). Lusk has just admitted that there are some people who have had Christ's atoning work applied to them but who end up lost. It is hard to imagine that Lusk has the audacity to even quote John Murray as one who is in support of this view! This is a gross dishonor to John Murray. I have shown in many other places in this book that one cannot trust at all Rich Lusk's quotations. He quotes the Reformed creeds and Reformed theologians, but he totally twists what they say. Does he not think that somebody will actually look up his quotes? Lusk references Romans 9:4 where the text states that physical or national Israel is said to be the adopted sons of God, and Lusk misreads the application totally. He thinks that this adoption is referring to the possession of spiritual blessings. It is not; it is clearly referring to the fact that physical Israel (the blood descendants of Abraham) was adopted in the sense that they were the custodians of the covenants of God, that they had the Mosaic Law, and the temple of God. However, the context clearly states that this did not help physical Israel to have all these things because they were not the inheritors of the promises.

What did John Murray teach about Romans 9? We must consult his commentary to see. Regarding 9:4 and the use of adoption here, Murray states:

> This adoption of Israel is to be distinguished from that spoken of as the apex of New Testament privileges (8:15; Gal. 4:5; Eph. 1:5; cf. John 1:12; I John 3:1). This is apparent from Galatians 4:5, for here the adoption is contrasted with the tutelary discipline of the Mosaic economy.[71]

---

[71] Murray, *Epistle to the Romans*, p.5.

Romans 9:5 states, *"Whose are the Fathers, and from whom is the Christ according to the flesh, who is over all, God blessed forever, amen."* Regarding this verse, Murray states:

> "Of whom is Christ as concerning the flesh," At this point there is a change in the relationship. After "Israelites" all the privileges mentioned are stated as belonging to the Jewish people. Even "the fathers" are represented thus. But when Paul reaches the climax he does not say that Christ belonged to them but that Christ came from the Jewish stock.[72]

John Murray is not saying in any shape, form, or fashion that physical Israel, the covenant people of God, were adopted in a saving sense. Being the recipients of special privileges does not make one the recipient of spiritual blessings as Murray will discuss in the following verses. In his comments on Romans 9:6-8 he will make the following points:

> In the other expression, "they are not all Israel," obviously the denotation is much more limited and the thought is that there is an "Israel" within ethnic Israel. This kind of distinction appears earlier in this epistle in connection with the term Jew and circumcision (2:28-29). If the terms of the present passage were applied to the earlier the formula would be, "they are not all Jews who are of the Jews" and "they are not all circumcised who are of the circumcision." The Israel distinguished from the Israel of natural descent is the **true Israel**. They are indeed "of Israel" but not coextensive with the latter...He distinguished between those who were disciples and those **truly** disciples (cf. John 8:30-32) ... If we use Paul's own language, this Israel is Israel "according to the Spirit" (Gal. 4:29) ..." (Emphasis Murray)

> The purpose of this distinction is to show that the covenantal promise of God did not have respect to Israel after the flesh but to this **true** Israel, and that, therefore, the unbelief and rejection of ethnic Israel as a whole in no way interfered with the fulfillment of God's covenantal purpose and promise.[73] (Emphasis Murray)

Regarding Romans 9:7, Murray continues:

---

[72] Murray, *Epistle to the Romans,* p. 6.

[73] Murray, *Epistle to the Romans*, p. 9.

He is still speaking of those "of Israel" and now draws the distinction in terms of that between "Abraham's seed" and "children." In this instance "Abraham's seed" denotes the natural posterity and "children" is equivalent to the **true** Israel, and that sense the **true** children as inheritors of the promise. Later on these children are called the "children of God" (v.8) and this fixes their identity even though in verse 7 are contemplated simply as the **true** children of Abraham.[74] (Emphasis Murray)

Regarding Romans 9:8 Murray states:

"The children of the flesh" has the same import and extent as "Abraham's seed" in verse 7. "The children of God" has the same reference as "children" in verse 7 ... The "children of the promise" are the same as the children of God and this designation is placed in contrast with "the children of the flesh." The latter are those born after the flesh but the children of the promise are those who derive their origin from the promise of God ... [75]

It is evident from the quotes of John Murray that he is anything but in agreement with the Federal Vision as Lusk thinks. Lusk has totally misunderstood everything Murray has said. Murray has championed a distinction that the Reformed Faith has championed for centuries. This is an example of the imposition of an unbiblical notion into the text, forcing it say nothing the Scripture intended. The very thing that Lusk, Schlissel and others complain about, they are guilty of themselves. Romans 9:4-8 is about as clear a passage together with Romans 2:28-29 as one will find to demonstrate this distinction between the outward and external covenant or the visible and invisible church respectively.

The Relationship of the Invisible Church to the Visible Church

It is very important that we understand the relationship between the visible and invisible church. Confusion here has led some to espouse serious errors, even heretical ones. Robert Shaw has stated very well this distinction when he says:

---

[74] Murray, *Epistle to the Romans*, p. 10.
[75] Murray, *Epistle to the Romans*, p. 11.

> When we speak of the visible and invisible Church, this is not
> to be understood as if there were two Churches, or as if one
> part of the Church were visible and another invisible. The
> former includes the latter, but they are not co-extensive; the
> same individuals, who constitute the Church considered as
> invisible, belong also to the Church considered as visible; but
> many who belong to the visible, are not comprehended in the
> invisible church.[76]

This statement clearly reflects biblical truth in that not everybody who is in the
visible church by profession of faith or as baptized children of professing
Christians is automatically in the invisible church. The invisible church consists only of the elect of God.

This fact is taught in such passages as Romans 9:6 which reads, *"But it is not
as though the word of God has failed. For they are not all Israel who are
descended from Israel."* In Galatians 6:15-16 we read, *"For neither is circumcision anything, nor uncircumcision, but a new creation. And those who
will walk by this rule, peace and mercy be upon them, and upon the Israel of
God."* And in Romans 2:28, 29 we read, *"for he is not a Jew who is one outwardly; neither is circumcision that which is outward in the flesh. But he is a
Jew who is one inwardly; and circumcision is that which is of the heart, by the
Spirit, not by the letter; and his praise is not from men, but from God."*

When we demonstrated from our study of words related to the church in the
Old Testament, a careful study of those passages revealed that "the assembly,"
"the congregation," and "Zion" for example were references to the entire
covenant community of which circumcision was the covenant sign of entrance
into this outward or visible community. Many times God judged "His people"
for their idolatry and wicked lifestyles. Esau was a circumcised member of the
covenant community, but as Malachi 1:2-3 and Romans 9:13 states, God
hated Esau.

In Matthew 3:7-9, John the Baptist was baptizing people in the Jordan River
with a baptism of repentance when some Pharisees and Sadducees came to him
for baptism. John rebuked them for their hypocrisy calling them to show fruits
of repentance. These Pharisees and Sadducees responded by saying that they
were Abraham's seed, as if this gave them automatic favor with God. John the
Baptist responded by saying that God could raise up children of Abraham from
stones. Being a physical descendant from Abraham does not make one a gen-

---

[76] Shaw, *An Exposition Of The Westminster Confession of Faith,* p. 261.

uine believer. It does not mean that one is of the faith of Abraham who trusted in Christ yet to come (Galatians 3:8-9). As Galatians 3:29 teaches, those of genuine faith in Christ are the only ones who are the spiritual seed of Abraham.

In John 8:31-59, Jesus also had an encounter with some physical descendants of Abraham who actually believed in Jesus to some extent, but their faith was a shallow, external faith that was hypocritical. Jesus said to this same group that their real father was the Devil (v.41, 44). Jesus said that if they were truly the seed of Abraham they would be doing the deeds of Abraham (v. 39).

In Hebrews 3 and 4, there were many who did not enter into God's rest, symbolized by Canaan, because of their unbelief that led to disobedience. As important as the covenant sign is (circumcision in the Old Testament and baptism in the New Testament) it does not guarantee that one is the elect of God, a spiritual heir of Abraham, a sheep of Christ for whom He shed His blood. The covenant sign of circumcision and baptism made one a member of the visible church, but it did not make one a member of the invisible church.

Even though the spiritual seed of Abraham, genuine Christians, constitutes the invisible church, this does not mean that the visible church is some unnecessary feature. Robert Shaw makes a very good point when he says:

> The ministry and ordinances of the gospel, which Christ has given to the visible Church, are designed for the gathering of sinners into the Church invisible, and for the perfecting of the saints, and, by the concurring influences of his Spirit, they are made effectual to these ends.[77]

Shaw continues in his comments about the relationship of the visible and invisible church:

> This visible Church comprehends hypocrites and formal professors, as well as those that are effectually called and regenerated. On this account the Church is compared to a **floor**, in which there is not only wheat but also chaff (Matthew 3:12); to a **field**, where tares as well as good seed are sown (Matt. 13:24, 25); to a **net** which gathers bad fish together with the good (v.47); to a **great house**, in which are vessels of every kind, some to honour and some to dishonour (II Timothy 2:20).

---

[77] Shaw, *An Exposition Of The Westminster Confession of Faith*, p. 261.

Such being the state of the visible Church, as exhibited in Scripture, there can be no warrant to exact from persons positive marks of their regeneration, as indispensable to their admission to the fellowship of the Church, and to require from them an account of their religious experience for the purpose of forming some judgment about their spiritual state. Christ has not authorized the office-bearers of the Church to make an entire separation between true believers and formal professors of religion- Matthew 13:30. This is a task to which they are altogether incompetent; for, as the servants of Christ cannot infallibly distinguish hypocrites from sincere believers. They can only judge of persons by their external deportment; and this cannot furnish evidence sufficient to enable them to pronounce an unerring judgment about their spiritual state before God. The ground of admission to the fellowship and privileges of the visible Church is a scriptural profession. Of this alone the office-bearers of the Church are capable of judging; and to proceed upon a judgment about their spiritual state as it is in the sight of God, would be to assume the prerogative of Him who alone "searcheth the heart."[78]

Steve Wilkins and his church session at Auburn Avenue Presbyterian Church (PCA) are very forthright in their denial of this Reformed distinction of the visible and invisible church. When Wilkins participated in the Christian Renewal magazine interviews, the question was put to him whether one could be in the church but not united to Christ. Wilkins' answer (see pages 203 and 204) clearly states that a distinction between an external covenant and real membership of the covenant is unbiblical and that being a member of the visible, historic church means that we are truly united to Christ. His statement went on to say that our baptism gives us Christ. The way that Wilkins phrased this is somewhat awkward. The historic Reformed Faith has always recognized that baptism does give us real membership in the **visible** church but not necessarily genuine union with Christ in a saving manner. The visible church is a real, true visible manifestation of Christ's church on earth. However, union with Christ that brings salvation is applicable only to the elect, to those who are in the invisible church. Of course, the visible church is comprised of those in the invisible church; yet, **the visible church is not synonymous with the invisible church.** It is at this point that Wilkins' church and others in the Federal

---

[78] Shaw, *An Exposition Of The Westminster Confession of Faith, pp. 262-263.*

Vision make their fatal error. One cannot equate the two lest one advocates an externalism that is ungodly. When Wilkins' church appeals to chapter 25:2 of the Westminster Confession to demonstrate that baptism into the church constitutes salvation, quoting Ephesians 5:30 as biblical justification, they totally misinterpret the Confession. If one looks at this section, it deals with the visible church. Yes, there is ordinarily no salvation outside the visible church. What did the writers of the confession mean by this phrase? For one, they used the word "ordinarily"meaning that one could be saved outside the confines of the visible local church. The visible church is the God ordained institution which has been authorized to proclaim the Word of God; it is the context whereby God comes in special ways during the assembly of the saints to minister. Throughout history, overwhelmingly more people have been converted in the context of the ministry of the local assembly of the saints than outside of it. When the Auburn session quotes Ephesians 5:30, it inappropriately uses this passage. In the context of Ephesians 5:30, the verses immediately preceding it clearly indicate that the church referred to is the **invisible church**, those who will be made blameless and who are in intimate union with Jesus. The Federal Vision makes a mess out of all the passages in the Bible relating to the church simply because they deny this biblical distinction of the visible and invisible church. They are guilty of quoting all of the passages that refer to salvation to all of those who are in the visible church as if to be in the visible church is salvation itself. Since they do this, they are forced into a position of denying the perseverance of the saints simply because they must explain apostates.

The Auburn Avenue Presbyterian Church session emphatically declared that the visible church "herself is God's new creation, the city He promised to build for Abraham. The Church is not merely a means to salvation, a stepping –stone to a more ultimate goal. Rather, the Church herself is the historic manifestation of God's salvation (WCF 25:1, 2)" (see top of page 221). For the Federal Vision, **the visible church itself is the salvation of God**. The fact that it quotes the Westminster Confession at chapter 25, which deals with the visible church, shows their corruption of this portion of the Confession. The Confession has explicitly made a distinction between the visible and invisible church.

The Federal Vision Distortion of John 15: 1-11

The text of Scripture states:

> I am the true vine, and My Father is the vinedresser. Every branch in Me that does not bear fruit, He takes away; and every branch that bears fruit, He prunes it, that it may bear more fruit. You are already clean because of the word which

> I have spoken to you. Abide in Me, and I in you. As the
> branch cannot bear fruit of itself, unless it abides in the vine,
> so neither can you, unless you abide in Me. I am the vine, you
> are the branches; he who abides in Me, and I in him, he bears
> much fruit; for apart from Me you can do nothing. If anyone
> does not abide in Me, he is thrown away as a branch, and
> dries up; and they gather them, and cast them into the fire,
> and they are burned. If you abide in Me, and My words abide
> in you, ask whatever you wish, and it shall be done for you.
> By this is My Father glorified, that you bear much fruit, and
> so prove to be My disciples. Just as the Father has loved Me,
> I have also loved you; abide in My love. If you keep My
> commandments, you will abide in My love; just as I have
> kept My Father's Commandments, and abide in His love.
> These things I have spoken to you, that My joy may be in
> you, and that your joy may be made full.

The Auburn Avenue Presbyterian Church's position paper in making reference to John 15 indicates that it is possible to have an initial salvation that the session calls "a glorious new creation in Christ" and "having been cleansed from their former sins" but because of the lack of fruitfulness as a branch one can be cut off from the source of salvation (see paragraph one on page 221).

Doug Wilson teaches a similar concept by insisting that Caiaphas, the high priest who presided over Christ's mock trial before the Sanhedrin, was in God's objective covenant (because he was a Jew) who had the sap flowing through his branch but who didn't bear fruit. In Wilson's thinking, Caiaphas would be saved, but because he refused to accept Christ as the Messiah and believe in Him, he was cut off and lost (see see first paragraph on page 224). Wilson denigrates the historic Reformed position of Romans 2: 28-29. Wilson says that we must not regard the outward Jew as someone who is not converted, who does not have his heart changed, and who is not a Christian. Wilson maintains that those in the covenant are genuinely in the covenant having been converted and having their hearts changed. Therefore, he says that we must recognize them as Christians by their baptisms. He says that the true church is the church in history; it is the church on the corner (see see first paragraph on page 225). In holding to this position, Wilson has departed from all the Reformed Standards and those Standards that he claims that he is in agreement with.

John Barach, in step with the other men of the Federal Vision, believes the same regarding John 15. Barach has boldly stated that baptism reveals the elect of God with all of God's saving promises. He says that at our baptism we have "redemption, righteousness, justification, sanctification, the Holy Spirit, glorification, and election" (see last paragraph on page 228). Barach asks, "But what about those who fall away?" He says that our election is unconditional, but for those who are in Christ and fall away, they are cut off and not elect. These people, Barach says, will hear Jesus say that He never knew them (see last paragraph on page 229). It is quite apparent that Barach has not thought very carefully about his comments because they are full of so much inherent contradictions. Barach told us that our baptism gives us everything, and one of those things is glorification. But how can that be if this person apostatizes? This means that the one who gets glorification does not get glorification! It means that the one who was truly redeemed is not really redeemed! The elect have become the non-elect! The justified have become unjustified! How can Jesus say to these former elect whom He knew intimately and savingly that "I never knew you?" Never means never. The men of the Federal Vision have been so deluded by their obsession with this "objective covenant" that they don't even stop to see how they often contradict themselves in the same paragraph just like Barach has done. All of this simply demonstrates that they are not proper stewards of God's Word, and they will pay a dear price for this betrayal.

The Federal Vision's interpretation of John 15 is completely skewed simply because of their principial commitment to their notion of the objectivity of the covenant. Reformed commentators do vary in their full understanding of John 15, but they all agree that the imagery **does not teach that one can fall from true union with Christ.**

One of the first things that we need to remember about this passage is that it is figurative language. John Calvin calls it a parable while Leon Morris calls it an allegory. It is meant to convey a general relationship; we must be careful about finding a point by point relationship in minute detail. The general thrust of the passage is that Jesus says that He is the true vine and that there are branches attached to Him. The branches are His disciples, His followers. Those branches that bear fruit are pruned in order to bear more fruit while those branches that bear no fruit are obviously worthless and dead and need to be cut off and burned. Now this is the overall thrust. We must be very careful about any other detail. The Federal Vision has argued for a very specific relationship such as discussing that the sap of the vine had to flow to all the branches indiscriminately since they are all attached to the vine. By this, they interpret that all the branches indiscriminately are in saving union with Christ. However, at some point due to the fault of some of the branches, some become fruitless and must be cut off. This means that they lost something very important that they once possessed – salvation in Christ! The Federal Vision would say that all the branches are objectively in Christ in a saving way because they were previously attached to the true vine. Of course, they would insist that they are referring to initial salvation, not necessarily final salvation. As I have pointed out elsewhere, this distinction between initial and final salvation is a totally foreign concept to the Bible. It is nowhere taught in the Reformed Standards. The only reason that the Federal Vision teaches this distinction is because their system demands it. Somehow they must preserve having all of God's saving graces at one's baptism – the point of entry objectively into the covenant. But then, they must account for the reality of apostasy; therefore, in order to sound somewhat biblical and not upset people in the Reformed community, they must insist that one is not really losing salvation. One can have initial justification or salvation, but until one apostatizes they haven't lost final justification or salvation. This is pure double talk on the part of the Federal Vision. No wonder people in the pews get thoroughly confused. If the Federal Vision was upfront with people, they would simply say, "Yes, one can lose his salvation if he does not persevere in good works." For those who understand the Reformed doctrine of the perseverance of the saints, they see through the Federal Vision's double talk. The Federal Vision is unequivocally in the Arminian camp on this point and in Roman Catholicism's camp as well. Their new concepts are passed off as nuances of their new theological paradigm.

There is no doubt that Jesus is seeking to teach that all who follow Him are similarly attached to Him as the branch is attached to the vine. But to teach that this relationship brings all of the Bible's redemptive truths to bear is a bit much. Calvin cautions us to be careful about reading too much into this parable, as he calls it. Calvin comments on verse 2 that says, "Every branch in Me that does not bear fruit, He takes away; and every branch that bears fruit, He prunes it, that it may bear more fruit." Calvin states:

> As some men corrupt the grace of God, others suppress it maliciously, and others choke it by carelessness. Christ intends by these words to awaken anxious inquiry, by declaring that all the branches which shall be unfruitful will be cut off from the vine. But here comes a question. Can any one who is engrafted into Christ be without fruit? I answer, many are supposed to be in the vine, according to the opinion of men, who actually have no root in the vine. Thus, in the writings of the prophets, the Lord calls the people of Israel his vine, because, by outward profession, they had the name of The Church.[79]

---

[79] Calvin, *Calvin's New Testament Commentaries: The Gospel According to John*, p. 94.

Calvin clearly states that those who do not bear fruit have never been truly attached to the vine. This would be consistent with the Bible's teaching elsewhere about trees and their fruit or lack thereof. A very helpful corrolary passage is Matthew 7:17-23 which reads:

> Even so, every good tree bears good fruit; but the bad tree bears bad fruit. A good tree cannot produce bad fruit, nor can a bad tree produce good fruit. Every tree that does not bear good fruit is cut down, and thrown into the fire. So then, you will know them by their fruits. Not everyone who says to Me, 'Lord, Lord,' will enter the kingdom of heaven: but he who does the will of My Father who is in heaven. Many will say to Me on that day, Lord, Lord, did we not prophesy in Your name, and in Your name cast out demons, and in Your name perform many miracle? And then I will declare to them, I never knew you; Depart from Me, you who practice lawlessness.

This passage sheds light on the meaning of the John 15 passage. The context of the Matthew 7 passage is that Jesus said there will come false prophets in sheep's clothing who will seek to lead people astray. Jesus said that you will know them by their fruit. And Jesus then quotes the section that I have just mentioned above. The whole point of Jesus' comments is that a tree is known by its fruit. Good trees, those trees that **really** belong to Him will bear good fruit, not bad fruit. If there is bad fruit, then the tree is bad and must be destroyed. Notice that Jesus said to the trees that claimed to bear fruit in His name but who did not obey Him that they **never belonged to Him.** Jesus said to them, **"I never knew you."** It is possible then to appear to be a good tree but not be one. Likewise, if a branch is not bearing fruit it means that it **never was truly attached to the vine.** If it really was attached to the true vine, which is Jesus, then it would have born fruit. Jesus said in John 15:7,8 that all those who **abide in Him** and who **bear much fruit prove to be His disciples.** It is very important that we understand Jesus' point. If a branch does not bear fruit, it means that the branch was diseased and did not receive the life sustaining sap from the vine. Since Jesus is giving this botanical analogy regarding His relationship to His followers, it means that not everyone who professes Jesus really belongs to Him. To be a true follower of Him, one must bear fruit, and Jesus has said that a good tree will bear fruit. The good tree is the elect of God, the only one who has God's saving graces applied to him. This fits well with what Jesus said in John 8:31-44. In this passage, there were Jews who it is said they believed in Him (v. 31). Jesus said that if you abide in My word then you are **truly** My disciples (v. 32). It is Jesus who uses the word "truly." Jesus said that if one continually abides in His word, then he shall know the truth that will make him free (v. 32). Free from what? Those followers who had believed in Him in some capacity said to Jesus that they were Abraham's seed, and they asked Jesus that question, *"How is it, that you say, You shall become free?"* (v. 33). Jesus answers them by saying that everyone who continually commits sin is a slave of sin and stands in need of being set free from the bondage of sin, and Jesus said that if the Son sets a man free, he is free indeed (verses 34-36). Now the shock begins. Jesus says to the very Jews who had believed in Him in some capacity, "I know that you are Abraham's offspring, yet you seek to kill Me, because my word has no place in you" (v. 37). These Jews, who by the way were objectively in the covenant by circumcision, said to Jesus that they were really the seed of Abraham. In other words, they were pleading for the objectivity of the covenant! Jesus said that if they were really Abraham's seed then they would not be seeking to kill him (verses 39 and 40). Jesus then declares to these Jews that their real father is not Abraham but the Devil! (verses 41-44). Let's understand something very important here. Jesus declares to some who are objectively in the covenant that they really are not **of** the covenant in a saving way. Jesus says that one is not really of the covenant, which means to be a true seed of Abraham, if one does not abide in His word. The one who is set free by the Son is the true seed of Abraham! This means that there is a visible church and an invisible church just like our Reformed Standards teach. Sorry Federal Vision. Jesus, the Lord of Glory, has Himself just refuted your objectivity of the covenant! The Federal Vision's belief that being objectively in the covenant means that one has all of God's saving graces such as justification, adoption, forgiveness of sins, etc. is pure myth and heresy! Paul clearly understood this point of Jesus when he wrote Romans 9:4-13. As we saw in this passage, Paul under the inspiration of the Holy Spirit, states that not every physical descendant of Abraham is truly of the seed of Abraham. Paul's object lesson? Jacob and Esau. Both were objectively in the covenant, but one was the real seed of Abraham and the other wasn't. Jacob was loved by God and Esau was hated by God. It really is not that difficult to understand, but if you deny the distinction between the visible and invisible church, then one finds himself in the biggest quagmire. Let's always remember that **Jesus is the one who made the distinction between the visible and invisible church!**

When the Federal Vision insists that the branch in John 15 must be interpreted that the branch is in true union with Jesus in a saving way, it has committed a terrible exegetical mistake – one that will lead them down a perilous path. They will then argue for the eradication of the distinction between the visible and invisible church. When they do this, they have found themselves at odds with the Lord Jesus Christ. They have quesioned the exegetical understanding of the Savior Himself!

The Federal Vision's concept of the church is their Achilles heel. Their presuppositional commitment to this perspective leads them down the road to all sorts of heresies. As we shall see in another chapter, this perspective on the nature of the church leads them to another error baptismal regeneration.

Chapter 7

Modern Day Judaizers

Rich Lusk, Steve Schlissel, and Doug Wilson

I refer to the proponents of the Federal Vision as modern day Judaizers. Their redefinition of faith as "the obedience of faith" is the reason for this designation. The Federal Vision advocates a works salvation paradigm. In redefining faith, the Federal Vision has sought to displace several of the great battle cries of the Reformation – *sola fide* (by faith alone), *sola gratia* (by grace alone), and *sola Christo* (by Christ alone). Steve Schlissel is really tired of hearing about all the solas of the Reformation. There are others in the Federal Vision camp say that they believe in *sola fide*, *sola gratia*, and *sola Christo*; they just don't believe them in the way that they have often been articulated. The Federal Vision thinks that its new paradigm is a theological advance. In thinking this, these men have deluded themselves, and they have introduced nothing new but the old Judaizing heresy.

I have already demonstrated that Norman Shepherd has explicitly denied the Biblical and Reformed understanding of justification by faith alone. Emphasis in this chapter will be upon the teachings of Rich Lusk, Steve Schlissel, and Doug Wilson. I find it most disheartening that these men still call themselves Reformed much less even orthodox.

Rich Lusk

He is presently the pastor of the Trinity Presbyterian Church in Birmingham, Alabama. I am not quite sure of the present denomination affiliation of that church, but the church's website indicates that the church will soon apply for membership into the Confederation of Reformed Evangelicals (CRE) of which

Doug Wilson's church in Moscow, Idaho is a member. The CRE claims that it accepts the Westminster Standards and the Three Forms of Unity. This admission is interesting because Rich Lusk's views are thoroughly incompatible with these Reformed documents.

Over the past three years, Rich Lusk has authored a series of articles that pertain to the relationship between justification and good works. I will quote extensively from these articles in order to demonstrate his denial of justification by faith alone. They constitute some of the most blatant and forthright denials of this precious doctrine that I have ever read. Those familiar with the Scripture and the Reformed Standards will find these comments utterly amazing for one who still claims to be orthodox and Reformed in doctrine. As you will see, **his views are another gospel, which stands condemned by the Word of God in Galatians 1:6-8.**

Lusk Says the Law can be Kept for Justification

The Federal Vision understands Romans 2:13 and James 2 completely different from what the Reformed Faith has understood it to mean for 500 years. Lusk really believes that the Mosaic Law could be kept for our justification. He states:

> Paul states just as emphatically as James that the doers of the law will be justified (Rom.2:13; James 2:14ff). But who are these doers of the law? Is Paul speaking hypothetically of a class of sinless people who do not really exist? Or does he have something in mind? Let's start by unpacking what it means to keep the law. **The law simply did not require perfect obedience.** It was not designed for the angels or sinless humans. It was given to a fallen-but-redeemed nation at Sinai, and was perfectly adapted to their maturity level and ability. (Emphasis mine)
>
> Law keeping in this context is not a matter of scoring 100% on an ethics test. It is not even a matter of scoring 51%. It simply doesn't work that way. Conformity to the law was a matter of relationship, not something mechanical. The law called for a life of faith (Hab. 2:4), a life of full-orbed loyalty to the Lawgiver. **If one sinned, one did not automatically become a "law breaker," except in a highly technical sense.** After all, the torah made provision for sin in the sacri-

ficial system. Law keeping included rituals for law breaking.[1]
(Emphasis is mine)

It is quite apparent that Lusk does not understand the Scripture, nor has he read very carefully the Reformed Standards. For Lusk, the breaking of the Law of God is not that horrendous. After all, one could go to the sacrificial system and find forgiveness. Lusk states that law keeping is a matter of relationship, not mechanical. What is this suppose to mean? Does he think that God just says, "Well, as long as you try hard that is okay, but you really don't need to score that high, not even 51%?" Contrary to Lusk's thinking, breaking one commandment just one time will condemn someone (James 2:10; Rom. 6:23).

In order to prove that God really did not require perfect obedience, Lusk gives several Old Testament people as those who were called "blameless" and "righteous" before God (Luke 1:6), implying that they were justified by keeping the commandments. Lusk is arguing exactly like a Romanist. Calvin has something to say about this kind of reasoning:

> They are accounted righteous and blameless, because their whole life testifies that they are devoted to righteousness, that the fear of God dwells in them, so long as they give a holy example. But as their pious endeavors fall very far short of perfection, they cannot please God without obtaining pardon. The righteousness which is commended in them depends on the gracious forbearance of God, who does not reckon to them their remaining unrighteousness.

> Those who explain it to mean that Zachariah and Elizabeth were righteous by faith, simply because they freely obtained the favor of God through the Mediator, torture and misapply the words of Luke. With respect to the subject itself, they state a part of the truth, but not the whole. I do own that the righteousness which is ascribed to them ought to be regarded as obtained, not by the merit of works, but by the grace of Christ; and yet, because the Lord has not imputed to them their sins, he has been pleased to bestow on their holy, though imperfect life, the appellation of righteousness. The folly of the Papists is easily refuted. With the righteousness of faith they contrast this righteousness, which is ascribed to

---

[1] Rich Lusk, *Future Justification To The Doers Of The Law,* (2003) <www. hornes.org/ Theologia:: Soteriology:: Future Justification to the Doers of the Law>.

Zachariah, which certainly springs from the former, and, therefore, must be subject, inferior, and, to use a common expression, subordinate to it, so that there is no collision between them.[2]

Rich Lusk is terribly confused by thinking that one can obtain justification by obeying the Law. He actually thinks that Jesus taught that we could keep the law for our justification. Lusk states:

The justification by works envisioned in Romans 2 cannot be any more hypothetical than the condemnation spoken of... Several other texts bear on Romans 2. In James 1:22, James speaks in non-hypothetical terms of doing the law. Jesus is not kidding or messing around when he speaks of a future justification according to our words (Matt. 12:37; 25:31ff). When Jesus describes two paths- one leading to life, the other to death- he isn't propounding a hypothetical way of salvation by walking the narrow path of obedience (Mt. 7:24). Rather, he is demanding obedience as a non-negotiable condition of salvation. When Hebrews says that without holiness, no man will see the Lord, it is not proposing holiness as a hypothetical plan of salvation by merit (Heb.12:14). When Jesus requires cross bearing and life-losing as a condition of eternal life in the gospels (e.g., Lk. 9:23, Jn. 12:25), he means exactly what he says. And on and on we could go.[3]

This quote is a tremendous denial of the gospel. It advocates that good works are not the fruit or evidence of justifying faith. Lusk has totally confused justification with sanctification, which is what Federal Vision theology consistently confuses. Lusk never mentions that any demand for obedience is intended to drive us to find grace and mercy in Christ; no, he thinks this is how we obtain salvation by bearing our cross. This is Romanism, pure and simple!

One of the most bizarre views that Lusk adopts is the idea of an initial justification and then a final justification. In his article, Lusk discusses Zechariah 3 and Revelation 3 where it talks about sinners receiving white robes in place of their sin-laden garments. Lusk states:

---

[2] Calvin, *Calvin's New Testament Commentaries, Matthew, Mark, and Luke*, p. 6-7.

[3] Lusk, *Future Justification To The Doers Of The Law.*

The initial clothing in white is received by faith alone. This is the beginning of Joshua's justification. But if Joshua is to remain justified- that is, if the garments he has received are not to become re-soiled with his iniquity- he must be faithful. **Thus, initial justification is by faith alone; subsequent justifications include obedience ... The fluidity of these symbols suggests a certain fluidity in our doctrine of justification. The white robes stand first and foremost for Christ's free gift to his people... But his forensic justification cannot be separated from the good works that make the saints worthy of their new apparel.** In other words, the poetic imagery points in the same direction as the theological prose of Paul (Rom. 2:13) and James (2:14ff): **those who will be vindicated in the end are those who have been faithfully obedient. There is not hint of merit theology in these passages, but there is no escaping the close nexus formed between priestly investiture, justification, and obedience.** To the question, "Are the saints robed in Christ's righteousness or their own obedience?", the imagery of Revelation answers, "Yes!" In other words, the word pictures drawn in this book do not support a rigid separation of justification from holy living. Justification and sanctification are of a piece, both symbolized by the same white robes.[4] (Emphasis mine)

Heresy abounds in this statement. It is an insult of immense proportions to the Lord Jesus Christ. The Bible never speaks of two types of justification, one that is initial and the other as final. Lusk talks about a fluidity in the doctrine of justification. This is simply saying that justification is a process, that it is not a one-time act of God in pardoning our sins in Christ alone. Where in the Reformed Standards is there a fluid doctrine of justification? Justification is **not** a process. Sanctification is a process. Lusk has flatly denied the Confessional statements, and then he wants us to believe that his doctrine is compatible with them?

This fluid form of justification, which has an initial and final justification, is purely fabricated in the minds of the Federal Vision in order to make way for a works salvation paradigm. Jesus, supposedly, grants initial justification, but then we must be very careful not to soil these white garments by failing to be obedient. Lusk unequivocally stated that it is our faithful obedience that guar-

---

[4] Lusk, *Future Justification To The Doers Of The Law.*

antees our final justification. It really does not matter what Jesus did for us initially; in the end it is our obedience. And then, Lusk has the audacity to say that this is not merit! Lusk tries to pull the same trick on us that Shepherd does. They both denounce the idea of "merit" but then turn around and advocate the necessity of obedience in order to be justified. I'm sorry but this is merit whether you like it or not, and it isn't the merit of Jesus given to us, but our own miserable merit that supposedly saves us. I don't know why Lusk even bothered to talk about Jesus' initial justification because it is absolutely irrelevant in the final analysis. According to him, what matters is our obedience that gets us final justification. And remember, since he says that the Law of God does not require perfect obedience and we can supposedly keep this law for our justification, then it is an imperfect obedience that gets us finally justified in the end.

This is heresy. This is not the gospel of the Lord Jesus Christ. This is an accursed gospel, which is no good news whatsoever. If my final justification depends upon my imperfect obedience, then I am hopelessly lost forever in Hell.

If Lusk hasn't made himself clear enough, he continues:

> The Bible is clear: obedience is necessary to receive eternal life. There is no justification apart from good works. But more needs to be said about final judgment. What role will faith play? What role will works play? Again, we find the Bible teaching that future justification is according to works. Final justification **is to the (faithful) doers of the law (Rom. 2:1ff) and by those good works which make faith complete** (James 2:14ff). Justification will not be fully realized until the resurrection. In fact, the main reason justification comes up at all in the Scriptures is because someday we will all stand before God's judgment seat an answer for our deeds done in the body. (Emphasis Lusk)

> In James 2, "justification" cannot be referring to a **demonstration** of justification, e.g., justification does and cannot mean something like "show to be justified." Rather, James has in view the same kind of justification as Paul- forensic, soteric justification. Good works justify **persons** in James 2, not **faith** or ones **status** as a justified sinner. James is not telling his readers how to "justify their justification" or how to "give evidence of a true and lively faith." Instead he says

their persons will **not** be justified by faith alone, but **also** by good works of obedience they have done. The use of the preposition "by" is important since it indicates a sort of dual instrumentality in justification. In other words, in some sense, James is speaking of a justification in which faith and works **combine together** to justify. Future justification is according to one's life pattern. No one dare claim these works to be meritorious, but they are necessary. There is congruence between the life we live and the destiny we will receive. (Emphasis is Lusk)

To unpack this a bit further, we can reconcile Paul and James by taking into account the factor of **time** (something systematic theology, with its abstract methodology, tends to leave out). Initial justification – the pole the Reformers focused on in their disputes with Rome- is by faith alone. Hence **sola fide** must stand unchallenged. Final justification, however, is according to works. This pole of justification takes into account the entirety of our lives- the obedience we've performed, the sins we've committed, the confession and repentance we've done. At the last day, our works will not have any meritorious value. In that sense, even before the great white judgment throne, we will plead nothing but the blood and resurrection of Jesus. We will place no confidence in anything we have accomplished- even what God has done in us and through us! Nevertheless, God's verdict over us will be in accord with, and therefore in some sense based upon, the life we have lived.[5] (Emphasis Lusk)

I trust that the reader will see the contradictions and blatant false theology in the previous paragraphs. The bold emphasis is Lusk's emphasis, not mine. He wants his reader to fully understand that final justification is based upon our faithful obedience. In keeping with others in the Federal Vision and Shepherd, in particular, Lusk tries to sound orthodox by saying that our justification will be by the blood and resurrection of Jesus and that our works are not meritorious. Notice, he never mentions the imputed righteousness of Christ, only His blood and union with Jesus' resurrection. At this point, this union with Jesus' resurrection remains nebulous. Second, his statements are inherently contradictory. He has been discussing at length the necessity of our faithful obedience in order to receive **final justification**; he then interjects something

---

[5] Lusk, *Future Justification To The Doers Of The Law.*

to the effect that it really is not meritorious, and he then immediately ends with saying that God's verdict is based on our obedient life.

The Federal Vision is always complaining that the rest of the Reformed world is simply misreading their statements. I believe this is either dishonesty or at best an inability to communicate clearly. Neo-orthodoxy was notorious for its ambiguity about the authority of the Word of God. It used evangelical words and redefined them; this is exactly what the Federal Vision does. It uses "faith," but it then redefines it to mean "faithful obedience." It uses the word "justification, "but it then redefines it as a process, not solely as a one time judicial act of pardon. It introduces a two-fold justification. It claims adherence to the Reformed Standards, but then it insists that we must read the Confessional documents in light of their presuppositions.

It is no wonder that the average Christian in the pew remains confused; however, Lusk is helping us to see the Federal Vision more clearly; he is quite explicit in his unorthodoxy. This is why I quote him so extensively. The bankruptcy of the Federal Vision's view of the atonement, the nature of the Law of God, and the holiness of God is brought out in this next quote:

> But the Bible nowhere says God will apply absolute justice at the last day. So why do we make that assumption? The only places where God enforces strict justice are the cross and hell. For the covenant people, at least, **it seems God will use "fatherly justice" in the final judgment, not "absolute justice."** He will judge us the way parents evaluate their child's art work, or the way a new husband assesses the dinner his beloved wife has made. **The standard will be soft and generous because God is merciful.** Our works will not have merit before God, but they will have worth precisely because of the covenant relationship we are in. (Again, compare this notion to those passages in Scripture which claim a particular saint is righteous, or has kept the law, or has done good, e.g., Jn. 5:29, Lk. 1:6, Ps. 7:8, Acts 13:22, etc. **These examples show the kind of "soft" evaluation God makes of his people.**[6] (Emphasis mine)

Note the bold assertion by Lusk that nowhere does the Bible apply justice at the last day. The idea of a "fatherly justice" that is a "soft" judgment is nowhere in the Bible. The work of Christ on behalf of sinners is completely undermined by Lusk. Apparently, the standard is not that high. We must remember that the

---

[6] Lusk, *Future Justification To The Doers Of The Law.*

Federal Vision has denied the truth that God's Law demands perfect obedience; it has denied that Christ's righteousness is imputed to us. According to them, we don't need it! After all, the standard is a "soft" judgment. This is another way of telling us that God supposedly accepts an imperfect obedience on our part. Lusk has already told us that the Law does not demand perfect obedience and that there are righteous men that the Bible recognizes.

Lusk refuses to understand what the Scripture maintains and one that is explicitly taught by our Confessional documents. Good works (sanctification), flow out of justification; they are not inherently part of it. This inability on the Federal Vision, or willful refusal to accept it, forces it into heretical positions.

I hope that everyone reading this recognizes the seriousness of these views of the Federal Vision. Trusting in them will not save you! I cannot conceive of going into the final judgment, trusting that I really do not need Jesus' righteousness, that my imperfect obedience will be good enough to pass judgment. As Lusk says, God doesn't demand 100% perfection or even 51% on His ethics test; God will judge us softly. This is frightening! The stakes are high – either Heaven or Hell. Is Lusk willing to stake his soul on this?

We must remember how God commended Abraham in Romans 4:3-5: *"For what does the Scripture say? And Abraham believed God, and it was reckoned to him as righteousness. Now to the one who works, his wage is not reckoned as a favor, but as what is due. But to the one who does not work, but believes in Him who justifies the ungodly, his faith is reckoned as righteousness."*

Rich Lusk and other Federal Vision proponents simply cannot understand this passage. Faith and works clearly are being contrasted. The one who works is earning a wage, but faith is not a work that gets rewarded with justification. Justification is rooted in a faith that rests **solely** in Christ. Jesus justifies the ungodly; he does not justify those who think their good works can save them. Where is an initial justification in this passage? Where is there a final justification based on our good works? The Federal Vision preaches a foreign gospel that will not save.

I know that Lusk and others would be very critical of me in making these comments and would insist that I don't understand. Again, are they willing to bet their souls on it? The fact that many in the Reformed community have condemned the doctrines of the Federal Vision should send a resounding warning to those in the Federal Vision and those who choose to believe their doctrines. Do not trust in a plan of salvation that cannot save. Take heed now while there is time for repentance. At Judgment Day there will be no chance of repentance. Are these people willing to cast aside the teaching of the Reformed Faith for the past 500 years and trust in an innovative teaching?

Lusk is clear that the "faith" that leads to justification should not be viewed independent of works:

> A judgment about works is really a judgment about faith, and vice versa. For example, it is **not** eisegesis to assume that the doers of the law in Romans 2 are those who have demonstrated the "obedience of faith," rather than those who have scored 100% on a moral exam ... God is not looking for perfection from his people; rather he desires a core commitment of loyalty that overshadows everything else we do, no matter how badly we may fail from time to time.[7] (Emphasis Lusk)

In discussing his view of Soteriology (the doctrines related to salvation), Lusk wants to tout his "soft" judgment theology:

> Third, the "softer" standard simply seems to be the teaching of Scripture. Pietistic Protestantism has created a sort of "holy worm" theology in which we are never allowed to "feel good" about anything we've done. We can never please God, no matter what Paul said we aim for (cf. 2 Cor. 5:9ff). Everything we do, no matter how noble or faithful, is tainted with sin and therefore worthy of condemnation ... However true that is in abstract, it's simply not the way Scripture evaluates things. The Bible repeatedly speaks of believers and their works as "good," as "worthy," and so forth.[8]

Is it not odd that Lusk failed to mention Luke 17. Jesus gives the parable of the unprofitable servant. In this parable, the servant who faithfully is tending the sheep expects special rewards for his work. Jesus gives the meaning of the parable in verses 9 and 10 – *"He does not thank the slave because he did the things which were commanded, does he? So you too, when you do all the things which are commanded you, say, 'We are unworthy slaves; we have done only that which we ought to have done."* Lusk simply cannot understand the Scripture.

It is interesting that Lusk figures that his view may seem out of accord with the Westminster Confession of Faith specifically at chapter 11 section 2 which speaks about faith as being the sole instrument for justification. Here is how he attempts to avoid the problem:

---

[7] Lusk, *Future Justification To The Doers Of The Law*, p. 5.

[8] Lusk, *Future Justification To The Doers Of The Law*.

This is not a denial of sola fide or WCF 11:2 (faith is the alone instrument ..."). For one thing, when Paul points to faith as the unique receptor of justifying righteousness, he is speaking of initial justification. But it is indisputable that the biblical data on final justification brings works into the picture. Faith is always the sole instrument of justification in that faith alone lays hold of Christ. Works cannot lay hold of anything. But faith's unique role in justification does not exclude other instruments functioning **in other senses**. Thus, works can become instrumental means (or "inferior causes") in a different sense, as Calvin pointed out. Similarly, in some sense, baptism is an instrument of justification since in the sacraments Christ is applied to the believer and the believer is not justified until that application takes place (cf WCF 11:4 and WSC 92).[9] (Emphasis Lusk)

I am sorry, but where is "initial justification" and "final justification" mentioned in the WCF 11:2? What Bible verse is there that speaks of "initial and final justification?" They don't exist! Lusk reinterprets the Confession; he inserts things into it that are simply not there, and he then says that his views are compatible with the Confession. The Federal Vision is notorious about doing this; this is why I have quoted the Reformed Standards at length in order to show that their views are contradictory to the Standards.

Notice from the quote that Lusk wants to speak of **other instruments of justification**. These are not mentioned in the Confession or Scripture, but his system demands it. Lusk tries to bring in the sacrament of baptism as one of these other instruments of justification and even tries to quote the Confession and Catechism as support of it. Of course, he is now advocating water baptism as a means of justification and is espousing baptismal regeneration.

The Westminster Confession of Faith in Chapter 11, section 4, does not mention baptism. It mentions that the elect will be justified, but they will not be justified until the Holy Spirit applies Christ to them. Lusk quotes the Westminster Shorter Catechism as support of his supposed additional instrument of justification, which does mention the sacraments. It is interesting that question number 92 mentions the benefits of the new covenant as being represented, sealed, and applied to **believers**. Question number 91 refers to the sacraments as effectual means of salvation **not from any virtue in them** but only by the blessing of Christ, and the working of his Spirit in them **that by faith receive them**.

---

[9] Lusk, *Future Justification To The Doers Of The Law,* p. 7.

No matter how you read the Shorter Catechism it does not teach a co-instrumentality of the sacraments in justification. Reading closely, the Catechism emphasizes the necessity of faith. Faith is the key. The Catechism does not speak of believer's baptism as Baptists would insist. The point is that faith must be present for the sacrament to be effectual. This could be present when the child is baptized or at a later time. This is why the Westminster Confession in Chapter 29, section 6, says that the efficacy is **not tied to that moment of time wherein it is administered.** The Holy Spirit confers it at God's appointed time. More will be said about baptism at a later point.

One thing is for sure about Lusk and company. They believe in co-instruments in justification, not in faith alone. Works and baptism are co-instruments. The fact that he considers baptism a co-instrument means that he does not view it as the historic Reformed Faith has understood it. Baptism without faith does no one any spiritual good.

In another article that Rich Lusk wrote in 2003 titled *"Why The Law/Gospel Paradigm Is Flawed,"* he further sets forth some aberrant theology. In discussing the Mosaic Law, Lusk states:

> Third, the law did not require perfect obedience. It was designed for sinners, not unfallen creatures. Thus, the core demand of the law was covenant loyalty and trust, not sinless perfection. This is why numerous sinful but redeemed people are regarded as law keepers in Scripture. Stretching back to the pre-Mosaic period and all the way forward to the New Testament, we find that Noah (Gen. 6:1-8), Jacob (Gen. 25:27), Job (1:1), Joseph (Mt.1:19), and Zachariah and Elizabeth (Lk 1:6) were all blameless in God's sight. **Moses was right; this law was not too hard to keep, for it was a law of faith (Dt. 30:11ff; cf Rom. 10:1-12. Even Dt. 27:26 ("Cursed is the one who does not confirm all the words of this law"), when read in covenantal context, does not insist on 100% obedience to be regarded a law keeper ...** If this strikes us as odd, it is because we have started out with our own ideas about what the law requires rather than letting Scripture itself shape our understanding of concepts like "law-keeping," "righteousness," "obedience," "goodness," "blamelessness," and "worthiness." [10] (Emphasis is mine)

---

[10] Rich Lusk, *Why The Law/Gospel Paradigm Is Flawed,* (2003), pp. 1-2.

Notice, the historic Reformed Faith for centuries has gotten it wrong and have imposed their faulty presuppositions upon Scripture. If we adopt Lusk's presuppositions, then we can come to the amazing conclusion that Moses taught that the Law was not really that hard to keep. After all, look at the parade of people in biblical history that were called righteous. Why, many people have been justified by a less than perfect obedience. No, it is Lusk's presuppositions that are terribly flawed, not those of the historic Reformed Faith. Lusk and the rest of the adherents to the Federal Vision simply cannot or refuse to see that all of these "righteous" people are said to be righteous because they first possessed saving faith, and their good works flowed out this saving faith. Just like all the Reformed Standards have taught from the Westminster Confession and its Catechism, to the Belgic Confession with its Heidelberg Catechism, to the Canons of Dordt, all the saving graces **accompany** the person who is first justified by faith alone (see WCF 11:2).

Lusk, just like Steve Schlissel as we shall soon see, equates the Law with the gospel, for Lusk writes:

> Fifth, the Law was a pre-Christian revelation of the gospel. Paul regarded the law as a witness to the gospel (Rom. 3:21) and a shadow of the good things to come in Christ (Heb. 10:1). John regarded the law as a type of the grace and truth that came in Christ Jesus, and (conversely) regarded Jesus as the Law incarnate, the Torah made flesh (Jn. 1:1-18). For John, the transition from Moses to Christ was a movement from grace to grace (Jn.1:17)…The law was a typological blueprint of the gospel; the gospel is the eschatological fulfillment of the law.[11]

The Law is **not** the gospel in typological form whatsoever! Lusk has made the gospel and the law identical in essence; only the Law in the OT was a type of precursor. Lusk cannot be more mistaken. Instead of honoring Jesus, he has insulted Jesus in the most emphatic way. Lusk commits the same terrible error that Norman Shepherd makes; he considers the law as grace in terms of our justification. The Federal Vision completely subverts the true gospel. Galatians 3:21-25 cannot be more clear (see my elaboration on this in chapter 5). The Law is a tutor to lead us to Christ to find grace! The Law is not gracious when it comes to justification. It condemns us; it shows that we cannot keep its perfect demands. That is why we need a savior! That is why we need Jesus, who is our righteousness for us! The gospel is that there is relief from

---

[11] Lusk, *Why The Law/Gospel Paradigm Is Flawed.*

our failure to keep perfectly God's holy Law. We can run to Jesus by faith. The Federal Vision does not need Jesus to save them. As Lusk has said, it is our works, done imperfectly as they may be, that will save us in final justification.

I must say that I have to exercise great restraint from being very angry at the men who espouse such a dishonoring theology. They have insulted my Savior; they advocate a gospel that cannot save from sin; they claim to be Reformed; they lead people down a soul destroying path; and they have the audacity to call this works salvation as grace. There is nothing gracious in it at all.

In the early days of this whole controversy over the 2002 Auburn Avenue Pastors' Conference, I made the comment to someone that if their view of the covenant is correct, then these men will be forced to deny the perseverance of the saints. Well, sure enough, this has happened. I will have an entire chapter dealing with the Federal Vision's denial of the perseverance of the saints, but for now, I will mention these comments that Lusk makes:

> Grace, conditions, and the possibility of genuine apostasy are not incompatible in God's covenant economy. In fact, we see that the transition from Old Covenant to New Covenant does not fundamentally alter the structure of the covenant. "Getting in" and "staying in" are predicated on the same basic conditions of faith and faithfulness.[12]

In other words, we can lose our justification! Our final justification depends upon our faithfulness, and if we are not faithful, then we can lose it all. More will be said on this later.

Steve Schlissel

Steve Schlissel is the pastor of Messiah's Congregation in New York City. He was one of the original speakers at the 2002 Auburn Avenue Pastors' Conference (AAPC). He spoke again at the AAPC in 2003. He participated in the Knox Theological Seminary Colloquium in 2003; he submitted papers in support of the Federal Vision. On his church's website, he has discussed the doctrines commonly associated with the Federal Vision. His church advertises that it subscribes to the Three Forms of Unity (the Belgic Confession, the Heidelberg Catechism, and the Canons of Dordt).[13] I shall demonstrate that Schlissel is in direct opposition to his own subscription Standards, and that he

---

[12] Lusk, *Why The Law/Gospel Paradigm Is Flawed.*

[13] One can find this on the internet at http://www.messiahnyc.org/beliefs.asp. Monday September 16, 2002, p. 1.

is unorthodox in his views of justification by faith as it relates to good works. He argues the same manner as others in the Federal Vision. His arguments are extremely close to those of Rich Lusk.

Steve Schlissel was the very first speaker of the 2002 AAPC which began the present controversy. I will never forget the incredible first words that Steve Schlissel spoke. He opened the conference stating - "*I'd like to know - I have been here many times by the grace of God in this pulpit and each time I am here Mr. Carter prays that the congregation be protected from false doctrine.*"[14] Those words have echoed almost prophetically down the corridors of modern Reformed thought.

It was this conference that began the controversy in the Reformed camp. Based upon all the lectures at this conference, Covenant Presbytery of the RPCUS condemned the teachings of these men as containing doctrines contrary to the Bible and to the Westminster Standards. I have no idea who this Mr. Carter is, but this man's prayers to protect the congregation from false doctrine still ring loudly. Unfortunately, this man's church and that particular conference opened up the door for false doctrine that has plagued the Reformed community for over three years. If this man is a godly man, then perhaps God will one day rid his own church of this hideous theology, but for the present, this church led by Steve Wilkins continues to be one of, if not the leading force in this false theology.

In his lecture Schlissel begins with a denunciation of people who want to look to the Westminster Confession as a guideline for doctrinal purity. (see his statements on the confessional documents covered in chapter 2.) In these quotes, Schlissel gives a scathing diatribe against a commitment to the solas of the Reformation. It is interesting that in this polemic of his against the Westminster Confession and the solas of the Reformation, he actually undermines his own church's subscription allegiance to the Three Forms of Unity, all of which predate the Westminster Confession. This means that his church, Messiah's Congregation, is really not interested in Confessional subscription. If so, they need to remove their statements to this fact. As we shall see, Schlissel adamantly opposes these Reformed expressions.

Why would Schlissel want us to be free from the restrictions of these Confessional documents? It is so that we can adopt the Federal Vision's new paradigm, which reinterprets faith as faithful obedience, which touts a different kind of covenant, which advocates baptismal regeneration, which redefines election, which advocates a denial of the perseverance of the saints, which denies justification by faith alone, and which denies the imputation of Christ's

---

[14] Schlissel, "*Covenant Reading.*"

righteousness to our account. This entire faulty theology of the Federal Vision is refuted by all of the historic Reformed Standards. The easiest way to promote a new theology is to convince people that the old expressions are archaic. We need to always be reforming. Under the guise of reforming the church, a hideous new paradigm is advanced, a different gospel is promoted – a justification by works of obedience.

Schlissel recognized that his ideas have been met with resistance when he said in his first lecture:

> Now to help people to move from where they are in asking the scriptures certain questions to go to hearing what the scripture would have us ask is a very difficult task and I don't know how to do it. I tried to do it up in Ontario recently, and I almost got killed. Not to mention that they had to put metal detectors at the doors but the response afterwards was very discouraging. People, one professor of a prominent reformed seminary wrote in reaction to this speech, "When it comes to the question upon what basis and for what reason am I right with God and an heir of eternal life, reformed believers have insisted as rigorously as Luther that the law is quote repugnant," and he says he is quoting Calvin here. Well you can quote Calvin to make him say anything you want and that is the problem with guys who write a lot.
>
> Well, of course, he said that, but wasn't it qualified? You know what Luther said, well he may have said that, but how was it qualified? How does the Bible speak and how does the Bible qualify itself? Is the law repugnant to how we are made right with God? How we stay right with God? Is the law truly repugnant, this law/gospel dichotomy is a false one. It is unbiblical.[15]

Schlissel calls Luther's law/gospel distinction regarding justification an unbiblical concept. In his lecture, Schlissel repeatedly sets up a straw man and then demolishes it. He criticizes those Christians who have problems with the Law of God, with the antinomians among us. While this is commonly true in today's Christian culture, this has nothing to do with the means of justification. It is at this juncture that Schlissel gets himself into theological quicksand.

---

[15] Schlissel, "*Covenant Reading,*" p. 6.

Schlissel insists that we are asking the wrong questions today. The wrong question is – What must I do to be saved? The right question, Schlissel says is – What does the Lord require? Schlissel states:

> The question has always been what does the Lord require? We've changed the question since Luther's day. Perhaps imperceptibly to some, but quite drastically if you look at it. The question is commonly, "What must I do to be saved?" But that's the wrong question. The question is, "What does the Lord require?" If we don't begin to retool our churches, to turn around from the, "What must I do to be saved?" "What does the Lord require?" we are going to die. Because in answering one, "What must I do to be saved?" you move in the idea of sola, sola, sola, and then you have the sola fide, and if you are only saved by faith apart from any activity or any response to God's word and then well, what kind of faith is that? Well there is the spurious faith and there is the pretentious faith and there is a certain quality to this faith and then the pulpits are devoted to examining your faith and then you have to bring up your faith and before you know it, everyone thinks they are not saved, the guy next to me is saved, she might be saved, I'm not saved. How can I be saved, I don't know how you can be saved, but you come here next week and I will make you feel guilty by golly, you just get here. And week after week, the people berate, are berated and bullied and tortured in their consciousness, make on the presupposition that God is really as niggardly as the preacher believes him to be and he only saves with the greatest possible reluctance. And when somebody manages to squeak into the kingdom, he almost snaps his fingers and says, shucks another one made it and I was hoping that he would be fooled and deceived into thinking that he had real faith when he didn't really have it.[16]

Schlissel seems to get twisted all out of shape by the simple phrase, "What must I do to be saved?" He makes this remark:

> So that when we ask only, "What must I do to be saved?" we end up with Baptistic Americana. But when we ask, "What

---

[16] Schlissel, *"Covenant Reading,"* p. 8.

does the Lord require?" we have the possibility of reaching the world.[17]

Has Schlissel forgotten that this is right out of inspired Scripture in Acts 16:30, where the Philippian jailer asks Paul and Silas, "What must I do to be saved?" In Acts 16:31, Paul did not tell the Philippian jailer that he had asked the wrong question. He did not tell the jailer to keep the commandments in order to be saved. Paul told him, *"Believe in the Lord Jesus, and you shall be saved, you and your household."* Luther was not the first one to ask the question. The inspired Paul answered the right question. I will take inspired Paul before Steve Schlissel any day.

Schlissel continues his assault on Martin Luther in the following comment:

> The difference is dramatic. The difference can be seen in the illustration of Archimedes' lever. You remember that he said, "Give me a place to stand upon and a lever long enough and I could move the entire earth." Luther had one foot on the Bible and used a broken lever and he shook the world. But imagine what he could have done if he had both feet on the Bible, that is the Old and the New Testament together without imagining an antipathy between them and that if he had a lever that was the covenant and not his mere personal salvation?[18]

According to Schlissel, what is Luther's broken lever? It is the recapturing of the biblical principle that we are justified by faith alone in Christ. This glorious gospel truth, which God brought back to His visible church dramatically affected the course of history, but according to Schlissel, it was a broken lever. According to Schlissel we need to rid ourselves of Greek ideas and categories, which Luther represents, and return to what he calls Hebraic categories. And what are these Hebraic categories? Schlissel states:

> If we have faltered, we have to go back where we made our mistakes. One of the falterings, one of the errors, has been in our antipathy to the law imagining that the Bible really says about it what Luther said about it.
>
> But the Lord told us in Micah, "Will the Lord be pleased with thousands of rams with ten thousand rivers of oil, shall I offer

---

[17] Schlissel, *"Covenant Reading"*.

[18] Schlissel, *"Covenant Reading"*.

my firstborn for my transgression, the fruit of my body for
the sin of my soul? He has shown you, o man, what is good
and what does the Lord require of you, to act justly and to
love mercy and to walk humbly with your God." Is that a
works religion? Is that legalism? That's what God told us that
he wants from us. "To do justice, to love mercy and to walk
humbly with our God." In Genesis 18 he tells us that as he is
musing within himself, that he chose Abraham so that he
would direct his children in his household after him to keep
the way of the Lord by doing what is right and just so that the
Lord will bring about for Abraham what he had promised
him.[19]

Schlissel is making the same terrible theological error that Norman Shepherd
and Rich Lusk have made. He thinks that these commands are the means by
which men are justified before God. Again, the inherent problem with Federal
Vision theology is their confusion of the doctrines of justification and sanctification. They completely blur the distinction, making them essentially identical.
There is no question that Micah 6 lays out God's commands for His covenant
people, but they are to be a loving response to His redeeming grace. They are
not the basis for man's justification.

Schlissel then goes on another tirade against some certain Southern
Presbyterians, calling them Baptists, as if there is something odious about
being a Baptist. Now, I am a committed Presbyterian, and a Southern one at
that, and while I am convinced that Presbyterianism is the most faithful understanding of Scripture, I do not consider my Baptist brothers, who are truly trusting in Christ alone for their salvation, as the dregs of the theological world.
Here is what Schlissel said:

> But this is the state of affairs because of our concern with our
> own personal salvation based upon a view that God really
> doesn't want to save anyone and that he is playing games and
> that if it is not by works which we have done then it's by a
> kind of faith which we can't identify. And we are always
> looking, you know you see this, no offense, but this is espe-
> cially prevalent in Southern Presbyterians for some reason
> who are essentially Baptists who don't refrain from sprin-
> kling their babies. They think like Baptists. They address
> their children as Baptists. They don't believe their children

---

[19] Schlissel, *"Covenant Reading,"* p. 9.

are saved by the grace of God, they believe they are waiting for a decision, some sort of cogent, confessable experience of personal regeneration and transition from death to life because they believe their children are born in death. They have bought into the Baptistic way of thinking and it is just an abomination.[20]

So what is the solution according to Schlissel? We must seek obedience. He says:

This is what the Lord Almighty, the God of Israel says, reform your ways and your actions and I will let you live. Don't trust in deceptive words, the temple of the Lord, the temple of the Lord, the temple of the Lord." Can I say something? Don't trust in deceptive words, we are reformed, we are reformed. Don't trust in deceptive words, Westminster Confession, Westminster Confession. You have to have the whole word of God and the fear of God in your heart and in your home. That's what God wants. If you really change your ways and your actions and deal with each other justly, if you don't oppress the alien, the fatherless or the widow and you don't shed innocent blood, if you don't follow other gods to your own harm, then I will let you live.

It is just as easy for God to say today, "I hate, I despise your confessions of faith. Take them out. I am disgusted by your solas." Why? Because they are not true? Of course they are true in a proper context. But they are not substitutes for the fear of the Lord. They are not substitutes for whole hearted, biblical, covenantal religion. Seek the Lord all you humble of the land and do what he commands, seek righteousness, seek humility, perhaps you will be sheltered on the day of the Lord's anger.[21]

The problem is that Schlissel is preaching against a straw man. The issue is not that many are trusting in the Confessional documents and an empty, hypocritical way of life. This has nothing to do with justification by faith alone in Christ. In expressing a truth against the false professors of the Faith, Schlissel is thinking that he is providing the right way in order to be right with God. He sees faithful obedience as the basis for justification, and he is dead wrong.

---

[20] Schlissel, "*Covenant Reading,*" pp. 10, 11.

[21] Schlissel, "*Covenant Reading,*" p. 11-12.

Schlissel paraphrases several stories of Jesus' encounter with a lawyer and the young rich ruler. Schlissel makes these comments:

> Jesus Christ said that the commandments of God can be summarized, they can be summarized in love to God and love to neighbor. He didn't say, I am going to trick you by telling you a command that is going to put in the same bind that Luther found himself in and then when you finally despair of any hope maybe you will come out the other side and you'll be saved by grace. It makes the transaction into something preposterous and fraudulent. Jesus looked at him and loved him. Jesus told him the truth. He didn't lie to him. He wasn't setting him up with the first use of the law or the second or the third.
>
> The very idea of a first, second and third use of the law is illegal and unbiblical. It demands that the law conform to what we want from it and if it doesn't do that, then we will have none of it. But the law itself is to be our life. This is your life, God said. **In the law I have given you atonement, in the law I have given you promises of forgiveness, in the law I have given you a way to live, in the law I have given you the key to life, in the law you will find grace abounding to the chief of sinners. But we turn it around and say, "No, we will have none of this. That is law as opposed to gospel."** [22] (Emphasis is mine)

It is here that we find Schlissel championing a works salvation exactly like Shepherd and Lusk. Schlissel even interprets the story of the young rich ruler as Lusk does. It completely escapes Schlissel what Jesus was doing. Schlissel completely rejects the idea that Jesus was trying to show these men that they could not live up to the perfect demands of the Law and that they needed to trust Jesus by faith. No, according to Schlissel, grace is found in the Law, which is exactly what Shepherd said in his book *The Call Of Grace* and what Lusk has said in his articles.

Steve Schlissel's Denial of Total Depravity

Steve Schlissel will reveal his further departure from orthodoxy and the Reformed Faith in his second lecture at the 2002 AAPC. Schlissel departs from

---

[22] Schlissel, *"Covenant Reading,"* pp. 12-13

the Reformed doctrine of total depravity, and he is going to challenges the French Confession and the Westminster Confession and Catechism on their use of Romans 3 to prove total depravity or inability. Schlissel states:

> I want to move this idea what I have called this problem into one particular manifestation of our difficulty and that is in the question of righteousness. Is it true that there are none right-eous? Now the reformed confessions generally say that is true and they generally use Romans chapter 3 to prove it. In the French Confession, the fourth section, it says, "from this original corruption, we are utterly indisposed, disabled and made opposite to all good and wholly inclined to all evil," and the proof text is Romans 3:10-12. The French Confession at eleven also says, "we believe that this evil is truly sin sufficient for the condemnation of the whole human race, even of little children in the mother's womb and God considers it as such," and the proof text is Romans 3:9-13. In the Westminster Larger Catechism it says, "that no man is able either of himself or by any grace received in this life per-fectly to keep the commandments of God but does daily break them in thought, word and deed." In the Shorter Catechism at twenty-five says, "that the sinfulness to the estate wherein two men fell consists in the guilt of Adam's first sin, the want of the righteousness wherein he was creat-ed and the corruption of his nature whereby he is utterly indisposed, disabled and made opposite unto all that is spiri-tually good and wholly inclined to all evil and that continual-ly." Now how do they prove that, Romans 3:10-19 alleged-ly prove these propositions and I hope that you see where we are going with this.

> Now Romans chapter 3 does not appear as directly from heaven without mediation, it appears as part of an argument that the holy spirit by Paul is making to a church in a partic-ular, historical circumstance. And it is in a section in which Paul is proving that the whole world is made up of sinners. Does that mean that each and every individual is what the confessions here say they are? Well, lets examine this a little bit.[23]

---

[23] Schlissel, "*Covenant Thinking,*" pp. 55-56.

Fundamentally, Schlissel refuses to accept that Romans 3:9-13 teaches total depravity. I personally don't find this denial surprising, but I actually believe that it is a logical necessity in the Federal Vision's new paradigm. As Lusk argued, there are righteous people out there, whose righteousness enabled them to imperfectly obey the law of God, but that is okay, because God doesn't demand 100% perfection to His Law. This theological perspective cannot have a total depravity that states that none can seek God; otherwise, how can you have all of these "righteous," "blameless," and "worthy" people who are justified before God?

The Federal Vision's denial of the historic doctrine of total depravity makes total sense. It is completely false, and is but another example of their intrusion or reinterpretation of texts to try to fit their works salvation paradigm. Schlissel then gives the following example to try to prove his point:

> We try to make it say things that fit what we believe must be the case in order for our system to hold together but we don't allow the bible to speak its own mind. And you can see this in the sort of sermons that will come from Romans. Now your sweet Christian grandmother becomes subject to this sort of abuse telling her that her throat is an open grave and her tongue practices deceit and the poison of vipers is on her lips. Though she may sing psalms from the time she wakes up until she goes to sleep. Though she may spend her time in prayer for her grandchildren, we are told that she is an evil, wicked witch who's entirely corrupt and no good. And this sort of brow beating goes on day after day after day. Is that really Paul's point? Is that what he is trying to say? What does Paul say here, there is no one righteous, not even one.[24]

Schlissel's reasoning is quite odd. The Reformed doctrine of total depravity has always meant that sin had affected all facets of a man's being - his mind, heart, and will. It has commonly been called original sin as the Westminster Larger Catechism #25 states. One of the proof texts is Romans 3:10. The Westminster delegates understood this passage to be applicable. In this fallen state, we are all seen as children of wrath and bond slaves to Satan as question #27 indicates.

It is hard to understand why Schlissel uses this illustration of the "sweet Christian grandmother." If she is indeed a Christian then she is no longer totally depraved. The genuine Christian, not merely a professing one who is a hypocrite, has been renewed in the whole man by Christ. The Reformed doctrine

---

[24] Schlissel, *"Covenant Thinking,"* p. 56.

of sanctification has maintained that the person has a new heart and a new spirit created in them. The bondage to sin and Satan is forever broken, and they are strengthened by the Spirit to put to death the remaining effects of sin and to live unto righteousness, although they will remain imperfect in this life.

The "sweet Christian grandmother" is a sanctified person, and she is capable of doing good works in the power of the Spirit, though not perfectly. She is considered "righteous" in the sense that she is a justified person who is being sanctified. The good deeds are the fruit of a justified life. Schlissel's illustration is pointless unless he is trying to argue for the fact that there are non-Christians, who if they seek to obey the Law they can become justified. Unfortunately, Schlissel is arguing precisely this. He reverses the doctrines of justification and sanctification. To argue that the two doctrines are essentially identical is basically saying the same thing as placing sanctification before justification. Doing this would be saying that one must seek to live a holy life in conformity with the Law of God in order to be declared pardoned from sin or justified.

The purpose of Romans 3 in Paul's argument against the Jews is that all men, be they Jew or Gentile are born totally depraved because of the guilt and pollution of sin due to Adam's transgression. If we are all totally depraved, then it is impossible to be justified by keeping the Law of God because we have no capacity to keep it. Only by believing in Jesus are we set free from sin's bondage and then enabled to do good.

Steve Schlissel believes that the Bible is full of people who are righteous. The following is a very lengthy quote, but it expresses very clearly his denial of total depravity. He states:

> We have to go meaning for meaning, context for context and eventually till we come to the whole scripture and the whole covenant and learn to retool ourselves to the way God has given us a word, not the way it has been Hellenized down to our time. Because the fact is and I have verses to prove this, nothing like playing both sides of the fence! There are plenty of righteous in the bible. Was not our ancestor Abraham considered righteous for what he did when he offered his son Isaac on the offer? If God rescued Lot, who was a righteous man, distressed by the filthy lives of lawless men, yes, Lot, a righteous man, living among these wicked people day after day tormented in his righteous soul by the lawless deeds he saw and heard his righteous soul? I want to hear a preacher

from the Netherlands Reformed Church tell me that Lot was a righteous man.

Dear children do not let anyone lead you astray. He who does what is right is righteous. **There is none righteous, no not one? The Bible says there are thousands of them, hundreds of thousands of them, millions of them throughout history**. Do not be like Cain who belonged to the evil one and murdered his brother and why did he murder him? Because his own actions were evil and his brother's were righteous.

Now you tell people that today, they will say, oh there is none righteous, there is none righteous. But God says there are righteous people ... The righteous man leads a blameless life, blessed are his children after him. Let the righteous rejoice in the Lord and take refuse in him, let all the upright in heart praise him. The righteous will flourish like a palm tree, they will grow like a cedar of Lebanon. The scepter of the wicked will not remain over the land allotted to the righteous, for the righteous might use their hands to do evil. Do good, o Lord, to those who are good, to those who are upright in heart. There is none good, no not one. So we just saw in that same psalm that there are people who do good. Those who turn to crooked ways, the Lord will banish with the evildoers, but peace be upon Israel.

This is the account of Noah. Noah was a righteous man, blameless among the people of his time and he walked with God. When Abraham was 99 years old, the Lord appeared to him and said, "I am God Almighty, walk before me and be blameless. To the faithful, God shows himself faithful, to the blameless, he shows himself blameless. To the pure, he shows himself pure. But to the crooked, he shows himself shrewd. You saved the humble, but your eyes are on the haughty to bring them low.

In the land of Uz there lived a man whose name was Job. This man was blameless and upright. He feared God and shunned evil. Then the Lord said to Satan, have you considered my servant Job, there is no one else on earth like him, he is blameless and upright, a man who fears God and shuns evil ... These verses are an embarrassment to those who would universalize the statements that we have in Romans chapter 3 and make them doctrines that have independent existence in the heavens theoretically, but when you come down to earth, you can't apply them. Because when we come down to earth in real history, we find in fact the righteous and the wicked, believers and unbelievers. Solomon said you have shown great kindness to your servant, my father David, because he was faithful to you and righteous and upright in heart. Remember, o lord how I have walked before you faithfully, Hezekiah said and with wholehearted devotion and have done what is good in your eyes.

Have we taught our people that they can pray this way if they keep covenant with God? That they can say to God, be merciful to me because I walk before you faithfully with wholehearted devotion and I have done what is good in your eyes? We have cut the legs off our own churches by berating our people and making the attainment and walking in righteousness a theoretical impossibility, whereas in the scripture it is an everyday reality. God says even if these three men, Noah, Daniel and Job were in it, they could save only themselves by their righteousness declares the sovereign lord, that seems to presuppose that they had righteousness and that they were righteous. Although he did not remove the high places from Israel, Asa's heart was fully committed to Jehovah all his life. He wasn't perfect, but he was perfect. As we heard Rev. Barach say before, Zachariah and Elizabeth were not perfect but they were perfect. They were blameless in obeying the law.

Consider the blameless, o God, observe the upright, there is a future for the man of peace. They are upright in the sight of God, observing the lord's commands and regulations blamelessly. And so we have an application of a simple principle that the scripture must interpret the scripture but that the scripture can't be reduced to a simple verse, no matter how many proof texts are provided in the Westminster Confession... If we don't look at the whole context, we have distorted the use of the word of God. We have made an illegal application of the word of God to support what we presuppose must be the case. And this has to run down the line and the way to resolve these things is the covenant. The covenant is God's gracious relationship that he has entered into with us in which are sins are forgiven and in which we are given new life, in which we are given a way to walk and to stay in that path of righteousness and not to depart from it. Not to depend on our own righteousness for eternal salvation but to stay in the path of righteousness for the glory of God.

Paul does not argue, does not maintain that every single person on the planet is equally wicked, there are converts. And to suggest otherwise is really to say that God's word has failed. To say there are none righteous and really mean that is to say that God's word has failed, it is to say that everyone is alike, that there is no covenant, no antithesis, no efficacy in God's grace. It is nearly blasphemous. For the whole work of God in this world is the bringing of a righteous people unto himself and setting them off from the world of the wicked, to be his and to act like it and he has done this throughout history. Even at the time of Noah, it was slim pickings, but there was one. There was one righteous. Even in Sodom and Gomorrah, there was one righteous and he was saved out of it. And at most times there has been more than one. The effect of this twisting of the scripture has been to distort and to put a blemish on the consciousness of the people of God. [25]

The problem with Schlissel is that he simply does not understand the relationship of justification with sanctification. Yes, there are people who are said to be righteous, but this is **not** the basis upon which God justifies them! The righteousness of all the people that Schlissel quoted is the **evidence** of their justified state, not the **cause** of it. We must remember the context of Schlissel's quote. He is challenging the interpretation that the Westminster Confession gives regarding Romans 3. He is challenging the universalization of Romans 3 in declaring all men depraved. When he challenges this, Schlissel is assaulting the idea that faith is that which is in contrast to the works of the Law. In keeping with others of the Federal Vision camp, Schlissel defines faith as "the obedience of faith." The point of Paul's argument in Romans 3:9-18 is in preparation for Romans 3:19-22. All men, be they Jew or Gentile, are sinners in need of a Savior. The Law was not given for men to keep in order to acquire salvation, for they cannot keep it. As verse 19 indicates, the Law shuts every man's mouth. The whole world stands condemned. Verse 20 indicates that by the works of the Law no man is justified. The Law brings knowledge of sin.

---

[25] Schlissel, *"Covenant Thinking,"* pp. 59-62.

We see the good news to this dilemma for all mankind in verses 21-22. The good news is that **apart from the works of the Law** the righteousness of God is manifested in Jesus Christ. The righteousness that men need is found in Jesus Christ Himself, and all those who have **faith in Him** obtain that righteousness found in Him alone.

Steve Schlissel stands in direct opposition to God's Word. He has become a modern day Judaizer. He believes that God justifies men by their obedience to God's Law. He believes that God grants justification to those men and women who choose to obey the Law that God graciously gave.

The Apostle Paul's Testimony Is A Direct Refutation To Schlissel

The apostle Paul's testimony is a refutation to Schlissel's view of the relationship of the Law to justification. In Paul's first epistle to Timothy, he is instructing young Timothy as to how he should deal with "self proclaimed teachers of the Law." There were some men in Ephesus who were engaging in fruitless discussions about myths and endless genealogies rather than being engaged in the proper goal of the apostle's instruction (I Timothy 1:4-6). These men wanted to be teachers of the Law, but Paul says they know nothing about what they confidently teach (I Timothy 1:7). Paul tells Timothy that the Law is good if one uses it lawfully (I Timothy 1:8). He then tells Timothy that the Law is made not for the righteous man but for the lawless. Paul proceeds to set forth a list of sins that are condemned in the Ten Commandments (I Timothy 1:9-10). In his epistle to Timothy, Paul is not giving an exhaustive use of the Law of God or stating the only use of the Law of God, but he is forthrightly stating that the Law was intended to convict sinners that they had fallen short of God's glory.

Any attempt to use the Law of God as the basis for one's justification is an unlawful use of the Law. In I Timothy 1:11-16, Paul uses himself as the great example of what he had just told Timothy. In contrast to the Law's condemnation, stands the gospel (verse 11). Paul says that God's mercy and grace found him in his miserable state. Paul views himself as the "chief of sinners" (verse 15). Rather than boasting in how righteous he was that earned God's favor, Paul boasts in God's marvelous patience toward him while he was such a sinner. In verse 16, Paul states that he is the premier example of God's saving grace to all who believe.

The immense problem for Schlissel is how Paul viewed himself while a Pharisee. Philippians 3 is most instructive. In Philippians 3:2 Paul warns the Philippians of the "dogs" or the "false circumcision." In verse 3, he contrasts himself now as a Christian with those of the false circumcision. Paul refers to himself now as being of the "true circumcision" who puts no confidence in the flesh. The false circumcision were the Judaizers that Paul confronted on several occasions. These men were insisting that one must submit to the Law of Moses in every regard in order to be a Christian. Faith in Jesus was not enough – one must have faith plus the works of the Law. Paul seeks to refute the Judaizers with his own past experience. In verses 5-6, he says that there was no better Jew than himself. There was no greater zealot for the Law than himself. Paul emphatically states that as a Pharisee he was blameless or righteous with reference to an outward conformity to the Law. In his zeal for Jehovah, he persecuted the Christians because he really saw them as blasphemers, not realizing that he was the true blasphemer and not them. In I Timothy 1:13, Paul said, *"I acted ignorantly in unbelief."* In other words, he had misplaced zeal. In Philippians 3:7-9, Paul says that all his supposed gains as a Pharisee was pure rubbish in view of the surpassing value of knowing Christ Jesus as Lord. Verse 9 is pivotal for it states, *"and be found in Him, not having a righteousness of my own derived from the Law, but that which is through faith in Christ, the righteousness which comes from God on the basis of faith."* Paul's former life as a Pharisee was not some allegiance to a subjective righteousness that had nothing to do with God's Law, but it was an attempt to justify himself with the Law. Paul is drawing a contrast between using the law to obtain personal righteousness as opposed to obtaining Christ's righteousness through faith. This biblical teaching is in direct opposition to Steve Schlissel and the rest of the proponents of the Federal Vision. Paul says that he was not justified by some kind of obedience to the Law; he was justified by faith in Jesus.

Schlissel's Views In The Knox Seminary Colloquium

Schlissel participated in the Knox Theological Seminary Colloquium in August 2003. One of the papers that he wrote was titled, *"A New Way of Seeing."* In trying to convey his understanding of the relationship of faith with obedience he said:

> The Book of Numbers reveals that the people of Israel, from the beginning, were not particularly inclined to abide by the conditions of the covenant. They provoked God continually because of their unbelief. In fact, Hebrews 4 tells us that the Gospel was preached to the Israelites just as it has been preached to us, but they didn't combine it with faith. We had better watch out and combine the Gospel with faith—and faith is identified with obedience (cf. Hebrews 4:2 with 4:6). **Nothing in the Bible teaches a kind of faith that does not**

> **obey. Obedience and faith are the same thing, biblically speaking. To submit to God's Word is what it means to believe. To believe is to obey.** [26] (Emphasis is mine)

Schlissel then openly falls into the camp of the New Perspective On Paul error when he says:

> Justification in Galatians and Romans deals with the status of the Gentiles. Trying to read the New Testament without understanding Paul's call as Christ's chosen ambassador to the Gentiles is like trying to understand mathematics without the use of numbers, or trying to describe snow without the word "white." Legal justification, far from being "the heart of the Gospel," let alone identical with it, is hardly ever in view when Paul speaks of justification. Paul's concern is the status of the Gentiles as Israelites indeed, through faith, not through ritual circumcision or the various identity markers uniquely connected with it.[27]

> The inclusion of the Gentiles is not an, "Oh yeah, that's also important" issue. It is THE issue occupying administrative center stage in the New Testament Scriptures. Aside from it, and its implications, there's nothing new in the New Testament. Those who obsess over the *ordo salutis* obsess over a manufactured problem. We must learn to ask the right questions, and that soon.[28]

These comments are virtually straight out of the New Perspective On Paul theology. It is a complete redefinition of the New Testament that refuses to see that Paul was dealing with the Judaizers and their vain attempts to justify themselves through attempts to keep the Law. To call the inclusion of the Gentiles THE most important issue of the New Testament is a very truncated understanding of the Bible. The center stage of the Bible at every point is Christ! The New Testament manifests the fulfillment of all of God's promises in Christ, who is the mediator of the new covenant. Justification is by faith alone in Christ, and this applies to all men whether they are Jew or Gentile.

---

[26] Schlissel, *"A New Way Of Seeing,"* pp. 26-27.

[27] Schlissel, *"A New Way Of Seeing,"* p. 33.

[28] Schlissel, *"A New Way Of Seeing,"* p. 35.

Schlissel's Views in the Christian Renewal Magazine [29]

In 2003 The Christian Renewal magazine out of Canada published two interviews conducted by Gerry Wisz on the Auburn Avenue Controversy (Federal Vision). The first interview featured "The Monroe Four." A follow-up response was given by Robert Godfrey, president of Westminster Seminary in California and a minister in the URC; Cornel Venema, president at Mid-America Reformed Seminary and a minister in the CRC; and two of the RPCUS presbyters who offered the resolutions against the Monroe teachings to their presbytery, Paul McDade, evangelist and pastor of West Tennessee Reformed Mission and Henry Johnson, pastor of Trinity Presbyterian Church, Tazewell, Virginia. (Dr. Venema's consent to this interview should not be understood to mean they necessarily concur with the resolutions of the RPCUS presbytery.) They are reprinted here as submitted to us by Mr. Wisz with their permission.[30] The following paragraphs are taken directly from this reprinted article on the internet.

In January 2002, four ministers — John Barach of the URC, Steve Schlissel of Messiah's Congregation, Steve Wilkins of the PCA, and Doug Wilson of Christ Church — delivered several lectures at a pastor's conference in Monroe, Louisiana, that precipitated the Reformed Presbyterian Church in the U.S. (RPCUS) to level a declamation against the four men and their teachings, declaring them heretics and calling them to repent.

Another Monroe conference was held in January 2003, where the four original speakers and other Reformed pastors, teachers and theologians were invited to speak. The disagreements still stand and there has not been reconciliation between the RPCUS and the Monroe four. Instead, Reformed ministers and churchmen of different churches have — to one degree or another — begun to take sides with either the RPCUS or with the four ministers.

Christian Renewal contributor Gerry Wisz spent several hours with Pastors Barach, Schlissel, Wilkins and Wilson in a conference call, asking them to respond to the RPCUS' declamation and to clarify their positions. The four agreed and the following is the completed interview.

Question: Steve, you suggest that law and gospel have been set up as an antithesis. Is this in your view what many Reformed churches and teachers do?
  S. Schlissel: Have Reformed folks gotten it wrong? Yes, to
  the extent that they've followed Luther in an imaginary

---

[29] *The Monroe Four Speak Out.*
[30] *The Monroe Four Speak Out.*

Law/Gospel antithesis. I'm surely not the only fellow to point that out. Cornelius Vander Wall has written powerfully on this in his book The Covenantal Gospel. Have the Reformed gotten it right? Yes, by affirming salvation by grace throughout history since the Fall, and not just in the New Testament.

The law as God gave it is the gospel. "The Law of the Lord is perfect, converting the soul," the Psalmist said. And the gospel as announced by Paul is the law as it had been conveyed by God and fulfilled in Messiah. Paul said, "I am saying nothing beyond what Moses and the Prophets said... (Acts 26:22)." Paul's beef was not with Moses, but with those who twisted him. The law given to Moses has the way of salvation; the gospel given by Paul has ethical requirements. And the requirements continue to abide. The gospel brings demands and law brings promise. There's no easy compartmentalization. People who suggest there is are distorting the Bible.

God did not give a ladder of merit in the Law; He gave Himself, just as He did in the gospel. Van der Waal said, "The texts of the covenant always mention the gospel first: I (AM) Yahweh! He came with His obligations for that reason alone." Paul sees the Law as in perfect conformity with his gospel (1 Tim 1:11). The Law is good. Always has been. The gospel has obligations. Always has. Luther at points imagined a Law/Gospel antipathy, but that antipathy was/is true only for those seeking merit from Law. Ironically, that is something the Law itself strictly forbids. Read it right and it's all one Book, one message: the Law is permeated with grace; the Gospel is permeated with God's good Law.

We must recognize that Luther's personal problem must not become the paradigm for interpreting Scripture wherein every verse or proposition is imagined to be Law or Gospel. That is a perversion of the Word of God; it is the source of many theological woes.

Question: You say in your address, "What must I do to be saved?" is the wrong question. Isn't this the question the rich young ruler asked Jesus, in his way, as the Jews in Jerusalem on Pentecost asked Peter and the Philippian jailer asked Paul, for which they each received answers?

S. Schlissel: "What must I do to be saved?" is a fine question — in context. I'm not opposed to the question. Every unbelieving Philippian jailer guarding apostles should ask it after an earthquake. But "What does the Lord require?" is better, more helpful, for many reasons. Chiefly, it includes the former question, but changes the orientation from self to the Savior, to God Almighty. The world revolves around Him and His will, not around me and my salvation. The right question puts us on the right track, helping us be concerned less with our salvation than God's glory. This is standard stuff from a Westminster perspective. Man's chief end is not to "get saved," but to glorify God.

Jesus' answer to the self-justifying expert mentioned in Luke 10:25 was not to introduce a Lutheran distinction between law and grace, or faith and works, but to illustrate how even a Samaritan can be more righteous than an Israelite, more righteous than a Levite or even a priest. Jesus taught in Luke 10 exactly what His disciple Paul taught in Romans 2: "Not the hearers of the Law are just before God, but the doers of the Law shall be justified," whether they be Jewish or Gentile. And the law demands faith in Jesus. Asking "What does the Lord require?" puts us on the only right track.

If Jesus believed in Lutheranism, I respectfully submit that He missed a grand opportunity to teach it in Luke 10. It is effrontery, an insult, to suggest that Jesus' answer, "Do this and you will live," was anything other than plain truth. The problem of the expert was not that he obeyed the Law. Such a notion is 180 degrees wrong. The expert's problem was that he didn't obey the Law. Jesus' answer to his question was not trickery, not an effort to first make the man frustrated by the Law so as to prepare him for the Gospel. What nonsense. Rather it was Christ teaching that obedience to the Law was something very do-able and that such obedience, which includes repentance and faith, does save. Such obedience is a turning away from self and toward God.

Jesus' words and Paul's reiteration of those words have been tortured by systematicians instead of believed. Why is it so hard to simply hear those words and believe them? Why are our Lord's own holy words an embarrassment to some of His followers; why are these words treated as words which must be explained away rather than trusted and treasured?

In Luke 18 we have no hint of a faith vs. works dichotomy, or law vs. grace. Rather we have Jesus pressing the Law as containing that which leads to eternal life. What is required to inherit life is simply the opposite of self-sufficiency, so often character-istic of the rich (compare James' teaching here, or the prophets). This has been the case since the Garden: one's own fig leaves (read self-merit) vs. God's provision of blood (read grace).

Excerpts from Schlissel's Church's Website

If anyone thinks that people are misunderstanding Schlissel's positions, they will soon realize that there is unanimity of thought in all of Schlissel's public statements, be they in lecture or in written form. There is no misunderstanding. He has maintained the same positions in all them.

In one of his articles on his website Schlissel states:

> Again, the Confession at 14:2 expounds saving faith as that which "yield(s) obedience to the commands" of God. While faith is extolled as the alone instrument of justification, it is freely and plainly admitted in the Westminster Confession (11:2) that such faith never appears on planet earth by itself … Faith is never "alone in the person justified, but is ever accompanied with all other saving graces, and is no dead faith, but worketh by love." Well, there ya go.[31]

> We ask you to remember John Owen's explicit statement of this very point. He said, "We absolutely deny that we can be justified by that faith which **can be alone;** that is, without a principle of spiritual life and **universal obedience,** operative in all the works of it, as duty doth require" (Justification By Faith, p.73; emphasis his). Owen categorically rejects the idea that justifying faith can be separated from "holy obedi-ence": "We allow no faith to be of the same kind or nature with that whereby we are justified, but what virtually and rad-ically contains in it universal obedience." **Note what Owen is asserting: Obedience is not merely a test or evidence of**

---

[31] Schlissel, "*True confessions.*" (Sept, 2002), p. 2 <www.messiahnyc.org/>.

saving faith; it is inseparably bond up in its character. There is no disobedient yet saving faith. It is not faith plus obedience, but the obedience of faith. [32] (Emphasis is mine)

Law-Gospel dichotomists ask us to believe that God showed His love for Israel by placing them under an un-bearable burden which He then commanded them to love! The thought comes close to blasphemy; it is certainly an insult to our God.[33]

For my bible knows nothing of a Law from God without Gospel, nor a Gospel from God without Law. Yet I am now told that these two things are in every way antithetical...Is the Law, as given by God, really our problem? IT is only if we seek to be justified by it apart from Christ...Luther and his sons seek to abstract, and set in opposition, the Christ from the Law He came to establish.[34]

Does the Lord delight in the solas as much as in obeying the voice of the Lord? To obey is better than sacrifice, and to heed is better than the systems of men. Do not trust in deceptive words and say, The solas of the Reformation, the solas of the Reformation, The solas of the Reformation. Rather, God says, "change you ways and your action and deal with each other justly (cf. Jeremiah 7). The Philippian jailer not withstanding, the question we must learn to ask is "What does God require?" because it is the most comprehensive question that a right reading of the Bible provokes. It includes the question, "What must I do to be saved?," but goes on to consider the glory and pleasure of God as man's chief end, not an optional byproduct.

Making the Law and the Gospel antithetical is not merely an error, it is an abomination...The writer of Hebrews tells us the same, and explains to all who would hear, that the difference is not Law vs. Gospel, but Faith vs. Unbelief. "For we also have had the gospel preached to us, just as they (in the Old Testament) did; but the message they heard was of no

---

[32] Schlissel, *"Living the Reformed Faith in the Real World: True confessions,"* p. 3.

[33] Schlissel, *"Living the Reformed Faith in the Real World: True confessions,"* p. 11.

[34] Schlissel, *"Faith Works."*

value to them, because those who heard did not combine it with faith.

It is no cause for stumbling when we read of the ruler asking Jesus, "What must I do to inherit eternal life?, and we find Jesus replying: "You know the commandments." Rather than being offended by Jesus' implication that the Law indeed revealed the path of life, we should be offended by those who impugn our Lord's integrity, suggesting He was anything but sincere and plain in pointing this man, whom He loved (Mark 10:21), to the commandments. The problem of the Jews, our Lord Jesus tells us, is not that they kept the Law, but that they didn't. "Has not Moses given you the law? Yet not one of you keeps the law" (John 7:19). The problem of the Jews was not that they believed Moses, but that they did not believe Moses.

To keep the Law as given by God is to believe Moses is to believe Jesus. Law-keepers are not hypothetical in Scripture: they really exist and they are the exact equivalent to believers. (Emphasis mine)

Salvation has always been by grace. The Law as it has come from God has always been gracious. Grace as it has come from God has always required the obedience of faith. Luther had a problem with this. I won't make Luther's problem mine. The Messiah won't let me. Remember his words: "Not every one that saith unto me, Lord, Lord, shall enter into the kingdom of heaven; but he that doth the will of my Father which is in heaven.[35]

Schlissel's Understanding of the Relationship of Justification To Sanctification

The Federal Vision position on the relationship of good works or sanctification to justification is one of their fundamental problems. Schlissel and Lusk, in particular, are thoroughly confused at this point. Actually, Steve Wilkins, Doug Wilson, and John Barach would all agree with Schlissel and Lusk.

---

[35] Schlissel, *"Faith Works"* p. 7.

The Westminster Standards are very clear on the distinction and the inseparable union of justification and sanctification, but they are very careful in their delineation. If the Federal Vision proponents had taken the time to carefully examine the Confessional documents, they would not have made these serious errors. But then again, they may have studied them carefully and found themselves in complete disagreement with the Standards and wanted to advance another "paradigm." If the latter is the case, then these men should have the integrity to openly say that they oppose the Standards and remove any comments from their literature and church websites stating that they subscribe to these Standards. Moreover, they need to leave the denominations that they are affiliated with that hold to these Standards. The problem is that all of these men still insist that their understanding is Reformed and true to the Standards.

Again, I have taken considerable time to quote the Reformed Standards in order for the reader to determine for himself whether the Federal Vision is in conformity or not. I insist that they have thoroughly misunderstood them or deliberately ignored them.

The Westminster Confession of Faith's Chapter 13 "Of Sanctification," Section 1 states:

> They who are once effectually called and regenerated, having a new heart and a new spirit created in them, are further sanctified, really and personally, through the virtue of Christ's death and resurrection, by His Word and Spirit dwelling in them: the dominion of the whole body of sin is destroyed, and the several lusts thereof are more and more weakened and mortified and they more and more quickened and strengthened in all saving graces, to the practice of true holiness, without which no man shall see the Lord.
>
> This sanctification is throughout, in the whole man; yet imperfect in this life, there abiding still some remnants of corruption in every part: whence ariseth a continual and irreconcilable war; the flesh lusting against the Spirit, and the Spirit against the flesh.
>
> In which war, although the remaining corruption, for a time, may much prevail; yet through the continual supply of strength from the sanctifying Spirit of Christ, the regenerate part doth overcome; and so, the saints grow in grace perfecting holiness in the fear of God.

Question 77 of the Westminster Larger Catechism delineates between justification and sanctification very carefully:

> Although sanctification be inseparably joined with justification, yet they differ, in that God in justification imputeth the righteousness of Christ; in sanctification of his Spirit infuseth grace, and enableth to the exercise thereof; in the former, sin is pardoned; in the other, it is subdued: the one doth equally free all believers from the revenging wrath of God, and that perfectly in this life, that they never fall into condemnation the other is neither equal in all, nor in this life perfect in any, but growing up to perfection.

Robert Shaw, in his exposition of the Westminster Confession of Faith makes some very good observations regarding the difference between justification and sanctification. He states:

> Romanists, as we formerly noticed, confound justification with sanctification; and, as this leads to various dangerous mistakes, we shall mention several points in which they differ. They differ in their **nature**: justification is a relative change of state; sanctification is a real change of the whole man, soul and body. They differ in their **order**: justification, in the order of nature, though not of time, precedes sanctification; for righteousness imputed is, in the order of nature, prior to holiness, implanted and inherent. They differ in their **matter**: the matter of justification is the righteousness of Christ imputed; the matter of sanctification is an inherent righteousness communicated. They differ in their **form**: justification is a judicial act, by which the sinner is pronounced righteous; sanctification is a physical or moral act, or rather a series of acts, by which a change is effected in the qualities of the soul. They differ in **properties:** justification is perfected at once, and is equal in all believers; sanctification is imperfect at first, and exists in different degrees of advancement in different individuals; hence the former is called an **act** and the latter a **work**. Other points of difference might be mentioned, but we only add, that in justification we receive a **title** to heaven; sanctification gives us **a meetness** for, and a capacity of, enjoying it.[36] (Emphasis is Shaw)

---

[36] Shaw, *An Exposition of The Westminster Confession of Faith*, pp. 142-143.

Schlissel and Lusk have the relationship of these two great doctrines thoroughly confused, or they are very conscious of their actions and are deliberately
seeking to advance a new theological paradigm, much like what Norman
Shepherd who has explicitly stated this in his book *The Call Of Grace.*
Previously, I quoted Shepherd stating that his covenant paradigm provides the
bridge between Roman Catholicism and Protestantism regarding salvation.
Schlissel and Lusk's comments are thoroughly in line with this kind of thinking.

Schlissel emphasizes the necessity of obedience to the Law of God in order to
receive God's blessings. The Reformed Faith has no problem with this whatsoever as long as we are referring to sanctification and not justification. Good
works are the evidences that flow out of justification, demonstrating the genuineness of the faith. As James says, a faith that is but a mere profession without substance, without obedience, is no saving faith. Obedience is necessary as
fruit, but Schlissel insists that faith and obedience are identical. This is his
heresy. In the above quotes, Schlissel says that the law keepers are identical
with the believers. He emphatically says that it is not faith plus obedience; it is
the obedience of faith. He commits the same heretical error that Shepherd,
Lusk, Wilkins, Wilson, and all the other Federal Vision proponents make.
Because Schlissel makes obedience identical with faith, he calls the Gospel as
Law and the Law as Gospel. Faith in Christ is merely seeking obedience to the
law of God. This is salvation by works because all of these men are referring
to justification and not sanctification.

I find it very upsetting that Schlissel would dare even mention the great John
Owen as one who supposedly agrees with his views. Schlissel's quote of Owen
is absolutely misrepresented. Apparently, Schlissel did not bother to read much
further in Owen. Owen is thoroughly in agreement with the Westminster
Confession which does not teach Schlissel's view whatsoever.

If the reader will refer back to Chapter 4 on the Federal Vision's denial of the
active obedience of Christ as our righteousness, I have that subsection dealing
with the Federal Vision and Socinianism. In that section, Owen thoroughly
condemns the idea of faith being defined as the obedience of faith. Owen called
this view – Socinian.

Allow me to give a few more quotes from Owen that clearly demonstrate that
Schlissel has totally corrupted Owen's views. The quote that Schlissel gives
from Owen does not support Schlissel's view. Owen is simply saying what the
Westminster Confession has always said: saving faith is always accompanied
by obedience. Schlissel even has this as part of the Owen quote, but Schlissel

is so blinded by his presuppositions that this statement is completely ignored by Schlissel. Schlissel even quotes the Westminster Confession where it says that saving faith **yields** obedience and that faith is never alone **in the person justified**, but is **ever accompanied** with all the other saving graces. How does Schlissel miss this? His own quotes contradict him!

If Schlissel had bothered to read further in Owen, he would have found Owen saying:

> Although saving faith, as it is described in general, **do not include obedience, not as its form or essence, but as the necessary effect is included in the cause, and the fruit-bearing juice.**[37] (Emphasis is mine)

We must remember that Schlissel has rejected the idea that obedience is the fruit or evidence of faith, but this is exactly what Owen says is the relationship between the two. Owen goes on to say:

> That God does require in and by the gospel a sincere obedience of all that do believe, to be performed in and by their own persons, though through the aids of grace supplied unto them by Jesus Christ ... **but the consideration of them which are performed before believing is excluded by all from any causality or interest in our justification before God ... It is wholly the obedience of faith, proceeding from true and saving faith in God by Jesus Christ: for, as it was said before, works before faith, are, as by general consent, excluded from any interest in our justification, and we have proved that they are neither conditions of it, dispositions unto it, nor preparations for it, properly so called; but every true believer is immediately justified on his believing.**[38] (Emphasis mine)

Owen cannot be clearer. Obedience to the Law has nothing to do with our justification, but it does have something with reference to us **after** we have been justified. The last statement by Owen thoroughly refutes the Federal Vision's idea that obedience is the essence of saving faith. No, says Owen, every true believer is immediately justified on his believing. Owen definitely does not see faith and works as identical.

---

[37] Owen, *"Justification of Faith."*

[38] Owen, *"Justification of Faith."*

Owen continues with comments that utterly refute Schlissel and Lusk's view of James 2:

> If faith and works are opposed as contrary and inconsistent, when considered as the means of attaining righteousness or justification before God, as plainly they are, then is it impossible we should be justified before God by them in the same sense, way, and manner. Wherefore, when the apostle James affirms that a man is justified by works, and not by faith only, he cannot intend our justification before God, where it is impossible they should both concur; for not only are they declared inconsistent by the apostle in this place, but it would introduce several sorts of righteousness into justification, that are inconsistent and destructive of each other. This was the first mistake of the Jew, whence this miscarriage ensued, - they sought not after righteousness by faith, but as it were by the works of the Law.[39]

Schlissel is faced with an incredible problem. The man who he quoted to give credence to his views has emphatically contradicted him. Note that Owen most emphatically separates faith from works as far as our justification is concerned. In fact, Owen devastates Schlissel's entire thesis. In keeping with the historic Reformed Faith, Owen understands that the Jews' problem was that they tried to keep the **moral law of God as a means to justification.** According to Owen, the Law is not the Gospel and neither is the Gospel the Law as Schlissel boldly asserts.

Owen makes remarks that are likewise devastating to Schlissel's interpretation of the young rich ruler and Schlissel's contention that Jesus was really teaching that this man was able to keep the Law if he really wanted to. Notice what Owen states about the Jews who tried to justify themselves by law keeping:

> Their second mistake was as unto the righteousness itself whereon a man might be justified before God; for this they judged was to be their own righteousness, chap. 10:3. Their own personal righteousness, consisting in their own duties of obedience, they looked on as the only righteousness whereon they might be justified before God. This, therefore, they went about to establish, as the Pharisee did, Luke 18:11,12: and this mistake, with their design thereon, "to establish their own

---

[39] Owen, "*Justification of Faith.*"

righteousness," was the principal cause that made them reject the righteousness of God; as it is with many this day.[40]

The Federal Vision, particularly Schlissel and Lusk, appeal to Abraham as a prime example of one who was justified by his faithful obedience. Here is what Owen says about Abraham:

> Those works must be understood which Abraham had then, when he is said to be justified in the testimony produced unto that purpose; but the works that Abraham then had were works of righteousness, performed in faith and love to God, works of new obedience under the conduct and aids of the Spirit of God, works required in the covenant of grace. These are the works excluded from the justification of Abraham. And these things are plain, express, and evident, not to be eluded by any distinctions or evasions. All Abraham's evangelical works are expressly excluded from his justification before God ... He was justified by faith in the way before described (for other justification by faith there is none), in opposition unto all his own works and personal righteousness thereby.[41]

Owen thoroughly refutes the Federal Vision notion that Abraham was justified by his obedience to God. Abraham's righteousness is his sanctified life flowing out of his justification! This is what the Reformed Faith has taught for 500 years, but apparently Schlissel and others think this was entirely wrong. Notice that Schlissel called this distinction between the Law and the Gospel taught by Luther and the Reformed Faith for all these centuries as an abomination. Schlissel says that his Bible doesn't teach this. As with Rich Lusk, if Steve Schlissel really and truly believes in his heart that law keeping is equal to faith in Christ, then he will have a rude awakening on Judgment Day.

John Owen speaks to men like Schlissel, Lusk, Wilkins, Shepherd and others when he says:

> All other disputes about qualifications, conditions, causes, "*aneu hoon ouk*," any kind of interest for our works and obedience in our justification before God, are but the speculations of men at ease.[42]

---

[40] Owen, "*Justification of Faith*"

[41] Owen, "*Justification of Faith*"

[42] Owen, "*Justification of Faith*"

Owen explains why seeking justification through law keeping is vanity when he says:

> This personal, inherent righteousness which, according to the Scripture, we allow in believers, is not that whereby or where-with we are justified before God; for it is not perfect, nor perfectly answers any rule of obedience that is given unto us: and so cannot be our righteousness before God unto our justification. Wherefore, we must be justified by the righteousness of Christ imputed to us, or be justified without respect unto any righteousness, or not be justified at all.[43]

Finally, Owen puts it all in the proper perspective which thoroughly refutes Federal Vision theology:

> We are justified, and in that exercise of it wherein we are so, by a looking unto Christ, under a sense of the guilt of sin and our lost condition thereby, for all, for our only help and relief, for deliverance, righteousness, and life, then is it therein, exclusive of all other graces and duties whatever; for by them we neither look, nor are they the things we look after … To come to Christ for life and salvation, is to believe on him unto the justification of life; but no other grace or duty is a coming unto Christ: and therefore have they no place in justification.[44]

Schlissel's gospel is not the gospel of the Bible! He totally blurs justification and sanctification, making them identical. Understanding the proper relationship between these two doctrines is essential to understanding the gospel. If one gets it wrong here, the souls of men are in jeopardy.

Schlissel seems to think that many in the Reformed community do not believe in holiness of life as something necessary. Sanctification is necessary, but it is only as the evidence of saving faith. Schlissel went through this long litany of biblical names whereby it said that they were "righteous" or "blameless." These people are righteous in terms of sanctification. This is entirely different than saying that they were justified by their righteousness. Robert Shaw states:

> Holiness, though it cannot give us a title to heaven, is indispensably necessary. It is necessary by a divine and unalter-

---

[43] Owen, *"Justification of Faith"*
[44] Owen, *"Justification of Faith"*

able constitution; for "without holiness no man shall see the Lord."- Heb. 12:14. God has enacted it as an immutable law, that nothing which defileth shall enter into the heavenly city, - Rev. 21:27. It is necessary, also as a preparative for heaven. It is the evidence of our title, and constitutes our meetness for enjoying the pleasures and engaging in the work of the heavenly world.[45]

In his lectures and on his website, Schlissel seems to think that mainline Reformed thinking seems to have lost a proper emphasis upon the Law of God. This is not true. For example, Chapter 19, Section 5, in the Westminster Confession of Faith states:

The moral law doth for ever bind all, as well justified persons as others, to the obedience thereof; and that, not only in regard of the matter contained in it, but also in respect of the authority of God the Creator, who gave it: neither doth Christ, in the Gospel, any way dissolve, but much strengthen this obligation.

The Confession makes very clear that everyone, be they unregenerate and justified persons are bound to obedience to God's Law. It says that Christ in the gospel does not abrogate that obligation. But notice, this section does **not** identify the law as the gospel.

One will notice in Schlissel's comments about the Law of God that he, like Shepherd and Lusk, says that the Law itself is the grace of God. Look again at the quote on top of page 320 and see that Schlissel says that law keepers and believers are exact equivalents. Schlissel says that grace has always required obedience, and he then takes a smack at Luther for not understanding this.

The real danger for the people in the pews who listen to men of the Federal Vision is that they hear what sounds like orthodox terminology, such as we are not saved by meritorious works but that we are saved by grace through faith. **The problem arises when these men totally redefined these terms. Meritorious works, they say, are works of our own, not works of obedience to God's Law. Grace is the giving of the Law for us to keep by faith, and faith is equivalent to the obedience to God's Law. The Federal Vision's gospel is actually a works salvation.**

Whereas orthodoxy and Reformed Christianity have said that the phrase – we are saved by grace through Christ by faith alone – means that grace has nothing to do with law keeping on our part. The grace of God is the gift of Jesus

---

[45] Shaw, *An Exposition of The Westminster Confession of Faith*, pp. 144- 145.

Christ, who kept the law for us, and his righteous law keeping grants us eternal life. This gracious gift from God must be received by faith alone. There are no works or Law keeping in faith itself. Faith is simply a look of trust unto Christ, our redeemer, independent of our works of righteousness.

The difference between the Federal Vision and Reformed, orthodox Christianity is that between night and day. The gospel of the Federal Vision is a false gospel that cannot save anyone from their sins. This is why the Reformed community must vehemently oppose the Federal Vision. A person who adopts the theology of the Federal Vision has placed his soul in a perilous position. Thinking that we don't need the righteousness of Christ for a supposed final justification is a disastrous belief. This person will hear Jesus' horrifying words, "Depart from me you **lawless ones.**" These condemned persons will protest that they sought to keep the Law, but Jesus says that He required **perfect obedience to His Law.** But these persons will insist that they were taught that the law did not teach perfect obedience and that God's judgment was going to be a "fatherly or soft judgment." But Jesus, is the judge on that Day, will say, "Without my perfect obedience credited to you, you are found wanting. Depart from me you lawless ones."

To all those who teach and who follow Federal Vision theology, you are gambling with your souls, and it is a bet that you are guaranteed to lose. Do not be deceived. Do not trust in your works of obedience to justify you. Run to Christ to find mercy and grace while there is time.

Doug Wilson on the Nature of Justification By Faith

Doug Wilson is the pastor of Christ Church in Moscow, Idaho. His church is affiliated with the Confederation of Reformed Evangelicals (CRE) and is a member in good standing with the CRE. Sometime between 2002 –2005, at the request of Doug Wilson the session of Christ Church agreed to ask for a special examination of Doug Wilson before the presbytery of the CRE in order to exonerate his name in light of the controversy over the Federal Vision. This was due to the serious charges leveled against him by Covenant Presbytery of the RPCUS and Covenant Presbytery's recommendation that the governing authorities over Doug Wilson bring charges against him for these views articulated at the 2002 AAPC.

A series of 105 questions was asked. The audio of this exam and a written form of this exam can be downloaded from Christ Church's website.[46] My purpose

---

[46] This website address is <www.christkirk.com> and one can click on the Doug Wilson presbytery exam to hear or read the exam questions and answers.

here is to evaluate as best as possible the theological views of Doug Wilson on the relationship of good works to justification by faith. In a later chapter, I will discuss his views regarding the perseverance of the saints and the nature of the church.

I will evaluate his views using some of his lectures over the past three years and his answers to the special presbytery exam. I will compare his lecture comments at the 2002 AAPC and his written articles for the Knox Theological Seminary Colloquium with his presbytery exam.

Regarding a presbytery question concerning his commitment to the Westminster Confession Of Faith, Wilson said:

> I currently subscribe to the Reformed Evangelical Confession. But Christ Church is in the process of adopting a Book of Confessions, which includes the 39 Articles, the Three Forms, and the original Westminster Confession of Faith. I have not yet subscribed to the Westminster Confession, but my subscription to the original Westminster Confession is therefore likely.[47]

On the website of Christ Church, we find these comments made:

> As a body of reformational evangelicals, we seek to display our unity in truth with other faithful churches, not only in the present, but also with the historic Christian church throughout the centuries. Although not included here, we are also in essential agreement with the historic confessions of the Reformation, including the Synod of Dordt, the Belgic Confession, the Heidelberg Catechism (together know as the Three Forms of Unity), the Westminster Confession of Faith of 1646, and the London Baptist Confession of 1689.[48]

On this basis, I will analyze Wilson's views. Let's begin with Wilson's statements at the 2002 AAPC. His view of the Reformed Standards is troubling:

> Well our problem, is that we assume that God has broken out of his word all of the truth that is to be broken out. Now we, of course, as conservative, as people who, you have sat at presbytery meetings where someone said something like that and all the yellow blinking lights in your head went off

---

[47] CRE's presbytery exam, question 3.
[48] Christ Church's website, "*Confessions.*"

because and you started thinking, ut oh, ut oh, ut oh, because what you know is the person, the person who says the Westminster Confession of Faith is not the high water mark of church history, the next thing is we need to be ordaining women or need to be doing, and you have just gotten to this reflex motion, well no, I am going to defend, I am going to go down fighting on this one, we are just going to go into rear guard defense action and that's all there is to it.[49]

The fact remains that this is an awfully big bluff. The fact remains that there is a awful lot of truth here that we still need to master. And the fact remains that when you try to fix something in history and when you try to hit the pause button and say, God, that's it, no more, no more, no more truth. What happens is that action winds up overturning the truth that you think you are, the truth that you think that you are defending, you find that you are the one that is overturning it. In Matthew 23, Jesus in chapter 23 is saying some very un-Christ like things. And the fact that makes sense to you, the fact that the joke worked, means that we have a whole host of tradition that we have substituted in for the word of God.[50]

I have a very difficult time squaring the above comments with what Wilson says in his presbytery exam. The above comments are those of one who is taking a very loose view of the Confession. While the Confession is a secondary document, subordinate to the Scripture, Reformed men would still acknowledge it as an accurate and thorough presentation of biblical truth. What truth has the Confession failed to convey about justification and other major doctrines? One cannot fit Lusk's and Schlissel's view of justification within the parameters of the Confession. Wilson was nebulous in his comments at the 2002 AAPC. He definitely implied that the Westminster Confession was not going to stop him from pushing some of his views. This is why a loose view of subscription to the Westminster Standards opens the doors for innovative teaching. A loose view opens the door for various and sometimes numerous exceptions being taken to the Confession. For example, the question was asked Wilson if he had any exceptions to the Westminster Confession. Wilson stated that he had seven such exceptions.[51] Some of these exceptions are rather significant as in the meaning of the covenant of works, the nature of religious wor-

---

[49] Wilson, *"Visible and Invisible Church Revisited,"*

[50] Wilson, *"Visible and Invisible Church Revisited,"* p. 21.

[51] The CRE's presbytery exam, question 3.

ship, and the nature of the sacraments. Wilson subscribes to paedocommunion, which is not taught in the Confession.

Wilson said that he did not take exception with the Confession on the nature of justification. The question remains however, is this actually true? Are his answers truly in conformity with the meaning that is given by the Confession to these terms and the proof texts that are used to formulate these statements I think it is noteworthy that on his church's website he lists the Confessions that his church is going to adopt. In their acceptance of the Westminster Confession with its Larger and Shorter Catechism, they say they accept them **without Scripture proofs.** What is significant about this? If the Confession is a truly secondary standard to the Word of God, then any statement from the Confession in order for it to be true must be substantiated by biblical support. These proof texts are necessary in understanding what the Westminster Standards mean by justification by faith and the relationship of good works to it. I noted earlier that Steve Schlissel does not like the proof texts of Romans 3:10ff to be given on the section dealing with original sin. This is because he does not believe this passage teaches total depravity as stated by the Confession. The Westminster Confession uses James 2 as Scriptural support when it speaks of good works that accompany saving faith, which are the fruits or evidences of it. Lusk and Schlissel do not believe that James 2 refers to a demonstrative faith but rather conditions for forensic, or declarative justification. They would oppose these Scripture proofs used in the Confession. Wilson does not like the wording of the covenant of works in the Westminster Confession in chapter 7:1. We know from others in the Federal Vision that they adamantly oppose the entire doctrine of the covenant of works. Wilson's statement of disagreement is – *"We would clarify that the 'covenant of works' was not meritorious and we deny that any covenant can be kept without faith. Good works, even in this covenant were a result of faith..."* [52] The Westminster Confession in its statement on the covenant of works in 7:1, uses Galatians 3:10 as a proof text, which says that everyone who does not keep the Law perfectly is cursed. Others in the Federal Vision have insisted that God never required perfect obedience in the covenant of grace; therefore, they do not think it is valid to use this proof text. It is disturbing that Wilson and his church do not want the Scripture proofs. This opens the doors for them to redefine terms and still claim adherence to the Confessional Standards.

In his 2002 lecture at the AAPC, Wilson makes the following comment about the Law's relationship with the Gospel:

---

[52] From the CRE presbytery exam of Wilson, p. 1.

When we say that all of God's word is perfect, converting the soul. When we don't divide it up into law and gospel, when we don't say law over here, gospel over there, when we say it's all gospel, it's all law, it's all good. When we say that, someone is going to accuse us of phariseeism or legalism. What does Jesus say about this pattern? Matthew 23, "then spake Jesus to the multitude and to his disciples saying, the scribes and the pharisees set in Moses' seat, all, therefore whatsoever they bid you observe, that observe and do, but do not ye after their works, for they say and do not."[53]

With this comment about the Law and the Gospel, Wilson is squarely in the camp with Lusk and Schlissel. To say that all is Gospel and Law is to commit the same errors of equating faithful obedience to God's law as the essence of saving faith.

In his interview with the Christian Renewal magazine, Wilson answers questions about the nature of faith as it relates to justification by faith. Gerry Wisz asked the following questions:

Question: The Jews in wilderness — wasn't their problem that they didn't combine being in the covenant and the blessings of the covenant with faith, and so were lost even though they were delivered from Egypt and God was their God? Does this not bolster the argument for justification by faith?

Doug Wilson: ...But if we allow for faith as a gift of God, then we're saved by faith from first to last. That we deny the necessity of faith is ludicrous. We all have a strong doctrine of apostasy. What drives apostasy is unbelief, and the engine that drives salvation is faith and only faith.[54]

Question: But not "faith only"?

Doug Wilson: Not bare bones faith. Not assent. Devils have that. True faith is more than assent. We are being accused of denying sola fide because we deny solus assensus. This is the rub, since we're all affirming this. Why are we heretics because we say faith cannot be separated from trust and obedience, and because we say saving faith cannot be separated from a life of obedience and trust?[55]

---

[53] Wilson, *"Visible and Invisible Church Revisited,"*

[54] Wilson, *The Monroe Four Speak Out*, p. 5.

[55] Wilson, *The Monroe Four Speak Out*, pp. 5-6.

Question: Has confessionalism replaced an active, living faith in Reformed churches? If so what is the solution?

> **Doug Wilson:** Yes, in many cases it has. In many other cases, non-confessionalism has replaced an active, living faith. In all cases, the problem is sin — not the confessions. When we make idols, we often do so out of innocent materials. The solution is to preach the Word like the house was burning down, sing the psalms like we believed them, learn how to incorporate wine and chocolate into the sabbath, come to the sacraments in humble reliance on the Holy Spirit, and pray for a tsunami reformation.
>
> We are in line with the Torah (the law) and the Talmud (the interpretation) of the Westminster Confession, but we have run afoul of the Midrash (oral tradition) of American Presbyterianism on what these phrases mean.[56]

Question: So, there's justification and ensuant to that is sanctification, a one-two step, whereas for you it's all of a piece?

> **Doug Wilson:** Justification to them is something that happens and has to be tied up with a bow, and then we can move on to sanctification. But when God gives faith, that faith doesn't immediately croak. It is a saving faith, and that same faith is the lone instrument for sanctification also. One can't be apprehended without the other. They are distinct but not separable. You can't make an ontological distinction. It is an organic whole for us.[57]

Question: Doug, when you cite "continuing in goodness" in Rom. 11 in your 2002 lecture, is that the cause of our salvation or the fruit of it?

> **Doug Wilson:** Yes (laughter all around).
> Look, in Colossians Paul says as you received Christ so walk in him. So the way we become Christians is the way we stay Christians is the way we finish as Christians — by faith from first to last. So we continue in God's goodness by trust. We stand by faith — they fell, but you stand — doing that to the end is how you come to your salvation. It's the gift of God

---

[56] Wilson, *The Monroe Four Speak Out*, pp. 6-7.

[57] From the CRE presbytery exam of Wilson, p. 7.

lest anyone boast. I believe we are saved by faith from first to
last, which is why I have been accused of denying sola fide.
Wisdom is vindicated by her children.[58]

Let's examine Wilson's statements in the context of his own statements and
those of his fellow speakers to the questions asked by Gerry Wisz. For one,
Doug Wilson does not disagree with any of Steve Schlissel's answers, even
though he could have said, "I don't believe Steve Schlissel at this point about
faith. I don't agree with Schlissel that the law is the gospel. I don't agree with
Schlissel's interpretation of the young rich ruler. I don't agree with Schlissel
that the most fundamental question is not "what must I do to be saved, but what
does the Lord require of me?" **Wilson did not refute any of the comments
Schlissel put forth in the same interview.** In fact, Wilson uses a virtual verbatim comment as Schlissel in his lecture at the 2002 AAPC where Wilson
says, *"When we say that all of God's word is perfect, converting the soul. When
we don't divide it up into law and gospel, when we don't say law over here,
gospel over there, when we say it's all gospel, it's all law, it's all good."*[59]
Schlissel's comment in the *Christian Renewal* interview was: *The Law as God
gave it is the Gospel. 'The Law of the Lord is perfect, converting the soul ...
The Law is good. Always has been."*[60]

Let's examine Wilson's direct comments in the *Christian Renewal* interview.
He does say that faith cannot be separated from trust and obedience. If he
emphatically qualified this statement that he clearly meant that obedience is the
fruit or evidence of faith and not the essence of faith or the cause of it, then
there would not be a problem; but, he made no qualification. In fact, his answer
to the question as to whether "continuing in goodness" is the cause of our salvation or the fruit of it, he said "yes" which brought laughter from his fellow
Monroe speakers. This means that Wilson does believe that obedience is the
cause of our salvation, that it is the cause of our justification. Wilson, made the
comment moments before he answered this question that others (namely the
RPCUS) like to have justification tied up with a bow that once completed we
can move on to sanctification. Wilson stated that he saw justification and sanctification as a one-step process, an organic whole. The fact that Wilson quotes
Colossians 2:6 in answer to the question demonstrates his true belief.
Colossians 2:6 states, *"As you therefore have received Christ Jesus the Lord,
so walk in Him,"* Wilson affirms that we cannot really make a fine distinction

---

[58] From the CRE presbytery exam of Wilson.

[59] Wilson, *"Visible and Invisible Church Revisited,"* p. 21.

[60] Schissel, *The Monroe Four Speak Out*, pp. 1, 2.

between justification and sanctification. When Wilson states that "continuing in goodness" is **the cause** of our salvation he has blurred the two great doctrines and made a heretical statement.

Wilson has stated that he totally agrees with the Westminster Standards in all that it states about justification. However, Larger Catechism question number 73 states:

> How does faith justify a sinner in the sight of God?
> **Answer:** Faith justifies a sinner in the sight of God, **not because of those other graces which do always accompany it, or of good works that are the fruits of it,** nor as if the grace of faith, or any act thereof, were imputed to him for his justification; but only as it is an instrument by which he receiveth and applieth Christ and his righteousness. (Emphasis mine)

Wilson is clearly out of accord with the Confession, and the fact that his church is not going to accept the Scripture proofs, means they will not accept the proof texts of Galatians 3:11 and Romans 3:28. The reason? Both texts make a clear distinction between works and faith, which the Federal Vision blurs.

Knowing all of this, let's go to his CRE presbytery exam, the purpose of which is to show that Wilson is in conformity with the historic Reformed Faith. Let's see how he qualifies his answers to specific questions.

When asked the question, "What is justification?" his answer is:

> The justification of an individual occurs when God imputes to that individual the complete obedience of Jesus Christ. This imputation reckons to a sinful and imperfect individual all the perfections of Jesus Christ. The ground of this imputation is the perfect obedience of Jesus Christ, both active and passive, and the instrument of receiving it is faith alone, a gift of God to be justified, given so that no one can boast.[61]

This statement seems okay, depending upon the meaning that one attaches to the terms; however, why did he not just emphasize what the Westminster Confession states? It is interesting that he does not mention a one time act of pardon completely divorced from our works.

---

[61] CRE's presbytery exam, question 3.

Wilson is asked these questions: "Do you believe that justification is by faith plus works? What is the relationship between works and justification? How are justification and sanctification related?"

> **His answer:** No, I do not believe that justification is by faith plus works. A man is justified by faith alone, and just in case someone might want to take credit for his faith (as though it were a work of his own), God even gives the gift of faith. Justification and sanctification are related in that faith is the instrument for receiving both. After a man has believed God to the saving of his soul, that man believes God to the ongoing renewal of his soul. We are justified by grace through faith. We are sanctified by that same grace through the same faith. God does not ever give His elect the gift of momentary faith. The faith that He gives remains with us, and so we continue to believe God.[62]

If one remembers Schlissel's former quotes, Schlissel says that there is no disobedient yet saving faith. **It is not faith plus obedience, but the obedience of faith**. Notice, Wilson says the same thing He does not ever mention that faith and obedience need to be separated in man's justification. Wilson's answer is a blending of justification and sanctification. The Federal Vision says that it believes in justification by faith alone, but it redefines "by faith alone." The Federal Vision speaks of faith as the "obedience of faith." Hence, obedience is the very essence of saving faith. So, when asked, "Do you believe in being justified by faith alone? They will say, "Of course." This is not the historic, orthodox Reformed Faith. The Reformed Faith makes a clear distinction between works and faith in terms of justification. Wilson also makes it a point to say that no credit should be taken for our faith, but he then has in parenthesis, (as though it were a work of his own). The Federal Vision never refers to its insistence on works for justification as "meritorious" because they define it to mean "works of our own." This is a clever way of introducing a works salvation into justification while maintaining these works as being non-meritorious. Works done by the Spirit in conformity with God's Law in order to cause our justification is totally acceptable in their way of thinking. This is why Schlissel and Lusk can call God's Law a gracious gift. I beg to differ. The Reformed Faith maintains that the Spirit uses the Law of God as a means to sanctify us, but the Law is not a gracious gift in order for us to gain justification.

---

[62] Doug Wilson's CRE presbytery exam, question 13.

Wilson was asked these questions, "Define "imputation," "active obedience," and "passive obedience." Do you uphold these concepts? Is Christ's active and passive obedience imputed to believers?"

> **His answer:** Imputation describes how God "reckons" with-
> in the confines of a covenant. He imputes the guilt of Adam's
> transgressions to us. He imputes the guilt of the elect to Jesus
> Christ. He imputes the righteousness of Jesus Christ to the
> elect. "Active obedience" refers to Christ's life of perfect
> obedience – His resistance to temptation, His obedience to
> the Law and so on. His "passive obedience" refers to His pas-
> sion, His suffering on the cross. Yes, I uphold these concepts
> as expressing the teaching of Scripture. Christ began to iden-
> tify with His elect before His suffering on the cross.[63]

In Wilson's answer he conveniently leaves out a very important point about Christ's active obedience. He defines it the same way that Shepherd and Lusk do. Rich Lusk stated that the "active obedience" consisted of Christ actively keeping the Law for Himself in order to qualify to be the redeemer; however, Lusk made it clear that this active obedience is not imputed to us as any kind of keeping of the law perfectly for us. The fact that Doug Wilson does not mention anything of the "merits" of Christ being given to us in terms of our failure to keep the Law perfectly speaks volumes about his position. He defined active obedience without having Christ credit anything to our account directly.

Wilson never once answered the question in the way that the Westminster Standards answers it. The Westminster Confession of Faith in Chapter 11:2 speaks of Christ discharging the debt of all those whom He justifies in addition to His being a full satisfaction for them. Wilson fails to speak like the Westminster Larger Catechism number 95 with reference to the moral law to all men. The Catechism speaks of all of mankind's failure to keep the moral law; the Law' purpose was given to drive men to have a sense of their sin and misery, driving them to see their need of Christ, and the **perfection of his obedience.** Wilson leaves all of this out when dealing with Christ's imputation.

Wilson avoids using the terminology of the Heidelberg Catechism in Lord's Day 23 question 60, which says:

> How are thou righteous before God?
> **Answer:** Only by a true faith in Jesus Christ; so that though
> my conscience accuse me, that I have grossly transgressed all

---

[63] CRE's presbytery exam, question 18.

the commandments of God, and kept none of them, and am still inclined to all evil; notwithstanding, God, without any merit of mine, but only of mere grace, grants and imputes to me, the perfect satisfaction, righteousness and holiness of Christ; even so, as if I never had had, nor committed any sin: yea, as if I had fully accomplished all that obedience which Christ has accomplished for me; inasmuch as I embrace such benefit with a believing heart.

When asked the question, "How did Christ "merit" our salvation?" Wilson says:

My skittishness about the word merit has to do with my rejection of certain medieval assumptions about merit, in which merit practically becomes a quasi-substance … The same is true of Christ's obedience. Christ purchased us, and it is just and right that this happen. My problem with merit is that it tends to drag autonomy behind it. Remove that, and I would not want to quibble over words.[64]

Wilson fundamentally avoided the purpose of the question. Not once did he say that Christ's merits discharged our debt to God. Not once did he say that we needed Christ's obedience because we failed to keep God's Law perfectly. He simply did not answer the question!

John Calvin, though he preferred another word due to Romanism's abuse of it, used the word and the idea of merit regarding Christ's imputation. Calvin said:

For if righteousness consists in the observance of the law, who will deny that Christ merited favor for us when, by taking that burden upon himself, he reconciled us to God as if we had kept the law? What he afterward taught the Galatians has the same purpose: "God sent forth his Son …subject to the law, to redeem those who were under the law" [Galatians 4:4-5 p.]. What was the purpose of this subjection of Christ to the law but to acquire righteousness for us, undertaking to pay what we could not pay?[65] (Emphasis mine)

---

[64] CRE's presbytery exam, question 44.

[65] Calvin, *The Institutes Of The Christian Religion,* Book 2, Chapter 17:5, p. 533.

If the presbytery exam questions were designed to settle once and for all Wilson's positions, then there would have been very specific questions regarding the "active obedience" of Christ. For example, no one asked, "By the active obedience of Christ do you understand this to specifically mean that Jesus kept the Law perfectly in our place **because** every person has failed to keep what the Law of God demands – perfect obedience?" No one asked, "Do you believe that the Mosaic Law demanded perfect obedience?" No one asked, "Is Jesus' righteousness credited to us to give us the title to eternal life because without it none of our works will justify us before God?"

When asked, "How is 'union with Christ' related to 'imputation'?" Wilson stated:

> For the elect, they amount to the same thing. For covenant members who are not elect, their union with Christi is distinct from the fruitful union enjoyed by the elect. One of the reasons for their fruitlessness is that they do not enjoy the benefits of imputation.[66]

Wilson states Christ's imputation exactly the same way that Rich Lusk states it. Imputation is with reference to this "union with Christ" and by resurrection with Christ, not by keeping the law perfectly for sinners who could not keep it. Wilson did not answer the question thoroughly, and his answer is not what the Westminster Standards teach. We must remember that he said that he did not disagree with any statement in the Confession regarding justification.

Wilson, just like the other Federal Vision proponents, denies the covenant of works. By failing to recognize that Jesus is the second Adam who perfectly keeps the law that Adam failed to perfectly keep as our representative head, Wilson has adopted a view of justification like all the rest. He blurs justification and sanctification, making justifying faith as covenant obedience to God's Law, not simply as the fruit or evidence that flows out of it. Wilson never reprimands Schlissel for saying that Law keepers are exact equivalents with believers. In fact, he agrees with Schlissel and Lusk that the Law is the Gospel and the Gospel is the Law.

Not one of the presbytery questions was specific enough to get Wilson to settle one of the major issues in this whole controversy. Knowing that many have been upset with the Federal Vision's definition of "faith" as "the obedience of faith," someone could have asked Wilson, "Do you believe that the faith that justifies us is a **one time act** that pardons all of our sins, **completely independ-**

---

[66] CRE's presbytery exam, question 19.

ent of any obedience that we might do?" No one turned to chapter 11 of the Westminster Confession dealing with "Of Justification" and took Wilson through it phrase by phrase, asking his understanding of each phrase.

One of the serious theological aberrations of Rich Lusk is his belief in two kinds of justification – an initial and final justification. Lusk, as with Norman Shepherd, speaks of a final justification that is tied to our perseverance in good works. Someone did ask Wilson during his presbytery exam as to whether there were past, present, and future aspects of justification. Wilson's answer:

> When we are talking about the theological justification of an individual sinner, we are talking about a punctiliar event in the life of that individual. But this is a particular stipulated (theological) definition of the word justification. If we want to talk about justification more broadly, we would have to include the demonstrative sense that James uses, the justification of Jesus in His resurrection, the apostates falling away from the "way of righteousness," and so on. I believe that Christ's resurrection was His vindication, His justification. I believe that we will have such a vindication in our resurrection, and that a biblical way of describing this would be to say that it will be our justification, our manifestation as the sons of God. But this use of the word, while not disconnected from individual justification, is certainly to be distinguished from it.[67]

This answer is a very muddled way of saying that he believes that justification is a process. No one asked Wilson where in the Westminster Confession do we find support for a process of justification? Where in chapter 11 does it come close to mentioning such a thing? Where in the Larger Catechism does it ever teach a process justification? Remember, Wilson claims that he does not disagree with any thing in the Westminster Standards on justification.

Where in the Westminster Standards or any of the Reformed Standards are their statements stating that Jesus was justified in His resurrection? Wilson speaks of Romans 1:4 as the justification of Jesus when the text states that He was declared to be the Son of God with power by His resurrection. This is not a Reformed interpretation of this passage. Where in any of the historic Reformed documents is there reference to the "justification" of Jesus, as if He needed anything?

---

[67] CRE's presbytery exam, question 23.

Federal Vision theology completely denies an imputation of Christ's righteousness to our account because we have failed to keep the Law perfectly. Any kind of imputation that the Federal Vision speaks of is a so-called imputation by virtue of our union with Christ. We are justified by imputation by union with Christ who was raised from the dead. Since Jesus was "justified" by His resurrection, then we are "justified" in Him by our resurrection from the dead. The problem is that the Scripture does not say that Jesus needed justification. By His incarnation, the Son of God assumes to Himself a human nature so that He can satisfy sin's curse by shedding real blood and by living a perfect life so that His perfect Law keeping can be imputed to us since God requires perfect obedience to His Law.

As I have shown before, John Calvin is very blunt about the viewpoint that Jesus merited anything for Himself. Calvin states:

> **But to ask whether Christ merited anything for himself, as Lombard and the Schoolmen do, is no less stupid curiosity than their temerity in making such a definition. What need was there for God's only Son to come down in order to acquire something new for himself?** For it is said not that the Father provided, in his Son's merits, for the needs of the Son; but that he delivered him over to death, and "did not spare him" [Romans 8:32] because he "loved the world" [John 3:16 p.; cf. Romans 8:35,37]. And we should note the prophets' expressions: "To us a child is born"[Isaiah 9:6]. "Rejoice ... O daughter of Zion! ... Lo, your king comes to you" [Zechariah 9:9, cf. Comm.]. Also, that confirmation of love which Paul commends would otherwise be barren: that Christ suffered death for his enemies [cf. Romans 5:10]. **From this we conclude that he had no regard for himself;** as he clearly affirms, "For their sake I sanctify myself" [John 17:19]. For he who gave away the fruit of his holiness to others testifies **that he acquired nothing for himself.** And this is indeed worth noting: to devote himself completely to saving us, Christ in a way forgot himself. But they absurdly apply Paul's testimony to this: "Therefore the Father has highly exalted him and bestowed on him the name," etc. [Philippians 2:9]. By what merits, they ask, could a man become judge of the world and head of the angels, acquire God's supreme dominion, and have abiding in himself that majesty, when all the power and virtue of men and angels

cannot attain even a thousandth part of it? But there is a ready and full answer: Paul is not there discussing the reason why Christ was exalted, but, for our example, is merely showing how Christ's exaltation follows his humiliation. And this means nothing else than what is said elsewhere: "It was necessary that the Christ should suffer ... and so enter into the glory of the Father" (Luke 24:26).[68] (Emphasis mine)

Calvin considers the views of Lombard, which are the views of the Federal Vision, as "stupid curiosity." John Owen considered this view as that of Socinianism. Jesus' incarnation was not for Himself but for us sinners.

There is a very good reason why Doug Wilson agrees with others in the Federal Vision when he speaks of Jesus' justification in His resurrection. They need to have some kind of imputation to appear evangelical. They devise an imputation and a justification that is tied to "union with Christ and His resurrection" apart from Jesus' perfect law keeping on our behalf. They deny the covenant of works because accepting this covenant implies that Jesus is the second Adam who perfectly keeps the Law for us. The Federal Vision must have its "obedience of faith." It must have its justification rooted in our good works that justifies us in the Day of Judgment.

The Federal Vision wants its "communion" with Jesus, but it is not the type of communion that the historic Reformed Standards speak of. The Belgic Confession states:

> Therefore we justly say with Paul, that we are justified by faith alone, or by faith without works. However, to speak more clearly, we do not mean, that faith itself justifies us, for it is only an instrument with which we embrace Christ our Righteousness. But Jesus Christ, imputing to us all his merits and so many holy works which he has done for us, and in our stead, is our Righteousness. And faith is an instrument that keeps us in communion with him in all his benefits, which, when become ours, are more than sufficient to acquit us of our sins.[69]

Having conducted this analysis, I find some troubling things remaining. While the special presbytery exam sought to be very specific in its questions about his views, I am not satisfied that Wilson has made his views clear enough. He has

---

[68] Calvin, *The Institutes Of The Christian Religion*, Book 2 Chapter 17:6.

[69] An excerpt from *The Belgic Confession*, Article 22.

used language that remains unspecified in certain details that is crucial in understanding his views of justification by faith. As I have noted in my critique of Rich Lusk and Steve Schlissel, these men have totally redefined the phrase, "justification by grace through faith." As I noted, these men state that the grace of God is the Law given for us to obey and that faith means faithful obedience to that Law.

Christ Church is sponsoring a ministerial conference on October 17-19, 2005 in Moscow, Idaho. The theme of the conference is "Great Deliverance: The Life of Justification." The speakers will be Doug Wilson, Peter Leithart, and Rich Lusk. The fact that Rich Lusk is being invited is most distressing and illuminating about Wilson's views on justification by faith. The fact that Rich Lusk is being invited to speak and not as an opposing view, means that Wilson and Christ Church are sanctioning Lusk's views. I am not aware of any public statement by Wilson that he disagrees with Rich Lusk on the issue of justification. Lusk and Schlissel are clearly outside the pale of the Reformed Faith and Christian orthodoxy on these issues. Unless Wilson openly distances himself by public statements that he opposes Lusk, Schlissel, and Shepherd, we must assume that he agrees with them. Is this guilt by association? Yes, to a large degree it is. If one does not openly renounce these other men's beliefs, then we must assume he agrees with them. Inviting one of them to speak at one's own conference implies such agreement.

Doug Wilson requested this special examination by his presbytery in order to clear his name from the stigma that many were attaching to him because of his alignment with the Federal Vision. A close examination of his answers combined with his previous statements, which he did not disavow, falls short of his goal. If he thinks that he is thoroughly Reformed then why not repudiate the views of Shepherd, Lusk, Shepherd, Wilkins, and Barach? Instead, he is inviting Rich Lusk to be one of the main speakers on justification at his ministerial conference in October of 2005. Once a person examines Rich Lusk's views on justification, then Wilson has "shown his hand." We have seen that Rich Lusk most explicitly denies the doctrine of justification by faith alone. A man is known by the company that he keeps.

Auburn Avenue's position on Justification

On September 26, 2002, the session put forth a position paper titled, "*Summary Statement of AAPC's Position on the Covenant, Baptism, and Salvation.*" On April 3, 2005, the session put forth a revised summary statement.

One of the attempts of the session in its revision is to sound more Confessional in its statement on justification; however, it fails to do so in light of the precise nature of the controversy. The session's statement is as follows:

> Salvation is by grace through faith in the Lord Jesus Christ and not of works. It is founded upon the obedience, death, and resurrection of the faithful Second Adam, Jesus Christ. Justification is an act of God's free grace wherein sinners are accepted as righteous in God's sight by virtue of the right-eousness of Christ imputed to them and received by faith alone (WSC Q. 33). This justifying faith is always accompanied by all other saving graces and virtues (WCF 11.2). Justifying faith, therefore, is never vain but one that works by love (Gal. 5:6).[70]

The fundamental difference between the revised statement and the original one in 2002 is the addition of the phrase "*Justification is an act of God's free grace wherein sinners are accepted as righteous in God's sight by virtue of the right-eousness of Christ imputed to them...*" Yes, this is almost a verbatim quote from the Westminster Shorter Catechism. The AAPC statement also quotes the Westminster Confession 11:2. The problem with the Federal Vision has been its redefinition of terms. When it speaks of the obedience of Christ and His righteousness it deliberately leaves out the imputation of Christ's perfect law keeping in our stead for having failed to keep the Law perfectly. The Auburn Avenue church wants to be vague just like all the others. The criticism of most of the Reformed community against the Federal Vision is its refusal to adhere to the active obedience of Christ in the way that it has historically been understood. I personally believe this is a deceptive maneuver. Those in the Federal Vision know that their views are not the historic Reformed position. Whenever someone says, "Oh yes, I believe in the active obedience of Christ," they never phrase it the way the historic Standards phrase it. They always leave out Christ's perfect law keeping in our stead because we cannot perfectly keep the Law. Their understanding is Christ's law keeping for Himself to be worthy to be the Redeemer.

The Auburn Avenue session's definition of justifying faith is **not complete.** The Westminster Confession at 11:2 makes it a point to state that these accompanying graces are not alone **"in the person justified."** It stresses that "faith" is the alone instrument that justifies, independent of works. This phrase clearly demonstrates that no one can misconstrue the graces that accompany faith

---

[70] Summary Statement of Auburn Avenue Presbyterian Church's Position on the Covenant, Baptism, and Salvation (Revised), April 3, 2005.

as the essence of that faith. The Federal Vision always conveniently leaves out this point, and therefore it leaves the impression that it is Confessional when it is really not. Graces that accompany faith are not the essence of faith! When the AAPC says, "Justifying faith, therefore, is never vain but one that works by love," it leaves itself maneuvering room on the precise relationship of works to justification.

One of the most damaging statements that the Auburn church has made in agreement with others of the Federal Vision are references to "**final salvation:**"

> The Bible often speaks of salvation in relational and covenantal categories. "Salvation" is a matter of being rightly related to God through Christ. But relationships are not static, unchanging entities. They are fluid and dynamic. Our salvation covenant with the Lord is like a marriage. If we continue to rest upon Christ in faith, we will live with Him happily ever after. If we break the marriage covenant, He will divorce us. It is probably unwise and pastorally inept, especially for tender consciences, to speak of this in terms of "losing one's salvation," but it seems contrary to Scripture to say that nothing at all is lost. To draw such a conclusion appears to deny the reality of the covenant and the blessedness that is said to belong even to those who ultimately prove themselves reprobate (Heb. 10:26ff).[71]

I will be devoting an entire chapter on the Federal Vision's denial of the perseverance of the saints, but this is one such explicit statement. Moreover, it acutely pertains to justification. When we are justified, we are saved. The works that accompany justifying faith are inevitable. Faith that really saves will always have good works as evidence of the genuineness of that faith. There is no such thing as a fluid or dynamic aspect of our justification or salvation in anyway whatsoever. The Auburn Avenue church sees justification as a marriage contract that can be broken by us, causing us to forfeit our eternal blessings.

The Auburn Avenue session, just like all the other Federal Vision proponents, betrays its "supposed" allegiance to the Reformed Standards. If justification and final salvation are dependent upon our good works, then justification is one and the same with sanctification. Further, if justification and final salvation are dependent upon our good works, then Christ died in vain and we are hopeless creatures indeed.

---

[71] Avenue Presbyterian Church's Position on the Covenant, Baptism, and Salvation (Revised), April 3, 2005.

Chapter 8

Baptismal Regeneration

The Federal Vision's concept of the nature of the church demands that they teach baptismal regeneration. What do we mean by this term? The historic Reformed Faith has always taught that baptism is a sacrament. I will give a definition of a sacrament using the Westminster Confession of Faith. I want to set forth what the Westminster Standards teach about the sacrament of baptism and demonstrate where the Federal Vision has corrupted this teaching.

Before I delineate the teaching of the Westminster Standards on the nature of baptism, I need to define the term "baptismal regeneration." This is the belief that we are regenerated or born again at our water baptism. It means that all of God's saving graces are present at our water baptism. Baptismal Regeneration teaches that at the ceremony of baptism one is in union with Christ in its truest sense, that at that moment there is a transition from death unto life, that one is justified, that one has forgiveness of sins, and that one is a new creation in Christ.

The view that a person is regenerated at water baptism carries some tremendous theological errors. Baptismal regeneration insists that saving faith is always present at water baptism; it makes salvation automatic for all who receive the sign and seal of baptism. It also impacts the biblical doctrine of apostasy. If one is a Christian in the fullest sense, a true seed of Abraham, then to apostatize and renounce Christ means that one loses his salvation.

The Reformed Standards do not teach baptismal regeneration. It is a very sad fact that the Federal Vision believes that the Westminster Standards teaches baptismal regeneration. This only demonstrates they are deceived and have forfeited any right to be in the ministry.

First, a sacrament conveys real spiritual blessings. Baptism, as one of the two sacraments of the Church, is no mere symbol. Christ is spiritually present in the ceremony. Unfortunately, you have Steve Wilkins criticizing Southern Presbyterians, particularly Robert Lewis Dabney and James Henley Thornwell, for what Wilkins calls - "a mere wet dedication service" (see first paragraph on page 203). Wilkins is critical is of these men because they hold to a biblical view that is in conformity with the Reformed Standards. Wilkins does not, even though he took an oath to uphold that view.

It is important that we take a look at the biblical teaching of baptism using the Westminster Standards. The Westminster Larger Catechism number 161 states:

> The sacraments become effectual means of salvation, not by
> any power in themselves, or any virtue derived from the piety
> or intention of him by whom they are administered, but only
> by the working of the Holy Ghost, and the blessing of Christ,
> by whom they are instituted.

The Westminster Confession of Faith brings out an important point about the relationship between the sacrament and that which it signifies and seals in Chapter 27, Section 2:

> There is in every sacrament a spiritual relation, or sacramen-
> tal union, between the sign and the thing signified: whence it
> comes to pass, that the names and effects of the one are attrib-
> uted to the other.

We noted earlier that the Westminster Confession emphasizes that the sacraments are holy signs and seals of the covenant of grace, which represent Christ and His benefits to us (Genesis 17:7 and Romans 4:4-13). Concerning signs, there are two parts of a sacrament – the sign and the thing signified. The sign is something visible that can be seen or handled. In baptism, we see the water being poured on the head of the infant or adult. In the Lord's Supper, we see the bread that we eat and the wine that we drink. The signs are visual reminders that something spiritual is happening. The signs point to Christ and the benefits of the new covenant.

Because of the sacramental union or spiritual relation between the sign and the thing signified, the Bible at times refers to the sacrament itself as being the blessing itself. For example, in the old covenant, the sign of the covenant was circumcision, and circumcision is called the covenant, which is sacramental language. We read in Genesis 17:10,11: *"This is My covenant, which you shall keep, between Me and you and your descendants after you: every male among you shall be circumcised. And you shall be circumcised. And you shall be circumcised in the flesh of your foreskin, and it shall be the sign of the covenant between Me and you."*

In Colossians 2:11-12 we read, *"and in Him you were also circumcised with a circumcision made without hands, in the removal of the body of the flesh by the circumcision of Christ; having been buried with Him in baptism in which you were also raised up with Him through faith in the working of God, who raised Him from the dead."* In this passage, baptism of the new covenant has replaced circumcision of the old covenant as the sign and seal of the covenant of God with His people. Here the work of the Holy Spirit is signified as the circumcision of Christ made without hands. This is sacramental language.

A very vivid example of sacramental language is expressed in I Peter 3:21 when it says, *"And corresponding to that, baptism now saves you – not the removal of dirt from the flesh, but an appeal to God for a good conscience-through the resurrection of Jesus Christ."* Without understanding that the Bible uses sacramental language to refer to the thing signified and sealed as the very thing itself, one can make some serious theological errors. This text does not teach in any shape or form that water baptism has any saving power. It does not teach baptismal regeneration, which is held by Roman Catholicism and others that one is spiritually born again at his water baptism. The text in I Peter clearly states that it is not the removal of dirt, that is, the water itself, which saves, but it is a good conscience before God that is conferred by the power of the resurrected Christ.

This sacramental language is used with reference to the Lord's Supper, when I Corinthians 5:7 states, *"Clean out the old leaven, that you may be a new lump, just as you are in fact unleavened. For Christ our Passover also has been sacrificed."* And in I Corinthians 11:24, the bread and wine are said to be the body and blood of Christ. Christ is not literally the Passover, nor is the bread and wine literally the body and blood of Christ.

Now let's turn our attention to **seals**. The difference between signs and seals is that seals not only remind us of invisible realities, but they authenticate these things to our consciences, making them more certain to us. A seal guarantees the authenticity of an important document. In I Corinthians 9:2, Paul informs the Corinthians that they are the seal of his apostleship in the Lord. In Ephesians 1:13-14 we read, *"In Him, you also, after listening to the message of truth, the gospel of your salvation having also believed, you were sealed in Him with the Holy Sprit of promise, who is given as a pledge of our inheritance, with a view to the redemption of God's own possession, to the praise of*

His glory." The seal authenticates a promise. Here, the Holy Spirit's presence in our lives is the seal, the guarantee, and the authentication that one day we will possess our inheritance in Christ.

In Romans 4:11-12 we read, *"and he received the sign of circumcision, a seal of the righteousness of the faith which he had while uncircumcised, that he might be the father of all who believe without being circumcised, that right-eousness might be reckoned to them, and the father of circumcision to those who not only are of the circumcision, but who also follow in the steps of the faith of our father Abraham which he had while uncircumcised."* In this passage, circumcision in the old covenant was said to be a seal of righteousness.

There is something very important in understanding the sacraments as seals. The guarantee or the authentication of the genuineness of that which is sealed is **not automatic**, but it is only effective if there is **faith.** Where there is true faith, then the sacrament as a seal finds its true fulfillment. For Abraham, his faith preceded the sacrament, which was a seal of authenticity that he already possessed before receiving the seal. In the Ephesians passage, the Holy Spirit is a seal of eternal life as a result of their belief or faith. Without faith nothing is guaranteed.

The Necessity of Baptism

Baptism is the sign and seal of the new covenant, replacing circumcision of the old covenant. This is clearly affirmed by Colossians 2:11-12 passage quoted earlier. While water baptism is not absolutely necessary in order for one to possess saving faith, it is a sin to neglect it as an adult and for parents to neglect baptizing their infant children.

In Matthew 28:18-20, the disciples were commanded by Jesus to go and disciple the nations, baptizing them in the name of the triune God. Whenever people exercised faith in Christ, they were baptized into the visible church. On the Day of Pentecost, when Peter preached a convicting sermon, the people asked what they should do, and Peter **commanded** them to repent and be baptized. On that day, 3000 people were baptized and added to the visible church (Acts 2:37-41). In Acts 8:12, Philip, the evangelist, preached to the Samaritans, and those who believed were baptized. In Acts 10: 34-48, Peter is sent by God to the Gentiles to preach the gospel. As a result of his preaching, those that believed received the Holy Spirit, and Peter commanded them to be baptized with water (verses 47-48). When Saul of Tarsus (to be renamed Paul) was converted on the road to Damascus, he was baptized (Acts 22:16). When Lydia heard the gospel preached by the apostle Paul, the Lord opened her heart to respond to the gospel. Consequently, she was baptized **with her household** (Acts 16:14-15). When the Philippian jailer was convicted of his sin and wanted to know what he must do to be saved, Paul and Silas said that he must believe in the Lord Jesus. He believed, and he and **his household** were baptized (Acts 16:30-34). When Paul was preaching in Corinth, Crispus, the leader of the synagogue in Corinth, believed in Jesus along with his household, and many others believed and were being baptized. When Paul preached to the disciples of John the Baptist in Ephesus who had only been baptized with John's baptism, Paul told them that John's baptism was one of repentance, but they needed to believe in the Messiah of whom John said was coming after him. Consequently, these disciples were baptized in the name of Jesus (Acts 19:1-12).

Baptism was clearly the sign of the new covenant, and it was commanded of all those who believed in Jesus. It would be a sin to refuse baptism. No one entered the local visible church without receiving baptism. Not only were adults commanded to be baptized, but these believing parents were to have their entire households, which would include children, to be baptized. This was totally consistent with the old covenant sign. In the Old Testament, God **commanded** believers to circumcise their infant children and all in their household (Genesis 17:10-14, 23-27). In Exodus 4:24-26, we learn that God was going to kill Moses for failing to circumcise his son, and Moses' wife, Zipporah, circumcises their son, but then she rebukes Moses for failing to act as the head of his household in obeying this commandment of God.

I have already established that baptism is clearly the sign of the new covenant, replacing circumcision of the old covenant. If God then commanded parents of the old covenant to obey Him by having their children receive the sign of the covenant, God commands believing parents in the new covenant to have their infant children baptized, and this is what the Bible teaches. The sermon that Peter preached on the Day of Pentecost where he commanded them to believe and be baptized, he immediately quotes from Genesis 17 that the promise of God was for their children as well (Acts 2:39). This explains why Lydia and the Philippian jailer had their entire households baptized. They were following the pattern that was said to be an everlasting covenant. The church, whether it was the church in the Old Testament or the church in the New Testament, was commanded to receive the sign of the covenant, which included children.

Earlier, I quoted I Corinthians 7:14, demonstrating how the unbelieving spouse is sanctified by the believing spouse. There is a very important phrase in this verse – *"For the unbelieving husband is sanctified through his wife, and* *the unbelieving wife is sanctified through her believing husband; **for otherwise your children are unclean, but now they are holy.***

Does this mean that the children of a Christian home (where at least one spouse is a Christian) are holy in the sense that they possess saving faith? No. To be unclean is to be outside the covenant, its life, and its blessings. To be holy is to be consecrated to God and to be inside his covenant, enjoying its life and blessings (Ezra 9:2; Isaiah 6:13). How does this covenantal holiness entitle an infant of even one believing parent to baptism? Covenantal holiness "necessarily supposes a being within the covenant, in virtue of the credible profession of the parent, and, consequently, a right to the initiatory seal of it."[1]

Therefore, it is a sin for Christian parents not to baptize all their children. One might ask, "If the sacrament of baptism is a sign and seal of the righteousness of faith, are all children who are baptized possessors of saving faith at the moment of their baptism? The answer is no. The Westminster Confession of Faith states it beautifully when it says in Chapter 28, Section 6:

> The efficacy of Baptism is not tied to that moment of time wherein it is administered; yet notwithstanding, by the right use of this ordinance, the grace promised is not only offered, but really exhibited and conferred, by the Holy Ghost, to such (whether of age or infants) as that grace belongeth unto, according to the counsel of God's own will, in His appointed time.

The grace promised in the sacrament is not only exhibited but conferred by the Holy Spirit to as many as **the grace belongs to in God's appointed time**. This means that the act of baptism does not automatically save the child, but the sign and seal are nonetheless real when there is **faith**, whenever God chooses to grant that faith. Hence, when a person who was baptized as an infant comes to repentance and faith at the age of 50, are they to be rebaptized? Absolutely not! The reality is that their baptism as an infant was made effectual 50 years later.

The Bible is clear that infants can possess saving faith as infants. We only have to look to David in the Old Testament and to John the Baptist in the New Testament. David could say the following in Ps. 22:9-10, "*Yet Thou art He who didst bring me forth from the womb; Thou didst **make me trust when upon my mother's breasts**. Upon Thee I was cast from birth; Thou hast been my God from my mother's womb.*" In speaking about John the Baptist, Luke

---

[1] Quoted in Joe Morecraft III's *"Word And Sacraments" Westminster Larger Catechism Questions 154-177,* p. 1738.

1:15 states, *"For he will be great in the sight of the Lord, and he will drink no wine or liquor, and he will be filled with the Holy Spirit, **while yet in his mother's womb.**"*

The promise of that which is signified and sealed in the sacrament of baptism is not tied to the moment of the baptism. Christian parents are obligated and commanded to have their children baptized. The elders of the church, who are the shepherds of the sheep watching over the souls of those entrusted to their care, also would be sinning by not insisting that those seeking to unite with the church, present all their children for baptism who have not previously been baptized.

Norman Shepherd Teaches Baptismal Regeneration

All that I have said in the previous pages regarding the meaning of the sacrament of baptism, is **not** what the Federal Vision believes. This movement is committed to a position of baptismal regeneration. Norman Shepherd has influenced the other men in the Federal Vision camp on this issue. Shepherd has made his views quite explicit in his book, *The Call of Grace.* Shepherd's commitment to his innovative objective covenant makes him propose a position of baptismal regeneration. In his chapter on covenant and regeneration, Shepherd explicitly states that **baptism marks the point of conversion, which is the transition from death to life and when a person is saved** (see second paragraph on page 247). To show the utter confusion and lack of clarity of this man's writing, Shepherd immediately states in a following paragraph that baptism does not accomplish the transition from death to life or that it causes a person to be born again. Shepherd says that would be teaching baptismal regeneration, which is rightly rejected by Reformed churches (see third paragraph on page 247). Shepherd says that the Holy Spirit works when and where He wants, not necessarily at the moment of baptism. So, it seems that Shepherd does not want to be known as espousing baptismal regeneration, but then in a few sentences after he tries to qualify himself, he makes this self-contradictory statement:

> From the perspective of election, regeneration is the point of conversion. Regeneration, however, is a secret work of the Holy Spirit, and so we do not know when it takes place. We do not have access to the moment of regeneration. What we hear from the converted sinner is a profession of faith, and what we see is his baptism into Christ. This covenant sign and seal marks his conversion and his entrance into the

church as the body of Christ. From the perspective of the
covenant, he is united to Christ when he is baptized.[2]

Shepherd says that baptism is the mark of conversion, but then he says that this
is not baptismal regeneration. He then immediately turns around and says that
this regeneration of the Holy Spirit is the mark of conversion when the person
is united to Christ in baptism. This is what I mean by the double talk found in
several of the Federal Vision documents. This "it is, no it isn't, but it is" language brings confusion to many trying to discern what these men are saying.
False teachers commonly use this practice of confusion. It only demonstrates
that these men are thoroughly confused themselves, or worse yet, they deliberately know what they are doing. They are doing this to confuse people, to teach
them a new paradigm. The claim that people do not understand their points is
quite disturbing. Who is causing the confusion? With statements like the one
quoted earlier, it is no wonder people are confused. However, if one takes the
time to carefully analyze their comments, there is no mystery.

Shepherd betrays his earlier comment that he does not believe in baptismal
regeneration when he says that the Great Commission pictures baptism as the
transition point from death to life. He says that a person is not really converted until he is baptized. Shepherd says that a person's baptism marks the time
when a person's sins were washed away, and he cites Acts 22:16 as a proof
text for that comment. Shepherd says that God seeks to remind men of their
baptism as the defining point of their conversion. See first paragraph on page
248 for these comments.

Shepherd states that the connection between baptism and regeneration comes
to vivid expression in Titus 3:5 where it says that we are saved through the
washing of rebirth and renewal of the Holy Spirit, who washes us, sanctifies
us, and justifies us at our baptism (see paragraph three on page 248) Now, I
thought Shepherd said that he does not believe in baptismal regeneration? Yet
he quotes Titus 3:5, which explicitly uses the phrase, "washing of
regeneration." As the old adage goes, "If it looks like a thorn and feels like a
thorn, then it is a thorn." If these comments do not teach baptismal regeneration, then I don't know what does. Shepherd makes the amazing comment that
the Great Commission does not specifically mention faith but only by implication. What is explicitly stated, says Shepherd, is repentance, obedience, and
baptism. Shepherd makes the heretical statement that when faith is isolated
from obedience to God's Law, as some supplement or evidence of salvation,
people are missing the point. Shepherd says obedience to the Law is no sup-

---

[2] Shepherd, *The Call of Grace*, p. 94.

plement of salvation or evidence of it – **it is salvation!** (see last paragraph on page 248). As I demonstrated in chapter 3, Norman Shepherd has denied the precious doctrine of justification by faith alone in Christ. If one recalls that chapter, I quoted Shepherd's book where he openly states that circumcision in the old covenant and baptism in the new covenant is **a condition of grace.** Where does the Bible teach that grace has conditions? Paul under the inspiration of the Holy Spirit says that faith is not a work (Rom. 7:4-5). Baptism, my friends, is a work. By Shepherd making baptism the condition of grace for salvation, he has just become a modern Judaizer.

Steve Wilkins Teaches Baptismal Regeneration

One of the most ardent advocates of baptismal regeneration is Steve Wilkins. I have noted already that Wilkins was critical of Dabney and Thornwell as Southern Presbyterians. In affirming that their view of baptism was a mere wet dedication service, Wilkins has "revealed his hand." Wilkins, obviously sees baptism as something much different. He says that baptism is much more than what most PCA Presbyterians believe it to be (see first paragraph on page 202). Wilkins faults the Puritans for draining all the scriptural significance regarding baptism. He says that the biblical teaching of salvation as it pertains to union with Christ in baptism was lost (see first paragraph on page 203). Wilkins says that infant baptism lost all its true significance; he says that it amounted to nothing more than a wet dedication service. What loss of significance? Wilkins will enlighten us supposedly with the fact that salvation is at one's baptism, just like Norman Shepherd. The truth is Dabney and Thornwell did not view baptism as some dedication service. These men were thoroughly Reformed in their understanding – only they did not believe in baptismal regeneration like Wilkins, which explains why he criticizes them.

When asked by the *Christian Renewal Magazine* interviewer what does baptism do for children, Wilkins said, "*to be a member of the church is to be a member of the body of Christ and biblically speaking, that means that the baptized are united to Christ*" (see Wilkins' answer to the question at the bottom of page 203). Wilkins makes no distinction between being in the visible and invisible church. He sees baptism as bringing us into the body of Christ in its fullest saving sense. The interviewer then became very specific by asking Wilkins as to whether one could be in the church but not united to Christ. Wilkins responded by saying that this distinction was unbiblical. Wilkins said that the visible church **is** the body of Christ and that baptism unites us to Christ (see Wilkins' answer to the question at the top of page 204). Now, Wilkins says that this gift must be received by faith; otherwise, everything is undermined. In saying this one might think that Wilkins is Confessional; however, the Westminster Confession makes a point that the sign and seal of baptism is not tied to the moment of baptism. Wilkins' position demands that it is present because he says that we are united to Christ in the fullest sense at the baptism. If Wilkins does not believe that one can be in the covenant without salvation, then he is tying salvation to the water baptism. Wilkins states that the apostle Paul teaches that baptism clothes us with Christ because we are in true union with Christ. Wilkins says that we have **all** the spiritual blessings, and we are members of Christ's flesh and bones as Ephesians 5:23-31 alludes to. At this point, Wilkins shows how he perverts the Westminster Confession. Westminster Confession Chapter 25, Section 2 states that outside the church there is ordinarily no salvation. In this section it is referring to the visible church. However, Wilkins applies Ephesians 5 to this concept, but the Westminster never does. Ephesians 5 is referring to the invisible church and, in fact, is used as the footnote to the previous section (25:1 on the invisible church) where the Westminster Divines properly placed it. This is the sort of twisting that occurs over and over in Federal Vision theology. The Federal Vision likes to appeal to the Westminster Confession when they think it serves their purposes and when they are trying to look Reformed. Wilkins completely distorts the Confession to teach that which it does not teach.

There should be no question whether Wilkins believes in baptismal regeneration because he stresses the idea of union with Christ. This union, he says, is at our water baptism. Wilkins states that it is at baptism that we receive the grace of God. This itself is an endorsement of baptismal regeneration. Wilkins says that grace is often seen as "unmerited favor," but he says that this designation is not the best way to understand grace. Wilkins says grace is "the favor of God." We receive God's grace by being found "in Him" (See Wilkins' comments on pages 206 and 207). Wilkins says that to be saved by grace then is to be united with Christ. Where has Wilkins said that union occurs? You guessed it, at our baptism. It doesn't take great intelligence to realize that Wilkins has just equated baptism with salvation by grace. In this regard, Wilkins is in total agreement with Norman Shepherd when Shepherd said that grace has conditions, and baptism is one of those conditions.

Wilkins, just like others, states that to be "elect" is to be baptized. He quotes Ephesians 1:3-5 as one of his proof texts to prove this (See fourth paragraph on page 208). Of course in all of Ephesians 1 baptism is never mentioned. Our Reformed Standards were very careful to restrict the term "elect" only to those who were part of the invisible church – the true Israel, the true seed of Abraham. Like Jesus said, being a physical seed of Abraham, does not necessarily save anyone. Wilkins has the audacity to quote 2 Thessalonians 2:13,

14 which specifies that the Thessalonians were chosen for salvation through sanctification to obtain the glory of God. Wilkins says, *"How could Paul say this? If someone insists that Paul was given special insight into whom God had chosen, then we must respond with John Barach, 'we suddenly discover that we cannot learn from the apostle Paul, who told us to imitate him, how to talk to our churches"* (See second paragraph on page 209).

I need to make a very important observation that the Federal Vision simply does not or refuses to understand. When Paul addresses the churches in his epistles, he addresses them with terminology that speaks of their election in Christ, their redemption and forgiveness in Him. In saying these things, they are applicable only to the invisible church, those who are genuine believers. We must remember that the visible church is comprised of the invisible church. They are not one and the same. God commands people who profess Christ to be a part of a local, visible church. Hence, when one addresses truths that are only applicable to the elect of God, they are publicly given to the entire group. Yes, Paul had no idea who is the elect of God, but how else is he going to address them other than in the context of the visible church? Is he going to say, "Okay, what I am about to say is only for the elect; therefore, I want all of you "elect" persons to go to the next room so I can be very specific." Of course not! God always spoke to covenant Israel, knowing full well that not all of Israel was truly Israel. When a preacher preaches the gospel, he has no idea who God is going to effectually call to Himself. Effectual calling means that people are born again by the Holy Spirit by having their hearts changed and enabled to believe the gospel. The effectual call goes out in the midst of the external, public call to repent and believe. The Federal Vision thinks that for Paul to write to the Ephesian church and call them "saints" means that all those in the visible church are really saints. Why the Federal Vision cannot see this simple fallacy is baffling to me. In making this error, the Federal Vision goes off onto a wild tangent that leads them to embrace heresies.

Wilkins makes a very bold statement that *"all of the members of the Church have been 'born again' by means of the word preached to them ... both Paul and Peter say this to the visible church"* (See fourth paragraph on page 210). Wilkins goes on to say in the same extended quote that the visible church has received a justifying and sanctifying **washing.** He says that the Greek grammar suggests that the Spirit instrumentally confers justification and sanctification through washing. Since Wilkins wants to talk about Greek grammar, let's talk about it. Why does Wilkins assume that baptism is the meaning of "washing" in I Corinthians 6:11? The Greek word for "washing" in this verse is the Greek word, *"apolouo."* The Greek word for baptism is the word *"baptizo."* There is nothing in the context of I Corinthians 6:11 for an exegete to think that water baptism is in view. This is but an example of how one's presuppositions are imposed on biblical texts to make them say what they do not say. There is no doubt that Wilkins sees the washing as a reference to water baptism because in a paragraph preceding it, he says that people have been "born" through the gospel and "*that they have been washed (or baptized) which has brought about sanctification and justification in the name of Christ, by the Spirit of God*" (See second paragraph on page 210). To be justified at one's water baptism is an emphatic endorsement of baptismal regeneration.

The public position paper of the Auburn Avenue Presbyterian Church states identical views regarding baptism as does their pastor Steve Wilkins. Wilkins is in full agreement with Norman Shepherd who teaches baptismal regeneration, and he will be in agreement with Wilson, Barach, and Lusk who also teach baptismal regeneration.

Doug Wilson Teaches Baptismal Regeneration

Doug Wilson has made it a major point that the term "Christian" applies in its fullest sense to all who are baptized in the Triune name (See bottom of page 221 and top of 222). If Wilson had said that with reference to the invisible church, there would be no real problem. The problem comes in when he like all his other Federal Vision associates blur the biblical distinction of the visible and invisible. Yes, all persons baptized in the name of the Triune God are **outwardly Christians**, but this does not mean that all outwardly baptized are baptized with the Spirit in a saving capacity. This is why Paul said in Romans 2:29 that circumcision is that which is of the heart, by the Spirit, not by the letter.

John Barach Teaches Baptismal Regeneration

John Barach is one of the most blatant proponents of baptismal regeneration. It is noteworthy that Steve Wilkins said in his paper for the Knox Theological Seminary Colloquium that he relied heavily on what Barach taught on this subject. John Barach was a speaker at the 2002 and 2003 Auburn Avenue Pastors' Conference. He was also a participant in the Knox Theological Seminary Colloquium.

John Barach says there are some people who have the privilege of already sharing in the beginnings of glorification. Who might these people be? That's right – all those who have been baptized into Christ. He says that every believing person with his children are in true union with Christ (See third paragraph on page 225). Barach has rejected the biblical notion of the distinction of the visible and invisible church. He says that the Bible speaks of the efficacy of baptism. This means that every baptized person shares new life in Christ (See third paragraph on page 225). Barach asks the question, "But then who is in Christ?" He answers the question by saying all who have been brought into Christ, those who have been baptized into Christ (See second paragraph on page 228). Moreover, Barach says that God has promised every covenant member that he or she is elect in Christ (See third paragraph on page 228). This means of course that every baptized person in the local church is elect. Barach explicitly states that God, in the gospel and through baptism, promises us that he unites us to Christ so that Paul "*can address the entire congregation men, women and children as those who are in Christ and who are chosen in Christ...In him you have redemption, righteousness, justification, sanctification, the Holy Spirit, glorification and election. The whole package of salvation you could say for eternity past to eternity future is all found in Christ*" (See fourth paragraph on page 228). Barach then immediately gives a quote equally famous now (not in a godly way) in the Reformed world. He says, "*But you don't need a special dramatic revivalistic conversion to let you know that you are elect, you had the special experience that God gives you, it was called baptism. That's the special experience that lets you know that you are one of God's chosen people*" (See first paragraph on page 229). There you have it, baptismal regeneration in its ugly glory.

Barach, like Steve Wilkins, has the audacity to go to the Reformed Standards and try to have them teach baptismal regeneration. Barach quotes the Heidelberg Catechism number 74 as proof for his view of baptismal regeneration. He says that the Catechism teaches all the church's children, who have been grafted into the church through baptism not to worry about their election but to confess with the whole church that they are now and always a living member of it. Heidelberg Catechism question number 74 asks:

> Are infants to be baptized?
> **Answer:** Yes: for since they, as well as the adult, are included in the covenant and church of God; and since redemption from sin by the blood of Christ, and the Holy Ghost, the author of faith, is promised to them no less than to the adult; they must therefore by baptism, as a sign of the covenant, be also admitted into the Christian church; and be distinguished from the children of unbelievers as was done in the old covenant or testament by circumcision, instead of which baptism is instituted in the new covenant.

Barach fallaciously thinks that this answer teaches baptismal regeneration. Since the answer states that children are included in the covenant and that redemption from sin is promised to them no less than an adult, this supposedly teaches baptismal regeneration. The Westminster Confession is very similar to this. All this is saying is that children are in the covenant and we do **presume** them to be Christians by their baptism. Presumption that faith is present in an infant **is not** the same as saying that it is there at that moment. This is why the Westminster Confession in Chapter 28, Sections 5 and 6 states:

> Although it be a great sin to contemn or neglect this ordinance, yet grace and salvation are not so inseparably annexed unto it, as that no person can be regenerated or saved without it; or, that all that are baptized are undoubtedly regenerated.

> The efficacy of Baptism is not tied to that moment of time wherein it is administered; yet notwithstanding, by the right use of this ordinance, the grace promised is not only offered, but really exhibited and conferred, by the Holy Ghost, to such (whether of age or infants) as that grace belongeth unto, according to the counsel of God's own will, in His appointed time.

Westminster was very careful not to say all baptized children are undoubtedly regenerated and that the grace signified and sealed is not tied to the moment of baptism. The grace belongs to all, even if they are infants, who are the recipients of God's saving faith. The Heidelberg is not as specific as Westminster; nonetheless, one could never deduce baptismal regeneration from question number 74. The reason being is that the Catechism states in question number 65 that it is only by faith alone in Christ that we share His blessings. It goes on to say that the Holy Spirit confirms that through the use of the sacraments. In question number 72 the Heidelberg asks:

> Is then the external baptism with water the washing away of sin itself?
> **Answer:** Not at all: for the blood of Jesus Christ only, and the Holy Ghost cleanse us from all sin.

Heidelberg Question number 73 states:

> Why then doth the Holy Ghost call baptism "the washing of regeneration," and "the washing away of sins"?
> **Answer:** God speaks thus not without great cause, to-wit, not only thereby to teach us, that as the filth of the body is purged away by water, so our sins are removed by the blood and Spirit of Jesus Christ; but especially that by this divine pledge

and sign he may assure us, that we are spiritually cleansed from our sins as really, as we are externally washed with water.

As long as we do not tie the promises signified and sealed to the very moment of baptism, and as long as we recognize that faith must be present of which the baptism signifies and seals, then we will not fall into the error of baptismal regeneration.

Steve Schlissel Teaches Baptismal Regeneration

Steve Schlissel falls squarely into the camp of those espousing baptismal regeneration when he derides Southern Presbyterians for being like Baptists when it comes to how they view their children. Outside of sprinkling their babies, Schlissel says that these Presbyterians address their children as Baptists. Schlissel says, *"They don't believe their children are saved by the grace of God, they believe they are waiting for a decision, some sort of cogent, confessable experience of personal regeneration and transition from death to life because they believe their children are born in death. They have bought into the Baptistic way of thinking and it is just an abomination"* (See last paragraph on page 233). Notice, Schlissel says that baptism is "being saved by the grace of God." While it is true that Presbyterians presume their baptized children to be elect, they do expect their children to give cogent, confessable professions of their own personal allegiance to Christ. This does not mean that Presbyterians expect their children to go through some dramatic conversion experience. Schlissel is arguing against a straw man here. Presbyterians do expect their baptized children to give cogent answers before they can partake of the Lord's Supper. Of course, the issue of paedocommunion is not being directly addressed in this book; it is interesting that all the major figures of the Federal Vision subscribe to paedocommunion (the belief that baptized children have a right to the Lord's Table regardless of their age or discernment). Schlissel uses the same terminology that Shepherd and Wilkins used about water baptism. He calls it a transition from death to life.

Schlissel relates "calling" with baptism. He says that "calling" is a purely objective thing that applies to every single baptized person. By calling, Schlissel clearly means what the Reformed Faith has understood to be the "effectual call." This is the call that regenerates a dead soul, that enables one to be transformed from death unto life. Schlissel makes reference to 2 Timothy 1:9 which talks about God saving us with a holy calling (See paragraph at top of page 239). The Reformed Standards **never** equate effectual calling to water baptism and never apply it to all those in the visible church; it relegates it only

to those in the invisible church, the elect of God. Of course, this is meaningless to Schlissel since he believes many Reformed people think that truth is
frozen in the 16th and 17th centuries with the Reformed Standards. Schlissel
gives lip service to these Confessional documents only when he thinks that
they will serve his purpose. There is a good reason why he does not want to be
bound to the system of doctrine taught in them. They refute his views.

Schlissel thinks that by not teaching our children that they are effectually called
in their baptism that we are teaching them to doubt the love of God for them.
As much as Schlissel accuses Southern Presbyterians of Baptistic thinking, he
is really saying the same thing as Baptists would say when it comes to all professing Christians – God loves all of you the same. Oh really? The Bible says
that God hated Esau who was a member of the covenant and saved for awhile
according to the Federal Vision. Schlissel says that the pastor needs to say to
the entire congregation that God loves them equally. He says that by virtue of
our baptism and being in the church, the whole congregation has turned from
darkness to light, from the power of Satan to God, has received forgiveness of
sins, are sanctified by faith in Christ, and are children of the light. Schlissel
mocks the attitude that he calls "the old scholastic unbelieving way of reading
the Bible." He says that we must accept that we **are** God's children by the fact
that we are objectively in the covenant via our baptisms (See paragraph at the
bottom of page 239 and top of 240). Schlissel thinks it is an affront to God to
get all wrapped up in this "mindless nonsense of assurance" as he calls it (See
second paragraph on page 240). Schlissel says that God has told us who we are
and we ought to say Amen.

In his paper presented at the Knox Theological Seminary Colloquium,
Schlissel denounces the critics of the Federal Vision for their idea that covenant
status essentially confers only proximity to grace, but not grace itself. Schlissel
maintains that there are those Reformed people who don't think that their children **are justified** in their baptism. He says, *"After all, one can only be justified by faith, and faith alone. Thus, for these men, the covenant status of children of believers is a halfway sort of thing"* (See paragraph on the top of page
241). For Schlissel, we Reformed people who do not see that our children are
emphatically justified are guilty of halfway believing God. For Schlissel, his
all the way covenant status is baptismal regeneration.

Rich Lusk Teaches Baptismal Regeneration

Rich Lusk has presented a most clever back door approach to try to get sym-
pathy for his position of baptismal regeneration. He admits that his view advo-

cates baptismal regeneration, but it is a kind that he says the Reformed creeds have been teaching for centuries. It is interesting how he gradually tries to lead one down the path to this false doctrine. He takes truths from various areas and tries to build a logical case for baptismal regeneration using the Westminster Confession. I will interact with his paper on baptismal regeneration, but I want to state from the outset that as much as Lusk seeks to come across as Reformed in some kind of baptismal regeneration, I must remind the reader of some of his other positions that I have documented in this book. First, he has openly denied the imputation of Christ's righteousness (See third paragraph on page 144). Second, he believes that God never demanded perfect obedience in the Mosaic Law (See first full paragraph on page 133). Third, he believes that God will deal with us with some kind of soft justice, accepting our sincere efforts at keeping the Law (See quote on page 292). Fourth, he believes in justification by works of the Law as demonstrated by his interpretation of the story of the young rich ruler. Lusk actually thinks that Jesus told the young man that the Law was keepable (See quote at the bottom of page 133 and top of 134). Fifth, he believes justification is a process because he says that it is a dynamic, fluid thing. Sixth, he believes that there is an initial justification and then a final justification . Seventh, he believes that this final justification is contingent upon our faithful obedience to the Law, imperfectly as it may be . Eighth, he believes that one can truly possess an initial justification and then lose it all (See quote on page 291). We need to keep in mind all of these facts as we examine Lusk's attempts to justify baptismal regeneration. His particular view of baptismal regeneration is subtle in many places. This is because he appeals regularly to the Reformed Standards, and many of his quotes do portray what several of the Reformers taught. However, we must not be fooled or lured into his trap. He seeks to use their accurate ideas but then manipulate them into a position that the Reformers did not hold, nor what the Reformed Standards taught.

To understand how Lusk approaches the subject of baptismal regeneration, we need to reiterate several key points in his understanding of the objectivity of the covenant. Lusk believes that all of the covenant people in the visible church are the elect of God. Lusk encourages pastors to openly declare from the pulpit to the congregation that their sins are forgiven, that Christ paid for their sins, and truly reconciled them to God - every single one of them (See Lusk's comments on pages 250 and 251). He states that those who will eventually apostatize were truly brought to Christ, united with Him, and loved by God for a time; they were part of the chosen, redeemed, Spirit indwelt people (See first paragraph on page 257).

Having considered all of the above beliefs of Rich Lusk, we will see that they have an important role to play in his case for an objective baptismal regeneration. Lusk gives us his meaning of baptismal regeneration:

> If I were going to speak of "baptismal regeneration," I would define "regeneration" as the new life situation entered into in baptism. This new life, in this carefully specified sense, is not so much a matter of ontology or subjectivity (Hodge's focus), as it a matter of new relationships, privileges, and responsibilities. It means one has a new family and a new story, a new citizenship and a new status.[3]

He states that the regeneration referred to in Titus 3:5 is not an inward regeneration but clearly a reference to the kingdom of God. He states:

> A good biblical case can be made for this objective understanding of regeneration. The "regeneration" of Mt. 19:28 (and Tit. 3:5, I would suggest) is clearly not an "inward spiritual renovation" but the new state of affairs brought about in the kingdom of God.[4]

Titus 3:5 says, *"He saved us, not on the basis of deeds which we have done in righteousness, but according to His mercy, by the washing of regeneration and renewing by the Holy Spirit."*

The fact that Lusk does not view the Titus passage as referring to an internal regeneration sets the tone for his erroneous views. Even though Lusk quotes Calvin in many places, it is Calvin who refutes Lusk's belief. Calvin says:

> Now the Apostles are wont to draw an argument from the Sacraments, to prove that which is there exhibited under a figure, because it ought to beheld by believers as a settled principle, that God does not sport with us by unmeaning figures, but **inwardly accomplishes by his power what he exhibits by the outward sign**; and therefore, baptism is fitly and truly said to be "the washing of regeneration." The efficacy and use of the sacraments will be properly understood by him who shall connect the sign and the thing signified, in such a manner as not to make the sign unmeaning and inefficacious, and who nevertheless shall not, for the sake of

---

[3] Rich Lusk, *Do I Believe In Baptismal Regeneration?* <www.auburnavenue.org/articles>.

[4] Lusk, *Do I Believe In Baptismal Regeneration?*

adorning the sign, take away from the Holy Spirit what belongs to him. Although by baptism wicked men are neither washed nor renewed, yet it retains that power, so far as relates to God, because, although they reject the grace of God, still it is offered to them.[5] (Emphasis mine)

Lusk bemoans what he calls an abandonment of an objective view of regeneration for a subjective one. He states:

For later Reformed scholastics after Dordt (1618-19), the meaning of the term "regeneration" narrowed to the moment of God's initiating grace in a person's life, resulting in life-long faith and repentance. It became almost exclusively subjective and individual, rather than corporate and cosmic.[6]

Of course Lusk believes that this supposed truth has been recaptured in biblical theology, and guess who has recaptured it – proponents of the Federal Vision of course. Lusk states:

In more recent biblical theology, "regeneration" has regained its full redemptive-historical overtones. Texts such as Mt. 19:28 and Tit. 3:5 have been read with their pregnant eschatological dimensions, in a more objective sense. Reformed writers such as Norm Shepherd, Peter Leithart, and Joel Garver have used "baptismal regeneration" language in this broader sense to describe entry into the "new creation" or the "new humanity.[7]

Lusk wants to elicit Calvin's view of baptism as support for his view of baptismal regeneration. He wants to view, for example, baptism as **an** instrument for forgiveness of sins. Lusk states, *"In other words, baptism is the instrument of forgiveness, and therefore of the assurance of forgiveness as well."*[8]

Lusk's great error is that he wants to link baptism itself (the moment it is applied) to the possession of those blessings that it signifies and seals. He tries to manipulate Calvin to say this, but this is a vain attempt. Calvin states:

Let us take as proof of this, Cornelius the centurion, who, having already received forgiveness of sins and the visible

---

[5] Calvin, *Calvin's New Testament Commentaries, The Epistle To Titus,* pp. 382- 383.

[6] Calvin, *Calvin's New Testament Commentaries, The Epistle To Titus.*

[7] Calvin, *Calvin's New Testament Commentaries, The Epistle To Titus.*

[8] Calvin, *Calvin's New Testament Commentaries, The Epistle To Titus.*

graces of the Holy Spirit, was nevertheless baptized [Acts
10:48]. He did not seek an ampler forgiveness of sins through
baptism, but a surer exercise of faith — indeed, increase of
assurance from a pledge. Perhaps someone will object: why,
then, did Ananias tell Paul to wash away his sins through baptism [Acts 22:16; cf. ch. 9:17-18] if sins are not washed
away by the power of baptism itself? I reply: we are said to
receive, obtain, and acquire what, according as our faith is
aware, is shown forth to us by the Lord, whether when he first
testifies to it, or when he confirms more fully and more surely what has been attested. Ananias meant only this: "To be
assured, Paul, that your sins are forgiven, be baptized. For the
Lord promises forgiveness of sins in baptism; receive it, and
be secure."[9]

One has to watch Lusk very carefully because he wants to make a direct association of the sign and seal of the covenant (baptism) with the actual graces. He
even makes this statement – "*Calvin affirms that regeneration – new life in
Christ – commences in baptism.*"[10] The problem is that Calvin does not make
the statement that regeneration commences in baptism. Calvin says:

Baptism also brings another benefit, for it **shows us** our mortification in Christ, and new life in him. Indeed (as the apostle says), "we have been baptized into his death," "buried
with him into death ... that we may walk in newness of life"
(Romans 6:3-4).[11] (Emphasis mine)

Stating that baptism **shows us** our new life in Christ is **not** the same as saying
that baptism **commences** new life. Again, we see that Lusk is attempting to
sneak in baptismal regeneration, passing it off as being Reformed. He mis-
quotes Calvin. I simply reiterate what the Westminster Confession of Faith
says in Chapter 28, Section 5: It says, "... *yet grace and salvation are not so
inseparably annexed unto it, as that no person can be regenerated or saved
without it; or that all that are baptized are undoubtedly regenerated.*" Lusk is
at odds with Westminster by insisting that regeneration commences in baptism.

---

[9] Calvin, *The Institutes of the Christian Religion*, Book 4 Chapter 15 section 15, p.
1315.

[10] Lusk, *Do I Believe In Baptismal Regeneration?*

[11] Calvin, *he Institutes of the Christian Religion*, Book 4, Chapter 15, Section 5,
p.1307.

Lusk believes that our union with Christ in its entire salvific sense occurs at our water baptism. Calvin makes this point:

> Paul **proves** that we are children of God from the fact that we put on Christ in baptism (Galatians 3:26-27) ... But we obtain regeneration by Christ's death and resurrection only if we are sanctified by the Spirit and imbued with a new and spiritual nature.[12] (Emphasis mine)

Proving or giving evidence that regeneration is present is not the same thing as regeneration commencing at baptism. The Federal Vision's errors often lie in the difference between evidences and the very nature of things. As noted earlier, the Federal Vision does say good works are the essence of saving faith. Likewise, the Federal Vision wants to make baptism not the evidence that regeneration **already** exists but the **very means** in causing the regeneration.

Lusk demonstrates his inability to understand this truth when he says:

> There is a parallel between the outward washing and the inward blessing, seen in the "just as" language. The objective and subjective are distinguished but not separated ... The Lord gives what he signifies when baptism is received in faith. Baptism is **the means** through which believers receive a new status and begin a new life.[13] (Emphasis mine)

Lusk does not believe that there is anything magical in the water, namely that it cleanses from sin. However, he does tie the inward blessing with the outward washing. He says that they are not separated! Hence, he is not presuming that people could have true faith at the moment of their baptism, he is emphatically declaring that they **do have** that faith at baptism. Lusk does some manipulating of the Westminster Confession to use it to support his view of baptismal regeneration. First, he makes the ridiculous statement – *"The Westminster Standards are compromise documents in the sense that several different parties had to be appeased. Thus, the fruit of the assembly has some internal tensions; nevertheless, the finished product exhibits a remarkable degree of self-consistency and self-harmony, despite harboring a variety of viewpoints within a single text."*[14] Lusk never fully explains all that he means by this statement; it appears that he says this to demonstrate that there were those who really had

---

[12] Calvin, *The Institutes of the Christian Religion,* Book 4, Chapter 15, Section 6, p.1308.

[13] Lusk, *Do I Believe In Baptismal Regeneration?*

[14] Lusk, *Do I Believe In Baptismal Regeneration?*

Lusk's views but who lost out to the majority at the Westminster Assembly. The cleverness of Lusk is seen in his statement about Westminster's statement about the "efficacy of the sacraments." Lusk appeals to Westminster's Shorter Catechism number 91, which says – "*The sacraments become effectual means of salvation, not from any virtue in them, or in him that doth administer them; but only by the blessing of Christ, and the working of his Spirit in them that by faith receive them.*" Lusk says that the blessings are sealed (WCF 28:1); the blessings are conferred (WCF 28:5); the blessings are exhibited (WCF 28:5); the blessings are applied (WSC 92); and the blessings are communicated (WSC 91). Additionally, Lusk says that these blessings are only intended for "worthy receivers" – those who believe. All of this sounds very Reformed doesn't it? Why, Lusk actually makes accurate statements about the individual blessings that baptism signs and seals. So, what is the problem? The problem is that he believes that these blessings **are tied automatically** to all at their baptism. To the unsuspecting person in the pew, this sounds biblical and even Reformed. But it is not Reformed whatsoever! This is why I reviewed all the other beliefs of Lusk earlier such as his belief that all in the visible church are the elect of God in a saving reality. The historic Reformed Faith does believe in the efficacy of the sacrament of baptism **only** when there is saving faith **already** present, and Westminster made it a special point to state that it is **not** tied to the moment of baptism but only when God decides to regenerate their souls by the power of the Holy Spirit whenever that may occur. It could be in the infant when the child is baptized, or it could be when the person is 100 years old. Let's suppose it was when the person was 100 years old. This simply means that effectual calling came a century later. The infant baptism was very real; the blessings that actually came 100 years later were still signified and sealed at the baptism.

Lusk further "reveals his hand" when he says the following:

> The blessings belong to the one baptized, regarded as a member of the visible church, not as someone who is "secretly elect" or "genuinely regenerate." (This just reiterates the earlier views of Calvin and Bucer, both of whom insisted that the promise of baptism has reference to the covenant as such, not to the secret decree. It's also just another way of "viewing election through the lens of the covenant," as Norm Shepherd was apt to put it.)[15]

---

[15] Lusk, *Do I Believe In Baptismal Regeneration?*

Several things need to be noted about this quote. First, this is not what Calvin taught! Calvin saw regeneration as a distinctively internal reality. He did not tie the internal reality with the external rite at the **moment** of baptism. Second, Lusk says that the saving blessings mistakenly (his opinion) associated with the "secret elect" or "genuinely regenerate" apply to **all** who are in the **visible** church. Westminster specifically says that these graces apply **only** to those who are in the **invisible** church (WCF 25:1; WLC 64 –68). This is where Lusk's commitment to this new paradigm of viewing election through the lens of the covenant that Norman Shepherd proposes, where there is no distinction between visible and invisible church, leads him inevitably to the error of baptismal regeneration.

Lusk wants to argue that the external rite of baptism adopts people into the family of God, the household of God in a **saving** way at the administration of the sacrament of baptism. Again, Lusk tries to manipulate the Westminster Standards to say what they do not teach. He appeals to the Westminster Confession 25:2 where it speaks about those who are in the visible church who are in the house and family of God. Lusk states:

> According to the Confession, God "lives" in the visible church, meaning he lives within its members. A baptized person is a mini-tabernacle; he may defile his house, such that God has to move out, as he did with the old covenant tabernacle (cf. Ezek. 8:1 Cor. 6), but baptism's objective meaning remains unstained by our pollution. **Even some kind of baptismal regeneration doctrine can be derived from this view of the visible church, since only those born again enter into the kingdom. Baptism marks the transition into a new life in the kingdom.** All the baptized are enrolled and sworn into Christ's army; we are obligated to fight manfully under the banner of our baptism into union with him as our Lord and King.[16] (Emphasis mine).

Lusk is forced into this position by virtue of his faulty view of the covenant. The fact that the Confession refers to the visible church as the family of God does not mean that each individual is adopted into God's family in a saving sense. There is a type of corporate election, and there is a soteric (saving) election. This is not an arbitrary designation. As noted in another chapter, Romans 9:4-6 is but one passage that clearly delineates between an adoption that corresponds with a corporate election that does not save from sins. Not all of Israel

---

[16] Lusk, *Do I Believe In Baptismal Regeneration?*

is Israel. John Murray recognizes this when he discusses Romans 9:4 where it says that physical Israel is adopted as a son to Jehovah. To physical Israel (the visible covenant community, the visible church) belong the covenants of God. To the nation as a whole was given the Mosaic Law. In Ephesians 2: 11-12, the Jews in contrast to the Gentiles are referred to as the "commonwealth of Israel" who have the covenants of promise. Not all who are physical descendants of Abraham are spiritual descendants as borne out in Jacob and Esau. Murray states:

> "Adoption" is the filial relation to God constituted by God's grace (cf. Exod. 4:22, 23; Deut. 14:1, 2; Isa. 63:16; 64:8; Hos. 11:1; Mal. 1:6; 2:10). This adoption of Israel is to be distinguished from that spoken of as the apex of New Testament privilege (8:15; Gal. 4:5; Eph. 1: 5; cf, John 1:12; I John 3:1). This is apparent from Galatians 4:5, for here the adoption is contrasted with the tutelary discipline of the Mosaic economy. Israel under the Old Testament were indeed children of God but they were as children under age (cf. Gal. 3:23; 4:1-3). The adoption secured by Christ in the fullness of time (Gal. 4:4) is the mature, full-fledged sonship in contrast with the pupilage of Israel under the ceremonial institution.[17]

Throughout the Old Testament Israel was known as "the children of God." Israel was called "Israel is My son, My first born" (Exodus 4:22-23). Speaking about the entire nation, Israel was referred to as "You are the sons of the Lord your God" (Deuteronomy 14:1). Israel would speak figuratively and say, "Thou art our Father" (Isaiah 64:8). Affectionate terms were used to refer to the entire nation such as "When Israel was a youth I loved him, And out of Egypt I called My son" (Hosea 11:1). Because God created the nation, Israel refers to God as its Father – "Do we not all have one father? Has not one God created us?"(Malachi 2:10)

In the New Testament, the term election predominately refers to God's soteric election. Hebrews 3 refers to Moses being faithful over his house and now in the new covenant Christ is faithful over His house of whom we are if we persevere in faith (verse 6). There were many Israelites who were forbidden to enter Canaan because of their unbelief. Hebrews 4:2 says – *"For indeed we have had good news preached to us, just as they also; but the word they heard*

---

[17] Murray, *The New International Commentary on the New Testament*, The Epistle To The Romans, pp. 4- 5.

did not profit them, because it was not united by faith in those who heard." Canaan was seen as a type of spiritual rest for Israel. In Hebrews 4, Jesus is seen as the new Israel's rest. Just because one was born a Jew and was circumcised bringing that person into the visible covenant community, did not make that person a spiritual recipient of God's covenant blessings. As John the Baptist and the Lord Jesus specifically said, there were many physical descendants of Abraham who were spiritually lost. In John 1:12-13, we see the term "adoption" take on a specific saving connotation – *"But as many as received Him, to them He gave the right to become children of God, even to those who believe in His name, who were born not of blood, nor of the will of the flesh, nor of the will of man, but of God."* It is clear from this text that the faith mentioned here is the result of a spiritual birth that is "born not of blood." In I John 3:1, the "love of God" is very specific, for it says – *"See how great a love the Father has bestowed upon us, that we should be called children of God; and such we are. For this reason the world does not know us, because it did not know Him."*

Lusk uses Galatians 3:27 as a proof text for his view of the objective covenant which pictures those baptized into Christ as being clothed with Christ. In doing this, Lusk commits a major theological error because he totally destroys the whole meaning of Galatians 3. Paul is writing some tough things to the Galatians because they have been bewitched by the Judaizers into thinking that they must keep the Mosaic Law, namely circumcision, in addition to believing Jesus in order to be saved. Paul makes a huge point that Abraham believed God apart from righteous law keeping, and it was this faith that was reckoned to him as righteousness (v. 6). In fact, the gospel was preached beforehand to Abraham so that he would be the father of all who would believe (v. 8). Paul goes into a long dissertation on how the Mosaic Law was given as a tutor to convict men of sin and lead them to Christ by faith. We are justified by faith and have become sons of God through faith in Christ Jesus (v. 26). This is the context of verse 27 where those who are baptized are clothed with Christ. As Galatians 3:29 indicates, *"And if you belong to Christ, then you are Abraham's offspring, heirs according to promise."* Rich Lusk's use of this passage to justify his objective covenant is a gross mishandling of Scripture.

Lusk continues to mislead people by advocating that baptism is a **co-instrument** in receiving God's covenantal blessings. He states:

> Baptism has reference to justification precisely because God
> has promised to make Christ available in the rite (as well as
> the other means of grace). But to receive forgiveness in bap-
> tism, one must receive Christ in faith. Acts 2:38 is very clear

regarding the instrumental role of baptism. The Greek grammar bears the point out well. Peter announces, "Repent, and let every one of you be baptized in the name of Jesus Christ for the remission of sins; and you shall receive the gift of the Holy Spirit." The preposition "for" in the phrase "for the remission of your sins" indicates instrumentality: baptism has reference to remission. While word order is not determinative in Greek, surely it is significant that baptism is sandwiched between repentance and forgiveness. Peter did not say, "Repent for the forgiveness of sins, and be baptized as a sign that this has happened." Instead he links repentance and baptism as a package deal: by repenting from sin, and submitting to God's act of baptism, they would receive the forgiveness of sins. If they repent, they will receive baptism, and in receiving baptism, they will receive (by faith) full remission. Baptism is instrumental in one way; faith/repentance in another.[18]

Lusk cannot be clearer. He would make a very good minister in the Church of Christ denomination, which insists that one must be water baptized in order to be saved. Actually, the Church of Christ would not want him because he believes in infant baptism, but in terms of believing that water baptism is a necessity for salvation, he would fit in very well. Lusk would fit very well in some kind of hybrid form of Roman Catholicism because Rome believes in baptismal regeneration. Of course, Lusk tries to pass himself off as being Reformed because he wrote an article titled "Rome Won't Have Me."[19] The only significant difference between the Federal Vision's view of baptism and Roman Catholicism's view is that the Federal Vision rejects the notion of "ex opera operatum." Other than that, the Federal Vision endorses baptism as a co-instrument in God's saving graces. Lusk continues in his downward spiral by stating:

> Thus, we have seen that baptism's efficacy is **objective**. Baptism, like the other outward means of grace through which Christ communicates himself and his benefits to us (cf. WSC 85, 88), is a genuine offer of new life and reconciliation. Baptism's efficacy is also instrumental; it has no power in its own right. There is nothing magical about it. God has

---

[18] Lusk, *Do I Believe In Baptismal Regeneration?*

[19] Lusk, Rich, *Rome Won't Have Me,* <www.hornes.org/theolgia/soteriology>

simply promised to work in it and through it. His Word makes it effective. Finally, baptism's efficacy is conditional. While baptism is what it is, even apart from our response, baptism's proffered blessings only come to realization in our lives if we respond in faith.[20] (Emphasis Lusk)

Lusk tries not to come off as being not Roman Catholic by saying that baptism accomplishes nothing apart from faith. However, notice that he calls baptism a condition, and he states that baptism is a genuine offer of new life and reconciliation. Lusk is not in the same camp as the Church of Christ nor is he squarely in the camp of Roman Catholicism. He is somewhere in between; however, he is still heretical. One recalls that Norman Shepherd called the sacraments of the old and new covenants as conditions for salvation in his book *The Call of Grace* (pages 14- 15). Lusk is desperate to try to find some way to bring in the Westminster Standards to buttress his argument. He makes this comment:

> But if baptism cannot give new life, why should we think that preaching can? Preaching is just as external as baptism. Preaching is words, baptism is water: the only reason either means is effectual is because of the Spirit's work (WSC 89, 91).[21]

In the preaching of the Word of God, God irresistibly brings his elect to saving faith. As Westminster Larger Catechism number 154 indicates, this is a means of grace. But saving faith is not always made a reality every time that the Word is preached. Not everyone who hears the preached Word is effectually called. When God saves a person, the Holy Spirit enlightens, convinces, and humbles sinners by driving them out of themselves and drawing them to Christ as Westminster Larger Catechism number 155 states. In the Westminster Confession's chapter on effectual calling Chapter 10, Section 4, the Confession states that there are some (the non-elect) who may have some common operations of the Spirit, yet they "**never truly come unto Christ, and therefore cannot be saved.**" This is the Confession's language.

Lusk has failed to keep everything in perspective. In his advocating of a co-instrumentality of baptism with faith as the means of entrance into God's family, he has failed to take seriously the Westminster Confession's insistence that justification is by faith alone. In Chapter 11, Section 2, of the Confession, emphasis is made that faith "**is the alone instrument of justification.**" The Westminster Confession, in keeping with the Scripture, was very serious about

---

[20] Lusk, *Rome Won't Have Me*

[21] Lusk, *Do I Believe in Baptismal Regeneration?*

this. There is no other instrument! To make anything else the instrument would be to add works into God's saving plan. Besides, I have already demonstrated that Rich Lusk agrees with all the other men of the Federal Vision that faith should be defined as "the obedience of faith." Lusk doesn't appreciate the fact that "baptism" as a condition for salvation is the introduction of a works paradigm. Lusk has indicated that he doesn't see how baptism could be considered a work. Well, the Scripture sees it as a work. This is the whole point of Romans 4 where Paul is refuting the Judaizers who were insisting on circumcision in addition to faith as instruments in salvation. When Lusk argues for a co-instrumentality for salvation, he argues the same way that the Judaizers argued. The major point of Romans 4 is that Abraham was justified by faith **before** he was circumcised, not after. He received the sign and seal of the covenant **after** he believed. The inward work of the Spirit in Abraham's life preceded the sign and seal of the covenant. For the Federal Vision to argue that grace has conditions (e.g. baptism) is to deny grace! Of course, I have noted previously, that the Federal Vision has accepted the New Perspective on Paul theology with its radical reinterpretation of the New Testament, namely that Paul was not dealing with the Judaizers in his epistles, but rather the inclusion of the Gentiles.

Lusk has accepted the views of Klass Schilder who advocates baptismal regeneration. Lusk states:

> Schilder himself emphasized that baptism came with promises, not predictions. The covenant was absolutely gracious, but also conditional. The elect are not mere "stocks and blocks;" they have to willingly and freely fulfill the obligations God has imposed upon them. Schilder is thoroughly pastoral in the way he frames the covenant-election relationship. He points out that we need is not a statement of facts about the elect, but a promise from God addressed to us as elect.[22]

> Schilder insists that the baptismal promise is always kept, though we must remember it is a two-sided promise. If a person fails to respond to baptism with faith, we should not conclude that God did not promise anything to that person; instead we should keep in mind that he promised nothing without the threat.[23]

In adopting the position that baptism is an objective means of entry into a saving relationship with God, Lusk realizes that Romans 2:25-29 presents a prob-

---

[22] Lusk, *Do I Believe In Baptismal Regeneration?*

[23] Lusk, *Do I Believe In Baptismal Regeneration?*

lem with the Federal Vision perspective. The historic Reformed interpretation has been that this is one of the classic passages in the Bible demonstrating a distinction between the visible and invisible church, between the external and the internal. Being in the external or visible covenant has its privileges, but ultimately, it is the internal reality that is preeminent. Paul says that one must be circumcised in the heart despite having received physical circumcision. In fact, even in the old covenant, God had always stressed internal circumcision. Jeremiah, in his prophetic exhortations to rebellious Judah, says – *"Circumcise yourselves to the Lord And remove the foreskins of your heart, Men of Judah and inhabitants of Jerusalem"* (Jer. 4:4). Jeremiah also prophesied – *"Behold, the days are coming", declares the Lord, that I will punish all who are circumcised and yet uncircumcised"* (Jer. 9:25). Centuries earlier Moses said to covenant Israel – *"Yet on your fathers did the Lord set His affection to love them, and He chose their descendants after them, even you above all peoples, as it is this day. Circumcise then your heart, and stiffen your neck no more"* (Deut. 10:15-16). Moses prophesies that God will internally work in the hearts of Israel after they have rebelled and brought a curse upon themselves, *"And the Lord your God will bring you into the land which your fathers possessed, and you shall possess it; and He will prosper you and multiply you more than your fathers. Moreover the Lord your God will circumcise your heart and the heart of your descendants, to love the Lord your God with all your heart and with all your soul, in order that you may live"* (Deut. 30:5-6). An important point for us to always remember is that the changed heart precedes any kind of faithful obedience. The circumcision of the heart enables spiritual Israel to love God! What we see in these passages on the circumcision of the heart is the interplay between effectual calling and sanctification. Notice in some of the passages quoted that God tells Israel to circumcise their hearts and in other instances, as in Deuteronomy 30, the text says that God will circumcise their hearts. Which is it? It is both! This is essentially stating the same truth that Philippians 2:12-13 mentions. In Philippians, we are told to work out our salvation with fear and trembling, for it is God at work in us to work for His good pleasure. Reformed theology maintains that effectual calling (regeneration) precedes sanctification. When God changes our hearts (circumcises our hearts), He then sets our wills free to voluntarily receive Christ as our Lord and Savior. The Westminster Confession of Faith in Chapter 10, Section 1, says:

> All those whom God hath predestinated unto life, and those
> only, He is pleased in His appointed and accepted time effec-
> tually to call, by His Word and Spirit, out of that state of sin
> and death, in which they are by nature, to grace and salvation
> by Jesus Christ; **enlightening their minds spiritually and**

savingly to understand the things of God; taking away
their heart of stone, and giving unto them a heart of flesh;
renewing their wills, and by His almighty power determining
them to that which is good, and effectually drawing them to
Jesus Christ: yet so, **as they come most freely, being made
willing by His grace.** (Emphasis mine)

Now how does Rich Lusk deal with Romans 2:25-29? Lusk states:

The strongest argument for severing water baptism from
Spirit baptism derives from a certain way of reading Rom.
2:25-29. The argument runs thus: Paul says circumcision is
only outward, not a circumcision of the heart; baptism is the
new covenant equivalent of circumcision; therefore baptism
is only outward. But this ignores the redemptive historical
nature of Paul's argument. Circumcision and baptism are not
equivalents. To be sure, baptism has replaced circumcision as
the sign of the covenant, and in that sense fulfills circumcision. But baptism has a much wider meaning; it fulfills several other rites and events of the old era in addition to circumcision. Or, to put it another way, circumcision was still a pre-
Messianic ritual, a sign of the coming Seed; baptism is an
eschatological sign, an indication that the Seed and Spirit
have now entered history. Therefore, baptism includes a
power and efficacy that circumcision could not possess.
Insofar as baptism is a sign and seal of the new and better
covenant (Jer. 31; Ezek. 36), it offers what circumcision
could not (namely the Spirit and full forgiveness). Indeed, if
anything, we might be driven to conclude from Col. 2:11-15
that baptism just is the offer of a circumcised heart (cf. Rom.
2:29), the thing Israel most needed (cf. Dt. 30; the circumcised heart was a promised, post-exilic, eschatological gift).

In Rom. 2, Paul is not drawing an absolute antithesis between
the inward and the outward. That would violate the unity of
body and soul found elsewhere in biblical theology. Rather,
Paul is showing that the Jews, by their stubborn unbelief and
rebellious idolization of Torah and their national privileges,
have pried apart the sign and thing signified. The efficacy of
the sacraments is conditional, after all – the offered blessings
must be received by faith, which then manifests itself in obedience. Paul is condemning Israel precisely for her lack of

faithfulness (cf. Rom. 3:1-4). And yet, Israel's unbelief puts God's own trustworthiness on the line; thus Paul must show throughout the letter that God has acted righteously and kept the promises. God has been true to the covenant; he has fulfilled what circumcision stood for by sending the Christ into the world as the promised Seed of the woman and Son of David.

Rom. 2, then, still stands as a warning to the baptized: be faithful to the covenant or face the wrath of God. But in context, it also provides hope: the old covenant was removed precisely because it could not bring about en masse faithfulness on the part of Israel. The new covenant, in the Spirit, will do what the old could not, in the letter. Thus, baptism should not be plugged into Rom. 2 in the place of circumcision in a simplistic manner; to get Paul's theology of baptism, we should fast forward ahead to Rom. 6. (It becomes obvious in that context that baptism are not absolutely interchangeable since no one would think of inserting circumcision for baptism in that passage.)

To come at this whole issue from another direction, we should not say that baptism joins some to the visible church and others to the invisible church. That might be true in a highly theoretical sense, but, again, our decisions and evaluations must be governed by what we can see, not by things that are known only by God (Dt. 29:29). In terms of the Westminster Confession, there is one church with two aspects: historical and eschatological. The invisible church is not a secret organization within the visible church, but the future church, the church in its final, glorified form, composed of all of the saved over the whole course of history (WCF 25.1; note the language: the catholic, or universal church is invisible because it contains the "whole number of the elect," including those not yet born).[24]

While several things that Lusk says is accurate in these quotes such as Israel's unfaithfulness to the covenant in that Israel had pried apart the sign and the thing signified, Lusk still does not realize that the emphasis of the text is the value of the **internal** work of the Holy Spirit over against trust in the **external**

---

[24] Lusk, *Do I Believe In Baptismal Regeneration?*

rite. The Jews believed that mere possession of the external rite was valuable in itself. The tendency was to neglect the weightier matters of the Law, as Jesus told the self righteous and blind Pharisees. The emphasis is on the internal work. This is why Paul says that the Gentiles who do not have circumcision but who keep the Law are actually circumcised (Rom. 2:26). How could they be circumcised, but not be circumcised? The answer is in verses 27-29. The real Jew is the one who is circumcised in heart! In fact, Paul says that a **real** Jew is not even one who is circumcised in the flesh (v. 28). Paul even says that circumcision is not even that which is outward in the flesh (v. 28). What? Circumcision is **"not even that which is outward in the flesh."** This is a devastating blow to the Federal Vision's objective covenant emphasis! The main thesis of the Federal Vision has been that Christianity, even Reformed believers, have put too much emphasis on individualism. According to the Federal Vision, modern Christianity emphasized this subjective regeneration to the demise of the church. Well, somebody forgot to tell inspired Paul. Paul says in verse 29 that the real Jew is the one who is **circumcised in the heart, which is by the Spirt, not by the letter.** The letter being the circumcision of the flesh or we could say, the objective sign of the covenant. If one will notice, Lusk hesitates to bring baptism into the text. The reason is obvious. It would be a devastating blow to the whole thesis of the Federal Vision's emphasis on the objective covenant, namely baptism. Lusk must sense that if one inserts baptism into the text as the new covenant counterpart to circumcision, then the Federal Vision is in real theological trouble. This would mean that Paul would be saying that the real Christian is one who is inwardly baptized by the Spirit, not by the letter of baptism. Now, this does not disparage the outward rite of baptism at all. It is still necessary. It simply means that the outward rite of baptism is a sign and seal of that which is **internally done by the Spirit of God.** We must remember that the Federal Vision believes that all of God's saving graces are given during the time of water baptism, that faith is not just presumed to be there but that it actually is there at that moment; otherwise, no one could say that at baptism one is passed out of death into life, that one has justification, adoption, sanctification, and glorification.

John Calvin understood Romans 2:25-29 as stressing the internal work of the Spirit, and Calvin did bring baptism into the picture, as he should. Calvin states the following about Romans 2:28, 29:

> The meaning is, that a real Jew is not to be ascertained, either by natural descent, or by profession, or by an external symbol; that the circumcision which constitutes a Jew, does not consist in an outward sign only, but that both are inward. And what he subjoins with regard to true circumcision, is

taken from various passages of Scripture, and even from its general teaching; for the people are everywhere commanded to circumcise their hearts, and it is what the Lord promises to do. The fore-skin was cut off, not indeed as the small corruption of one part, but as that of the whole nature. Circumcision then signified the mortification of the whole flesh.

What he then adds, **in the spirit, not in the letter**, understand thus: He calls the outward rite, without piety, the letter, and the spiritual design of this rite, the spirit; for the whole importance of signs and rites depends on what is designed; when the end in view is not regarded, the letter alone remains, which in itself is useless. And the reason for this mode of speaking is this, — where the voice of God sounds, all that he commands, except it be received by men in sincerity of heart, will remain in the letter, that is, in the dead writing; but when it penetrates into the heart, it is in a manner transformed into spirit. And there is an allusion to the difference between the old and the new covenant, which Jeremiah points out in Jeremiah 31:33; where the Lord declares that his covenant would be firm and permanent when engraven on the inward parts. Paul had also the same thing in view in another place, (2 Corinthians 3:6) where he compares the law with the gospel, and calls the former "the letter," which is not only dead but killeth; and the latter he signalizes with the title of "spirit." But extremely gross has been the folly of those who have deduced a double meaning from the "letter," and allegories from the "spirit."[25] (Emphasis Calvin)

John Murray saw the emphasis in Romans 2:28, 29:

He shows who is **true** Jew and what is **true** circumcision ... The contrast instituted is that between what is outward and what is inward. The outward in the case of the Jew is, ostensibly, natural descent from Abraham and the possession of the privileges which that relation entailed ... the inward as it pertains to the Jew is not explained any further than as that which is "in the secret," that is to say, in that which is hidden from external observation (cf. 2:16; I Cor. 4:5; 14:25; II Cor. 4:2; I Pt.. 3:4), the hidden man of the heart, and is to be

---

[25] John Calvin, Commentary to the Romans, pp. 56-57.

understood of that which a man is in the recesses of the heart in distinction from external profession.[26]

When Rich Lusk says that the invisible church is not some secret organization within the visible church, he is in opposition to the Reformed Standards. Reformed theology has always maintained that within the visible church the elect (the invisible church) are found. Lusk advocates that the elect are synonymous with the visible church. When Lusk uses Doug Wilson's terms as referring to the historical and eschatological church, he is affirming that the elect is that which is in process. We really don't know who the elect will be until the end of their lives. Remember, Lusk believes that men are initially justified or initially elect via their baptism, but these people can apostatize and not reach final justification and salvation. Lusk would say with the rest of those in the Federal Vision camp that God knows ahead of time who these people will be that persevere in faith and make it to final justification. However, I will demonstrate in Chapter 9 on the Federal Vision's denial of the perseverance of the saints, that this doctrine of the Federal Vision is essentially identical with traditional Arminianism. Arminian doctrine says that one can initially be saved but lose it. And, God looks down the corridors of history and knows who of their own free will apostatize from the faith.

Rich Lusk has a section titled in his article – "Church Membership as a Soteriological Fact." He says:

> Some might think: so, baptism joins the one baptized to the church – big deal! After all, church membership is just an outward thing, unrelated to the deepest core of a person's being. It's an external relationship, one more thing to strip away (like layers of onion) in getting at the real core of someone's personality ... Peter Leithart has argued quite effectively against this view, showing that church membership is in fact a soteriological fact. [27]

> I think a key reason high views of baptismal efficacy have proved controversial in American Presbyterianism is that we have drifted into a rather low ecclesiology. We have pried apart the church and salvation. Most of our time spent debating over the "efficacy of the sacraments" should probably be spent exegeting NT texts on the nature of the church. To put it in confessional terms, I do not think we have taken serious-

---

[26] Murray, *Epistle to the Romans,* p. 88.

[27] Lusk, *Do I Believe In Baptismal Regeneration?*

ly enough WCF 25.2. The visible church into which one is admitted in baptism is no mere human organization. Rather, it is, "the kingdom of the Lord Jesus Christ, the house and family of God." These categories are clearly soteriological, even if we must add that bare membership in the church is not enough to save apart from a corresponding life of faithfulness (keep in mind the objective/subjective distinction). Kingdom subjects can rebel, the house can become defiled, and family members can be disinherited. Nevertheless, to be in the church is to be in the place of grace and salvation.[28]

I have noted previously that Lusk and the entire Federal Vision camp does not understand and twists the Westminster Confession in its chapter "Of the Church." When Lusk says that American Presbyterianism hasn't taken seriously WCF 25:2, I respond that he has not taken WCF 25: 2 seriously in light of WCF 25:1. Section 1 of chapter 25 states that the elect are the invisible church. Section 2 deals with the visible church. I have already made comments why WCF 25:2 uses the terms house and family of God. It is the Federal Vision that twists the Westminster Confession.

Lusk wants us to think that the Westminster Confession teaches some kind of baptismal regeneration in WCF 25:2. He states:

> Every person baptized is "automatically" (or "irresistibly") put into the kingdom, house, and family. So viewing baptism as an adoption rite into the Triune family, for example, is entirely confessional, even though the Standard's teaching on baptism does not make that very explicit. I would think some kind of baptismal regeneration is bound up in viewing the church as the "kingdom of Christ." After all, only those born again can enter the kingdom, but everyone baptized is inserted into the kingdom in at least some sense. Some form of the gift of the Spirit must also be conferred in baptism. If the one baptized is made a member of God's house, surely God dwells in that house by his Spirit!
>
> Can we then sum up how all this fits together? In baptism we are brought covenantally and publicly out of union with Adam and into union with Christ. When this occurs, one is "born again," not in the sense we have come to speak of "regeneration" as an irresistible, irreversible change of heart,

---

[28] Lusk, *Do I Believe In Baptismal Regeneration?*

but in the covenantal sense of being brought out of Adam's family into God's family. In baptism, we are united to Christ by faith, and therefore to the Triune God. Having been admitted to the fellowship of Father, Son, and Spirit, this new relationship, like any other relationship, requires fidelity and love. This doesn't mean we maintain our end of the covenant in our own strength; God provides that as well. But it does mean that there is such a thing as covenant keeping and covenant breaking. All covenant members are encouraged to rely on God's promises and trust him for the gift of perseverance.

In this relationship, one has, in principle, all the blessings and benefits in the heavenly places delivered over to him as he is "in Christ." We've already noted that baptism is like an adoption ceremony. The adopted child is brought into a new relationship, given a new name, new blessings, a new future, new opportunities, a new inheritance – in short, a new life. And yet these blessings, considered from the standpoint of the covenant rather than the eternal decree, are mutable. The child is a full member of the family and has everything that comes with sonship. But, if he grows up and rejects his Father and Mother (God and the church), if refuses to repent and return home when warned and threatened, then he loses all the blessings that were his. It would not be accurate to say that he never had these things; he did possess them, even though he never experienced or enjoyed some of them. By refusing to abide in covenant, he faces a more severe judgment than others who were never admitted to the family, or given such rich and gracious promises.[29]

Lusk admits to holding to a form of baptismal regeneration. At least he admits it. He must sincerely think that baptismal regeneration is an acceptable doctrine of the Reformed Faith. He desperately tries to get the Westminster Confession to teach his view of baptismal regeneration. He has miserably failed of course because that is not what is taught, as I have demonstrated. The Federal Vision has adopted a form of baptismal regeneration that is not identical to Roman Catholicism but is closely akin to it. The theological damage done by this view is tremendous! It robs Jesus and the Holy Spirit of their due glory. It focuses attention on an external rite. It encourages people to look to their baptism in the wrong way. Yes, we are to look to our baptism and remember God's promises,

---

[29] Lusk, *Do I Believe In Baptismal Regeneration?*

but we are not to look to our baptism as the defining moment of our transition from death unto life, that in the outward rite we have all of God's saving graces at that moment. Steve Schlissel says that we must divest ourselves of this morbid introspection of asking ourselves if we are really in the faith. He and the rest of his cohorts say, "Look to your objective proof – you were baptized!" On the other hand, II Corinthians 13: 5 states – "Test yourselves to see if you are in the faith; examine yourselves! Or do you not recognize this about yourselves that Jesus Christ is in you – unless indeed you fail the test?" No thank you Federal Vision, I will take the Word of God over your heresies any day.

Chapter 9

A Denial of the Perseverance of the Saints

I indicated in another chapter that the Federal Vision has virtually denied all of the five points of Calvinism, and the last point of the popular Reformed acronym TULIP, is the perseverance of the saints. The Federal Vision's denial of this precious doctrine of the Christian Faith is rooted in its doctrine of the objectivity of the covenant. As previously mentioned, this innovative concept of the nature of the church is the fulcrum upon which the whole Federal Vision understands the Christian life. Since the Federal Vision denies the Reformed distinction of the visible and invisible church, seeing them as identical, then it is forced to a position of denying the perseverance of the saints. The reason being is that this theology must account for the reality of apostates. The Federal Vision's attempt to be consistent has forced them into this position. The historic Reformed Faith has understood apostates as those who were obviously professing Christians, who were members of the visible church, but who were never genuine Christians, that is, members of the invisible church, the elect of God who will persevere to the end. I John 2:19 indicates that those who do apostatize went out because they never were really part of them – "*They went out from us, but they were not really of us; for if they had been of us, they would have remained with us; but they went out, in order that it might be shown that they all are not of us.*" Moreover, there will be those who professed Jesus and who cast out demons, prophesied in Jesus' name, and performed many miracles in His name but who will hear Jesus say to them, "I never knew you" (Matthew 7:21-23).

The Federal Vision's obsession with their objective covenant has blinded their minds from understanding the Word of God. Believing that all of God's saving graces are really and truly present in one's water baptism necessitates an unbiblical view of apostasy. The Federal Vision does not like to use the phrase, "lose your salvation;" however, it does insist that one must lose something. This is just another example of how the Federal Vision distorts words in order to sound acceptable. It is ridiculous to say that baptism marks the point of conversion, the transition from death to life, being a new creation in Christ, having forgiveness of sins, being reconciled, and justified without saying that this constitutes salvation. If someone has all of these things, then he is saved! This is the insidiousness of this theology. It uses common words that evangelicals use but then reinterprets them. To lose this, is to lose salvation! To say that their view is not a "losing of salvation but a loss of initial justification" is an inherent contradiction. Again, the Federal Vision wants to operate within the parameters of the Reformed community; therefore, it must come across sounding Reformed. Rich Lusk stated, "*This, then is the biblical picture. The TULIP is still in place, but has been enriched by a nuanced covenant theology*" (See second paragraph on page 258). I don't think so; it has been supplanted by a new paradigm.

What is the historic Reformed position on the perseverance of the saints? The Westminster Confession states in Chapter 17 "Of the Perseverance of the Saints," Section 1-3:

> They, whom God hath accepted in His Beloved, effectually called, and sanctified by His Spirit, can neither totally, nor finally, fall away from the state of grace: but shall certainly persevere therein to the end, and be eternally saved.

> This perseverance of the saints depends not upon their own free will, but upon the immutability of the decree of election, flowing from the free and unchangeable love of God the Father; upon the efficacy of the merit and intercession of Jesus Christ; the abiding of the Spirit, and of the seed of God within them; and the nature of the covenant of grace: from all which ariseth also the certainty and infallibility thereof.

> Nevertheless, they may, through the temptations of Satan and of the world, the prevalency of corruption remaining in them, and the neglect of the means of their preservation, fall into grievous sins; and, for a time, continue therein: whereby they incur God's displeasure, and grieve His Holy Spirit, come to be deprived of some measure of their graces and comforts, have their hearts hardened, and their consciences wounded, hurt and scandalize others, and bring temporal judgments upon themselves.

The Westminster Larger Catechism states in Question number 79:

> May not true believers, by reason of their imperfections, and
> the many temptations and sins they are overtaken with, fall
> away from the state of grace?
> **Answer:** True believers, by reason of the unchangeable love
> of God, and his decree and covenant to give them persever-
> ance, their inseparable union with Christ, his continual inter-
> cession for them, and the Spirit and seed of God abiding in
> them, can neither totally nor finally fall away from the state
> of grace, but are kept by the power of God through faith unto
> salvation.

The Synod of Dordt (1618-1619) dealt in detail with the errors of the
Arminians (also known as the Remonstrants). The Arminians submitted to the
Synod their positions on various doctrinal points. Regarding its fifth article
concerning perseverance, the Arminians said:

> True believers can fall from true faith and fall into such sins
> as cannot be consistent with true and justifying faith; and not
> only can this happen, but it also not infrequently occurs. True
> believers can through their own fault fall into sins and blas-
> phemies, persevere and die in the same; and accordingly they
> can finally fall away and go lost.[1]

Whereas the Belgic Confession and Heidelberg Catechism do not deal much
at all with this subject, the Westminster Standards and the Canons of Dordt
have significant statements on the subject. I have already quoted from the
Westminster Standards. The Canons of Dordt had 15 articles regarding what it
called the Fifth Head of Doctrine: The Perseverance of the Saints. I will not
quote all 15 articles but only a select number that would be pertinent to show
the errors of the Federal Vision.

Various Articles of the Canons of Dordt [2]

> **Article 1:** Whom God calls, according to his purpose, to the
> communion of his Son, our Lord Jesus Christ, and regener-
> ates by the Holy Spirit, he delivers also from the dominion
> and slavery of sin in this life; though not altogether from the

---

[1] Hoeksema, *The Voice of Our Fathers,* p. 108.
[2] Hoeksema, *Voice of our Fathers*, p. 633.

body of sin, and from the infirmities of the flesh, so long as they continue in this world.

Article 3: By reason of these remains of indwelling sin, and the temptations of sin and of the world, those who are converted could not persevere in a state of grace, if left to their own strength. But God is faithful, who having conferred grace, mercifully confirms, and powerfully preserves them herein, even to the end.

Article 4: Although the weakness of the flesh cannot prevail against the power of God, who confirms and preserves true believers in a state of grace, yet converts are not always so influenced and actuated by the Spirit of God, as not in some particular instances sinfully to deviate from the guidance of divine grace, so as to be seduced by, and to comply with the lusts of the flesh; they must, therefore, be constant in watching and in prayer, that they be not led into temptation. When these are neglected, they are not only liable to be drawn into great and heinous sins, by Satan, the world and the flesh, but sometimes by the righteous permission of God actually fall into these evils. This, the lamentable fall of David, Peter, and other saints described in Holy Scripture, demonstrates.

Article 5: By such enormous sins, however, they very highly offend God, incur a deadly guilt, grieve the Holy Spirit, interrupt the exercise of faith, very grievously wound their consciences, and sometimes lose the sense of God's favor, for a time, until on their returning into the right way of serious repentance, the light of God's fatherly countenance again shines upon them.

Article 6: But God, who is rich in mercy, according to his unchangeable purpose of election, does not wholly withdraw the Holy Spirit from his own people, even in their melancholy falls; nor suffers them to proceed so far as to lose the grace of adoption, and forfeit the state of justification, or to commit sins unto death; nor does he permit them to be totally deserted, and to plunge themselves into everlasting destruction.

Article 8: Thus, it is not in consequence of their own merits, or strength, but of God's free mercy, that they do not totally fall from faith and grace, nor continue and perish finally in their backslidings; which, with respect to themselves, is not only possible, but would undoubtedly happen; but with respect to God, it is utterly impossible, since his counsel cannot be changed, nor his promise fail, neither can the call according to his purpose be revoked, nor the merit, intercession and preservation of Christ be rendered ineffectual, nor the sealing of the Holy Spirit be frustrated or obliterated.

Article 9: Of this preservation of the elect to salvation, and of their perseverance in the faith, true believers for themselves may and ought to obtain assurance according to the measure of their faith, whereby they arrive at the certain persuasion, that they ever will continue true and living members of the church; and that they experience forgiveness of sins, and will at last inherit eternal life.

Article 15: The carnal mind is unable to comprehend this doctrine of the perseverance of the saints, and the certainty thereof; which God hath most abundantly revealed in his Word, for the glory of his name, and the consolation of pious souls, and which he impresses upon the hearts of the faithful. Satan abhors it; the world ridicules it; the ignorant and hypocrite abuse, and heretics oppose it; but the spouse of Christ hath always most tenderly loved and constantly defended it, as an inestimable treasure; and God, against whom neither counsel nor strength can prevail, will dispose her to continue this conduct to the end. Now, to this one God, Father, Son, and Holy Spirit, be honor and glory, forever. AMEN. (Emphasis mine)

As if there was any doubt as to what the Canons of Dordt were affirming, the Synod stated exactly the errors that the Arminians were committing when the Synod wrote their "Rejection of Errors" into various paragraphs.

Rejection of Errors, Paragraph 3 states:

Who teach: That the true believers and regenerate not only can fall from justifying faith and likewise from grace and salvation wholly and to the end, but indeed often do fall from this and are lost forever. For this conception makes powerless the grace, justification, regeneration, and continued keeping by Christ, contrary to the expressed words of the Apostle

Paul: "That while we were yet sinners Christ died for us. Much more then, being justified by his blood, shall we be saved from the wrath of God through him," Romans 5:8, 9. And contrary to the Apostle John: "Whosoever is begotten of God doeth no sin, because his seed abideth in him; and he cannot sin, because he is begotten of God," I John 3:9. And also contrary to the words of Jesus Christ: "I give unto them eternal life; and they shall never perish, and no one shall snatch them out of my hand. My Father who hath given them to me, is greater than all; and no one is able to snatch them out of the Father's hand," John 10:28,29.[3]

Rejection of Errors, Paragraph 7 states:

Who teach: That the faith of those, who believe for a time, does not differ from justifying and saving faith except only in duration. For Christ himself, in Matthew 13:20, Luke 8:13, and in other places, evidently notes, besides this duration, a threefold difference between those who believe only for a time and true believers, when he declares that the former receive the seed in stony ground, but the latter in the good ground or heart; that the former are without root, but that the latter have a firm root; that the former are without fruit, but that the latter bring forth their fruit in various measure, with constancy and steadfastness.[4]

The Reformed Standards on the Perseverance of the Saints

For the Christian, the doctrine of the perseverance of the saints is one of the most precious, comforting, and inspiring doctrines of the Faith. Arminianism and its doctrinal cohort, the Federal Vision, robs God of His glorious majesty and drags God's glorious majesty down through the dregs of human effort. The spiritual bankruptcy of the Federal Vision is unmasked revealing the ugliness of this man-centered theology when it comes to an understanding of the perseverance of the saints. The Federal Vision insults the Triune God. It despises the efficacy of the redemptive work of the Savior. It exalts man's imperfect, puny efforts above the power of God.

---

[3] Hoeksema, *Voice of our Fathers.*

[4] Hoeksema, *Voice of our Fathers.*

The heresy of the Federal Vision reaches its zenith in its denial of the persever-ance of the saints. What many do not realize is that the doctrine of the perse-verance of the saints brings the nature of God, His sovereign, eternal decrees, and His eternal redemptive plan all together. In the doctrine of the perseverance of the saints, God's glory and His unmatchless love is seen in all of its pristine beauty. All of this, the Federal Vision denies. Of course, proponents of this the-ology will flatly deny this characterization. Again, I will let the reader decide if the Federal Vision stands guilty as charged.

Regarding the Westminster Standards, we must remember that the Confession in its earlier chapters has explicitly limited "effectual calling" to only the elect, to only those in the invisible church (See WCF chapter 10; WLC # 64-66, 68). The Westminster Confession emphatically states that those whom God has accepted in his Beloved, effectually called and sanctified by the Holy Spirit **cannot totally fall away from the state of grace, but that they will perse-vere to the end and be eternally saved.** The elect will be saved eternally because their perseverance depends not upon man's will but upon the unchangeability of God's decree of election. The Federal Vision has corrupted the doctrine of "effectual calling" because it believes that **all** who are in the vis-ible church (that is all baptized, professing Christians) are effectually called, meaning that all of God's saving graces are given at baptism. The Federal Vision does not believe in the unchangeability of God's decree of election because it affirms that a person can forfeit (implies a change) his salvation given him at his baptism. This clearly means that God's decree to save initial-ly has been overruled by man's rule. The moment that the Federal Vision speaks of an initial justification and election in contrast to a final justification and election it has just espoused a dependency upon man's will as the decid-ing factor as to who obtains final justification and salvation. Rich Lusk and oth-ers explicitly state that man's covenant obedience determines his final justifi-cation (See Lusk's comments on pages 290 and 291). If man can lose what he once possessed, this implies change, and it implies that man's will is the basis for bringing about this change. This is just one of many reasons that I refer to the Federal Vision as a man-made religion. The denial of the perseverance of the saints is a direct attack upon the nature of God's perfections. If man can lose the saving graces that he initially possessed because of his own unfaithful-ness, then God's decree to save is not immutable but mutable. It means that God's election is not unchangeable and unconditional but changeable and con-ditional. After all, the Federal Vision believes that all are elect at their entrance into the objective covenant by water baptism.

The Federal Vision gets very upset once somebody starts using terms like "genuine Christian," and "true believer." It considers this symptomatic of the problem with the present status of the Reformed community, especially Southern Presbyterians. Well, I suppose they need to consider the Westminster Assembly and the Synod of Dordt theologically deficient, since both Reformed documents use the phrase, "true believers."

The Westminster Confession stresses the point that the doctrine of the perseverance of the saints depends upon the efficacy and merit and intercession of Jesus Christ. Here is another word that is forbidden in Federal Vision vocabulary - the word "merit." Both Shepherd and Lusk do not believe that is a proper word applied to Christ. They think that it smacks of Roman Catholicism, which is really ironic because it is the Federal Vision that advocates an hybrid form of Catholicism. Since the Westminster Confession links the perseverance of the saints to Christ's atoning work, we have a very serious theological problem with the Federal Vision. If Christ's redemptive work is really and truly applied at water baptism and marks the person's entrance into the objective covenant, the church, then when a person apostatizes from the Faith, this means that the death of Christ becomes ineffective for that person. Like Arminianism, the Federal Vision must believe that there are some people in Hell for whom Christ really died. This is an insult to the Savior as we noted previously. In another chapter, I stated that the Federal Vision must likewise deny the Reformed doctrine of limited or particular atonement. The renowned John Owen in his masterpiece work, *The Death of Death In The Death of Christ* forever dispelled the absurdity of the belief that a person could be in Hell for whom Christ's atoning work was applied. The Federal Vision has fallen into a quicksand pit from which there is no escape.

The Westminster Confession stresses another reason that all elect will be eternally saved; it is because of the presence of the Holy Spirit in their lives. The proof texts that provide the biblical justification for such a statement are: John 14:16,-17; I John 2:27; and I John 3:9 all of which refer to the fact that Christians have the Holy Spirit abiding in them. Of course, the proof texts mean nothing to the Federal Vision because as Doug Wilson has stated, his church says that it subscribes to the Westminster Standards **without** the proof texts. As noted earlier, this makes it very convenient to say at any time that their views are within the parameters of the Reformed Standards because there is no basis to refute it. The Reformed Faith has always understood that the application of Christ's redemptive work is performed by the third person of the Trinity – the Holy Spirit. So, in apostasy, the Federal Vision is advocating that the decretive plan of the Father can be set aside by man; that the redemptive work of Christ Himself can be made ineffectual to save to the uttermost those for whom He died, and that the Spirit can be resisted to the point that the Spirit must depart, leaving the wretched man to go to Hell.

The reason that Westminster Confession 17:2 states that the covenant of grace provides the **certainty and infallibility** of the perseverance of the saints is because the covenant, in its ultimate spiritual reality, is made only with the elect of God, the invisible church. Since the Federal Vision rejects the covenant of grace being made with the invisible church only, then it rejects any certainty of one's perseverance to the end. The real tragedy is that the Federal Vision wants to play trickery with words on this doctrine too. Rich Lusk speaks about God withholding the gift of perseverance to those who apostatize; hence, Lusk will talk about a perseverance of saints, and he will seek to quote the Westminster Standards. Lusk states that all who persevere by being loyal to the covenant and obeying the Law will achieve final election, final justification. This is not the assurance of the saints taught in the Westminster Confession.

The Canons of Dordt, which is part of the Three Forms of Unity of which several of the men in the Federal Vision camp pledged to support, strongly favors the perseverance of the saints. Therefore, these men who say that they support these Reformed statements are betraying their oaths when they deny the perseverance of the saints.

In The Fifth Head Article 1 of the Canons of Dordt, the Synod made it very clear that God's calling, the communion of the Son, being in union with Christ, and the regenerating work of the Holy Spirit do indeed deliver a person from the dominion of sin **in this life.** Article 4 stresses the fact that the flesh's weakness cannot override the power of God to preserve "true believers," as it calls them. In the rest of Article 4 and in Article 5, the Synod states that Christians can commit some very grievous sins; however, the loss of God's favor is only for a time at which point God will grant repentance to His elect. Article 6 emphatically states that God in His rich mercy never **wholly withdraws the Holy Spirit from His people.** But the Federal Vision believes in an apostasy whereby the Spirit that really saved a man can be withdrawn. Article 6 goes on to state that His people, referred to as His elect, can never lose the grace of adoption nor forfeit the state of justification, which would plunge them into everlasting destruction. But, the Federal Vision believes that men who are genuinely adopted into the family of God and who receive initial justification can be lost forever. The word "initial" is the Federal Vision's innovative word in the realm of Reformed theology. In a vain attempt to try to circumvent the obvious problem, the Federal Vision says, "Oh, the apostate only loses initial justification, initial adoption. Those who are faithful all their lives to keep the Law the best they can in the name of Jesus, of course, can achieve final justification.

Article 8 clearly states that it is the **mercy** of God that keeps any of us from totally falling away from the Faith. It is not contingent upon my faithfulness as the Federal Vision contends; it is all, from start to last, the mercy of God. The intercession of Christ cannot be made ineffectual, nor is the Spirit sealing frustrated or obliterated. Yet, the Federal Vision in its view of apostasy maintains that the adopted in Christ, the justified, and sealed in Him can lose it all! This is why the Federal Vision's theology exalts man and makes him the superior to Almighty God. This is one of the reasons why the Federal Vision is a heresy, for it strips God of all His glory.

Notice in Article 15, the Synod states that the **carnal mind** cannot comprehend the perseverance of the saints, nor can this carnal mind comprehend the **certainty** of it. Rightly, the Synod noted that Satan abhors the doctrine of the perseverance of the saints. Why does Satan relish in theologies that deny the perseverance of the saints? It is because true assurance of salvation cannot be maintained. Of course, I have debated with Arminians on this point, and they say, "Well, one can have assurance as long as one is sure to be faithful." Is that exhortation really comforting, knowing that it is possible in this system of thought to be fully accepted and then feasibly to lose it all? I think not! Those of us that understand our sinfulness and propensity towards sin can at times struggle with doubts about our salvation. If one's theology holds that you can lose your salvation, then Satan can and does come in and wreck havoc with one's emotions. Moreover, any time that Satan can shift our trust in God alone to our own efforts, then he rejoices in that. I don't know if Rich Lusk ever stopped to think about the implications of his horrendous belief that God doesn't require perfect obedience to His holy Law. If God accepts imperfect obedience, then just how much is that? According to Lusk, God really does not even require a 51% grade on an ethics test (See bottom paragraph on page 288). Now, Satan enjoys that concept as well because he can then delude men into a sense of false security. After all, Lusk did say that God judges according to "soft justice" on the final Day of Judgment (See quote on page 294). Satan would love to have men think that their salvation is contingent upon their works for final salvation and a standard that really is not all that hard to keep. This is the ultimate deception! I said it before, and I will restate it. I would not want to be in Lusk's and his sheep's position that listen to and trust in his preaching. They both will get the shock of their lives on Judgment Day.

Notice in Article 15 that the Synod also states that with the ignorant and the hypocrites, **heretics oppose the doctrine of the perseverance of the saints.** The contrast is made between the heretics that oppose the doctrine and the spouse of Christ (the church) that Christ has always tenderly loved and defended as a precious gem.

As I noted in another chapter, John Barach summarized the view of the Federal Vision on baptismal regeneration when he said that a pastor can assure all those who are baptized in his church – "*In him you have redemption, righteousness, justification, sanctification, the Holy Spirit, glorification and election. The whole package of salvation you could say from eternity past to eternity future is all found in Christ*" (See last paragraph on page 228). All of this is at water baptism; all of which can be lost in apostasy.

Having set forth what the Reformed Standards actually teach on the doctrine of the perseverance of the saints, let's now take a look at the exact quotes by proponents of the Federal Vision that demonstrate just how far they have fallen themselves. I will not necessarily repeat the lengthy quotes from chapter 6, but I will simply refer the reader to the appropriate footnotes in that chapter that demonstrates their denial of the perseverance of the saints.

Wilkins and His Session Deny the Perseverance of the Saints

Wilkins makes an incredible statement about who constitutes the elect of God. He states:

> The elect are those who are faithful in Christ Jesus. If they later reject the Savior, they are no longer elect–they are cut off from the Elect One and thus, lose their elect standing. But their falling away doesn't negate the reality of their standing prior to their apostasy. They were really and truly the elect of God because of their relationship with Christ.[5]

This statement is totally out of accord with the Reformed Standards. There is no unconditional election in this statement. It openly states that man can undo what God had previously done. Wilkins says that one can be cut off from election. I don't understand the value of the statement that apostasy doesn't change prior election. What good was a prior election, if it doesn't guarantee us anything? The concept of "election" is rendered meaningless. Election means that God sets His love upon a people that guarantees their salvation from start to finish. Romans 9 is the classic passage that demonstrates the unconditional nature of God's election.

In commenting on the spiritual status of the Corinthian church in I Corinthians 10, Wilkins states that the entire church, all individual members by their baptism, have been joined to Christ in a saving way. Wilkins states that Paul says to them that Christ died for their sins. Wilkins indicates that Paul knew this,

---

[5] Colloquium on the Federal Vision, p. 261.

not because he was privy to God's secret decrees, but because of their objective union with Christ in the covenant. However, each must be faithful to persevere in faith; otherwise, the blessings could sink into everlasting fire (See second paragraph on page 211). The Reformed Faith demands that men must persevere in faith, and there is no question that those "elect" and those for whom Christ died will unquestionably persevere. Wilkins clearly denies this. He continues to state that if church members fail to persevere they lose all the blessings they once were given. Supposedly all this is according to God's decree ordained from the foundation of the world (See bottom paragraph on page 211 and top of 212). What does Wilkins mean here about God's decree? He has just denied the Reformed understanding of God's decrees. The Westminster Confession Chapter 3, Section 1 affirms the unconditionality of God's decrees. It states that God's decree is unchangeable! Chapter 3, Section 2 also affirms that God foreordains whatsoever comes to pass neither on the basis of any supposed conditions, nor because of what He foresaw as future that could come to pass upon such conditions. Wilkins argues for the condition of human faithfulness as the basis of continuing in the initial state of blessing. When Wilkins states that this condition is what God has foreordained from all eternity, he refutes the Confession of Faith. He has adopted a classic Arminian interpretation, which states that God plans according to what He knows men will do in space and time. What has the apostate given up according to Wilkins? He has *"forfeited life, forgiveness, and salvation ... had real communion with Christ, had the Spirit's work within them ... had been sanctified by the blood of Christ, had been made members of the heavenly city, had been sprinkled by the blood of Jesus, had been cleansed from former sins, were bought by the Lord, escaped the pollutions of the world ..., and had the adoption."* (See quote on page 212). Wilkins says that the apostate fails to persevere in all of these blessings and has his name removed from the book of life (See quote on page 212-213). This is pure, unadulterated Arminianism. Wilkins stresses that this falling away is not a hypothetical impossibility but a very real possibility for those in covenant with God and members of His Church. He says that the apostates enjoy for a season all of these blessings but eventually fall short of the grace of God (See quotes on page 213). He wants us to be sure that we understand what he is affirming. Wilkins states:

> The apostate, thus, forsakes the grace of God that was given to him by virtue of his union with Christ. It is not accurate to say that they only "appeared" to have these things but did not actually have them–if that were so, there would be nothing to "forsake" and apostasy is bled of its horror and severity. That which makes apostasy so horrendous is that these blessings

actually belonged to the apostates–though they only had them temporarily they had them no less truly. The apostate doesn't forfeit "apparent blessings" that were never his in reality, but real blessings that were his in covenant with God.[6]

Wilkins quotes John 15:1-8 as support for his Arminian view of apostasy. He says that that the branches are in true saving union with Christ and that when they are cut off and burned for being fruitless; they are eternally lost. Wilkins wants us to realize that there is genuine loss of salvation. He states:

> Often this passage is interpreted along these lines: There are two kinds of branches. Some branches are not really in Christ "in a saving way," but only in an external sense–whatever fruit they bear is not genuine and they will eventually be destroyed. Other branches are truly joined to Christ inwardly and savingly, and they bear more and more fruit as they are pruned and cultivated by the Father." As Norman Shepherd has noted, "If this distinction is in the text, it is difficult to see what the point of the warning is. The outward ("external") branches cannot profit from it, because they cannot in any case bear genuine fruit. They are not related to Christ inwardly and draw no life from him. The inward branches do not need the warning, because they are vitalized by Christ and therefore cannot help but bear good fruit. Cultivation by the Father, with its attendant blessing, is guaranteed."[7]

Wilkins' denial of the unconditional nature of God's decree is explicit, when he says:

> Covenant, therefore, is a gracious relationship, not a potentially gracious relationship. To be in covenant is to have the treasures of God's mercy and grace and the love which He has for His own Son given to you. But the covenant is not unconditional. It requires persevering faithfulness.[8]

Here it is in glaring clarity. Wilkins denies the unconditional nature of God's decrees, making God's decree contingent upon man's faithfulness, and then he clearly states that God's mercy and grace can be nullified if the person is

---

[6] *Colloquium on the Federal Vision*, p. 264.

[7] *Colloquium on the Federal Vision*, pp. 264- 265.

[8] *Colloquium on the Federal Vision*, pp. 265-266.

unfaithful. So much for the faithfulness of God that preserves us to the end. It is all gone in Federal Vision theology.

The position statement by the session of Auburn Avenue Presbyterian Church is one of the most convoluted statements that one can ever read (See quote at the bottom of page 220 and top of 221). If someone did not study thoroughly all that the Federal Vision teaches, then one may have a tendency to think that Auburn Avenue has not denied the Reformed doctrine of the perseverance of the saints. After all, the statement says that it would be improper to speak of anyone "losing their salvation." But if one reads the statement carefully, one will notice that the statement says, "none of the elect unto **final** salvation can lose that salvation." This is not Reformed terminology. There is no such thing as initial or final salvation; either one is saved thoroughly at the start or he is not saved at all. The statement wants to preserve the appearance of some kind of predestination when it says that God has ordained all to eternal life that He has determined, but this final salvation is contingent upon man himself. The position statement clearly refers to the phrases "glorious new creation in Christ," "have been delivered out of the world," "been cleansed from their former sins" and "have known the way of righteousness" as things that indicate "salvation." The statement continues to acknowledge that not all persevere in that "salvation." The problem is that the Federal Vision maintains **two kinds of salvation.** What the Federal Vision attributes to initial salvation, the Bible attributes to the only salvation that God provides, which cannot be lost. Does it make any sense to say that a person can have his former sins forgiven, but there remains a possibility for this person to be lost in the future? This would mean that there are sins that can be committed after this initial forgiveness and salvation that would forfeit all that one previously had. This is why the position statement was careful to say - "been cleansed from their **former** sins." In Federal Vision theology there is a death of Jesus initially for the forgiveness of sins, but then the efficacy of Jesus' death will not guarantee final forgiveness simply because the person may apostatize from the Faith. This is an outright challenge to the nature of Christ's atoning work.

The session of Auburn Avenue Presbyterian Church actually seeks to quote Westminster Confession chapter 18: 1-2 as a proof text for its statements. This is amazing, for there is no similarity between Westminster and the Federal Vision. The session speaks of those who persevere to the end can have assurance but others have false hopes. The fact that the Federal Vision believes that all the saving graces are present at baptism changes everything. The Confession says that those who have false hopes are the "unregenerate." The assurance of salvation is reserved for those who "truly believe in the Lord" as the Confession states in 18:1. WCF 18:2 states that this assurance is a

certainty, which is based on "the divine truth of the promises of salvation." The Confession does not say "initial salvation" or "final salvation." This distinction is pure fabrication in the minds of the Federal Vision. WCF 18:2 continues to add that this certainty of the promise of salvation is due to the inward testimony of the Holy Spirit that we are children of God. The Federal Vision believes that all persons baptized are "the children of God."

Doug Wilson Denies the Perseverance of the Saints

Doug Wilson follows the interpretation of John 15 that all the other men of the Federal Vision camp purport. The basic thrust is that there is no distinction between an external and an internal covenant. The branches that are attached to the vine are in vital union with the vine. In his understanding of the church, Wilson has said that the term "Christian" is a fitting term for all those who are objectivity of the covenant, having been sealed in the covenant through baptism.

Wilson has made some remarkable comments regarding the doctrine of the perseverance of the saints, remarkable, in that Wilson says that he is Reformed. He states:

> In an exegetical debate between an average Arminian, who has checked out in the scripture, and the average Calvinist, who is checked out on his system, the average Arminian is going to eat that Calvinist's lunch when it comes to the perseverance of the saints ... Now perseverance, this is difficult because the perseverance of the saints is the one point of Calvinism that is popular. All right, all the rest we hate. Oh, yes, we hate them. Perseverance, you mean I can't loose my salvation once I get saved, I can't lose it? That's right. Cool! Cool! That's Cool. Well, but that is the most popular tenant of Calvinism and when you are looking at the scriptures as they present themselves to us in the light of our system, it is the least defensible.[9]

Doug Wilson, mentioned above, believes that the average Arminian who has done his Bible study on the topic would eat the Calvinist's lunch in a debate! All this says is that Wilson doesn't understand his Bible. As I mentioned in the opening paragraphs of this chapter, the great, precious, and comforting doctrines find their culmination in the doctrine of the perseverance of the saints.

---

[9] Wilson, *Visible and Invisible Church Revisited*.

Wilson apparently really believes that the biblical texts better support an Arminian interpretation rather than a Reformed interpretation. Wilson continues:

> The New Testament talks about apostasy all the time and when people apostatize they are falling from grace, they are being cut out of the vine, they are being cut out of the olive tree. People fall away. Well, you have to understand, says the astute Calvinist commentator, these are hypothetical warnings. These are hypothetical warnings. There is a big "stay away from the cliff" sign in the middle of Kansas. And all the eternally secure people out in the middle of Kansas who can't fall off of anything and there is nothing to do in Kansas, so they gather around the sign and debate what it means. Well I think it is referring to this, what does "cliff" actually mean? Well these are not hypothetical warnings. Apostasy is a real sin committed by real people, baptized people, who are real members and the grace of God was involved in their life, they had tasted the heavenly gift. They were partakers of the powers of the coming age. Sap flowed to them. They were partakers and they really lost something when they fell away.
>
> Our system has to submit to scripture. Our system has to be brought back regularly to scripture and I believe that when it does, there are questions that our Arminian brethren can't answer and I believe there are far more questions that they can't answer. But I would submit plainly, there are questions that reformed exegetes have been dishonest with. All right, there are questions that reformed exegetes have been dishonest with and perseverance of the saints is one of the prime areas where we say these are hypothetical warnings and they are plainly in the text very, very real warnings.[10]

This reasoning is but another example of how false presuppositions become a snare. Wilson and the entire Federal Vision's presupposition is that external membership into the covenant constitutes real, saving union with Christ. Wilson recoils at the idea that there can be two membership rolls in the church – one for the visible church and one for the invisible church. Consequently, he thinks that there is a real problem for Reformed Theology regarding the texts commonly associated with apostasy such as Hebrews 6:4-6 and Hebrews

---

[10] Wilson, *Visible and Invisible Church Revisited.*

10:26-31. These texts among others have been dealt with very responsibly for centuries. Who says that the warnings are hypothetical? They are real warnings. The warnings that Paul gives in his epistles are real warnings. The warnings are addressed to the visible church, which comprises the invisible church. The Scripture maintains that there are false professors of Christ. It maintains that not everyone in the covenant is of the covenant (Romans 9:4-6). As Hebrews 3 and 4 brings out, there were always those Israelites (circumcised) who needed to be warned of failing to believe in the Lord. If I am a pastor, and I have a congregation of which I know that there may be someone in it who has not truly embraced Christ as Lord and Savior, then a warning against apostasy is a real warning. The Federal Vision has ridiculed the viewpoint that I have just mentioned. Wilkins, Barach, and Schlissel have greatly criticized this as the problem in our churches. They think this to be an unbiblical emphasis on a subjective experience. No, the problem is with the Federal Vision's false doctrine of the objectivity of the covenant. Reasoning like a Federal Vision proponent, there would be an exegetical problem about the warnings being only hypothetical. If I have all of God's saving graces at my baptism as a member of the covenant, then, yes, I have fallen from salvation if I apostatize. But this is the problem! The Federal Vision has created this monstrous theological system that is resting on a false foundation. Being in the covenant **does not mean that I possess salvation automatically.** The warnings are meant for all in the visible church. In 2 Corinthians 13:5, Paul exhorted the Corinthian church to examine themselves and to test themselves to see if Christ was in them, unless indeed they fail the test. Talk about a passage that presents a real exegetical problem for the Federal Vision - here it is. Paul is addressing the church for the members to examine themselves to see if they are in Christ. The Federal Vision believes that all members are already in union with Christ in a saving way at their baptism. Then, if this is true, why does Paul exhort people in Christ to see if they are in Christ?

Wilson thinks that the warnings that Jesus gave in John 15 are real warnings. I agree; they are genuine warnings to those in the visible church to be sure they really abide in Jesus. As Jesus said in John 15: 8, those who do not bear fruit **are not His true disciples.** There is no exegetical problem for the Reformed Faith here.

Concerning this imagery in John 15, Wilson states:

> You can be on the tree, someone can be on the tree right next
> to you and he is as much on the tree as you are, he's as much
> a partaker of Christ as you are, he is as much a member of

Christ as you are and he is cut away and you are not and you
stand by faith, so don't be haughty, but fear.[11]

Wilson adds to the confusion when he says that the elect cannot lose their salvation. He is not as elaborate in his explanations as others, but he means that
those who persevere to the end are the elect. The problem is this: everyone who
is in the visible church is the elect of God. Wilson has said, *"So what is the true
church? The true church is the church in history. The true church is the church
on the corner."*[12] This means that some in the true church do apostatize. I ask,
"How is it that the elect don't lose their salvation?" Yes, the elect are those who
do persevere to the end, but there are none who are in the invisible church that
can fall away, and our Confessional documents equate the invisible church
with only the elect.

John Barach Denies The Perseverance of the Saints

John Barach anticipates that there are some who are going to have potential
problems with his idea of the covenant. Barach states:

> What kind of election is that that he talks about when he says
> he chose us in him before the foundation of the world?
> People say well this covenant election that Israel enjoyed,
> that certainly didn't mean that everybody in Israel was going
> to be saved automatically. By the way, watch that word, auto-
> matically, that is a bit of a weasel word. People use that in odd
> ways. But they will say, well look, covenant election, that
> doesn't guarantee that you are going to heaven no matter
> what. Covenant people fall away. And so they say what Paul
> was talking about here is the election of individuals to eternal
> life, special election, Paul says, you are going to be holy, you
> are going to be blameless. And this is not the same kind of
> election that Moses was talking about when he said God
> chose you.[13]

John Barach affirms that in water baptism a person has redemption, righteousness, justification, sanctification, the Holy Spirit, glorification and election. He
says that we have the whole package of salvation at baptism (See quote on the

---

[11] Wilson, *Visible and Invisible Church Revisited.*

[12] Wilson, *Visible and Invisible Church Revisited.*

[13] Barach, *Covenant and Election.*

bottom of page 228). To demonstrate how confusing and self-contradictory Barach can be, notice the following quote:

> But what about those who fall away? Our election is unconditional. God doesn't choose us due to something in us. But our life in God's covenant including our enjoyment of that promise of election does have conditions, not everybody responds in faith. John 15 says that some in Christ are cut off and burned, there is no room in the covenant for presumption, "well I am elect, I can sin all I like." But those who fall away will be cut off from the church.[14]

Barach says that election is unconditional, but he then immediately states that the promise of election has conditions! Barach is making God's sovereign decree contingent upon man's faith. He says that there are some who are cut off and never experience the promise of election even though they were unconditionally elected. Barach says that God doesn't choose us due to something in us, but he says that securing the blessings of the election is conditional upon us. This is the double talk that is so common in the Federal Vision. These men do not hold to the historic Reformed Faith, but they want to be recognized as being Reformed, which explains why they like to use Reformed terminology and make references to the Reformed Standards.

Rich Lusk Denies The Perseverance of the Saints

Rich Lusk falls into the same pit, as his comrades in the Federal Vision. He says that God addresses covenant members consistently as God's eternally elect, even though some of these may apostatize and prove themselves to not be elected to eternal salvation (See paragraph at the bottom of page 249). We must consider the inherent contradiction of his statement, which seems to completely escape him. Lusk says that God addresses covenant members as His **eternally elect.** But he then says that some of these persons will apostatize and prove to **not be eternally elect.** This is what I mean by the delusion that has blinded the men of the Federal Vision. How can an eternally elect person not be eternally elect? Eternal means forever! He refutes himself. Moreover, the idea of an "eternal election" implies an unconditional election since who can undo what God foreordains? When Lusk states that the apostates prove themselves to be non-elect, this means that their "eternal" election is conditional after all – it is contingent upon man's faithfulness. Just like so many other biblical words, the Federal Vision redefines "eternal" to be "not eternal," or maybe

---

[14] Barach, *Covenant and Election.*

"almost eternal," or maybe "for a limited time." Lusk also says that election in Ephesians 1 applies to all members of the church and that this election is from the foundation of the world; however, not all of these elect members will achieve final salvation, as he puts it (See second paragraph on page 250). Here again the idea of elect before the foundation of the world means only elect for a time. It is amazing how many false doctrines that one is forced to hold in order to believe in the Federal Vision's objective covenant. All of the precious doctrines associated with the salvation of men are robbed of their majesty and efficacy. Regeneration is only for a limited time. Pardon of sin is only for a limited time. God's mercy and grace can be thwarted by man's actions. God's faithfulness is not faithful enough to see all of the elect to glorification in heaven. All of God's actions are contingent upon man's faithfulness. Eternal does not mean forever. There are people in Hell for whom Jesus died and redeemed. If they were redeemed then how did they end up in Hell? Redemption means deliverance. They are supposedly redeemed but then not totally redeemed. It is all a tragedy of immense proportions. This is why the Federal Vision is a heresy that stands under the curse of God.

Lusk uses King Saul as an example of his view of apostasy:

> Saul and David look alike in the early phases of their careers; Judas looked like the other disciples for a time. No appeal to the decree can be allowed to soften or undercut this covenantal perspective on our salvation. It is only as history is lived, as God's plan unfolds, that we come to know who will persevere and who won't... This means that at the outset of Saul's career, the biblical narrative itself draws no distinction between his initial experience of the Spirit and the experience of those who would enter into final salvation. Saul's apostasy was not due to any lack in God's grace given to him, but was his own fault... Saul received the same initial covenantal grace that David, Gideon, and other saved men received, though God withheld from him continuance in that grace. At the same time, his failure to persevere was due to his own rebellion. Herein lies the great mystery of God's sovereignty and human responsibility (cf. WCF 3.1, 8).[15]

He says that Saul **initially** had an experience with the Spirit but that experience would not give him **final** salvation. Lusk states that the Bible draws no distinction of the initial workings of the Spirit and of those who make it to final sal-

---

[15] Barach, *Covenant and Election.*

vation. Lusk says that Saul's apostasy was his own fault and not God's. He says that Saul had the same initial grace that David, Gideon, and other saved men. Notice that Lusk uses the word "saved." This means that Lusk views Saul as one who was saved but who would later apostatize and fall out of a saved condition. Lusk says that God withheld from Saul continuance in that grace. It is baffling to see Lusk quoting the Westminster Confession's chapter on God's eternal decree. This chapter utterly refutes his position. Lusk references 3:1 where I suppose that he is referring to the fact that despite God's decree being eternal and unchangeable, God's decree does no violence to man's will and that God is not responsible for the sinful actions of men. Lusk has argued that Saul was a saved man initially just like David and others; however, Saul, of his own free will, apostatized and lost his initial salvation. This contradicts the fact that God's decree is eternal and unchangeable. To lose a previous salvation is a change! Lusk also quotes 3:8 of the Confession where it refers to the doctrine of predestination as a mystery. Lusk states that the mystery is between divine sovereignty and human responsibility pertaining to how one could be initially saved but then lost because God withheld continuance of grace. This is not what 3:8 teaches. This section refers to the fact that men can be assured of their eternal election flowing from the **"certainty of their effectual vocation."** The concept that God withholds continuing grace from those whom He elects is an impossibility. The Federal Vision completely rejects Philippians 1:6 – *"For I am confident of this very thing, that He who began a good work in you will perfect it until the day of Christ Jesus."* There is no contingency here. There is no withholding a continuance of grace. Why will God complete what he has started? It is because God is faithful. Lusk is stating that for some unknown reason (mystery) God stops his act of electing grace and allows the person to apostatize and go to Hell. What an insult to God. Is there any comfort in this doctrine of the Federal Vision? None whatsoever. While Lusk maintains that it is the fault of the apostate who apostatizes, he turns around and blames God for the fact that God withheld continuance of grace to keep this person saved. The Federal Vision does not understand nor appreciate I Thessalonians 5:23, 24 – *"Now may the God of peace Himself sanctify you entirely; and may your spirit and soul and joy be preserved complete without blame at the coming of our Lord Jesus Christ. Faithful is He who calls you, and He also will bring it to pass."* The comfort for the Christian is in God's faithfulness. If God elects you, God will provide sustaining grace all your life. Assurance of salvation flows out of the promise of God's unconditional election. The Federal Vision gives no real comfort; it hangs over our heads a threat of eternal damnation to everyone who does not continue in obedience, as if this obedience ultimately depended upon us. Yes, as Hebrews 12:14 states, no one will see God without holiness of life. There must be a sanctified life, but God always provides what

He promises. This is why the Westminster Confession states in Chapter 11, Section 2 that justifying faith is **always accompanied with all other saving graces.** Since Lusk says that God is the one who withheld continuing grace from Saul, who is to say that God will not withhold continuing grace from any of us? How do I know that any kind of backsliding isn't the beginning of the end of my salvation? The Westminster Confession in its chapter on assurance of grace and salvation clearly teaches that we who truly believe in Jesus, who love Him in sincerity, and who endeavor to walk in Him, can be **certainly assured** that we are in the state of grace. And what is the basis of this confident assurance? Our determined wills? No. Chapter 18, Section 2 of The Westminster Confession says that this certainty is grounded upon the divine truth of the **promise of salvation and the inward evidence of those graces unto which the promises are made, and the testimony of the Spirit of adoption witnessing with our spirits that we are the children of God.** The Confession uses Ephesians 1:13-14 as a proof text that all who believe in Jesus as a result of their election are **sealed with the Holy Spirit of promise.** This sealing of the Holy Spirit is viewed by Scripture as a pledge of our inheritance. What the Federal Vision tells us is that God reneges on His election by withholding His sustaining grace. Lusk says it is a mystery why God does this.

Lusk likens our covenant relationship with God as a marriage (See first three paragraphs on page 255). In his analogy, Lusk states that our water baptism is like the wedding ceremony, and as long as we remain faithful, Christ will keep us under His protection. Yet, if we become unfaithful (adulterous), then Christ will divorce us. Lusk then asks, "What constitutes unfaithfulness leading to Christ's divorcing of us?" Lusk's answer to his own question is quite odd. He says that God does not demand perfection from us, only loyalty. He says that God is concerned with our direction, not perfection. He says that sustained faithfulness is what counts, however numerous our failings may be. Does this mean that if we cheat on Jesus only once that is okay? How about twice? Lusk's analogy is not that sound. He wants us to understand that there is a real wedding with Christ. We are His bride, and the relationship is a true union with Him. The problem with Lusk's analogy is that it breaks down seriously because he makes the wedding applicable to the visible church in its entirety. Lusk says that all baptized persons are married to Christ and in full union with Him. Jesus is married to His bride, the church, according to Ephesians 5:22-33. But this marriage is to His elect, the invisible church! Christ promises to have a **spotless bride.** Christ sanctifies His bride and presents her to Himself **as holy and blameless.** There is no divorcing of His bride! Ephesians 5:25-27 states:

> Husbands, love your wives, just as Christ also loved the
> church and gave Himself up for her; that He might present to
> Himself the church in all her glory, having no spot or wrinkle
> or any such thing; but that she should be holy and blameless.

Notice that Christ preserves and guarantees the faithfulness of His bride! It never puts the onus of responsibility on the bride, the church, to maintain the relationship. Lusk's illustration totally breaks down and insults the Lord Jesus Christ. This means that when those who are in the visible church apostatize, it simply demonstrates that they were **never** married to Christ. If they had been married to Him, they would not have apostatized just as Ephesians 5 states. As I John 2:19 states, those that go out from the body of believers as apostates only showed that they were never really part of the body in terms of a spiritual reality. The Federal Vision simply cannot accept this because of its obsession to maintain its objective covenant. Once a person buys into the Federal Vision's covenant concept, then he begins a downward spiral of immense proportions. One precious doctrine after another must be denied, such as the Reformed doctrine of the perseverance of the saints.

Lusk, just like other proponents of the Federal Vision, want to avoid using the phrase "lose one's salvation." This would be too openly Arminian. To solve his dilemma, Lusk asks the question, "What do you mean by salvation?" (See paragraph at the bottom of page 255). He says that biblical writers view salvation as an eschatological concept, meaning that no one is saved until the last day. I wonder who these biblical writers are that he never mentions? They don't exist because this is nowhere taught in Scripture. Not once is the term "eschatological salvation" ever used. His attempts to explain this are one huge convoluted mess. He says that salvation can be understood as a past reality, meaning that it is in eternity past when God chose us or when Christ died for us on the cross, or when the Spirit converted us. I am using Lusk's verbatim statements from his quote. Lusk continues to say that no elect person can lose his salvation, and he quotes John 10:27-28. However, he says that the biblical language is much more complicated. By complicated, Lusk means that "*in one sense all those in the covenant are saved. They have been delivered out of the world and brought into the glorious new creation of Christ. But not all will persevere.*"[16] Lusk then quotes Jude 5 as support for the fact that people can be saved but then lost. If we look at Jude 5 we read – "*Now I desire to remind you, though you know all things once for all, that the Lord, after saving a people of the land of Egypt, subsequently destroyed those who did not believe.*" The word does not carry the connotation of "saving" in a soteriological sense.

---

[16] Lusk, *Covenant & Election FAQ's (Version 6.4).*

It simply means "deliverance" in this context. It is obvious that there is no sote-riological meaning for this word here because the verse clearly states that those whom God destroyed after "saving" **did not believe.** We must remember that the terms "adoption" and "children of God" can simply have an external mean-ing as John Murray has pointed out as in Romans 9. Lusk totally misunder-stands because he is looking through his tinted lens of this erroneous objective covenant.

Lusk says that the Reformed community cannot hide behind the doctrine of election, or the "invisible church" and say these warnings are for other people, but not for us (See middle paragraph on page 256). He is in outright defiance of the very Standards that he swore to uphold. Chapter 18 of the Westminster Confession again affirms that everyone effectually called and sanctified cannot totally fall away from the Faith (18:1). The perseverance is rooted in God's immutable decree and unchangeable love. Westminster Larger Catechism number 68 affirms that only the elect are effectually called while others only receive "common operations of the Spirit" but who never truly come to Christ. Like Barach and Wilkins he makes absolutely no sense when he says that "*no elect person can be lost and no non-elect person can attain salvation*" (See last paragraph on page 256). He then turns around and says that non-elect persons are truly brought to Christ and united to Him. He says, "*In some sense, they were really joined to the elect people, really sanctified by Christ's blood, real-ly recipients of new life by the Holy Spirit. But God withholds from them the gift of perseverance and all is lost. They break the gracious new covenant they entered into at baptism*" (See second paragraph on page 257). It is hard to see how Lusk can immediately state: "*The covenant really is gospel – good news-through and through. Yet only those who continue to persevere in loyalty to the covenant and the Lord of the covenant inherit final salvation…those who fall away lose the temporary covenantal blessings they had enjoyed. Ultimately, this is because God decreed that these covenant breakers would not share in the eschatological salvation of Christ*" (See third paragraph on page 257). It is not good news to those whom God supposedly decides to deny sustaining grace.

Scriptures refuting the Federal Vision's views

I do not intend to list many of the passages that support the Reformed doctrine of the perseverance of the saints, but a few will suffice.

Romans 8:28-39

> And we know that God causes all things to work together for good to those who love God, to those who are called according to His purpose. For whom He foreknew, He also predestined to become conformed to the image of His Son, that He might be the first-born among many brethren; and whom He predestined, these He also called; and whom He called, these He also justified; and whom He justified, these He also glorified. What then shall we say to these things? If God is for us, who is against us? He who did not spare His own Son, but delivered Him up for us all, how will He not also with Him freely give us all things? Who will bring a charge against God's elect? God is the one who justifies; who is the one who condemns? Christ Jesus is He who died, yes, rather who was raised who is at the right hand of God, who also intercedes for us. Who shall separate us from the love of Christ? Shall tribulation, or distress, or persecution, or famine, or nakedness, or peril, or sword? Just as it is written, 'For Thy sake we are being put to death all day long; we were considered as sheep to be slaughtered.' But in all these things we overwhelmingly conquer through Him who loved us. For I am convinced that neither death, nor life, nor angels, nor principalities, nor things present, nor things to come, nor powers, nor height, nor depth, nor any other created thing, shall be able to separate us from the love of God, which is in Christ Jesus our Lord.

This passage commonly has been called "the ordo salutis," a Latin phrase meaning "the order of salvation." This is one of the most glorious passages in all of God's Word. It sets forth for us the plan of salvation from start to finish. It is one of the most comforting and awe inspiring passages for the Christian. However, it is not for those of the Federal Vision, for they deny this passage, and in so doing they rob God of His glorious mercy and grace, and they leave the professing Christian in the realm of his own feeble efforts.

In verse 28 we see that God causes all things to work together for good to those who love God and are called according to His purpose. One might ask, "What purpose is that?" The answer is found in the succeeding verses. The word "for" is a transitional word linking verse 28 with all that follows. The Greek word is "oti," which can be translated as "because." Verse 29 begins with those whom God has "foreknown." A word study on this word, and its usage in this context refers to a love that God has shown to a certain group of persons from all eternity. Paul is now going to link together several great biblical concepts in an unbreakable chain. Those whom God has foreknown, these He also predestines, meaning that He foreordains them. To what does God predestine those whom He foreknew? It is to the goal of becoming conformed to the image of His Son. This is very important for us to understand in our analysis of the Federal Vision. Predestination is to holiness of life in all whom God has predestined. Verse 30 indicates that those whom God predestines, these He also calls. This is effectual calling. The only ones who are called by God are those whom He foreknew and predestined to reach holiness of life. Those who are called are those whom God has loved from all eternity according to God's sovereign choice. Verse 30 continues to add that all those whom God called, these He also justified. The people who are justified are those who have been loved from all eternity and called. To be justified means that one is declared innocent, not for anything done in them but for the righteousness of Christ imputed to them. To be justified means to be pardoned of sins once and for all. Then, we are told that all whom God justified, He glorified. Glorification is pictured in the Bible as that state when we are made perfect both in body and soul. This occurs at the Second coming of Jesus, which is at the last Day, when Jesus raises up all those whom God justified. Now this is the unbroken sequence of the plan of salvation. Does anyone see an election according to our faithful obedience? Does anyone see reference to an initial election or justification in some but who do not make it to glorification because God decided to withhold His sovereign, sustaining grace? Election, which is foreknowledge combined with predestination, always culminates in glorification in those whom God foreloves and predestines. In verse 31 we need to ask, "Who is the "us"?" Moving on to verse 32, we see that God did not spare His own Son for "us." The Son of God was delivered up for "us all." God freely gave "us" all things in the Son. In verse 33, we are told who the "us" are. It is the "elect." Verse 33 and 34 emphasize that God justifies the elect! No charge can be brought against the elect, and who can condemn these elect? Verse 34 affirms that Jesus died for the elect and that He intercedes for the elect. This is no minor point! Jesus intercedes for all the elect. If a person has Jesus continually interceding for them, how can any such person ever fail to be glorified? Paul then asks the glorious question, "Who shall separate us from the love of Christ?" In verses 35–39, he gives this litany of things that cannot separate us from Christ's love for us. The "love of Christ" in verse 35 is not our love for Christ but Christ's love for us! The conclusion to verses 35- 39 is that **absolutely nothing can separate the elect of God from God's love for them in Jesus Christ.**

The ordo salutis is God's unconditional love for an undeserving people. It begins in eternity past and will continue into eternity future. There are no conditions pending to some initially elect who must persevere or else. God promised that all whom He foreknew and predestined **will be conformed to Christ's image, not maybe.** If someone apostatizes, it is simply because they were **never foreknown, never predestined, never called, never justified, and never glorified.** As Jesus said in Matthew 7:23, there will be those whom Jesus **never knew.** These are people who were members of the visible church! Jesus knows savingly only those in the invisible church.

The Federal Vision's gospel is no gospel. It can save no man. Trusting in such a theology will be disastrous for the souls of such persons.

Hebrews 6:4-9

> For in the case of those who have once been enlightened and have tasted of the heavenly gift and have been made partakers of the Holy Spirit, and have tasted the good word of God and the powers of the age to come, and then have fallen away, it is impossible to renew them again to repentance, since they again crucify to themselves the Son of God, and put Him to open shame. For ground that drinks the rain which often falls upon it and brings forth vegetation useful to those for whose sake it is also tilled, receives a blessing from God; but if it yields thorns and thistles, it is worthless and close to being cursed and it ends up being burned. But, beloved, we are convinced of better things concerning you, and things that accompany salvation, though we are speaking in this way.

This is one of the classic passages that Arminianism has used to attempt to prove that one can lose his salvation. It is interesting this is also one of the passages that the Federal Vision uses to agree with the Arminians that one can lose his salvation. Doug Wilson said that it is such passages that Calvinists have been dishonest with, and remember, Wilson said that Arminians would eat the Calvinist's lunch with passages like this.

Wilson makes a fatal assumption because of his commitment to a false view of the covenant. Like all the men of the Federal Vision, he believes that entrance into the covenant via baptism is accompanied by God's saving graces at that moment. When we are in covenant we are in Christ in all respects. As Rich Lusk and John Barach say, the whole package of salvation is present at baptism. Hence, it is assumed that all the characteristics mentioned in this passage must be indicative of someone who is saved initially. The assumption is that the warnings are directed toward genuine Christians to keep them alert, lest they should lose it all.

The pivotal verse in the entire passage is verse 9. Verse 9 begins with the conjunction "but," which is a transitional word. In verses 4 through 8, the writer has been setting forth a list of traits of certain persons. Now, in verse 9 the writer says that he thinks of better things concerning them – things that **accompany salvation.** This means that all the traits listed in verses 4-8 are things that may look like salvation or that may be closely associated with salvation but fall short of true saving faith.

Simon Kistemaker makes some helpful comments on this passage. He states:

> Throughout the epistle the writer has admonished his readers to accept the Word of God in faith and not to fall into the sin of unbelief that results in eternal judgment (2:1; 3:12-14; 4:1, 6, 11; 10:25, 27, 31; 12:16-17, 25, 29). In 6:4-6 he does not address the recipients of his letter, but instead he states a truth that emerges from an earlier reference to the Israelites persishing in the desert because of their unbelief. The truth also applies to the Hebrews, even though the author omits the personal reference in 6:4-6.[17]

Regarding this passage, John Calvin, has made these comments:

> But here arises a new question, how can it be that he who has once made such a progress should afterwards fall away? For God, it may be said, calls none effectually but the elect, and Paul testifies that they are really his sons who are led by his Spirit, (Romans 8:14) and he teaches us, that it is a sure pledge of adoption when Christ makes us partakers of his Spirit. The elect are also beyond the danger of finally falling away; for the Father who gave them to be preserved by Christ his Son is greater than all, and Christ promises to watch over them all so that none may perish. To all this I answer, That God indeed favors none but the elect alone with the Spirit of regeneration, and that by this they are distinguished from the reprobate; for they are renewed after his image and receive the earnest of the Spirit in hope of the future inheritance, and by the same Spirit the Gospel is sealed in their hearts. But I

---

[17] Simon J. Kistemaker, *New Testament Commentary, Exposition of the Epistle to the Hebrews,* (Grand Rapids, Michigan: Baker Book House, 1984), pp. 157-158.

cannot admit that all this is any reason why he should not grant the reprobate also some taste of his grace, why he should not irradiate their minds with some sparks of his light, why he should not give them some perception of his goodness, and in some sort engrave his word on their hearts. Otherwise, where would be the temporal faith mentioned by Mark 4:17? There is therefore some knowledge even in the reprobate, which afterwards vanishes away, either because it did not strike roots sufficiently deep, or because it withers, being choked.[18]

Calvin is very clear to state that only the elect are effectually called and that those led of the Holy Spirit are truly His sons. Calvin is the one who uses the word "truly" to describe God's sons. The Federal Vision vehemently objects to this kind of verbiage because it views all in the covenant as sons in a saving sense. Calvin emphatically states that the elect are beyond the danger of finally falling away because God the Father who gave the elect His Son is greater than all and that Christ promises (John 17:12) that He will care for them all, so that none perishes. There is no discussion of an **initial** elect as opposed to a **final** elect as the Federal Vision insists. There is no contingency based upon man's efforts. Calvin states that God bestows His Spirit of regeneration only on the elect and that they are distinguished from the reprobate. This is a key point in demonstrating the spiritual bankruptcy of the Federal Vision. Calvin recognizes an antithesis between the elect and the reprobate. The Federal Vision states that the reprobate are initially elect because of their baptism into the covenant community. This is why the Federal Vision must create a "final elect" or a "final salvation." Calvin states that only the elect have the Spirit of God sealed to their hearts as the earnest of their inheritance. This completely refutes the Federal Vision's comments that all baptized persons are regenerated and have the Holy Spirit, of whom some apostatize. The point of Calvin is clear. **It is impossible for any elect to apostatize.**

There are several things that characterize the persons of Hebrews 6:4-6. They have once been enlightened; they have tasted the heavenly gift; they have been made partakers of the Holy Spirit; and they have tasted the good word of God and the powers of the age to come. If these things are not references to genuine Christians, then how are they to be explained? What does it mean to be enlight-

---

[18] John Calvin, *Calvin's New Testament Commentaries, Hebrews,* Translated by W. B. Johnston (Grand Rapids, Michigan: Eerdman's Publishing Co. 1963), p. 76.

ened? The Scripture does maintain that illumination does not always mean a saving enlightenment to the truth. In John 1:5 we read: *"And the light shines in the darkness, and the darkness did not comprehend it."* This is a reference about the eternal Word who has come into the world, who John tells us is Jesus Christ. In John 1:9 we read: *"There was the true light which, coming into the world, enlightens every man."* What is meant by the phrase, "enlightens every man?" Of all the various interpretations that could attempt to explain this, William Hendrikson gives his analysis:

> He illumines every man who hears the Gospel; i.e., he imparts a degree of understanding concerning spiritual matters (not necessarily resulting in salvation) to all those who ears and minds are reached by the message of salvation. The majority, however, do not respond favorably. Many who have the light prefer the darkness. Some, however, due entirely to the sovereign, saving grace of God, receive the word with the proper attitude of heart and mind, and obtain everlasting life.[19]

There are those in the world who have been enlightened to the gospel message but who have never truly come to the light. Jesus said on several occasions that He is the true light and that men must come unto Him if they are to be saved. We know from the Scripture in doing word studies that words often can change their meanings according to the context. The word "flesh" can mean material body in one context and then mean "sinful living" in another context. The word "world" can mean everyone without exception in one context but then refer only to believers in another context, and even refer to a sinful system of thought in another context.

How can certain men taste the heavenly gift and be made partakers of the Holy Spirit, taste the goodness of the Word of God, and taste of the powers of the coming age and not be genuinely saved? Let's suppose we have someone who has professed Christ, who has been baptized, who has taken part actively in the local church, and who has participated in the Lord's Supper (eaten and drank the gift of God pictured in the sacrament). Is this person automatically a Christian? The Federal Vision would emphatically say yes, but the Bible has false professors. Why should we assume that the word "partake in" must mean saving union? Is it possible to be associated with the Holy Spirit and not be saved? Of course it is. Let's consider some notable figures in the New Testament. First, we have Judas Iscariot who was Jesus' disciple for three

---

[19] William Hendrikson, *New Testament Commentary on John.*

years. Was he in close association with the Holy Spirit? He sure was. He was in the presence of Jesus in whom the Spirit of God abode. He saw the miracles of Jesus. He heard the word of God consistently as Jesus preached and taught. Did this do Judas any good? Absolutely not. John 6:70-71 states that Jesus knew all along from the outset when He chose His disciples that Judas Iscariot was a devil and would betray Him, but He permitted him to be with the true believers. Jesus did this because in fulfillment of prophecy, the Messiah must be betrayed for 30 pieces of silver, and the betrayer would throw it into a potter's field (Zechariah 11: 12-13). We then have Simon Magus, the magician in Samaria, who saw the great signs and wonders performed by Philip and the apostles. He saw those who believed and who were baptized speak in tongues. Simon Magus was in very close association with the Holy Spirit, and he saw the powers of the coming age. Simon was said to have believed and was baptized (Acts 8:13). Is everyone who believes a true participant in God's saving work? No. We are told in Acts 8:18-24 that when Simon Magus wanted to buy from Peter the gift of the laying on of hands to do miracles that Peter had some very strong words to say to him. Peter says that Simon has no portion in this matter and that he is in the bondage of sin. This is said to one who "believed and was baptized." Not everyone who professes Christ is necessarily a true disciple. In chapter 6, I dealt in some detail with those "believers" in John 8 who Jesus declared to be the children of the Devil. We are told in John 6:1-2 that there was a multitude that followed Jesus because of *"seeing the signs which He was performing on those who were sick."*

How can men be closely associated with the Word of God, see miraculous things and not be genuinely saved? Matthew 7:21-23 is the vivid proof. In that passage we see men who profess Christ, who prophesy in Jesus' name, who cast out demons in Jesus' name, and who performed many miracles in Jesus' name. To these persons, Jesus says, *"I never knew you; depart from Me, you who practice lawlessness."* The key words are – **"I never knew you."**

To answer Doug Wilson who stated that Arminians would eat the Calvinist's lunch on such passages and that Calvinists have been dishonest with them, "My lunch was not eaten, and neither have the lunches of Calvinists for centuries been eaten." It is Doug Wilson and his fellow Federal Vision proponents who have no lunch to offer.

Chapter 10

A Hybrid Form of Roman Catholicism

In this chapter I will seek to demonstrate that Federal Vision theology is closely akin to Roman Catholicism. It is a hybrid form of Roman Catholicism. Rich Lusk wrote an article in 2004 titled, "Rome Won't Have Me," in response to accusations that his view was leading men back to Rome. He states:

> Rome holds no allure for me. I can easily and sharply distinguish my own position on key theological topics from Rome's perspective. Thus, it is deeply distressing when I find myself accused of heading in a Romeward direction. I have no such desire or inclination (nor do any other people I know associated with the so-called Auburn Avenue Theology). The purpose of this essay, however, is to show that even if I wanted to go to Rome, Rome wouldn't take me.[1]

Lusk is responding to an article by Michael Horton in the July/August 2004 edition of *Modern Reformation* magazine. In this article Lusk says that Horton accuses him of having strong parallels with Rome's soteriology as set forth in the Council of Trent. Lusk's primary argument that his views do not lead people back to Rome is because he totally rejects Rome's commitment to the idea of "merit." Lusk states:

> I offer a barrage of arguments against merit. Roman theology requires merit; I reject it categorically. Hence, my theology and Rome's theology mix about as well as fire and water.[2]

---

[1] Rich Lusk, *Rome Won't Have Me.* <www.hornes.org/theologia/soteriology>

[2] Lusk, *Rome Won't Have Me.*

Despite Lusk's insistence that his theology is the antithesis of Roman Catholicism, the fact is, this is not true. In the Federal Vision's denial of any kind of merit, even that of the Lord Jesus Christ imputed to believers, it has not divorced itself from the fundamental notion of merit. We can quibble over words all day long, but merit conveys the idea of something earned. Something that is meritorious is something that is seen as acceptable, commendable, and rewardable. The Federal Vision can claim all it wants that its view of justification is not the espousing of Romish "merit;" however, it is still meritorious. It is not called "merit" but "the obedience of faith."

Lusk says that he differs from Rome. Rome sees justification as a process or moral renewal; he sees justification as a forensic or declarative act whereby we are once and for all united to Christ by faith. He emphatically states:

> In no way do I believe that our works produce or cause our justification. In no way do I suggest our works satisfy God's justice or form the ground of the favorable verdict we receive.[3]

This statement by Rich Lusk is simply not true whatsoever. He has stated that there is an initial and final justification. *"The initial justification is by faith alone; subsequent justification includes obedience ... The fluidity of these symbols suggests a certain fluidity in our doctrine of justification"* (See bottom paragraph on page 291). Lusk stated, *"The Bible is clear; obedience is necessary to receive eternal life. There is no justification apart from good works ... Final justification is to the (faithful) doers of the law (Rom. 2:1ff) and by those good works which make faith complete ... In James 2, 'justification' cannot be referring to a demonstration of justification, e.g., justification does and cannot mean something like 'show to be justified.' Rather James has in view the same kind of justification as Paul – forensic, soteric justification ... In other words, in some sense, James is speaking of a justification in which faith and works combine together to justify. Future justification is according to one's life pattern* (See Lusk's quote on pages 292 and 293).

Rich Lusk's other essays have betrayed him. The quotes that I have just referred to clearly puts him into Rome's view of justification. He implied in his negation statement that if he really did believe that justification is a process and that works cause justification, then the accusation against him would be accurate. Well, Lusk has just espoused Rome's view of justification.

Lusk is also deceptive in his comments about the active obedience of Christ. In his essay *Rome Won't Have Me*, he says that he never denied Christ's active

---

[3] Lusk, *Rome Won't Have Me.*

obedience. He says that Christ's active obedience was necessary for Jesus to be worthy to be our Redeemer. This is not the Reformed understanding of Christ's active obedience. Calvin and John Owen both insist that Jesus did not perfectly keep the Law for His sake but that He kept it so as to impute righteousness to those who needed it – us sinners. Lusk restates in his essay that it is not *Jesus' thirty-three years of obedience that gets reckoned to our account. Rather, it is the verdict the Father passed over him. The Father declared Jesus righteous; that verdict took the shape of the resurrection.*[4]

It is imperative that I emphasize the following quote from Norman Shepherd's quote from his book, *The Call of Grace.* He said:

> Is there any hope for a common understanding between Roman Catholicism and evangelical Protestantism regarding the way of salvation? May I suggest that there is at least a glimmer of hope if both sides are willing to embrace a covenantal understanding of the way of salvation.[5]

I have found this comment both perplexing and troublesome. It is perplexing because how does one reconcile two theological views that are on opposite ends of the spectrum? One of the positions must seriously compromise. Rome insists on works being necessary for justification while Protestantism has insisted that justification is by faith alone, completely void of any works. It is troublesome because Shepherd somehow thinks that his covenantal paradigm is that bridge. I have said earlier that the bridge is really a one-way street back to Rome. The differences in Roman Catholicism and Federal Vision theology is only in semantics. While Shepherd and Lusk say that Rome is wrong because she advocates merit theology, the Federal Vision fundamentally offers the same thing; it just calls it "the obedience of faith." Shepherd states that Rome believes that James 2 clearly teaches that justification is not by faith alone but that faith expresses itself through love. But this is what the Federal Vision teaches! I have demonstrated this over and over throughout my book from all of the various quotes of proponents of the Federal Vision. I just quoted Lusk in the first part of this chapter. Shepherd teaches in his book that his covenant paradigm seeks to find salvation exclusively in Jesus Christ through faith in Him. Shepherd states – *"It is the biblical doctrine of covenant that challenges Roman Catholicism at its root."*[6]

---

[4] Lusk, *Rome Won't Have Me.*

[5] Shepherd, *The Call of Grace,* p. 59.

[6] Shepherd, *The Call of Grace,* p. 61.

This is very upsetting to me because I know this comment to be very deceptive. Shepherd has made explicit comments that faith is obedience to God's
Law, that the grace God has shown man is the giving of the Mosaic Law for
him to keep out of love for Jesus. As I have illustrated in previous chapters, this
is works salvation! This is essentially Romanism. Shepherd and Lusk can
refuse to call it "merit," but it is still tying works to justification, which is what
Rome has always done.

One of the best ways to demonstrate that there is essentially no difference
between Roman Catholicism's view of justification and the Federal Vision's
view of justification is to quote from the Council of Trent. The Council of Trent
was Rome's official response to the Reformation. Rome declared the teachings
of the Reformation on the nature of justification as anathema. This is still
Rome's official position on justification. The bulk of Trent's decree centered
on the nature of justification.

My procedure will be to quote segments from the Council of Trent and then
immediately demonstrate the similarity of Catholic doctrine with the Federal
Vision.

In 1547 the Council issued its decree on justification. In chapter 4 we find an
emphasis upon the necessity of water baptism. Trent states:

> By which words, a description of the Justification of the
> impious is indicated,-as being a translation, from that state
> wherein man is born a child of the first Adam, to the state of
> grace, and of the adoption of the sons of God, through the
> second Adam, Jesus Christ, our Saviour. And this translation,
> since the promulgation of the Gospel, cannot be effected,
> without the laver of regeneration, or the desire thereof, as it is
> written; unless a man be born again of water and the Holy
> Ghost, he cannot enter into the Kingdom of God.[7]

In chapter 8, I demonstrated that the Federal Vision stresses the necessity of
water baptism as the point of conversion, that all of God's saving graces are
present at the moment of baptism. Whereas Rome would see some special significance with the water itself, the Federal Vision does say that faith needs to
be present. This is why the Federal Vision is a hybrid form of Catholicism. The
Federal Vision sees water baptism as the act of regeneration. Steve Wilkins
went to great lengths to stress that we are in full union with Christ at our bap-

---

[7] The information on *The Council of Trent* can be found at
<history.hanover.edu/early/trent.htm.>

tisms. Steve Schlissel chided Presbyterians to quit looking for some inward proof in some kind of subjective experience. He says we have our baptisms to see that we are Christians.

Trent states in its chapter 5:

> The Synod furthermore declares, that in adults, the beginning of the said Justification is to be derived from the prevenient grace of God, through Jesus Christ, that is to say, from His vocation, whereby, without any merits existing on their parts, they are called; that so they, who by sins were alienated from God, may be disposed through His quickening and assisting grace, to convert themselves to their own justification, by freely assenting to and co-operating with that said grace: in such sort that, while God touches the heart of man by the illumination of the Holy Ghost, neither is man himself utterly without doing anything while he receives that inspiration, forasmuch as he is also able to reject it; yet is he not able, by his own free will, without the grace of God, to move himself unto justice in His sight.

In this statement, Trent is stressing man's cooperation in his justification. Trent emphasizes that it begins with the grace of God, but it then says that man is quickened or assisted by grace to cooperate with that grace in his justification. How is this essentially any different than what the Federal Vision purports? The redefinition of "faith" as "the obedience of faith" and the insistence that works are not simply the fruit or evidence of saving faith is making man do something in order to be justified. How is this not cooperation in justification?

In chapter 6, "The Manner of Preparation for Justification," the Council stated:

> … by that penitence which must be performed before baptism: lastly, when they purpose to receive baptism, to begin a new life, and to keep the commandments of God. Concerning this disposition it is written; He that cometh to God, must believe that he is, and is a rewarder to them that seek him; and, Be of good faith, son, thy sins are forgiven thee; and, The fear of the Lord driveth out sin; and, Do penance, and be baptized every one of you in the name of Jesus Christ, for the remission of your sins, and you shall receive the gift of the Holy Ghost; and, Going, therefore, teach ye all nations, baptizing them in the name of the Father, and of the Son, and of the Holy Ghost; finally, Prepare your hearts unto the Lord.

It was Norman Shepherd who made the comment that the Great Commission only infers faith; he says the stress is on baptism and obedience to Jesus' commandments. The Federal Vision has explicitly stated that there is remission of sins actually present at all baptisms. It was Steve Wilkins who chided Southern Presbyterians for believing in their infant baptisms as only wet dedication services. He stated that we have full pardon of sins at our water baptisms. The only difference is that I have not read where any Federal Vision proponent is calling for penance in terms of preparation for justification.

The Council of Trent declared in chapter 7:

> Of this Justification the causes are these: the final cause indeed is the glory of God and of Jesus Christ, and life everlasting; while the efficient cause is a merciful God who washes and sanctifies gratuitously, signing, and anointing with the holy Spirit of promise, who is the pledge of our inheritance; but the meritorious cause is His most beloved only-begotten, our Lord Jesus Christ, who, when we were enemies, for the exceeding charity wherewith he loved us, merited Justification for us by His most holy Passion on the wood of the cross, and made satisfaction for us unto God the Father; the instrumental cause is the sacrament of baptism, which is the sacrament of faith, without which (faith) no man was ever justified; lastly, the alone formal cause is the justice of God, not that whereby He Himself is just, but that whereby He maketh us just, that, to wit, with which we being endowed by Him, are renewed in the spirit of our mind, and we are not only reputed, but are truly called, and are, just, receiving justice within us, each one according to his own measure, which the Holy Ghost distributes to every one as He wills, and according to each one's proper disposition and co-operation.

Trent emphasizes that the cause of our justification is the Passion of Jesus Christ with His merits given to us. It says that the instrumental cause in justification is the sacrament of baptism, which it calls the sacrament of faith. This is almost identical to the teaching of the Federal Vision. Rich Lusk called water baptism a co-instrument with faith in our justification!

Trent's chapter 8 is a most interesting declaration, for it stresses faith as the root of all justification:

> And whereas the Apostle saith, that man is justified by faith and freely, those words are to be understood in that sense

which the perpetual consent of the Catholic Church hath held and expressed; to wit, that we are therefore said to be justified by faith, because faith is the beginning of human salvation, the foundation, and the root of all Justification; without which it is impossible to please God, and to come unto the fellowship of His sons: but we are therefore said to be justified freely, because that none of those things which precede justification-whether faith or works-merit the grace itself of justification. For, if it be a grace, it is not now by works, otherwise, as the same Apostle says, grace is no more grace.

It is uncanny how similar this statement is to the Federal Vision's position. Schlissel and others have clamored against the Reformation's obsession with the word "alone" as it relates to justification. Schlissel insists that this is not the real meaning of justification. He states that James 2 declares that works are not simply fruit or evidence of faith but that it is the essence of faith. Norman Shepherd said, *"In fact, Genesis 15:6 says that Abraham's faith was so significant that it was credited to him as righteousness! If so, then righteousness was a condition to be met, and faith met that condition."*[8] The Federal Vision wants to emphasize "faith" without attaching the word "alone" to it. Notice, Rome does the same thing. Rome and the Federal Vision's interpretation of James 2 is identical, both believe that works are the very essence of faith.

In Trent's decree, justification is increased by keeping the commandments:

Having, therefore, been thus justified, and made the friends and domestics of God, advancing from virtue to virtue, they are renewed, as the Apostle says, day by day; that is, by mortifying the members of their own flesh, and by presenting them as instruments of justice unto sanctification, they, through the observance of the commandments of God and of the Church, faith co-operating with good works, increase in that justice which they have received through the grace of Christ, and are still further justified, as it is written; He that is just, let him be justified still; and again, Be not afraid to be justified even to death; and also, Do you see that by works a man is justified, and not by faith only. And this increase of justification holy Church begs, when she prays, "Give unto us, O Lord, increase of faith, hope, and charity."

---

[8] Shepherd, *The Call of Grace*, p. 15.

It was Norman Shepherd as far back as the 1970's who stated in his thesis 23 on justification the following relationship between obedience and justification:

> Because faith which is not obedient faith is dead faith, and because repentance is necessary for the pardon of sin included in justification, and because abiding in Christ by keeping his commandments (John 15:5, 10; I John 3:13; 24) are all necessary for continuing in the state of justification, good works, works done from true faith, according to the law of God, and for his glory, being the new obedience wrought by the Holy Spirit in the life of the believer united to Christ, though not the ground of his justification, are nevertheless necessary for salvation from eternal condemnation and therefore for justification (Rom. 6:16, 22; Gal. 6:7-9).[9]

Rather startling isn't it? Shepherd just like Rome states that keeping the commandments is necessary for continuing in the state of justification. Of course, these good works do not originate from ourselves but from the Holy Spirit. Rome would not really argue with the fact that it is the Holy Spirit who is empowering the person to keep the commandments.

Trent's chapter 11 emphasizes persevering in good works to remain justified:

> For God forsakes not those who have been once justified by His grace, unless he be first forsaken by them. Wherefore, no one ought to flatter himself up with faith alone, fancying that by faith alone he is made an heir, and will obtain the inheritance, even though he suffer not with Christ, that so he may be also glorified with him. For even Christ Himself, as the Apostle saith, Whereas he was the son of God, learned obedience by the things which he suffered, and being consummated, he became, to all who obey him, the cause of eternal salvation.

This statement by Trent on the nature of apostasy is identical to that of the Federal Vision. Trent says that God will not forsake the justified ones if they don't forsake Christ first. The Federal Vision even uses the same Bible reference as does Rome in obeying Jesus who had to learn obedience Himself. Rome believes that apostates forfeit justification; the Federal Vision totally agrees.

---

[9] Shepherd, *Thirty-four Theses on Justification.*

In Trent's chapter 12, Rome tells its disciples not to trust in predestination as if it gave absolute certainty of salvation:

> No one, moreover, so long as he is in this mortal life, ought so far to presume as regards the secret mystery of divine predestination, as to determine for certain that he is assuredly in the number of the predestinate; as if it were true, that he that is justified, either cannot sin any more, or, if he do sin, that he ought to promise himself an assured repentance; for except by special revelation, it cannot be known whom God hath chosen unto Himself.

The Federal Vision has no problem with this statement. When the Federal Vision speaks of justification it refers to initial justification or initial election; however, final justification is a mystery. Lusk stated that it is a mystery why God withholds sustaining grace from some people and they apostatize.

The Council of Trent summarized its teaching on justification by making declaration of what it considered anathema. There are several that are pertinent to us.

CANON 9.

> If any one saith, that by faith alone the impious is justified; in such wise as to mean, that nothing else is required to co-operate in order to the obtaining the grace of Justification, and that it is not in any way necessary, that he be prepared and disposed by the movement of his own will; let him be anathema.

CANON 11

> If any one saith, that men are justified, either by the sole imputation of the justice of Christ, or by the sole remission of sins, to the exclusion of the grace and the charity which is poured forth in their hearts by the Holy Ghost, and is inherent in them; or even that the grace, whereby we are justified, is only the favour of God; let him be anathema.

CANON 12

> If any one saith, that justifying faith is nothing else but confidence in the divine mercy which remits sins for Christ's sake; or, that this confidence alone is that whereby we are justified; let him be anathema.

CANON 14

If any one saith, that man is truly absolved from his sins and justified, because that he assuredly believed himself absolved and justified; or, that no one is truly justified but he who believes himself justified; and that, by this faith alone, absolution and justification are effected; let him be anathema.

CANON 18

If any one saith, that the commandments of God are, even for one that is justified and constituted in grace, impossible to keep; let him be anathema.

CANON 23

If any one saith, that a man once justified can sin no more, nor lose grace, and that therefore he that falls and sins was never truly justified; or, on the other hand, that he is able, during his whole life, to avoid all sins, even those that are venial,-except by a special privilege from God, as the Church holds in regard of the Blessed Virgin; let him be anathema.

CANON 24

If any one saith, that the justice received is not preserved and also increased before God through good works; but that the said works are merely the fruits and signs of Justification obtained, but not a cause of the increase thereof; let him be anathema.

The similarities between the Canons of Trent and Federal Vision theology are uncanny. Take out references to the Blessed Virgin Mary and fundamentally there is agreement. Trent anathematizes the idea that "faith alone" is all that is necessary for justification. It anathematizes the belief that Christ's imputation is all that is necessary for justification. Canon 12 insists that there must be love coming from the Holy Spirit in the life of the justified person for there to be justification. Trent would argue for faith plus works. Trent insists that one cannot be justified by simply trusting only in God's mercy for the forgiveness of sins. Canon 18 teaches that one is cursed who believes that it is impossible to keep God's Law. Canon 24 states that one who insists that works are only the fruits or signs of justification and not the cause or the increase of justification is accursed of God. Moreover, Trent in Canon 23 insists that to teach that one cannot lose salvation after being justified is accursed.

Let's consider what the proponents of the Federal Vision have taught about the Law of God as it relates to the Gospel. Rich Lusk has taught that the doers of the Law will be justified. He says that the Law did not require perfect obedience. What is so important about that? If God emphatically states the doers of the Law will be justified, then this means that the Law cannot demand perfect obedience; otherwise, no one could keep it for justification. Lusk goes on to say that God doesn't demand 100% on an ethics test; God is only concerned about the direction of our lives and that God will judge us according to "soft justice" or "fatherly justice." He says that the Bible teaches that there have been righteous people throughout the Bible. Zacahrias and Elizabeth (the parents of John the Baptist) are showcased as examples of those who God favors because of their holy but imperfect lives. In other words, it was good enough for God to accept them as righteous. Lusk goes on to speak of an initial justification which is through Christ, but we then need an obedient life in order to obtain final justification. He is emphatic that James 2 does not teach that works simply demonstrate justification but that works are necessary for justification. All of these statements that I have just made about Lusk have been documented from his direct quotes (See footnotes 1-10 in chapter 7). Lusk states that the Law was a pre-Christian revelation of the Gospel, that it was a witness to the Gospel, that the Law was a type of grace that came later in Christ, and that the transition from Moses to Christ was a transition from grace to grace (See quote on page 299). He agrees totally with Trent that one can lose his salvation after being justified. Rich Lusk stated that his views and Rome's views fit together like fire and water. I am sorry but Rich Lusk stands convicted of all charges. Lusk and Rome are identical in their salient points.

Let's now consider Steve Schlissel and his views as they stack up with Rome. He has been quite adamant about his opposition to Luther's law/gospel dichotomy as it pertains to justification. Schlissel considered this dichotomy a false teaching (See quote on page 302). He doesn't like "what must I do to be saved?" He likes "what does the Lord require of me?" Schlissel then goes into a long discussion of what it means to keep the Law. He has emphatically said that the Law is the gospel. He made this comment in his *Christian Renewal* magazine interview. He has said that the Law promised forgiveness, that in the Law we find grace abounding to sinners (See quote on page 307). Schlissel does not believe that Romans 3 teaches total depravity. Now why did Schlissel assault this doctrine? He must have righteous people in the Old Testament who can keep the Law in order to be justified. Schlissel says that nothing in the Bible teaches a kind of faith that does not obey. Obedience and faith, he says, are the same thing (See quote on top of page 316). He would probably insist that he is not a Romanist, but the only difference between him and Rome is in the definition of faith. Rome speaks of works plus faith; while Schlissel says works is the essence of faith. One could call Schlissel's views a hybridization of Roman Catholic doctrine, but in the final analysis, they fundamentally agree. Both systems teach a works salvation paradigm. Schlissel made it a point on his website that obedience is not merely a test or evidence of saving faith; it is inseparably bound up in its character (See quote on pages 320-321). Schlissel and Canon 24 of Trent totally agree. Schlissel has taught that the story of the young rich ruler is not that Jesus was showing that he could not keep the Law but that he could keep the Law. This fits in very well with Canon 18. Schlissel emphatically states that law keepers and believers are exact equivalents. Those are Schlissel's precise words (See quote on page 322). Steve Schlissel stands guilty as charged of promoting a form of Romanism.

We can conclude that the Federal Vision is not a precise rendition of Roman Catholic doctrine on justification, but it is a definite hybridization of it. Fundamentally, both systems advocate a works salvation. Both systems view works as intricately linked with justification. Both systems believe that men are justified at their water baptisms. Both systems believe that the imputation of Christ's righteousness is not what totally saves us. Both systems believe that the Law of God does not demand perfect obedience. Both systems believe that justified men can lose their salvation. Is there any wonder that some people who have bought into Federal Vision theology have gone back to Romanism? I am afraid that the defection will continue unless the Reformed world deals decisively with the cancerous growth within its body. Federal Vision theology must be eradicated from our Reformed communities before it destroys our churches and the souls of men.

Chapter 11

Greg Bahnsen is Not in the Federal Vision Camp

This may seem to be an odd chapter in this book. Why a chapter dealing with Greg Bahnsen? He died in 1995 long before this controversy arose in the Reformed community. My main reason for including this as a chapter is to vindicate the name of Greg Bahnsen for various reasons. First, his son, David Bahnsen, has publicly stated that his father, if still alive, would be sympathetic to the Federal Vision. Second, the institution that he was associated with in California has been captured by the Federal Vision camp; therefore, when people think of this institution and Bahnsen's name, they will think that Bahnsen held the same theological views. And third, some critics of the Federal Vision think that a presuppositional apologetic approach lends one to be given to Federal Vision theology.

Unfortunately, in August 2003, the Southern California Center for Christian Studies sponsored a summer conference and invited Norman Shepherd to be one of its speakers. In the lectures that Shepherd gave, from which I have quoted significant portions in chapter 4, he openly denied the active obedience of Christ in the imputation of Christ's righteousness to the believer. This was a major further development in the view of the Federal Vision. To deny the imputation of Christ's righteousness is a heretical position. This is the study center that Bahnsen started many years ago. This institution was a tremendous champion for the Reformed Faith during Bahnsen's lifetime. For me to see this institution under the flag of the Federal Vision is quite disheartening. David Bahnsen enthusiastically introduced Norman Shepherd at this conference. It was at Bahnsen's institution that this heresy of the Federal Vision was further propagated.

I am desirous of defending Greg Bahnsen's good name. I personally benefited from Bahnsen's teaching over the past 30 years. When I was a student at

Reformed Theological Seminary during the mid to late 1970's, I took apologetics and ethics under Greg Bahnsen. In subsequent years, I benefited greatly from his brilliant scholarship. He was truly one of the greatest theological minds of the 20th Century. In his later years just prior to his death, I had the privilege to be a personal friend of Greg Bahnsen. Even those who did not agree with him in several of his teachings (e.g. theonomy), still recognized that there were few men who could match his intellect and his ability to bring to bear the Scripture on virtually any issue. For his son to champion the cause of the Federal Vision is discouraging to me, for Bahnsen's institution to be in the Federal Vision camp is distressing, and for Covenant Media Foundation (the organization handling the distribution of Bahnsen's audio tapes) to be in the Federal Vision camp is equally disheartening. It is most discouraging because I **know** that Greg Bahnsen would not have been sympathetic in any way with the theology of the Federal Vision. If he were alive today, he probably would have written a book similar to mine, exposing the heresies of the Federal Vision. Why do I say that I know this to be the case? Before I answer that question, let me quote his son David Bahnsen. In 2003 David Bahnsen wrote an article titled "*Greg Bahnsen and the Auburn Avenue Controversy.*" In this article, David Bahnsen writes:

> To begin, I suppose of the truly difficult things in writing this article, is that in one very real sense, the answer to how my late father "would have felt" about the current controversy should be, "Who cares?" He was a mere man, albeit a bright one, and he did not have any divine intercessions when he was alive, and if he were here today he would have none. Nonetheless, I have received over 250 emails in the last year regarding people's opinion on what my father would feel, should feel, did feel, etc. There is a sense in which I can relate to the people that have wondered about such a thing, because I do know that I hold him in such high regard (not **just** as a father, but also as a thinker), that whenever I do feel confused on some theological, ethical, philosophical, or political issue I often find myself wondering "WWDD" (i.e. what would dad do?)... I especially get tempted to think this way when it comes to matters of division amongst people whom I deeply respect. There is a naïve and tender part of me that just wishes to myself, "Dad, come down here and straighten this thing out."[1]

---

[1] David Bahnsen, *Greg Bahnsen and the Auburn Avenue Controversy,* February 2003. Found at www.cmfnow.com/AAPC/Bahnsen.html.

In the 1990's I had the privilege to meet Greg Bahnsen's sons. I had met several of them briefly when they were very young children when Greg Bahnsen had his short tenure at Reformed Theological Seminary in Jackson, Mississippi. I have had the opportunity to meet David Bahnsen when I was living in Atlanta, Georgia. I felt for David and his other siblings when their father died in 1995 at the relatively young age of 46. I sensed with many other Reformed friends that the world had lost a great champion for the Christian Faith. I too greatly miss Greg Bahnsen's physical presence with us. He was truly a unique, gifted man. David, if I could speak directly to you, I would say to you, "You don't need to have your daddy come down from heaven to help us sort out this controversy; your daddy left a legacy behind. He left his books and his audio tapes as a legacy for us to appreciate, just like several other great Reformers of the past like Calvin and Owen." All we need to do is read Greg Bahnsen's books and listen to his audiotapes and we would know what he thought. This is why I am including this chapter in this book. There is no mystery what Greg Bahnsen taught on the issues surrounding the Federal Vision. My primary source will be quotes from his magnum opus, *Theonomy In Christian Ethics*. In his book, Greg Bahnsen, unmistakably sets forth his understanding of the nature of the gospel as it relates to the law of God.

I **cannot agree** with the conclusion that his son David Bahnsen draws when he writes:

> I have no pretensions that there are not serious theological matters here that need to be addressed, further clarified, and continually exegeted. However, I feel that were my father alive, he would want that exegesis, that discussion, that clarification, etc. to take place in a context of love, and grace, and benefit of the doubt...I do not deny that the Monroe men are endorsing a paradigm shift. As a matter of fact, I embrace it and am certain my father would as well.[2]

Before I demonstrate that Greg Bahnsen would not have embraced Federal Vision theology, I want to quote from some others who think that he did endorse it. In April 2003, Randy Booth (who heads Covenant Media Foundation), wrote an article titled *"Caution and Respect in Controversy."* In this article Randy Booth quotes Greg Bahnsen from one of Bahnsen's lectures on Calvin's Institutes. The purpose of Booth quoting from Bahnsen is to demonstrate that Bahnsen agreed with Norman Shepherd on James 2. Booth quotes Bahnsen as saying:

---

[2] Bahnsen, *Greg Bahnsen and the Auburn Avenue Controversy.*

I think (this) is rather convoluted … let me very briefly point out, some people will say James can't mean the word justify in a forensic sense, because then he would contradict Paul. Paul says we are justified by faith, not works. James says we are justified by works. So if they both mean "justify" in the forensic sense, there is a contradiction. Well, I don't think so, because in Galatians 5:6 Paul teaches exactly what James does. Paul says we are justified by faith working by love. We are justified by working, active, living faith. I think that's what James is teaching. They mean exactly the same thing. But nevertheless some people have insisted- and this has been a bone of controversy in my denomination even, because a professor at Westminster Seminary insisted James means this in the forensic sense.

Now … people who don't like that say, It is to be taken in the demonstrative sense. The problem is, the demonstrative sense of the word justify means "to show someone to be righteous," and that doesn't relieve the contradiction between James and Paul, because Paul in Romans 4 looks at Abraham as an example of how God justifies the ungodly. James is say-ing, Look at how God justifies someone demonstrated as godly. The contradiction is not relieved. And so what you really get – and this is crucial, this is a crucial point- modern interpreters who don't like what I am suggesting and what Professor Shepherd is suggesting end up saying that to justi-fy in James 2 really means "to demonstrate justification," not to "demonstrate righteousness." That is, they make the word to justify mean "to justify the fact that I'm justified." And the word never means that. That's utterly contrived. It means either "to declare righteous" or "to demonstrate righteous" It does not mean "to justify that one's justified."

… Am I making myself clear? I'm suggesting that the reason Paul and James are not contrary to one another is because the only kind of faith that will justify us is working faith, and the only kind of justification ever presented in the Bible after the Fall is a justi-fication by working faith, a faith that receives its merit from God and proceeds to work as a regenerated, new person.[3]

---

[3] Randy Booth, *"Caution and Respect In Controversy,"* Booth quotes Greg Bahnsen's 1986 audio tape on Calvin's Institutes. <www.cmf.com/AAPC/controversy.html>

Greg Bahnsen attended a class with Roger Wagner that was taught by Norman Shepherd at Westminster Seminary. Because of this, Booth interviewed Wagner to see what he thought Bahnsen would believe about the Federal Vision controversy. Booth quotes Roger Wagner's reply:

> I'm absolutely sure if Greg were still with us, he'd be square-ly on the "Shepherd side" of this issue (if I may use that short-hand in a "non-partisan" sense), and trying to get Joe M. and others of his opinion to erase the "line in the sand" they've drawn among the confessionally Reformed Reconstructionists.[4]

Those in the Federal Vision camp think that this comment from Greg Bahnsen demonstrates that if alive he would be clearly on the Federal Vision side of the controversy. I do not think this to be the case at all. The Greg Bahnsen quote that Randy Booth is referring to is not how Shepherd views James 2 in his book *The Call of Grace*. Bahnsen does mention in his quote that Shepherd was teaching that the meaning of the word "justified" was still a forensic meaning. Let's assume that is the case. This still does not mean that Bahnsen's quote supports Shepherd's views that reemerged in the late 1990's and to the present. The way that Shepherd now expresses his views on works as they relate to jus-tification is not what Bahnsen stated in the above quote and are not in conform-ity with what Bahnsen wrote in *Theonomy In Christian Ethics*. Let's examine closely Bahnsen's quote. When Bahnsen states that justification is a justifica-tion by working faith, a faith that receives its merit from God and proceeds to work as a regenerated, new person, this is not what Shepherd and the rest of the Federal Vision has said about justification. Shepherd has defined saving faith as "the obedience of faith." In his book *The Call of Grace* Shepherd made the comment about James 2 that *"the faith credited to Abraham as righteous-ness was a living and active faith."*[5] Shepherd also stated, *"In fact, Genesis 15:6 says that Abraham's faith was so significant that it was credited to him as righteousness! If so, then righteousness was a condition to be met, and faith met that condition."*[6]

Bahnsen speaks about a faith that **proceeds to work as a regenerated, new person.** When he said the word "proceed" Bahnsen separated himself in what Shepherd came to articulate. Bahnsen has said nothing different than what the Westminster Confession of Faith says in chapter 11:2. This section states: *"Faith, thus receiving and resting on Christ and his righteousness, is the alone*

---

[4] Booth, *"Caution and Respect In Controversy."*

[5] Shepherd, *The Call of Grace*, p. 16.

[6] Shepherd, *The Call of Grace*, p. 15.

instrument of justification, yet is it not alone in the person justified, but is ever accompanied with all other saving graces, and is no dead faith, but worketh by love." The proof texts given for the last phrases in this section are James 2:17, 22, 26 and Galatians 5:6. Bahnsen was saying that saving faith is a living, active faith. Now, when Shepherd says that faith is a living, active faith he means something different because he means that the essence of faith is obedience to God's law. This is a view that Bahnsen utterly rejects in *Theonomy in Christian Ethics.*

Let's consider what Greg Bahnsen said on James 2 in *Theonomy in Christian Ethics.* Bahnsen states:

> James 2:23 says, "The scripture was fulfilled saying, Abraham believed God, and it was imputed to him for righteousness." The quotation from the older Testament to which James alludes is Genesis 15:6; yet the activity of Abraham that James has in mind is Abraham's willingness to offer up Isaac (James 2:21), and this does not occur in Genesis until chapter 22. Abraham's activity does not fulfill a prophecy, for the statement in Genesis 15:6 is an assertion, not a prediction. What James tells us, therefore, is that Abraham **confirmed** his imputed righteousness by obedience to God; this is the theme of James 2:14-26.[7] (Emphasis Bahnsen)

There is a very glaring difference between Bahnsen, Shepherd, and Schlissel. Bahnsen says that Abraham's obedience was not the essence of faith; it was not "the obedience of faith" as the Federal Vision purports. Bahnsen says that Abraham's faith was an **imputed righteousness.** I have demonstrated in this book that Shepherd and the rest of the Federal Vision emphatically denies the imputation of Christ's righteousness to the believer. Bahnsen says that Abraham's obedience **confirms** his imputed righteousness. He did not say that the essence of Abraham's faith was obedience, which was the cause of his justification. What did Bahnsen say was the meaning of justification in James 2 that Randy Booth quotes from? Bahnsen says that justification means either "to declare righteous" or "to demonstrate righteous." Bahnsen is saying that Abraham's obedience demonstrated the imputed righteousness that he possessed. Bahnsen is clearly within the parameters of the Reformed Faith. Bahnsen is clearly Confessional. Shepherd is not!

---

[7] Greg Bahnsen, *Theonomy In Christian Ethics.* (Nutley, N.J: The Craig Press, 1977), p. 69.

In my book, I have set forth the Federal Vision's understanding of Romans 4:5-8 which is a complete distortion of this portion of Scripture. The Federal Vision maintains that Abraham's faith was fundamentally obedience to the covenant demands which is why he was justified. Is this what Bahnsen believes? I don't think so. Bahnsen states:

> So important is the law in our salvation that our justification is grounded in Christ's obedience to it (Rom. 5:17-19); we're saved by grace no doubt, but by a grace made possible through the lawful obedience of God's Son. Our **faith in Christ** is counted for righteousness, thereby justifying us freely by God's grace **through Christ's righteousness**, which is declared for the remission of sins (Rom. 4: 5-8; 3:22-25; 5:17-19)...Christ's atoning work, then, does not entail the relaxation of the law's demand for righteousness, but rather accentuates it. Christ, who suffered as the righteous for the unrighteous (I Pet. 3:18), is the believer's righteousness (I Cor. 1:30).[8] (Emphasis Bahnsen)

This quote is absolutely devastating to the Federal Vision. Every one of the major figures that I have quoted from in the Federal Vision camp would disagree with Bahnsen's quote. Remember, the Federal Vision has denied the active obedience of Christ imputed to the sinner. Bahnsen champions the Reformed doctrine of Christ's active obedience as good as any one has expressed. Would Bahnsen be siding with the Federal Vision if he were alive? Absolutely not!

Bahnsen continues to make very helpful comments about the relationship of the law to the justified man. Bahnsen says:

> It is the **condemning** aspect of the law which is nullified by Christ's perfect obedience to that law; the law itself with all its integrity, remains in force while our **guilt** is removed...Furthermore, the Holy Spirit causes the believer in his sanctification to grow in **likeness** and obedience to Christ...Union with Christ, which underlies our salvation, entails the requirement of sharing His righteous character – of **identifying** with His lawful obedience.[9] (Emphasis Bahnsen)

---

[8] Bahnsen, *Theonomy In Christian Ethics,* p. 154.

[9] Bahnsen, *Theonomy In Christian Ethics*, pp. 154-155.

Just like the Westminster Confession of Faith states, Bahnsen agrees that sanctification flows out of justification as an inevitable reality. He does not blur the distinction between justification and sanctification. Just what role does the Law of God play in our justification according to Bahnsen? We know what the Federal Vision says. Schlissel and Lusk openly stated that the law is the gospel, and the Gospel is Law. Schlissel derided Luther for what he calls Luther's false dichotomy between the Law and the Gospel. We recall that Schlissel stated that good works are not the fruit or evidence of justifying faith but that it is the very essence of faith. This is why Schlissel stated that the Law keeper and the believer are identical. Let's see what Bahnsen has to say about this.

Bahnsen states, *"Using the law as a means of salvation is high handed flattery and disdain for God's grace."*[10] Bahnsen describes the fundamental problem of the Pharisees. *"The Pharisees attempted to justify* **themselves** *by means of the law"...Justification was not by the law in the Older Testament, and the scribes of the law should have known this fact well."* [11] (Emphasis Bahnsen) Bahnsen discusses people like Abel, Enoch, Noah, and Abraham. The Federal Vision has told us that there were righteous people that God recognized and rewarded with justification. Steve Schlissel and Rich Lusk make a big point of this. The Federal Vision says that men can keep the Mosaic Law, and God expected them to keep it for their justification. The Federal Vision interpreted the story of the young rich ruler as one where the failure of the rich young ruler as an example of one who failed to keep the law as he should. Jesus was encouraging him to keep the Law in order to gain eternal life as if he could really keep it. Bahnsen states:

> Abel, Enoch, and Noah were all clear illustrations that man gains favor with God, not by works, but by faith (Gen. 4:4; 5:24; 6:8,9 with Heb. 11:4-7)...Genesis 15:6 clearly teaches that righteousness was **imputed by faith**: "then he believed in God, and it was imputed to him for righteousness." [12] (Emphasis Bahnsen)

According to some, Bahnsen would support the Federal Vision if he were here. This says that he totally disagrees with the Federal Vision. These same historical figures that the Federal Vision point toward as examples of righteous who are justified because of their righteous works, Bahnsen uses to demonstrate that they were justified by faith and not by works. Bahnsen says, "The law does **not**

---

[10] Bahnsen, *Theonomy In Christian Ethics*, p. 90.

[11] Bahnsen, *Theonomy In Christian Ethics*, p. 125.

[12] Bahnsen, *Theonomy In Christian Ethics*, p. 126.

save a man, but it **does** show him **why** he needs to be saved and **how** he is to walk after he is saved."[13] (Emphasis Bahnsen)

We know from Federal Vision theology that the Mosaic Law never demanded perfection. We learned from Rich Lusk that Moses even said that the Law was easy to keep. We learned that God, on Judgment Day, will judge with "soft justice" being concerned not that we score a 100% on an ethics test but that we are loyal. What would Bahnsen say to this? He says:

> As the sinner compares his life to the demands of the law he finds himself sold under sin and lost. The magnitude of his sinfulness is glaring because "it stands written that accursed is everyone who continues not in **all** the things having been written in the book of the law to do them" (Gal. 3:10 and "whoever keeps all the law, but stumbles in **one point** has become guilty of all" (James 2:10). The law, then, works wrath against the sinner (Rom. 4:15). Hence it should be plain that "no man is justified by the law in the sight of God (Gal. 3:11; cf. 2:16). To use the law as a means of justification is an unlawful use of the law (cf. I Tim. 1:8).[14] (Emphasis Bahnsen)

Bahnsen says that the sinner is overwhelmed by his inability to keep the law because the law **demands perfect obedience.** No, the Federal Vision cannot claim Bahnsen on this one either. Bahnsen continues:

> Christ's perfect obedience to the law of God secures our release for the necessity of personally keeping the law as a condition of justification. "And may be found in Him, not having a righteousness of my own derived from the law, but that which is through faith in Christ, the righteousness which comes from God on the basis of faith" (Phil. 3:9, NASV). Our righteousness before God must be that which is **imputed** to us, the righteousness of Christ who was sinless before the law ... Christ justifies us from all the things which the **Mosaic law was not able** to justify us (Acts 13:38f; cf. Rom. 3:28; 10:4; Acts 2:38; 10:43).[15] (Emphasis Bahnsen)

---

[13] Bahnsen, *Theonomy In Christian Ethics*, p. 127.

[14] Bahnsen, *Theonomy In Christian Ethics*, p. 128

[15] Bahnsen, *Theonomy In Christian Ethics*, pp. 128- 129.

Again, Bahnsen expresses his belief in the active obedience of Christ; he is not supposed to believe this because the Federal Vision denies it, and Bahnsen is supposed to be in their camp. Moreover, Bahnsen is supposed to believe that the Mosaic Law is easy to keep. Why does Bahnsen say that the Mosaic Law was not able to justify us? It is because the Bible teaches that the law cannot justify us. Bahnsen continues:

> Justification must be **by the law** according to the **Pharisaical** converts (v.5); this squares with what we know about the doctrine of the Pharisees.[16] (Emphasis Bahnsen)

This statement by Bahnsen would indicate that my chapter 7, "Modern Day Judaizers," would be appropriate for the Federal Vision proponents. Remember, the Law is the Gospel, and the Gospel is the Law according to the Federal Vision. Bahnsen discusses Paul's attitude about the Law and the Holy Spirit's role in Law obedience:

> The law had executed Paul because he was unable to keep it; the letter killed him (cf. 2 Cor. 3:6) ... Now the law can no longer manipulate him, for he is a dead servant; nothing more can be exacted of him. It did not supply the power to obey...Only the Holy Spirit of God can bring power to obey to the sinner, and that Holy Spirit was received not by law-works but by faith (3:2). The law is simply not a quickening power; it is without power because of sin (Rom. 8:3), and therefore unable to impart life and righteousness (Gal. 3:21). Thus anyone who seeks justification before God out of obedience to the law lies under the law's curse. Paul directs this comment against the self-righteous legalism of the Judaziers and Jewish rabbis. They should have known that nobody shall be justified by the law, for the Older Testament clearly said that the righteous shall live by **faith...** If those individuals who want to be under the law as a way of salvation would truly **listen to the law**, then they would not submit to the Judaizers and their slave principle ... Galatians 5:4 make it unmistakably clear that Paul has been dealing in this epistle with the way of **justification**; if one takes the law as his salvation, then he has precluded grace.[17] (Emphasis Bahnsen)

---

[16] Bahnsen, *Theonomy In Christian Ethics*, p. 130.

[17] Bahnsen, *Theonomy In Christian Ethics*, pp. 132- 133.

This sounds like Bahnsen would agree with my assessment of the Federal Vision as a heresy since he viewed the Judaizers as heretics. And what was a Judaizer? Someone who believed the Law could be kept for our justification, which is identical to what the Federal Vision teaches. Bahnsen is drawing a distinction between Law and faith, which Schlissel says was Luther's broken lever. The moment that Bahnsen drew a contrast between Law and faith, he has distanced himself from the Federal Vision's meaning of faith as "the obedience of faith." Bahnsen further distances himself from Federal Vision theology when he says:

> Scripture uniformly views the law as a standard of righteousness after which we should pattern our sanctification and Christian life, but **justification** is never by our obedience to the law (after the fall of Adam and Eve). The Pharisees and Judaizers both missed this important truth and thereby unlawfully abused the law of God. It is necessary for us to **distinguish** between **two types** of forensic religion: that of Judaistic legalism and that of the Scriptures. In the former **self-righteousness** is generated. In the latter Christ perfectly obeys the law's demands and qualifies as an atoning substitute for those who have violated the law, and then in gratitude to God for His grace Christians pattern their lives after the laws as the expression of God's holy will. Before the law the sinner is guilty and powerless to obey its demands, but in the gospel he is forgiven and empowered (cf. Rom. 3:19-26; 8:1). When Paul says that we are not under the law but under the Spirit, he has in mind that we are no longer obligated to the law in regard to the accomplishment of righteousness or doing of God's commandments; instead, we are dependent upon the Spirit who renders us capable of doing what God demands (cf. Gal. 5:18 with Rom. 8:4). A proper understanding of the law's abiding **validity** must be accompanied with a recognition of the law's **inabilities**.[18] (Emphasis Bahnsen)

According to the Federal Vision the Mosaic Law can be kept. Again, Lusk says it is not that hard to keep (See last paragraph on page 296). Bahnsen said that justification is **never** by obedience to the law. Shepherd, in his thesis 23, said that obedience to the commandments is necessary for continuing in the state of justification (See last quote on page 45). Bahnsen's quote should shed much

---

[18] Bahnsen, *Theonomy In Christian Ethics*, pp. 135- 136.

light on Randy Booth's assertion that Bahnsen would have been a supporter of the Federal Vision if he were alive today. This is nonsense! Bahnsen has clearly stated that obedience to the law has **nothing** to do with justification but everything to do with sanctification. He made it very clear that we have a choice between two types of forensic justification: we can choose the self-righteousness of the Judaizers, or we can choose the imputation of Christ's perfect obedience. The Federal Vision believes in the first according to Bahnsen – the self righteousness of the Judaizers. If it isn't clear enough yet, Bahnsen in speaking about Paul's statements in Romans 7 says this:

> He refutes his antinomian opponents who would make him as a minister of the new covenant a despiser for grace. But since the law came from God, Paul appropriately states that it came in glory. Nevertheless, the law is not to be exalted at the expense of the gospel. The gospel far **excels** in glory because it has renewing **power.** Although Moses' glory faded, the glory of the good news in the face of Jesus Christ does not (2 Cor. 4:6).[19] (Emphasis Bahnsen)

Schlissel called Luther's view as false, but Bahnsen has just affirmed Luther's dichotomy of Law and Gospel in terms of justification; thereby, he is implicated by inference in Schlissel's condemnation. Greg Bahnsen's son, David said that his father thought very highly of Steve Schlissel's ministry in New York City. Does this mean that Bahnsen would have agreed with Schlissel on this controversy? Absolutely not! There is no question that Bahnsen would have called Schlissel and all of the Federal Vision proponents to repentance for having betrayed the Gospel. Bahnsen stated:

> Consequently we glory in the gospel of Christ and His Spirit as accomplishing what the law could not; that is, we magnify the gospel as the **power of God unto salvation** unto all who believe, for therein is revealed the **righteousness of God unto our justification (Rom. 1:16f).**[20] (Emphasis Bahnsen)

I have proved that Bahnsen believed in the active obedience of Christ in that Christ's righteousness is imputed to us as our righteousness. This contradicts the Federal Vision. As I pointed out in earlier chapters, the Federal Vision is very deceptive in this regard because they will say that they believe in an active

[19] Bahnsen, *Theonomy In Christian Ethics*, p. 136.
[20] Bahnsen, *Theonomy In Christian Ethics*, p. 137.

obedience too. They believe that Jesus actively kept the Law for Himself in order to qualify as the Redeemer. The Federal Vision does not believe in an active obedience of Jesus in **our stead.** Rich Lusk said that Dr. Morton Smith was entirely wrong when Dr. Smith said – "*It is Christ's active fulfillment of the law that becomes the ground of our acceptance with God. It is this righteousness that is imputed to us*" (See last paragraph on page 145). Lusk said that Smith's view was problematic, and went on to say that Jesus' thirty-three years of Law keeping being imputed to us was unnecessary. Lusk said that there is no notion of this in the Bible (See second and third paragraphs on page 146).

Greg Bahnsen has something quite explicit to say about the Federal Vision's concept of no need of Christ's righteousness being imputed to as. Bahnsen states:

> We have no reason to hope that God, who immutably righteous, will lower His ethical norms in order to accommodate our unrighteousness. However, God does credit the perfect obedience of Christ to our account, thereby being just and the justifier of His people (cf. Rom. 3:26). Herein the law takes on a two-fold significance for Christians; **first,** obedience to the law by the Messiah plays an integral part in the accomplishment of salvation, and **second** followers of Christ thus have set before them the example and goal of lawful living by their Lord.[21] (Emphasis Bahnsen)

Bahnsen has just refuted Rich Lusk's views that God doesn't require a 100% on an ethics test, and that God's final judgment will be a "soft judgment." He continues:

> God could only forgive sins in a manner which is consistent with His holiness; in salvation righteousness and peace must kiss each other (Ps. 85:9f). Consequently, salvation with justification is impossible, and justification without righteousness is inconceivable. There must be perfect righteousness in the reign of God's grace for our salvation. Therefore, Scripture centers on the **obedience** of Christ- both active and passive – because it is the necessary requirement for the full justification of sinners.[22] (Emphasis Bahnsen)

---

[21] Bahnsen, *Theonomy In Christian Ethics*, p. 149.

[22] Bahnsen, *Theonomy In Christian Ethics*, p. 152.

The extent of Christ's righteous obedience is seen in the fact
that He both actively obeyed the prescriptive as well as pas-
sively obeying the penal requirements of the law, the former
in order to qualify as a substitute, the latter in order to atone
for sin. Having obeyed the law in its moral requirements in
order that His perfect righteousness might be imputed to us.
He came under the law's curse and condemnation so that our
transgressions could be forgiven.[23]

Therefore, although **our own** obedience to the law cannot be
used as a way of justification, we are saved by the **imputed**
obedience of the Messiah (I Cor. 1:30; Phil. 3:9), an obedience to **both** the prescriptive and penal requirements of
God's law. With its customary accuracy the Westminster
Confession states: The Lord Jesus, by His perfect obedience,
and sacrifice of Himself, which He through the eternal Spirit,
once offered up unto God, hath fully satisfied the justice of
His father; and purchased, not only reconciliation, but an
everlasting inheritance in the kingdom of heaven, for all
those whom the Father hath given unto Him" (Chapter 8, section 5).[24] (Emphasis Bahnsen)

So important is the law in our salvation that our justification
is grounded in Christ's obedience to it (Rom. 5:17-19); we
are saved by grace no doubt, but by a grace made possible
through the lawful obedience of God's Son. Our **faith in
Christ** is counted for righteousness, thereby justifying us
freely by God's grace **through Christ's righteousness,**
which is declared for the remission of our sins (Rom. 4:5-8;
3:22-25; 5:17-19).[25] (Emphasis Bahnsen)

Metaphorically speaking, Bahnsen just put the "blow torch" to the Federal
Vision's denial of Christ's active obedience. Bahnsen has clearly expressed the
historic Reformed view, which is not the view of the Federal Vision. Bahnsen
probably would have led the charge in the condemnation of the Federal Vision
if he were still alive. Bahnsen moves on to discuss the role of obedience in the
Christian life as a means of sanctification, not justification. Bahnsen states:

---

[23] Bahnsen, *Theonomy In Christian Ethics*, p. 152.

[24] Bahnsen, *Theonomy In Christian Ethics*, p. 153.

[25] Bahnsen, *Theonomy In Christian Ethics*, p. 154.

Furthermore, the Holy Spirit causes the believer in his sanctification to grow in **likeness** and obedience to Christ, "to the measure of the stature which belongs to the fullness of Christ (Eph. 4:13; cf. v. 15; Gal. 4:19) ... Union with Christ, which underlies our salvation, entails the requirement of sharing His righteous character – of **identifying** with His lawful obedience...**Those who have been saved by Christ's obedience must strive to imitate the same obedient spirit**. "Hereby we know that we are in him: he that saith that he abideth in him ought himself also to walk even as he walked.[26] (Emphasis Bahnsen)

There is much in this quote that refutes Federal Vision theology. First, Bahnsen distinguishes justification from sanctification. Our obedience in keeping the commandments is the fruit or evidence of our justification. Notice that Bahnsen says that the believer must strive to imitate Christ's obedience. Union with Christ entails being found righteous in Christ and then obeying Him by the power of the Holy Spirit. Our obedience flows out of Christ's obedience. Bahnsen is in total agreement with the Westminster Confession's statement that obedience on our part is the accompanying grace that flows out of our justification (WCF 11:2). Bahnsen makes it crystal clear when he says:

The removal of man's guilt and his securing of a right standing in the sight of God comes, not by his own personal works of the law, but only through the imputation of Christ's righteousness (His perfect obedience, both active and passive, to every demand of God's law). The sinner's legal condition is changed by God's judicial act, grounded in the "alien" righteousness of Christ, so that God's people are entitled to the eternal enjoyments of God presence.[27]

To summarize what has been said to this point, we can say that salvation is not exhaustively circumscribed by God's pardon of, and imputation of Christ's righteousness to, the sinner, salvation continues beyond the **point** of justification into the **process** of sanctification, a process which begins with a **definitive break** with the bondage of sinful depravity and matures by **progressively preparing** the Christian to enjoy the internal purifying of his moral condition ... It is the

---

[26] Bahnsen, *Theonomy In Christian Ethics*, p. 155.

[27] Bahnsen, *Theonomy In Christian Ethics*, p. 157.

perfect obedience of God's Son that is imputed to the
Christian in justification, and sanctification can be understood as a progressive growth toward the **personal realization** of that level of righteousness which has been imputed to
the believer.[28] (Emphasis Bahnsen)

I have demonstrated in earlier chapters that the Federal Vision believes in a
process justification. It argues for an **initial** justification and a **final** justification. Rich Lusk said that justification is a dynamic fluid concept. Bahnsen
utterly refutes this false theology. Bahnsen affirms the historic Reformed position as set forth in the Westminster Confession when he emphasizes that justification is a **point** reality while sanctification is a **process.** He would have been
appalled with the Federal Vision's blurring of this distinction. Bahnsen continued to emphasize over and over that our justification is rooted in the imputation
of Christ's righteousness to us. He understood that we can't be saved without
this imputation. The Federal Vision, namely Norman Shepherd, insists that it
is only the passive obedience of Christ that saves us. Bahnsen continues to dif-
ferentiate between justification and sanctification:

This inescapable requirement of holiness or sanctification is
not contradictory to salvation by grace through faith (Eph.
2:8, 9); we are not saved **by** obedience, but **unto** obedience.[29]
(Emphasis Bahnsen)

David Bahnsen and others in the Federal Vision believed that Greg Bahnsen
would have enthusiastically endorsed Steve Schlissel's views of the Law. This
is categorically incorrect. Greg Bahnsen just stated that we are not saved **by**
obedience, but **unto** obedience. Steve Schlissel has said:

Obedience is not merely a test or evidence of saving faith; it
is inseparably bound up in its character. There is no disobedient yet saving faith. It is not faith plus obedience, but the obedience of faith.[30]

Bahnsen would also take great exception to Schlissel's comments that the law
and the gospel are identical. Bahnsen was careful to relate the two but make a
fine distinction:

---

[28] Bahnsen, *Theonomy In Christian Ethics*, pp. 160- 161.

[29] Bahnsen, , *Theonomy In Christian Ethics* p. 162.

[30] Steve Schlissel *"Living the Reformed Faith in the Real World: True Confessions,"*

In Biblical perspective, grace and promise are not antithetical
to law and demand. The law and the gospel both aim at the
same thing; what the law was unable to bestow upon us, the
gospel has the power to grant. Hence, Paul can say, "Is the
law contrary to the promises of God? May it never be! (Gal.
3:21).[31]

It is Schlissel who believes that the law can be kept. He insists that this is the
real lesson of the story of the young rich ruler. This is why Schlissel says that
we are asking the wrong question if we ask, "What must I do to be saved?"
Rather Schlissel insists that we must rather ask, "What does the Lord require
of me?" He then says that the Law tells us what we must do to be saved – obey
it. If Bahnsen were alive with us today, he would surely say that Schlissel is a
modern day Judaizer.

Before I close this chapter on Bahnsen's views, I want to quote from a sermon
that Bahnsen gave on Romans 3:21-30. Regarding the necessity for righteousness outside of us, Bahnsen said:

All mankind comes under the judgment of God. And so if
your righteousness is that which is geared to the law, you are
lost. But now another kind of righteousness has been manifested. What a glorious mercy. "But now apart from the law
of God has manifested a righteousness' being witnessed by
the law and the prophets."[32]

And what is this righteousness that God has shown apart
from the law, apart from our efforts, apart from our obedience? He tells us in the next verse. "Even the righteousness
of God through faith in Jesus Christ unto all them that
believe...This is God's provision of the righteousness that He
requires. We said as we began this morning, God will not
change His mind. **God demands perfect righteousness**. He
won't violate His own justice. And so how can He possibly
justify sinners?[33] (Emphasis mine)

---

[31] Bahnsen, *Theonomy In Christian Ethics*, p. 183.

[32] Bahnsen, A sermon preached titled *Paul's View of the Law: Justified by Faith –
Romans 3:21-30.* Transcribed by Wayne Rogers for *The Counsel of Chalcedon.*
(April 2005), p. 3.

[33] Bahnsen's sermon on Romans 3:21-30.

Here is another source from Bahnsen that indicates that God's standard is a perfect standard. So much for Bahnsen agreeing with the Federal Vision on its view of the Law. To answer his own question, Bahnsen continues:

> Here is God's own provision of a righteousness that He requires, a righteousness apart from the law, apart from all of our effort – all of our effort – a righteousness that has nothing to do with any merit in you or in me, a righteousness that does not come because you have even in a small way lived up to what God wants... "But now apart from the law, a righteousness of God has been made manifest even the righteousness of God has been made manifest even the righteousness of God through faith in Jesus Christ unto all them that believe being justified freely by his grace." How utterly gracious on the part of God to save sinners. Vs 26 tells us, however, God accomplished that; this is the amazing thing. God accomplished giving this gift to sinners without violating His justice. He didn't send forth a righteousness which is contrary to the law.
>
> What God did was to supply His own Son. He provided a substitute. And He said "Instead of doing it on your own, trust My Son who did it for you. You didn't have to live up to the law. You cannot live up to the law. By the law you will be cursed. Instead of trying then to keep the law and gain my favor, then completely give up your own effort, and turn rather and trust simply in the accomplishment of My Son."[34]

Again, Bahnsen destroys forever the idea that the Law can be kept by us. The Federal Vision insists that it can be kept for our justification; it insists that Moses' Law was not that hard. Bahnsen recognizes the trouble with our sinful thinking when he says that we have a tendency to think that there must be something for us to do. Bahnsen states, "*You know sometimes we find that hard to do. Its kind of strange, there is this kind of works righteousness that's really got its tangles around our heart.*"[35] Yes, I totally sympathize with Bahnsen's statement. It's too bad that the Federal Vision doesn't realize this fact. It wants to resurrect that old works salvation mentality, which is what every other religion in the world does. The great demarcation between Christianity and other world religions is that Christianity is God reaching down to us rather than our

---

[34] Bahnsen's sermon on Romans 3:21-30.

[35] Bahnsen's sermon on Romans 3:21-30.

feeble attempts to please Him with our sin tainted efforts. The Federal Vision utterly destroys this demarcation and reduces Christianity to the level of all other pagan religions. Bahnsen makes a statement in his sermon that every Federal Vision teacher and sympathizer better heed:

> But, you see, if you approach going to church, if you approach a daily time of reading the word and prayer, if you approach witnessing, or works of mercy, or any obedience that you offer to God, and you should offer as much as you can give, but if you approach any of that in the attitude that somehow this will show that I am worthy rather than simply saying "My only hope is in Jesus Christ," **then you will be lost.**[36] (Emphasis mine)

I cannot get more serious in echoing what Bahnsen has just exhorted. In another chapter I mentioned that any of the Federal Vision preachers that really believe in their heart that obedience to the law is what maintains our justification are in serious trouble. Any person in their congregations who really believes this lie is in serious trouble. I mentioned that I don't want to be in Rich Lusk's shoes on Judgment Day who claims that God will render "soft justice." I don't want to be in Steve Schlissel's shoes either on Judgment Day who says that we have asked the wrong question, "What must I do to be saved?" but believed Schlissel's alternative – "What does the Lord require of me?" This is why Paul in Galatians 1:6-9 says that those who preach another gospel of works stand under the anathema of God. I know that if any Federal Vision teacher or sympathizer reads this, he may scoff saying, "Why that judgmental Otis ought to be ashamed for calling us heretics; he is totally wrong." Are you willing to bet your soul on it? I say with all seriousness; I plead with all who have come to embrace this false theology, please repent before its too late. Do not let your pride get in the way. If you don't, then on that great and terrible day, you will hear the horrendous words of Jesus – "Depart from Me; I never knew you."

Greg Bahnsen died in 1995 before the Federal Vision theology was unloaded publicly upon the Reformed world in January 2002. This does not mean that there were no instances prior to 2002. Shepherd's book was published in 2000, and Steve Schlissel mentions that he was met with resistance in Canada in late 2001. It was at the 2002 Auburn Avenue Pastors' Conference that major emphasis was given to this theology. Prior to Bahnsen's death in 1995 there were occasions where there were defections from Protestantism back to

---

[36] Bahnsen's sermon on Romans 3:21-30.

Roman Catholicism. Bahnsen warned us back then of Romanizing tendencies floating around in Protestantism. He says:

> This is important now and it's important for two reasons: first, in the most general use, the issues in the Protestant Reformation have not been fully resolved even yet and we have in our day and age, and I need to tell you this to warn you to protect your own souls, we have in our day and age people who at one time knew the grace of God, at least knew how to teach it, had been taught it, who knew that justification is by grace through faith in Christ, who have nevertheless left the Presbyterian church and gone back into Roman Catholicism ... How can any explanation be given to that kind of thing? Of course, I do pray with all my might that God will take away their confusion and restore the truth in the lives of these men who have done this, if that truth was ever there, genuinely there, in their hearts. But if there is self-conscious affirmation of the teaching of the Roman Catholic church, these men cannot be saved and neither can you and that's why I have to set this out very plainly for you this morning.[37]

I can only imagine what Bahnsen would think today. I have demonstrated in chapter 10 that the Federal Vision is a hybridization of Roman Catholicism. I mentioned in an earlier chapter that I know of at least three persons who have gone back into Roman Catholicism due to Federal Vision influence. The casualties will be even greater if we don't stop this movement in its tracks. Bahnsen talked about the errors of Rome:

> Justification is not causing someone to have sanctifying grace in his heart. The Roman Catholic church is simply wrong about this. For God to justify the sinner is for God to act as a judge and to declare the sinner righteous. God will also make the sinner righteous. You say, "Well then what difference does it make, Dr. Bahnsen; you admit what the Roman Catholics do, that those who are going to be saved need to lead new lives." Absolutely, But that isn't what the Roman Catholic church teaches. It teaches that those who lead new lives will be saved. Don't think that I am just drawing a very minor point in English grammar when I put it to you that way

---

[37] Bahnsen's sermon on Romans 3:21-30.

because on that point rests your salvation. It is a matter of eternal consequences that you get this right. God does make saved people to be holy but He does not save them by making them holy.[38]

This is what so many of us in the Reformed world have been trying to tell those in the Federal Vision. If you simply relegated good works as necessary evidence of a justified life then there would be no controversy. However, because the Federal Vision links obedience to God's Law to faith itself and to the act of justification, even calling justification a process, we have a controversy on our hands. Those in the Federal Vision have been somewhat dismayed by many sectors of the Reformed world who have reacted so strongly to their teaching. One Federal Vision proponent referred to my denomination, the RPCUS, as "those who came out swinging," after hearing the tapes at the 2002 AAPC. What did he expect? Did he think that we would not see their teaching as a direct challenge to the gospel? Obviously not.

In commenting about Romans 3:21, Bahnsen has said:

> And the reason why He maintains His justice in declaring you righteous though you yourself are not, is because in Christ your record has changed. You mustn't think that in Christ God has simply ignored your record. He has changed your record. Amazingly God now looks upon you as Jesus. He looks upon you as righteous. That's the point of verse 21, now apart from the law a righteousness of God has been manifested. God has set forth a different righteousness, not your own. Luther called it an "alien righteousness," and he had that right. It's alien because it doesn't belong to me; I have not earned it. It's not mine by right. It's the righteousness of Jesus Christ. But here's the point, in Christ it's not alien to me, it is now mine; not my accomplishment. Oh, it's a big theological word but I think maybe you would appreciate it, it's by "imputation." God has now imputed to you the righteousness of Jesus Christ by faith so that in your record, as He opens the folder up, and read what is there, He sees the righteousness of Christ now constituted as your own.[39]

---

[38] Bahnsen's sermon on Romans 3:21-30.

[39] Bahnsen's sermon on Romans 3:21-30.

One thing is for sure. Steve Schlissel would not be happy that Bahnsen agrees with Martin Luther on the view of "alien righteousness." As noted previously, Schlissel believes Luther was wrong. Rich Lusk would not rejoice either that Bahnsen says that the imputed righteousness of Jesus is credited to our account, which makes us righteous. After all, Lusk said that "*final justification is to the (faithful) doers of the law (Rom. 2:1ff) and that by those good works which make faith complete (James 2:14ff). Justification will not be fully realized until the resurrection.*"[40]

Bahnsen rejects the fundamental notion of the Federal Vision that justifying faith be defined as "the obedience of faith." He states:

> He calls on us to have faith in Christ but he doesn't make faith the basis of our justification. Now this may call for some quick explanation because you have probably heard the expression, which is true and precious to Protestants, that "We are justified by faith." But you have to understand we are not justified on the basis of faith. We are justified by faith, or if you will, through faith, but not on the basis of faith ... The basis of God's justifying work is the redemption that is brought to me in Jesus Christ.[41]

This statement of Bahnsen utterly refutes those who think that Bahnsen is teaching what Norman Shepherd has taught. Shepherd said:

> In fact, Genesis 15:6 says that Abraham's faith was so significant that it was credited to him as righteousness! If so, then righteousness was a condition to be met, and faith met that condition.[42]

As I conclude this chapter, it should be evident from Greg Bahnsen's writings that he is not even in the same ballpark as the Federal Vision men. I want to address David Bahnsen: "David, please forsake the Federal Vision camp. Your father left you the means for you to have discernment; he left you his great book *Theonomy In Christian Ethics* and other valuable tools. You don't need to wish that your daddy would come down to you and speak to you; your daddy has said, "Son, I have shown you the way."

---

[40] Lusk, *Future Justification To The Doers of the Law,"* p. 8.

[41] Bahnsen's sermon on Romans 3:21-30.

[42] Norman Shepherd, The Call of Grace, p. 15.

Chapter 12

Conclusion

We Have a Responsibility

The head of the church is the Lord Jesus Christ. He is the chief Shepherd of the sheep. We are told in Ephesians 5 that the church is His bride who He will present to Himself as holy and blameless. God's love reaches back into eternity past. God the Father has determined to have a people for Himself, His elect. Upon these He showers His grace and mercy. They are "vessels of mercy" according to Romans 9. To this undeserving mass of humanity, the Father sent His only begotten Son to redeem these elect out of their sin and misery. The eternal Son assumed to Himself a real human nature; He became flesh in order to purchase these elect out of their sinful bondage. The eternal Son of God became the God/Man Jesus. He became the last Adam to do what the first Adam failed to do. Jesus fulfilled all righteousness; He purchased his church with the price of his own blood (Acts 20:28).

Prior to His death, Jesus prayed that His church throughout all the ages would be one (John 17:20-26). We are to strive to be of the same mind, maintaining the same love, united in spirit, and intent on one purpose (Philippians 2:2). One of the great desires of the Lord of the church is that His church be unified. Combined with the desire for His church to be unified, Jesus desires His church to be pure. Pure in what way? Pure in doctrine. Unless the church is nourished in sound doctrine she will never become mature. Ephesians 4:14-15 exhorts us to not be tossed here and there, carried about by every wind of doctrine, by the trickery of men, by craftiness in deceitful scheming. Verse 15 exhorts us to "speak the truth in love" in order for the church to grow up in all respects unto Him who is the head, even Christ. When Paul was with the Ephesian elders for the last time, he said that they were to guard themselves and the flock against wolves who would not spare the flock. These wolves were in sheep's clothing; they were teachers who would seek to draw away disciples after their lies. Jesus told His disciples to beware of the false prophets who would come in sheep's clothing (Matthew 7:15). The apostle Paul had to instruct the young pastor Timothy to deal with the false teaching that arose so quickly in the Ephesian church. In the fight against these false teachers, Paul told Timothy to pay close attention to his teaching (I Timothy 4:16). He told Timothy to beware of those conceited men who would come and advocate a different doctrine that does not agree with sound words (I Timothy 6:3-4). Paul pled with Timothy to guard that which was entrusted to him (I Timothy 6:20). Just what was he to guard? Jude 3 illumines us with that answer: We are to contend earnestly for the Faith which was once for all delivered to the saints.

Upon whom does this responsibility fall to earnestly contend for the Faith? It is the responsibility of the elders of the church. One of the qualifications for an elder is found in Titus 1:9-11 which states, *"holding fast the faithful word which is in accordance with the teaching, that he may be able both to exhort in sound doctrine and to refute those who contradict. For there are many rebellious men, empty talkers and deceivers, especially those of the circumcision, who must be silenced because they are upsetting whole families, teaching things they should not teach, for the sake of sordid gain."* To the elders of the church Jesus has given the keys to the kingdom (Matthew 16:19). The elders of Christ's church, as under shepherds, have a two-fold responsibility. They must preserve the purity and peace of Christ's church. False doctrine will do two things: It will foster unrest, disunity in Christ's church, and if unchecked, it will destroy men's souls. This is why God says that such men must be silenced. A faithful elder must do is to expose the false shepherds to be the wolves that they really are. False doctrine must be exposed. The infection must be identified, and then it must be eliminated. If elders do not do this, then the church can be severely damaged. A little leaven leavens the entire lump (I Corinthians 5:6). One of the worse things that elders can do is to pretend that there is not an infection, hoping that it will go away on its own. An untreated infection becomes a raging threat to the body.

I have titled my book *"Danger In The Camp"* for a deliberate purpose. The Reformed church faces a serious challenge to its effectiveness in our time. Wolves in sheep's clothing have permeated our camp and have brought a false doctrine that will destroy men's souls. Those men who refer to their new paradigm theology as the Federal Vision have infiltrated our churches and infected them with their destructive theology. As Greg Bahnsen stated in one of his sermons, to believe that one can achieve eternal life by seeking to obey the commandments of God for one's justification is to trust in a false hope – it will destroy men's souls in Hell forever. Salvation is by grace through faith alone. The righteousness that we must present to a Holy God on Judgment Day is a perfect, holy, and righteous life. No man can achieve this in himself; He needs the righteousness of another who obeyed those commandments perfectly. That perfect substitute is the Lord Jesus Christ. Without His righteousness none of us will make it into Heaven. Federal Vision theology repudiates this glorious doctrine that the Reformation recaptured. May the Reformed church of the 21st Century rise and defend the great cause once again.

What Should be Done to Those in The Federal Vision?

They should be exposed for the false teachers that they are. It is the earnest prayer of this author that this book will aid the church to understand Federal Vision theology for the spiritual cancer that it is. I assure you that if we don't eradicate this theology from our churches, then we will pay a dear price, and we will incur the displeasure of the Lord of the church who will say to us – "Why did you not discharge your duty as stewards of the mysteries of God?"

The Responsibility of Local Sessions

It is the responsibility of each church session (the elders) to staunchly protect its own flock from this damaging Federal Vision theology. As noted previously, the church elders are obligated to guard the flock against false doctrine (Acts 20:28-31; Titus 1:9-11). The elders must guard the pulpit. The elders foremost must not allow their teacher elder (preacher/pastor) to hold these views. The preacher is to be the herald of the gospel, and if that heralding is a false gospel, then the congregation is put in serious spiritual danger. The elders must not tolerate any one in the congregation propagating this theology. This means that the elders must not allow any Sunday school teacher to propagate Federal Vision theology. As with any class, all educational instruction must be under the oversight of the elders. There must be unanimity of doctrine in all that that is taught in the church. If there is a person who is seeking to persuade members of the congregation to embrace Federal Vision theology, the elders must immediately stop it; otherwise, factions can arise, and the unity of the visible body of Christ will be disrupted.

Overall, the elders must inform their congregation of any deviant theology when it arises in the church at large. Position papers, if necessary, should be formulated for distribution to the congregation, warning them of dangerous theologies that may be circulating in the Reformed community. The pastor should occasionally have special sermons, dealing with these dangerous theologies.

The Responsibility of Presbyteries and General Assemblies

As faithful Presbyterian elders, the presbytery must guard against those of the Federal Vision who would infiltrate various churches within its jurisdictional boundaries. The elders at large must hold local church sessions accountable. It is the responsibility of presbytery to guard the doctrinal integrity of the presbytery. Local churches cannot be allowed to teach doctrines out of accord with the doctrinal position of the presbytery. Most, if not all, conservative Presbyterian bodies in the United States acknowledge the Westminster Standards as their constitution. When presbyteries examine prospective ministers for its churches, they require these ministers to take various vows. One such vow reads:

> Do you sincerely receive and adopt the Confession of Faith
> of this Church, as containing the system of doctrine taught in
> the Holy Scriptures; and do you further promise that if at any
> time you find yourself out of accord with any of the funda-
> mentals of this system of doctrine, you will, on your own ini-
> tiative, make known to your Session the change which has
> taken place in your views since the assumption of this ordi-
> nation vow? [1]

It is incumbent upon a presbytery to hold its ministers accountable to this vow. If a minister does not voluntarily make known any such change in his doctrinal conformity to the Westminster Standards, then presbytery must intervene and insist that these ministers comply or face discipline.

I have written this book in order to demonstrate that Federal Vision theology is totally out of accord with the Westminster Standards. It is my opinion that any presbytery that has a minister who is promoting Federal Vision theology instructs this minister to appear before it for clarification. The presbytery is obligated to thoroughly examine the minister in order to determine if the minister is out of accord with the Westminster Standards. If this minister is found out of accord, then presbytery must instruct him to immediately desist from such teaching or face disciplinary measures.

---

[1] Derived from *The Book of Church Order of the Presbyterian Church In America*, Chapter 21 on "Ordination and Installation of Ministers."

Of course, it is the responsibility of every presbytery to be thoroughly acquainted with Federal Vision theology in order to know where it deviates from the Westminster Standards. One of the primary purposes for my book is to provide documentation that the Federal Vision is indeed out of accord with our Confessional documents.

As I mentioned in my introduction, the Reformed Presbyterian Church In the United States (RPCUS) is not the only denomination that has condemned the Federal Vision for teaching aberrant views. The Reformed Church in the United States (RCUS) has also condemned its teachings. Mississippi Valley Presbytery of the Presbyterian Church in America (PCA) issued its final report in February 2005, finding the teaching of the Federal Vision to be out of accord with the Westminster Standards.

Of key interest is the report of Louisiana Presbytery of the Presbyterian Church in America. Steve Wilkins and Auburn Avenue Presbyterian Church are members of this presbytery. In July 2005, Louisiana Presbytery responded to its Ad Hoc Committee's final report on the Federal Vision. The teachings of Rev. Steve Wilkins were examined in several areas: 1) sacramental efficacy, 2) the centrality of the visible Church, 3) the importance of a lived out faith to Christ, and 4) "real" covenantal union with Christ.[2]

While the report raised some concerns with various expressions of Rev. Wilkins, it did not find him at this particular time to be out of acceptable bounds of the Confession. The study committee recommended:

> 2. Having thoroughly examined Rev. Steve Wilkins as to his views on these and other related issues, we find him to be within the bounds of the Confession at this time. However particular written expressions especially on the issue of baptism still have led to confusion, both on the part of those troubled by these writings as well as those who embrace what was written. We exhort him to clarify/reformulate his teachings to define them more precisely, especially as they relate to the Confession's use of language and to take more care when communicating these things in the future. Nonetheless, we do believe that Rev. Steve Wilkins should be exonerated as the charges and inquiries that our Presbytery has received

---

[2] Report of the *LA Presbytery Ad Hoc Committee on Federal Vision Theology Final Report and Recommendations.* <www.louisianapresbytery.com/AAT-FV_final.htm.>

about him, as he appears to be within the Confession and the System of doctrine contained therein.

3. That Rev. Steve Wilkins be publicly exonerated by Louisiana Presbytery, and declared to be faithful to the Confessional standards of the PCA.[3]

While it is commendable of Louisiana Presbytery of the PCA to address the issue, I am not the only one to be troubled by the presbytery's response. Of course, each presbytery has the right to conduct its own investigation. As noted earlier, Mississippi Valley Presbytery of the PCA found the teaching of the Federal Vision to be out of accord with the Westminster Standards, and that the Federal Vision gave evidence of "another gospel."[4]

On July 27, 2005, several prominent men of the Reformed community responded to the Louisiana presbytery report. These men were: Dr. Calvin Beisner (associate professor at Knox Theological Seminary, RE Christopher Hutchinson, Rev. Richard D. Phillips, Dr. Joseph Pipa (president of Greenville Theological Seminary), Rev. Carl Robbins, TE Dr. Morton Smith (professor, Greenville Theological Seminary and former stated clerk of the PCA General Assembly), and TE Dr. R. Fowler White. While these men commended Louisiana Presbytery for addressing concerns, they were disappointed in the committee's lack of thoroughness. These men thought that Louisiana Presbytery should have found Rev. Wilkins' views on baptism and assurance of salvation as unacceptable and contrary to the Westminster Standards. These distinguished gentlemen also were disappointed with the Louisiana Presbytery committee recommendations. They said:

> Finally, we were disappointed in the Report's recommenda-
> tions. A. As is clear from some of our comments above, we
> believe that Mr. Wilkins has said and written some things that
> are clearly outside the bounds of the Confession, whatever he
> might believe "at this time." B. While we were pleased that
> the Report exhorted Mr. Wilkins to "clarify/reformulate his
> teachings... and to take more care when communicating
> these things in the future," it 1) badly disserved him by fail-
> ing to list specific quotations from his writings or speeches
> that are the basis for the exhortation and that need retraction,

---

[3] Report of the *LA Presbytery Ad Hoc Committee on Federal Vision Theology Final Report and Recommendations*

[4] Ad Hoc Committee Report of Mississippi Valley Presbytery (PCA), February 1, 2005, pp. 4-5.

clarification, or reformulation, 2) said nothing of how and in what forums it ought to be done, 3) gave him no time frame within which to get it done, and 4) said nothing of what sanctions might follow if it were not done.

In light of all the foregoing, we believe, despite the Report's assertion to the contrary, that Mr. Wilkins has taught or written contrary to the Westminster Standards on at least the following matters: 1) the doctrine of assurance, 2) the relations of water baptism, covenant, union with Christ, and eternal salvation, 3) the biblical use of "proorizo", and 4) apostasy.

For the preservation of the purity of the gospel and of the Presbyterian Church in America, we therefore call upon the Committee and the Presbytery to: 1) reconsider their findings, identifying specific statements (such as those quoted above) by which Mr. Wilkins has in the past contradicted the Standards, 2) instruct Mr. Wilkins that he must clearly, publicly, and in forums likely to reach audiences similar to those exposed to the statements quoted above, retract those statements and correct them with Confessionally sound teaching on the same subjects, 3) set deadlines by which he is to have fulfilled those requirements, and 4) inform him clearly of sanctions that will be imposed of he fails to comply with those instructions.[5]

Finally, the General Assembly or Synods of Reformed churches must be willing to courageously stand for the truth against this theology. These great bodies of elders must carry out their responsibility as did the Council of Jerusalem in Acts 15. What is ironic is that the issue of the Jerusalem Council is virtually the same as the Reformed church faces today in the theology of the Federal Vision. It had to deal with the Judaizers who were adding works to faith in Jesus Christ for the saving of men's souls. The battle cries of the Reformation of "*sola fide*" (by faith alone) and "*sola Christo*" (by Christ alone) and "*sola gratia*" (by grace alone) must be shouted from the rooftops. The trumpet must sound to rally the defenders of the Faith. Who will say? "Lord, here am I; I will fight for your church."

---

[5] A response to Louisiana Presbytery's report on the Federal Vision from Calvin Beisner, Christopher Hutchinson, Richard Phillips, Joseph Pipa, Carl Robbins, Morton H. Smith, and R. Fowler White. The full response can be found on the internet at http://www.ecalvinbeisner.com/farticles/LA.Pres_Response.pdf.

Appendex A

Presbytery Questions for ministerial candidates

If the Reformed church is to guard against the spread of Federal Vision theology, it begins at the presbytery level. Presbyteries have the responsibility of examining prospective ministers. Presbytery examinations must be geared to reveal if prospective ministers espouse Federal Vision theology. It is very important the kinds of questions that are asked. In my book, I trust that I demonstrated how deceptive those can be in the Federal Vision camp. For example, Doug Wilson's request for a presbytery exam to determine his orthodoxy was deficient. Though the questions appeared to reveal his position on key areas, the questions were not precise enough. Wilson would skirt around the questions frequently and phrase his answers so that it appeared that he was Reformed. Often, the questioner would not follow up with the necessary questions to pin point Wilson.

It is imperative that presbyters be equipped to know what to ask and what to look for in an answer. More damage has been done in Presbyterian denominations over the years because certain men, holding to false doctrine, were able to pass presbytery examinations. These men then introduced their destructive heresies into their churches, and certain heretics have been approved to be seminary professors, which augments the problem. These false teachers educate prospective ministers with false theology.

The following questions are not an exhaustive list, but they should serve as a guide to elders. I will give a question and then make a comment on the kind of answer that one needs to hear. The answer does not need to be exactly like I specify, but it needs to incorporate the general idea.

Are you familiar with the writings of Norman Shepherd, N.T. Wright, Steve Wilkins, Doug Wilson, Steve Schlissel, Rich Lusk, Peter Leithart, James Jordan, and John Barach? And do you agree with their writings?

Answer: This should be an obvious question but vital. If the candidate says that he is not familiar with their teachings, the presbytery still needs to be very careful. However, if he says that he is familiar and that there are some things that he agrees with, then presbytery must proceed with extreme caution. Presbytery must assume that the candidate has accepted some of their teachings. It must probe to determine what areas the candidate agrees with Federal Vision theology.

Do you accept the Westminster Standards with their proof texts as containing the system of doctrine revealed in Holy Scripture? And how do you understand subscription to the Westminster Standards?

Answer: The candidate must indicate that he holds to the doctrines as delineated in the Confessional documents. It is important that the candidate accept the proof texts because the proof texts set the parameters for the meaning of the doctrine. For example, the Federal Vision men do not often accept the proof texts in the area of total depravity and man's ability to keep the Law of God. The Federal Vision also wants to redefine the meaning of Christ's imputation.

Regarding subscription to the Westminster Standards, the candidate must not adopt a loose view, whereby he accepts general terminology but is unwilling to accept the precise wording of the Standards. This is not to say that the precise wording is inerrant or inspired. The Westminster divines did a masterful job of choosing words, phrases, etc. to reflect accurately the doctrines of Scripture. For example, when the Confession speaks of Christ's **perfect** obedience to the Law's demands and our obligation to **personal, entire, exact, and perpetual** obedience to the same Law, these adjectives are absolutely critical to maintain the integrity of God's Word in this area.

Do you believe in the covenant of works?

Answer: The candidate must accept the covenant of works. The Federal Vision denies the covenant of works. This is because it does not accept the imputation of Christ's righteousness for the believer the way that the Bible specifies. A denial of the covenant of works also reveals the eventual denial of justification by faith alone. The covenant of works sets forth God's demand for perfect and personal obedience, as our Westminster Confession specifies. An understanding of the covenant of works is the basis for understanding Christ's work as the last Adam, who is able to merit eternal life for all whom He represents.

Do you believe that the Mosaic Law demands perfect obedience for all men?

Answer: The candidate must say, "Absolutely." The Federal Vision does not believe that the Mosaic Law demands perfect obedience of us. The reason is that the Federal Vision advocates an imperfect obedience that God accepts. As Rich Lusk believes, God judges us with "soft justice."

Do you believe that there are any "righteous" men who God justifies because they are righteous?

Answer: The candidate must say, "No." This question is designed to reveal whether he believes "personal good works" is tied to our justification. The Federal Vision believes that the imperfect obedience that God accepts for justification is possible because some people do seek to obey God's commandments.

Do you believe that justification is a one time act or is it a process?

Answer: The candidate must affirm that it is a one time act. The Federal Vision believes that justification is a process.

Do you believe that there is such a thing as an "initial" justification and a "final justification.?

Answer: The Federal Vision uses the terminology "initial" and "final" regarding justification. This reveals the belief that justification is a process and not a one time act. The heretical view is that justification is a process. The candidate must not seek to refer to justification with any kind of division.

Does "justifying faith" itself entail personal obedience to God's commandments?

Answer: The candidate must say "Absolutely not."

How do you understand the Reformed concept, "justified by faith **alone?** Define for us, the meaning of the term, **"alone."**

Answer: This question forces the candidate to deal with the precise nature of faith. This question's design also reveals if the candidate is committed to the Bible's teaching that there are no good works attached to the doctrine of justification itself. If the man vacillates or is hesitant to use the term, "alone," this is a red flag, indicating that presbytery needs to delve deeply into this area.

Is it permissible to define "saving or justifying faith" as "the obedience of faith?"

Answer: The term "the obedience of faith" has become a common catch phrase for the Federal Vision in its definition of "saving or justifying faith." If a man says that he believes that this kind of definition is correct, this is also a red flag. If a candidate says that he agrees with this definition, an important follow up question is:

By believing that justifying faith can be defined as "the obedience of faith" do you mean that keeping the commandments is part of the **essence** of justifying faith? Do you mean that a man must keep the commandments of God **in order** to be justified?

Answer: The candidate must never equate "justifying faith" with the keeping of the commandments. He must not associate our obedience to God's commandments at all with reference to the doctrine of justification. The only obedience to God's commandments that he ought to reference is Christ's perfect obedience to the Law in our stead.

Do you believe that good works are the **fruit** or **evidence** of justification, or do you believe that good works are the essence of saving faith?

Answer: The candidate must view good works as **fruit or evidence** of justification but never as part of justification itself. The Federal Vision refuses to state that good works are **only** the fruit that flows out of a justified state. It believes that good works are the very essence of saving faith. Steve Schlissel made it a specific point that good works are not merely the fruit of saving faith but the essence of it. Any kind of human works attached to the doctrine of justification itself is a heretical view. By attached, I mean good works that are involved with the **act** of justification, with our good works as the **cause** or **basis** for God's pardon.

Do you believe that there is such a thing as a Law/Gospel dichotomy?

Answer: The candidate must recognize the distinction between the Gospel and the Law, never equating the two. The Federal Vision disdains this kind of terminology. It wants to equate the two terms; therefore, it would be helpful to follow up with the following question.

Is a keeper of the Law identical to a believer?

Answer: The candidate must not equate the two. While a true believer will evidence a life of Law keeping, though imperfectly, law keeping is not the essence of "faith."

Do you believe in the "active obedience of Christ," meaning that Christ credits His righteousness to the believer so that Christ's perfect Law keeping becomes the righteousness of the believer?

Answer: The candidate **must** state that the believer needs the righteousness of Christ because he has been condemned by a failure to keep the law perfectly. Federal Vision proponents are very deceptive, and I believe dishonest by how they answer this question about Christ's active obedience. These men will say that they believe in the active obedience of Christ, but it is not what the Scripture teaches. It is important to follow up with the following question.

By the "active obedience" of Christ you don't mean that Christ kept the Law for Himself **only** so that He would qualify to be our Redeemer?

Answer: The Federal Vision believes that Jesus' perfect Law keeping was for Him **only.** The Federal Vision says that our union with Christ in His resurrection makes us righteous, but Jesus' righteousness is not credited to me personally as something that I need.

Did Abraham's personal righteousness have anything to do with his justification?

Answer: The candidate must say, "Absolutely not." The Federal Vision does believe that Abraham's righteousness was his justification because it believes that obedience is the essence of saving faith. But to believe that is heresy, for that is a works salvation scheme.

Does justification have any conditions?

Answer: The candidate must say that there are no conditions to be met except for "faith." And this faith does not imply obedience to the Law as being part and parcel with the nature of this faith.

Can you distinguish between justification and sanctification?

Answer: The candidate must make a clear distinction between the two while maintaining that sanctification will always **flow out** of justification.

There is an inseparable union of the two only in the sense that a justified man will be a sanctified man. The candidate must refer to justification as a **one time act** while referring to sanctification as a **process**. The candidate must **never** refer to justification as a process. The Federal Vision blurs the distinction between justification and sanctification, making the two essentially the same.

Have you ever heard the phrase, "the objectivity of the covenant?" If so, what is your understanding of this phrase?

Answser: This phrase is another common one of Federal Vision theology. The phraseology reveals a man's understanding of the nature of one's entrance into the covenant community. The Federal Vision uses the term, "objective covenant," as a way of denying the distinction between the Reformed and biblical idea of the visible and invisible church. This phraseology also is used by the Federal Vision to express their fidelity to baptismal regeneration.

Do you believe in the distinction of the "visible" and "invisible" church?

Answer: It is very important that the candidate make this distinction. The Federal Vision refuses to make this distinction. To help determine this distinction, a follow up question can be:

What do you believe is the meaning of the "invisible church?"

Answer: He must say that the invisible church is comprised **only** of the elect of God and that Christ died **only** for the invisible church. His bride, for whom He died, is restricted to the invisible church, to only the elect.

What do you believe is the meaning of the "visible church?"

Answer: He must say that the visible church is comprised of all who **profess** the Christian faith together with their children.

Is it possible to be in the "visible church" but not be a genuine Christian?

Answer: He must say "Yes." The Federal Vision believes that one is the elect of God in a saving sense by virtue of being in the visible church. Of course, a Federal Vision adherent is one who will not accept that distinction of "visible" and "invisible."

What is your understanding of John 15:1-10?

Answer: The historic Reformed interpretation of this passage is that the branches that do not abide in the Vine, who bear no fruit and are cut off and burned are not genuine Christians. They are in the visible church by profession only. They are not in the invisible church, the elect of God. In other words, it is possible to be in the visible church but not in the invisible church. The Federal Vision rejects this interpretation. It believes that all who are joined to the vine are joined to it in a saving sense. The Federal Vision believes that the failure to bear fruit, which leads to its destruction, signifies the loss of "initial salvation or initial justification."

Is it possible for someone in the "invisible church" to permanently apostatize from the faith and lose his salvation?

Answer: This brings out the man's view of apostasy. Apostasy is a permanent condition that a "professing Christian" can commit, but it is impossible for someone in the invisible church to apostatize or lose his salvation. The Federal Vision believes that one can lose what he initially had. It wants to avoid using the terminology, "lose one's salvation." Hence, it speaks of losing **initial salvation.**

What is your understanding of the perseverance of the saints?

Answer: The biblical and Reformed answer is that all the elect will surely persevere in the faith to the end of their lives. The Holy Spirit seals the elect, making it impossible for them to permanently fall away. The Federal Vision believes that only those granted "final justification or final salvation" will persevere.

What is your understanding of "union with Christ?"

Answer: The biblical answer is that union with Christ is brought about by the presence of true, saving faith. Our union with Christ is fundamentally an internal reality brought about by the Holy Spirit. This internal reality is pictured in the external rite of water baptism. The Federal Vision rejects the notion of an internal and external union with Christ. It pictures union with Christ in its saving sense at one's water baptism.

Do you believe that all of God's saving graces are present at the **moment** of baptism into the covenant community?

Answer: He must say, "No." While it is possible for saving faith to be present at the moment of baptism, it cannot be viewed as **always** being the case. A follow up question should be:

Do you believe in "baptismal regeneration?"

Answer: The candidate must never be vague in this answer. If he says, "yes," or if he is vague, then a follow up question should be:

Do you believe that everyone baptized is redeemed, justified, sanctified, has full union with Christ, and has passed out of death unto life by virtue of his entrance into the covenant community by baptism?

Answer: The candidate must never say that these things are **always** present at baptism. The Federal Vision believes that they are.

Is water baptism an instrument in any way in justification?

Answer: He must never say that water baptism is an instrument in justification. He must never say it is a co-instrument in justification like Rich Lusk contends.

As I noted earlier, these are only a few questions that can be used to discern if a man adheres to Federal Vision theology or not.

Scripture Index

Genesis

1-2	144
2:17	85
4:4; 5:24; 6:8,9	438
6:1-8	298
8:9	19
12:3	59
15	59, 60
15: 5-6	58, 59, 60, 62
15:6	55, 62, 182, 197, 425, 435, 436, 438, 452
17:7	350
17:10,11	350
17:10-14, 23-27	353
18	305
18:19	244
22:18	63
25:27	298
26:4-5	63

Exodus

4:22, 23	372
4:24-26	353
32: 8-10	87
32:11-14	87
32:31-33	212

Leviticus

11:44	85
18:5	114, 150, 165, 167, 175

Numbers

21:7	183

Deuteronomy

4:1	43, 158
7	250
9:4-6	161
9:25-29	87
10:15-16	377
14:1	372
14:1, 2	372
17:26	111
27:26	43, 85, 298
27:27	138
29:29	216, 379
30	165, 377, 378
30:1ff	133
30:5-6	377
30:11ff	298
30:19	118
30:19-20	165

Job

1:1	298

Psalms

6:1	87
7:8	294
7:11	87
22:9-10	354
38:1	87
80:8-16	214
85:9f	443
135:4	208

Proverbs

2:3-6	2
11:14-15	12
15: 31-33	12

Isaiah

5:1-7	214
6:13	354
9:6	344
45:4	208
53:7	84
59:2	85, 86

63:16	372
64:6	161
64:6-7	85
64:8	372

Jeremiah

2:21	214
4:4	377
7	321
9:25	377
31	378
31:33	381

Ezekiel

8:1	371
9:2	354
36	378

Hosea

6:7	96
11:1	372

Amos

9	24

Micah

6:7-8	160
7:18-19	87

Habbakuk

2:4	174, 288

Zechariah

9:9	344
11: 12-13	417

Malachi

1:2-3	276
1:6	372
2:10	372

Matthew

1:19	298
3:12	277
3:7-9	276

6:33	244
7	283
7:15	454
7:17-23	283
7:21-23	271, 387, 417
7:21-23	44, 77
7:22-23	3
7:23	413
7:24	290
10:22	217
11:11	146
13:20	212, 392
13:30	278
12:37; 25:31ff	290
13:20-22	219
13:24, 25	277
15:14	3
15:1-9	14
16:18	15
16:19	23, 454
18	4
18:15-20	23
19:16	134
19:16-26	134, 168
19:17	114
19:17-19	134
19:20	134
19:21	134
19:22	135
19:28	366, 367
21:42-45	212
23	333, 335
24:13	217
25	267
25:14ff	212
25:31-46	44, 77
28:19, 20	70
28:18-20	352
28:20	244

Mark

1:35	215
4:17	415
7:5-8	25
10:21	322
10:45	88
13:13	217

Luke

1:6	289, 294, 298
1:15	354
8:13	392
8:13	212
8:13-14	219
8:14	212
8:21	43, 158
9:23	290
10: 25-29	170
10:25	134, 319
10:27	137
10:37	171
17	296
18	320
18:11,12	327
23:46	215
24:26	345

John

1:5	416
1:9	416
1:1-18	299
1:12	273, 372
1:12-13	373
1:17	299
5:29	294
8:56-59	59
10	220
10:11, 15	267
10:16	267
10:17	84
10:26	267
10:27	267
10:27-28	409
10:28	270
10:28,29	267, 392
12:25	290
14:12	146
15	212, 220, 281, 401, 403, 405
15:1-8	246, 399
15: 1-11	279
15: 8	403
15:10	70
15:1-8	213
15:5, 10	45, 77, 426
15:14	70
16:13-15	1
17	215
17:12	415
17:17	1
17:17-24	1
17:19	344
17:20-26	453
17:21, 24	270
3:14-16	183
3:16	265, 344
3:16, 36	172
3:36	85
6:1-2	417
6:37, 44	267
6:70-71	417
7:19	322
8	417
8:30-32	274
8:31-32	216
8:31-44	283
8:31-59	277

Acts

2:37-41	352
2:38	373
2:38; 10:43	439
2:39	353

3:15	125
3:19	48
6:7	72
8:12	352
8:13	417
8:18-24	417
9:17-18	368
9:18	248
10: 34-48	352
11:23	217
13:22	294
13:38f	439
13:39	150
13:43	208
13:43	217
14:22	217
15	23
15:1-2	23
15:13-16	24
16:14-15	353
16:30	304
16:30-34	353
16:31	304
19:1-12	353
20: 29-31	24
20:28	28, 84, 268, 453
20:28-30	250
20:28-31	14, 27, 455
22:16	248, 352, 356, 368
24:14	14
26:22	318

Romans

1:5	72, 244
1:16-17	148
1:17	69, 174
2	290, 296, 319, 379,
2:1ff	292, 452
2:11-13	158
2:13	43, 158, 288, 291
2:25-29	376, 378, 380

2:26	380
2:28, 29	230, 246, 271, 275,
	276, 280, 380, 381
2:29	360, 378
3	81, 308, 310, 313
3:1-4	379
3:9-18	85
3:10	309
3:10ff	334
3:10-12	308
3:10-19	308
3:19- 20	85
3:19-22	313
3:19-26	441
3:19-31	159, 162
3:20	137
3:21	299, 451
3:21-30	447, 449, 448,
	450, 451, 452
3:22-25	437
3:22-25	444
3:24	88
3:24-25	87
3:23	85
3:26	443
3:27	98
3:28	69, 439
3:28	338
3:9-13	309
3:9-13	308
3:9-18	313
4	58, 62, 150, 434
4:1-5	63, 65
4:2 ff.	69
4:3	60, 62
4:3-5	295
4:3-6	165
4:4	61, 66
4:4-13	350
4:5-8	437
4:9-16	64

4:5-8	44, 437	8:29	206
4:6-8	89	8:32	344
4:11	72, 244	8:35,37	344
4:11-12	352	9	397, 410, 453
4:13	65	9:4	212, 273, 372
4:14	65	9:4-6	371, 403
4:15	439	9:4, 18	220, 251
4:16	65	9:4-8	275
4:25	147	9:5	274
5:8	86	9:6	250, 266, 276
5:8, 9	392	9:6-8	272, 274
5:9	88	9:7	274
5:10	344	9:8	275
5:12-14	84	10:4	439
5:12-19	86	9:13	276
5:12-21	94, 96	9:30-33	163, 164
5:14	96	9:30ff	133
5:15-21	265	9:32	163
5:16-19	84, 92	10:1-12	298
5:17-19	437, 444	10:1-12	133
5:19	118	10:9	175
6	379	11	249
6:1ff	219, 255	11:1f	220, 251
6:1-11	248	11:6	266
6:16, 22	45, 46, 426	11: 7	266
6:23	85, 289	12:7	26
7	166, 442	13:8-10	172
7:4-5	357	16:26	72, 244
7:5-11	85		
7:7	166	**1 Corinthians**	
7:8-12	176	1:30	437, 444
7:12	171	1:30, 31	93
7:14	171	2:4	206
8:1	441	4:5	381
8:1-3	250	5:6	454
8:3	440	5:7	351
8:3-4	117	6:11	210, 248, 359
8:4	441	6:11	210
8:14	414	6:20	88
8:28-30	269	7:14	353
8:28-39	411	9:2	351

10	249
10:1ff	219
10:1-5	220
10:4-5	212
11:18-19	15
11:19	14
11:24	351
12	220
12:13	206
14:25	381
15:1-2	216
15:45, 47	96

2 Corinthians

1:19-20	206
1:20	219
3:6	381, 440
4:6	442
5:9ff	296
5:21	172
6:1	252
10:3-5	15
11:13, 14	16
13:5	403

Galatians

1:6-8	288
1:6-9	449
1:8	79
1:8, 9	40, 58
2:11	4
2:15-21	176, 178
2:16	172, 177, 439
2:21	150
3:8	59
3:8-9	277
3:10	85, 97, 111, 138, 439
3:10-12	173
3:11	338, 439
3:11-12	67
3:12	133, 171
3:13	172

3:15-29	177
3:16	265
3:16, 29	59
3:21	166, 440, 447
3:21	440
3:21-25	299
3:21-26	165
3:22-24	164
3:23	133, 372
3:24	99
3:26-27	369
3:27	219, 373
3:29	265, 277, 373
4:1-3	372
4:4	88, 372
4:4-5	150, 341
4:5	273, 372
4:19	445
4:29	274
5:1-6	179
5:4	220, 440
5:6	68, 73, 180, 181, 242, 347, 434, 436
5:18	441
6:7	201
6:7-9	45, 426
6:15-16	276

Ephesians

1:3ff	249
1:3-5	208, 358
1:5	273, 372
1:5-6	208
1:7	88
1:10; 22-23	267
1:11	208
1:13	88
1:13-14	266, 351, 408
1:18-20	271
2:5-6	208, 270
2:8-9	180, 446

2: 11-12	372	2:13	249
2:18	265	2:13, 14	209, 358
3:26-28	206		
4:13; cf. v. 15	445	**1 Timothy**	
4:14-15	453	1: 3-7	17
4:14-16	26	1:4-6	314
5:30	219	1:7	314
5	358, 409, 453	1:8	314, 439
5:22ff	255	1:9-10	314
5:22-33	408	1:11-16	314
5:23-27	270, 408	1:11	318
5:23-31	358	1: 13	315
5:30	207, 279	4:16	454
		6:1-5	26
Philippians		6:3-4	454
1:6	407	6:3-5	22
2:2	453		
2:6-8	84	**2 Timothy**	
2:8	244	1:8-9	271
2:9	149, 344	1:9	363
2:12-13	377	2:15	1, 2, 22
3:2	14, 314	2:20	277
3:7-9	315	3:14-17	22
3:8-9	93	**Titus**	
3:9	439, 444	1:9-10	27
		1:9-11	454, 455
Colossians		3:4-5	271
1:13-14	88	3:4-7	264
1:15	206	3:5	248, 356, 366, 367
1:16-19	25	3:9-11	16
1:21-23	216	3:10	14
2:3	25		
2:4-8	25	**Hebrews**	
2:6	337	2:10	215
2:11-12	351, 352	2:13	215
2:11-15	378	2:17	87
3:12	208	3 and 4	403
		3 and 4	277
1 Thessalonians		3:6,14	44
5:23, 24	407	4:15	215
		4:2	372
2 Thessalonians			

4:2 with 4:6	315
5:7-9	215
5:8-9	145
6:4ff	212
6:4-6	402, 415
6:4-9	413
6:4-5	252
6:4-6	219
7:27	84
9:14, 22	88
10:1	299
10: 5-7	86
10:26 26	212
10:26-30	269
10:26-31	269, 402
10:29	212, 219
11	133
11:4-7	438
11:6	249
11:8	81
12:14	44, 50, 77, 191, 290, 330, 407
12:22ff	212

James

James 1:22	290
1:22-25	43, 158
2	53, 55, 81, 78, 288, 327, 334, 420, 421, 425, 429, 433, 435, 436
James 2:10	85, 289
2:14ff	291, 292, 452
2:14, 22	73
2:14-26	436
2:17	78
2:17, 22, 26	436
2:18	79
2:18: 9, 22	265
2:19	81
2:21	79, 80, 436
2:22-23	80

2:24	181, 242
3:22	186
4:6	12

1 Peter

1:1-2	208
1:16	85, 97
1:19	88
2:9	208
3	256
3:4	381
3:18	437
3:21	351
5:13	208

2 Peter

1:9	212
2	256
2:1	14, 212
2:1- 2	16
2:13, 18-19	24
2:20	212
2:21	212

1 John

1:7	46
2:1-2	87
2:4	70
2:6	70
2:18–24	20
2:19	387, 409
I2:27	394
3:1	273, 372, 373
3:13; 24	45, 77, 426
3:23	70
3:4	85, 166
3:9	392, 394
4:10	87
5:11-12	265

2 John

1:13	208

Jude

3	31, 454
5	409

Revelation

2:7, 11, 17, 26	218
3:5	212
3:5, 12, 21	218
5:9	88
13:8	212
17:8	212
20:12, 15	212
21:7	218
21:27	212, 330
22:19	213

Subject Index

A

A Call to Repentance, 4-12

A New Way of Seeing, 36

A Response to The Biblical Plan of Salvation, 130

a return to Rome, 52

AAPC, 39, 225, 226, 229, 230, 231, 232, 236, 237, 241, 258, 259, 300, 301, 307, 331, 332, 333, 334, 337, 346, 347, 348, 432, 434, 451

AAPC pastors' conference,, 37

Abaddon, the destroyer, 16-32

abide in Him, 208, 213, 219, 283

abiding in Christ, 45, 77

abiding in Him, 213, 246

Abraham, 165, 166, 182, 187, 197, 295, 305, 310, 311, 328, 349, 352, 358, 372, 373, 376, 381, 434, 435, 436, 437, 438, 452

Abraham, children of, 275, 276

Abraham, descendants of, 372, 373

Abraham, faith of our father, 352

Abraham, seed of, 244, 265, 266, 277, 284

Abraham, true seed of, 349, 358

Abraham's seed, 275, 276, 284

Abrahamic, 54, 56, 57, 58, 63, 64, 66, 168

Abram, 60, 61, 62

accompanied, 11, 31-32, 42, 75, 77, 320, 325, 326, 347

accompanied by other saving graces, 42

accompanied with all other saving graces, 320

accompany, 75, 81, 159, 180, 182, 186, 191, 193, 299, 334, 338, 347, 348

accompany salvation, 159, 414

accompanying, 42, 75

accompanying faith, 188

accompanying graces, 157

accursed, 3-12, 14-32, 174, 428

active faith, 435, 436

active obedience, 162, 169, 172, 184, 194, 325, 340, 342, 347, 420, 421, 431, 437, 440, 442, 443, 444

active obedience of Christ, 8-12

ad hoc study committee's report, 10-12

Adam, first, 96, 453

Adam, last, 96

Adam, second, 86, 94, 97, 106, 132

Adam's guilt, 84

Adam's transgression, 48

adopted, 202, 223, 251, 268, 273, 274

adoption, 199, 212, 213, 264, 272, 273, 284, 371, 372, 373, 380, 383, 384, 390, 395, 398, 408, 410, 414

adoption of Israel, 273

adoption of sons, 86, 90

advocate, 83, 87, 145

alien righteousness, 451, 452

all other saving graces, 320, 347

alone instrument, 185, 186, 188, 189, 190

alone instrument of justification, 320, 375

American Presbyterianism, 382, 383

Ames, William, 131

Ananias, 368

anathema, 20-32, 51, 79, 422, 427, 428

anathematized, 13-32

Antichrist, 20-32

antinomian, 53, 54, 162, 442

antinomianism, 53, 54, 242

antinomians, 53, 302

apostasy, 29-32, 33, 209, 212, 213, 250, 251, 256, 258, 269, 282, 300, 335, 387, 394, 395, 396, 397, 398, 399, 402, 403, 406, 407, 459

apostasy, Saul's, 251

apostate, 212, 213, 252, 395, 398, 399, 407

Apostates, 212, 213, 257, 267, 271, 273, 279, 387, 398, 399, 405, 409, 426

apostatize, 29-32, 212, 213, 218, 231, 249, 250, 260, 266, 267, 270, 271, 273, 349, 365, 382, 387, 395, 400, 402, 403, 404, 405, 407, 409, 415, 427

apostatized, 407, 409

apostatizes, 394, 407, 413

apostatizing, 267, 268

apostle James, 24-32

appointed time, 354, 362

approvingly of the necessity of good works for salvation, 49

Archimedes' lever, 304

Arianism, 21-32

Arians, modern day, 21-32

Arius, 21-32

Arminian, 10-12, 126, 128, 129, 201, 269, 282, 382, 398, 399, 401, 402, 409

Arminianism, 16-32, 128, 130, 199, 267, 382, 392, 394, 398, 413

Arminians, 16-32, 128, 130, 208, 389, 391, 396, 413, 417

Article 15, 391, 396

Article 3, 390

Article 4, 390, 395

Article 5, 390, 395

Article 6, 390, 395

Article 8, 390, 396

Article 9, 391

assent, 192

assurance, 118, 142, 148, 165, 188, 221, 232, 237, 238, 239, 243, 250, 252, 253, 256, 391, 395, 396, 400, 407, 408

assurance of forgiveness, 367

assured, 407, 408

atonement, 99, 102, 126, 128, 140, 183, 184, 206, 244, 268, 294, 307

atonement of Christ, 17-32

atonement, definite, 244

atoning, 84, 96, 121

atoning work, 21-32

Auburn, 156, 162

Auburn Avenue, 130, 141, 143, 156, 162

Auburn Avenue Controversy, 317

Auburn Avenue Pastors' Conference, 30-32, 33, 39, 141, 143, 201, 203, 221, 225, 226, 229, 231, 236, 237, 259, 300, 449

Auburn Avenue Presbyterian Church, 4, 39, 156, 162, 218, 221, 278, 279, 280, 346, 347, 360, 400

Auburn Avenue session, 347, 348

Auburn Avenue Theology, 419

Auburn proponents, 8-12

Auburn Theology, 3-12

Auburn views, 38

Augustine, 21-32, 68

automatic, 349, 352

automatically, 41, 74, 354, 370, 383

B

backslidings, 391

bad fruit, 283

bad tree, 283

Bahnsen, David, 431, 432, 433, 446, 452

baptism a condition, 375

baptism of repentance, 107

baptism unites us to Christ, 204, 206

baptism you are clothed with Christ Jesus, 204

baptism, A faulty view of, 28-32

baptism, adult, 29-32

baptism, efficacy of, 354, 360, 362

baptism, God's testimony in, 238

baptism, infant, 29-32

baptism, mode of, 21-32

baptism, moment of, 355, 358, 362, 363, 370, 371

baptism, water, 29-32

baptism's efficacy is conditional, 375

baptismal regeneration, 11-12, 297, 301, 397

Baptistic Americana, 303

Baptistic thinking, 364

Baptistic way of thinking, 306, 363

Baptists, 202, 233, 298, 305

baptized into his death, 368

Barach, John, 4-12, 39, 41, 156, 194, 209, 225, 226, 229, 230, 231, 232, 260, 271, 280, 281, 312, 317, 322, 346, 359, 360, 361, 397, 403, 404, 405, 406, 410, 413

Barnabas, 23-32

Beisner, Calvin, 8-12, 458, 459

Belgic Confession, 33, 40, 124, 127, 130, 153, 184, 194, 195, 299, 300, 332, 345, 389

believe for a while, 212, 219, 220

Berkhof, Louis, 115, 131

Betrayal, 7-12, 14-32

bewitched, 373

bewitching, 14

blameless, 289, 298, 309, 311, 312, 315, 329

blamelessness, 298

blasphemies, 389

blessings, 57, 58, 59, 63, 64, 65, 71, 144, 157, 181, 182, 204, 206, 207, 209, 211, 213, 216, 218, 219, 225, 242, 251, 252, 257, 270, 271, 272, 273, 274

blood, 46, 84, 86, 87, 88, 103, 107, 140, 159, 198, 211, 212, 219, 234, 235, 238, 256, 257, 268, 269, 273, 277

body of Christ, 356, 357

Booth, Randy, 433, 434, 435, 436, 442

born, 202, 207, 210, 233, 247, 275, 283

born of God, 48

Boston, Thomas, 131

Brakel, Wilhelmus a, 94

branch, 224, 279, 280, 282, 283, 284

branches, 212, 213, 214, 219, 246, 280, 281, 282, 399, 401

broken lever, 233

bronze serpent, 183, 192

Bucer, 370

burned, 399, 405, 413

by faith alone, 13-32

C

Caiaphas, 224, 280

Cain, 311

calling, 214, 217, 218, 235, 238, 239, 240, 248, 263, 269, 271, 276, 359, 363, 370, 375, 377

Calvin, John, 18, 19, 17-32, 43, 44, 47, 48, 60, 61, 62, 63, 66, 67, 68, 69, 72, 78, 79, 80, 81, 83, 93, 94, 100, 103, 104, 105, 115, 116, 117, 118, 119, 123, 124, 125, 126, 134, 135, 149, 150, 151, 158, 159, 163, 166, 167, 168, 170, 173, 175, 176,

177, 178, 179, 180, 182, 201, 205, 281, 282, 283, 289, 290, 297, 302, 341, 344, 345, 366, 367, 368, 369, 370, 371, 380, 381, 414, 415, 421, 433, 434

Calvinism, 387, 401

Calvinist, 214, 250, 401, 402, 413, 417

Calvinist's lunch, 401, 413, 417

Calvinists, 252, 413, 417

Canaan, 372, 373

CANON 11, 427

CANON 12, 427, 428

CANON 14, 428

CANON 18, 428, 430

CANON 23, 428

CANON 24, 428, 430

CANON 9, 427

Canons, 127, 128, 129, 130

Canons of Dordt, 40, 127, 128, 130, 153, 184, 194, 197, 198, 299, 300, 389, 391, 395

carnal mind, 391, 396

Carter, Mr., 301

catechism, 86, 95, 100, 102, 103, 104, 105, 107, 108, 109, 110, 111, 115, 116, 122, 123, 127, 130, 135, 136, 137, 138, 139, 140, 143, 153, 154, 184, 191, 192, 193, 194, 195, 196, 197, 219, 230, 232, 261, 262,

263, 264, 265, 266, 267, 269, 270, 271, 272

Catechisms, 7-12, 37, 200, 217

Catholic capital, 33

Catholic Church, 425

Catholicism, 170, 176, 178, 180, 182, 199, 201, 241, 242, 258, 282

cause, 41, 46, 47, 48, 55, 61, 62, 79, 80

cause of our salvation, 336, 337, 338

Caution and Respect in Controversy, 433, 434, 435

Central Carolina Presbytery, 10-12

certain, 420, 427

certainty, 388, 391, 395, 396, 401, 407, 408

certainty of their effectual vocation, 407

children are unclean, 354

children of God, 273, 275

children of the flesh, 273, 275

children of the promise, 273, 275

Christ also loved the church, 409

Christ Church, 317, 331, 332, 346

Christ died to save you, 245

Christ is the elect One, 217

Christ our Passover, 351

Christ paid for your sins, 250

Christ, baptized into, 204, 225, 228, 231

Christ, glorious new creation of, 220, 256

Christ, the merits of, 121, 127, 131

Christ's atonement, 17-32

Christ's atoning work, 28-32

Christ's blood, 256, 257

Christ's bone and flesh of his flesh, 219, 254

Christ's keeping of the Law, 109

Christ's merit, 125

Christ's merits, 39

Christ's obedience, 29-32

Christ's righteousness, 21-32

Christian, 200, 203, 204, 205, 212, 220, 221, 222, 224, 226, 236, 237, 248, 250, 278, 280

Christian Reformed, 40

Christian Renewal, 317, 335, 337

Christian Renewal magazine, 6-12, 30-32, 203, 204, 278, 317, 335, 357, 429

church invisible, 262, 277

church member, 227

church membership, 223, 382

church membership rolls, 223

church roll on earth, 272

church rolls, 272

church, A faulty view of the, 28-32

church, eschatological, 199, 223, 224

church, historical, 223, 224

church, invisible, 29-32

church, real, 223, 272

church, true, 223, 225, 265, 280

circumcise, 353, 377, 381

Circumcise then your heart, 377

circumcise your heart, 377

Circumcise yourselves, 377

circumcised, 64, 351, 352, 373, 376, 377, 378, 380

circumcised in the heart, 377, 380

circumcises, 353, 377

circumcises our hearts, 377

circumcision, 27-32, 157, 179, 180, 182, 230, 244, 266, 267, 269, 274, 276, 277, 284, 314, 315, 316, 350, 351, 352, 353, 357, 360, 361, 373, 376, 377, 378, 379, 380, 381, 454

circumcision of the heart, 377, 378

circumcision, covenant sign of, 277

circumcision, true, 380, 381

cleansed, 398, 400

co-instrument, 373, 374, 424

co-instrumentality, 298

co-instruments, 298

colloquium, 5-12, 36, 37, 131, 132, 133, 135, 141, 142, 143, 144, 145,

146, 147, 148, 149, 156, 170, 200, 205, 210, 212, 214, 216, 218, 225, 231, 240, 241, 259

commandments, 21-32

commonwealth of Israel, 372

communion, 206, 209, 210, 211, 212, 217, 243, 262, 263, 264, 269, 272, 345

communion in grace, 264, 272

condemnation, 43, 45, 58, 73, 92, 96, 112, 167, 193, 426

condition, 43, 48, 54, 55, 56, 60, 63, 76, 89, 95, 98, 114, 119, 123, 127, 182, 188, 189, 192, 197, 290, 329, 357, 375, 376, 398, 407, 425

conditions, 54, 56, 60, 65, 71, 72, 81, 89, 128, 129, 156, 157, 181, 182, 183, 184, 185, 186, 187, 189, 192, 195, 229, 242, 269, 300, 315, 326, 328, 334, 398, 405, 413

Confederation of Reformed Evangelicals, 287, 331

Confession, 33, 34, 37, 38, 40, 41, 42, 46, 47, 75, 76, 95, 96, 97, 98, 99, 105, 115, 119, 120, 121, 122, 124, 127, 130, 131, 132, 135, 153, 154, 184, 185, 186, 187, 188, 189, 190, 191, 194, 195, 293, 296, 297, 298, 299, 300, 301, 306, 308, 312, 313, 320, 323, 324, 325, 326, 330, 332, 333, 334, 336, 338, 340, 342, 343, 345, 347

confessional, 33, 35, 36, 37, 38, 40, 41, 46, 48, 56, 74, 153, 154, 157, 200, 222, 224

Confessional documents, 294, 295, 301, 306, 323

confessional formulations, 127

Confessional Standards, 7-12, 33, 36, 46, 48, 56, 74, 132, 143

Confessions, 7-12, 24-32, 35, 36-37

confident assertions, 17-32

consummation, 50

Contemporary Perspectives on Covenant Theology, 9-12

contend earnestly, 454

contend earnestly for the faith, 32

continue in the faith, 216

continuing in the state of justification, 45, 77

controversies, 16-32

controversy, 13-32, 40, 47, 49, 431, 432, 433, 434, 435, 442, 451

conversion, 202, 229, 236, 247, 248, 252, 264

converting the soul, 318, 335, 337

Corinth, 353

Cornelius the centurion, 367

Council, 13-32

Council of Jerusalem, 24-32, 459

Council of Nicea, 21-32

Council of Trent, 13, 51, 104, 241, 419, 422, 424, 427

councils, 23-32

covenant, 28-32

Covenant breakers, 255, 257, 258, 410

covenant breaking, 231, 255

covenant keeping, 231

Covenant Media Foundation, 432, 433

covenant members, 218, 221, 224, 228, 230, 239, 249, 250, 251, 255, 257

covenant of grace, 350

covenant of life, 95

Covenant of Works, 83, 89, 94, 95, 96, 97, 98, 99, 106, 121, 122, 130, 131, 132, 133, 136, 141, 143, 144, 145

Covenant Presbytery, 4-12

Covenant Reformed Church, 225

covenant sign, 247, 276, 277

covenant, A faulty view of the, 28-32

Covenant, Abrahamic, 54, 56, 57, 58, 63, 64, 66

covenant, external, 231, 275, 278

Covenant, Federal Vision and the Objectivity of the, 201

covenant, marriage, 254, 348

covenant, Mosaic, 99, 141

Covenant, New, 157, 182, 183, 197

Covenant, Objectivity of the, 199, 201, 221, 225, 232, 237, 240, 241, 244, 246, 249, 258, 259, 281, 284

Covenant, Old, 157, 182

Covenantal election, 227, 228

covenantal faithfulness, 94, 165, 182, 196

covenantal holiness, 354

covenantal loyalty, 54, 57

covenantal obedience, 52, 60, 75

covenantal paradigm is that bridge, 421

covenantal scheme, 144

CRC, 40, 317

CRE, 287, 288, 331, 332, 334, 336, 337, 338, 339, 340, 341, 342, 343

credited, 41, 55, 56, 57, 65, 78, 169, 172, 182, 197

creedal formulations, 33

creeds, 24-32

Crispus, 353

crucify to themselves the Son of God, 413

curse, 19-32, 85, 89, 90, 98, 136, 139, 145, 159, 166, 167, 173, 174, 183, 206, 207, 239, 256

curse, under the, 85, 98, 136

cursed, 43, 97, 138, 173, 174, 213, 298, 334

curses, 167

cursing, 20-32

D

Dabney, 203, 350, 357

Dabney, R.L., 131

daddy, 433, 452

danger of finally falling away, 414, 415

David, 251, 252, 390, 406, 407

Day of Judgment,, 84

Day of Pentecost, 352, 353

dead faith, 426

deceived, 34, 37

deceptiveness, 56

declare righteous, 434, 436

decree is unchangeable, 398

decrees, 56, 63, 165

decrees of God, 211, 216

dedication service, 203

definite, 244

demand perfect obedience, 170

demanded perfect obedience, 171, 172, 197, 198

demands of the law, 99, 101, 112, 115, 140

demands perfect obedience, 439

demonstrate, 40, 41, 45, 54, 56, 57, 58, 63, 66, 72, 78, 81

demonstrate justification, 434

demonstrate righteous, 434, 436

demonstrate righteousness, 434

demonstration, 420

deny the covenant of works, 94, 132

depravity, 134

depravity, A faulty view of man's, 28-32

depravity, man's, 28-32

devil, 103, 138

dichotomy, 34, 36

Dick, John, 90, 103, 104

didaskalia, 25-32

different Gospel, 10-12

disaskalos, 25-32

disciple, 159, 170

disciples, 43, 57, 70, 156, 158, 169, 170, 178, 251, 274, 280, 281, 283

disciples are saved because they did sell all to follow Jesus., 170

disciples, truly, 274

disciples, truly My, 283

discipleship, 133

discipline, 4-12

disobedience, 91, 92, 100, 110, 117, 118, 138

distinction between justification and sanctification., 45

distinction between the visible and invisible church, 260, 264, 268, 270, 279, 284

distinction between visible and invisible church, 231

divine grace, 52

division, 15-32

division in the Church, 17-32

divisive, 24-32

divorcing, 408

doctrine, 14-32, 39, 41, 44, 60, 62, 69, 71, 72, 78, 83, 91, 94, 95, 103, 104, 105, 106, 115, 116, 119, 121, 124, 126, 128, 129, 131, 134, 144, 146, 147, 148, 174, 179, 181, 190, 194, 198, 349, 357, 364, 365, 371, 382, 384, 387, 389, 391, 392, 393, 394, 395, 396, 397, 400, 401, 403, 407, 409, 410, 420, 421, 422, 429, 430, 453, 454, 455, 456, 458, 459

doctrine conforming to godliness, 22-32

doctrine, false, 14-32

doctrine, Roman Catholic, 30-32

doctrine, sound, 25-32

doctrines, 13-32, 44, 47, 126, 130, 199, 201, 237, 242, 268, 295, 296, 300, 301, 305, 310, 312, 325, 329, 333, 338

doers of the law, 158, 159, 175

double imputation, 110, 122, 146, 147

dramatic revivalistic conversion, 229, 361

Dutch Reformed, 131

E

easy-believism, 81, 162

eat that Calvinist's lunch, 401

Edwards, President, 91

effectual call, 359, 363

effectual calling, 214, 217, 263, 269, 271, 393, 412

effectually called, 121, 263, 271, 272, 277

efficacious, 17-32

efficacy, 86, 121, 146, 225, 258, 354, 360, 362, 366, 370, 374, 375, 378, 382, 388, 392, 394, 400, 406

efficacy of the sacraments, 370, 378, 382

elders, 14, 22, 23, 24, 25, 27, 28, 31, 453, 454, 455, 456, 459

elect, 29-32, 88, 121

elect for a time, 406

elect in Christ, 228, 250

elect of God, 208, 209, 229, 245, 246, 265, 266, 267, 271, 272, 276, 277, 280, 283

Elect One, 207, 208, 209, 217, 221, 228

elect only, 202, 226, 263

election, 28-32, 121, 199, 200, 205, 208, 214, 216, 218, 226, 227, 228, 229, 230, 231, 232, 242, 243, 244, 245, 246, 247, 249, 250, 251, 253, 254, 255, 256, 258, 260, 268, 269, 271, 272, 281, 388, 390, 393, 395, 397, 404, 405, 406, 407, 408, 409, 410, 412, 427

election, A faulty view of, 28-32

election, corporate, 227, 250

election, final, 269

Elizabeth, 289, 298, 312, 429

endless genealogies, 314

enemies of Christ, 15-32

enlightened, 212, 413, 415, 416

enlightening, 377

enlightens, 416

enlightens every man, 416

entire congregation, 361, 364

Ephesian elders, 14-32

equivalent to believers, 322

Esau, 229, 271, 276, 284, 364, 372

eschatological, 50, 133, 144, 145, 148, 199, 220, 223, 224, 255, 257, 272, 367, 378, 379, 382, 409, 410

essence, 42, 52, 55, 64, 68, 70, 72, 73, 78, 81, 156, 157, 165, 172, 173, 179, 180, 182, 186, 187, 188, 193, 299, 326, 335, 337, 339, 348

essence of faith, 29-32, 436, 438

essence of saving faith, 52, 369

essential form of faith, 127

eternal life, 84, 89, 92, 94, 100, 102, 103, 105, 106, 107, 109, 110, 112, 114, 115, 116, 118, 119, 120, 121, 129, 130, 134, 141, 142

eternal security, 28-32

eternally elect, 405

ethics test, 288, 295, 429, 439, 443

Evangel Presbytery, 10-12

Evangelical, 100, 101, 105, 112, 113, 120, 124, 181, 184, 185

evangelicals, 52, 182, 194

evangelism, 107, 199, 242, 243, 247, 248

ever accompanied, 320, 326

evidence, 29-32, 41, 42, 47, 56, 70, 73, 74, 75, 79, 81, 159, 179, 290, 292, 313, 320, 326, 329, 330, 337, 342, 348, 356, 357, 369, 423, 425, 430, 438, 445, 446, 451

evidence of faith, 74, 75, 79

evidence of justifying faith, 75

evidence of saving faith, 29-32

evidences, 42, 47, 157, 188

exact equivalent to believers, 322

exaltation, 345

examine yourselves, 385

examining your faith, 303

exhort in sound doctrine, 454

expiated, 93, 116

expiation, 89

external, 203, 213, 214, 231, 236, 272, 275, 277, 278, 399, 401, 402, 410

external rite, 371, 379, 380, 384

external symbol, 380

externally, 225, 230, 271, 272

F

faction, 15-32

factions, 15-32

factious, 15-32

factious Christians, 15-32

faith alone, 153, 157, 179, 180, 184, 190, 196

faith and works, 40, 52, 65, 66

faith only, 327, 335

faith plus obedience, 321, 325, 339

faith plus works, 339

faith without works is dead, 127

faith working through love, 68, 179

Faith Works, 36

faith, Abraham's, 55

faith, dead, 42, 45, 77, 320

faith, demonstration of a man's, 81

faith, essence of, 42, 55, 70, 78, 127, 156, 165, 172, 173, 179, 180, 188

faith, external, 277

faith, fruits of, 193

faith, fullness of, 70, 71

faith, good works accompany or cooperate with, 180

faith, obedience of, 287, 296, 313, 321, 322, 325, 326, 339, 342, 345

faith, obedient, 45, 56, 71, 100, 103, 110, 111, 121, 132

faith, true saving, 201

faithful, 43, 57, 61, 62, 63, 64, 87, 103, 107, 121, 130, 153, 154, 156, 157, 158, 159, 165, 178, 196, 207, 209, 211, 215, 216, 245, 255, 257, 268, 269, 291, 292, 293, 294, 296, 300, 301, 305, 306, 311, 312, 328, 332, 335, 346, 347, 390, 391, 395, 396, 397, 398, 406, 407, 408, 412

Faithful disciples will be justified, 156

faithful obedience, 29-32, 157

faithfulness, 29-32, 70, 71, 76, 77, 94, 107, 160, 163, 164, 165, 182, 186, 192, 196, 201, 214, 216, 220, 221, 227, 231, 255, 258, 379, 383, 396, 398, 399, 400, 405, 406, 407, 408, 409

faithfulness, covenant, 29-32

faithfulness, lack of, 378

fall away, 388, 389, 393, 402, 404, 405, 410, 414

fall from grace, 220

fallen from grace, 20-32

false apostles, 16-32

false beliefs, 2-12

false circumcision, 314, 315

false doctrine, 270, 301, 454, 455

false gospel, 455

false pastors, 27-32

false presuppositions, 402

false prophets, 16-32

false shepherds, 200, 201, 259, 454

false teachers, 16-32

false teachings, 51, 201

false theology, 293, 301

Falsehoods, 100, 107

federal representative, 98

Federal Vision's theology, 216

fiery serpent, 183

final, 50

final fulfillment, 219, 254

final justification, 365, 382, 393, 395, 420, 427, 429

final salvation, 348, 396, 400, 401, 406, 410, 415

first Adam, 206, 207, 215

flesh, 204, 207, 219, 254, 270, 273, 274, 275, 276

flock, 14-32, 453, 454, 455

fluidity, 291, 420

fluidity in our doctrine of justification, 420

foolish controversies, 16-32

foresaw, 398

forfeit, 390, 393, 395, 399, 400, 426

forfeited life, forgiveness, and salvation, 398

forgiveness, 88, 101, 102, 103, 105, 106, 107, 108, 115, 117, 148, 428, 429

forgiveness of sin, 45

forgiveness of sins, 349, 364, 367, 368, 374, 388, 391, 400

Form of Concord, 115

foundation of the world., 218

freed from sin, 46

French Confession, 308

fruit, 29-32, 55, 56, 66, 68, 74, 75, 79, 81, 95, 149, 157, 159, 161, 179, 188, 195, 212, 213, 214, 219, 220, 224, 229, 246, 257, 279, 280, 281, 282, 283, 392, 399, 403, 438, 445

fruitful branches, 246

fruitless, 399

fruitless discussion, 17-32

fruits, 42, 76, 79, 81, 188, 193, 276, 283

fruits and evidences, 42

full satisfaction of Christ, 123

Future justification, 420

G

Galatians, 18, 19, 14-32

Garver, Joel, 367

gates of Hell, 15-32

General Assembly, 155, 458, 459

Geneva, 17-32, 126

Gentile, 85, 146, 148, 310, 313, 316, 319

Gentiles, 43, 58, 59, 142, 160, 163, 164, 176, 177, 352, 372, 376, 380

genuine Christian, 30-32

genuine Christians, 246, 269, 277, 387, 414, 415

genuinely regenerate, 370, 371

Gideon, 406, 407

gift of God, 41, 47, 71

glorification, 225, 228, 268, 270, 271, 281, 360, 361, 380, 397, 404, 406, 412

glorified, 120, 145, 146, 147, 411, 412, 413, 426

glorious new creation, 400, 409

goat, 267

goats, 267

God demands perfect righteousness, 447

God foreordains, 398, 405

God's appointed time, 354

God's judgment, 42

God's Law, 85, 92, 116, 123, 134, 139

God's new creation, 219, 254, 279

God's own possession, 351

God's sovereignty, 406

Godfrey, Robert, 317

good fruit, 214, 283

good news preached, 372

good Samaritan, 170

good tree, 283

Good works, 29-32, 41, 42, 43, 45, 49, 50, 52, 57, 66, 68, 73, 74, 77, 78, 79, 81, 156, 158, 159, 165, 175, 179, 180, 182, 184, 185, 188, 189, 190, 191, 193, 194, 195, 196, 420, 425, 426, 428

good works in relation to justification, 49

gospel contrary, 18-32

Gospel of grace, 10-12

gospel of the Lord Jesus, 70

gospel, another, 18-32

gospel, different, 18-32

gospel, genuine, 19-32

gospel, hear the, 262

gospel, spurious, 18-32

gospel, subvert his, 19-32

grace and merit, 52

Grace is not without conditions, 156, 181, 182, 187

grace through faith, 52, 53, 54, 58, 65

grace with conditions, 72

grace, act of God's free, 46, 77

grace, condition of, 357

grace, free, 46, 58, 65, 71, 77

grace, irresistible, 269

grace, law as a type of the, 299

grace, state of, 388, 389, 390, 393, 408

grace, work of God's free, 77

graces, 42, 49, 75, 77, 157, 186, 193

gracious relationship, 399

great "deceiver", 16-32

Great Commission, 55, 57, 70, 73-81, 107, 244, 248, 249, 356

Greek categories, 36, 233

Greek ideas, 233

Greek mindset, 36, 222

Greeks, 204, 211

Greenville Theological Seminary, 5-12, 458

Greg Bahnsen and the Auburn Avenue Controversy, 432, 433

ground, 41, 44, 45, 46, 51, 80, 84, 85, 90, 101, 102, 103, 104, 105, 106, 124, 129, 131, 145, 338, 392, 413, 420, 426

ground of his justification, 45

ground of the believer's justification, 44

ground of the justification, 44

grounded, 103, 108, 148

grounds, 56, 71, 81, 162

guilty, 85, 86, 92, 108, 112, 142, 144

H

had union with Christ, 212

haireomai, 14-32

hairesis, 14-32

hairetikos, 14-32

hearers of the Law, 158

Hebraic biblical way of thinking, 223

Hebraic categories, 304

Hebrew mindset, 36

Heidelberg, 100, 102, 103, 104, 105, 107, 108, 109, 110, 111, 115, 116, 127, 130, 137, 138, 139, 140, 361, 362

Heidelberg Catechism, 9-12, 33, 40, 100, 102, 103, 104, 105, 107, 108, 109, 110, 111, 115, 116, 127, 130, 137, 138, 139, 140, 153, 184, 194, 195, 196, 197, 230, 232, 299, 300, 332, 340, 361, 389

Hellenistic, 222, 223

Hellenized, 310

Hendrikson, William, 171, 172

Heresies, 13-32, 39, 51, 71, 96, 151, 359, 385

Heresy, 13, 15, 17, 19, 21, 23, 25, 27, 29, 13-32, 37, 38, 45, 56, 75, 83,

94, 121, 124, 133, 134, 141, 159, 170, 172, 182, 287, 291, 292, 325, 393, 396, 406, 431, 441

Heretic, 13-32

heretical, 13-32, 201, 259, 275, 295, 325, 338, 431

heretics, 13-32, 317, 335, 391, 396

His law keeping, 97, 102

his obedience and death, 120, 123

His obedience and satisfaction, 120

historic creeds, 24-32

historic Reformed confessional faith, 31-32

History of the Christian Church, 126

Hodge, Charles, 84, 85, 89, 91, 92, 112, 116

Hoeksema, Anthony, 128, 129, 130, 131

holiness, 96, 102, 106, 108, 109, 110, 111, 127, 135, 149

holy signs, 350

household, 353, 371

Hughes, Phillip, 49, 50

human effort, 58, 67

human merit, 241

human responsibility, 406, 407

humiliation, 89, 102, 115, 122

Hutchinson, Christopher, 8-12, 458, 459

hybrid form of Catholicism, 394, 422

hypocrisy, 81

hypothetical, 398, 402, 403

hypothetical warnings, 402

I

I never knew you, 387, 417

immutable, 393, 410

imperfect obedience, 292, 295, 396

impossible for any elect to apostatize, 415

impossible to renew them again to repentance, 413

imputation, 21-32, 39, 46, 57, 60, 67, 80, 83, 84, 85, 87, 89, 90, 91, 101, 105, 108, 109, 110, 114, 115, 116, 117, 118, 120, 122, 123, 124, 126, 130, 132, 140, 146, 147, 148, 149, 150, 162, 172, 189, 192, 193, 196, 301, 338, 340, 341, 342, 344, 345, 347, 431, 436, 442, 445, 446, 451

imputation, Christ's, 84, 86, 89, 110, 114, 124, 147

imputation, Christ's Work of, 83, 120

imputations, 120

impute, 85, 101, 108

imputed, 46, 50, 58, 60, 61, 80, 81, 85, 90, 92, 93, 96, 100, 101, 103, 106, 107, 110, 112, 115, 116, 121, 123, 124, 131, 132, 142, 144, 145, 146, 147, 148, 162, 173, 176, 184, 189, 192, 193, 196, 289, 293, 295, 324, 329, 338, 340, 344, 347, 420,

436, 437, 438, 439, 442, 443, 444, 446, 451, 452

imputed righteousness, 436, 452

imputes, 338, 340, 341

imputeth, 324

imputing, 41, 108, 120, 123, 170, 184, 192, 194

imputing his righteousness to them, 192

in Christ, 87, 88, 91, 93, 96, 98, 101, 106, 108, 112, 113, 114, 117, 118, 130, 136, 142, 148, 150

in the person justified, 320, 326, 347

in the spirit, not in the letter, 381

individual election, 228

ineffectual, 391, 394, 396

inerrant, 22-32

infant children, 352, 353

infants, 354, 361, 362

infusing, 41

inheritance, 161, 165, 166, 191, 424, 426

iniquity, 87

initial, 50

initial clothing, 291

initial election, 427

initial justification, 365, 388, 393, 395

initial salvation, 400, 401, 407

inseparable, 48, 74

inseparably linked, 47, 48

Institutes, 115, 116, 117, 118, 119, 124, 125, 134, 135, 149, 150, 151

Institutes of the Christian Religion, 115, 117, 118, 119, 125, 134, 135, 149, 150, 151

instrument, 41, 42, 48, 75, 296, 297, 298, 320, 336, 338, 339, 345, 347, 367, 373, 374, 375, 376

instrument of justification, 42, 48, 75

instrumental cause, 424

intercession, 86, 117, 121, 122

internal, 214, 237, 366, 369, 371, 377, 379, 380

internal work of the Holy Spirit, 379

internally, 225, 271, 272

internally done by the Spirit of God., 380

invisible, 29-32

invisible church, 201, 221, 222, 223, 224, 225, 231, 254, 256, 260, 263, 264, 265, 266, 267, 268, 269, 270, 271, 272, 275, 276, 277, 278, 279, 284, 357, 358, 359, 360, 364, 371, 377, 379, 382, 383, 387, 393, 395, 401, 402, 403, 404, 408, 410, 413

inward, 214, 231, 246, 366, 369, 376, 378, 380, 381

inward evidence of those graces, 408

inward regeneration, 366

inwardly, 213, 214, 224, 230, 231, 246, 276, 366, 380

Isaiah, 25-32

Israel, 208, 209, 210, 211, 214, 227, 234, 239, 250, 256, 266, 270, 273, 274, 275, 276, 282, 358, 359, 371, 372, 373, 377, 378, 379

Israel, ethnic, 274

Israel, physical, 273, 274

Israel, true, 274, 275

Israelite, 208, 209, 227

Israelites, 161, 165, 183, 372

J

Jacob, 298, 372

Jehovah's Witnesses, 21-32

Jeremiah, 377, 381

Jesus, 199, 204, 208, 209, 210, 212, 213, 214, 215, 216, 217, 219, 220, 221, 225, 226, 228, 229, 234, 235, 238, 239, 241, 244, 245, 246, 248, 252, 255, 260, 261, 262, 263, 264, 265, 266, 267, 268, 271, 277, 279, 281, 282, 283, 284, 285

Jesus purchased the church, 268

Jesus' resurrection, 293

Jesus' thirty-three years of Law keeping, 443

Jesus' thirty-three years of law-keeping, 145

Jesus' thirty-three years of obedience, 421

Jew, 85, 224, 230, 274, 276, 280, 310, 313, 315, 316, 327, 373, 380, 381

Jew, true, 381

Jews, 43, 58, 59, 158, 160, 163, 164, 165, 176, 204, 211, 214, 234, 246, 274, 283, 284, 372, 378, 380

Job, 311, 312

Joe M, 435

John the Baptist, 276

Johnson, Henry, 30-32, 317

joined to the people of God, 216

Jordan, James B., 6-12

Joseph, 298

Judaizer, 179, 441, 447

Judaizers, 14-32, 58, 65, 142, 143, 373, 376, 440, 441, 442

Judaizers, modern, 28-32

Judaizing, 287

Judas, 251

Judas Iscariot, 417

Judaziers, 440

Judgment, 24-32, 42, 44, 50, 77, 84, 92, 101, 104, 116, 117, 118, 121, 138, 139, 148, 292, 293, 294, 295, 296, 328, 331, 345, 396, 414

Judgment Day, 190, 197, 439, 449

Judgment, Day of, 29-32

judgment, final, 292, 294, 295

jurisdiction, 4-12

justice, 46, 85, 86, 87, 88, 89, 104, 120, 123, 139, 140, 141, 146, 167, 187, 192, 294, 305, 420, 423, 424, 425, 427, 428, 429

justice, absolute, 294

justice, fatherly, 294

justification a process, 77

justification by faith alone, 13-32, 49, 50, 51, 74, 75, 77

justification by works, 365

Justification is a life long process, 157

justification of Abraham, 328

justification, A faulty view of, 28-32

justification, baptism is an instrument of, 297

justification, basis of, 48, 56

justification, demonstration of, 292

justification, final, 29-32, 290, 291, 292, 293, 295, 297, 300, 331, 343

justification, fluid doctrine of, 291

justification, fluid form of, 291

justification, forensic, 291

justification, Future, 289, 290, 291, 292, 293, 294, 296, 297

justification, Good works are the evidences that flow out of, 325

justification, initial, 29-32, 290, 291, 292, 293, 295, 297

Justification, Law can be Kept for, 288

justification, Legal, 316

justification, necessary element in, 156

justification, obedient faith is necessary for, 156

justification, other instruments of, 297

justification, Socinianism's view of, 100

justification, sole instrument for, 296

justification, two-fold, 294

justification, What is, 338

justifications, 291

justified, 4-12, 13-32

justified by imputation, 344

justified by works, 61, 63, 79, 80, 81, 327

justified on his believing, 326

justified person, 75

justified state, 47

justifieth, 41, 120

justify, 59, 61, 68, 76, 101

justifying, 83, 94, 103, 104, 123

justifying faith is always accompanied with all other saving graces, 408

K

Kansas, 402

Katekomen, 8-12

keeper of the law, 135

keeping of the Law, 109

keeping the law, 161, 162, 169, 268

kept in custody under the law, 166

kept the Law, 234

Kistemaker, Simon, 414

Knight, George, III, 8-12

Knox Seminary Colloquium, 36, 37, 156, 205, 225, 300, 315, 332, 360, 364

Knox Theological Seminary, 5, 8-12, 130, 131, 199, 205, 231, 240, 259, 458

L

Larger and Shorter Catechisms, 40, 130, 131, 153, 184

Larger Catechism, 44, 74, 184, 191, 192, 193, 261, 262, 263, 264, 265, 266, 267, 269, 270, 271, 272, 308, 309, 324, 338, 340, 343, 389, 410

last day, 44, 77, 208, 219, 224, 229, 255

Law, 43, 44, 45, 53, 54, 62, 64, 65, 67, 69, 71, 74, 76, 81

Law always condemns, 141

law and gospel, 317, 335, 337

law as opposed to gospel, 307

law breaker, 288

Law is a tutor, 299

Law is conditioned by strict justice, 141

law keeper, 298

law keeping, 161, 163, 164, 171, 172, 189, 190, 288, 289, 327, 328, 329, 330, 331, 344, 345, 347

Law keeping in conformity with the Mosaic Law, 161

law makes clear, 168

law must be fulfilled, 158

law of God, 45, 53, 71, 85, 89, 92, 97, 116, 118, 137, 138, 139, 141, 160, 182, 185, 192, 193, 195, 196, 197

Law of the Ten Commandments, 98, 99

law reveals our sin, 168, 176

law simply did not require perfect obedience., 288

law was designed to counter, 168

Law was keepable, 365

Law with the gospel, 299

law, bondage of the, 18-32

Law, doers of the, 288, 289, 290, 291, 292, 293, 294, 296, 297, 319

law, faithful doers of the, 292

law, fulfilled the, 159

law, God's moral, 94

Law, hearers of the, 319

law, in custody under the, 166

law, moral, 94, 97, 99, 118, 135, 136, 137

Law, Mosaic, 132, 137, 142, 143

Law, nature of the, 294

law, performed obedience to the, 122

Law, Under the, 85, 88, 89, 150

law, works of the, 98, 130, 150

Law/Gospel, 298, 299, 300, 318

law/gospel dichotomy, 302

law/gospel distinction, 302

law's curse, 440, 444

law's inabilities, 441

lawbreaker, 133

Law-keepers, 322

lawless ones, 331

laws, 56, 63, 75

laws of Moses, 20-32

legalism, 242

Leithart, Peter, 6-12, 205, 346, 367, 382

Lenski, R.C.H., 72, 73

Levite, 319

liar, 20-32

limited, 244, 268, 274

Linden, David, 75, 76, 77

lively faith, 42

living and active, 55, 58, 65, 71, 78

living and active faith, 55, 58, 65, 71, 78

Lombard, 67, 68

London Baptist Confession of 1689, 332

Lord of the covenant, 257

Lord's Day, 100, 102, 108, 109, 110, 137, 138, 139, 140, 195

Lord's Supper, 202, 350, 351, 363

lose, 387, 388, 390, 393, 395, 396, 397, 398, 400, 401, 404, 407, 409, 410, 413, 414

lose his salvation, 16-32

lose salvation, 388, 428

losing of salvation, 388

Lot, 302, 310, 311, 333

Louisiana Presbytery, 10-12, 457, 458, 459

Lusk, Rich, 6, 8, 130, 131, 132, 133, 134, 135, 137, 139, 140, 141, 142, 143, 144, 145, 146, 147, 148, 149, 150, 154, 156, 162, 169, 170, 172, 189, 190, 205, 249, 251, 252, 253, 254, 255, 256, 258, 269, 273, 275, 287, 288, 289, 290, 291, 292, 293, 294, 295, 296, 297, 298, 299, 300, 301, 305, 307, 309, 322, 325, 327, 328, 330, 333, 334, 335, 339, 340, 342, 343, 346, 360, 364, 365, 366, 367, 368, 369, 370, 371, 373, 374, 375, 376, 378, 379, 380, 382, 383, 384, 388, 393, 394, 395, 396, 405, 406, 407, 408, 409, 410, 413, 419,

420, 421, 422, 424, 427, 429, 438, 439, 441, 443, 446, 449, 452

Luther, Martin, 12, 22-32, 52, 53, 74, 103, 104, 131, 141, 142, 189, 190, 302, 303, 304, 307, 317, 318, 321, 322, 328, 330, 438, 441, 442, 451, 452

Lutheran, 103, 115

Lutheran church, 115

Lutheranism, 319

Lydia, 352, 353

M

Machen, Gresham, 147

made partakers of the Holy Spirit, 212

Magus, Simon, 417

man made traditions, 14-32

man, first, 96, 97, 98, 145

man, second, 96

man's justification, 83, 85, 94, 108, 120

man-made religion, 393

Marcion, 21-32

mark of conversion, 356

Marks of a Heretic, 24-32

McDade, Paul, 317

Mediator, 86, 87, 91, 99, 111, 116, 122, 125, 140, 149, 165, 206, 235, 261, 289, 316

members, 204, 207, 208, 210, 211, 212, 213, 217, 218, 221, 224, 226, 228, 230, 231, 239, 249, 250, 251, 255, 257, 260, 262, 263, 264, 266, 271, 272

members of the invisible church, 263, 264, 266, 272

members, true, 262, 266

membership rolls, 402

mercy, 125, 138, 139, 160, 163, 171, 390, 395, 396, 399, 406, 411

merit, 42, 52, 53, 54, 58, 61, 62, 67, 69, 70, 71, 92, 93, 103, 104, 105, 106, 107, 108, 109, 112, 118, 120, 121, 122, 124, 125, 126, 127, 128, 129, 132, 134, 135, 141, 143, 146, 149, 154, 160, 161, 162, 163, 174, 177, 178, 180, 181, 182, 188, 190, 195, 196, 289, 290, 291, 292, 294, 318, 320, 341, 388, 391, 394, 419, 420, 421, 422, 425, 434, 435, 448

merit theology, 154, 291

merit, man's, 93

merited, 52, 57, 66, 112, 125, 128, 149, 150

meritorious, 49, 50, 57, 62, 66, 67, 70, 71, 72, 104, 127, 131, 145, 181, 182, 189, 293, 294, 330, 334, 339, 420, 424

meritorious achievement, 57, 66, 70, 71, 72, 241, 242

meritorious conditions, 71

meritorious value, 293

meritorious works, 29-32, 330

merits, 39, 46, 61, 66, 67, 114, 121, 124, 126, 127, 128, 129, 130, 131, 132, 141, 142, 144, 146, 149, 162, 163, 171, 172, 176, 194, 195, 197, 198, 340, 341, 344, 345

merits of Christ, 121-151

Merits of Christ's Work, 127, 131

Messiah's congregation, 35, 36, 194, 300, 301, 317

Mid-America Reformed Seminary, 317

Mississippi Valley presbytery, 10, 10-12, 156, 457, 458

mixed multitude, 201, 226

modern day Judaizer, 447

moment of baptism, 247

moment of regeneration, 355

moment of time wherein it is administered, 298

Monroe, 30-32

Monroe Doctrine, 36

Monroe Four, 33, 156, 157, 194, 203, 204, 218, 231

Monroe, Louisiana, 4-12

moral exam, 296

moral law, 327, 330, 340

Mormons, 21-32

Morris, Leon, 281

Mosaic covenant, 160, 161, 163, 168, 177

Mosaic Law, 160, 161, 163, 166, 168, 171, 172, 173, 176, 177, 179, 182, 184, 187, 365, 372, 373, 422, 438, 439, 440, 441

Mosaic Law demanded perfect obedience, 342

Moses, 60, 61, 63, 65, 80, 84, 87, 118, 133, 141, 150, 161, 164, 168, 175, 183, 192, 227, 228, 298, 299, 315, 318, 322, 335

Mount Sinai, 97, 98, 136

Murray, John, 72, 73, 131, 147, 154, 162, 251, 273, 274, 275, 372, 381, 382, 410

myths, 17-32

N

nature of justifying faith, 51, 76, 77

necessary, 43, 44, 45, 46, 47, 48, 50, 61, 71, 77

necessary conditions for the blessings of the Covenant, 157

necessary for salvation, 45

Neo-orthodoxy, 294

never belonged to Him, 283

never demanded perfect obedience, 365

never knew you, 229, 271, 281, 283

Nevin, 205

new birth, 206, 210, 247, 248

new citizenship, 366

New Covenant, 129, 133

new obedience, 45, 57, 66

new paradigm, 5-12

New Perspective on Paul, 36, 58, 138, 141, 142, 143, 316

New Perspective on Paul theology, 376

New Perspectives on Paul, 11-12

new status, 366, 369

no salvation apart from union with Christ, 209

Noah, 298, 311, 312, 313

non-confessional, 31-32

nonelect, 245

nothing can separate the elect of God, 412

numerous as the stars, 56, 59, 63, 65

O

obedience of Christ, 16-32

obedience of faith, 162, 163, 179, 186, 194, 196, 197, 198

obedience of the One, 92

obedience to the law, 159, 162, 164, 165, 168, 177, 189, 192, 193, 195, 196

obedience to the Law of God, 200

obedience, Abraham's, 56, 63

obedience, Christ's perfect, 92, 94, 113, 121, 122, 123

Obedience, Denial of Christ's Active, 83, 100

obedience, evangelical, 41, 42

obedience, faithful, 291, 293, 294, 301, 306, 328, 335, 346

obedience, Jesus learned, 84

obedience, Law requires perfect, 85

obedience, law's requirement of perfect, 113

obedience, perfect, 85, 86, 87, 88, 89, 90, 92, 94, 97, 98, 113, 114, 119, 121, 122, 123, 129, 132, 133, 135, 137, 138, 139, 145

obedience, personal, 91, 95

Obedience, Prescriptive, 89

obedient, 84, 100, 103, 110, 111, 114, 121, 132

obedient disciple, 57

obedient faith, 29-32, 156, 157, 160, 161, 162, 165, 170, 178, 179, 192, 197, 426

obey, 92, 94, 106, 107, 112, 122, 138

obeyed, 84, 91, 145

obeying, 110, 111, 117

objective, 16-32, 355, 363, 366, 367, 369, 371, 373, 374, 376, 380, 383, 385

objective covenant, 387, 393, 394, 406, 409, 410

objectivity of the covenant, 387, 401, 403

offspring, 56, 59, 61, 63

once been enlightened, 413, 415

one time act, 44, 338, 342

Ontario, 302

ontological distinction, 336

OPC, 40

order of salvation, 411

ordination vow, 456

ordo salutis, 77, 316, 411, 413

organic whole, 336, 337

orthodox, 40, 41, 42, 51, 54, 55, 71

orthodox Christianity, 7-12, 28-32, 40, 54, 71

Orthodox position, 11-12

Orthodox Presbyterian Church, 42, 51

orthodoxy, 36, 55

our justification can only be effected by fulfilling the law, 113

outward, 214, 230, 231, 246, 264, 268, 275, 276, 280, 282, 366, 369, 374, 378, 380, 381, 382, 385

outward in the flesh, 380

outwardly, 230, 231, 246, 263, 272, 276

outwardly baptized, 360

outwardly Christians, 360

Owen, John, 83, 89, 90, 96, 100, 126, 127, 131, 320, 325, 326, 327, 328, 329, 345, 394, 421, 433

P

package of salvation, 228, 230, 271

paedocommunion, 37, 363

Papist, 68

Papists, 18-32, 67, 126, 174, 177, 178, 179, 180, 289

paradigm, 83, 99, 103, 104, 105, 106, 107, 108, 112, 124, 132, 135, 142, 143, 157, 159, 170, 178, 181, 182, 184, 191, 199, 200, 201, 215, 241, 242, 253, 258, 272, 282, 287, 291, 298, 299, 300, 301, 302, 309, 318, 323, 325

paradigm shift, 7-12

paradigms, 153, 154

pardon, 42, 45, 46, 47, 48, 167, 185, 190, 192, 193, 424, 426

pardoned, 45, 47, 310, 324

pardoning, 41, 42, 45, 47, 48, 184, 185, 193

pardons, 41, 87, 89

partaker of Christ, 403

partakers, 117, 127, 212, 261, 262

partakers of the Holy Spirit, 212, 413, 415, 416

passive, 84, 86, 89, 91, 93, 101, 102, 103, 108, 111, 112, 120, 140

passive and active obedience of Christ, 84, 89

passive obedience, 30-32, 84, 91, 93, 101, 102, 103, 108, 111, 112, 120, 340

Passover, 351

pastors' conference, 4-12

pattern, 187

pay the penalty, 86, 101, 102, 108, 112, 117

PCA, 10, 10-12, 155, 156, 194, 202, 222, 278, 457, 458

PCA Presbyterians, 202, 357

Pelagian, 144

Pelagians, 95, 151, 186

Pelagius, 21-32

penalty, 85, 86, 87, 88, 90, 91, 101, 102, 106, 108, 111, 112, 115, 117, 125, 148

penance, 47, 423, 424

penitent, 100, 103, 110, 111, 114, 121, 132

Pentecost, 107

perfect demands of the Law, 198

perfect obedience, 396, 437, 439, 442, 443, 444, 445, 446

perfect obedience to His Law, 331, 344

perfect righteousness of Christ, 50

perfection of His obedience, 122, 136

perfection of works, 158

perfection, sinless, 298

perseverance of the saints, 44, 71, 78, 121, 193, 199, 214, 268, 279, 282, 300, 301, 332, 348

persevere, 71, 121

persevering, 44

persevering faithfulness, 214, 399

perversion, 58, 64, 318

pervert, 43

Peter, 178, 390, 417

Pharisaical, 440

Pharisee, 15-32, 314, 315, 327

Pharisees, 3-12, 25-32, 173, 380, 438, 440, 441

Philadelphia, 40, 42, 49, 66

Philip, 352, 417

Philippian jailor, 304, 318, 319, 321

Phillips, Richard D., 8-12, 458

physical descendant, 276, 284

Pipa, Joseph, 5-12, 458, 459

Platonist, 223

point of conversion, 247, 355

Pollyanna notion, 34

power of Satan, 364

power of the Holy Spirit, 206, 216, 266

powers of the world to come, 212

Preaching, 352, 353, 375

precepts of men, 25-32

pre-Christian revelation of the gospel, 299

Predestination, 400, 407, 412, 427

predestined, 208, 217, 220, 231, 411, 412, 413

predestines, 412

Presbyterian, 4-12, 33, 39, 42, 51, 287, 305, 317, 347, 348

Presbyterian and Reformed churches, 200

Presbyterian Church In America, 10-12, 155

Presbyterianism, 203, 305, 336

Presbyterians, 202, 203, 233, 423, 424

presbytery, 456, 457, 458, 459

prescriptive, 84, 89

presume, 362, 363

Presumption, 362

presupposition, 237

presuppositions, 294, 299, 326, 402

presuppositions, faulty, 299

prevenient grace, 423

Princeton Seminary, 91

Professing Christians, 15-32, 224, 246, 266, 276

promise, 56, 58, 59, 60, 61, 63, 64, 65, 66, 71, 72, 78, 165, 166, 168, 181, 182, 192, 197, 209, 219, 226, 227, 228, 229, 230, 242, 243, 267, 273, 274, 275

promised, 54, 57, 59, 70, 78, 154, 161, 163, 165

promises, 54, 55, 56, 57, 58, 60, 61, 64, 65, 66, 71, 76

promises, Abrahamic, 56

proof text, 400, 408

proof texts, 264, 265, 266, 267, 270, 271, 309, 312, 334, 338

Propitiated, 87, 147

propitiation, 87, 159, 198

propitiatory, 109

proponent, 58, 74, 83, 170

proponents, 124, 131, 132, 144, 393, 397, 409, 417

proponents of the Federal Vision, 4-12

proposition, 35

Prostestantism, 296

Protestant, 37, 128, 242

Protestant Reformation, 4-12, 52, 53, 54, 450

Protestantism, 51, 52, 54, 68, 132, 178, 180, 182, 203, 241, 242, 421, 449, 450

Protestantism, evangelical, 51

Protestants, 17-32, 52, 452

providence of God, 95

purchased by Christ, 216

purchased salvation, 207

Pure in doctrine, 453-459

Puritans, 201, 202, 203, 357

R

ransom, 88

RCUS, 9, 10, 31-32, 49, 112, 113, 114, 115, 457

RCUS study report, 112, 115

real Jew, 380

real warnings, 402, 403

really sanctified by Christ's blood, 410

reckoned, 59, 60, 64, 65, 80, 92, 116, 118, 150, 295

Reconciled, 86, 150, 365, 388

Reconciled To God, 86

reconciliation, 52, 86, 87, 117

reconciling, 87

redeem, 88, 109, 150

redeemed, 210, 256, 257, 266, 281, 406

redeemer, 16-32

redemption, 87, 88, 91, 93, 103, 106, 140, 150, 159, 198, 206, 228, 257, 261, 262, 265, 266, 268, 271, 281, 351, 359, 361, 362, 397, 404, 406

Redemption through Christ's Blood, 88

redemptive work of Christ, 24-32

Reformation, 31-32, 34, 35, 36, 38, 52, 53, 54, 74, 75, 104, 105, 108, 124, 131, 157, 162, 287, 301, 321, 332, 336, 419, 422, 425

Reformation and Revival, 157

Reformation, solas of the, 287, 301, 321

Reformational, 104, 105, 107

Reformed, 13, 199, 200, 201, 208, 215, 218, 222, 225, 226, 232, 234, 242, 243, 244, 245, 246, 247, 248, 249, 251, 252, 253, 258, 259, 260, 268, 269, 270, 271, 272, 273, 275, 278, 280, 281, 282, 284

Reformed camp, 28-32

Reformed Church in the United States, 9, 40, 126

Reformed churches, 3-12, 317, 336

Reformed community, 13

Reformed confessional documents, 153, 157

Reformed Confessions, 123

Reformed creeds, 12

Reformed doctrine, 44, 71, 72, 308, 309

Reformed documents, 288, 343

Reformed faith, 4-12, 52, 54, 288, 295, 298, 299, 307, 321, 325, 327, 328, 338, 339, 346, 387, 394, 398, 403, 405

Reformed Presbyterian Church in the United States, 4, 457

Reformed Standards, 6-12, 29-32, 40, 83, 100, 107, 130, 132, 137, 153, 154, 155, 184, 199, 201, 258, 259, 260, 264, 265, 268, 280, 282, 284, 288, 289, 291, 294, 297, 299, 302, 323, 332, 343, 345, 348, 349, 350, 358, 361, 363, 364, 365, 382, 392, 394, 397, 405

Reformed Theological Seminary, 432, 433

Reformers, 35, 83, 84, 100, 108, 114, 132, 142, 151

reforming, 153

refute those who contradict, 454

regenerate, 135, 136, 202, 219, 248, 252, 254, 323

regenerated, 48, 216, 248, 265, 268, 277, 349, 362, 368

regeneration, 28-32, 48, 66, 77, 101, 180, 297, 301, 306, 422

regeneration, A faulty view of, 28-32

Rejection of Errors, 128, 129, 391, 392

relationship, 39, 41, 43, 44, 45, 47, 49, 77

relationship of sanctification to justification, 47

remained with us, 387

Remonstrants, 389

renew them again to repentance, 413

repent, 4-12, 48, 216, 247, 352, 359, 374, 384, 449

Repent for the forgiveness of sins, 374

repentance, 4-12, 106, 107, 156, 157, 158, 181, 185, 186, 216, 217, 242, 243, 248, 276, 390, 395, 413, 426, 427

repentance is necessary for justification, 47

repentance is necessary for the pardon of sin, 426

repentance necessary to justification, 46

representatives, 122, 130

reprobate, 201, 213, 220, 229, 243, 246, 251

resolutions, 4-12

resolutions of Covenant Presbytery, 7-12

resurrection, 101, 103, 106, 107, 112, 115, 126, 144, 145, 146, 147, 148, 206, 207, 211, 224, 227, 292, 293, 323, 342, 343, 344, 345, 347

resurrection of Jesus Christ, 351

revivalistic, 229

rich young ruler, 133, 318, 438

right with God, 100, 109, 110, 111

righteousness, 453, 455

righteousness of Christ, 41, 45, 50, 68

righteousness of Jesus Christ, 44, 56, 57

righteousness of the law consists in the perfection of works, 158

righteousness, Abraham's, 55

righteousness, covenantal, 56

righteousness, credited to us as, 87

righteousness, doctrine of the imputation of Christ's, 91

righteousness, imputation of, 90, 117, 150

righteousness, imputation of Christ's, 301, 344

righteousness, imputed to us for, 93, 116

righteousness, law was the rule of, 158

righteousness, Legal, 100, 101, 104, 105, 111, 112

righteousness, one act of, 92, 93

Robbins, Carl, 8-12, 458, 459

Robertson, O Palmer, 157

Roman Catholic, 4-12, 47, 52, 101, 104, 124, 132, 181, 199, 205, 241, 450

Roman Catholic Church, 13, 30-32

Roman Catholic teaching, 241

Roman Catholicism, 4-12, 22-32, 45, 51, 68, 78, 104, 108, 121, 124, 132, 170, 176, 178, 180, 182, 199, 201, 241, 242, 258, 282, 351, 374, 375, 384, 394, 450

Roman Catholics, 17-32, 52, 450

Romanism, 31-32, 52, 68, 78, 124, 132, 170, 258, 290, 341, 422, 430

Romanist, 105, 121, 124, 132, 178, 429

Romanists, 186, 324

Romanizing, 31-32, 450

Rome, 51, 52, 53, 54, 68, 103, 104, 105, 111, 124, 142, 180, 181, 182, 241, 242, 258, 419, 420, 421, 422, 425, 426, 427, 429, 430, 450

Rome Won't Have Me, 374

Romish, 126, 142

RPCUS, 4-12, 28-32, 126, 143, 225, 226, 229, 231, 236, 237, 259, 301, 317, 331, 337, 451, 457

S

sacrament, 65, 189, 424

sacramental language, 350, 351

sacraments, 17-32, 102, 126, 219, 258, 297, 298, 334, 336, 350, 352, 354, 362, 366, 370, 375, 378, 382

sacrifice, 84, 86, 87, 96, 102, 109, 122, 125

saints, 157, 193

salvation by grace through faith, 53, 54

Salvation is relational, 208

salvation, A faulty view of eternal security and assurance of, 28-32

salvation, assurance of, 28-32

salvation, eternal, 208, 215, 218, 220, 221, 235, 249, 252, 256, 258

salvation, final, 219, 220, 250, 251, 252, 256, 257, 266, 267, 268, 272, 282

salvation, inherit final, 257

salvation, losing their, 220

salvation, plan of, 22-32

salvation, receive final, 257

salvation, Rome's doctrine of, 241

sanctification, 425

sanctification flows out of justification, 438

sanctification, process of, 77, 157

Sanctified, 154, 195, 212, 219, 238, 240, 248, 257, 268, 269

sanctifying, 210, 217, 270

sap, 224, 280, 281, 283, 402

Satan, 15-32, 388, 390, 391, 396

satisfaction, 41, 46, 47, 87, 90, 91, 102, 103, 108, 109, 110, 111, 112, 113, 117, 120, 123, 125, 127, 128, 139, 140, 185, 187, 192, 196

satisfaction of Christ, 41

satisfaction of Christ unto them, 120

satisfaction, Christ's, 91, 108, 110, 111, 120

Saul, 251, 253, 406, 407, 408

Saul initially had an experience with the Spirit, 406

Saul of Tarsus, 352

saved, 208, 215, 219, 220, 227, 233, 239, 247, 248, 251, 252, 255, 256, 262, 263, 265, 266, 268, 270, 271, 272, 279, 280

saved automatically, 227

saved by Christ's obedience, 445

saving faith, 46, 48, 52, 54, 69, 76, 77, 81, 199, 201, 202, 216, 265

saving graces, 349, 374, 380, 385, 387, 393, 400, 403, 408, 413

saving graces are present at baptism, 400

Schaff, Philip, 17, 126

schemes, 174

scheming, 26-32

Schilder, 376

Schlissel, Steve, 4-12, 33, 34, 35, 36, 41, 74, 134, 141, 153, 156, 172, 194, 200, 215, 216, 232, 234, 235, 236, 237, 238, 240, 241, 258, 259, 260, 275, 287, 299, 300, 301, 302, 303, 304, 305, 306, 307, 308, 309, 310, 313, 314, 315, 316, 317, 319, 320, 321, 322, 325, 326, 327, 328, 329, 330, 333, 334, 335, 337, 339, 342, 346, 363, 364, 385, 403, 423, 425, 429, 430, 436, 438, 441, 442, 446, 447, 449, 452

schoolmaster, 99, 166, 167

Schwertley, Brian, 31-32, 90, 91, 94

Scottish Covenanters, 13-32

seal, 349, 351, 352, 354, 355, 358, 368, 376, 378, 380

seal of the righteousness of the faith, 352

sealed, 235, 351, 352, 355, 362, 363, 370

sealed with the Holy Spirit of promise, 408

sealing, 391, 396, 408

seals, 350, 351, 352, 363, 367, 370

second Adam, 206, 207, 215, 261, 265

sect, 14-32

seed, 57, 59, 60, 63, 64, 65, 66, 96, 99, 121, 165

Seed of the woman, 379

self righteous, 380

self-deception, 243

self-denial, 170

self-examination, 243

self-righteousness, 441, 442

Shaw, Robert, 46, 47, 95, 96, 97, 98, 99, 185, 186, 187, 188, 189, 190, 191, 275, 276, 277, 278, 324, 329, 330

Shedd, W.G.T., 90

sheep, 3, 12, 14-32, 200, 259, 267, 268, 271, 277, 283

sheep's clothing, 37, 454-459

Shepherd, Norman, 6-12, 27-32, 39, 40, 41, 42, 43, 44, 45, 46, 47, 48, 49, 50, 51, 52, 53, 54, 55, 56, 57, 58, 59, 60, 62, 63, 64, 65, 66, 67, 68, 69, 70, 71, 72, 73, 74, 75, 76, 77, 78, 81, 83, 90, 99, 100, 106, 107, 108, 109, 110, 111, 112, 113, 114, 115, 116, 117, 119, 121, 123, 124, 126, 127, 130, 132, 153, 154, 155, 156, 157, 158, 159, 160, 161, 162, 163, 164, 165, 168, 172, 173, 176, 178, 180, 181, 182, 184, 185, 187, 188, 189, 190, 192, 197, 199, 213, 215, 225, 241, 242, 243, 244, 245, 246, 247, 248, 249, 267, 268, 269, 287, 292, 293, 299, 305, 307, 325, 328, 330, 340, 343, 346, 355, 356, 357, 358, 360, 363, 367, 370, 371, 375, 394, 399, 421, 422, 424, 425, 426, 431, 433, 434, 435, 436, 441, 446, 449, 452

Shepherd's, 83, 99, 100, 106, 107, 109, 110, 111, 112, 114, 115, 121, 123, 124

Shorter Catechism, 297, 298, 308, 347

sign, 230, 244, 247, 269, 276, 277, 349, 350, 351, 352, 353, 354, 355, 358, 361, 363, 366, 367, 368, 374, 376, 378, 379, 380

sign and seal, 349, 351, 352, 354, 355, 358, 368, 376, 378, 380

sign and seal of baptism, 230, 349, 358

sign of the covenant, 350, 351, 353, 361, 378, 380

sign, outward, 366, 380

signs, 350, 351, 370, 381

Silas, 304, 353

sin is pardoned, 45

sin, merit pardon of, 120

Sinai, 97, 98, 99, 136, 288

sinned, 84, 92, 96, 140, 144, 145

sinned under the Law, 158

sinner, 84, 90, 91, 102, 109, 123, 138, 140, 141

slaves, 46

Smith, Morton, 8-12, 130, 131, 143, 145, 443, 458, 459

Socinian, 10-12, 126, 325

Socinianism, 100, 126, 127, 325, 345

Socinianism, The Federal Vision and, 126

Socinians, 95, 96, 126, 127, 186

Socinus, 17-32, 126, 127, 198

soft judgment, 443

soft justice, 439, 449

softer standard, 296

sola, 35, 287, 293, 297, 303, 335, 337

sola Christo, 287, 459

sola fide, 50, 287, 293, 297, 303, 335, 337, 459

sola gratia, 287, 459

solas, 34, 35

sole instrument, 296, 297

Son of David, 379

Son of Man, 183

Son of Man being lifted up, 183

Sophistry, 67, 158

Sophists, 66, 67, 69, 78, 79, 80

soteric, 105, 115, 292, 420

soteriological, 409, 410

Soteriology, 289, 296

Southern California Center for Christian Studies, 9-12, 100, 130, 431

Southern California Christian Studies Conference, 123

Southern Presbyterians, 233, 305, 350, 357, 363, 364, 394, 424

special experience, 229, 361

Spirit, 154, 155, 161, 172, 179, 180, 187, 190, 192, 193

spiritual blessings, 204, 209, 273, 274, 350, 358

Sproul, R.C., 104, 107

standard, 97

Standards, 6-12, 29-32, 83, 100, 107, 124, 130, 131, 132, 137, 143, 144, 153, 154, 155, 184, 194, 288, 289, 291, 294, 297, 299, 300, 301, 302, 323, 332, 333, 334, 338, 340, 342, 343, 345, 347, 348

state of justification, 44, 45, 77

stepping-stone, 219, 254

stony ground, 392

strange doctrines, 17-32

strict subscription, 33

stumbles in one point, 439

substitute, 86, 87, 90, 91, 93, 94, 130, 143, 148

substitution, 88

substitutionary, 102, 172, 183, 194, 196, 211

suffering, 84, 101, 102, 103, 105, 108, 109, 110, 111, 113, 115, 116, 122, 145

Summary Statement of AAPC's Position on the Covenant, Baptism, and Salvation, 346

superior covenant, 96

sweet Christian grandmother, 309, 310

Synod, 389, 391, 394, 395, 396, 423

Synod of Dordt, 33, 128, 332, 389, 394

synods, 23-32

T

Talmud, 336

tasted of the heavenly gift, 212, 220, 413

tasted the good word of God, 413, 415

tasted the Word, 212

teachers of the Law, 17-32, 314

temporary covenantal blessings, 410

ten commandments, 97, 98, 99, 136, 137, 233, 256

The Auburn Avenue Theology, 36

The Auburn Avenue Theology, Pros and Cons: Debating the Federal Vision, 130

The Banner Of Truth, 9-12

The Belgic Confession, 9-12

The Call Of Grace, 39, 41, 51, 52, 53, 54, 55, 56, 57, 58, 63, 65, 67, 70, 71, 72, 74, 99, 123, 132, 153, 156, 157, 160, 161, 163, 165, 168, 178, 180, 182, 187, 189, 197, 199, 241, 242, 243, 244, 245, 246, 247, 248, 249, 307, 325, 355, 356, 375, 421, 425, 435, 452

the Canons of Dordt, 9-12

The Death of Death In The Death of Christ, 394

the doers of the Law, 43

the law did not require perfect obedience, 133, 135

The Law of the Lord is perfect, 318, 337

the law's demand, 437

The Monroe Four, 5-12, 317, 335, 336, 337

the obedience of faith, 70, 71, 72, 73, 376, 420, 421, 423, 435, 436, 441, 446, 452

the RCUS, 9-12

The Relation of Good Works to Justification in the Westminster Standards, 49

the way of salvation, 51, 53, 54

The Westminster Assembly, 153, 154

The whole package of salvation, 228

theological errors, 2

Theonomy In Christian Ethics, 433, 435, 436, 437, 438, 439, 440, 441, 442, 443, 444, 445, 446, 447, 452

Thesis, 156, 157, 158, 178, 185, 187, 190, 192

They deny particular atonement, 268

things that accompany salvation, 413, 414

Thirty-four Theses, 42, 43, 44, 45, 51, 57, 77, 156, 158

Thornwell, James Henly, 203, 350, 357

Three Forms of Unity, 33, 36, 127, 131, 194, 288, 300, 301, 332, 395

title to eternal life, 84, 89, 92, 102, 103, 105, 109, 116

Torah, 142, 144, 146, 288, 299, 336

Torah made flesh, 299

Torah-keeping, 146

total depravity, 268, 307, 308, 309, 310, 334

transformed from death unto life, 363

transgressions, 165, 166, 168, 186

transgressor, 176

transgressors of the law, 246

transition, 349, 355, 356, 363, 371, 385

transition point from death to life, 356

Trent, 419, 422, 423, 424, 425, 426, 427, 428, 429, 430

Trinity Presbyterian Church, 287, 317

Trouwborst, Tom, 8-12

true and lively faith, 42

true believer, 122

True believers, 389, 390, 391, 392, 394, 395, 417

true children, 275

true church, 404

true circumcision, 315

True Confessions, 36

true disciple, 417

true disciples, 403

true faith, 185, 190, 195, 196, 426

true Gospel, 10-12

true Israel, 358

true Jew, 224

true living faith, 31-32

true union, 270, 281, 284

true union with Christ, 270, 281

truly converted, 216

TULIP, 253, 258, 269, 387, 388

Turretin, Francis, 114, 115, 131

tutor, 166

twisting of the Scripture, 11-12

two kinds of branches, 213

two kinds of salvation, 400

typological, 299

U

unchangeable love of God, 388, 389

uncircumcised, 64, 352, 377

uncircumcised hearts, 239

uncircumcision, 179, 276

unconditional, 393, 397, 399, 405, 407, 413

unconditionally elected, 405

unfaithful, 216, 231, 255, 271, 400, 408

unfaithfulness, 267, 393, 408

union, 203, 204, 206, 207, 208, 209, 211, 212, 213, 214, 215, 217, 219, 221, 225, 243, 254, 263, 264, 269, 270, 272, 278, 279, 281, 284

union with Christ, 29-32, 37, 103, 106, 148, 149, 203, 204, 342, 344, 345, 349, 357, 358, 360, 369, 383, 389, 395, 398, 399, 402, 403, 437, 445, 457, 459

union with Him, 206, 207

Unitarianism, 17-32

United Reformed Churches In North America, 194, 225

united to Christ, 45, 76, 204, 208, 209, 217, 219, 227, 247, 255, 278, 420, 426

united to Him, 206, 213, 214, 217, 220, 228, 246, 257

united with Him, 365

unites, 204, 206, 228

unites us to Christ, 357, 361

Unity, 14

universal contempt, 43, 44

unmerited favor, 207

unregenerate, 135, 136, 330, 400

unregenerate men, 136

unworthy slaves, 296

upsetting whole families, 454

URC, 317

URCNA, 225

Ursinus, 100, 101, 102, 103, 104, 105, 108, 110, 111, 112, 113, 114, 115, 116, 123

V

Vander Wall, 318

various vows, 456

Venema, 317

Venema, Cornel, 317

vicarious atonement, 126

vine, 212, 213, 214, 219, 246, 279, 280, 281, 282, 283, 401, 402

vineyard, 214

visible, 23-32

visible church, 1-12, 23-32, 201, 210, 218, 222, 223, 224, 231, 254, 260, 262, 264, 265, 266, 267, 268, 270, 272, 275, 276, 277, 278, 279, 284, 352, 353, 357, 358, 359, 363, 365, 370, 371, 372, 379, 382, 383, 387, 393, 402, 403, 404, 408, 409, 413, 457-459

vow, 456

W

W`gner, Roger, 435

wage, 295

Wall, Cornelius Vander, 318

warnings, 402, 403, 410, 414

was once for all delivered to the saints, 454

washing, 356, 359, 360, 362, 366, 369

washing of rebirth, 248

washing of regeneration, 356, 362, 366

water baptism a co-instrument with faith in our justification, 424

went out, 387

West Tennessee Reformed Mission, 317

Westminster, 40, 41, 42, 44, 46, 47, 49, 51, 66, 74, 75, 76

Westminster Assembly, 105, 115, 121, 124, 370, 394

Westminster Confession, 23-32, 34, 37, 40, 41, 42, 46, 47, 75, 76, 95, 96, 97, 98, 99, 105, 115, 119, 120, 121, 122, 130, 131, 135, 153, 184, 185, 186, 187, 188, 189, 190, 191, 194, 200, 205, 207, 217, 222, 234, 253, 258, 260, 276, 277, 278, 279, 296, 297, 298, 299, 301, 306, 308, 312, 313, 320, 323, 324, 325, 326, 330, 332, 333, 334, 336, 338, 340, 343, 347, 349, 350, 354, 358, 362, 365, 368, 369, 371, 375, 377, 379, 383, 384, 388, 393, 394, 395, 398, 400, 407, 408, 410, 435, 438, 444, 445, 446

Westminster Confession of Faith, 23-32, 95, 96, 98, 99, 119, 130, 296, 297, 323, 324, 330, 332, 333, 340, 435, 438

Westminster Confession of Faith of 1646, 332

Westminster delegates, 119, 120, 154, 216, 265

Westminster Divines, 131, 358

Westminster Larger Catechism, 44, 86, 95, 122, 123, 135, 136, 140, 143

Westminster Larger Catechism number, 350, 375

Westminster Seminary, 41, 51, 317, 434, 435

Westminster Standards, 33, 49, 74, 124, 131, 144, 154, 155, 194, 200, 216, 218, 221, 260, 264, 266, 270, 288, 301, 323, 333, 334, 338, 340, 342, 343, 349, 350, 369, 371, 375, 389, 393, 394, 395, 456, 457, 458, 459

Westminster Theological Seminary, 40, 49

wet dedication service, 203

wet dedication services, 424

What does God require, 321

What does the Lord require, 303, 305, 319, 337

What must I do to be saved, 303, 304, 318, 319, 321, 337

white robes, 290, 291

White, Dr. R. Fowler, 458

White, R. Fowler, 8-12

whole package of salvation, 397, 404, 413

Wilkins, Steve, 4-12, 30-32, 37, 38, 39, 41, 156, 162, 194, 200, 201, 202, 203, 204, 205, 210, 212, 215, 216, 218, 260, 269, 278, 279, 301, 317, 322, 325, 328, 346, 350, 357, 358, 359, 360, 361, 363, 397, 398, 399, 403, 410, 422, 424, 457, 458, 459

Wilson, Doug, 4-12, 30-32, 36, 37, 41, 156, 194, 199, 221, 225, 236, 264, 265, 270, 272, 280, 287, 288, 317, 322, 325, 331, 332, 333, 334, 335, 336, 337, 338, 339, 340, 341, 342, 343, 345, 346, 360, 382, 394, 401, 402, 403, 404, 413, 417

Wisz, Gerry, 30-32, 317, 335, 337

without Scripture proofs, 334

without the proof texts, 265

wolves, 3-12, 14-32, 37, 200, 259, 454-459

worketh by love, 42, 77

works paradigm, 99, 135, 142, 376

works salvation, 58, 63, 70, 83, 99, 132, 134, 287, 291, 300, 307, 309, 330, 339

works salvation paradigm, 83, 132, 287, 291, 309

works, meritorious, 49

works/merit paradigm, 103, 104, 105, 106, 107, 108, 124

worthiness, 298

Wright, N.T., 8-12, 58, 141, 148

WWDD, 432

Y

young rich ruler, 133-151, 170, 307, 327, 337

Z

Zacahrias, 429

Zacharias, 289, 290, 298, 312

Zipporah, 353

Bibliography

A Response to Louisiana Presbytery's report on the Federal Vision from Calvin Beisner, Christopher Hutchinson, Richard Phillips, Joseph Pipa, Carl Robbins, Morton H. Smith, and R. Fowler White. July 2005. www.calbeisner.com/farticles/LA Pres_Response.pdf.

Ad Hoc Committee Report: *"The New Perspectives on Paul."* Mississippi Valley Presbytery (PCA), February 1, 2005.

Auburn Avenue Presbyterian Church. *Summary Statement on Covenant, Baptism, and Salvation,* passed September 26, 2002.

Auburn Avenue Presbyterian Church. *Summary Statement on Covenant, Baptism, and Salvation* (Revised), passed April 3, 2005.

Bahnsen, David. "Greg Bahnsen and the Auburn Avenue Controversy." February 2003. www.cmfnow.com/AAPC/Bahnsen.html.

Bahnsen, Greg. Sermon titled "Paul's View of the Law: Justified by Faith – Romans 3:21-30" Transcribed by Wayne Rogers for the *Counsel of Chalcedon.* April 2005.

Bahnsen, Greg. *Theonomy In Christian Ethics.* Nutley, New Jersey: The Craig Press, 1977.

Barach, John. "Covenant and Election," lecture. Auburn Avenue Pastors' Conference, January 2002.

Barach, John. "Covenant and History," lecture. Auburn Avenue Pastors' Conference, January 2002.

Berhof, Louis. *Systematic Theology.* Grand Rapids, Michigan: Eerdman's Publishing Co., 1939.

Booth, Randy. "Caution and Respect In Controversy." www.cmf.com/AAPC/controversy.html.

Calvin, John. *Calvin's New Testament Commentaries.* Translated by T.H.L. Parker. Grand Rapids, Michigan: Eerdman's Publishing Co., 1965.

Calvin, John. *The Comprehensive John Calvin Collection.* Commentary on Genesis . Albany, Oregon: Sages Software, 1998.

Calvin, John. *Institutes of the Christian Religion.* Translated by Ford Lewis Battles, ed. John T. McNeil. Philadelphia: The Westminster Press, 1975.

Donnelly, Edward. "By Faith Alone," *The Banner of Truth.* August-September 2003.

Hendrikson, William. *New Testament Commentaries.* Grand Rapids, Michigan: Baker Book House, 1980.

Hoeksema, Homer C. *The Voice of Our Fathers.* Grand Rapids, Michigan: Reformed Free Publishing Association, 1980.

Hodge, Charles. *Systematic Theology, Vol. 3.* Grand Rapids, Michigan: Eerdman's Publishing Co., 1977.

Kistemaker, Simon. *New Testament Commentary, Exposition of the Epistle to the Hebrews.* Grand Rapids, Michigan: Baker Book House, 1984.

Lenski, R.C.H. *Interpretation of Romans.* Minneapolis, Minnestoa: Augsburg Publishing House, 1961.

Linden, David. "Review by Faith Alone," *Reformation and Revival Journal Vol. 11,* Number 2, Spring 2002.

Lusk, Rich. "Covenant and Election FAQ's (Version 6.4) <www.hornes.org/theologia/Soteriology>

Lusk, Rich. "Do I Believe In Baptismal Regeneration?" www.auburnavenue.org/articles

Lusk, Rich. "Future Justification To The Doers of the Law." <www.hornes.org/Theologia/Soteriology>

Lusk, Rich. "Rome Won't Have Me." www.hornes.org/Theologia/soteriology

Lusk, Rich. "Why The Law/Gospel Paradigm Is Flawed." www.hornes.org/Theologia/Soteriology

Morecraft III, Joe. "Faith and Works." *The New Southern Presbyterian Review,* Summer 2002.

Morecraft III, Joe. "The Covenant of Works." *The New Southern Presbyterian Journal,* Vol. 1, Number 2, Fall 2002.

Morecraft III, Joe. "Word and Sacraments: Westminster Larger Catechism Questions 154-177."

Murray, John. *The New International Commentary on the New Testament, Epistle to the Romans.* Grand Rapids, Michigan: Eerdman's Publishing Co., 1968.

Murray, John. "The Work of the Westminster Assembly." www.members.aol.com/RSICHURCH/assemble2. html.

Overture 14 to the General Assembly of the PCA from Mississippi Valley Presbytery regarding its Ad Hoc Committee Report: *"The New Perspectives on Paul,"* May 11, 2005.

Pipa, Joseph. "A Response to 'Covenant, Baptism, and Salvation.'" In *The Knox Theological Seminary Colloquium on the Federal Vision,* August 11-13, 2003.

"Question and Answer Session # 1. Auburn Avenue Pastors' Conference, January 2002.

Report of the Louisiana Presbytery (PCA) Ad Hoc Committee on Federal Vision Theology Final Report and Recommendations, July 2005. www.louisianapresbytery.com/AATFV_final.htm.

Report of the Special Committee To Study Justification in Light of the Current Justification Controversy. Presented to the 258th Synod of the Reformed church of the united States, May 10-13, 2004.

Schaff, Philip. *History of the Christian Church.* Grand Rapids, Michigan: Eerdmans Publishing Co., 1974.

Schlissel, Steve. "A New Way of Seeing." In the *Knox Theological Seminary Colloquium on the Federal Vision,* August 11-13, 2003.

Schlissel, Steve. "Covenant Hearing," lecture. Auburn Avenue Pastors' Conference, January 2002.

Schlissel, Steve. "Covenant Reading" lecture. Auburn Avenue Pastors' Conference, January 2002.

Schlissel, Steve. "Covenant Thinking," lecture. Auburn Avenue Pastors' Conference, January 2002.

Schlissel, Steve. "Faith Works." March 24, 2002 www.messiah-nyc.org/Articles

Schlissel, Steve. "Questions and Answers Session # 2. Auburn Avenue Pastors' Conference, January 2002.

Schlissel, Steve. "True Confessions."September 21,2002 www.messiah-nyc.org/Articles

Schwertley, Brian. "A Defense of the Active Obedience of Jesus Christ in the Justification of Sinners: A Biblical Refutation of Norman Shepherd on the Preceptive Obedience of the Savior," *The New Southern Presbyterian Review,* Fall 2004.

Shaw, Robert. *An Exposition of the Westminster Confession of Faith.* Scotland: Christian Focus Publications, 1992.

Shepherd, Norman. "Justification By Faith Alone," *Reformation and Revival,* Spring 2002.

Shepherd, Norman. "Justification By Faith and Pauline Theology" and "Justification by Works in Reformed Theology" lectures. Southern California Center for Christian Studies, Summer Conference, 2003.

Shepherd, Norman. *The Call of Grace: How The Covenant Illuminates Salvation and Evangelism.* Phillipsburg, New Jersey: Presbyterian and Reformed Publishing, 2000.

Shepherd, Norman. *"Thirty-four Theses on Justification in Relation to Faith, Repentance, and Good Works."* www.hornes.org/theologia/content/norman_shepherd/the 34theses. Htm

The Belgic Confession and Heidelberg Catechism. <www.messiah-nyc.org/belgic.htm.

The Book of Church Order of the Presbyterian Church in America.

The Canons of Dordt. Hoeksema, Homer C. *The Voice of Our Fathers.* Grand Rapids, Michigan: Reformed Free Publishing Association, 1980.

"The Monroe Four Speak Out (with a Response)" *The Counsel of Chalcedon,* May 2004 Volume 1.

The Westminster Confession of Faith: Glasgow, Scotland: Free Presbyterian Publications, 1985.

Turretin, Francis, *Institutes of ElencticTheology, 3 Vols.* Translated by George M. Giger, James T. Dennison ed. Phillipsburg, New Jersey: Presbyterian and Reformed Publishing , 1992.

Ursinus, Zacharias. *The Commentary of Dr. Zacharias Ursinus on the Heidelberg Catechism.* Translated by Rev. G.W. Willard. Phillipsburg, New Jersey: Presbyterian and Reformed Publishing Co.

Wilkins, Steve. "The Legacy of the Half-Way Covenant" lecture. Auburn Avenue Pastors' Conference, January 2002.

Wilson, Douglas. "Confederation of Reformed Evangelicals' Presbytery exam."

Wilson, Douglas. *A Serrated Edge: A Brief Defense of Biblical and Trinitarian Skylarking.* Moscow, Idaho: Canon Press, 2003.

Wilson, Douglas. "Union with Christ." In the *Knox Theological Seminary Colloquium on the Federal Vision,* August 11-13, 2003.

Wilson, Douglas. "Visible and Invisible Church Revisted," lecture. Auburn Avenue Pastors' Conference, January 2002.

Triumphant Publications' Books

Triumphant Publications is dedicated to publishing and distributing literature consistent with the theology of the Westminster Confession of Faith. It firmly believes that the Lord Jesus Christ is King of kings and Lord of lords, whose kingdom will be triumphant in history – *"For the earth will be filled With the knowledge of the glory of the Lord, As the waters cover the sea"* (Habakkuk 2:14).

These books by John M. Otis are available from:
Triumphant Publications
4253 Mulligan Dr.
Corpus Christi, TX 78413
(361) 225-2339
www.westminster-rpcus.org

DISTINCTIVES OF BIBLICAL PRESBYTERIANISM

"The purpose of this work is to set forth the major distinctives of Biblical Presbyterianism in order that those who are members of a Presbyterian Church might know in a somewhat concise way what their church believes and that curious persons might know what Presbyterians generally believe." Softcover $3.00

THE NECESSITY FOR JOINING THE LOCAL CHURCH

This booklet, sets forth fourteen biblical principles demonstrating the necessity for people to be a part of a Bible believing Presbyterian church. This is a great tool to give those considering joining your church. It is ideal for new member classes. Softcover $3.00

THE PRAYING CHRISTIAN: GOD'S WARRIOR

"This booklet's purpose is to make available a concise piece of literature, which sets forth the basic principles of prayer. Many Christians are living a powerless and ineffective life because of a poor prayer life. They have feeble expectations because they have a feeble concept of a sovereign God, who eagerly awaits to pour out His blessings to a people, who are bold enough to pray as they are commanded in Scripture." Softcover $3.00

BOOK 1 - GOD'S SOVEREIGNTY: WHO'S IN CONTROL - GOD OR MAN?

This 72 page book is unique in its revolutionary method of training people to defend God's sovereignty. The unique methodology utilizes 48 memory reference cards that come with the book. Now you can systematically argue your case and confidently demonstrate to others the truth of God's sovereignty. It deals with difficult questions: Has God predetermined all events? Is man a mere puppet in a universe governed by a sovereign God? If God predestines all things does this make God the author of evil? Does God use Satan as a tool in His eternal plan? Does God's sovereignty nullify the use of prayer? Softcover $3.00

BOOK 2 - TOTAL DEPRAVITY: MAN'S HEART HELD CAPTIVE

This book contains the same method of training found in Book 1 of the series - God's Sovereignty: Who's in control - God or Man? Dealing with the first point in the five points of Calvinism, that of Total Depravity, this book deals with the primary arguments between Arminianism and Calvinism. Some other topics dealt with in this book are: the nature of the human will, the thoroughness of sin's pollution, natural man's slavery to sin and the devil and the necessity for God's supernatural power in the work of salvation. Softcover $3.00

A BIBLICAL UNDERSTANDING OF DIVORCE

"There is a tremendous need for a biblical approach to divorce and remarriage in American society. Divorce is an immense problem facing our culture. Presently, one in two marriages ends in divorce-a statistic reflecting the American population in general. Though the overwhelming numbers of these divorces are among non-Christians, divorces among professing Christians are growing at an alarming rate." This booklet presents a concise Biblical look at this very important issue in today's culture. It even gives precise examples of what does and does not constitute a Biblical divorce. Softcover $3.00

WHO IS THE GENUINE CHRISTIAN?

"This booklet's purpose is to set forth the biblical teaching concerning what it means to be a genuine Christian. It is sad that one has to use the word "genuine" when referring to a Christian. It is because there is great confusion in the Christian community regarding this issue. Who is the genuine Christian? What are the distinguishing characteristics of this person? Can we have assurance of our salvation in light of the fact that we can make a false profession of faith? This booklet seeks to give these answers." Softcover $1.00

NECESSITY FOR THE CHRISTIAN SCHOOL

"The purpose of this tract is to help the Christian parent to realize his Biblical responsibility for his child's education, to comprehend the kind of education his child likely is receiving, to understand what is Christian education, to imagine the tremendous implications a genuine Christian education can have on a generation and a future culture, and to challenge the parent that a Christian school is not just a viable alternative but an absolute necessity." Softcover $1.00

Danger in the Camp

The Reformed Bookshelf

This CD is one of the most useful Reformed tools available. David Martinez of Corpus Christi, Texas has done a marvelous job of creating this powerful tool.

Free with the purchase of *Danger In the Camp*

What Does It Have?

- The Westminster Confession of Faith with Scripture proofs.
- The Westminster Larger and Shorter Catechisms with Scripture proofs.
- The Belgic Confession
- The Heidelberg Catechism with Scripture proofs
- The Canons of Dordt with Scripture proofs
- The Apostles, Athanasian, Chalcedon, and Nicene Creeds
- Matthew Henry's Bible Commentary
- Calvin's Institutes of the Christian Religion (Beveridge Translation)
- The Ten Commandments
- The King James Bible
- An Introduction to the RPCUS
- The RPCUS' Resolutions of 2002 Regarding the Federal Vision
- The RPCUS' transcription of the 2002 Auburn Avenue Pastors' Conference
- The New Southern Presbyterian Review – Summer and Fall 2002 editions
- Multitudes of articles dealing with the Federal Vision controversy
- Distinctives of Biblical Presbyterianism booklet by John M. Otis
- The Limitation of Congregational Voting To Male Heads of Household by John M. Otis
- RPCUS Distinctives and the Westminster Standards by John M. Otis

The Reformed Bookshelf is continually expanding. Check our website at www.westminster-rpcus.org.

Danger in the Camp

About the Author

John M. Otis is a graduate of East Tennessee State University, receiving a B.S. degree in 1973. He is a graduate of Reformed Theological Seminary in Jackson, Mississippi, receiving a Master of Divinity and a Master of Christian Education degree in 1979. He was ordained in 1979 by Westminster Presbytery (PCA) and served as pastor of the Coeburn Presbyterian Church in Coeburn, Virginia from 1982-1987. From 1988-2004, John was associated with Chalcedon Presbyterian Church (RPCUS) where he served as one of its elders for fifteen years, and he was the moderator of Covenant Presbytery of The Reformed Presbyterian Church in the United States (RPCUS) for several years.

He is presently an evangelist of Covenant Presbytery (RPCUS), serving as the evangelist and church planter of its mission work (Westminster Presbyterian) in Corpus Christi, Texas.

He is a contributing editor for the *Counsel of Chalcedon* magazine, and he has written several booklets that are listed in the back of this book. He is founder and president of Triumphant Publications located in Corpus Christi, Texas.

John is married to the former Christine Weagly of Columbia, South Carolina. John and Christine have three adult sons: Jason, Brian, and Derrick.